JAVA™
EXAMPLES
IN A NUTSHELL

*A Tutorial Companion
to Java in a Nutshell*

THE JAVA™ SERIES

Learning Java™

Java™ Threads

Java™ Network Programming

Java™ Virtual Machine

Java™ AWT Reference

Java™ Language Reference

Java™ Fundamental Classes Reference

Database Programming with JDBC™ and Java™

Java™ Distributed Computing

Developing Java Beans™

Java™ Security

Java™ Cryptography

Java™ Swing

Java™ Servlet Programming

Java™ I/O

Java™ 2D Graphics

Enterprise JavaBeans™

Creating Effective JavaHelp™

Java™ and XML

Java™ Performance Tuning

Also from O'Reilly

Java™ in a Nutshell

Java™ Examples in a Nutshell

Java™ Enterprise in a Nutshell

Java™ Foundation Classes in a Nutshell

Java™ Power Reference: A Complete Searchable Resource on CD-ROM

JAVA™
EXAMPLES
IN A NUTSHELL

A Tutorial Companion
to Java in a Nutshell

Second Edition

David Flanagan

O'REILLY®

Beijing • Cambridge • Farnham • Köln • Paris • Sebastopol • Taipei • Tokyo

Java™ Examples in a Nutshell, Second Edition

by David Flanagan

Copyright © 2000, 1997 O'Reilly & Associates, Inc. All rights reserved.
Printed in the United States of America.

Published by O'Reilly & Associates, Inc., 101 Morris Street, Sebastopol, CA 95472.

Editor: Paula Ferguson

Production Editor: Mary Anne Weeks Mayo

Cover Designer: Edie Freedman

Printing History:

September 1997: First Edition.

September 2000: Second Edition.

Library of Congress Cataloging-in-Publication Data

Flanagan, David.
    Java examples in a nutshell / David Flanagan.--2nd ed.
        p.cm.-- (A Nutshell handbook) (The Java series)
    Includes index.
    ISBN 1-596-00039-1
    1.Java (Computer program language) I.Title. II.Series. III.Java series (O'Reilly & Associates)
    QA76.73.J38 F5518 2000
    005.13'3--dc21   00-045274

ISBN: 0-596-00039-1
[M]   [4/03]

Table of Contents

Part II: Graphics and GUIs

Part III: Enterprise Java

Preface

This book is a companion volume to my previous books *Java in a Nutshell*, *Java Foundation Classes in a Nutshell*, and *Java Enterprise in a Nutshell*. While those books are quick-references at heart, they also include accelerated introductions to various Java™ programming topics and small sets of example programs. I wrote *Java Examples in a Nutshell* to pick up where those books leave off, providing a suite of example programs for novice Java programmers and experts alike.

This book was a lot of fun to write. The first edition came about when Java 1.1 was released at more than double the size of Java 1.0. While I was busy writing additional examples for the second edition of *Java in a Nutshell*, the engineers at Sun were busy turning Java into something that could no longer quite fit in a nutshell. With its quick-reference section expanding so much, *Java in a Nutshell* could no longer hold many examples. We were able to include some examples of new Java 1.1 features, but we had to cut many more than we could include. This was a hard decision; the examples in *Java in a Nutshell* were one of its most popular features.

This book is the result of those cuts, and I am glad that we made the decision we did. Given the freedom to devote an entire book to examples, I was able to write the examples I really wanted to write. I was able to go into more depth than I ever would have before, and I found myself really enjoying the exploration and experimentation that went into developing the examples. For the second edition of the book, I had the pleasure of exploring and experimenting with new parts of the Java API: Swing™, Java 2D™, servlets, and XML. I hope you will use these examples as a starting point for your own explorations, and that you get a taste of the same excitement I felt while writing them.

As its name implies, this book teaches by example, which is how many people learn best. There is not a lot of hand-holding, nor will you find detailed documentation of the exact syntax and behavior of Java statements. This book is designed to work in tandem with *Java in a Nutshell*, *Java Foundation Classes in a Nutshell*, and *Java Enterprise in a Nutshell*. You'll probably find those volumes quite useful while studying the examples here. You may also be interested in a the other books in the O'Reilly Java series. Those books are listed at *http://java.oreilly.com*.

This book is organized into three parts. Chapters 1 through 9 cover the core non-graphical parts of the Java API. The APIs covered in these chapters are documented in *Java in a Nutshell*. Chapters 10 through 15 form the second part of the book. These chapters demonstrate Java's graphics and graphical user interface APIs, which are documented in *Java Foundation Classes in a Nutshell*. Finally, Chapters 16 through 19 contain examples of Java enterprise APIs and complement the book *Java Enterprise in a Nutshell*.

You can read the chapters in this book in more or less whatever order they strike your interest. There are some interdependencies between the chapters, however, and some chapters really ought to be read in the order they are presented. For example, it is important to read Chapter 3, *Input/Output*, before you read Chapter 5, *Networking*. Chapter 1, *Java Basics*, and Chapter 2, *Objects, Classes, and Interfaces*, are aimed at programmers just starting out with Java. Seasoned Java programmers will probably want to skip them.

Java Examples Online

The examples in this book are available online, so you don't have to type them all in yourself! You can download them from the author's web site, *http://www.davidflanagan.com/javaexamples2*, or from the publisher's site, *http://www.oreilly.com/catalog/jenut2*. As typos and bugs are reported, you will also find an errata list at the publisher's site. The examples are free for noncommercial use. If you want to use them commercially, however, I ask that you pay a nominal commercial licensing fee. Visit *http://www.davidflanagan.com/javaexamples2* for licensing details.

Related Books from O'Reilly

O'Reilly publishes an entire series of books on Java. These books include *Java in a Nutshell*, *Java Foundation Classes in a Nutshell*, and *Java Enterprise in a Nutshell*, which, as mentioned earlier, are companions to this book.

A related reference work is the *Java Power Reference*. It is an electronic Java quick reference on CD-ROM that uses the *Java in a Nutshell* style. But since it is designed for viewing in a web browser, it is fully hyperlinked and includes a powerful search engine. It is wider in scope but narrower in depth than the *Java in a Nutshell* books. The *Java Power Reference* covers all the APIs of the Java 2 platform, plus the APIs of many standard extensions. But it does not include tutorial chapters on the various APIs, nor does it include descriptions of the individual classes.

You can find a complete list of Java books from O'Reilly at *http://java.oreilly.com*. Individual chapters in this book refer to specific books that may help you understand that material in more detail.

Conventions Used in This Book

The following formatting conventions are used in this book:

Italic

> Used for emphasis and to signify the first use of a term. Italic is also used for commands, email addresses, web sites, FTP sites, file and directory names, and newsgroups.

Bold

> Occasionally used to refer to particular keys on a computer keyboard or to portions of a user interface, such as the **Back** button or the **Options** menu.

`Letter Gothic`

> Used in all Java code and generally for anything that you would type literally when programming, including keywords, data types, constants, method names, variables, class names, and interface names. Also used for command lines and options that should be typed verbatim on the screen, as well as tags that might appear in an HTML document.

`Letter Gothic Oblique`

> Used for the names of method parameters and generally as a placeholder to indicate an item that should be replaced with an actual value in your program. Also used for variable expressions in command-line options.

Request for Comments

The information in this book has been tested and verified, but you may find that features have changed (or even find mistakes!). You can send any errors you find, as well as suggestions for future editions, to:

> O'Reilly & Associates, Inc.
> 101 Morris Street
> Sebastopol, CA 95472
> (800) 998-9938 (in the United States or Canada)
> (707) 829-0515 (international/local)
> (707) 829-0104 (fax)

You can also send messages electronically. To be put on the mailing list or request a catalog, send email to:

> *info@oreilly.com*

To ask technical questions or comment on the book, send email to:

> *bookquestions@oreilly.com*

There is a web site for the book, where examples, errata, and any plans for future editions are listed. Before sending a bug report, you may want to check the errata list to see if the bug has already been submitted. You can access this page at:

> *http://www.oreilly.com/catalog/jenut2*

For more information about our books, conferences, software, Resource Centers, and the O'Reilly Network, see our web site at:

http://www.oreilly.com

Acknowledgments

My thanks, as always, to my editor Paula Ferguson for pulling everything together into one coherent book and for putting up with my repeated schedule slippages. Thanks also to Frank Willison and Tim O'Reilly for being willing and enthusiastic to try this all-example book format.

I've had the help of a number of O'Reilly's other Java authors with this book. Jonathan Knudsen, author of several Java books from O'Reilly, reviewed the graphics and the printing chapters. Bob Eckstein, coauthor of *Java Swing*, reviewed the Swing chapter. Jason Hunter, author of *Java Servlet Programming*, reviewed the servlets chapter. Hans Bergsten, author of a forthcoming book on JavaServer Pages™', also reviewed the servlets chapter but focused his review on the JSP examples in particular. Brett McLaughlin, author of *Java and XML*, reviewed the XML chapter. George Reese, author of *Database Programming with JDBC and Java*, was kind enough to look over the database chapter. Jim Farley, author of *Java Distributed Computing* and coauthor of *Java Enterprise in a Nutshell*, reviewed the RMI examples. The expertise contributed by these reviewers has dramatically improved the quality of my examples. I am indebted to them all and recommend their books highly!

The production team at O'Reilly & Associates has again done a great job of turning the manuscript I submitted into a honest-to-goodness book. As usual, I am grateful to and awestruck by them.

Finally, I want to thank Christie, for reasons too numerous to list here.

David Flanagan
http://www.davidflanagan.com
July 2000

PART I

Core Java APIs

Part I contains examples that demonstrate basic Java functionality and essential Java APIs. These examples correspond to the portion of Java that is covered in *Java in a Nutshell.*

CHAPTER 1

Java Basics

This chapter contains examples that demonstrate the basic syntax of Java; it is meant to be used in conjunction with Chapter 2 of *Java in a Nutshell*. If you have substantial programming experience with C or C++, you should find the material in this chapter straightforward. If you are coming to Java from another language, however, you may need to study the examples here more carefully.

The most important step in learning a new programming language is mastering the basic control statements of the language. With Java, this means learning the if/ else branching statement and the while and for looping statements. Learning to program well is like learning to do word problems in high-school algebra class: you have to translate the problem from an abstract description into the concrete language of algebra (or, in this case, the language of Java). Once you learn to think in if, while, and for statements, other Java statements, such as break, continue, switch, and try/catch/finally, should be easy to pick up. Note that although Java is an object-oriented language, we won't discuss objects until Chapter 2, *Objects, Classes, and Interfaces*.

So, with that as an introduction, and with mastery of basic syntax as our goal, let's jump right in and start writing Java programs.

Hello World

As long ago as 1978, Brian Kernighan and Dennis Ritchie wrote, in their classic book *The C Programming Language*, that "the first program to write is the same for all languages." They were referring, of course, to the "Hello World" program. The Java implementation of "Hello World" is shown in Example 1-1.

Example 1-1: Hello.java

```
package com.davidflanagan.examples.basics;   // A unique class name prefix
public class Hello {                          // Everything in Java is a class
    public static void main(String[] args) {  // All programs must have main()
```

Example 1–1: Hello.java (continued)

```
System.out.println("Hello World!");   // Say hello!
  }                                    // This marks the end of main()
}                                      // Marks the end of the class
```

The first line of this program is the package declaration. It specifies the name of the *package* of which this program is part. The program's name (as we'll see in the second line) is Hello. The package name is com.davidflanagan.examples.basics. We can combine these two names to produce a fully qualified name, com.davidflanagan.examples.basics.Hello. Using packages provides a unique namespace for every Java program. By placing this Hello program in a package, I've ensured that no naming conflict will arise if someone else defines a program that is also named Hello. To ensure that the package name I've chosen is unique, I've followed the convention of reversing the components of my Internet domain name to produce a package name prefix.* Each chapter of this book has its own package that begins with the prefix com.davidflanagan.examples. In this case, since this is the basics chapter, the package name is com.davidflanagan.examples.basics.

The value of "Hello World" is that it is a template that you can expand on in your later experiments with Java. The second and third lines lines of Example 1-1 are a required part of the template. Every program—every piece of Java code, really—you write is a class. The second line of the example says that we're writing a class named Hello. It also says the class is public, which means it can be used by anyone.

Every standalone Java program requires a main() method. This is where the Java interpreter begins running a Java program. The third line of the example declares this main() method. It says that the method is public, that it has no return value (i.e., its return value is void), and that it is passed an array of strings as its argument. The name of the array is args. The line also says that main() is a static method. (In this chapter, we work exclusively with static methods. In Chapter 2, when we start working with objects, you'll learn what a static method is, and you'll see that non-static methods are actually the norm.)

In any case, you might as well go ahead and memorize this line:

```
public static void main(String[] args)
```

Every standalone Java program you ever write contains a line that looks exactly like this one. (Actually, you can name the array of strings anything you want, but it is usually called args.)

The fifth and sixth lines of Example 1-1 simply mark the end of the main() method and of the Hello class. Like most modern programming languages, Java is a block-structured language. This means that such things as classes and methods have bodies that comprise a "block" of code. In Java, the beginning of a block is marked by a {, and the end is marked by a matching }. Method blocks are always defined within class blocks, and as we'll see in later examples, methods blocks can contain such things as if statements and for loops that form subblocks within the

---

* My web site is *http://www.davidflanagan.com*, so my package name begins com.davidflanagan.

method. Furthermore, these sorts of statement blocks can be nested arbitrarily deep within each other.

The first three lines and the last two lines of Example 1-1 are part of the basic framework of a Java application. It is the fourth line of the example that is of primary interest to us. This is the line that prints the words "Hello World!" The `System.out.println()` method sends a line of output to "standard output," which is usually the screen. This method is used throughout this chapter and in many other chapters in this book. It isn't until Chapter 3, *Input/Output*, however, that you'll really understand what it is doing. If you are curious before then, look up the `java.lang.System` and `java.io.PrintStream` classes in *Java in a Nutshell* (or some other Java reference manual).

One final point to note about this program is the use of comments. Example 1-1 uses C++-style comments that begin with `//` and continue until the end of the line. Thus, anything between the `//` characters and the end of a line is ignored by the Java compiler. You'll find that the examples in this book are thoroughly commented. The code and the comments are worth studying because the comments often draw your attention to points that are not mentioned in the main text of the book.

Running "Hello World"

The first step in running our program is to type it in.* Using a text editor, type in the `Hello` program as shown in Example 1-1. For now, however, omit the `package` declaration on the first line. Save the program in a file named *Hello.java*.

The second step is to compile the program. If you are using the Java Software Development Kit (SDK) from Sun, you compile code with the *javac* command.† *cd* to the directory that contains your *Hello.java* file, and type this command (assuming that *javac* is in your path):

```
% javac Hello.java
```

If the Java SDK has been properly installed, *javac* runs for a short while and then produces a file named *Hello.class*. This file contains the compiled version of the program. As I said earlier, everything you write in Java is a class, as the *.class* extension on this file indicates. One important rule about compiling Java programs is that the name of the file minus the *.java* extension must match the name of the class defined in the file. Thus, if you typed in Example 1-1 and saved it in a file named *HelloWorld.java*, you would not be able to compile it.

To run the program (again using the Java SDK) type:

```
% java Hello
```

---

* Although this example is included in the online example archive, I'm suggesting that you type it in so that you start imprinting basic Java idioms in your brain. I'm also going to have you modify the example, in order to explain certain aspects of running the program.

† If you are using some other Java programming environment, read and follow the vendor's instructions for compiling and running programs.

This command should produce the output:

```
Hello World!
```

The *java* command is the Java interpreter; it runs the Java Virtual Machine. You pass *java* the name of the class that you want to run. Note that you are specifying the class name, Hello, not the name of the file, *Hello.class*, that contains the compiled class.

The previous steps have shown you how to compile and run Java programs that don't have package declarations. If you omitted the package declaration when you typed in *Hello.java*, these instructions should have worked for you (if they didn't, check that you typed the program in correctly). In practice, however, all nontrivial Java programs (including the examples in this book) do have package declarations. Using packages makes compiling and running Java programs a bit more complicated. As I just noted, a Java program must be saved in a file that has a name that matches the class name. When a class is in a package, there is a further requirement that the class be saved in a directory that matches the name of the package.

Go ahead and reinsert the package declaration into *Hello.java*:

```
package com.davidflanagan.examples.basics;
```

Now make yourself a new directory (or folder) in which you'll do all your work with the examples from this book. For example, on a Windows system, you might create a folder named *c:\jenut2*. On a Linux system, you might use *~/jenut2*. Within this directory, create a subdirectory named *com*. Then create a subdirectory of *com* named *davidflanagan*. Then create an *examples* subdirectory of *davidflanagan*. Finally, create a subdirectory in *examples* named *basics*. Now copy your *Hello.java* program (with the package declaration) into this directory. On a Windows system, the resulting file might be:

```
c:\jenut2\com\davidflanagan\examples\basics\Hello.java
```

After you've created the directory structure and put your Java program in it, the next step is to tell the Java compiler and interpreter where to find it. The compiler and interpreter simply need to know the base directory you've chosen; they will look for the *Hello.class* file in subdirectories of this base directory, based on the package name. To tell Java where to look, you have to set the CLASSPATH environment variable in the manner appropriate for your operating system. If you used the suggested name for your base directory on a Windows system (*c:\jenut2*), you can use a command like the following:

```
C:\> set CLASSPATH=.;c:\jenut2
```

This tells Java to look first for classes in the current directory (.), followed by the *c:\jenut2* directory.

On a Unix system using the *csh* shell, you can use the following command:

```
% setenv CLASSPATH .:/home/david/jenut2
```

With the *sh* or *bash* shell, the command is:

```
$ CLASSPATH=.:/home/david/jenut2; export CLASSPATH
```

You may want to automate this process by setting CLASSPATH in a startup file, such as *autoexec.bat* on Windows systems or *.cshrc* on Unix systems (under *csh*).

With your CLASSPATH set, you can now go ahead and compile and run the Hello program. To compile, change directories to the *examples/basics* directory that holds *Hello.java*. Compile the program as before:

```
% javac Hello.java
```

This creates the *Hello.class* file.

To run the program, you invoke the Java interpreter as before, but now you must specify the fully qualified name of the program, so that the interpreter knows exactly which program you want to run:

```
% java com.davidflanagan.examples.basics.Hello
```

Because you've set the CLASSPATH, you can run the Java interpreter from any directory on your system, and it will always find the correct program. If you get tired of typing such long class names, you may want to write yourself a batch file or shell script that automates the process for you.

Note that all Java programs are compiled and run in this way, so we won't go through these individual steps again. Of course, one step you don't have to repeat is typing in all the examples. You can download the example source code from *http://www.davidflanagan.com/javaexamples2*.

FizzBuzz

FizzBuzz is a game I learned long ago in elementary-school French class, as a way to practice counting in that language. The players take turns counting, starting with one and going up. The rules are simple: when your turn arrives, you say the next number. However, if that number is a multiple of five, you should say the word "fizz" (preferably with a French accent) instead. If the number is a multiple of seven, you should say "buzz." And if it is a multiple of both, you should say "fizzbuzz." If you mess up, you're out, and the game continues without you.

Example 1-2 is a Java program named FizzBuzz that plays a version of the game. Actually, it isn't a very interesting version of the game because the computer plays by itself, and it doesn't count in French! What is interesting to us is the Java code that goes into this example. It demonstrates the use of a for loop to count from 1 to 100 and the use of if/else statements to decide whether to output the number or one of the words "fizz", "buzz", or "fizzbuzz". (In this case, the if/else statement is used as an if/elseif/elseif/else statement, as we'll discuss shortly.)

This program introduces System.out.print(). This method is just like System.out.println(), except that it doesn't terminate the line of output. Whatever is output next appears on the same line.

The example also shows another style for comments. Anything, on any number of lines, between the characters /* and the characters */ is a comment in Java and ignored by the compiler. When one of these comments begins with /**, as the one in this example does, then it is additionally a *doc comment*, which means its contents are used by the *javadoc* program that automatically generates API documentation from Java source code.

Example 1-2: FizzBuzz.java

```java
package com.davidflanagan.examples.basics;

/**
 * This program plays the game "Fizzbuzz".  It counts to 100, replacing each
 * multiple of 5 with the word "fizz", each multiple of 7 with the word "buzz",
 * and each multiple of both with the word "fizzbuzz".  It uses the modulo
 * operator (%) to determine if a number is divisible by another.
 **/
public class FizzBuzz {                          // Everything in Java is a class
    public static void main(String[] args) { // Every program must have main()
        for(int i = 1; i <= 100; i++) {          // count from 1 to 100
            if (((i % 5) == 0) && ((i % 7) == 0)) // Is it a multiple of 5 & 7?
                System.out.print("fizzbuzz");
            else if ((i % 5) == 0)                // Is it a multiple of 5?
                System.out.print("fizz");
            else if ((i % 7) == 0)                // Is it a multiple of 7?
                System.out.print("buzz");
            else System.out.print(i);             // Not a multiple of 5 or 7
            System.out.print(" ");
        }
        System.out.println();
    }
}
```

The `for` and `if/else` statements may require a bit of explanation for programmers who have not encountered them before. A `for` statement sets up a loop, so that some code can be executed multiple times. The `for` keyword is followed by three Java expressions that specify the parameters of the loop. The syntax is:

```
for(initialize ; test ; update)
    body
```

The *initialize* expression does any necessary initialization. It is run once, before the loop starts. Usually, it sets an initial value for a loop counter variable. Often, as in this example, the loop counter is used only within the loop, so the *initialize* expression also declares the variable.

The *test* expression checks whether the loop should continue. It is evaluated before each execution of the loop body. If it evaluates to true, the loop is executed. When it evaluates to false, however, the loop body is not executed, and the loop terminates.

The *update* expression is evaluated at the end of each iteration of the loop; it does anything necessary to set up the loop for the next iteration. Usually, it simply increments or decrements the loop counter variable.

Finally, the *body* is the Java code that is run each time through the loop. It can be a single Java statement or a whole block of Java code, enclosed by curly braces.

This explanation should make it clear that the `for` loop in Example 1-2 counts from 1 to 100.

The `if/else` statement is simpler than the `for` statement. Its syntax is:

```
if (expression)
    statement1
else
    statement2
```

When Java encounters an `if` statement, it evaluates the specified *expression*. If the expression evaluates to `true`, *statement1* is executed. Otherwise, *statement2* is evaluated. That is all `if/else` does; there is no looping involved, so the program continues with the next statement following `if/else`. The `else` clause and *statement2* that follows it are entirely optional. If they are omitted, and the *expression* evaluates to `false`, the `if` statement does nothing. The statements following the `if` and `else` clauses can either be single Java statements or entire blocks of Java code, contained within curly braces.

The thing to note about the `if/else` statement (and the `for` statement, for that matter) is that it can contain other statements, including other `if/else` statements. This is how the statement was used in Example 1-2, where we saw what looked like an `if/elseif/elseif/else` statement. In fact, this is simply an `if/else` statement within an `if/else` statement within an `if/else` statement. This structure becomes clearer if the code is rewritten to use curly braces:

```
if (((i % 5) == 0)&& ((i % 7) == 0))
    System.out.print("fizzbuzz");
else {
    if ((i % 5) == 0)
        System.out.print("fizz");
    else {
        if ((i % 7) == 0)
            System.out.print("buzz");
        else
            System.out.print(i);
    }
}
```

Note, however, that this sort of nested `if/else` logic is not typically written out with a full set of curly braces in this way. The `else if` programming construct is a commonly used idiom that you will quickly become accustomed to. You may have also noticed that I use a compact coding style that keeps everything on a single line wherever possible. Thus, you'll often see:

```
if (expression) statement
```

I do this so that the code remains compact and manageable, and therefore easier to study in the printed form in which it appears here. You may prefer to use a more highly structured, less compact style in your own code.

The Fibonacci Series

The Fibonacci numbers are a sequence of numbers in which each successive number is the sum of the two preceding numbers. The sequence begins 1, 1, 2, 3, 5, 8, 13, and goes on from there. This sequence appears in interesting places in nature. For example, the number of petals on most species of flowers is one of the Fibonacci numbers.

Example 1-3 shows a program that computes and displays the first 20 Fibonacci numbers. There are several things to note about the program. First, it again uses a for statement. It also declares and uses variables to hold the previous two numbers in the sequence, so that these numbers can be added together to produce the next number in the sequence.

Example 1-3: Fibonacci.java

```
package com.davidflanagan.examples.basics;
/**
 * This program prints out the first 20 numbers in the Fibonacci sequence.
 * Each term is formed by adding together the previous two terms in the
 * sequence, starting with the terms 1 and 1.
 **/
public class Fibonacci {
    public static void main(String[] args) {
        int n0 = 1, n1 = 1, n2;          // Initialize variables
        System.out.print(n0 + " " +      // Print first and second terms
                        n1 + " ");       // of the series

        for(int i = 0; i < 18; i++) {    // Loop for the next 18 terms
            n2 = n1 + n0;                // Next term is sum of previous two
            System.out.print(n2 + " ");  // Print it out
            n0 = n1;                     // First previous becomes 2nd previous
            n1 = n2;                     // And current number becomes previous
        }
        System.out.println();            // Terminate the line
    }
}
```

Using Command-Line Arguments

As we've seen, every standalone Java program must declare a method with exactly the following signature:

```
public static void main(String[] args)
```

This signature says that an array of strings is passed to the main() method. What are these strings, and where do they come from? The args array contains any arguments passed to the Java interpreter on the command line, following the name of the class to be run. Example 1-4 shows a program, Echo, that reads these arguments and prints them back out. For example, you can invoke the program this way:

```
% java com.davidflanagan.examples.basics.Echo this is a test
```

The program responds:

```
this is a test
```

In this case, the args array has a length of four. The first element in the array, args[0], is the string "this" and the last element of the array, args[3], is "test". As you can see, Java arrays begin with element 0. If you are coming from a language that uses one-based arrays, this can take quite a bit of getting used to. In particular, you must remember that if the length of an array a is n, the last element in the array is a[n-1]. You can determine the length of an array by appending .length to its name, as shown in Example 1-4.

This example also demonstrates the use of a while loop. A while loop is a simpler form of the for loop; it requires you to do your own initialization and update of the loop counter variable. Most for loops can be rewritten as a while loop, but the compact syntax of the for loop makes it the more commonly used statement. A for loop would have been perfectly acceptable, and even preferable, in this example.

Example 1-4: Echo.java

```
package com.davidflanagan.examples.basics;

/**
 * This program prints out all its command-line arguments.
 **/
public class Echo {
    public static void main(String[] args) {
        int i = 0;                              // Initialize the loop variable
        while(i < args.length) {                // Loop until the end of array
            System.out.print(args[i] + " ");    // Print each argument out
            i++;                                // Increment the loop variable
        }
        System.out.println();                   // Terminate the line
    }
}
```

Echo in Reverse

Example 1-5 is a lot like the Echo program of Example 1-4, except that it prints out the command line arguments in reverse order, and it prints out the characters of each argument backwards. Thus, the Reverse program can be invoked as follows, with the following output:

```
% java com.davidflanagan.examples.basics.Reverse this is a test
tset a si siht
```

This program is interesting because its nested for loops count backward instead of forward. It is also interesting because it manipulates String objects by invoking methods of those objects and the syntax starts to get a little complicated. For example, consider the expression at the heart of this example:

```
args[i].charAt(j)
```

This expression first extracts the ith element of the args[] array. We know from the declaration of the array in the signature of the main() method that it is a

String array; that is, it contains String objects. (Strings are not a primitive type, like integers and boolean values in Java: they are full-fledged objects.) Once you extract the ith String from the array, you invoke the charAt() method of that object, passing the argument j. (The . character in the expression refers to a method or a field of an object.) As you can surmise from the name (and verify, if you want, in a reference manual), this method extracts the specified character from the String object. Thus, this expression extracts the jth character from the ith command-line argument. Armed with this understanding, you should be able to make sense of the rest of Example 1-5.

Example 1–5: Reverse.java

```java
package com.davidflanagan.examples.basics;

/**
 * This program echos the command-line arguments backwards.
 **/
public class Reverse {
    public static void main(String[] args) {
        // Loop backwards through the array of arguments
        for(int i = args.length-1; i >= 0; i--) {
            // Loop backwards through the characters in each argument
            for(int j=args[i].length()-1; j>=0; j--) {
                // Print out character j of argument i.
                System.out.print(args[i].charAt(j));
            }
            System.out.print(" ");  // Add a space at the end of each argument.
        }
        System.out.println();       // And terminate the line when we're done.
    }
}
```

FizzBuzz Switched

Example 1-6 is another version of the FizzBuzz game. This version uses a switch statement instead of nested if/else statements to determine what its output should be for each number. Take a look at the example first, then read the explanation of switch.

Example 1–6: FizzBuzz2.java

```java
package com.davidflanagan.examples.basics;

/**
 * This class is much like the FizzBuzz class, but uses a switch statement
 * instead of repeated if/else statements
 **/
public class FizzBuzz2 {
    public static void main(String[] args) {
        for(int i = 1; i <= 100; i++) { // count from 1 to 100
            switch(i % 35) {       // What's the remainder when divided by 35?
            case 0:                        // For multiples of 35...
                System.out.print("fizzbuzz "); // print "fizzbuzz".
                break;                         // Don't forget this statement!
            case 5: case 10: case 15:  // If the remainder is any of these
            case 20: case 25: case 30: // then the number is a multiple of 5
                System.out.print("fizz ");     // so print "fizz".
```

Example 1-6: FizzBuzz2.java (continued)

```
            break;
        case 7: case 14: case 21: case 28:   // For any multiple of 7...
            System.out.print("buzz ");       // print "buzz".
            break;
        default:                             // For any other number...
            System.out.print(i + " ");       // print the number.
            break;
        }
    }
    System.out.println();
    }
}
```

The `switch` statement acts like a switch operator at a busy railyard, switching a train (or the execution of a program) to the appropriate track (or piece of code) out of many potential tracks. A `switch` statement is often an alternative to repeated `if/else` statements, but it only works when the value being tested is a primitive integral type (e.g., not a `double` or a `String`) and when the value is being tested against constant values. The basic syntax of the `switch` statement is:

```
switch(expression) {
    statements
}
```

The `switch` statement is followed by an *expression* in parentheses and a block of code in curly braces. After evaluating the *expression*, the `switch` statement executes certain code within the block, depending on the integral value of the expression. How does the `switch` statement know where to start executing code for which values? This information is indicated by `case:` labels and with the special `default:` label. Each `case:` label is followed by an integral value. If the *expression* evaluates to that value, the `switch` statement begins executing code immediately following that `case:` label. If there is no `case:` label that matches the value of the expression, the `switch` statement starts executing code following the `default:` label, if there is one. If there is no `default:` label, `switch` does nothing.

The `switch` statement is an unusual one because each case doesn't have its own unique block of code. Instead, `case:` and `default:` labels simply mark various entry points into a single large block of code. Typically, each label is followed by several statements and then a `break` statement, which causes the flow of control to exit out of the block of the `switch` statement. If you don't use a `break` statement at the end of the code for a label, the execution of that case "drops through" to the next case. If you want to see this in action, remove the `break` statements from Example 1-6 and see what happens when you run the program. Forgetting `break` statements within a `switch` statement is a common source of bugs.

Computing Factorials

The factorial of an integer is the product of that number and all of the positive integers smaller than it. Thus the factorial of 5, written 5!, is the product 5*4*3*2*1, or 120. Example 1-7 shows a class, `Factorial`, that contains a method, `factorial()`, that computes factorials. This class is not a program in its own right, but the method it defines can be used by other programs. The method itself is quite simple; we'll see several variations of it in the following sections. As a exercise, you might think about how you could rewrite this example using a while loop instead of a for loop.

Example 1–7: Factorial.java

```
package com.davidflanagan.examples.basics;
/**
 * This class doesn't define a main() method, so it isn't a program by itself.
 * It does define a useful method that we can use in other programs, though.
 **/
public class Factorial {
    /** Compute and return x!, the factorial of x */
    public static int factorial(int x) {
        if (x < 0) throw new IllegalArgumentException("x must be >= 0");
        int fact = 1;
        for(int i = 2; i <= x; i++)    // loop
            fact *= i;                 // shorthand for: fact = fact * i;
        return fact;
    }
}
```

Recursive Factorials

Example 1-8 shows another way to compute factorials. This example uses a programming technique called *recursion*. Recursion happens when a method calls itself, or in other words, invokes itself recursively. The recursive algorithm for computing factorials relies on the fact that $n!$ is equal to $n*(n-1)!$. Computing factorials in this fashion is a classic example of recursion. It is not a particularly efficient technique in this case, but there are many important uses for recursion, and this example demonstrates that it is perfectly legal in Java. This example also switches from the int data type, which is a 32-bit integer, to the long data type, which is a 64-bit integer. Factorials become very large, very quickly, so the extra capacity of a long makes the factorial() method more useful.

Example 1–8: Factorial2.java

```
package com.davidflanagan.examples.basics;
/**
 * This class shows a recursive method to compute factorials.  This method
 * calls itself repeatedly based on the formula: n! = n * (n-1)!
 **/
public class Factorial2 {
    public static long factorial(long x) {
        if (x < 0) throw new IllegalArgumentException("x must be >= 0");
        if (x <= 1) return 1;                // Stop recursing here
        else return x * factorial(x-1);      // Recurse by calling ourselves
    }
}
```

Caching Factorials

Example 1-9 shows a refinement to our previous factorial examples. Factorials are ideal candidates for caching because they are slightly time consuming to compute, and more importantly, there are few factorials you actually can compute, due to the limitations of the `long` data type. So, in this examples, once a factorial is computed, its value is stored for future use.

Besides introducing the technique of caching, this example demonstrates several new things. First, it declares static fields within the `Factorial3` class:

```
static long[] table = new long[21];
static int last = 0;
```

A static field is kind of like a variable, but it retains its value between invocations of the `factorial()` method. This means that static fields can cache values computed in one invocation for use by the next invocation.

Second, this example shows how to create an array:

```
static long[] table = new long[21];
```

The first half of this line (before the = sign) declares the static field `table` to be an array of `long` values. The second half of the line actually creates an array of 21 `long` values using the `new` operator.

Finally, this example demonstrates how to throw an exception:

```
throw new IllegalArgumentException("Overflow; x is too large.");
```

An exception is a kind of Java object; it is created with the `new` keyword, just as the array was. When a program throws an exception object with the `throw` statement, it indicates that some sort of unexpected circumstance or error has arisen. When an exception is thrown, program control transfers to the nearest containing `catch` clause of a `try/catch` statement. This clause should contain code to handle the exceptional condition. If an exception is never caught, the program terminates with an error.

Example 1-9 throws an exception to notify the calling procedure that the argument it passed is too big or too small. The argument is too big if it is greater than 20, since we can't compute factorials beyond 20!. The argument is too small if it is less than 0, as factorial is only defined for nonnegative integers. Examples later in the chapter demonstrate how to catch and handle exceptions.

Example 1-9: Factorial3.java

```
package com.davidflanagan.examples.basics;

/**
 * This class computes factorials and caches the results in a table for reuse.
 * 20! is as high as we can go using the long data type, so check the argument
 * passed and "throw an exception" if it is too big or too small.
 **/
public class Factorial3 {
    // Create an array to cache values 0! through 20!.
    static long[] table = new long[21];
    // A "static initializer": initialize the first value in the array
```

Example 1–9: Factorial3.java (continued)

```
static { table[0] = 1; }  // factorial of 0 is 1.
// Remember the highest initialized value in the array
static int last = 0;

public static long factorial(int x) throws IllegalArgumentException {
    // Check if x is too big or too small.  Throw an exception if so.
    if (x >= table.length)   // ".length" returns length of any array
        throw new IllegalArgumentException("Overflow; x is too large.");
    if (x<0) throw new IllegalArgumentException("x must be non-negative.");

    // Compute and cache any values that are not yet cached.
    while(last < x) {
        table[last + 1] = table[last] * (last + 1);
        last++;
    }
    // Now return the cached factorial of x.
    return table[x];
}
}
```

Computing Big Factorials

In the previous section, we learned that 20! is the largest factorial that can fit in a 64-bit integer. But what if you want to compute 50! or 100!? The java.math.Big-Integer class represents arbitrarily large integer values and provides methods to perform arithmetic operations on these very large numbers. Example 1-10 uses the BigInteger class to compute factorials of any size. It also includes a simple main() method that defines a standalone test program for our factorial() method. This test program says, for example, that 50! is the following 65-digit number:

```
30414093201713378043612608166064768844377641568960512000000000000
```

Example 1-10 introduces the import statement. This statement must appear at the top of a Java file, before any class is defined (but after the package declaration). It provides a way to tell the compiler what classes you are using in a program. Once a class like java.math.BigInteger has been imported, you no longer have to type its full name; instead you can refer to it simply as BigInteger. You can also import an entire package of classes, as with the line:

```
import java.util.*
```

Note that the classes in the java.lang package are automatically imported, as are the classes of the current package, which, in this case, is com.davidflana-gan.examples.basics.

Example 1-10 uses the same caching technique Example 1-9 did. However, because there is no upper bound on the number of factorials that can be computed with this class, you can't use a fixed-sized array for the cache. Instead, use the java.util.ArrayList class, which is a utility class that implements an array-like data structure that can grow to be as large as you need it to be. Because an ArrayList is an object, rather than an array, you use such methods as size(), add(), and get() to work with it. By the same token, a BigInteger is an object rather than a primitive value, so you can't simply use the * operator to multiply BigInteger objects. Use the multiply() method instead.

Example 1-10: Factorial4.java

```
package com.davidflanagan.examples.basics;

// Import some other classes we'll use in this example.
// Once we import a class, we don't have to type its full name.
import java.math.BigInteger; // Import BigInteger from java.math package
import java.util.*; // Import all classes (including ArrayList) from java.util

/**
 * This version of the program uses arbitrary precision integers, so it does
 * not have an upper-bound on the values it can compute.  It uses an ArrayList
 * object to cache computed values instead of a fixed-size array.  An ArrayList
 * is like an array, but can grow to any size.  The factorial() method is
 * declared "synchronized" so that it can be safely used in multi-threaded
 * programs.  Look up java.math.BigInteger and java.util.ArrayList while
 * studying this class.  Prior to Java 1.2, use Vector instead of ArrayList.
 **/
public class Factorial4 {
    protected static ArrayList table = new ArrayList(); // create cache
    static { // Initialize the first element of the cache with !0 = 1.
        table.add(BigInteger.valueOf(1));
    }

    /** The factorial() method, using BigIntegers cached in a ArrayList */
    public static synchronized BigInteger factorial(int x) {
        if (x<0) throw new IllegalArgumentException("x must be non-negative.");
        for(int size = table.size(); size <= x; size++) {
            BigInteger lastfact = (BigInteger)table.get(size-1);
            BigInteger nextfact = lastfact.multiply(BigInteger.valueOf(size));
            table.add(nextfact);
        }
        return (BigInteger) table.get(x);
    }

    /**
     * A simple main() method that we can use as a standalone test program
     * for our factorial() method.
     **/
    public static void main(String[] args) {
        for(int i = 0; i <= 50; i++)
            System.out.println(i + "! = " + factorial(i));
    }
}
```

Handling Exceptions

Example 1-11 shows a program that uses the Integer.parseInt() method to convert a string specified on the command line to a number. The program then computes and prints the factorial of that number, using the Factorial4.factorial() method defined in Example 1-10. That much is simple; it takes only two lines of code. The rest of the example is concerned with exception handling, or, in other words, taking care of all of the things that can go wrong. You use the try/catch statement in Java for exception handling. The try clause encloses a block of code from which exceptions may be thrown. It is followed by any number of catch clauses; the code in each catch clause takes care of a particular type of exception.

In Example 1-11, there are three possible user-input errors that can prevent the program from executing normally. Therefore, the two main lines of program code are wrapped in a try clause followed by three catch clauses. Each clause notifies the user about a particular error by printing an appropriate message. This example is fairly straightforward. You may want to consult Chapter 2 of *Java in a Nutshell*, as it explains exceptions in more detail.

Example 1-11: FactComputer.java

```java
package com.davidflanagan.examples.basics;

/**
 * This program computes and displays the factorial of a number specified
 * on the command line.  It handles possible user input errors with try/catch.
 **/
public class FactComputer {
    public static void main(String[] args) {
        // Try to compute a factorial.
        // If something goes wrong, handle it in the catch clause below.
        try {
            int x = Integer.parseInt(args[0]);
            System.out.println(x + "! = " + Factorial4.factorial(x));
        }
        // The user forgot to specify an argument.
        // Thrown if args[0] is undefined.
        catch (ArrayIndexOutOfBoundsException e) {
            System.out.println("You must specify an argument");
            System.out.println("Usage: java FactComputer <number>");
        }
        // The argument is not a number.  Thrown by Integer.parseInt().
        catch (NumberFormatException e) {
            System.out.println("The argument you specify must be an integer");
        }
        // The argument is < 0.  Thrown by Factorial4.factorial()
        catch (IllegalArgumentException e) {
            // Display the message sent by the factorial() method:
            System.out.println("Bad argument: " + e.getMessage());
        }
    }
}
```

Interactive Input

Example 1-12 shows yet another program for computing factorials. Unlike Example 1-11, however, it doesn't just compute one factorial and quit. Instead, it prompts the user to enter a number, reads that number, prints its factorial, and then loops and asks the user to enter another number. The most interesting thing about this example is the technique it uses to read user input from the keyboard. It uses the readLine() method of a BufferedReader object to do this. The line that creates the BufferedReader may look confusing. For now, take it on faith that it works; you don't really need to understand how it works until we reach Chapter 3. Another feature of note in Example 1-12 is the use of the equals() method of the String object line to check whether the user has typed "quit".

The code for parsing the user's input and computing and printing the factorial is the same as in Example 1-11, and again, it is enclosed within a `try` clause. In Example 1-12, however, there is only a single `catch` clause to handle the possible exceptions. This one handles any exception object of type `Exception`. `Exception` is the superclass of all exception types, so this one `catch` clause is invoked no matter what type of exception is thrown.

Example 1-12: FactQuoter.java

```java
package com.davidflanagan.examples.basics;
import java.io.*; // Import all classes in java.io package.  Saves typing.

/**
 * This program displays factorials as the user enters values interactively
 **/
public class FactQuoter {
    public static void main(String[] args) throws IOException {
        // This is how we set things up to read lines of text from the user.
        BufferedReader in=new BufferedReader(new InputStreamReader(System.in));
        // Loop forever
        for(;;) {
            // Display a prompt to the user
            System.out.print("FactQuoter> ");
            // Read a line from the user
            String line = in.readLine();
            // If we reach the end-of-file,
            // or if the user types "quit", then quit
            if ((line == null) || line.equals("quit")) break;
            // Try to parse the line, and compute and print the factorial
            try {
                int x = Integer.parseInt(line);
                System.out.println(x + "! = " + Factorial4.factorial(x));
            }
            // If anything goes wrong, display a generic error message
            catch(Exception e) { System.out.println("Invalid Input"); }
        }
    }
}
```

Using a StringBuffer

One of the things you may have noticed about the `String` class that is used to represent strings in Java is that it is immutable. In other words, there are no methods that allow you to change the contents of a string. Methods that operate on a string return a new string, not a modified copy of the old one. When you want to operate on a string in place, you must use a `StringBuffer` object instead.

Example 1-13 demonstrates the use of a `StringBuffer`. It interactively reads a line of user input, as Example 1-12 did, and creates a `StringBuffer` to contain the line. The program then encodes each character of the line using the *rot13* substitution cipher, which simply "rotates" each letter 13 places through the alphabet, wrapping around from Z back to A when necessary. Because a `StringBuffer` object is being used, you can replace each character in the line one-by-one. A session with this Rot13Input program might look like this:

```
% java com.davidflanagan.examples.basics.Rot13Input
> Hello there.  Testing, testing!
Uryyb gurer.  Grfgvat, grfgvat!
> quit
%
```

The main() method of Example 1-13 calls another method, rot13(), to perform the actual encoding of a character. This method demonstrates the use of the primitive Java char type and character literals (i.e., characters that are used literally in a program within single quotes).

Example 1-13: Rot13Input.java

```java
package com.davidflanagan.examples.basics;
import java.io.*;  // We're doing input, so import I/O classes

/**
 * This program reads lines of text from the user, encodes them using the
 * trivial "Rot13" substitution cipher, and then prints out the encoded lines.
 **/
public class Rot13Input {
    public static void main(String[] args) throws IOException {
        // Get set up to read lines of text from the user
        BufferedReader in = new BufferedReader(new InputStreamReader(System.in));
        for(;;) {                                    // Loop forever
            System.out.print("> ");                  // Print a prompt
            String line = in.readLine();             // Read a line
            if ((line == null) || line.equals("quit")) // If EOF or "quit"...
                break;                               // ...break out of loop
            StringBuffer buf = new StringBuffer(line); // Use a StringBuffer
            for(int i = 0; i < buf.length(); i++)    // For each character...
                buf.setCharAt(i, rot13(buf.charAt(i)));// ..read, encode, store
            System.out.println(buf);                 // Print encoded line
        }
    }

    /**
     * This method performs the Rot13 substitution cipher.  It "rotates"
     * each letter 13 places through the alphabet.  Since the Latin alphabet
     * has 26 letters, this method both encodes and decodes.
     **/
    public static char rot13(char c) {
        if ((c >= 'A') && (c <= 'Z')) {  // For uppercase letters
            c += 13;                     // Rotate forward 13
            if (c > 'Z') c -= 26;        // And subtract 26 if necessary
        }
        if ((c >= 'a') && (c <= 'z')) {  // Do the same for lowercase letters
            c += 13;
            if (c > 'z') c -= 26;
        }
        return c;                        // Return the modified letter
    }
}
```

Sorting Numbers

Example 1-14 implements a simple (but inefficient) algorithm for sorting an array of numbers. This example doesn't introduce any new elements of Java syntax, but it is interesting because it reaches a real-world level of complexity. The sorting algorithm manipulates array entries using an if statement within a for loop that is itself within another for loop. You should take the time to study this short program carefully. Make sure that you understand exactly how it goes about sorting its array of numbers.

Example 1-14: SortNumbers.java

```java
package com.davidflanagan.examples.basics;

/**
 * This class demonstrates how to sort numbers using a simple algorithm
 **/
public class SortNumbers {
    /**
     * This is a very simple sorting algorithm that is not very efficient
     * when sorting large numbers of things
     **/
    public static void sort(double[] nums) {
        // Loop through each element of the array, sorting as we go.
        // Each time through, find the smallest remaining element, and move it
        // to the first unsorted position in the array.
        for(int i = 0; i < nums.length; i++) {
            int min = i;  // holds the index of the smallest element
            // find the smallest one between i and the end of the array
            for(int j = i; j < nums.length; j++) {
                if (nums[j] < nums[min]) min = j;
            }
            // Now swap the smallest one with element i.
            // This leaves all elements between 0 and i sorted.
            double tmp;
            tmp = nums[i];
            nums[i] = nums[min];
            nums[min] = tmp;
        }
    }

    /** This is a simple test program for the algorithm above */
    public static void main(String[] args) {
        double[] nums = new double[10];       // Create an array to hold numbers
        for(int i = 0; i < nums.length; i++)  // Generate random numbers
            nums[i] = Math.random() * 100;
        sort(nums);                           // Sort them
        for(int i = 0; i < nums.length; i++)  // Print them out
            System.out.println(nums[i]);
    }
}
```

Computing Primes

Example 1-15 computes the largest prime number less than a specified value, using the Sieve of Eratosthenes algorithm. The algorithm finds primes by eliminating multiples of all lower prime numbers. Like Example 1-14, this example introduces no new Java syntax, but is a nice, nontrivial program with which to end this chapter. The program may seem deceptively simple, but there's actually a fair bit going on, so be sure you understand how it is ruling out prime numbers.

Example 1-15: Sieve.java

```
package com.davidflanagan.examples.basics;

/**
 * This program computes prime numbers using the Sieve of Eratosthenes
 * algorithm: rule out multiples of all lower prime numbers, and anything
 * remaining is a prime.  It prints out the largest prime number less than
 * or equal to the supplied command-line argument.
 **/
public class Sieve {
    public static void main(String[] args) {
        // We will compute all primes less than the value specified on the
        // command line, or, if no argument, all primes less than 100.
        int max = 100;                          // Assign a default value
        try { max = Integer.parseInt(args[0]); } // Parse user-supplied arg
        catch (Exception e) {}                  // Silently ignore exceptions.

        // Create an array that specifies whether each number is prime or not.
        boolean[] isprime = new boolean[max+1];

        // Assume that all numbers are primes, until proven otherwise.
        for(int i = 0; i <= max; i++) isprime[i] = true;
        // However, we know that 0 and 1 are not primes.  Make a note of it.
        isprime[0] = isprime[1] = false;

        // To compute all primes less than max, we need to rule out
        // multiples of all integers less than the square root of max.
        int n = (int) Math.ceil(Math.sqrt(max));  // See java.lang.Math class

        // Now, for each integer i from 0 to n:
        //    If i is a prime, then none of its multiples are primes,
        //    so indicate this in the array.  If i is not a prime, then
        //    its multiples have already been ruled out by one of the
        //    prime factors of i, so we can skip this case.
        for(int i = 0; i <= n; i++) {
            if (isprime[i])                          // If i is a prime,
                for(int j = 2*i; j <= max; j = j + i) // loop through multiples
                    isprime[j] = false;              // they are not prime.
        }

        // Now go look for the largest prime:
        int largest;
        for(largest = max; !isprime[largest]; largest--) ;  // empty loop body
        // Output the result
        System.out.println("The largest prime less than or equal to " + max +
                           " is " + largest);
    }
}
```

Exercises

1-1. Write a program that counts from 1 to 15, printing out each number, and then counts backwards by twos back to 1, again printing out each number.

1-2. Each term of the Fibonacci series is formed by adding the previous two terms. What sort of series do you get if you add the previous three terms? Write a program to print the first 20 terms of this series.

1-3. Write a program that takes two numbers and a string as command-line arguments and prints out the substring of the string specified by the two numbers. For example:

```
% java Substring hello 1 3
```

should print out:

```
ell
```

Handle all possible exceptions that might arise because of bad input.

1-4. Write a program that interactively reads lines of input from the user and prints them back out, reversed. The program should exit if the user types "tiuq".

1-5. The SortNumbers class shows how you can sort an array of doubles. Write a program that uses this class to sort an array of 100 floating-point numbers. Then, interactively prompt the user for numeric input and display the next larger and next smaller number from the array. You should use an efficient binary search algorithm to find the desired position in the sorted array.

CHAPTER 2

Objects, Classes, and Interfaces

This chapter provides examples that highlight the object-oriented nature of Java. It is designed to be read in conjunction with Chapter 3 of *Java in a Nutshell*. That chapter offers a complete introduction to the object-oriented concepts and syntax you must understand to program in Java. The following paragraphs give a quick summary of Java's object-oriented terminology.

An *object* is a collection of data values, or *fields*, plus *methods* that operate on that data. The data type of an object is called a *class*; an object is often referred to as an *instance* of its class. The class defines the type of each field in an object, and it provides the methods that operate on data contained in an instance of the class. An object is created using the new operator, which invokes a *constructor* of the class to initialize the new object. The fields and methods of an object are accessed and invoked using the . operator.

Methods that operate on the fields of an object are known as instance methods. They are different from the static, or class, methods that we saw in Chapter 1, *Java Basics*. Class methods are declared static; they operate on the class itself, rather than on an individual instance of the class. Fields of a class may also be declared static, which makes them class fields instead of instance fields. While each object has its own copy of each instance field, there is only one copy of a class field and it is shared by all instances of the class.

The fields and methods of a class may have different visibility levels, including public, private, and protected. These different levels of visibility allow fields and methods to be used in different contexts. Every class has a *superclass*, from which it *inherits* fields and methods. When a class inherits from another class, it is called a *subclass* of that class. Classes in Java form a *class hierarchy*. The java.lang.Object class is root of this hierarchy; Object is the ultimate superclass of all other classes in Java.

An *interface* is a Java construct that defines methods, like a class, but doesn't provide any implementations for those methods. A class can *implement* an interface by defining an appropriate implementation for each method in the interface.

A Rectangle Class

Example 2-1 shows a class that represents a rectangle. Each instance of this Rect class has four fields, x1, y1, x2, and y2, that define the coordinates of the corners of the rectangle. The Rect class also defines a number of methods that operate on those coordinates.

Note the toString() method. This method overrides the toString() method of java.lang.Object, which is the implicit superclass of the Rect class. toString() produces a String that represents a Rect object. As you'll see, this method is quite useful for printing out Rect values.

Example 2-1: Rect.java

```
package com.davidflanagan.examples.classes;
/**
 * This class represents a rectangle.  Its fields represent the coordinates
 * of the corners of the rectangle.  Its methods define operations that can
 * be performed on Rect objects.
 **/
public class Rect {
    // These are the data fields of the class
    public int x1, y1, x2, y2;

    /**
     * The is the main constructor for the class.  It simply uses its arguments
     * to initialize each of the fields of the new object.  Note that it has
     * the same name as the class, and that it has no return value declared in
     * its signature.
     **/
    public Rect(int x1, int y1, int x2, int y2) {
        this.x1 = x1;
        this.y1 = y1;
        this.x2 = x2;
        this.y2 = y2;
    }

    /**
     * This is another constructor.  It defines itself in terms of the above
     **/
    public Rect(int width, int height) { this(0, 0, width, height); }

    /** This is yet another constructor. */
    public Rect() { this(0, 0, 0, 0); }

    /** Move the rectangle by the specified amounts */
    public void move(int deltax, int deltay) {
        x1 += deltax; x2 += deltax;
        y1 += deltay; y2 += deltay;
    }

    /** Test whether the specified point is inside the rectangle */
    public boolean isInside(int x, int y) {
        return ((x >= x1) && (x <= x2) && (y >= y1) && (y <= y2));
    }

    /**
     * Return the union of this rectangle with another.  I.e. return the
     * smallest rectangle that includes them both.
```

Example 2-1: Rect.java (continued)

```
    **/
    public Rect union(Rect r) {
        return new Rect((this.x1 < r.x1) ? this.x1 : r.x1,
                        (this.y1 < r.y1) ? this.y1 : r.y1,
                        (this.x2 > r.x2) ? this.x2 : r.x2,
                        (this.y2 > r.y2) ? this.y2 : r.y2);
    }

    /**
     * Return the intersection of this rectangle with another.
     * I.e. return their overlap.
     **/
    public Rect intersection(Rect r) {
        Rect result =  new Rect((this.x1 > r.x1) ? this.x1 : r.x1,
                                (this.y1 > r.y1) ? this.y1 : r.y1,
                                (this.x2 < r.x2) ? this.x2 : r.x2,
                                (this.y2 < r.y2) ? this.y2 : r.y2);
        if (result.x1 > result.x2) { result.x1 = result.x2 = 0; }
        if (result.y1 > result.y2) { result.y1 = result.y2 = 0; }
        return result;
    }

    /**
     * This is a method of our superclass, Object.  We override it so that
     * Rect objects can be meaningfully converted to strings, can be
     * concatenated to strings with the + operator, and can be passed to
     * methods like System.out.println()
     **/
    public String toString() {
        return "[" + x1 + "," + y1 + "; " + x2 + "," + y2 + "]";
    }
}
```

Testing the Rect Class

Example 2-2 is a standalone program named RectTest that puts the Rect class of Example 2-1 through its paces. Note the use of the new keyword and the Rect() constructor to create new Rect objects. The program uses the . operator to invoke methods of the Rect objects and to access their fields. The test program also relies implicitly on the toString() method of Rect when it uses the string concatenation operator (+) to create strings to be displayed to the user.

Example 2-2: RectTest.java

```
package com.davidflanagan.examples.classes;

/** This class demonstrates how you might use the Rect class */
public class RectTest {
    public static void main(String[] args) {
        Rect r1 = new Rect(1, 1, 4, 4);    // Create Rect objects
        Rect r2 = new Rect(2, 3, 5, 6);
        Rect u = r1.union(r2);             // Invoke Rect methods
        Rect i = r2.intersection(r1);

        if (u.isInside(r2.x1, r2.y1))   // Use Rect fields and invoke a method
            System.out.println("(" + r2.x1 + "," + r2.y1 +
```

Example 2–2: RectTest.java (continued)

```
                              ") is inside the union");

        // These lines implicitly call the Rect.toString() method
        System.out.println(r1 + " union " + r2 + " = " + u);
        System.out.println(r1 + " intersect " + r2 + " = " + i);
    }
}
```

A Rect Subclass

Example 2-3 is a simple subclass of the Rect class of Example 2-1. This DrawableRect class inherits the fields and methods of Rect and adds its own method, draw(), that draws a rectangle using a specified java.awt.Graphics object. (We'll see more of the Graphics object in Chapter 11, *Graphics*.) DrawableRect also defines a constructor that doesn'thing more than pass its arguments on to the corresponding Rect constructor. Note the use of the extends keyword to indicate that Rect is the superclass of DrawableRect.

Example 2–3: DrawableRect.java

```
package com.davidflanagan.examples.classes;
/**
 * This is a subclass of Rect that allows itself to be drawn on a screen.
 * It inherits all the fields and methods of Rect
 * It relies on the java.awt.Graphics object to perform the drawing.
 **/
public class DrawableRect extends Rect {
    /** The DrawableRect constructor just invokes the Rect() constructor */
    public DrawableRect(int x1, int y1, int x2, int y2) { super(x1,y1,x2,y2); }

    /** This is the new method defined by DrawableRect */
    public void draw(java.awt.Graphics g) {
        g.drawRect(x1, y1, (x2 - x1), (y2-y1));
    }
}
```

Another Subclass

Example 2-4 shows another subclass. ColoredRect is a subclass of DrawableRect (see Example 2-3), which makes it a sub-subclass of Rect (see Example 2-1). This class inherits the fields and methods of DrawableRect and of Rect (and of Object, which is the implicit superclass of Rect). ColoredRect adds two new fields that specify the border color and fill color of the rectangle when it is drawn. (These fields are of type java.awt.Color, which we'll learn about in Chapter 11.) The class also defines a new constructor that allows these fields to be initialized. Finally, ColoredRect overrides the draw() method of the DrawableRect class. The draw() method defined by ColoredRect draws a rectangle using the specified colors, rather than simply using the default colors as the method in DrawableRect did.

Example 2–4: ColoredRect.java

```java
package com.davidflanagan.examples.classes;
import java.awt.*;

/**
 * This class subclasses DrawableRect and adds colors to the rectangle it draws
 **/
public class ColoredRect extends DrawableRect {
    // These are new fields defined by this class.
    // x1, y1, x2, and y2 are inherited from our super-superclass, Rect.
    protected Color border, fill;

    /**
     * This constructor uses super() to invoke the superclass constructor, and
     * also does some initialization of its own.
     **/
    public ColoredRect(int x1, int y1, int x2, int y2,
                       Color border, Color fill)
    {
        super(x1, y1, x2, y2);
        this.border = border;
        this.fill = fill;
    }

    /**
     * This method overrides the draw() method of our superclass so that it
     * can make use of the colors that have been specified.
     **/
    public void draw(Graphics g) {
        g.setColor(fill);
        g.fillRect(x1, y1, (x2-x1), (y2-y1));
        g.setColor(border);
        g.drawRect(x1, y1, (x2-x1), (y2-y1));
    }
}
```

Complex Numbers

Example 2-5 shows the definition of a class that represents complex numbers. You may recall from algebra class that a complex number is the sum of a real number and an imaginary number. The imaginary number i is the square root of -1. This ComplexNumber class defines two double fields, which represent the real and imaginary parts of the number. These fields are declared private, which means they can be used only within the body of the class; they are inaccessible outside the class. Because the fields are inaccessible, the class defines two accessor methods, real() and imaginary(), that simply return their values. This technique of making fields private and defining accessor methods is called *encapsulation*. Encapsulation hides the implementation of a class from its users, which means that you can change the implementation without it affecting the users.

Notice that the ComplexNumber class doesn't define any methods, other than the constructor, that set the values of its fields. Once a ComplexNumber object is created, the number it represents can never be changed. This property is known as *immutability*; it is sometimes useful to design objects that are immutable like this.

ComplexNumber defines two add() methods and two multiply() methods that perform addition and multiplication of complex numbers. The difference between the two versions of each method is that one is an instance method and one is a class, or static, method. Consider the add() methods, for example. The instance method adds the value of the current instance of ComplexNumber to another specified ComplexNumber object. The class method doesn't have a current instance; it simply adds the values of two specified ComplexNumber objects. The instance method is invoked through an instance of the class, like this:

```
ComplexNumber sum = a.add(b);
```

The class method, however, is invoked through the class itself, rather than through an instance:

```
ComplexNumber sum = ComplexNumber.add(a, b);
```

Example 2-5: ComplexNumber.java

```
package com.davidflanagan.examples.classes;

/**
 * This class represents complex numbers, and defines methods for performing
 * arithmetic on complex numbers.
 **/
public class ComplexNumber {
    // These are the instance variables.  Each ComplexNumber object holds
    // two double values, known as x and y.  They are private, so they are
    // not accessible from outside this class.  Instead, they are available
    // through the real() and imaginary() methods below.
    private double x, y;

    /** This is the constructor.  It initializes the x and y variables */
    public ComplexNumber(double real, double imaginary) {
        this.x = real;
        this.y = imaginary;
    }

    /**
     * An accessor method.  Returns the real part of the complex number.
     * Note that there is no setReal() method to set the real part.  This means
     * that the ComplexNumber class is "immutable".
     **/
    public double real() { return x; }

    /** An accessor method.  Returns the imaginary part of the complex number */
    public double imaginary() { return y; }

    /** Compute the magnitude of a complex number */
    public double magnitude() { return Math.sqrt(x*x + y*y); }

    /**
     * This method converts a ComplexNumber to a string.  This is a method of
     * Object that we override so that complex numbers can be meaningfully
     * converted to strings, and so they can conveniently be printed out with
     * System.out.println() and related methods
     **/
    public String toString() { return "{" + x + "," + y + "}"; }

    /**
```

Example 2–5: ComplexNumber.java (continued)

```
 * This is a static class method.  It takes two complex numbers, adds
 * them, and returns the result as a third number.  Because it is static,
 * there is no "current instance" or "this" object.  Use it like this:
 * ComplexNumber c = ComplexNumber.add(a, b);
 **/
public static ComplexNumber add(ComplexNumber a, ComplexNumber b) {
    return new ComplexNumber(a.x + b.x, a.y + b.y);
}

/**
 * This is a non-static instance method by the same name.  It adds the
 * specified complex number to the current complex number.  Use it like
 * this:
 * ComplexNumber c = a.add(b);
 **/
public ComplexNumber add(ComplexNumber a) {
    return new ComplexNumber(this.x + a.x, this.y+a.y);
}

/** A static class method to multiply complex numbers */
public static ComplexNumber multiply(ComplexNumber a, ComplexNumber b) {
    return new ComplexNumber(a.x*b.x - a.y*b.y, a.x*b.y + a.y*b.x);
}

/** An instance method to multiply complex numbers */
public ComplexNumber multiply(ComplexNumber a) {
    return new ComplexNumber(x*a.x - y*a.y, x*a.y + y*a.x);
}
}
```

Computing Pseudo-Random Numbers

So far, all the classes we've defined have represented real-world objects. (A complex number is an abstract mathematical concept, but it's not too hard to think of it as a real-world object.) In some cases, however, you need to create a class that doesn't represent some kind of object, or even an abstract concept. Example 2-6, which defines a class that can compute pseudo-random numbers, is just this kind of class.

The Randomizer class obviously doesn't implement some kind of object. It turns out, however, that the simple algorithm used to generate pseudo-random numbers requires a state variable, seed, that stores the random-number seed. Because you need to keep track of some state, you can't simply define a static random() method, as you did for methods such as Factorial.factorial() in Chapter 1. When a method requires state to be saved between one invocation and the next, the method typically needs to be an instance method of an object that contains the necessary state, even if the object itself has no obvious real-world or abstract counterpart.

Thus, our Randomizer class defines a single instance variable, seed, that saves the necessary state for generating pseudo-random numbers. The other fields in Randomizer are declared static and final, which makes them constants in Java. In other words, for each static final field, there is a field associated with the class itself whose value never changes.

Example 2-6: Randomizer.java

```
package com.davidflanagan.examples.classes;
/**
 * This class defines methods for computing pseudo-random numbers, and defines
 * the state variable that needs to be maintained for use by those methods.
 **/
public class Randomizer {
    // Carefully chosen constants from the book "Numerical Recipes in C".
    // All "static final" fields are constants.
    static final int m = 233280;
    static final int a = 9301;
    static final int c = 49297;

    // The state variable maintained by each Randomizer instance
    int seed = 1;

    /**
     * The constructor for the Randomizer() class.  It must be passed some
     * arbitrary initial value or "seed" for its pseudo-randomness.
     **/
    public Randomizer(int seed) { this.seed = seed; }

    /**
     * This method computes a pseudo-random number between 0 and 1 using a very
     * simple algorithm.  Math.random() and java.util.Random are actually a lot
     * better at computing randomness.
     **/
    public float randomFloat() {
        seed = (seed * a + c) % m;
        return (float) Math.abs((float)seed/(float)m);
    }

    /**
     * This method computes a pseudo-random integer between 0 and specified
     * maximum.  It uses randomFloat() above.
     **/
    public int randomInt(int max) {
        return Math.round(max * randomFloat());
    }

    /**
     * This nested class is a simple test program: it prints 10 random ints.
     * Note how the Randomizer object is seeded using the current time.
     **/
    public static class Test {
        public static void main(String[] args) {
            Randomizer r = new Randomizer((int)new java.util.Date().getTime());
            for(int i = 0; i < 10; i++) System.out.println(r.randomInt(100));
        }
    }
}
```

Example 2-6 introduces an important new feature. The Randomizer class defines a static inner class named Test. This class, Randomizer.Test, contains a main() method and is thus a standalone program suitable for testing the Randomizer class. When you compile the *Randomizer.java* file, you get two class files,

Randomizer.class and *Randomizer$Test.class.* Running this nested Random-izer.Test class is a little tricky. You *ought* to be able to do so like this:

```
% java com.davidflanagan.examples.classes.Randomizer.Test
```

However, current versions of the Java SDK don't correctly map from the class name Randomizer.Test to the class file *Randomizer$Test.class.* So, to run the test program, you must invoke the Java interpreter using a $ character instead of a . character in the class name:

```
% java com.davidflanagan.examples.classes.Randomizer$Test
```

On a Unix system, however, you should be aware that the $ character has special significance and must be escaped. Therefore, on such a system, you have to type:

```
% java com.davidflanagan.examples.classes.Randomizer\$Test
```

or:

```
% java 'com.davidflanagan.examples.classes.Randomizer$Test'
```

You need to use this technique whenever you need to run a Java program that is defined as an inner class.

Computing Statistics

Example 2-7 shows a class that computes some simple statistics for a set of numbers. As numbers are passed to the addDatum() method, the Averager class updates its internal state so that its other methods can easily return the average and standard deviation of the numbers that have been passed to it so far. Like Randomizer, the Averager class doesn't represent any kind of real-world object or abstract concept. Nevertheless, Averager does maintains some state (this time as private fields), and it has methods that operate on that state, so it is implemented as a class.

Like Example 2-6, Example 2-7 defines an inner Test class that contains a main() method that implements a test program for Averager.

Example 2–7: Averager.java

```
package com.davidflanagan.examples.classes;
/**
 * A class to compute the running average of numbers passed to it
 **/
public class Averager {
    // Private fields to hold the current state.
    private int n = 0;
    private double sum = 0.0, sumOfSquares = 0.0;

    /**
     * This method adds a new datum into the average.
     **/
    public void addDatum(double x) {
        n++;
        sum += x;
        sumOfSquares += x * x;
    }
```

Example 2-7: Averager.java (continued)

```
/** This method returns the average of all numbers passed to addDatum() */
public double getAverage() { return sum / n; }

/** This method returns the standard deviation of the data */
public double getStandardDeviation() {
    return Math.sqrt(((sumOfSquares - sum*sum/n)/n));
}

/** This method returns the number of numbers passed to addDatum() */
public double getNum() { return n; }

/** This method returns the sum of all numbers passed to addDatum() */
public double getSum() { return sum; }

/** This method returns the sum of the squares of all numbers. */
public double getSumOfSquares() { return sumOfSquares; }

/** This method resets the Averager object to begin from scratch */
public void reset() { n = 0; sum = 0.0; sumOfSquares = 0.0; }

/**
 * This nested class is a simple test program we can use to check that
 * our code works okay.
 **/
public static class Test {
    public static void main(String args[]) {
        Averager a = new Averager();
        for(int i = 1; i <= 100; i++) a.addDatum(i);
        System.out.println("Average: " + a.getAverage());
        System.out.println("Standard Deviation: " +
                            a.getStandardDeviation());
        System.out.println("N: " + a.getNum());
        System.out.println("Sum: " + a.getSum());
        System.out.println("Sum of squares: " + a.getSumOfSquares());
    }
}
}
```

A Linked List Class

Example 2-8 displays a class, LinkedList, that implements a linked-list data structure. The example also defines a Linkable interface. If an object is to be "linked" to a LinkedList, the class of that object must implement the Linkable interface. Recall that an interface defines methods but doesn't provide any bodies for those methods. A class implements an interface by providing an implementation for each method in the interface and by using the implements keyword in its declaration. Any instance of a class that implements Linkable can be treated as an instance of Linkable. A LinkedList object treats all objects in its list as instances of Linkable, and therefore doesn't need to know anything about their true types.

Note that this example was written for Java 1.1. Java 1.2 introduces a similar, but unrelated class: java.util.LinkedList. This new LinkedList collection class is more useful than the class developed in Example 2-8, but Example 2-8 is a better example of the use of interfaces.

LinkedList defines a single state field, head, that refers to the first Linkable item in the list. The class also defines a number of methods for adding items to and removing items from the list. Note that the Linkable interface is nested within the LinkedList class. While this is a convenient and useful way to define the interface, it is by no means necessary to nest things in this way. Linkable could just as easily be defined as an ordinary, top-level interface.

The LinkedList class also defines an inner Test class that, once again, is a stand-alone program for testing the class. In this example, however, the inner Test class itself contains an inner class, LinkableInteger. This class implements Linkable; instances of it are linked into a list by the test program.

Example 2-8: LinkedList.java

```
package com.davidflanagan.examples.classes;

/**
 * This class implements a linked list that can contain any type of object
 * that implements the nested Linkable interface.  Note that the methods are
 * all synchronized, so that it can safely be used by multiple threads at
 * the same time.
 **/
public class LinkedList {
    /**
     * This interface defines the methods required by any object that can be
     * linked into a linked list.
     **/
    public interface Linkable {
        public Linkable getNext();      // Returns the next element in the list
        public void setNext(Linkable node); // Sets the next element in the list
    }

    // This class has a default constructor: public LinkedList() {}

    /** This is the only field of the class.  It holds the head of the list */
    Linkable head;

    /** Return the first node in the list */
    public synchronized Linkable getHead() { return head; }

    /** Insert a node at the beginning of the list */
    public synchronized void insertAtHead(Linkable node) {
        node.setNext(head);
        head = node;
    }

    /** Insert a node at the end of the list */
    public synchronized void insertAtTail(Linkable node) {
        if (head == null) head = node;
        else {
            Linkable p, q;
            for(p = head; (q = p.getNext()) != null; p = q) /* no body */;
            p.setNext(node);
        }
    }

    /** Remove and return the node at the head of the list */
    public synchronized Linkable removeFromHead() {
        Linkable node = head;
```

Example 2–8: LinkedList.java (continued)

```
            if (node != null) {
                head = node.getNext();
                node.setNext(null);
            }
            return node;
    }

    /** Remove and return the node at the end of the list */
    public synchronized Linkable removeFromTail() {
        if (head == null) return null;
        Linkable p = head, q = null, next = head.getNext();
        if (next == null) {
            head = null;
            return p;
        }
        while((next = p.getNext()) != null) {
            q = p;
            p = next;
        }
        q.setNext(null);
        return p;
    }

    /**
     * Remove a node matching the specified node from the list.
     * Use equals() instead of == to test for a matched node.
     **/
    public synchronized void remove(Linkable node) {
        if (head == null) return;
        if (node.equals(head)) {
            head = head.getNext();
            return;
        }
        Linkable p = head, q = null;
        while((q = p.getNext()) != null) {
            if (node.equals(q)) {
                p.setNext(q.getNext());
                return;
            }
            p = q;
        }
    }

    /** This nested class defines a main() method that tests LinkedList */
    public static class Test {
        /**
         * This is a test class that implements the Linkable interface
         **/
        static class LinkableInteger implements Linkable {
            int i;           // The data contained in the node
            Linkable next;   // A reference to the next node in the list
            public LinkableInteger(int i) { this.i = i; }  // Constructor
            public Linkable getNext() { return next; }      // Part of Linkable
            public void setNext(Linkable node) { next = node; } // Linkable
            public String toString() { return i + ""; }    // For easy printing
            public boolean equals(Object o) {              // For comparison
                if (this == o) return true;
                if (!(o instanceof LinkableInteger)) return false;
```

Example 2–8: LinkedList.java (continued)

```
                if (((LinkableInteger)o).i == this.i) return true;
                return false;
            }
    }


    /**
     * The test program.  Insert some nodes, remove some nodes, then
     * print out all elements in the list.  It should print out the
     * numbers 4, 6, 3, 1, and 5
     **/
    public static void main(String[] args) {
        LinkedList ll = new LinkedList();            // Create a list
        ll.insertAtHead(new LinkableInteger(1));  // Insert some stuff
        ll.insertAtHead(new LinkableInteger(2));
        ll.insertAtHead(new LinkableInteger(3));
        ll.insertAtHead(new LinkableInteger(4));
        ll.insertAtTail(new LinkableInteger(5));
        ll.insertAtTail(new LinkableInteger(6));
        System.out.println(ll.removeFromHead()); // Remove and print a node
        System.out.println(ll.removeFromTail()); // Remove and print again
        ll.remove(new LinkableInteger(2));         // Remove another one

        // Now print out the contents of the list.
        for(Linkable l = ll.getHead(); l != null; l = l.getNext())
            System.out.println(l);
    }
    }
}
```

Advanced Sorting

In Chapter 1, we saw an example of a simple, unsophisticated algorithm for sorting an array of numbers. Example 2-9 defines a class, Sorter, that supports more efficient and general-purpose sorting. Sorter defines a multitude of static sort() methods that each take slightly different arguments. A number of these methods sort strings in various ways, while others sort other types of objects. The last of these sort() methods implements the quicksort algorithm to efficiently sort an array of objects. All other methods are variants; each one ultimately invokes the general sorting method.

The sort() methods that sort strings take advantage of some of the internationalization features introduced in Java 1.1. In particular, they use the java.util.Locale, java.text.Collator, and java.text.CollationKey classes. We examine these classes in more detail in Chapter 7, *Internationalization*.

To sort an array of objects, Sorter needs some way to compare two objects to determine which one should come before the other in the sorted array. Sorter defines two nested interfaces, Sorter.Comparer and Sorter.Comparable, that provide two different ways of implementing this comparison. You can sort arbitrary objects by passing a Comparer object to one of the sort() methods. A Comparer object defines a compare() method that compares arbitrary objects. Alternatively, the object classes you need to sort can implement the Sorter.Comparable interface. In this case, the objects themselves have compareTo() methods, so they can be compared directly.

Note that in Java 1.2 and later, the java.util.Arrays class defines a number of sort() methods for sorting arrays of objects or primitive values. Also, java.util.Collections defines sort() methods to sort java.util.List objects (these classes are part of the Java collection framework introduced in Java 1.2). These classes and methods are preferred over the sorting methods developed here. Nevertheless, Example 2-9 is still an interesting and useful example. Note also that the sorting methods in Arrays and Collections use java.util.Comparator and java.lang.Comparable interfaces, which are similar to the Comparer and Comparable interfaces in this example.

Example 2-9 rounds out this chapter. If you've skimmed ahead and looked at the program, you probably noticed that it is a rather complex example. As such, it is worth studying carefully. In particular, the program makes heavy use of inner classes, so you should be sure you understand how inner classes work before you examine this code in detail. As usual, there is an inner Test class at the end of the example, but inner classes and interfaces are used throughout the program.

Example 2-9: Sorter.java

```java
package com.davidflanagan.examples.classes;
// These are some classes we need for internationalized string sorting
import java.text.Collator;
import java.text.CollationKey;
import java.util.Locale;

/**
 * This class defines a bunch of static methods for efficiently sorting
 * arrays of Strings or other objects.  It also defines two interfaces that
 * provide two different ways of comparing objects to be sorted.
 **/
public class Sorter {
    /**
     * This interface defines the compare() method used to compare two objects.
     * To sort objects of a given type, you must provide a Comparer
     * object with a compare() method that orders those objects as desired
     **/
    public static interface Comparer {
        /**
         * Compare objects, return a value that indicates their relative order:
         * if (a > b) return > 0;
         * if (a == b) return 0;
         * if (a < b) return < 0.
         **/
        public int compare(Object a, Object b);
    }

    /**
     * This is an alternative interface that can be used to order objects.  If
     * a class implements this Comparable interface, then any two instances of
     * that class can be directly compared by invoking the compareTo() method.
     **/
    public static interface Comparable {
        /**
         * Compare objects, return a value that indicates their relative order:
         * if (this > other) return > 0
```

Example 2-9: Sorter.java (continued)

```
        * if (this == other) return 0
        * if (this < other) return < 0
        **/
       public int compareTo(Object other);
}


/**
 * This is an internal Comparer object (created with an anonymous class)
 * that compares two ASCII strings.
 * It is used in the sortAscii methods below.
 **/
private static Comparer ascii_comparer = new Comparer() {
        public int compare(Object a, Object b) {
             return ((String)a).compareTo((String)b);
        }
    };


/**
 * This is another internal Comparer object.  It is used to compare two
 * Comparable objects.  It is used by the sort() methods below that take
 * Comparable objects as arguments instead of arbitrary objects
 **/
private static Comparer comparable_comparer = new Comparer() {
        public int compare(Object a, Object b) {
             return ((Comparable)a).compareTo(b);
        }
    };


/** Sort an array of ASCII strings into ascending order */
public static void sortAscii(String[] a) {
    // Note use of the ascii_comparer object
    sort(a, null, 0, a.length-1, true, ascii_comparer);
}


/**
 * Sort a portion of an array of ASCII strings into ascending or descending
 * order, depending on the argument up
 **/
public static void sortAscii(String[] a, int from, int to, boolean up) {
    // Note use of the ascii_comparer object
    sort(a, null, from, to, up, ascii_comparer);
}


/** Sort an array of ASCII strings into ascending order, ignoring case */
public static void sortAsciiIgnoreCase(String[] a) {
    sortAsciiIgnoreCase(a, 0, a.length-1, true);
}


/**
 * Sort an portion of an array of ASCII strings, ignoring case.  Sort into
 * ascending order if up is true, otherwise sort into descending order.
 **/
public static void sortAsciiIgnoreCase(String[] a, int from, int to,
                                       boolean up) {
    if ((a == null) || (a.length < 2)) return;
    // Create a secondary array of strings that contains lowercase versions
    // of all the specified strings.
    String b[] = new String[a.length];
```

Example 2-9: Sorter.java (continued)

```
            for(int i = 0; i < a.length; i++) b[i] = a[i].toLowerCase();
            // Sort that secondary array, and rearrange the original array
            // in exactly the same way, resulting in a case-insensitive sort.
            // Note the use of the ascii_comparer object
            sort(b, a, from, to, up, ascii_comparer);
        }


        /**
         * Sort an array of strings into ascending order, using the correct
         * collation order for the default locale
         **/
        public static void sort(String[] a) {
            sort(a, 0, a.length-1, true, false, null);
        }


        /**
         * Sort a portion of an array of strings, using the collation order of
         * the default locale.  If up is true, sort ascending, otherwise, sort
         * descending.  If ignorecase is true, ignore the capitalization of letters
         **/
        public static void sort(String[] a, int from, int to,
                               boolean up, boolean ignorecase) {
            sort(a, from, to, up, ignorecase, null);
        }


        /**
         * Sort a portion of an array of strings, using the collation order of
         * the specified locale.  If up is true, sort ascending, otherwise, sort
         * descending.  If ignorecase is true, ignore the capitalization of letters
         **/
        public static void sort(String[] a, int from, int to,
                               boolean up, boolean ignorecase,
                               Locale locale) {
            // Don't sort if we don't have to
            if ((a == null) || (a.length < 2)) return;

            // The java.text.Collator object does internationalized string compares
            // Create one for the specified, or the default locale.
            Collator c;
            if (locale == null) c = Collator.getInstance();
            else c = Collator.getInstance(locale);

            // Specify whether or not case should be considered in the sort.
            // Note: this option does not seem to work correctly in JDK 1.1.1
            // using the default American English locale.
            if (ignorecase) c.setStrength(Collator.SECONDARY);

            // Use the Collator object to create an array of CollationKey objects
            // that correspond to each of the strings.
            // Comparing CollationKeys is much quicker than comparing Strings
            CollationKey[] b = new CollationKey[a.length];
            for(int i = 0; i < a.length; i++) b[i] = c.getCollationKey(a[i]);

            // Now define a Comparer object to compare collation keys, using an
            // anonymous class.
            Comparer comp = new Comparer() {
                    public int compare(Object a, Object b) {
                        return ((CollationKey)a).compareTo((CollationKey)b);
```

Example 2-9: Sorter.java (continued)

```
                }
            };

        // Finally, sort the array of CollationKey objects, rearranging the
        // original array of strings in exactly the same way.
        sort(b, a, from, to, up, comp);
    }

    /** Sort an array of Comparable objects into ascending order */
    public static void sort(Comparable[] a) {
        sort(a, null, 0, a.length-1, true);
    }

    /**
     * Sort a portion of an array of Comparable objects.  If up is true,
     * sort into ascending order, otherwise sort into descending order.
     **/
    public static void sort(Comparable[] a, int from, int to, boolean up) {
        sort(a, null, from, to, up, comparable_comparer);
    }

    /**
     * Sort a portion of array a of Comparable objects.  If up is true,
     * sort into ascending order, otherwise sort into descending order.
     * Re-arrange the array b in exactly the same way as a.
     **/
    public static void sort(Comparable[] a, Object[] b,
                            int from, int to, boolean up) {
        sort(a, b, from, to, up, comparable_comparer);
    }

    /**
     * Sort an array of arbitrary objects into ascending order, using the
     * comparison defined by the Comparer object c
     **/
    public static void sort(Object[] a, Comparer c) {
        sort(a, null, 0, a.length-1, true, c);
    }

    /**
     * Sort a portion of an array of objects, using the comparison defined by
     * the Comparer object c.  If up is true, sort into ascending order,
     * otherwise sort into descending order.
     **/
    public static void sort(Object[] a, int from, int to, boolean up,
                            Comparer c)
    {
        sort(a, null, from, to, up, c);
    }

    /**
     * This is the main sort() routine. It performs a quicksort on the elements
     * of array a between the element from and the element to.  The up argument
     * specifies whether the elements should be sorted into ascending (true) or
     * descending (false) order.  The Comparer argument c is used to perform
     * comparisons between elements of the array.  The elements of the array b
     * are reordered in exactly the same way as the elements of array a are.
     **/
```

Example 2-9: Sorter.java (continued)

```java
public static void sort(Object[] a, Object[] b,
                        int from, int to,
                        boolean up, Comparer c)
{
    // If there is nothing to sort, return
    if ((a == null) || (a.length < 2)) return;

    // This is the basic quicksort algorithm, stripped of frills that can
    // make it faster but even more confusing than it already is.  You
    // should understand what the code does, but don't have to understand
    // just why it is guaranteed to sort the array...
    // Note the use of the compare() method of the Comparer object.
    int i = from, j = to;
    Object center = a[(from + to) / 2];
    do {
        if (up) {  // an ascending sort
            while((i < to) && (c.compare(center, a[i]) > 0)) i++;
            while((j > from) && (c.compare(center, a[j]) < 0)) j--;
        } else {    // a descending sort
            while((i < to) && (c.compare(center, a[i]) < 0)) i++;
            while((j > from) && (c.compare(center, a[j]) > 0)) j--;
        }
        if (i < j) {
            Object tmp = a[i];  a[i] = a[j];  a[j] = tmp; // swap elements
            if (b != null) { tmp = b[i]; b[i] = b[j]; b[j] = tmp; } // swap
        }
        if (i <= j) { i++; j--; }
    } while(i <= j);
    if (from < j) sort(a, b, from, j, up, c); // recursively sort the rest
    if (i < to) sort(a, b, i, to, up, c);
}

/**
 * This nested class defines a test program that demonstrates several
 * ways to use the Sorter class to sort ComplexNumber objects
 **/
public static class Test {
    /**
     * This subclass of ComplexNumber implements the Comparable interface
     * and defines a compareTo() method for comparing complex numbers.
     * It compares numbers based on their magnitude. I.e. on their distance
     * from the origin.
     **/
    static class SortableComplexNumber extends ComplexNumber
        implements Sorter.Comparable {
        public SortableComplexNumber(double x, double y) { super(x, y); }
        public int compareTo(Object other) {
            return sign(this.magnitude()-((ComplexNumber)other).magnitude());
        }
    }

    /** A a test program that sorts complex numbers in various ways. */
    public static void main(String[] args) {
        // Define an array of SortableComplexNumber objects.  Initialize it
        // to contain random complex numbers.
        SortableComplexNumber[] a = new SortableComplexNumber[5];
        for(int i = 0; i < a.length; i++)
            a[i] = new SortableComplexNumber(Math.random()*10,
```

Example 2–9: Sorter.java (continued)

```
                                          Math.random()*10);

        // Now sort it using the SortableComplexNumber compareTo() method,
        // which sorts by magnitude, and print the results out.
        System.out.println("Sorted by magnitude:");
        Sorter.sort(a);
        for(int i = 0; i < a.length; i++) System.out.println(a[i]);

        // Sort the complex numbers again, using a Comparer object that
        // compares them based on the sum of their real and imaginary parts
        System.out.println("Sorted by sum of real and imaginary parts:");
        Sorter.sort(a, new Sorter.Comparer() {
                public int compare(Object a, Object b) {
                    ComplexNumber i = (ComplexNumber)a;
                    ComplexNumber j = (ComplexNumber)b;
                    return sign((i.real() + i.imaginary()) -
                                (j.real() + j.imaginary()));
                }
            });
        for(int i = 0; i < a.length; i++) System.out.println(a[i]);

        // Sort them again using a Comparer object that compares their real
        // parts, and then their imaginary parts
        System.out.println("Sorted descending by real, then imaginary:");
        Sorter.sort(a, 0, a.length-1, false, new Sorter.Comparer() {
                public int compare(Object a, Object b) {
                    ComplexNumber i = (ComplexNumber) a;
                    ComplexNumber j = (ComplexNumber) b;
                    double result = i.real() - j.real();
                    if (result == 0) result = i.imaginary()-j.imaginary();
                    return sign(result);
                }
            });
        for(int i = 0; i < a.length; i++) System.out.println(a[i]);
    }

    /** This is a convenience routine used by comparison routines */
    public static int sign(double x) {
        if (x > 0) return 1;
        else if (x < 0) return -1;
        else return 0;
    }
  }
}
```

Exercises

2-1. Write a `Circle` class that is similar to the `Rect` class. Define a `move()` method and an `isInside()` method. (Recall that a circle is defined as all points within a given radius from the center. Test for insideness by using the Pythagorean theorem to compute the distance between a point and the center of the circle.) Also, define a `boundingBox()` method that returns the smallest `Rect` that encloses the complete `Circle`. Write a simple program to test the methods you've implemented.

2-2. Write a class that represents a person's mailing address. It should have separate fields for the name, street address, city, state, and ZIP code. Define a toString() method that produces nicely formatted output.

2-3. Using the Sort.Comparer and/or the Sort.Comparable interfaces, write a static search() method for a class named Search that performs an efficient binary search for a specified object within a sorted array of objects. If the object is found in the array, search() should return the array index at which it is located. Otherwise, it should return –1.

CHAPTER 3

Input/Output

A computer program isn't much good unless it can communicate with the outside world. This communication often takes the form of input/output (I/O); I/O capabilities are a fundamental feature of any programming platform. In Java, I/O is done with the classes and interfaces of the java.io package. This chapter demonstrates many of the input/output capabilities of java.io. The examples here show you how to:

- Read and write files

- List directories and obtain file size and date information

- Use various Java stream classes

- Define customized stream subclasses

The techniques introduced in this chapter are also used in other places in this book. We'll see many examples that use streams for input and output in Chapter 5, *Networking*, and we'll see a specialized kind of I/O in Chapter 9, *Object Serialization*.

Files and Streams

One of the commonly used classes in the java.io package is File. This class is somewhat misleadingly named, as it represents a filename (or directory name), rather than a file itself. Because files (and directories) have different naming conventions under different operating systems, Java provides the File class to try to hide some of those differences. The File class also defines various methods for operating on files as a whole: deleting files, creating directories, listing directories, querying the size and modification time of a file, and so on.

While the File class provides methods to manipulate directories and the files within those directories, it doesn't provide any methods that manipulate the contents of the files. In other words, it doesn't provide any way to read or write the bytes or characters that are contained in files. In Java, sequential file I/O is performed through a stream abstraction. (Random-access file I/O is performed with the RandomAccessFile class, but sequential I/O is much more common.)

A *stream* is simply an object from which data can be read sequentially or to which data can be written sequentially. The bulk of the java.io package consists stream classes: there are 40 of them. InputStream and OutputStream and their respective subclasses are objects for reading and writing streams of bytes, while Reader and Writer and their subclasses are objects for reading and writing streams of Unicode characters. In addition to these stream classes, the java.util.zip package defines another eight input and output byte streams for data compression and decompression. Table 3-1 through Table 3-4 summarize the stream classes available in java.io and java.util.zip.

Table 3-1. Byte Input Streams

Byte Input Stream	Description
BufferedInputStream	Reads a buffer of bytes from an InputStream, and then returns bytes from the buffer, making small reads more efficient.
ByteArrayInputStream	Reads bytes sequentially from an array.
CheckedInputStream	This java.util.zip class computes a checksum of the bytes it reads from an InputStream.
DataInputStream	Reads binary representations of Java primitive types from an InputStream.
FileInputStream	Reads bytes sequentially from a file.
FilterInputStream	The superclass of byte input stream filter classes.
GZIPInputStream	This java.util.zip class uncompresses GZIP-compressed bytes it reads from an InputStream.
InflaterInputStream	The superclass of GZIPInputStream and ZipInputStream.
InputStream	The superclass of all byte input streams.
LineNumberInputStream	This class is deprecated as of Java 1.1; use LineNumberReader instead.
ObjectInputStream	Reads binary representations of Java objects and primitive values from a byte stream. This class is used for the deserialization of objects.
PipedInputStream	Reads bytes written to the PipedOutputStream to which it is connected. Used in multithreaded programs.
PushbackInputStream	Adds a fixed-size pushback buffer to an input stream, so that bytes can be unread. Useful with some parsers.
SequenceInputStream	Reads bytes sequentially from two or more input streams, as if they were a single stream.

Table 3-1. Byte Input Streams (continued)

Byte Input Stream	Description
StringBufferInputStream	This class is deprecated as of Java 1.1; use StringReader instead.
ZipInputStream	This java.util.zip class uncompresses entries in a ZIP file.

Table 3-2. Character Input Streams

Character Input Stream	Description
BufferedReader	Reads a buffer of characters from a Reader, and then returns characters from the buffer, making small reads more efficient.
CharArrayReader	Reads characters sequentially from an array.
FileReader	Reads characters sequentially from a file. An InputStreamReader subclass that reads from an automatically-created FileInputStream.
FilterReader	The superclass of character input stream filter classes.
InputStreamReader	Reads characters from a byte input stream. Converts bytes to characters using the encoding of the default locale, or a specified encoding.
LineNumberReader	Reads lines of text and keeps track of how many have been read.
PipedReader	Reads characters written to the PipedWriter to which it is connected. Used in multithreaded programs.
PushbackReader	Adds a fixed-size pushback buffer to a Reader, so that characters can be unread. Useful with some parsers.
Reader	The superclass of all character input streams.
StringReader	Reads characters sequentially from a string.

Table 3-3. Byte Output Streams

Byte Output Stream	Description
BufferedOutputStream	Buffers byte output for efficiency; writes to an OutputStream only when the buffer fills up.
ByteArrayOutputStream	Writes bytes sequentially into an array.
CheckedOutputStream	This java.util.zip class computes a checksum of the bytes it writes to an OutputStream.

Table 3-3. Byte Output Streams (continued)

Byte Output Stream	Description
DataOutputStream	Writes binary representations of Java primitive types to an OutputStream.
DeflaterOutputStream	The superclass of GZIPOutputStream and ZipOutputStream.
FileOutputStream	Writes bytes sequentially to a file.
FilterOutputStream	The superclass of all byte output stream filters.
GZIPOutputStream	This java.util.zip class outputs a GZIP-compressed version of the bytes written to it.
ObjectOutputStream	Writes binary representations of Java objects and primitive values to an OutputStream. Used for the serialization of objects.
OutputStream	The superclass of all byte output streams.
PipedOutputStream	Writes bytes to the PipedInputStream to which it is connected. Used in multithreaded programs.
PrintStream	Writes a textual representation of Java objects and primitive values. Deprecated except for use by the standard output stream System.out as of Java 1.1. In other contexts, use PrintWriter instead.
ZipOutputStream	This java.util.zip class compresses entries in a ZIP file.

Table 3-4. Character Output Streams

Character Output Stream	Description
BufferedWriter	Buffers output for efficiency; writes characters to a Writer only when the buffer fills up.
CharArrayWriter	Writes characters sequentially into an array.
FileWriter	Writes characters sequentially to a file. A subclass of OutputStreamWriter that automatically creates a FileOutputStream.
FilterWriter	The superclass of all character output stream filters.
OutputStreamWriter	Writes characters to a byte output stream. Converts characters to bytes using the encoding of the default locale, or a specified encoding.
PipedWriter	Writes characters to the PipedReader to which it is connected. Used in multithreaded programs.
PrintWriter	Writes textual representations of Java objects and primitive values to a Writer.

Input/Output

Table 3–4. *Character Output Streams (continued)*

Character Output Stream	Description
StringWriter	Writes characters sequentially into an internally-created StringBuffer.
Writer	The superclass of all character output streams.

Working with Files

Example 3-1 is a relatively short program that deletes a file or directory specified on the command line. It demonstrates a number of the methods of the File class—methods that operate on a file (or directory) as a whole, but not on its contents. Other useful File methods include getParent(), length(), mkdir(), and renameTo().

Example 3–1: Delete.java

```
package com.davidflanagan.examples.io;
import java.io.*;

/**
 * This class is a static method delete() and a standalone program that
 * deletes a specified file or directory.
 **/
public class Delete {
    /**
     * This is the main() method of the standalone program.  After checking
     * its arguments, it invokes the Delete.delete() method to do the deletion
     **/
    public static void main(String[] args) {
        if (args.length != 1) {     // Check command-line arguments
            System.err.println("Usage: java Delete <file or directory>");
            System.exit(0);
        }
        // Call delete() and display any error messages it throws.
        try { delete(args[0]); }
        catch (IllegalArgumentException e) {
            System.err.println(e.getMessage());
        }
    }

    /**
     * The static method that does the deletion.  Invoked by main(), and
     * designed for use by other programs as well.  It first makes sure that
     * the specified file or directory is deleteable before attempting to
     * delete it.  If there is a problem, it throws an
     * IllegalArgumentException.
     **/
    public static void delete(String filename) {
        // Create a File object to represent the filename
        File f = new File(filename);

        // Make sure the file or directory exists and isn't write protected
        if (!f.exists()) fail("Delete: no such file or directory: " +filename);
        if (!f.canWrite()) fail("Delete: write protected: " + filename);
```

Example 3-1: Delete.java (continued)

```
    // If it is a directory, make sure it is empty
    if (f.isDirectory()) {
        String[] files = f.list();
        if (files.length > 0)
            fail("Delete: directory not empty: " + filename);
    }

    // If we passed all the tests, then attempt to delete it
    boolean success = f.delete();

    // And throw an exception if it didn't work for some (unknown) reason.
    // For example, because of a bug with Java 1.1.1 on Linux,
    // directory deletion always fails
    if (!success) fail("Delete: deletion failed");
}

/** A convenience method to throw an exception */
protected static void fail(String msg) throws IllegalArgumentException {
    throw new IllegalArgumentException(msg);
}
}
```

Copying File Contents

Example 3-2 shows a program that copies the contents of a specified file to another file. This example uses the `File` class, much as Example 3-1 did, to check that the source file exists, that the destination is writable, and so on. But it also introduces the use of streams to work with the contents of files. It uses a `FileInputStream` to read the bytes of the source file and a `FileOutputStream` to copy those bytes to the destination file.

The `copy()` method implements the functionality of the program. This method is heavily commented, so that you can follow the steps it takes. First, it performs a surprisingly large number of checks to verify that the copy request is a legitimate one. If all those tests succeed, it then creates a `FileInputStream` to read bytes from the source and a `FileOutputStream` to write those bytes to the destination. Notice the use of a byte array buffer to store bytes during the copy. Pay particular attention to the short `while` loop that actually performs the copy. The combination of assignment and testing in the condition of the `while` loop is a useful idiom that occurs frequently in I/O programming. Also notice the `finally` statement that ensures the streams are properly closed before the program exits.

This program uses streams to do more than read from and write to files, however. Before overwriting an existing file, this example asks for user confirmation. It demonstrates how to read lines of text with a `BufferedReader` that reads individual characters from an `InputStreamReader`, which in turn reads bytes from `System.in` (an `InputStream`), which itself reads keystrokes from the user's keyboard. Additionally, the program displays textual output with `System.out` and `System.err`, which are both instances of `PrintStream`.

The static FileCopy.copy() method can be called directly by any program. The FileCopy class also provides a main() method, however, so that it can be used as a standalone program.

Example 3-2: FileCopy.java

```
package com.davidflanagan.examples.io;
import java.io.*;

/**
 * This class is a standalone program to copy a file, and also defines a
 * static copy() method that other programs can use to copy files.
 **/
public class FileCopy {
    /** The main() method of the standalone program.  Calls copy(). */
    public static void main(String[] args) {
        if (args.length != 2)     // Check arguments
            System.err.println("Usage: java FileCopy <source> <destination>");
        else {
            // Call copy() to do the copy; display any error messages
            try { copy(args[0], args[1]); }
            catch (IOException e) { System.err.println(e.getMessage()); }
        }
    }

    /**
     * The static method that actually performs the file copy.
     * Before copying the file, however, it performs a lot of tests to make
     * sure everything is as it should be.
     */
    public static void copy(String from_name, String to_name)
        throws IOException
    {
        File from_file = new File(from_name);  // Get File objects from Strings
        File to_file = new File(to_name);

        // First make sure the source file exists, is a file, and is readable.
        if (!from_file.exists())
            abort("no such source file: " + from_name);
        if (!from_file.isFile())
            abort("can't copy directory: " + from_name);
        if (!from_file.canRead())
            abort("source file is unreadable: " + from_name);

        // If the destination is a directory, use the source file name
        // as the destination file name
        if (to_file.isDirectory())
            to_file = new File(to_file, from_file.getName());

        // If the destination exists, make sure it is a writeable file
        // and ask before overwriting it.  If the destination doesn't
        // exist, make sure the directory exists and is writeable.
        if (to_file.exists()) {
            if (!to_file.canWrite())
                abort("destination file is unwriteable: " + to_name);
            // Ask whether to overwrite it
            System.out.print("Overwrite existing file " + to_file.getName() +
                             "? (Y/N): ");
            System.out.flush();
            // Get the user's response.
```

Example 3-2: FileCopy.java (continued)

```java
            BufferedReader in=
                new BufferedReader(new InputStreamReader(System.in));
            String response = in.readLine();
            // Check the response.  If not a Yes, abort the copy.
            if (!response.equals("Y") && !response.equals("y"))
                abort("existing file was not overwritten.");
        }
        else {
            // If file doesn't exist, check if directory exists and is
            // writeable.  If getParent() returns null, then the directory is
            // the current dir.  so look up the user.dir system property to
            // find out what that is.
            String parent = to_file.getParent();  // The destination directory
            if (parent == null)       // If none, use the current directory
                parent = System.getProperty("user.dir");
            File dir = new File(parent);           // Convert it to a file.
            if (!dir.exists())
                abort("destination directory doesn't exist: "+parent);
            if (dir.isFile())
                abort("destination is not a directory: " + parent);
            if (!dir.canWrite())
                abort("destination directory is unwriteable: " + parent);
        }

        // If we've gotten this far, then everything is okay.
        // So we copy the file, a buffer of bytes at a time.
        FileInputStream from = null;  // Stream to read from source
        FileOutputStream to = null;   // Stream to write to destination
        try {
            from = new FileInputStream(from_file);  // Create input stream
            to = new FileOutputStream(to_file);     // Create output stream
            byte[] buffer = new byte[4096];         // To hold file contents
            int bytes_read;                         // How many bytes in buffer

            // Read a chunk of bytes into the buffer, then write them out,
            // looping until we reach the end of the file (when read() returns
            // -1).  Note the combination of assignment and comparison in this
            // while loop.  This is a common I/O programming idiom.
            while((bytes_read = from.read(buffer)) != -1) // Read until EOF
                to.write(buffer, 0, bytes_read);          // write
        }
        // Always close the streams, even if exceptions were thrown
        finally {
            if (from != null) try { from.close(); } catch (IOException e) { ; }
            if (to != null) try { to.close(); } catch (IOException e) { ; }
        }
    }

    /** A convenience method to throw an exception */
    private static void abort(String msg) throws IOException {
        throw new IOException("FileCopy: " + msg);
    }
}
```

Reading and Displaying Text Files

Example 3-3 shows the `FileViewer` class. It combines the use of the `File` class and I/O streams to read the contents of a text file with GUI techniques to display those contents. `FileViewer` uses a `java.awt.TextArea` component to display file contents, as shown in Figure 3-1. Example 3-3 uses graphical user interface techniques that are introduced in Chapter 10, *Graphical User Interfaces*. If you have not yet read that chapter or do not already have AWT programming experience, you probably won't understand all the code in the example. That's okay; just concentrate on the I/O code, which is the main focus of this chapter.

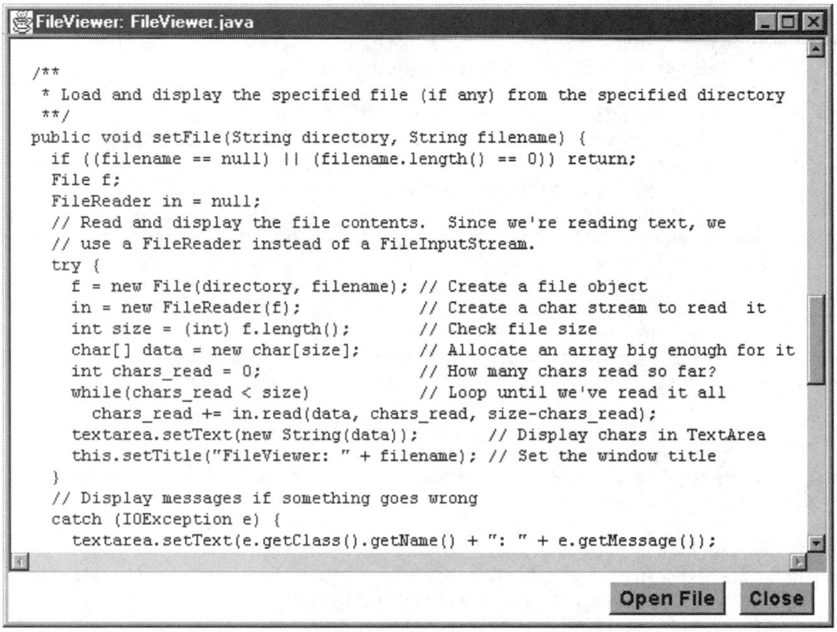

```
FileViewer: FileViewer.java                                    _ □ X

/**
 * Load and display the specified file (if any) from the specified directory
 **/
public void setFile(String directory, String filename) {
    if ((filename == null) || (filename.length() == 0)) return;
    File f;
    FileReader in = null;
    // Read and display the file contents. Since we're reading text, we
    // use a FileReader instead of a FileInputStream.
    try {
        f = new File(directory, filename); // Create a file object
        in = new FileReader(f);            // Create a char stream to read  it
        int size = (int) f.length();       // Check file size
        char[] data = new char[size];      // Allocate an array big enough for it
        int chars_read = 0;                // How many chars read so far?
        while(chars_read < size)           // Loop until we've read it all
            chars_read += in.read(data, chars_read, size-chars_read);
        textarea.setText(new String(data));        // Display chars in TextArea
        this.setTitle("FileViewer: " + filename); // Set the window title
    }
    // Display messages if something goes wrong
    catch (IOException e) {
        textarea.setText(e.getClass().getName() + ": " + e.getMessage());

                                                      Open File    Close
```

Figure 3-1. A FileViewer window

The `FileViewer` constructor concerns itself mainly with the mechanics of setting up the necessary GUI. There are some interesting uses of the `File` object at the end of this constructor, however. The heart of this example is the `setFile()` method. This is where the file contents are loaded and displayed. Because the file contents are to be displayed in a `TextArea` component, the legitimate assumption is that the file contains characters. Thus, you use a character input stream, a `File-Reader`, instead of the byte input stream used in the `FileCopy` program of Example 3-2. Once again, use a `finally` clause to ensure that the `FileReader` stream is properly closed.

The `actionPerformed()` method handles GUI events. If the user clicks on the **Open File** button, this method creates a `FileDialog` object to prompt for a new file to display. Note how the default directory is set before the dialog is displayed and then retrieved after the user makes a selection. This is possible because the `show()` method actually blocks until the user selects a file and dismisses the dialog.

The `FileViewer` class is designed to be used by other classes. It also has its own `main()` method, however, so that it can be run as a standalone program.

Example 3-3: FileViewer.java

```java
package com.davidflanagan.examples.io;
import java.awt.*;
import java.awt.event.*;
import java.io.*;

/**
 * This class creates and displays a window containing a TextArea,
 * in which the contents of a text file are displayed.
 **/
public class FileViewer extends Frame implements ActionListener {
    String directory;  // The default directory to display in the FileDialog
    TextArea textarea; // The area to display the file contents into

    /** Convenience constructor: file viewer starts out blank */
    public FileViewer() { this(null, null); }
    /** Convenience constructor: display file from current directory */
    public FileViewer(String filename) { this(null, filename); }

    /**
     * The real constructor.  Create a FileViewer object to display the
     * specified file from the specified directory
     **/
    public FileViewer(String directory, String filename) {
        super();  // Create the frame

        // Destroy the window when the user requests it
        addWindowListener(new WindowAdapter() {
                public void windowClosing(WindowEvent e) { dispose(); }
            });

        // Create a TextArea to display the contents of the file in
        textarea = new TextArea("", 24, 80);
        textarea.setFont(new Font("MonoSpaced", Font.PLAIN, 12));
        textarea.setEditable(false);
        this.add("Center", textarea);

        // Create a bottom panel to hold a couple of buttons in
        Panel p = new Panel();
        p.setLayout(new FlowLayout(FlowLayout.RIGHT, 10, 5));
        this.add(p, "South");

        // Create the buttons and arrange to handle button clicks
        Font font = new Font("SansSerif", Font.BOLD, 14);
        Button openfile = new Button("Open File");
        Button close = new Button("Close");
        openfile.addActionListener(this);
        openfile.setActionCommand("open");
        openfile.setFont(font);
        close.addActionListener(this);
        close.setActionCommand("close");
        close.setFont(font);
        p.add(openfile);
        p.add(close);

        this.pack();
```

Example 3-3: FileViewer.java (continued)

```java
        // Figure out the directory, from filename or current dir, if necessary
        if (directory == null) {
            File f;
            if ((filename != null) && (f = new File(filename)).isAbsolute()) {
                directory = f.getParent();
                filename = f.getName();
            }
            else directory = System.getProperty("user.dir");
        }

        this.directory = directory;    // Remember the directory, for FileDialog
        setFile(directory, filename); // Now load and display the file
    }

    /**
     * Load and display the specified file from the specified directory
     **/
    public void setFile(String directory, String filename) {
        if ((filename == null) || (filename.length() == 0)) return;
        File f;
        FileReader in = null;
        // Read and display the file contents.  Since we're reading text, we
        // use a FileReader instead of a FileInputStream.
        try {
            f = new File(directory, filename); // Create a file object
            in = new FileReader(f);            // And a char stream to read it
            char[] buffer = new char[4096];    // Read 4K characters at a time
            int len;                           // How many chars read each time
            textarea.setText("");              // Clear the text area
            while((len = in.read(buffer)) != -1) { // Read a batch of chars
                String s = new String(buffer, 0, len); // Convert to a string
                textarea.append(s);                     // And display them
            }
            this.setTitle("FileViewer: " + filename);  // Set the window title
            textarea.setCaretPosition(0);              // Go to start of file
        }
        // Display messages if something goes wrong
        catch (IOException e) {
            textarea.setText(e.getClass().getName() + ": " + e.getMessage());
            this.setTitle("FileViewer: " + filename + ": I/O Exception");
        }
        // Always be sure to close the input stream!
        finally { try { if (in!=null) in.close(); } catch (IOException e) {} }
    }

    /**
     * Handle button clicks
     **/
    public void actionPerformed(ActionEvent e) {
        String cmd = e.getActionCommand();
        if (cmd.equals("open")) {               // If user clicked "Open" button
            // Create a file dialog box to prompt for a new file to display
            FileDialog f = new FileDialog(this, "Open File", FileDialog.LOAD);
            f.setDirectory(directory);          // Set the default directory

            // Display the dialog and wait for the user's response
            f.show();
```

Example 3-3: FileViewer.java (continued)

```
            directory = f.getDirectory();      // Remember new default directory
            setFile(directory, f.getFile()); // Load and display selection
            f.dispose();                       // Get rid of the dialog box
        }
        else if (cmd.equals("close"))        // If user clicked "Close" button
            this.dispose();                    //    then close the window
    }

    /**
     * The FileViewer can be used by other classes, or it can be
     * used standalone with this main() method.
     **/
    static public void main(String[] args) throws IOException {
        // Create a FileViewer object
        Frame f = new FileViewer((args.length == 1)?args[0]:null);
        // Arrange to exit when the FileViewer window closes
        f.addWindowListener(new WindowAdapter() {
                public void windowClosed(WindowEvent e) { System.exit(0); }
            });
        // And pop the window up
        f.show();
    }
}
```

Listing Directory and File Information

Just as the `FileViewer` class of Example 3-3 displays the contents of a file in a `TextArea` component, the `FileLister` class, shown in Example 3-4, displays the contents of a directory in a `java.awt.List` component. When you select a file or directory name from the list, the program displays information (size, modification date, etc.) about the file or directory in a `TextField` component. When you double-click on a directory, the contents of that directory are displayed. When you double-click on a file, it displays the contents of the file in a `FileViewer` object. Figure 3-2 shows a `FileLister` window. Again, if you are not already familiar with GUI programming in Java, don't expect to understand all of the code until you've read Chapter 10; instead, just pay attention to the various uses of the `File` object that are demonstrated in this example.

The GUI mechanics of making the `FileLister` work form a large part of this example. The `listDirectory()` method lists the contents of a directory, using an optionally specified `FilenameFilter` object passed to the `FileLister()` constructor. This object defines an `accept()` method that is called for every entry in a directory to determine whether it should be listed.

The `itemStateChanged()` method is invoked when an item in the list is selected. It obtains information about the file or directory and displays it. The `actionPerformed()` method is another event listener method. This one is invoked when the user clicks either of the `Button` objects or double-clicks on an item in the list. If the user double-clicks on a directory, the program lists the contents of that directory. If the user double-clicks on a file, however, it creates and display a `FileViewer` window to list the contents of the file.

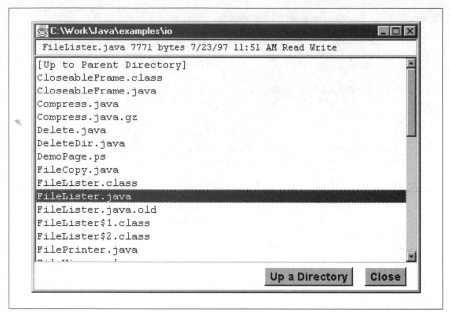

Figure 3–2. A FileLister window

Like the FileViewer class, the FileLister can be used by other classes, or it can be invoked as a standalone program. If you invoke it standalone, it lists the contents of the current directory. You can also invoke it with an optional directory name to see the contents of that directory. Using the optional -e flag followed by a file extension causes the program to filter the list of files and displays only the ones that have the specified extension. Note how the main() method parses the command-line arguments and uses an anonymous class to implement the FilenameFilter interface.

Example 3–4: FileLister.java

```java
package com.davidflanagan.examples.io;
import java.awt.*;
import java.awt.event.*;
import java.io.*;
import java.text.DateFormat;
import java.util.Date;

/**
 * This class creates and displays a window containing a list of
 * files and sub-directories in a specified directory.  Clicking on an
 * entry in the list displays more information about it. Double-clicking
 * on an entry displays it, if a file, or lists it if a directory.
 * An optionally-specified FilenameFilter filters the displayed list.
 **/
public class FileLister extends Frame implements ActionListener, ItemListener {
    private List list;                  // To display the directory contents in
    private TextField details;          // To display detail info in.
    private Panel buttons;              // Holds the buttons
    private Button up, close;           // The Up and Close buttons
    private File currentDir;            // The directory currently listed
```

Example 3-4: FileLister.java (continued)

```java
    private FilenameFilter filter;     // An optional filter for the directory
    private String[] files;            // The directory contents
    private DateFormat dateFormatter = // To display dates and time correctly
        DateFormat.getDateTimeInstance(DateFormat.SHORT, DateFormat.SHORT);

    /**
     * Constructor: create the GUI, and list the initial directory.
     **/
    public FileLister(String directory, FilenameFilter filter) {
        super("File Lister");          // Create the window
        this.filter = filter;          // Save the filter, if any

        // Destroy the window when the user requests it
        addWindowListener(new WindowAdapter() {
                public void windowClosing(WindowEvent e) { dispose(); }
            });

        list = new List(12, false);      // Set up the list
        list.setFont(new Font("MonoSpaced", Font.PLAIN, 14));
        list.addActionListener(this);
        list.addItemListener(this);

        details = new TextField();       // Set up the details area
        details.setFont(new Font("MonoSpaced", Font.PLAIN, 12));
        details.setEditable(false);

        buttons = new Panel();           // Set up the button box
        buttons.setLayout(new FlowLayout(FlowLayout.RIGHT, 15, 5));
        buttons.setFont(new Font("SansSerif", Font.BOLD, 14));

        up = new Button("Up a Directory"); // Set up the two buttons
        close = new Button("Close");
        up.addActionListener(this);
        close.addActionListener(this);

        buttons.add(up);                 // Add buttons to button box
        buttons.add(close);

        this.add(list, "Center");        // Add stuff to the window
        this.add(details, "North");
        this.add(buttons, "South");
        this.setSize(500, 350);

        listDirectory(directory);        // And now list initial directory.
    }

    /**
     * This method uses the list() method to get all entries in a directory
     * and then displays them in the List component.
     **/
    public void listDirectory(String directory) {
        // Convert the string to a File object, and check that the dir exists
        File dir = new File(directory);
        if (!dir.isDirectory())
            throw new IllegalArgumentException("FileLister: no such directory");

        // Get the (filtered) directory entries
        files = dir.list(filter);
```

Example 3–4: FileLister.java (continued)

```
        // Sort the list of filenames.  Prior to Java 1.2, you could use
        // com.davidflanagan.examples.classes.Sorter.sort() to sort instead.
        java.util.Arrays.sort(files);

        // Remove any old entries in the list, and add the new ones
        list.removeAll();
        list.add("[Up to Parent Directory]");  // A special case entry
        for(int i = 0; i < files.length; i++) list.add(files[i]);

        // Display directory name in window titlebar and in the details box
        this.setTitle(directory);
        details.setText(directory);

        // Remember this directory for later.
        currentDir = dir;
    }

    /**
     * This ItemListener method uses various File methods to obtain information
     * about a file or directory. Then it displays that info.
     **/
    public void itemStateChanged(ItemEvent e) {
        int i = list.getSelectedIndex() - 1;  // minus 1 for Up To Parent entry
        if (i < 0) return;
        String filename = files[i];                 // Get the selected entry
        File f = new File(currentDir, filename);  // Convert to a File
        if (!f.exists())                            // Confirm that it exists
            throw new IllegalArgumentException("FileLister: " +
                                               "no such file or directory");

        // Get the details about the file or directory, concatenate to a string
        String info = filename;
        if (f.isDirectory()) info += File.separator;
        info += " " + f.length() + " bytes ";
        info += dateFormatter.format(new java.util.Date(f.lastModified()));
        if (f.canRead()) info += " Read";
        if (f.canWrite()) info += " Write";

        // And display the details string
        details.setText(info);
    }

    /**
     * This ActionListener method is invoked when the user double-clicks on an
     * entry or clicks on one of the buttons. If they double-click on a file,
     * create a FileViewer to display that file. If they double-click on a
     * directory, call the listDirectory() method to display that directory
     **/
    public void actionPerformed(ActionEvent e) {
        if (e.getSource() == close) this.dispose();
        else if (e.getSource() == up) { up(); }
        else if (e.getSource() == list) {  // Double click on an item
            int i = list.getSelectedIndex(); // Check which item
            if (i == 0) up();                 // Handle first Up To Parent item
            else {                            // Otherwise, get filename
                String name = files[i-1];
                File f = new File(currentDir, name);    // Convert to a File
                String fullname = f.getAbsolutePath();
```

Example 3-4: FileLister.java (continued)

```
                if (f.isDirectory()) listDirectory(fullname);  // List dir
                else new FileViewer(fullname).show();           // display file
        }
    }
}

/** A convenience method to display the contents of the parent directory */
protected void up() {
    String parent = currentDir.getParent();
    if (parent == null) return;
    listDirectory(parent);
}

/** A convenience method used by main() */
public static void usage() {
    System.out.println("Usage: java FileLister [directory_name] " +
                       "[-e file_extension]");
    System.exit(0);
}

/**
 * A main() method so FileLister can be run standalone.
 * Parse command line arguments and create the FileLister object.
 * If an extension is specified, create a FilenameFilter for it.
 * If no directory is specified, use the current directory.
 **/
public static void main(String args[]) throws IOException {
    FileLister f;
    FilenameFilter filter = null;  // The filter, if any
    String directory = null;       // The specified dir, or the current dir

    // Loop through args array, parsing arguments
    for(int i = 0; i < args.length; i++) {
        if (args[i].equals("-e")) {
            if (++i >= args.length) usage();
            final String suffix = args[i];  // final for anon. class below

            // This class is a simple FilenameFilter.  It defines the
            // accept() method required to determine whether a specified
            // file should be listed.  A file will be listed if its name
            // ends with the specified extension, or if it is a directory.
            filter = new FilenameFilter() {
                    public boolean accept(File dir, String name) {
                        if (name.endsWith(suffix)) return true;
                        else return (new File(dir, name)).isDirectory();
                    }
                };
        }
        else {
            if (directory != null) usage();  // If already specified, fail.
            else directory = args[i];
        }
    }

    // If no directory specified, use the current directory
    if (directory == null) directory = System.getProperty("user.dir");
    // Create the FileLister object, with directory and filter specified.
    f = new FileLister(directory, filter);
```

Example 3–4: FileLister.java (continued)

```
        // Arrange for the application to exit when the window is closed
        f.addWindowListener(new WindowAdapter() {
            public void windowClosed(WindowEvent e) { System.exit(0); }
        });
        // Finally, pop the window up up.
        f.show();
    }
}
```

Compressing Files and Directories

Example 3-5 demonstrates an interesting application of stream classes: compressing files and directories. The classes of interest in this example are not actually part of the java.io package, but instead part of the java.util.zip package. The Compress class defines two static methods, gzipFile(), which compresses a file using GZIP compression format, and zipDirectory(), which compresses the files (but not directories) in a directory using the ZIP archive and compression format. gzipFile() uses the GZIPOutputStream class, while zipDirectory() uses the ZipOutputStream and ZipEntry classes, all from java.util.zip.

This example demonstrates the versatility of the stream classes and shows again how streams can be wrapped around one another so that the output of one stream becomes the input of another. This technique makes it possible to achieve a great variety of effects. Notice again the while loop in both methods that does the actual copying of data from source file to compressed file. These methods do not attempt to handle exceptions; instead they just pass them on to the caller, which is often exactly the right thing to do.

Compress is meant to be used as a utility class by other programs, so it doesn't itself include a main() method. The example does include an inner Compress.Test class, however, which has a main() method that can test the gzipFile() and zipDirectory() methods.

Example 3-5: Compress.java

```
package com.davidflanagan.examples.io;
import java.io.*;
import java.util.zip.*;

/**
 * This class defines two static methods for gzipping files and zipping
 * directories.  It also defines a demonstration program as a nested class.
 **/
public class Compress {
    /** Gzip the contents of the from file and save in the to file. */
    public static void gzipFile(String from, String to) throws IOException {
        // Create stream to read from the from file
        FileInputStream in = new FileInputStream(from);
        // Create stream to compress data and write it to the to file.
        GZIPOutputStream out = new GZIPOutputStream(new FileOutputStream(to));
        // Copy bytes from one stream to the other
        byte[] buffer = new byte[4096];
        int bytes_read;
        while((bytes_read = in.read(buffer)) != -1)
```

Example 3-5: Compress.java (continued)

```
            out.write(buffer, 0, bytes_read);
        // And close the streams
        in.close();
        out.close();
    }

    /** Zip the contents of the directory, and save it in the zipfile */
    public static void zipDirectory(String dir, String zipfile)
        throws IOException, IllegalArgumentException {
        // Check that the directory is a directory, and get its contents
        File d = new File(dir);
        if (!d.isDirectory())
            throw new IllegalArgumentException("Compress: not a directory:  " +
                                                dir);
        String[] entries = d.list();
        byte[] buffer = new byte[4096];  // Create a buffer for copying
        int bytes_read;

        // Create a stream to compress data and write it to the zipfile
        ZipOutputStream out =
            new ZipOutputStream(new FileOutputStream(zipfile));

        // Loop through all entries in the directory
        for(int i = 0; i < entries.length; i++) {
            File f = new File(d, entries[i]);
            if (f.isDirectory()) continue;          // Don't zip sub-directories
            FileInputStream in = new FileInputStream(f); // Stream to read file
            ZipEntry entry = new ZipEntry(f.getPath());  // Make a ZipEntry
            out.putNextEntry(entry);                     // Store entry
            while((bytes_read = in.read(buffer)) != -1)  // Copy bytes
                out.write(buffer, 0, bytes_read);
            in.close();                                  // Close input stream
        }
        // When we're done with the whole loop, close the output stream
        out.close();
    }

    /**
     * This nested class is a test program that demonstrates the use of the
     * static methods defined above.
     **/
    public static class Test {
        /**
         * Compress a specified file or directory.  If no destination name is
         * specified, append .gz to a file name or .zip to a directory name
         **/
        public static void main(String args[]) throws IOException {
            if ((args.length != 1) && (args.length != 2)) {  // check arguments
                System.err.println("Usage: java Compress$Test <from> [<to>]");
                System.exit(0);
            }
            String from = args[0], to;
            File f = new File(from);
            boolean directory = f.isDirectory(); // Is it a file or directory?
            if (args.length == 2) to = args[1];
            else {                               // If destination not specified
                if (directory) to = from + ".zip";   //  use a .zip suffix
                else to = from + ".gz";              //  or a .gz suffix
```

Compressing Files and Directories 61

Example 3–5: Compress.java (continued)

```
        }

        if ((new File(to)).exists()) { // Make sure not to overwrite
            System.err.println("Compress: won't overwrite existing file: "+
                               to);
            System.exit(0);
        }

        // Finally, call one of the methods defined above to do the work.
        if (directory) Compress.zipDirectory(from, to);
        else Compress.gzipFile(from, to);
    }
  }
}
```

Filtering Character Streams

FilterReader is an abstract class that defines a null filter; it reads characters from a specified Reader and returns them with no modification. In other words, Filter-Reader defines no-op implementations of all the Reader methods. A subclass must override at least the two read() methods to perform whatever sort of filtering is necessary. Some subclasses may override other methods as well. Example 3-6 shows RemoveHTMLReader, which is a custom subclass of FilterReader that reads HTML text from a stream and filters out all of the HTML tags from the text it returns.

In the example, you implement the HTML tag filtration in the three-argument version of read(), and then implement the no-argument version in terms of that more complicated version. The example includes an inner Test class with a main() method that shows how you might use the RemoveHTMLReader class.

Note that you can also define a RemoveHTMLWriter class by performing the same filtration in a FilterWriter subclass. Or, to filter a byte stream instead of a character stream, you can subclass FilterInputStream and FilterOutputStream. RemoveHTMLReader is only one example of a filter stream. Other possibilities include streams that count the number of characters or bytes processed, convert characters to uppercase, extract URLs, perform search-and-replace operations, convert Unix-style LF line terminators to Windows-style CRLF line terminators, and so on.

Example 3–6: RemoveHTMLReader.java

```
package com.davidflanagan.examples.io;
import java.io.*;

/**
 * A simple FilterReader that strips HTML tags (or anything between
 * pairs of angle brackets) out of a stream of characters.
 **/
public class RemoveHTMLReader extends FilterReader {
    /** A trivial constructor.  Just initialize our superclass */
    public RemoveHTMLReader(Reader in) { super(in); }
```

Example 3-6: RemoveHTMLReader.java (continued)

```
boolean intag = false;    // Used to remember whether we are "inside" a tag

/**
 * This is the implementation of the no-op read() method of FilterReader.
 * It calls in.read() to get a buffer full of characters, then strips
 * out the HTML tags. (in is a protected field of the superclass).
 **/
public int read(char[] buf, int from, int len) throws IOException {
    int numchars = 0;        // how many characters have been read
    // Loop, because we might read a bunch of characters, then strip them
    // all out, leaving us with zero characters to return.
    while (numchars == 0) {
        numchars = in.read(buf, from, len); // Read characters
        if (numchars == -1) return -1;      // Check for EOF and handle it.

        // Loop through the characters we read, stripping out HTML tags.
        // Characters not in tags are copied over previous tags
        int last = from;                    // Index of last non-HTML char
        for(int i = from; i < from + numchars; i++) {
            if (!intag) {                   // If not in an HTML tag
                if (buf[i] == '<') intag = true; // check for tag start
                else buf[last++] = buf[i];       // and copy the character
            }
            else if (buf[i] == '>') intag = false;  // check for end of tag
        }
        numchars = last - from; // Figure out how many characters remain
    }                           // And if it is more than zero characters
    return numchars;            // Then return that number.
}


/**
 * This is another no-op read() method we have to implement.  We
 * implement it in terms of the method above.  Our superclass implements
 * the remaining read() methods in terms of these two.
 **/
public int read() throws IOException {
    char[] buf = new char[1];
    int result = read(buf, 0, 1);
    if (result == -1) return -1;
    else return (int)buf[0];
}

/** This class defines a main() method to test the RemoveHTMLReader */
public static class Test {
    /** The test program: read a text file, strip HTML, print to console */
    public static void main(String[] args) {
        try {
            if (args.length != 1)
                throw new IllegalArgumentException("Wrong number of args");
            // Create a stream to read from the file and strip tags from it
            BufferedReader in = new BufferedReader(
                    new RemoveHTMLReader(new FileReader(args[0])));
            // Read line by line, printing lines to the console
            String line;
            while((line = in.readLine()) != null)
                System.out.println(line);
            in.close();  // Close the stream.
        }
```

Example 3-6: RemoveHTMLReader.java (continued)

```
                catch(Exception e) {
                    System.err.println(e);
                    System.err.println("Usage: java RemoveHTMLReader$Test" +
                                        " <filename>");
                }
            }
        }
    }
```

Filtering Lines of Text

Example 3-7 defines GrepReader, another custom input stream. This stream reads lines of text from a specified Reader and returns only those lines that contain a specified substring. In this way, it works like the Unix *fgrep* command; it performs a "grep" or search. GrepReader performs filtering, but it filters text a line at a time, rather than a character at a time, so you extend BufferedReader instead of FilterReader.

The code for this example is straightforward. The example includes an inner Test class with a main() method that demonstrates the use of the GrepReader stream. You might invoke this test program as follows:

```
% java com.davidflanagan.examples.io.GrepReader\$Test needle haystack.txt
```

Example 3-7: GrepReader.java

```java
package com.davidflanagan.examples.io;
import java.io.*;

/**
 * This class is a BufferedReader that filters out all lines that
 * do not contain the specified pattern.
 **/
public class GrepReader extends BufferedReader {
    String pattern;  // The string we are going to be matching.

    /** Pass the stream to our superclass, and remember the pattern ourself */
    public GrepReader(Reader in, String pattern) {
        super(in);
        this.pattern = pattern;
    }

    /**
     * This is the filter: call our superclass's readLine() to get the
     * actual lines, but only return lines that contain the pattern.
     * When the superclass readLine() returns null (EOF), we return null.
     **/
    public final String readLine() throws IOException {
        String line;
        do { line = super.readLine(); }
        while ((line != null) && line.indexOf(pattern) == -1);
        return line;
    }

    /**
     * This class demonstrates the use of the GrepReader class.
```

Example 3-7: GrepReader.java (continued)

```
    * It prints the lines of a file that contain a specified substring.
    **/
    public static class Test {
        public static void main(String args[]) {
            try {
                if (args.length != 2)
                    throw new IllegalArgumentException("Wrong number of args");
                GrepReader in=new GrepReader(new FileReader(args[1]), args[0]);
                String line;
                while((line = in.readLine()) != null) System.out.println(line);
                in.close();
            }
            catch (Exception e) {
                System.err.println(e);
                System.out.println("Usage: java GrepReader$Test" +
                                    " <pattern> <file>");
            }
        }
    }
}
```

A Custom HTML Output Stream

One of the first common uses of Java was to run applets—miniature programs delivered over the Internet—within web browsers. (We'll discuss applets in more detail in Chapter 15, *Applets*.) Because applets run within web browsers, and browsers are powerful tools for displaying HTML documents, it seems logical that there should be some way to use the HTML display capabilities of the browser from within an applet.

Example 3-8 shows a custom output stream named HTMLWriter that provides exactly this capability. When a new HTMLWriter stream is created, it communicates with the web browser using JavaScript commands and tells the browser to open a new window. Then, when HTML-formatted text is written to this stream, it passes that text, through JavaScript, to the new web-browser window, which parses and displays it. This class relies on Navigator's LiveConnect technology and the netscape.javascript.JSObject class. It is designed for use with Netscape Navigator 4.0 or later, although Microsoft has implemented a version of this technology, and this example should also work with recent versions of Internet Explorer.

Note the implementation of the write() and close() methods, and the no-op implementation of the flush() method. These are the three abstract methods of Writer that must be implemented by every concrete subclass. Note also the closeWindow() method that this class adds.

You are not expected to understand the JSObject class or the JavaScript commands sent to the browser through it. If you are interested in learning about these things, I recommend my JavaScript book, *JavaScript: The Definitive Guide*, also published by O'Reilly.

The example includes an inner applet class named Test that demonstrates how to use the HTMLWriter class. This applet reads a URL specified in an applet parameter (i.e., with a <PARAM> tag) and creates an HTMLWriter to display the contents of that URL. You can test out this applet with an HTML tag like the following:

```
<APPLET CODE="HTMLWriter$Test.class" WIDTH=10 HEIGHT=10 MAYSCRIPT>
  <PARAM NAME="url" VALUE="HTMLWriter.java">
</APPLET>
```

Note the MAYSCRIPT attribute of the <APPLET> tag. This gives the Java applet permission to invoke JavaScript commands in the browser. The <PARAM> tag specifies the value of the parameter named url—the URL of the file the applet will display.

To compile this example, you need to have the netscape.javascript.JSObject class in your CLASSPATH. You can usually find this class in a file like *java/classes/java40.jar* in your Netscape installation. Since the example is designed to run as an applet within a web browser, it should automatically be able to find the JSObject class when you run it.

For another example of a custom output stream like this, see Example 12-3 in Chapter 12, *Printing*.

Example 3–8: HTMLWriter.java

```java
package com.davidflanagan.examples.io;
import java.io.*;
import java.net.*;
import java.applet.Applet;
import netscape.javascript.JSObject;     // A special class we need

/**
 * An output stream that sends HTML text to a newly created web browser window.
 * It relies on the netscape.javascript.JSObject class to send JavaScript
 * commands to the Web browser, and only works for applets running in
 * the Netscape Navigator Web browser.
 **/
public class HTMLWriter extends Writer {
    JSObject main_window;      // the initial browser window
    JSObject window;           // the new window we create
    JSObject document;         // the document of that new window
    static int window_num = 0; // used to give each new window a unique name

    /**
     * When you create a new HTMLWriter, it pops up a new, blank, Web browser
     * window to display the output in.  You must specify the applet
     * (this specifies the main browser window) and the desired size
     * for the new window.
     **/
    public HTMLWriter(Applet applet, int width, int height) {
        // Verify that we can find the JSObject class we need.  Warn if not.
        try { Class c = Class.forName("netscape.javascript.JSObject"); }
        catch (ClassNotFoundException e) {
            throw new NoClassDefFoundError("HTMLWriter requires " +
                "Netscape Navigator 4.0 or higher " +
                "or a browser that supports LiveConnect technology");
        }

        // Get a reference to the main browser window from the applet.
        main_window = JSObject.getWindow(applet);

        // Create a new window to display output in.  This command sends a
```

Example 3-8: HTMLWriter.java (continued)

```
            // string of JavaScript to the web browser
            window = (JSObject)
                main_window.eval("self.open('','" +
                                "'HTMLWriter" + window_num++ + "','," +
                                "'menubar,status,resizable,scrollbars," +
                                "width=" + width + ",height=" + height + "')");

            // Obtain the Document object of this new window, and open it.
            document = (JSObject) window.getMember("document");
            document.call("open", null);
    }

    /**
     * This is the write() method required for all Writer subclasses.
     * Writer defines all its other write() methods in terms of this one.
     **/
    public void write(char[] buf, int offset, int length) {
        // If no window or document, do nothing.  This occurs if the stream
        // has been closed, or if the code is not running in Navigator.
        if ((window == null) || (document == null)) return;
        // If the window has been closed by the user, do nothing
        if (((Boolean)window.getMember("closed")).booleanValue()) return;
        // Otherwise, create a string from the specified bytes
        String s = new String(buf, offset, length);
        // And pass it to the JS document.write() method to output the HTML
        document.call("write", new String[] { s });
    }

    /**
     * There is no general way to force JavaScript to flush all pending output,
     * so this method does nothing.  To flush, output a <P> tag or some other
     * HTML tag that forces a line break in the output.
     **/
    public void flush() {}

    /**
     * When the stream is closed, close the JavaScript Document object
     * (But don't close the window yet.)
     **/
    public void close() { document.call("close", null); document = null; }

    /**
     * If the browser window is still open, close it.
     * This method is unique to HTMLWriter.
     **/
    public void closeWindow() {
        if (document != null) close();
        if (!((Boolean)window.getMember("closed")).booleanValue())
            window.call("close", null);
        window = null;
    }

    /** A finalizer method to close the window in case we forget. */
    public void finalize() { closeWindow(); }

    /**
     * This nested class is an applet that demonstrates the use of HTMLWriter.
     * It reads the contents of the URL specified in its url parameter and
```

Example 3–8: HTMLWriter.java (continued)

```
 * writes them out to an HTMLWriter stream.  It will only work in
 * Netscape 4.0 or later.  It requires an <APPLET> tag like this:
 *    <APPLET CODE="HTMLWriter$Test.class" WIDTH=10 HEIGHT=10 MAYSCRIPT>
 *    <PARAM NAME="url" VALUE="HTMLWriter.java">
 *    </APPLET>
 * Note that MAYSCRIPT attribute.  It is required to enable the applet
 * to invoke JavaScript.
 **/
public static class Test extends Applet {
    HTMLWriter out;
    /** When the applet starts, read and display specified URL */
    public void init() {
        try {
            // Get the URL specified in the <PARAM> tag
            URL url =
                new URL(this.getDocumentBase(), this.getParameter("url"));
            // Get a stream to read its contents
            Reader in = new InputStreamReader(url.openStream());
            // Create an HTMLWriter stream for out output
            out = new HTMLWriter(this, 400, 200);
            // Read buffers of characters and output them to the HTMLWriter
            char[] buffer = new char[4096];
            int numchars;
            while((numchars = in.read(buffer)) != -1)
                out.write(buffer, 0, numchars);
            // Close the streams
            in.close();
            out.close();
        }
        catch (IOException e) {}
    }
    /** When the applet terminates, close the window we created */
    public void destroy() { out.closeWindow(); }
}
}
```

Exercises

3-1. Write a program named Head that prints out the first 10 lines of each file specified on the command line.

3-2. Write a corresponding program named Tail that prints out the last 10 lines of each file specified on the command line.

3-3. Write a program that counts and reports the number of lines, words, and characters in a specified file. Use static methods of the java.lang.Character class to determine whether a given character is a space (and therefore the boundary between two words).

3-4. Write a program that adds up and reports the size of all files in a specified directory. It should recursively scan any subdirectories, summing and reporting the size of the files that they contain, and incorporate those directory sizes into its final output.

3-5. Write a program that lists all of the files and subdirectories in a specified directory, along with their sizes and modification dates. By default, the output should be sorted by name. If invoked with the -s option, however, output should be sorted by size from largest to smallest. If invoked with the -d option, output should be sorted by date, from most recent to least. Use the sort() method of java.util.Collections to help with the sorting.

3-6. Write a program named Uncompress that uncompresses files and directories compressed by the Compress example in this chapter.

3-7. Write a subclass of OutputStream named TeeOutputStream that acts like a T joint in a pipe; the stream sends its output to two different output streams, specified when the TeeOutputStream is created. Write a simple test program that uses two TeeOutputStream objects to send text read from System.in to System.out and to two different test files.

3-8. Write a simple subclass of Reader named TestReader that returns the same character (a character passed to the constructor) over and over. The stream should never reach EOF. Write a trivial subclass of Writer named NullWriter that simply discards any output sent to it. Streams like these are occasionally useful for testing and other purposes. Write a test program that reads from the TestReader and sends its output to a PrintWriter wrapped around a NullWriter.

CHAPTER 4

Threads

A *thread* is a unit of program execution that runs independently from other threads. Java programs may consist of multiple threads of execution that behave as if they were running on independent CPUs, even when the host computer actually has only a single CPU. In many programming languages, multithreading capabilities are added on as an afterthought. In Java, however, they are integrated tightly with the language and its core packages:

- The java.lang.Runnable interface defines a run() method that serves as the block of code a thread executes. When that method exits, the thread stops running.

- The java.lang.Thread class represents a thread; it defines methods for setting and querying thread properties (such as execution priority level) and for starting the execution of a thread.

- The synchronized statement and modifier can be used to write blocks of code and entire methods, respectively, that require a thread to obtain a lock before executing the block or method. This mechanism ensures that two threads can't run the block or method at the same time, to avoid problems with different threads putting shared data in an inconsistent state.

- The wait() and notify() methods of java.lang.Object can be used to suspend threads and wake them up again.

The use of threads is common in Java programming; it is not possible to confine a discussion of them to just one chapter. We'll start with some simple examples here. We'll see threads again in Chapter 5, *Networking*, where they are quite useful for writing network server programs that can respond to multiple client requests simultaneously. Threads also appear in Chapter 11, *Graphics*, and Chapter 15, *Applets*, where they are used to produce animation effects.

Thread Basics

Example 4-1 is a simple program that demonstrates how to define, manipulate, and run threads. The bulk of the program is the main() method; it is run by the initial thread created by the Java interpreter. This main() method defines two additional threads, sets their priorities, and starts them running. The two threads are defined using two different techniques: the first is defined by subclassing the Thread class, while the second implements the Runnable interface and passes a Runnable object to the Thread() constructor. The example also demonstrates how you might use the important sleep(), yield(), and join() methods. Finally, Example 4-1 demonstrates the java.lang.ThreadLocal class, which has been added as of Java 1.2.

Example 4-1: ThreadDemo.java

```
package com.davidflanagan.examples.thread;

/**
 * This class demonstrates the use of threads.  The main() method is the
 * initial method invoked by the interpreter.  It defines and starts two
 * more threads and the three threads run at the same time.  Note that this
 * class extends Thread and overrides its run() method.  That method provides
 * the body of one of the threads started by the main() method
 **/
public class ThreadDemo extends Thread {
    /**
     * This method overrides the run() method of Thread.  It provides
     * the body for this thread.
     **/
    public void run() { for(int i = 0; i < 5; i++) compute(); }

    /**
     * This main method creates and starts two threads in addition to the
     * initial thread that the interpreter creates to invoke the main() method.
     **/
    public static void main(String[] args) {
        // Create the first thread: an instance of this class.  Its body is
        // the run() method above
        ThreadDemo thread1 = new ThreadDemo();

        // Create the second thread by passing a Runnable object to the
        // Thread() construtor.  The body of this thread is the run() method
        // of the anonymous Runnable object below.
        Thread thread2 = new Thread(new Runnable() {
                public void run() { for(int i = 0; i < 5; i++) compute(); }
            });

        // Set the priorities of these two threads, if any are specified
        if (args.length >= 1) thread1.setPriority(Integer.parseInt(args[0]));
        if (args.length >= 2) thread2.setPriority(Integer.parseInt(args[1]));

        // Start the two threads running
        thread1.start();
        thread2.start();

        // This main() method is run by the initial thread created by the
        // Java interpreter.  Now that thread does some stuff, too.
        for(int i = 0; i < 5; i++) compute();
```

Example 4-1: ThreadDemo.java (continued)

```
            // We could wait for the threads to stop running with these lines
            // But they aren't necessary here, so we don't bother.
            // try {
            //      thread1.join();
            //      thread2.join();
            // } catch (InterruptedException e) {}

            // The Java VM exits only when the main() method returns, and when all
            // threads stop running (except for daemon threads--see setDaemon()).
        }

    // ThreadLocal objects respresent a value accessed with get() and set().
    // But they maintain a different value for each thread.  This object keeps
    // track of how many times each thread has called compute().
    static ThreadLocal numcalls = new ThreadLocal();

    /** This is the dummy method our threads all call */
    static synchronized void compute() {
        // Figure out how many times we've been called by the current thread
        Integer n = (Integer) numcalls.get();
        if (n == null) n = new Integer(1);
        else n = new Integer(n.intValue() + 1);
        numcalls.set(n);

        // Display the name of the thread, and the number of times called
        System.out.println(Thread.currentThread().getName() + ": " + n);

        // Do a long computation, simulating a "compute-bound" thread
        for(int i = 0, j=0; i < 1000000; i++) j += i;

        // Alternatively, we can simulate a thread subject to network or I/O
        // delays by causing it to sleep for a random amount of time:
        try {
            // Stop running for a random number of milliseconds
            Thread.sleep((int)(Math.random()*100+1));
        }
        catch (InterruptedException e) {}

        // Each thread politely offers the other threads a chance to run.
        // This is important so that a compute-bound thread does not "starve"
        // other threads of equal priority.
        Thread.yield();
    }
}
```

Threads and Thread Groups

Every Java Thread belongs to some ThreadGroup and may be constrained and controlled through the methods of that ThreadGroup. Similarly, every ThreadGroup is itself contained in some parent ThreadGroup. Thus, there is a hierarchy of thread groups and the threads they contain. Example 4-2 shows a ThreadLister class, with a public listAllThreads() method that displays this hierarchy by listing all threads and thread groups currently running on the Java interpreter. This method displays the name and priority of each thread, as well as other information about threads and thread groups. The example defines a main() method that creates a simple Swing user interface and uses it to display a listing of its own threads. Figure 4-1 shows such a listing.

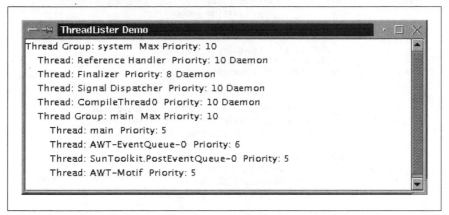

Figure 4–1. The threads and thread groups of a Swing application

The listAllThreads() method uses the static Thread method currentThread() to obtain the current thread and then calls getThreadGroup() to find the thread group of that thread. The method then uses the ThreadGroup.getParent() method to move up through the thread-group hierarchy until it finds the root thread group, the thread group that contains all other threads and thread groups.

Now listAllThreads() calls the private ThreadLister.printGroupInfo() method to display the contents of the root thread group and then recursively display the contents of all the thread groups it contains. printGroupInfo(), and the printThreadInfo() method it calls, use various Thread and ThreadGroup methods to obtain information about the threads and their groups. Note that the isDaemon() method returns whether a thread is a daemon thread or not. Daemon threads are background threads that are not expected to exit. The Java interpreter exits when all nondaemon threads have quit.

The ThreadLister class has a main() method, so it can be run as a standalone program. It is more interesting, of course, to invoke the listAllThreads() method from within another program; it can also help you to diagnose problems you are having with threads.

Example 4–2: ThreadLister.java

```
package com.davidflanagan.examples.thread;
import java.io.*;
import java.awt.*;      // AWT classes for the demo program
import javax.swing.*;   // Swing GUI classes for the demo

/**
 * This class contains a useful static method for listing all threads
 * and threadgroups in the VM.  It also has a simple main() method so it
 * can be run as a standalone program.
 **/
public class ThreadLister {
    /** Display information about a thread. */
```

Example 4-2: ThreadLister.java (continued)

```java
    private static void printThreadInfo(PrintWriter out, Thread t,
                                        String indent) {
        if (t == null) return;
        out.println(indent + "Thread: " + t.getName() +
                    " Priority: " + t.getPriority() +
                    (t.isDaemon()?" Daemon":"") +
                    (t.isAlive()?"":" Not Alive"));
    }

    /** Display info about a thread group and its threads and groups */
    private static void printGroupInfo(PrintWriter out, ThreadGroup g,
                                       String indent) {
        if (g == null) return;
        int num_threads = g.activeCount();
        int num_groups = g.activeGroupCount();
        Thread[] threads = new Thread[num_threads];
        ThreadGroup[] groups = new ThreadGroup[num_groups];

        g.enumerate(threads, false);
        g.enumerate(groups, false);

        out.println(indent + "Thread Group: " + g.getName() +
                    " Max Priority: " + g.getMaxPriority() +
                    (g.isDaemon()?" Daemon":""));

        for(int i = 0; i < num_threads; i++)
            printThreadInfo(out, threads[i], indent + "    ");
        for(int i = 0; i < num_groups; i++)
            printGroupInfo(out, groups[i], indent + "    ");
    }

    /** Find the root thread group and list it recursively */
    public static void listAllThreads(PrintWriter out) {
        ThreadGroup current_thread_group;
        ThreadGroup root_thread_group;
        ThreadGroup parent;

        // Get the current thread group
        current_thread_group = Thread.currentThread().getThreadGroup();

        // Now go find the root thread group
        root_thread_group = current_thread_group;
        parent = root_thread_group.getParent();
        while(parent != null) {
            root_thread_group = parent;
            parent = parent.getParent();
        }

        // And list it, recursively
        printGroupInfo(out, root_thread_group, "");
    }

    /**
     * The main() method creates a simple graphical user interface to display
     * the threads in.  This allows us to see the "event dispatch thread" used
     * by AWT and Swing.
     **/
    public static void main(String[] args) {
```

Example 4-2: ThreadLister.java (continued)

```
            // Create a simple Swing GUI
            JFrame frame = new JFrame("ThreadLister Demo");
            JTextArea textarea = new JTextArea();
            frame.getContentPane().add(new JScrollPane(textarea),
                                    BorderLayout.CENTER);
            frame.setSize(500, 400);
            frame.setVisible(true);

            // Get the threadlisting as a string using a StringWriter stream
            StringWriter sout = new StringWriter();  // To capture the listing
            PrintWriter out = new PrintWriter(sout);
            ThreadLister.listAllThreads(out);        // List threads to stream
            out.close();
            String threadListing = sout.toString();  // Get listing as a string

            // Finally, display the thread listing in the GUI
            textarea.setText(threadListing);
    }
}
```

Deadlock

Multithreaded programming requires a programmer to take special care in several areas. For example, if multiple threads can be changing the state of an object at the same time, you must typically use synchronized methods or the synchronized statement to ensure that only one thread changes the object's state at a time. If you do not, two threads could end up overwriting each other's edits, leaving the object in an inconsistent state.

Unfortunately, using synchronization can itself cause problems. Thread synchronization involves acquiring an exclusive lock. Only the one thread that currently holds the lock can execute the synchronized code. When a program uses more than one lock, however, a situation known as deadlock can arise. Deadlock occurs when two or more threads are all waiting to acquire a lock that is currently held by one of the other waiting threads. Because each thread is waiting to acquire a lock, none ever releases the lock or locks it already holds, which means that none of the waiting threads ever acquires the lock it is waiting for. The situation is a total impasse; all the threads involved come to a halt, and the program can't continue.

Example 4-3 is a simple program that creates a deadlock situation in which two threads attempt to acquire locks on two different resources. It is pretty easy to see how deadlock can arise in this simple program. It might not be as clear, however, if there were synchronized methods involved, instead of a simple symmetrical set of synchronized statements. More complicated situations also arise with multiple threads and multiple resources. In general, the problem of deadlock is a deep and nasty one. One good technique for preventing it, however, is for all threads always to acquire all the locks they need in the same order.

Example 4–3: Deadlock.java

```
package com.davidflanagan.examples.thread;

/**
 * This is a demonstration of how NOT to write multi-threaded programs.
 * It is a program that purposely causes deadlock between two threads that
 * are both trying to acquire locks for the same two resources.
 * To avoid this sort of deadlock when locking multiple resources, all threads
 * should always acquire their locks in the same order.
 **/
public class Deadlock {
    public static void main(String[] args) {
        // These are the two resource objects we'll try to get locks for
        final Object resource1 = "resource1";
        final Object resource2 = "resource2";
        // Here's the first thread.  It tries to lock resource1 then resource2
        Thread t1 = new Thread() {
            public void run() {
                // Lock resource 1
                synchronized(resource1) {
                    System.out.println("Thread 1: locked resource 1");

                    // Pause for a bit, simulating some file I/O or
                    // something.  Basically, we just want to give the
                    // other thread a chance to run.  Threads and deadlock
                    // are asynchronous things, but we're trying to force
                    // deadlock to happen here...
                    try { Thread.sleep(50); }
                    catch (InterruptedException e) {}

                    // Now wait 'till we can get a lock on resource 2
                    synchronized(resource2) {
                        System.out.println("Thread 1: locked resource 2");
                    }
                }
            }
        };

        // Here's the second thread.  It tries to lock resource2 then resource1
        Thread t2 = new Thread() {
            public void run() {
                // This thread locks resource 2 right away
                synchronized(resource2) {
                    System.out.println("Thread 2: locked resource 2");

                    // Then it pauses, just like the first thread.
                    try { Thread.sleep(50); }
                    catch (InterruptedException e) {}

                    // Then it tries to lock resource1.  But wait!  Thread
                    // 1 locked resource1, and won't release it 'till it
                    // gets a lock on resource2.  This thread holds the
                    // lock on resource2, and won't release it 'till it
                    // gets resource1.  We're at an impasse. Neither
                    // thread can run, and the program freezes up.
                    synchronized(resource1) {
                        System.out.println("Thread 2: locked resource 1");
                    }
                }
```

Example 4–3: Deadlock.java (continued)

```
                }
        };

        // Start the two threads. If all goes as planned, deadlock will occur,
        // and the program will never exit.
        t1.start();
        t2.start();
    }
}
```

Timers

Java 1.3 introduces the `java.util.Timer` class and the abstract `java.util.TimerTask` class. If you subclass `TimerTask` and implement its `run()` method, you can then use a `Timer` object to schedule invocations of that `run()` method at a specified time or at multiple times at a specified interval. One `Timer` object can schedule and invoke many `TimerTask` objects. `Timer` is quite useful, as it simplifies many programs that would otherwise have to create their own threads to provide the same functionality. Note that `java.util.Timer` is not at all the same as the Java 1.2 class `javax.swing.Timer`.

Example 4-4 and Example 4-5 are simple implementations of the `TimerTask` and `Timer` classes that can be used prior to Java 1.3. They implement the same API as the Java 1.3 classes, except that they are in the `com.davidflanagan.examples.thread` package, instead of the `java.util` package. These implementations are not intended to be as robust as the official implementations in Java 1.3, but they are useful for simple tasks and are a good example of a nontrivial use of threads. Note in particular the use of `wait()` and `notify()` in Example 4-5. After studying these examples, you may be interested to compare them to the implementations that come with Java 1.3.*

Example 4–4: TimerTask.java

```
package com.davidflanagan.examples.thread;

/**
 * This class implements the same API as the Java 1.3 java.util.TimerTask.
 * Note that a TimerTask can only be scheduled on one Timer at a time, but
 * that this implementation does not enforce that constraint.
 **/
public abstract class TimerTask implements Runnable {
    boolean cancelled = false;   // Has it been cancelled?
    long nextTime = -1;          // When is it next scheduled?
    long period;                 // What is the execution interval
    boolean fixedRate;           // Fixed-rate execution?

    protected TimerTask() {}

    /**
     * Cancel the execution of the task.  Return true if it was actually
     * running, or false if it was already cancelled or never scheduled.
```

---

* If you have the Java SDK™ from Sun, look in the *src.jar* archive that comes with it.

Example 4-4: TimerTask.java (continued)

```java
     **/
    public boolean cancel() {
        if (cancelled) return false;              // Already cancelled;
        cancelled = true;                         // Cancel it
        if (nextTime == -1) return false;         // Never scheduled;
        return true;
    }

    /**
     * When is the timer scheduled to execute? The run() method can use this
     * to see whether it was invoked when it was supposed to be
     **/
    public long scheduledExecutionTime() { return nextTime; }

    /**
     * Subclasses must override this to provide the code that is to be run.
     * The Timer class will invoke this from its internal thread.
     **/
    public abstract void run();

    // This method is used by Timer to tell the Task how it is scheduled.
    void schedule(long nextTime, long period, boolean fixedRate) {
        this.nextTime = nextTime;
        this.period = period;
        this.fixedRate = fixedRate;
    }

    // This will be called by Timer after Timer calls the run method.
    boolean reschedule() {
        if (period == 0 || cancelled) return false; // Don't run it again
        if (fixedRate) nextTime += period;
        else nextTime = System.currentTimeMillis() + period;
        return true;
    }
}
```

Example 4-5: Timer.java

```java
package com.davidflanagan.examples.thread;
import java.util.Date;
import java.util.TreeSet;
import java.util.Comparator;

/**
 * This class is a simple implementation of the Java 1.3 java.util.Timer API
 **/
public class Timer {
    // This sorted set stores the tasks that this Timer is responsible for.
    // It uses a comparator (defined below) to sort the tasks by execution time.
    TreeSet tasks = new TreeSet(new TimerTaskComparator());

    // This is the thread the timer uses to execute the tasks
    TimerThread timer;

    /** This constructor create a Timer that does not use a daemon thread */
    public Timer() { this(false); }

    /** The main constructor: the internal thread is a daemon if specified */
    public Timer(boolean isDaemon) {
```

Example 4–5: Timer.java (continued)

```
        timer = new TimerThread(isDaemon);  // TimerThread is defined below
        timer.start();                      // Start the thread running
    }

    /** Stop the timer thread, and discard all scheduled tasks */
    public void cancel() {
        synchronized(tasks) {      // Only one thread at a time!
            timer.pleaseStop();    // Set a flag asking the thread to stop
            tasks.clear();         // Discard all tasks
            tasks.notify();        // Wake up the thread if it is in wait().
        }
    }

    /** Schedule a single execution after delay milliseconds */
    public void schedule(TimerTask task, long delay) {
        task.schedule(System.currentTimeMillis() + delay, 0, false);
        schedule(task);
    }

    /** Schedule a single execution at the specified time */
    public void schedule(TimerTask task, Date time) {
        task.schedule(time.getTime(), 0, false);
        schedule(task);
    }

    /** Schedule a periodic execution starting at the specified time */
    public void schedule(TimerTask task, Date firstTime, long period) {
        task.schedule(firstTime.getTime(), period, false);
        schedule(task);
    }

    /** Schedule a periodic execution starting after the specified delay */
    public void schedule(TimerTask task, long delay, long period) {
        task.schedule(System.currentTimeMillis() + delay, period, false);
        schedule(task);
    }

    /**
     * Schedule a periodic execution starting after the specified delay.
     * Schedule fixed-rate executions period ms after the start of the last.
     * Instead of fixed-interval executions measured from the end of the last.
     **/
    public void scheduleAtFixedRate(TimerTask task, long delay, long period) {
        task.schedule(System.currentTimeMillis() + delay, period, true);
        schedule(task);
    }

    /** Schedule a periodic execution starting after the specified time */
    public void scheduleAtFixedRate(TimerTask task, Date firstTime,
                                    long period)
    {
        task.schedule(firstTime.getTime(), period, true);
        schedule(task);
    }


    // This internal method adds a task to the sorted set of tasks
    void schedule(TimerTask task) {
```

Example 4-5: Timer.java (continued)

```
        synchronized(tasks) {  // Only one thread can modify tasks at a time!
            tasks.add(task);   // Add the task to the sorted set of tasks
            tasks.notify();    // Wake up the thread if it is waiting
        }
    }

    /**
     * This inner class is used to sort tasks by next execution time.
     **/
    static class TimerTaskComparator implements Comparator {
        public int compare(Object a, Object b) {
            TimerTask t1 = (TimerTask) a;
            TimerTask t2 = (TimerTask) b;
            long diff = t1.nextTime - t2.nextTime;
            if (diff < 0) return -1;
            else if (diff > 0) return 1;
            else return 0;
        }
        public boolean equals(Object o) { return this == o; }
    }

    /**
     * This inner class defines the thread that runs each of the tasks at their
     * scheduled times
     **/
    class TimerThread extends Thread {
        // This flag is set true to tell the thread to stop running.
        // Note that it is declared volatile, which means that it may be
        // changed asynchronously by another thread, so threads must always
        // read its true value, and not used a cached version.
        volatile boolean stopped = false;

        // The constructor
        public TimerThread(boolean isDaemon) { setDaemon(isDaemon); }

        // Ask the thread to stop by setting the flag above
        public void pleaseStop() { stopped = true; }

        // This is the body of the thread
        public void run() {
            TimerTask readyToRun = null;  // Is there a task to run right now?

            // The thread loops until the stopped flag is set to true.
            while(!stopped) {
                // If there is a task that is ready to run, then run it!
                if (readyToRun != null) {
                    if (readyToRun.cancelled) {  // If it was cancelled, skip.
                        readyToRun = null;
                        continue;
                    }
                    // Run the task.
                    readyToRun.run();
                    // Ask it to reschedule itself, and if it wants to run
                    // again, then insert it back into the set of tasks.
                    if (readyToRun.reschedule())
                        schedule(readyToRun);
                    // We've run it, so there is nothing to run now
                    readyToRun = null;
```

Example 4-5: Timer.java (continued)

```
                    // Go back to top of the loop to see if we've been stopped
                    continue;
                }

                // Now acquire a lock on the set of tasks
                synchronized(tasks) {
                    long timeout;  // how many ms 'till the next execution?

                    if (tasks.isEmpty()) {  // If there aren't any tasks
                        timeout = 0;  // Wait 'till notified of a new task
                    }
                    else {
                        // If there are scheduled tasks, then get the first one
                        // Since the set is sorted, this is the next one.
                        TimerTask t = (TimerTask) tasks.first();
                        // How long 'till it is next run?
                        timeout = t.nextTime - System.currentTimeMillis();
                        // Check whether it needs to run now
                        if (timeout <= 0) {
                            readyToRun = t;  // Save it as ready to run
                            tasks.remove(t); // Remove it from the set
                            // Break out of the synchronized section before
                            // we run the task
                            continue;
                        }
                    }

                    // If we get here, there is nothing ready to run now,
                    // so wait for time to run out, or wait 'till notify() is
                    // called when something new is added to the set of tasks.
                    try { tasks.wait(timeout); }
                    catch (InterruptedException e) {}

                    // When we wake up, go back up to the top of the while loop
                }
            }
        }
    }

    /** This inner class defines a test program */
    public static class Test {
        public static void main(String[] args) {
            final TimerTask t1 = new TimerTask() { // Task 1: print "boom"
                    public void run() { System.out.println("boom"); }
                };
            final TimerTask t2 = new TimerTask() { // Task 2: print "BOOM"
                    public void run() { System.out.println("\tBOOM"); }
                };
            final TimerTask t3 = new TimerTask() { // Task 3: cancel the tasks
                    public void run() { t1.cancel(); t2.cancel(); }
                };

            // Create a timer, and schedule some tasks
            final Timer timer = new Timer();
            timer.schedule(t1, 0, 500);      // boom every .5sec starting now
            timer.schedule(t2, 2000, 2000);  // BOOM every 2s, starting in 2s
            timer.schedule(t3, 5000);        // Stop them after 5 seconds
```

Example 4-5: Timer.java (continued)

```
// Schedule a final task: starting in 5 seconds, count
// down from 5, then destroy the timer, which, since it is
// the only remaining thread, will cause the program to exit.
timer.scheduleAtFixedRate(new TimerTask() {
        public int times = 5;
        public void run() {
            System.out.println(times--);
            if (times == 0) timer.cancel();
        }
    },
                            5000,500);
    }
  }
}
```

Exercises

4-1. Write a Java program that takes a list of filenames on the command line and prints out the number of lines in each file. The program should create one thread for each file and use these threads to count the lines in all the files at the same time. Use java.io.LineNumberReader to help you count lines. You'll probably want to define a LineCounter class that extends Thread or implements Runnable. Now write a variant of your program that uses your LineCounter class to read the files sequentially, rather than at the same time. Compare the performance of the multithreaded and single-threaded programs, using System.currentTimeMills() to determine elapsed time. Compare the performance of the two programs for two, five, and ten files.

4-2. Example 4-3 demonstrates how deadlock can occur when two threads each attempt to obtain a lock held by the other. Modify the example to create deadlock among three threads, where each thread is trying to acquire a lock held by one of the other threads.

4-3. Example 4-3 uses the synchronized statement to demonstrate deadlock. Write a similar program that causes two threads to deadlock, but use synchronized methods instead of the synchronized statement. This sort of deadlock is a little more subtle and harder to detect.

4-4. Example 4-5 shows an implementation of the Java 1.3 java.util.Timer API. Java 1.2 introduced another Timer class, the javax.swing.Timer class. This class has a similar purpose but a different API. It invokes the actionPerformed() method of any number of registered ActionListener objects one or more times after a specified delay and at a specified interval. Read the documentation for this Timer class, then create your own implementation of it. If you've read Chapter 10, *Graphical User Interfaces*, you know that the methods of event listeners, such as the actionPerformed() method, are supposed to be invoked only by the event dispatch thread. Therefore, your implementation of the Timer class should not invoke actionPerformed() directly, but should instead use java.awt.EventQueue.invokeLater() or javax.swing.SwingUtilities.invokeLater() to tell the event dispatch thread to invoke the method.

4-5. Once you have read Chapter 5, you may want to come back to this chapter to try this exercise. The Server class of Chapter 5 is a multithreaded, multiservice network server. It demonstrates important networking techniques, but it also makes heavy use of threads. One particular feature of this program is that it creates a ThreadGroup to contain all the threads it creates. Modify Server so that in addition to creating this one master thread group, it also creates a nested thread group for each of the individual services it provides. Place the thread for each individual client connection within the thread group for its service. Also, modify the program so that each service can have a thread priority specified and use this priority value when creating connection threads. You will probably want to store the thread group and priority for each service as fields of the nested Listener class.

CHAPTER 5

Networking

Sun Microsystems has long used the slogan "The Network is the Computer." It's no surprise, therefore, that they designed Java to be a network-centric language. The java.net package provides powerful and easy-to-use networking capabilities. The examples in this chapter demonstrate those capabilities at a number of different levels of abstraction. They show you how to:

- Use the URL class to parse URLs and download the network resources specified by a URL

- Use the URLConnection class to gain more control over the downloading of network resources

- Write client programs that use the Socket class to communicate over the network

- Use the Socket and ServerSocket classes to write servers

- Send and receive low-overhead datagram packets

Downloading the Contents of a URL

Example 5-1 shows how you can download the network resource referred to by a URL using the URL class. This class serves mainly to represent and parse URLs but also has several important methods for downloading URLs. The most high-level of these methods is getContent(), which downloads the content of a URL, parses it, and returns the parsed object. This method relies on special content handlers having been installed to perform the parsing. By default, the Java SDK has content handlers for plain text and for several common image formats. When you call the getContent() method of a URL object that refers to a plain text or GIF or JPEG image file, the method returns a String or Image object. More commonly, when getContent() doesn't know how to handle the data type, it simply returns an InputStream so that you can read and parse the data yourself.

Example 5-1 doesn't use the getContent() method. Instead, it calls openStream() to return an InputStream from which the contents of the URL can be downloaded. This InputStream is connected, through the network, to the remote resource named by the URL, but the URL class hides all the details of setting up this connection. (In fact, the connection is set up by a protocol handler class; the Java SDK has default handlers for the most common network protocols, including *http:*, *ftp:*, *mailto:* and *file:*.)

Example 5-1 is a simple standalone program that downloads the contents of a specified URL and saves it in a file or writes it to the console. You'll note that most of this program looks like it belongs in Chapter 3, *Input/Output.* In fact, as we'll see in this and other examples in this chapter, almost all networking involves the use of the I/O techniques we learned about in that chapter.

Example 5-1: GetURL.java

```
package com.davidflanagan.examples.net;
import java.io.*;
import java.net.*;

/**
 * This simple program uses the URL class and its openStream() method to
 * download the contents of a URL and copy them to a file or to the console.
 **/
public class GetURL {
    public static void main(String[] args) {
        InputStream in = null;
        OutputStream out = null;
        try {
            // Check the arguments
            if ((args.length != 1) && (args.length != 2))
                throw new IllegalArgumentException("Wrong number of args");

            // Set up the streams
            URL url = new URL(args[0]);    // Create the URL
            in = url.openStream();         // Open a stream to it
            if (args.length == 2)          // Get an appropriate output stream
                out = new FileOutputStream(args[1]);
            else out = System.out;

            // Now copy bytes from the URL to the output stream
            byte[] buffer = new byte[4096];
            int bytes_read;
            while((bytes_read = in.read(buffer)) != -1)
                out.write(buffer, 0, bytes_read);
        }
        // On exceptions, print error message and usage message.
        catch (Exception e) {
            System.err.println(e);
            System.err.println("Usage: java GetURL <URL> [<filename>]");
        }
        finally {  // Always close the streams, no matter what.
            try { in.close(); out.close(); } catch (Exception e) {}
        }
    }
}
```

Using a URLConnection

The URLConnection class establishes a connection to a URL. The openStream() method of URL we used in Example 5-1 is merely a convenience method that creates a URLConnection object and calls its getInputStream() method. By using a URLConnection object directly, instead of relying on openStream(), you have much more control over the process of downloading the contents of a URL.

Example 5-2 is a simple program that shows how to use a URLConnection to obtain the content type, size, last-modified date, and other information about the resource referred to by a URL. If the URL uses the HTTP protocol, it also demonstrates how to use the HttpURLConnection subclass to obtain additional information about the connection.

Note the use of the java.util.Date class to convert a timestamp (a long that contains the number of milliseconds since midnight, January 1, 1970 GMT) to a human-readable date and time string.

Example 5-2: GetURLInfo.java

```
package com.davidflanagan.examples.net;
import java.net.*;
import java.io.*;
import java.util.Date;

/**
 * A class that displays information about a URL.
 **/
public class GetURLInfo {
    /** Use the URLConnection class to get info about the URL */
    public static void printinfo(URL url) throws IOException {
        URLConnection c = url.openConnection();  // Get URLConnection from URL
        c.connect();                             // Open a connection to URL

        // Display some information about the URL contents
        System.out.println("  Content Type: " + c.getContentType());
        System.out.println("  Content Encoding: " + c.getContentEncoding());
        System.out.println("  Content Length: " + c.getContentLength());
        System.out.println("  Date: " + new Date(c.getDate()));
        System.out.println("  Last Modified: " +new Date(c.getLastModified()));
        System.out.println("  Expiration: " + new Date(c.getExpiration()));

        // If it is an HTTP connection, display some additional information.
        if (c instanceof HttpURLConnection) {
            HttpURLConnection h = (HttpURLConnection) c;
            System.out.println("  Request Method: " + h.getRequestMethod());
            System.out.println("  Response Message: " +h.getResponseMessage());
            System.out.println("  Response Code: " + h.getResponseCode());
        }
    }

    /** Create a URL, call printinfo() to display information about it. */
    public static void main(String[] args) {
        try { printinfo(new URL(args[0])); }
        catch (Exception e) {
            System.err.println(e);
            System.err.println("Usage: java GetURLInfo <url>");
        }
```

Example 5-2: GetURLInfo.java (continued)

```
    }
}
```

Sending Email Through a URLConnection

As I mentioned earlier, Java includes support for different URL protocols through protocol handlers that are implemented internally to the Java SDK. These handlers include support for the *mailto:* protocol. Example 5-3 shows a program that uses a *mailto:* URL to send email. The program prompts the user to enter the sender, recipient or recipients, subject, and body of the message, and then creates an appropriate *mailto:* URL and obtains a URLConnection object for it. The program uses the setDoInput() and setDoOutput() methods to specify that it is writing data to the URLConnection. It obtains the appropriate stream with getOutput-Stream() and then writes the message headers and body to that stream, closing the stream when the message body is complete. The program uses the user.name system property and the InetAddress class to attempt to create a valid return address for the sender of the email, though this doesn't actually work correctly on all platforms.

In order for the *mailto:* protocol handler to send mail, it must know what computer, or mailhost, to send it to. By default, it attempts to send it to the machine on which it is running. Some computers, particularly Unix machines on intranets, work as mailhosts, so this works fine. Other computers, such as PCs connected to the Internet by a dialup connection, have to specify a mailhost explicitly on the command line. For example, if your Internet service provider has the domain name *isp.net*, the appropriate mailhost is often *mail.isp.net*. If you specify a mailhost, it is stored in the system property mail.host, which is read by the internal *mailto:* protocol handler.

Note that Example 5-3 uses the println() method to display messages to the console but uses the print() method and explicit "\n" line terminator characters to send text over the network. Different operating systems use different line terminators, and println() uses whatever terminator is expected on the local system. Since most network services originated in the Unix world, however, they typically use the Unix line terminator, which is the "\n" newline character. We use it explicitly here, so that this client program works correctly when run on Unix, Windows, or Macintosh systems.

Example 5-3: SendMail.java

```
package com.davidflanagan.examples.net;
import java.io.*;
import java.net.*;

/**
 * This program sends e-mail using a mailto: URL
 **/
public class SendMail {
    public static void main(String[] args) {
        try {
            // If the user specified a mailhost, tell the system about it.
```

Example 5–3: SendMail.java (continued)

```
            if (args.length >= 1)
                System.getProperties().put("mail.host", args[0]);

            // A Reader stream to read from the console
            BufferedReader in =
                new BufferedReader(new InputStreamReader(System.in));

            // Ask the user for the from, to, and subject lines
            System.out.print("From: ");
            String from = in.readLine();
            System.out.print("To: ");
            String to = in.readLine();
            System.out.print("Subject: ");
            String subject = in.readLine();

            // Establish a network connection for sending mail
            URL u = new URL("mailto:" + to);        // Create a mailto: URL
            URLConnection c = u.openConnection();    // Create its URLConnection
            c.setDoInput(false);                     // Specify no input from it
            c.setDoOutput(true);                     // Specify we'll do output
            System.out.println("Connecting...");     // Tell the user
            System.out.flush();                      // Tell them right now
            c.connect();                             // Connect to mail host
            PrintWriter out =                        // Get output stream to host
                new PrintWriter(new OutputStreamWriter(c.getOutputStream()));

            // Write out mail headers.  Don't let users fake the From address
            out.print("From: \"" + from + "\" <" +
                    System.getProperty("user.name") + "@" +
                    InetAddress.getLocalHost().getHostName() + ">\n");
            out.print("To: " + to + "\n");
            out.print("Subject: " + subject + "\n");
            out.print("\n");  // blank line to end the list of headers

            // Now ask the user to enter the body of the message
            System.out.println("Enter the message. " +
                            "End with a '.' on a line by itself.");
            // Read message line by line and send it out.
            String line;
            for(;;) {
                line = in.readLine();
                if ((line == null) || line.equals(".")) break;
                out.print(line + "\n");
            }

            // Close (and flush) the stream to terminate the message
            out.close();
            // Tell the user it was successfully sent.
            System.out.println("Message sent.");
        }
        catch (Exception e) {  // Handle any exceptions, print error message.
            System.err.println(e);
            System.err.println("Usage: java SendMail [<mailhost>]");
        }
    }
}
```

Connecting to a Web Server

Example 5-4 shows a program, HttpClient, that downloads the contents of a URL from a web server and writes it to a file or to the console. It behaves just like the GetURL program from Example 5-1 does. Despite the similarity in behavior, however, the implementation of these two programs is entirely different. While GetURL relies on the URL class and its protocol handlers to handle protocol details, Http-Client connects directly to a web server and communicates with it using the HTTP protocol. (It uses an old and extremely simple version of the protocol, which keeps the program very simple.) As a consequence, HttpClient is restricted to downloading URLs that use the *http:* protocol. It can't handle *ftp:* or other network protocols. Note that HttpClient does use the URL class but only to represent a URL and to parse it, not to connect to it.

The main point of interest in this example is the introduction of the Socket class, which creates a stream-based network connection between a client and a server. To create a network connection to another host, you simply create a Socket, specifying the desired host and port. If there is a program (a server) running on the specified host and listening for connections on the specified port, the Socket() constructor returns a Socket object you can use to communicate with the server. (If there is not a server listening on the specified host and port, or if anything goes wrong—and many things can go wrong with networking—the Socket() constructor throws an exception).

If you are not familiar with hosts and ports, think of the host as a post office and the port as a post-office box. Just as a post office has many different post-office boxes, any host on the network can run many different servers at a time. Different servers use different ports for their addresses. To establish a connection, you must specify both the correct host and the correct port. Many services have standard default ports. Web servers run on port 80, POP email servers run on port 110, and so on.

Once you have a Socket object, you are connected, across the network, to a server. The getInputStream() method of the socket returns an InputStream you can use to read bytes from the server, and getOutputStream() returns an Output-Stream you can use to write bytes to the server. This is exactly what the Http-Client program does. It establishes a connection to the web server, sends an HTTP GET request to the server through the output stream of the socket, and then reads the server's response through the input stream of the socket. Note once again that the GET request is explicitly terminated with a "\n" newline character, rather than relying on the platform-dependent line terminator provided by the println() method.

Example 5-4: HttpClient.java

```
package com.davidflanagan.examples.net;
import java.io.*;
import java.net.*;

/**
 * This program connects to a Web server and downloads the specified URL
 * from it.  It uses the HTTP protocol directly.
 **/
```

Example 5-4: HttpClient.java (continued)

```java
public class HttpClient {
    public static void main(String[] args) {
        try {
            // Check the arguments
            if ((args.length != 1) && (args.length != 2))
                throw new IllegalArgumentException("Wrong number of args");

            // Get an output stream to write the URL contents to
            OutputStream to_file;
            if (args.length == 2) to_file = new FileOutputStream(args[1]);
            else to_file = System.out;

            // Now use the URL class to parse the user-specified URL into
            // its various parts.
            URL url = new URL(args[0]);
            String protocol = url.getProtocol();
            if (!protocol.equals("http")) // Check that we support the protocol
                throw new IllegalArgumentException("Must use 'http:' protocol");
            String host = url.getHost();
            int port = url.getPort();
            if (port == -1) port = 80; // if no port, use the default HTTP port
            String filename = url.getFile();

            // Open a network socket connection to the specified host and port
            Socket socket = new Socket(host, port);

            // Get input and output streams for the socket
            InputStream from_server = socket.getInputStream();
            PrintWriter to_server = new PrintWriter(socket.getOutputStream());

            // Send the HTTP GET command to the Web server, specifying the file
            // This uses an old and very simple version of the HTTP protocol
            to_server.print("GET " + filename + "\n\n");
            to_server.flush();  // Send it right now!

            // Now read the server's response, and write it to the file
            byte[] buffer = new byte[4096];
            int bytes_read;
            while((bytes_read = from_server.read(buffer)) != -1)
                to_file.write(buffer, 0, bytes_read);

            // When the server closes the connection, we close our stuff
            socket.close();
            to_file.close();
        }
        catch (Exception e) {    // Report any errors that arise
            System.err.println(e);
            System.err.println("Usage: java HttpClient <URL> [<filename>]");
        }
    }
}
```

A Simple Web Server

Example 5-5 shows a very simple web server, HttpMirror. Instead of returning a requested file, however, this server simply "mirrors" the request back to the client as its reply. This can be useful when debugging web clients and can be interesting if you are just curious about the details of HTTP client requests. To run the program, you specify the port that it should listen on as an argument. For example, I can run the server on the host *oxymoron.oreilly.com* like this:

```
oxymoron% java com.davidflanagan.examples.net.HttpMirror 4444
```

Then, in my web browser, I can load *http://oxymoron.oreilly.com:4444/testing.html*. The server ignores the request for the file *testing.html*, but it echoes back the request that my web browser sent. It might look something like this:

```
GET /testing.html HTTP/1.0
Connection: Keep-Alive
User-Agent: Mozilla/3.01Gold (X11; I; Linux 2.0.18 i486)
Host: 127.0.0.1:4444
Accept: image/gif, image/x-xbitmap, image/jpeg, image/pjpeg, */*
```

The main new feature introduced in Example 5-5 is the ServerSocket class. This class is used by a server, or any other program, that wants to sit and wait for a connection request from a client. When you create a ServerSocket, you specify the port to listen on. To connect to a client, call the accept() method of the ServerSocket. This method blocks until a client attempts to connect to the port that the ServerSocket is listening on. When such a connection attempt occurs, the ServerSocket establishes a connection to the client and returns a Socket object that can communicate with the client. Your code can then call the getInput-Stream() and getOutputStream() methods of the socket to get streams for reading bytes from the client and for writing bytes to the client.

Note that the ServerSocket is not used for communication between the server and its client; it is used only to wait for and establish the connection to the client. Typically, a single ServerSocket object is used over and over again to establish connections to any number of clients.

Example 5-5 is quite straightforward. It creates a ServerSocket and calls its accept() method, as outlined previously. When a client connects, it sets up the streams and then sends some HTTP headers to the client, telling it that the request has been received successfully and that the reply is text/plain data. Next, it reads all the HTTP headers of the client's request and sends them back to the client as the body of its reply. When it reads a blank line from the client, this indicates the end of the client's headers, so it closes the connection.

Note that the body of the HttpMirror program is a big infinite loop. It connects to a client, handles the request, and then loops and waits for another client connection. Although this simple server works perfectly well for the testing purposes for which it is designed, there is one flaw in it: it is a single-threaded server and can talk to only one client at a time. Later in this chapter, we'll see examples of servers that use multiple threads and can maintain connections to any number of clients.

Example 5-5: HttpMirror.java

```
package com.davidflanagan.examples.net;
import java.io.*;
import java.net.*;

/**
 * This program is a very simple Web server.  When it receives a HTTP request
 * it sends the request back as the reply.  This can be of interest when
 * you want to see just what a Web client is requesting, or what data is
 * being sent when a form is submitted, for example.
 **/
public class HttpMirror {
    public static void main(String args[]) {
        try {
            // Get the port to listen on
            int port = Integer.parseInt(args[0]);
            // Create a ServerSocket to listen on that port.
            ServerSocket ss = new ServerSocket(port);
            // Now enter an infinite loop, waiting for & handling connections.
            for(;;) {

                // Wait for a client to connect.  The method will block;
                // when it returns the socket will be connected to the client
                Socket client = ss.accept();

                // Get input and output streams to talk to the client
                BufferedReader in = new BufferedReader(
                            new InputStreamReader(client.getInputStream()));
                PrintWriter out = new PrintWriter(client.getOutputStream());

                // Start sending our reply, using the HTTP 1.0 protocol
                out.print("HTTP/1.0 200 \n");        // Version & status code
                out.print("Content-Type: text/plain\n"); // The type of data
                out.print("\n");                      // End of headers

                // Now, read the HTTP request from the client, and send it
                // right back to the client as part of the body of our
                // response.  The client doesn't disconnect, so we never get
                // an EOF.  It does sends an empty line at the end of the
                // headers, though.  So when we see the empty line, we stop
                // reading.  This means we don't mirror the contents of POST
                // requests, for example.  Note that the readLine() method
                // works with Unix, Windows, and Mac line terminators.
                String line;
                while((line = in.readLine()) != null) {
                    if (line.length() == 0) break;
                    out.print(line + "\n");
                }

                // Close socket, breaking the connection to the client, and
                // closing the input and output streams
                out.close();     // Flush and close the output stream
                in.close();      // Close the input stream
                client.close();  // Close the socket itself
            } // Now loop again, waiting for the next connection
        }
        // If anything goes wrong, print an error message
        catch (Exception e) {
            System.err.println(e);
```

Example 5–5: HttpMirror.java (continued)

```
            System.err.println("Usage: java HttpMirror <port>");
        }
    }
}
```

A Proxy Server

Example 5-6 shows another network server: a simple, single-threaded proxy server. A proxy server is one that acts as a proxy for some other real server. When a client connects to a proxy server, the proxy forwards the client's requests to the real server, and then forwards the server's responses to the client. To the client, the proxy looks like the server. To the real server, the proxy looks like a client.

Why bother with a proxy server at all? Why can't a client just connect directly to the real server? First and foremost, there are firewall-related reasons to use proxy servers. There are also interesting filtering applications of such servers; a sophisticated proxy web server might strip advertising out of the web pages it downloads, for example. There is yet another reason to use proxy servers that arises when using Java networking capabilities with applets, as the following scenario makes clear.

Suppose that I have developed a nifty new server that runs on my computer *oxymoron.oreilly.com*. Now I write an applet client for my service and make the applet available on the Web by publishing it on the *www.oreilly.com* web server. Right away there is a problem. Applet security restrictions allow an applet to establish network connections to only one host: the host from which it was downloaded. So my applet client downloaded from *www.oreilly.com* can't communicate with my incredibly useful server on *oxymoron.oreilly.com*. What can I do? The system administrator won't let me install my new server on *www.oreilly.com*, and I don't want the overhead of running Apache or some other web server on my desktop workstation, *oxymoron*. So instead, I run a simple proxy server, like the one in Example 5-6, on *oxymoron*. I set it up so that it listens for connections on port 4444 and acts as a proxy for the web server running on port 80 of *www.oreilly.com*. I publish my applet at *http://www.oreilly.com/staff/david/nifty.html*, but tell people to load it from *http://oxymoron.oreilly. com:4444/staff/david/nifty.html*.* This solves the problem. As far as the applet is concerned, it has been loaded from *oxymoron.oreilly.com*, so it can connect to my nifty service running on that host.

There are not really any new features in Example 5-6. It is an interesting example because it combines the features of both client and server into one program. When studying this code, remember that the proxy server mediates the connection between a client and a server. It acts like a server to the client and like a client to the server. SimpleProxyServer is a single-threaded server; it can only handle one client connection at a time. Nevertheless, you'll notice that it does use a thread (implemented in an anonymous inner class) so that the proxy can transfer data from client to server and from server to client at the same time. In this example,

---

* This is a fictitious example; these URLs don't really do anything!

the main thread reads bytes from the server and sends them to the client. A separate thread reads bytes from the client and sends them to the server. In Java 1.3 and earlier, if you want to monitor multiple streams, as we do here, you have to use multiple threads: Java doesn't support nonblocking I/O, nor does it define any way to block on multiple streams at the same time. Using one thread per stream can cause scalability problems for busy servers, however, so this limitation may be remedied in Java 1.4.

Example 5–6: SimpleProxyServer.java

```java
package com.davidflanagan.examples.net;
import java.io.*;
import java.net.*;

/**
 * This class implements a simple single-threaded proxy server.
 **/
public class SimpleProxyServer {
    /** The main method parses arguments and passes them to runServer */
    public static void main(String[] args) throws IOException {
        try {
            // Check the number of arguments
            if (args.length != 3)
                throw new IllegalArgumentException("Wrong number of args.");

            // Get the command-line arguments: the host and port we are proxy
            // for and the local port that we listen for connections on.
            String host = args[0];
            int remoteport = Integer.parseInt(args[1]);
            int localport = Integer.parseInt(args[2]);
            // Print a start-up message
            System.out.println("Starting proxy for " + host + ":" +
                               remoteport + " on port " + localport);
            // And start running the server
            runServer(host, remoteport, localport);   // never returns
        }
        catch (Exception e) {
            System.err.println(e);
            System.err.println("Usage: java SimpleProxyServer " +
                               "<host> <remoteport> <localport>");
        }
    }

    /**
     * This method runs a single-threaded proxy server for
     * host:remoteport on the specified local port.  It never returns.
     **/
    public static void runServer(String host, int remoteport, int localport)
        throws IOException {
        // Create a ServerSocket to listen for connections with
        ServerSocket ss = new ServerSocket(localport);

        // Create buffers for client-to-server and server-to-client transfer.
        // We make one final so it can be used in an anonymous class below.
        // Note the assumptions about the volume of traffic in each direction.
        final byte[] request = new byte[1024];
        byte[] reply = new byte[4096];

        // This is a server that never returns, so enter an infinite loop.
```

Example 5-6: SimpleProxyServer.java (continued)

```
while(true) {
    // Variables to hold the sockets to the client and to the server.
    Socket client = null, server = null;
    try {
        // Wait for a connection on the local port
        client = ss.accept();

        // Get client streams.  Make them final so they can
        // be used in the anonymous thread below.
        final InputStream from_client = client.getInputStream();
        final OutputStream to_client = client.getOutputStream();

        // Make a connection to the real server.
        // If we cannot connect to the server, send an error to the
        // client, disconnect, and continue waiting for connections.
        try { server = new Socket(host, remoteport); }
        catch (IOException e) {
            PrintWriter out = new PrintWriter(to_client);
            out.print("Proxy server cannot connect to " + host + ":"+
                      remoteport + ":\n" + e + "\n");
            out.flush();
            client.close();
            continue;
        }

        // Get server streams.
        final InputStream from_server = server.getInputStream();
        final OutputStream to_server = server.getOutputStream();

        // Make a thread to read the client's requests and pass them
        // to the server.  We have to use a separate thread because
        // requests and responses may be asynchronous.
        Thread t = new Thread() {
            public void run() {
                int bytes_read;
                try {
                    while((bytes_read=from_client.read(request))!=-1) {
                        to_server.write(request, 0, bytes_read);
                        to_server.flush();
                    }
                }
                catch (IOException e) {}

                // the client closed the connection to us, so close our
                // connection to the server.  This will also cause the
                // server-to-client loop in the main thread exit.
                try {to_server.close();} catch (IOException e) {}
            }
        };

        // Start the client-to-server request thread running
        t.start();

        // Meanwhile, in the main thread, read the server's responses
        // and pass them back to the client.  This will be done in
        // parallel with the client-to-server request thread above.
        int bytes_read;
        try {
```

Networking

Example 5–6: SimpleProxyServer.java (continued)

```
            while((bytes_read = from_server.read(reply)) != -1) {
                to_client.write(reply, 0, bytes_read);
                to_client.flush();
            }
        }
        catch(IOException e) {}

        // The server closed its connection to us, so we close our
        // connection to our client.
        // This will make the other thread exit.
        to_client.close();
    }
    catch (IOException e) { System.err.println(e); }
    finally {  // Close the sockets no matter what happens.
        try {
            if (server != null) server.close();
            if (client != null) client.close();
        }
        catch(IOException e) {}
    }
    }
    }
}
```

Networking with Applets

As I just described, untrusted applets have strict restrictions placed on the kind of networking they can do. They are allowed to connect to and accept connections only from the one host from which they were loaded. No other networking is allowed. This still leaves open some interesting applet networking possibilities, though, and Example 5-7 illustrates one of them. We'll discuss applets and the graphical user interfaces they display in Chapter 15, *Applets*, and Chapter 10, *Graphical User Interfaces*. You shouldn't expect to understand all of this example until you've read those chapters. Nevertheless, this example does contain interesting networking code, primarily in its run( ) method.

finger is a program and network service that used to be run on almost all Unix machines. It allows a client to connect over the network and obtain a list of the users logged on to another system. It may also allow a client to obtain detailed information (such as telephone numbers) for individual users. Nowadays, with heightened security concerns, many Unix machines don't provide this service.

The applet shown in Example 5-7 is a client for the *finger* service. Suppose that I'm an old Unix hacker, and I think that the *finger* service is a great thing. I run the *finger* server on my workstation and encourage my friends to use it to find out when I'm logged on. Unfortunately, my friends work on PCs, so they don't have access to the old-fashioned, text-based *finger* client that all Unix machines have. The Who applet in Example 5-7 solves this problem. It connects to the appropriate port on my host and tells them whether I'm logged on or not. Of course, for this to work, the applet has to be served from my host as well. I might use the SimpleProxyServer program from Example 5-6 to make my computer into a proxy web server. (Or, of course, I could use `SimpleProxyServer` to set up a proxy *finger* server for my host on the host that runs the web server.)

If your system doesn't run the *finger* server itself, trying out this applet may be a little tricky. What you can do is find some host out on the Net that does provide the *finger* service. (I've used *rtfm.mit.edu*, for example.) Then use `SimpleProxy-Server` to run a local proxy for that finger server and run the applet locally on your machine. You have to modify the applet slightly to make it connect to the desired proxy port, instead of the reserved *finger* port, 79, however.

Example 5-7: Who.java

```java
package com.davidflanagan.examples.net;
import java.applet.*;
import java.awt.*;
import java.awt.event.*;
import java.io.*;
import java.net.*;

/**
 * This applet connects to the "finger" server on the host
 * it was served from to determine who is currently logged on.
 * Because it is an untrusted applet, it can only connect to the host
 * from which it came.  Since web servers do not usually run finger
 * servers themselves, this applet will often be used in conjunction
 * with a proxy server, to serve it from some other host that does run
 * a finger server.
 **/
public class Who extends Applet implements ActionListener, Runnable {
    Button who;  // The button in the applet

    /**
     * The init method just creates a button to display in the applet.
     * When the user clicks the button, we'll check who is logged on.
     **/
    public void init() {
        who = new Button("Who?");
        who.setFont(new Font("SansSerif", Font.PLAIN, 14));
        who.addActionListener(this);
        this.add(who);
    }

    /**
     * When the button is clicked, start a thread that will connect to
     * the finger server and display who is logged on
     **/
    public void actionPerformed(ActionEvent e) { new Thread(this).start(); }

    /**
     * This is the method that does the networking and displays the results.
     * It is implemented as the body of a separate thread because it might
     * take some time to complete, and applet methods need to return promptly.
     **/
    public void run() {
        // Disable the button so we don't get multiple queries at once...
        who.setEnabled(false);

        // Create a window to display the output in
        Frame f = new Frame("Who's Logged On: Connecting...");
```

Example 5–7: Who.java (continued)

```
    f.addWindowListener(new WindowAdapter() {
        public void windowClosing(WindowEvent e) {
            ((Frame)e.getSource()).dispose();
        }
    });
    TextArea t = new TextArea(10, 80);
    t.setFont(new Font("MonoSpaced", Font.PLAIN, 10));
    f.add(t, "Center");
    f.pack();
    f.show();

    // Find out  who's logged on
    Socket s = null;
    PrintWriter out = null;
    BufferedReader in = null;
    try {
        // Connect to port 79 (the standard finger port) on the host
        // that the applet was loaded from.
        String hostname = this.getCodeBase().getHost();
        s = new Socket(hostname, 79);
        // Set up the streams
        out = new PrintWriter(new OutputStreamWriter(s.getOutputStream()));
        in = new BufferedReader(new InputStreamReader(s.getInputStream()));

        // Send a blank line to the finger server, telling it that we want
        // a listing of everyone logged on instead of information about an
        // individual user.
        out.print("\n");
        out.flush();    // Send it now!

        // Now read the server's response and display it in the textarea
        // The server should send lines terminated with \n.  The
        // readLine() method will detect these lines, even when running
        // on a Mac that terminates lines with \r
        String line;
        while((line = in.readLine()) != null) {
            t.append(line);
            t.append("\n");
        }
        // Update the window title to indicate we're finished
        f.setTitle("Who's Logged On: " + hostname);
    }
    // If something goes wrong, we'll just display the exception message
    catch (IOException e) {
        t.append(e.toString());
        f.setTitle("Who's Logged On: Error");
    }
    // And finally, don't forget to close the streams!
    finally {
        try { in.close(); out.close(); s.close(); } catch(Exception e) {}
    }

    // And enable the button again
    who.setEnabled(true);
  }
}
```

A Generic Client

The HttpClient class of Example 5-4 was a special-purpose client. Example 5-8 defines a class, GenericClient, that can serve as a client for a variety of text-based services. When you run this program, it connects to the host and port you have specified on the command line. From that point on, it simply sends the text you type to the server and then outputs the text the server sends in response to the console.

You can use GenericClient to download files from a web server by sending a simple HTTP protocol GET command, as HttpClient does. For big files, however, the server's output scrolls by too quickly for this to be useful. GenericClient is more useful for text-based interactive protocols. The Post Office Protocol (POP) is such a protocol. You can use GenericClient to preview any email you have waiting for you at your ISP (or elsewhere). An interaction, using GenericClient, with a POP server might look as follows (The lines in bold are those typed by the user):

```
oxymoron% java com.davidflanagan.examples.net.GenericClient mail.isp.net 110
Connected to mail.isp.net/208.99.99.251:110
+OK QUALCOMM Pop server derived from UCB (version 2.1.4-R3) at mail.isp.net
starting.
user djf
+OK Password required for djf.
pass notrealpassword
+OK djf has 3 message(s) (2861 octets).
retr 3
+OK 363 octets
Received: from obsidian.oreilly.com (obsidian.oreilly.com [207.144.66.251])
        by mail.isp.net (8.8.5/8.8.5) with SMTP id RAA11654
        for djf@isp.net; Wed, 21 Jun 2999 17:01:50 -0400 (EDT)
Date: Wed, 25 Jun 1997 17:01:50 -0400 (EDT)
Message-Id: <199706252101.RAA11654@mail.isp.net>
From: "Paula Ferguson" <pf@oreilly.com>
To: djf@isp.net
Subject: schedule!

Aren't you done with that book yet?

.
dele 3
+OK Message 3 has been deleted.
quit
+OK Pop server at mail.isp.net signing off.
Connection closed by server.
oxymoron%
```

The GenericClient class is fairly similar in structure to the SimpleProxyServer class shown in Example 5-6. Like SimpleProxyServer, GenericClient uses an anonymous second thread. This thread transfers data from server to client in parallel with the main thread, which transfers data from client to server. Note that the thread that transfers data from the server to the client translates "\n" line terminators from the server into whatever the local line terminator is. By using two threads, user input and server output can occur asynchronously, which, in fact, it does in some protocols. The only complication in GenericClient is that the two threads must have different priorities, because with some Java implementations, a thread can't write to the console while another thread of the same priority is blocked waiting to read from the console.

Example 5-8: GenericClient.java

```java
package com.davidflanagan.examples.net;
import java.io.*;
import java.net.*;

/**
 * This program connects to a server at a specified host and port.
 * It reads text from the console and sends it to the server.
 * It reads text from the server and sends it to the console.
 **/
public class GenericClient {
    public static void main(String[] args) throws IOException {
        try {
            // Check the number of arguments
            if (args.length != 2)
                throw new IllegalArgumentException("Wrong number of args");

            // Parse the host and port specifications
            String host = args[0];
            int port = Integer.parseInt(args[1]);

            // Connect to the specified host and port
            Socket s = new Socket(host, port);

            // Set up streams for reading from and writing to the server.
            // The from_server stream is final for use in the inner class below
            final Reader from_server=new InputStreamReader(s.getInputStream());
            PrintWriter to_server = new PrintWriter(s.getOutputStream());

            // Set up streams for reading from and writing to the console
            // The to_user stream is final for use in the anonymous class below
            BufferedReader from_user =
                new BufferedReader(new InputStreamReader(System.in));
            // Pass true for auto-flush on println()
            final PrintWriter to_user = new PrintWriter(System.out, true);

            // Tell the user that we've connected
            to_user.println("Connected to " + s.getInetAddress() +
                            ":" + s.getPort());

            // Create a thread that gets output from the server and displays
            // it to the user.  We use a separate thread for this so that we
            // can receive asynchronous output
            Thread t = new Thread() {
                public void run() {
                    char[] buffer = new char[1024];
                    int chars_read;
                    try {
                        // Read characters until the stream closes
                        while((chars_read = from_server.read(buffer)) != -1) {
                            // Loop through the array of characters, and
                            // print them out, converting all \n characters
                            // to the local platform's line terminator.
                            // This could be more efficient, but it is probably
                            // faster than the network is, which is good enough
                            for(int i = 0; i < chars_read; i++) {
                                if (buffer[i] == '\n') to_user.println();
                                else to_user.print(buffer[i]);
                            }
```

Example 5-8: GenericClient.java (continued)

```
                        to_user.flush();
                }
            }
            catch (IOException e) { to_user.println(e); }

            // When the server closes the connection, the loop above
            // will end.  Tell the user what happened, and call
            // System.exit(), causing the main thread to exit along
            // with this one.
            to_user.println("Connection closed by server.");
            System.exit(0);
        }
    };

    // We set the priority of the server-to-user thread above to be
    // one level higher than the main thread.  We shouldn't have to do
    // this, but on some operating systems, output sent to the console
    // doesn't appear when a thread at the same priority level is
    // blocked waiting for input from the console.
    t.setPriority(Thread.currentThread().getPriority() + 1);

    // Now start the server-to-user thread
    t.start();

    // In parallel, read the user's input and pass it on to the server.
    String line;
    while((line = from_user.readLine()) != null) {
        to_server.print(line + "\n");
        to_server.flush();
    }

    // If the user types a Ctrl-D (Unix) or Ctrl-Z (Windows) to end
    // their input, we'll get an EOF, and the loop above will exit.
    // When this happens, we stop the server-to-user thread and close
    // the socket.

    s.close();
    to_user.println("Connection closed by client.");
    System.exit(0);
}
// If anything goes wrong, print an error message
catch (Exception e) {
    System.err.println(e);
    System.err.println("Usage: java GenericClient <hostname> <port>");
}
    }
}
```

Networking

A Generic Multithreaded Server

Example 5-9 is a long and fairly complex example. The Server class it defines is a
multithreaded server that provides services defined by implementations of a nested
Server.Service interface. It can provide multiple services (defined by multiple
Service objects) on multiple ports, and it has the ability to dynamically load and
instantiate Service classes and add (and remove) new services at runtime. It logs

its actions to a specified stream and limits the number of concurrent connections to a specified maximum.

The Server class uses a number of inner classes. The Server.Listener class is a thread that waits for connections on a given port. There is one Listener object for each service the Server is providing. The Server.ConnectionManager class manages the list of current connections to all services. There is one ConnectionManager shared by all services. When a Listener gets a connection from a client, it passes it to the ConnectionManager, which rejects it if the connection limit has been reached. If the ConnectionManager doesn't reject a client, it creates a Server.Connection object to handle the connection. Connection is a Thread subclass, so each service can handle multiple connections at a time, making this a multithreaded server. Each Connection object is passed a Service object and invokes its serve() method, which is what actually provides the service.

The Service interface is a nested member of the Server class; Server includes a number of implementations of this interface. Many of these implementations are trivial, demonstration services. The Control class, however, is a nontrivial Service. This service provides password-protected runtime access to the server, allowing a remote administrator to add and remove services, check the server status, and change the current connection limit.

Finally, the main() method of Server is a standalone program that creates and runs a Server. By specifying the -control argument on the command line, you can tell this program to create an instance of the Control service so that the server can be administered at runtime. Other arguments to this program specify the names of Service classes to be run and the ports that they should use. For example, you could start the server with a command like this:

```
% java com.davidflanagan.examples.net.Server -control secret 3000 \
      com.davidflanagan.examples.net.Server\$Time 3001 \
      com.davidflanagan.examples.net.Server\$Reverse 3002
```

This command starts the Control service on port 3000 with the password "secret", the Server.Time service on port 3001, and the Server.Reverse service on port 3002. Once you have started the server program, you can use GenericClient (see Example 5-8) to connect to each of the services it provides. Using the Control service is the most interesting, of course, and you can use it to add (and remove) other services.

The best way to understand the Server class and its inner classes and interfaces is to dive in and study the code. It is heavily commented. I recommend that you skim it, reading comments first, and then go back through and study each class in detail.

Example 5-9: Server.java

```
package com.davidflanagan.examples.net;
import java.io.*;
import java.net.*;
import java.util.*;

/**
 * This class is a generic framework for a flexible, multi-threaded server.
 * It listens on any number of specified ports, and, when it receives a
```

Example 5-9: Server.java (continued)

```
 * connection on a port, passes input and output streams to a specified Service
 * object which provides the actual service.  It can limit the number of
 * concurrent connections, and logs activity to a specified stream.
 **/
public class Server {
    /**
     * A main() method for running the server as a standalone program.  The
     * command-line arguments to the program should be pairs of servicenames
     * and port numbers.  For each pair, the program will dynamically load the
     * named Service class, instantiate it, and tell the server to provide
     * that Service on the specified port.  The special -control argument
     * should be followed by a password and port, and will start special
     * server control service running on the specified port, protected by the
     * specified password.
     **/
    public static void main(String[] args) {
        try {
            if (args.length < 2)  // Check number of arguments
                throw new IllegalArgumentException("Must specify a service");

            // Create a Server object that uses standard out as its log and
            // has a limit of ten concurrent connections at once.
            Server s = new Server(System.out, 10);

            // Parse the argument list
            int i = 0;
            while(i < args.length) {
                if (args[i].equals("-control")) {  // Handle the -control arg
                    i++;
                    String password = args[i++];
                    int port = Integer.parseInt(args[i++]);
                    // add control service
                    s.addService(new Control(s, password), port);
                }
                else {
                    // Otherwise start a named service on the specified port.
                    // Dynamically load and instantiate a Service class
                    String serviceName = args[i++];
                    Class serviceClass = Class.forName(serviceName);
                    Service service = (Service)serviceClass.newInstance();
                    int port = Integer.parseInt(args[i++]);
                    s.addService(service, port);
                }
            }
        }
        catch (Exception e) { // Display a message if anything goes wrong
            System.err.println("Server: " + e);
            System.err.println("Usage: java Server " +
                               "[-control <password> <port>] " +
                               "[<servicename> <port> ... ]");
            System.exit(1);
        }
    }

    // This is the state for the server
    Map services;                // Hashtable mapping ports to Listeners
    Set connections;             // The set of current connections
    int maxConnections;          // The concurrent connection limit
```

Example 5-9: Server.java (continued)

```java
    ThreadGroup threadGroup;          // The threadgroup for all our threads
    PrintWriter logStream;            // Where we send our logging output to

    /**
     * This is the Server() constructor.  It must be passed a stream
     * to send log output to (may be null), and the limit on the number of
     * concurrent connections.
     **/
    public Server(OutputStream logStream, int maxConnections) {
        setLogStream(logStream);
        log("Starting server");
        threadGroup = new ThreadGroup(Server.class.getName());
        this.maxConnections = maxConnections;
        services = new HashMap();
        connections = new HashSet(maxConnections);
    }

    /**
     * A public method to set the current logging stream.  Pass null
     * to turn logging off
     **/
    public synchronized void setLogStream(OutputStream out) {
        if (out != null) logStream = new PrintWriter(out);
        else logStream = null;
    }

    /** Write the specified string to the log */
    protected synchronized void log(String s) {
        if (logStream != null) {
            logStream.println("[" + new Date() + "] " + s);
            logStream.flush();
        }
    }
    /** Write the specified object to the log */
    protected void log(Object o) { log(o.toString()); }

    /**
     * This method makes the server start providing a new service.
     * It runs the specified Service object on the specified port.
     **/
    public synchronized void addService(Service service, int port)
        throws IOException
    {
        Integer key = new Integer(port);  // the hashtable key
        // Check whether a service is already on that port
        if (services.get(key) != null)
            throw new IllegalArgumentException("Port " + port +
                                                " already in use.");
        // Create a Listener object to listen for connections on the port
        Listener listener = new Listener(threadGroup, port, service);
        // Store it in the hashtable
        services.put(key, listener);
        // Log it
        log("Starting service " + service.getClass().getName() +
            " on port " + port);
        // Start the listener running.
        listener.start();
    }
```

Example 5-9: Server.java (continued)

```java
/**
 * This method makes the server stop providing a service on a port.
 * It does not terminate any pending connections to that service, merely
 * causes the server to stop accepting new connections
 **/
public synchronized void removeService(int port) {
    Integer key = new Integer(port);  // hashtable key
    // Look up the Listener object for the port in the hashtable
    final Listener listener = (Listener) services.get(key);
    if (listener == null) return;
    // Ask the listener to stop
    listener.pleaseStop();
    // Remove it from the hashtable
    services.remove(key);
    // And log it.
    log("Stopping service " + listener.service.getClass().getName() +
        " on port " + port);
}

/**
 * This nested Thread subclass is a "listener".  It listens for
 * connections on a specified port (using a ServerSocket) and when it gets
 * a connection request, it calls the servers addConnection() method to
 * accept (or reject) the connection.  There is one Listener for each
 * Service being provided by the Server.
 **/
public class Listener extends Thread {
    ServerSocket listen_socket;    // The socket to listen for connections
    int port;                      // The port we're listening on
    Service service;               // The service to provide on that port
    volatile boolean stop = false; // Whether we've been asked to stop

    /**
     * The Listener constructor creates a thread for itself in the
     * threadgroup.  It creates a ServerSocket to listen for connections
     * on the specified port.  It arranges for the ServerSocket to be
     * interruptible, so that services can be removed from the server.
     **/
    public Listener(ThreadGroup group, int port, Service service)
        throws IOException
    {
        super(group, "Listener:" + port);
        listen_socket = new ServerSocket(port);
        // give it a non-zero timeout so accept() can be interrupted
        listen_socket.setSoTimeout(600000);
        this.port = port;
        this.service = service;
    }

    /**
     * This is the polite way to get a Listener to stop accepting
     * connections
     ***/
    public void pleaseStop() {
        this.stop = true;            // Set the stop flag
        this.interrupt();            // Stop blocking in accept()
        try { listen_socket.close(); } // Stop listening.
        catch(IOException e) {}
```

Example 5-9: Server.java (continued)

```java
    }

    /**
     * A Listener is a Thread, and this is its body.
     * Wait for connection requests, accept them, and pass the socket on
     * to the addConnection method of the server.
     **/
    public void run() {
        while(!stop) {        // loop until we're asked to stop.
            try {
                Socket client = listen_socket.accept();
                addConnection(client, service);
            }
            catch (InterruptedIOException e) {}
            catch (IOException e) {log(e);}
        }
    }
}


/**
 * This is the method that Listener objects call when they accept a
 * connection from a client.  It either creates a Connection object
 * for the connection and adds it to the list of current connections,
 * or, if the limit on connections has been reached, it closes the
 * connection.
 **/
protected synchronized void addConnection(Socket s, Service service) {
    // If the connection limit has been reached
    if (connections.size() >= maxConnections) {
        try {
            // Then tell the client it is being rejected.
            PrintWriter out = new PrintWriter(s.getOutputStream());
            out.print("Connection refused; " +
                    "the server is busy; please try again later.\n");
            out.flush();
            // And close the connection to the rejected client.
            s.close();
            // And log it, of course
            log("Connection refused to " +
                s.getInetAddress().getHostAddress() +
                ":" + s.getPort() + ": max connections reached.");
        } catch (IOException e) {log(e);}
    }
    else {  // Otherwise, if the limit has not been reached
        // Create a Connection thread to handle this connection
        Connection c = new Connection(s, service);
        // Add it to the list of current connections
        connections.add(c);
        // Log this new connection
        log("Connected to " + s.getInetAddress().getHostAddress() +
            ":" + s.getPort() + " on port " + s.getLocalPort() +
            " for service " + service.getClass().getName());
        // And start the Connection thread to provide the service
        c.start();
    }
}

/**
```

Example 5-9: Server.java (continued)

```
 * A Connection thread calls this method just before it exits.  It removes
 * the specified Connection from the set of connections.
 **/
protected synchronized void endConnection(Connection c) {
    connections.remove(c);
    log("Connection to " + c.client.getInetAddress().getHostAddress() +
        ":" + c.client.getPort() + " closed.");
}

/** Change the current connection limit */
public synchronized void setMaxConnections(int max) {
    maxConnections = max;
}

/**
 * This method displays status information about the server on the
 * specified stream.  It can be used for debugging, and is used by the
 * Control service later in this example.
 **/
public synchronized void displayStatus(PrintWriter out) {
    // Display a list of all Services that are being provided
    Iterator keys = services.keySet().iterator();
    while(keys.hasNext()) {
        Integer port = (Integer) keys.next();
        Listener listener = (Listener) services.get(port);
        out.print("SERVICE " + listener.service.getClass().getName()
                + " ON PORT " + port + "\n");
    }

    // Display the current connection limit
    out.print("MAX CONNECTIONS: " + maxConnections + "\n");

    // Display a list of all current connections
    Iterator conns = connections.iterator();
    while(conns.hasNext()) {
        Connection c = (Connection)conns.next();
        out.print("CONNECTED TO " +
                c.client.getInetAddress().getHostAddress() +
                ":" + c.client.getPort() + " ON PORT " +
                c.client.getLocalPort() + " FOR SERVICE " +
                c.service.getClass().getName() + "\n");
    }
}

/**
 * This class is a subclass of Thread that handles an individual
 * connection between a client and a Service provided by this server.
 * Because each such connection has a thread of its own, each Service can
 * have multiple connections pending at once.  Despite all the other
 * threads in use, this is the key feature that makes this a
 * multi-threaded server implementation.
 **/
public class Connection extends Thread {
    Socket client;      // The socket to talk to the client through
    Service service;    // The service being provided to that client

    /**
     * This constructor just saves some state and calls the superclass
```

Example 5-9: Server.java (continued)

```
    * constructor to create a thread to handle the connection.  Connection
    * objects are created by Listener threads.  These threads are part of
    * the server's ThreadGroup, so all Connection threads are part of that
    * group, too.
    **/
    public Connection(Socket client, Service service) {
        super("Server.Connection:" +
                client.getInetAddress().getHostAddress() +
                ":" + client.getPort());
        this.client = client;
        this.service = service;
    }

    /**
     * This is the body of each and every Connection thread.
     * All it does is pass the client input and output streams to the
     * serve() method of the specified Service object.  That method is
     * responsible for reading from and writing to those streams to
     * provide the actual service.  Recall that the Service object has
     * been passed from the Server.addService() method to a Listener
     * object to the addConnection() method to this Connection object, and
     * is now finally being used to provide the service.  Note that just
     * before this thread exits it always calls the endConnection() method
     * to remove itself from the set of connections
     **/
    public void run() {
        try {
            InputStream in = client.getInputStream();
            OutputStream out = client.getOutputStream();
            service.serve(in, out);
        }
        catch (IOException e) {log(e);}
        finally { endConnection(this); }
    }
}

/**
 * Here is the Service interface that we have seen so much of.  It defines
 * only a single method which is invoked to provide the service.  serve()
 * will be passed an input stream and an output stream to the client.  It
 * should do whatever it wants with them, and should close them before
 * returning.
 *
 * All connections through the same port to this service share a single
 * Service object.  Thus, any state local to an individual connection must
 * be stored in local variables within the serve() method.  State that
 * should be global to all connections on the same port should be stored
 * in instance variables of the Service class.  If the same Service is
 * running on more than one port, there will typically be different
 * Service instances for each port.  Data that should be global to all
 * connections on any port should be stored in static variables.
 *
 * Note that implementations of this interface must have a no-argument
 * constructor if they are to be dynamically instantiated by the main()
 * method of the Server class.
 **/
public interface Service {
    public void serve(InputStream in, OutputStream out) throws IOException;
```

Example 5-9: Server.java (continued)

```
    }

    /**
     * A very simple service.  It displays the current time on the server
     * to the client, and closes the connection.
     **/
    public static class Time implements Service {
        public void serve(InputStream i, OutputStream o) throws IOException {
            PrintWriter out = new PrintWriter(o);
            out.print(new Date() + "\n");
            out.close();
            i.close();
        }
    }

    /**
     * This is another example service.  It reads lines of input from the
     * client, and sends them back, reversed.  It also displays a welcome
     * message and instructions, and closes the connection when the user
     * enters a '.' on a line by itself.
     **/
    public static class Reverse implements Service {
        public void serve(InputStream i, OutputStream o) throws IOException {
            BufferedReader in = new BufferedReader(new InputStreamReader(i));
            PrintWriter out =
                new PrintWriter(new BufferedWriter(new OutputStreamWriter(o)));
            out.print("Welcome to the line reversal server.\n");
            out.print("Enter lines.  End with a '.' on a line by itself.\n");
            for(;;) {
                out.print("> ");
                out.flush();
                String line = in.readLine();
                if ((line == null) || line.equals(".")) break;
                for(int j = line.length()-1; j >= 0; j--)
                    out.print(line.charAt(j));
                out.print("\n");
            }
            out.close();
            in.close();
        }
    }

    /**
     * This service is an HTTP mirror, just like the HttpMirror class
     * implemented earlier in this chapter.  It echos back the client's
     * HTTP request
     **/
    public static class HTTPMirror implements Service {
        public void serve(InputStream i, OutputStream o) throws IOException {
            BufferedReader in = new BufferedReader(new InputStreamReader(i));
            PrintWriter out = new PrintWriter(o);
            out.print("HTTP/1.0 200 \n");
            out.print("Content-Type: text/plain\n\n");
            String line;
            while((line = in.readLine()) != null) {
                if (line.length() == 0) break;
                out.print(line + "\n");
            }
```

Networking

Example 5-9: Server.java (continued)

```
            out.close();
            in.close();
        }
    }


    /**
     * This service demonstrates how to maintain state across connections by
     * saving it in instance variables and using synchronized access to those
     * variables.  It maintains a count of how many clients have connected and
     * tells each client what number it is
     **/
    public static class UniqueID implements Service {
        public int id=0;
        public synchronized int nextId() { return id++; }
        public void serve(InputStream i, OutputStream o) throws IOException {
            PrintWriter out = new PrintWriter(o);
            out.print("You are client #: " + nextId() + "\n");
            out.close();
            i.close();
        }
    }


    /**
     * This is a non-trivial service.  It implements a command-based protocol
     * that gives password-protected runtime control over the operation of the
     * server.  See the main() method of the Server class to see how this
     * service is started.
     *
     * The recognized commands are:
     *    password: give password; authorization is required for most commands
     *    add:      dynamically add a named service on a specified port
     *    remove:   dynamically remove the service running on a specified port
     *    max:      change the current maximum connection limit.
     *    status:   display current services, connections, and connection limit
     *    help:     display a help message
     *    quit:     disconnect
     *
     * This service displays a prompt, and sends all of its output to the user
     * in capital letters.  Only one client is allowed to connect to this
     * service at a time.
     **/
    public static class Control implements Service {
        Server server;              // The server we control
        String password;            // The password we require
        boolean connected = false;  // Whether a client is already connected

        /**
         * Create a new Control service.  It will control the specified Server
         * object, and will require the specified password for authorization
         * Note that this Service does not have a no argument constructor,
         * which means that it cannot be dynamically instantiated and added as
         * the other, generic services above can be.
         **/
        public Control(Server server, String password) {
            this.server = server;
            this.password = password;
        }
```

Example 5-9: Server.java (continued)

```java
/**
 * This is the serve method that provides the service.  It reads a
 * line from the client, and uses java.util.StringTokenizer to parse it
 * into commands and arguments.  It does various things depending on
 * the command.
 **/
public void serve(InputStream i, OutputStream o) throws IOException {
    // Setup the streams
    BufferedReader in = new BufferedReader(new InputStreamReader(i));
    PrintWriter out = new PrintWriter(o);
    String line;  // For reading client input lines
    // Has the user has given the password yet?
    boolean authorized = false;

    // If there is already a client connected to this service, display
    // a message to this client and close the connection.  We use a
    // synchronized block to prevent a race condition.
    synchronized(this) {
        if (connected) {
            out.print("ONLY ONE CONTROL CONNECTION ALLOWED.\n");
            out.close();
            return;
        }
        else connected = true;
    }

    // This is the main loop: read a command, parse it, and handle it
    for(;;) {  // infinite loop
        out.print("> ");            // Display a prompt
        out.flush();                // Make it appear right away
        line = in.readLine();       // Get the user's input
        if (line == null) break;    // Quit if we get EOF.
        try {
            // Use a StringTokenizer to parse the user's command
            StringTokenizer t = new StringTokenizer(line);
            if (!t.hasMoreTokens()) continue;  // if input was empty
            // Get first word of the input and convert to lower case
            String command = t.nextToken().toLowerCase();
            // Now compare to each of the possible commands, doing the
            // appropriate thing for each command
            if (command.equals("password")) {  // Password command
                String p = t.nextToken();      // Get the next word
                if (p.equals(this.password)) { // Is it the password?
                    out.print("OK\n");         // Say so
                    authorized = true;         // Grant authorization
                }
                else out.print("INVALID PASSWORD\n"); // Otherwise fail
            }
            else if (command.equals("add")) {  // Add Service command
                // Check whether password has been given
                if (!authorized) out.print("PASSWORD REQUIRED\n");
                else {
                    // Get the name of the service and try to
                    // dynamically load and instantiate it.
                    // Exceptions will be handled below
                    String serviceName = t.nextToken();
                    Class serviceClass = Class.forName(serviceName);
                    Service service;
```

Example 5-9: Server.java (continued)

```
                    try {
                        service = (Service)serviceClass.newInstance();
                    }
                    catch (NoSuchMethodError e) {
                        throw new IllegalArgumentException(
                                        "Service must have a " +
                                        "no-argument constructor");
                    }
                    int port = Integer.parseInt(t.nextToken());
                    // If no exceptions occurred, add the service
                    server.addService(service, port);
                    out.print("SERVICE ADDED\n");    // acknowledge
                }
            }
            else if (command.equals("remove")) { // Remove service
                if (!authorized) out.print("PASSWORD REQUIRED\n");
                else {
                    int port = Integer.parseInt(t.nextToken());
                    server.removeService(port); // remove the service
                    out.print("SERVICE REMOVED\n"); // acknowledge
                }
            }
            else if (command.equals("max")) { // Set connection limit
                if (!authorized) out.print("PASSWORD REQUIRED\n");
                else {
                    int max = Integer.parseInt(t.nextToken());
                    server.setMaxConnections(max);
                    out.print("MAX CONNECTIONS CHANGED\n");
                }
            }
            else if (command.equals("status")) { // Status Display
                if (!authorized) out.print("PASSWORD REQUIRED\n");
                else server.displayStatus(out);
            }
            else if (command.equals("help")) {  // Help command
                // Display command syntax.  Password not required
                out.print("COMMANDS:\n" +
                            "\tpassword <password>\n" +
                            "\tadd <service> <port>\n" +
                            "\tremove <port>\n" +
                            "\tmax <max-connections>\n" +
                            "\tstatus\n" +
                            "\thelp\n" +
                            "\tquit\n");
            }
            else if (command.equals("quit")) break; // Quit command.
            else out.print("UNRECOGNIZED COMMAND\n"); // Error
        }
        catch (Exception e) {
            // If an exception occurred during the command, print an
            // error message, then output details of the exception.
            out.print("ERROR WHILE PARSING OR EXECUTING COMMAND:\n" +
                        e + "\n");
        }
    }
}
// Finally, when the command loop ends, close the streams
// and set our connected flag to false so that other clients can
// now connect.
```

Example 5–9: Server.java (continued)

```
                connected = false;
                out.close();
                in.close();
        }
    }
}
```

A Multithreaded Proxy Server

Example 5-6 demonstrated how to write a simple, single-threaded proxy server. Example 5-10 uses the Server class and Server.Service interface defined in Example 5-9 to implement a multithreaded proxy server. It demonstrates how you can use the generic Server class to implement your own custom servers without using the main() method of Server. The body of the inner Proxy class (which is what implements the Service interface) is reminiscent of the SimpleProxyServer class but creates two anonymous threads instead of just one. The main thread uses the join() method of the Thread class to wait for these two anonymous threads to finish.

Example 5–10: ProxyServer.java

```
package com.davidflanagan.examples.net;
import java.io.*;
import java.net.*;

/**
 * This class uses the Server class to provide a multi-threaded server
 * framework for a relatively simple proxy service.  The main() method
 * starts up the server.  The nested Proxy class implements the
 * Server.Service interface and provides the proxy service.
 **/
public class ProxyServer {
    /**
     * Create a Server object, and add Proxy service objects to it to provide
     * proxy service as specified by the command-line arguments.
     **/
    public static void main(String[] args) {
        try {
            // Check number of args.  Must be a multiple of 3 and > 0.
            if ((args.length == 0) || (args.length % 3 != 0))
                throw new IllegalArgumentException("Wrong number of args");

            // Create the Server object
            Server s = new Server(null, 12); // log stream, max connections

            // Loop through the arguments parsing (host, remoteport, localport)
            // tuples.  For each, create a Proxy, and add it to the server.
            int i = 0;
            while(i < args.length) {
                String host = args[i++];
                int remoteport = Integer.parseInt(args[i++]);
                int localport = Integer.parseInt(args[i++]);
                s.addService(new Proxy(host, remoteport), localport);
            }
        }
```

Example 5-10: ProxyServer.java (continued)

```
            catch (Exception e) {  // Print an error message if anything goes wrong
                System.err.println(e);
                System.err.println("Usage: java ProxyServer " +
                                   "<host> <remoteport> <localport> ...");
                System.exit(1);
            }
        }

    /**
     * This is the class that implements the proxy service.  The serve() method
     * will be called when the client has connected.  At that point, it must
     * establish a connection to the server, and then transfer bytes back and
     * forth between client and server.  For symmetry, this class implements
     * two very similar threads as anonymous classes.  One thread copies bytes
     * from client to server, and the other copies them from server to client.
     * The thread that invokes the serve() method creates and starts these
     * threads, then just sits and waits for them to exit.
     **/
    public static class Proxy implements Server.Service {
        String host;
        int port;

        /** Remember the host and port we are a proxy for */
        public Proxy(String host, int port) {
            this.host = host;
            this.port = port;
        }

        /** The server invokes this method when a client connects. */
        public void serve(InputStream in, OutputStream out) {
            // These are some sockets we'll use.  They are final so they can
            // be used by the anonymous classes defined below.
            final InputStream from_client = in;
            final OutputStream to_client = out;
            final InputStream from_server;
            final OutputStream to_server;

            // Try to establish a connection to the specified server and port
            // and get sockets to talk to it.  Tell our client if we fail.
            final Socket server;
            try {
                server = new Socket(host, port);
                from_server = server.getInputStream();
                to_server = server.getOutputStream();
            }
            catch (Exception e) {
                PrintWriter pw = new PrintWriter(new OutputStreamWriter(out));
                pw.print("Proxy server could not connect to " + host +
                        ":" + port + "\n");
                pw.flush();
                pw.close();
                try { in.close(); } catch (IOException ex) {}
                return;
            }

            // Create an array to hold two Threads.  It is declared final so
            // that it can be used by the anonymous classes below.  We use an
            // array instead of two variables because given the structure of
```

Example 5-10: ProxyServer.java (continued)

```
            // this program two variables would not work if declared final.
            final Thread[] threads = new Thread[2];

            // Define and create a thread to copy bytes from client to server
            Thread c2s = new Thread() {
                    public void run() {
                        // Copy bytes 'till EOF from client
                        byte[] buffer = new byte[2048];
                        int bytes_read;
                        try {
                            while((bytes_read=from_client.read(buffer))!=-1) {
                                to_server.write(buffer, 0, bytes_read);
                                to_server.flush();
                            }
                        }
                        catch (IOException e) {}
                        finally {
                            // When the thread is done
                            try {
                                server.close();      // close the server socket
                                to_client.close();   // and the client streams
                                from_client.close();
                            }
                            catch (IOException e) {}
                        }
                    }
            };

            // Define and create a thread to copy bytes from server to client.
            // This thread works just like the one above.
            Thread s2c = new Thread() {
                    public void run() {
                        byte[] buffer = new byte[2048];
                        int bytes_read;
                        try {
                            while((bytes_read=from_server.read(buffer))!=-1) {
                                to_client.write(buffer, 0, bytes_read);
                                to_client.flush();
                            }
                        }
                        catch (IOException e) {}
                        finally {
                            try {
                                server.close(); // close down
                                to_client.close();
                                from_client.close();
                            } catch (IOException e) {}
                        }
                    }
            };

            // Store the threads into the final threads[] array, so that the
            // anonymous classes can refer to each other.
            threads[0] = c2s; threads[1] = s2c;

            // start the threads
            c2s.start(); s2c.start();
```

Example 5–10: ProxyServer.java (continued)

```
            // Wait for them to exit
            try { c2s.join(); s2c.join(); } catch (InterruptedException e) {}
        }
    }
}
```

Sending Datagrams

Now that we've thoroughly covered the possibilities of networking with sockets and streams, let's examine how low-level networking can be done using datagrams and packets. Example 5-11 and Example 5-12 show how you can implement simple network communication using datagrams. Datagram communication is sometimes called UDP, for Unreliable Datagram Protocol. Sending datagrams is fast, but the tradeoff is that that they are not guaranteed to reach their destination. In addition, multiple datagrams are not guaranteed to travel to their destination by the same route or to arrive at their destination in the order in which they were sent. Datagrams are useful when you want low-overhead communication of non-critical data and when a stream model of communication is not necessary. For example, you might implement a multiuser chat server for a local area network using datagrams.

To send and receive datagrams, you use the DatagramPacket and DatagramSocket classes. These objects are created and initialized differently depending on whether they send or receive datagrams. Example 5-11 shows how to send a datagram; Example 5-12 shows how to receive a datagram and how to find who sent it.

To send a datagram, you first create a DatagramPacket, specifying the data to be sent, the length of the data, the host to send it to, and the port on that host where it is to be sent. You then use the send() method of a DatagramSocket to send the packet. The DatagramSocket is a generic one, created with no arguments. It can be reused to send any packet to any address and port.

Example 5–11: UDPSend.java

```
package com.davidflanagan.examples.net;
import java.io.*;
import java.net.*;

/**
 * This class sends the specified text or file as a datagram to the
 * specified port of the specified host.
 **/
public class UDPSend {
    public static final String usage =
        "Usage: java UDPSend <hostname> <port> <msg>...\n" +
        "   or: java UDPSend <hostname> <port> -f <file>";

    public static void main(String args[]) {
        try {
            // Check the number of arguments
            if (args.length < 3)
                throw new IllegalArgumentException("Wrong number of args");
```

Example 5-11: UDPSend.java (continued)

```
                // Parse the arguments
                String host = args[0];
                int port = Integer.parseInt(args[1]);

                // Figure out the message to send.
                // If the third argument is -f, then send the contents of the file
                // specified as the fourth argument.  Otherwise, concatenate the
                // third and all remaining arguments and send that.
                byte[] message;
                if (args[2].equals("-f")) {
                    File f = new File(args[3]);
                    int len = (int)f.length();    // figure out how big the file is
                    message = new byte[len];       // create a buffer big enough
                    FileInputStream in = new FileInputStream(f);
                    int bytes_read = 0, n;
                    do {                           // loop until we've read it all
                        n = in.read(message, bytes_read, len-bytes_read);
                        bytes_read += n;
                    } while((bytes_read < len) && (n != -1));
                }
                else { // Otherwise, just combine all the remaining arguments.
                    String msg = args[2];
                    for (int i = 3; i < args.length; i++) msg += " " + args[i];
                    message = msg.getBytes();
                }

                // Get the internet address of the specified host
                InetAddress address = InetAddress.getByName(host);

                // Initialize a datagram packet with data and address
                DatagramPacket packet = new DatagramPacket(message, message.length,
                                                 address, port);

                // Create a datagram socket, send the packet through it, close it.
                DatagramSocket dsocket = new DatagramSocket();
                dsocket.send(packet);
                dsocket.close();
            }
            catch (Exception e) {
                System.err.println(e);
                System.err.println(usage);
            }
        }
    }
```

Receiving Datagrams

Example 5-12 is a program that sits and waits to receive datagrams. When it receives one, it prints out the contents of the datagram and the name of the host that sent it.

To receive a datagram, you must first create a DatagramSocket that listens on a particular port of the local host. This socket can receive packets sent only to that particular port. Then, you must create a DatagramPacket with a byte buffer into which datagram data is stored. Finally, you call the DatagramSocket.receive() method to wait for a datagram to arrive on the specified port. When it does, the data it contains is transferred into the specified buffer, and receive() returns. If the datagram contains more bytes than fit to the specified buffer, the extra bytes are discarded. When a datagram arrives, receive() also stores the host and port that the datagram was sent from into the packet.

Example 5–12: UDPReceive.java

```java
package com.davidflanagan.examples.net;
import java.io.*;
import java.net.*;


/**
 * This program waits to receive datagrams sent the specified port.
 * When it receives one, it displays the sending host and prints the
 * contents of the datagram as a string.  Then it loops and waits again.
 **/
public class UDPReceive {
    public static final String usage = "Usage: java UDPReceive <port>";
    public static void main(String args[]) {
        try {
            if (args.length != 1)
                throw new IllegalArgumentException("Wrong number of args");

            // Get the port from the command line
            int port = Integer.parseInt(args[0]);

            // Create a socket to listen on the port.
            DatagramSocket dsocket = new DatagramSocket(port);

            // Create a buffer to read datagrams into.  If anyone sends us a
            // packet containing more than will fit into this buffer, the
            // excess will simply be discarded!
            byte[] buffer = new byte[2048];

            // Create a packet to receive data into the buffer
            DatagramPacket packet = new DatagramPacket(buffer, buffer.length);

            // Now loop forever, waiting to receive packets and printing them.
            for(;;) {
                // Wait to receive a datagram
                dsocket.receive(packet);

                // Convert the contents to a string, and display them
                String msg = new String(buffer, 0, packet.getLength());
                System.out.println(packet.getAddress().getHostName() +
                                   ": " + msg);

                // Reset the length of the packet before reusing it.
                // Prior to Java 1.1, we'd just create a new packet each time.
                packet.setLength(buffer.length);
            }
        }
        catch (Exception e) {
            System.err.println(e);
            System.err.println(usage);
        }
    }
}
```

Exercises

5-1. Using the `URLConnection` techniques demonstrated in Example 5-2, write a program that prints the modification date of a specified URL.

5-2. Modify the `HttpClient` program of Example 5-4 so that it uses a newer version of the HTTP protocol. To do this, you have to send a somewhat more complicated `GET` request to the web server. Use the `HttpMirror` program of Example 5-5 to find what form this request should take. HTTP Versions 1.0 and later add a version number to the `GET` request and follow the `GET` line with a number of header lines followed by a blank line that serves to terminate the request.

For this exercise, the only header you need to include is the User-Agent line, which should identify the web client that you are using. Since you are writing your own web client, you can give it any name you like! Be sure to follow your `GET` request and User-Agent header with a blank line, or the web server will keep waiting for more headers and will never respond to your request. When you get this program working, you should notice that web servers respond differently to requests from it than they did to requests from the original `HttpClient` program. When a client requests data using HTTP 1.0 or 1.1, the server sends a version number, a status code, and a number of response header lines before it sends the actual requested file.

5-3. Write a simple server that reports the current time (in textual form) to any client that connects. Use Example 5-5, `HttpMirror`, as a framework for your server. This server should simply output the current time and close the connection, without reading anything from the client. You need to choose a port number that your service listens on. Use the `GenericClient` program of Example 5-8 to connect to this port and test your program. Alternatively, use the `HttpClient` program of Example 5-4 to test your program. To do this, encode the appropriate port number into the URL. `HttpClient` sends an extraneous `GET` request to the time server, but it still displays the server's response.

5-4. In the discussion of Example 5-8, `GenericClient`, there is an example of using that program to communicate with a POP (Post Office Protocol) server to retrieve email. The POP protocol is a simple one; a little experimentation with `GenericClient` should allow you to figure out how it works. (Be careful not to delete any important email!)

For this exercise, write a client program named `Checkmail` that uses the POP protocol to check a user's mail. It should output the number of messages that are waiting to be retrieved and display the From line of each message. This client should *not* use the POP `dele` command to delete mail messages from the server; it should simply display a summary of the messages waiting to be retrieved. In order to read mail messages, this client has to know the hostname of the POP server and has to send a username and password to the server. Your program may obtain the hostname, username, and password from the command line or by prompting the user, but should ideally get this information by reading a configuration file. Consider a `java.util.Properties` object to implement such a configuration file.

Networking

5-5. Write a simple web server that responds to GET requests like those generated by the program you wrote in Exercise 5-2. You may want to use Example 5-5 HttpMirror, as a framework for your server. Alternatively, you can implement your server as a Service subclass for use with the Server program developed in Example 5-9.

Your server should use the HTTP 1.0 protocol or a later version. This means that the server expects GET requests to be followed by header lines and terminated by a blank line. And it means that the responses to GET requests should begin with a version number and status code. This status line is followed by header lines, which are terminated with a blank line. The content of the response follows the blank line. Use the client you wrote in Exercise 5-2 to experiment with existing web servers to see how they respond to various GET requests.

The web server you write should be started with a directory specified on the command line and should serve files relative to this directory. When a client requests a file in or beneath the directory, the server should return the contents of the file, but should first output Content-Type, Content-Length, and Last-Modified header lines. For this exercise, assume that files with an extension of *.html* or *.htm* have a content type of text/html, and that all other files are text/plain. If a client requests a file that doesn't exist, your server should return an appropriate error code and message. Again, use the client you developed in Exercise 5-2 to figure out how existing web servers respond to requests for nonexistent files.

5-6. Modify the UDPSend and UDPReceive programs of Example 5-11 and Example 5-12 so that UDPReceive sends an acknowledgment when it receives a datagram, and so that UDPSend doesn't exit until it receives the acknowledgment. The acknowledgment should itself be a datagram and can contain any data you desire. (You could use the checksum classes of the java.util.zip package, for example, to compute a checksum of the received data and send this back in the acknowledgment packet.) Use the setSoTimeout() method of DatagramSocket so that UDPSend doesn't wait for more than a few seconds to receive the acknowledgment. If the acknowledgment packet is not received before the timeout, UDPSend should assume that the original packet got lost and was not received. Your modified UDPSend should try to resend the packet once or twice, and if it still doesn't receive an acknowledgment, it should exit with an error message.

CHAPTER 6

Security and Cryptography

Security is one of the key features that has made Java as successful as it has been. The Java security architecture includes access control mechanisms that allows untrusted programs, such as applets, to be executed safely, without fear that they will cause malicious damage, steal company secrets, or otherwise wreak havoc. The access control mechanisms used by Java have changed substantially between Java 1.0 and 1.2; we'll discuss the Java 1.2 mechanisms in this chapter.

Access control is only one half of the Java security architecture, however. The other half is authentication. The java.security package and its subpackages allow you to create and verify cryptographic checksums and digital signatures to prove whether a Java class file (or any other file) is authentic; that is whether it truly comes from the source that it purports to be from. The authentication API has also changed as Java has evolved, and I cover the Java 1.2 API here.

The access control and authentication aspects of the Java security architecture are closely coupled. Access control is about granting privileges only to trusted code. But what code should you trust? If you know which people and organizations to trust (which is ultimately a social, not a technological, problem), you can use authentication technologies, such as digital signatures, to allow you to trust the Java class files from those people and organizations.

Cryptography is clearly an important piece of the Java security architecture. Because of strict U.S. export regulations, however, encryption and decryption technologies are not part of the standard Java distribution. The Java Cryptography Extension™ (JCE) is available as an extension, though, to support encryption and decryption.

This chapter contains examples that show how you can use the access control, authentication, and cryptographic APIs of Java and the JCE.

Running Untrusted Code

Recall the `Server` example of Chapter 5, *Networking*. That generic server class dynamically loaded and ran `Service` implementations. Suppose that you are a system administrator in charge of the `Server` program, and that you don't trust the programmers who are developing the `Service` implementations; you're afraid that they'll accidentally (or maliciously) include damaging code in their `Service` classes. Java makes it easy to run these untrusted classes with access-control mechanisms in place, to prevent them from doing anything they shouldn't.

Access control in Java is performed by the `SecurityManager` and `AccessController` classes. When a security manager has been registered, Java checks with it every time it is asked to perform any operation, such as reading or writing a file or establishing a network connection, that might be restricted. In Java 1.2 and later, the `SecurityManager` class uses the `AccessController` class to perform these access-control checks, and the `AccessController` in turn refers to a `Policy` file that describes exactly what `Permission` objects are granted to what code.

As of Java 1.2, it is quite simple to run code under the watchful eye of a security manager. Simply run the Java interpreter using the `-D` option to set the `java.security.manager` property. For example, to run the `Server` class under a security manager, start it like this:

```
% java -Djava.security.manager com.davidflanagan.examples.net.Server \
-control password 4000
```

When you do this, both the `Server` class and the control service class it loads are subject to the access-control checks of a security manager that uses the system's default security policy.

If you try running `Server` using the default security policy shipped by Sun, the server will fail when the first client attempts to connect to it, and you'll see the following message:

```
java.security.AccessControlException:
    access denied (java.net.SocketPermission 127.0.0.1:1170 accept,resolve)
```

This message tells you that the security manager has not allowed your `Server` class to accept a network connection from the client. The reason is that the default security policy is too restrictive for our server. Fortunately, there is an easy way to allow the server to accept connections. Create a file with the following contents (except replace the directory name with the name of the directory where you have your classes installed) and name it *Server.policy*:

```
// These lines grant permissions to any code loaded from the directory shown.
// Edit the directory to match the installation on your system.
// On Windows systems, change the forward slashes to double backslashes: "\\".
grant codeBase "file:/home/david/Books/JavaExamples2/Examples" {
    // Allow the server to listen for and accept network connections
    // from any host on any port > 1024
    permission java.net.SocketPermission "*:1024-", "listen,accept";
};
```

Once you've created the *Server.policy* file, run the server class again but add another `-D` option to specify that the interpreter should use this policy file:

```
% java -Djava.security.manager -Djava.security.policy=Server.policy \
  com.davidflanagan.examples.net.Server -control password 4000
```

When you use this command line, the Java interpreter takes the default security policy and augments it with the policy specified on the command line. Note that if you use == instead of = in the command line, the interpreter ignores the default policy and uses only the policy you've specified. Our *Server.policy* file should work either way.

The moral of the story is that if you write a Java application, and you want people who don't trust you to run it, you should figure out exactly what kind of restricted actions it takes and develop a policy file for it. Then your users can study the policy file to see what permissions the application requires. If they're willing to grant those permissions to your code, they can run your program using the -D options shown earlier, secure in the knowledge that your code can't take any dangerous actions other than those explicitly allowed by your policy file.

To fully understand Java's access control mechanisms, you'll want to read about the java.security.Permission class and its many subclasses. You should also read about the java.security.Policy class. To be able to create policy files of your own, you'll want to read about the *policytool* program that ships with the Java SDK from Sun. See *Java in a Nutshell*. If you want to edit policy files by hand (which is often easiest), see the security documentation that comes with the SDK for details on the file format.

Loading Untrusted Code

Let's continue our Server example. Suppose now that you want to modify the server so that it can load Service classes over the network from an arbitrary URL. Suppose also that you want to give Service classes the ability to read and write files from a "scratch" directory on the local system. You can accomplish this by writing a simple class that uses URLClassLoader to load service classes and pass them to an instance of the Server class. To make it work, however, you also have to develop an appropriate security policy file.

Example 6-1 shows our SafeServer class. Like the original Server class, this one expects a list of Service classes and port numbers on the command line. But the first command-line argument it expects is the URL from which the service classes should be downloaded.

Example 6-1: SafeServer.java

```
package com.davidflanagan.examples.security;
import com.davidflanagan.examples.net.Server;
import java.io.*;
import java.net.*;
import java.security.*;

/**
 * This class is a program that uses the Server class defined in Chapter 5.
 * Server would load arbitrary "Service" classes to provide services.
 * This class is an alternative program to start up a Server in a similar
 * way.  The difference is that this one uses a SecurityManager and a
 * ClassLoader to prevent the Service classes from doing anything damaging
```

Example 6–1: SafeServer.java (continued)

```
 * or malicious on the local system.  This allows us to safely run Service
 * classes that come from untrusted sources.
 **/
public class SafeServer {
    public static void main(String[] args) {
        try {
            // Install a Security manager, if the user didn't already install
            // one with the -Djava.security.manager argument
            if (System.getSecurityManager() == null) {
                System.out.println("Establishing a security manager");
                System.setSecurityManager(new SecurityManager());
            }

            // Create a Server object
            Server server = new Server(null, 5);

            // Create the ClassLoader that we'll use to load Service classes.
            // The classes should be stored in the JAR file or the directory
            // specified as a URL by the first command-line argument
            URL serviceURL = new URL(args[0]);
            ClassLoader loader =
                new java.net.URLClassLoader(new URL[] {serviceURL});

            // Parse the argument list, which should contain Service name/port
            // pairs.  For each pair, load the named Service using the class
            // loader, then instantiate it with newInstance(), then tell the
            // server to start running it.
            int i = 1;
            while(i < args.length) {
                // Dynamically load the Service class using the class loader
                Class serviceClass = loader.loadClass(args[i++]);
                // Dynamically instantiate the class.
                Server.Service service =
                    (Server.Service)serviceClass.newInstance();
                int port = Integer.parseInt(args[i++]);  // Parse the port #
                server.addService(service, port);         // Run service
            }
        }
        catch (Exception e) { // Display a message if anything goes wrong
            System.err.println(e);
            System.err.println("Usage: java " + SafeServer.class.getName() +
                            " <url> <servicename> <port>\n" +
                            "\t[<servicename> <port> ... ]");
            System.exit(1);
        }
    }
}
```

A Policy for SafeServer

The SafeServer class creates and establishes a SecurityManager even if the user doesn't do this with the -Djava.security.manager argument. This means that the program is not able to run without a security policy that grants it the permissions it needs. Example 6-2 shows a policy file you can use to make it work.

There are a couple of things to note about the *SafeServer.policy* file. First, the policy file reads system properties named service.dir and service.tmp. These are not standard system properties; they are properties that you must specify to the Java interpreter when you run the `SafeServer` program. `service.dir` specifies the directory from which the service classes are to be loaded. Assume here that they are loaded via a local *file:* URL, not through an *http:* or other network URL. The `service.tmp` property specifies a directory in which the service classes are allowed to read and write temporary scratch files. *SafeServer.policy* demonstrates a syntax that replaces the name of a system property with the value of that property. In this way, the security policy file can be made somewhat independent of the installation location of the application.

Example 6–2: SafeServer.policy

```
// This file grants the SafeServer class the permissions it needs to load
// Service classes through a URLClassLoader, and grants the Service classes
// permission to read and write files in and beneath the directory specified
// by the service.tmp system property.  Note that you'll need to edit the
// URL that specifies the location of the SafeServer class, and that for
// Windows systems, you'll need to replace "/" with "\\"

// Grant permissions to the SafeServer class.
// Edit the directory for your system.
grant codeBase "file:/home/david/Books/JavaExamples2/Examples" {
    // Allow the server to listen for and accept network connections
    // from any host on any port > 1024
    permission java.net.SocketPermission "*:1024-", "listen,accept";

    // Allow the server to create a class loader to load service classes
    permission java.lang.RuntimePermission "createClassLoader";

    // Give the server permission to read the directory that contains the
    // service classes.  If we were using a network URL instead of a file URL
    // we'd need to add a SocketPermission instead of a FilePermission
    permission java.io.FilePermission "${service.dir}/-", "read";

    // The server cannot grant permissions to the Service classes unless it
    // has those permissions itself. So we give the server these two Service
    // permissions.
    permission java.util.PropertyPermission "service.tmp", "read";
    permission java.io.FilePermission "${service.tmp}/-", "read,write";
};

// Grant permissions to classes loaded from the directory specified by the
// service.dir system property.  If we were using a network URL instead of a
// local file: URL, this line would have to be different.
grant codeBase "file:${service.dir}" {
    // Services can read the system property "service.tmp"
    permission java.util.PropertyPermission "service.tmp", "read";
    // And they can read and write files in the directory specified by
    // that system property
    permission java.io.FilePermission "${service.tmp}/-", "read,write";
};
```

Testing SafeServer

To demonstrate that `SafeServer` runs its services safely, you need a demonstration service. Example 6-3 shows one such service that attempts various restricted actions and reports its results. Note that since you're going to load this class with a custom class loader, rather than from the class path, I haven't bothered to give it a package statement.

Example 6-3: SecureService.java

```java
import com.davidflanagan.examples.net.*;  // Note no package statement here.
import java.io.*;

/**
 * This is a demonstration service.  It attempts to do things that may
 * or may not be allowed by the security policy and reports the
 * results of its attempts to the client.
 **/
public class SecureService implements Server.Service {
    public void serve(InputStream i, OutputStream o) throws IOException {
        PrintWriter out = new PrintWriter(o);

        // Try to install our own security manager.  If we can do this,
        // we can defeat any access control.
        out.println("Trying to create and install a security manager...");
        try {
            System.setSecurityManager(new SecurityManager());
            out.println("Success!");
        }
        catch (Exception e) { out.println("Failed: " + e); }

        // Try to make the Server and the Java VM exit.
        // This is a denial of service attack, and it should not succeed!
        out.println();
        out.println("Trying to exit...");
        try { System.exit(-1); }
        catch (Exception e) { out.println("Failed: " + e); }

        // The default system policy allows this property to be read
        out.println();
        out.println("Attempting to find java version...");
        try { out.println(System.getProperty("java.version")); }
        catch (Exception e) { out.println("Failed: " + e); }

        // The default system policy does not allow this property to be read
        out.println();
        out.println("Attempting to find home directory...");
        try { out.println(System.getProperty("user.home")); }
        catch (Exception e) { out.println("Failed: " + e); }

        // Our custom policy explicitly allows this property to be read
        out.println();
        out.println("Attempting to read service.tmp property...");
        try {
            String tmpdir = System.getProperty("service.tmp");
            out.println(tmpdir);
            File dir = new File(tmpdir);
            File f = new File(dir, "testfile");

            // Check whether we've been given permission to write files to
            // the tmpdir directory
            out.println();
            out.println("Attempting to write a file in " + tmpdir + "...");
            try {
                new FileOutputStream(f);
```

Example 6-3: SecureService.java (continued)

```
            out.println("Opened file for writing: " + f);
        }
        catch (Exception e) { out.println("Failed: " + e); }

        // Check whether we've been given permision to read files from
        // the tmpdir directory
        out.println();
        out.println("Attempting to read from " + tmpdir + "...");
        try {
            FileReader in = new FileReader(f);
            out.println("Opened file for reading: " + f);
        }
        catch (Exception e) { out.println("Failed: " + e); }
    }
    catch (Exception e) { out.println("Failed: " + e); }

    // Close the Service sockets
    out.close();
    i.close();
  }
}
```

To test `SafeServer` with the `SecureService` class, you have to decide which directories you'll use for storing the service classes and for the scratch directory. In the material that follows, I've used */tmp/services* and */tmp/scratch* as the directory names.

First, compile `SecureService` using the -d option to tell *javac* where to put the resulting class file:

```
% javac -d /tmp/services SecureService.java
```

It is important that you make sure there isn't a copy of the *SecureService.class* file in the current directory or anywhere else that Java might find it in the local class path. If the `URLClassLoader` can find the class locally, it won't bother loading it through the URL you specify.

Now, to run the `SafeServer` class, specify the name of the `SecureService` class, the URL to load it from, the port to listen for connections on, and four different system properties with -D options:

```
% java -Djava.security.manager -Djava.security.policy=SafeServer.policy \
    -Dservice.dir=/tmp/services -Dservice.tmp=/tmp/scratch \
    com.davidflanagan.examples.security.SafeServer file:/tmp/services/ \
    SecureService 4000
```

This is a complicated command line, but it produces the desired results. When you connect to port 4000, you get the following output from the service:

```
% java com.davidflanagan.examples.net.GenericClient localhost 4000
Connected to localhost/127.0.0.1:4000
Trying to create and install a security manager...
Failed: java.security.AccessControlException: access denied
  (java.lang.RuntimePermission createSecurityManager)

Trying to exit...
Failed: java.security.AccessControlException: access denied
```

```
(java.lang.RuntimePermission exitVM)

Attempting to find java version...
1.3.0

Attempting to find home directory...
Failed: java.security.AccessControlException: access denied
  (java.util.PropertyPermission user.home read)

Attempting to read service.tmp property...
/tmp/scratch

Attempting to write a file in /tmp/scratch...
Opened file for writing: /tmp/scratch/testfile

Attempting to read from /tmp/scratch...
Opened file for reading: /tmp/scratch/testfile
Connection closed by server.
```

Message Digests and Digital Signatures

The authentication portion of the Java Security API includes support for message digests (also known as cryptographic checksums), digital signatures, and simple key management tasks through a "keystore" abstraction. Example 6-4 shows a program named Manifest that demonstrates the use of message digests, digital signatures, and keystores. The Manifest program provides the following functionality:

- When you pass a list of filenames on the command line, the program reads each file, computes a message digest on the contents of the file, and then writes an entry in a manifest file (named *MANIFEST* by default) that specifies each of the filenames and its digest.

- If you use the optional -s flag to specify a signer and the -p flag to specify a password, the program signs the contents of the manifest file and includes a digital signature within the manifest.

- When you invoke the program with the -v option, it verifies an existing manifest file. First, it checks the digital signature, if any. If the signature is valid, it then reads each file named in the manifest and verifies that its digest matches the one specified in the manifest.

Using the Manifest program to create a signed manifest file and then later verify it accomplishes two goals. First, the message digests prove that the named files have not been maliciously or inadvertently modified or corrupted since the digests were computed. And second, the digital signature proves that the manifest file itself has not been modified since it was signed. (Attaching a digital signature to a file is like signing a legal document. By signing a manifest file, you are making the implicit assertion that the contents of the manifest are true and valid, and that you are willing to stake your trustworthiness on it.)

Digital signatures use public-key cryptography technology. A *private key* can create a digital signature and the corresponding *public key* verifies the signature. The classes of the java.security package rely on a keystore in which they can look up these keys. This database stores keys for various entities, which may be people, corporations, or other computers or programs.

In order to make this example work, you need to generate a public and private key pair for yourself (or for some test entity) and add those keys to the keystore. The Java SDK includes a program named *keytool* you can use to generate keys and perform other operations on a keystore. Use *keytool* as follows to generate a key pair for yourself. Note that the program prompts you for the information, including passwords, that it needs. See *Java in a Nutshell* for documentation on *keytool*.

```
% keytool -genkey -alias david
Enter keystore password:  secret
What is your first and last name?
  [Unknown]:  David Flanagan
What is the name of your organizational unit?
  [Unknown]:
What is the name of your organization?
  [Unknown]:  davidflanagan.com
What is the name of your City or Locality?
  [Unknown]:  Bellingham
What is the name of your State or Province?
  [Unknown]:  WA
What is the two-letter country code for this unit?
  [Unknown]:  US
Is <CN=David Flanagan, OU=Unknown, O=davidflanagan.com, L=Bellingham, ST=WA,
C=US> correct?
  [no]:  yes

Enter key password for <david>
        (RETURN if same as keystore password):  moresecret
```

Example 6-4 uses the `MessageDigest` and `DigestInputStream` classes to compute and verify message digests. It uses the `Signature` class with a `PrivateKey` to compute digital signatures and uses `Signature` with a `PublicKey` to verify digital signatures. The `PrivateKey` and `PublicKey` objects are obtained from the `KeyStore` object. The manifest file itself is created and read by a `java.util.Properties` object, which is ideal for this purpose. Message digests and digital signatures are stored in the manifest file using a simple hexadecimal encoding implemented by convenience methods that appear at the end of the example. (This is one shortcoming of the `java.security` package; it doesn't provide an easy way to convert an array of bytes to a portable textual representation.)

Example 6-4: Manifest.java

```java
package com.davidflanagan.examples.security;
import java.security.*;
import java.io.*;
import java.util.*;

/**
 * This program creates a manifest file for the specified files, or verifies
 * an existing manifest file.  By default the manifest file is named
 * MANIFEST, but the -m option can be used to override this.  The -v
 * option specifies that the manifest should be verified.  Verification is
 * also the default option if no files are specified.
 **/
public class Manifest {
```

Example 6-4: Manifest.java (continued)

```java
public static void main(String[] args) throws Exception {
    // Set the default values of the command-line arguments
    boolean verify = false;              // Verify manifest or create one?
    String manifestfile = "MANIFEST";    // Manifest file name
    String digestAlgorithm = "MD5";      // Algorithm for message digests
    String signername = null;            // Signer. No sig. by default
    String signatureAlgorithm = "DSA";   // Algorithm for digital sig.
    String password = null;              // Private keys are protected
    File keystoreFile = null;            // Where are keys stored
    String keystoreType = null;          // What kind of keystore
    String keystorePassword = null;      // How to access keystore
    List filelist = new ArrayList();     // The files to digest

    // Parse the command-line arguments, overriding the defaults above
    for(int i = 0; i < args.length; i++) {
        if (args[i].equals("-v")) verify = true;
        else if (args[i].equals("-m")) manifestfile = args[++i];
        else if (args[i].equals("-da") && !verify)
            digestAlgorithm = args[++i];
        else if (args[i].equals("-s") && !verify)
            signername = args[++i];
        else if (args[i].equals("-sa") && !verify)
            signatureAlgorithm = args[++i];
        else if (args[i].equals("-p"))
            password = args[++i];
        else if (args[i].equals("-keystore"))
            keystoreFile = new File(args[++i]);
        else if (args[i].equals("-keystoreType"))
            keystoreType = args[++i];
        else if (args[i].equals("-keystorePassword"))
            keystorePassword = args[++i];

        else if (!verify) filelist.add(args[i]);
        else throw new IllegalArgumentException(args[i]);
    }

    // If certain arguments weren't supplied, get default values.
    if (keystoreFile == null) {
        File dir = new File(System.getProperty("user.home"));
        keystoreFile = new File(dir, ".keystore");
    }
    if (keystoreType == null) keystoreType = KeyStore.getDefaultType();
    if (keystorePassword == null) keystorePassword = password;

    if (!verify && signername != null && password == null) {
        System.out.println("Use -p to specify a password.");
        return;
    }

    // Get the keystore we'll use for signing or verifying signatures
    // If no password was provided, then assume we won't be dealing with
    // signatures, and skip the keystore.
    KeyStore keystore = null;
    if (keystorePassword != null) {
        keystore = KeyStore.getInstance(keystoreType);
        InputStream in =
            new BufferedInputStream(new FileInputStream(keystoreFile));
        keystore.load(in, keystorePassword.toCharArray());
```

Example 6–4: Manifest.java (continued)

```
        }

        // If -v was specified or no file were given, verify a manifest
        // Otherwise, create a new manifest for the specified files
        if (verify || (filelist.size() == 0)) verify(manifestfile, keystore);
        else create(manifestfile, digestAlgorithm,
                    signername, signatureAlgorithm,
                    keystore, password, filelist);
    }

    /**
     * This method creates a manifest file with the specified name, for
     * the specified vector of files, using the named message digest
     * algorithm.  If signername is non-null, it adds a digital signature
     * to the manifest, using the named signature algorithm.  This method can
     * throw a bunch of exceptions.
     **/
    public static void create(String manifestfile, String digestAlgorithm,
                              String signername, String signatureAlgorithm,
                              KeyStore keystore, String password,
                              List filelist)
        throws NoSuchAlgorithmException, InvalidKeyException,
               SignatureException, KeyStoreException,
               UnrecoverableKeyException, IOException
    {
        // For computing a signature, we have to process the files in a fixed,
        // repeatable order, so sort them alphabetically.
        Collections.sort(filelist);
        int numfiles = filelist.size();

        Properties manifest = new Properties(), metadata = new Properties();
        MessageDigest md = MessageDigest.getInstance(digestAlgorithm);
        Signature signature = null;
        byte[] digest;

        // If a signer name was specified, then prepare to sign the manifest
        if (signername != null) {
            // Get a Signature object
            signature = Signature.getInstance(signatureAlgorithm);

            // Look up the private key of the signer from the keystore
            PrivateKey key = (PrivateKey)
                keystore.getKey(signername, password.toCharArray());

            // Now prepare to create a signature for the specified signer
            signature.initSign(key);
        }

        // Now, loop through the files, in a well-known alphabetical order
        System.out.print("Computing message digests");
        for(int i = 0; i < numfiles; i++) {
            String filename = (String)filelist.get(i);
            // Compute the digest for each, and skip files that don't exist.
            try { digest = getFileDigest(filename, md); }
            catch (IOException e) {
                System.err.println("\nSkipping " + filename + ": " + e);
                continue;
            }
```

Security

Example 6–4: Manifest.java (continued)

```java
            // If we're computing a signature, use the bytes of the filename
            // and of the digest as part of the data to sign.
            if (signature != null) {
                signature.update(filename.getBytes());
                signature.update(digest);
            }
            // Store the filename and the encoded digest bytes in the manifest
            manifest.put(filename, hexEncode(digest));
            System.out.print('.');
            System.out.flush();
        }

        // If a signer was specified, compute signature for the manifest
        byte[] signaturebytes = null;
        if (signature != null) {
            System.out.print("done\nComputing digital signature...");
            System.out.flush();

            // Compute the digital signature by encrypting a message digest of
            // all the bytes passed to the update() method using the private
            // key of the signer.  This is a time consuming operation.
            signaturebytes = signature.sign();
        }

        // Tell the user what comes next
        System.out.print("done\nWriting manifest...");
        System.out.flush();

        // Store some metadata about this manifest, including the name of the
        // message digest algorithm it uses
        metadata.put("__META.DIGESTALGORITHM", digestAlgorithm);
        // If we're signing the manifest, store some more metadata
        if (signername != null) {
            // Store the name of the signer
            metadata.put("__META.SIGNER", signername);
            // Store the name of the algorithm
            metadata.put("__META.SIGNATUREALGORITHM", signatureAlgorithm);
            // And generate the signature, encode it, and store it
            metadata.put("__META.SIGNATURE", hexEncode(signaturebytes));
        }

        // Now, save the manifest data and the metadata to the manifest file
        FileOutputStream f = new FileOutputStream(manifestfile);
        manifest.store(f, "Manifest message digests");
        metadata.store(f, "Manifest metadata");
        System.out.println("done");
    }

    /**
     * This method verifies the digital signature of the named manifest
     * file, if it has one, and if that verification succeeds, it verifies
     * the message digest of each file in filelist that is also named in the
     * manifest.  This method can throw a bunch of exceptions
     **/
    public static void verify(String manifestfile, KeyStore keystore)
        throws NoSuchAlgorithmException, SignatureException,
               InvalidKeyException, KeyStoreException, IOException
    {
```

Example 6–4: Manifest.java (continued)

```
Properties manifest = new Properties();
manifest.load(new FileInputStream(manifestfile));
String digestAlgorithm =
    manifest.getProperty("__META.DIGESTALGORITHM");
String signername = manifest.getProperty("__META.SIGNER");
String signatureAlgorithm =
    manifest.getProperty("__META.SIGNATUREALGORITHM");
String hexsignature = manifest.getProperty("__META.SIGNATURE");

// Get a list of filenames in the manifest.
List files = new ArrayList();
Enumeration names = manifest.propertyNames();
while(names.hasMoreElements()) {
    String s = (String)names.nextElement();
    if (!s.startsWith("__META")) files.add(s);
}
int numfiles = files.size();

// If we've got a signature but no keystore, warn the user
if (signername != null && keystore == null)
    System.out.println("Can't verify digital signature without " +
                       "a keystore.");

// If the manifest contained metadata about a digital signature, then
// verify that signature first
if (signername != null && keystore != null) {
    System.out.print("Verifying digital signature...");
    System.out.flush();

    // To verify the signature, we must process the files in exactly
    // the same order we did when we created the signature.  We
    // guarantee this order by sorting the filenames.
    Collections.sort(files);

    // Create a Signature object to do signature verification with.
    // Initialize it with the signer's public key from the keystore
    Signature signature = Signature.getInstance(signatureAlgorithm);
    PublicKey publickey =
        keystore.getCertificate(signername).getPublicKey();
    signature.initVerify(publickey);

    // Now loop through these files in their known sorted order For
    // each one, send the bytes of the filename and of the digest to
    // the signature object for use in computing the signature.  It is
    // important that this be done in exactly the same order when
    // verifying the signature as it was done when creating the
    // signature.
    for(int i = 0; i < numfiles; i++) {
        String filename = (String) files.get(i);
        signature.update(filename.getBytes());
        signature.update(hexDecode(manifest.getProperty(filename)));
    }

    // Now decode the signature read from the manifest file and pass
    // it to the verify() method of the signature object.  If the
    // signature is not verified, print an error message and exit.
    if (!signature.verify(hexDecode(hexsignature))) {
        System.out.println("\nManifest has an invalid signature");
```

Example 6–4: Manifest.java (continued)

```
                    System.exit(0);
            }

            // Tell the user we're done with this lengthy computation
            System.out.println("verified.");
        }

        // Tell the user we're starting the next phase of verification
        System.out.print("Verifying file message digests");
        System.out.flush();

        // Get a MessageDigest object to compute digests
        MessageDigest md = MessageDigest.getInstance(digestAlgorithm);
        // Loop through all files
        for(int i = 0; i < numfiles; i++) {
            String filename = (String)files.get(i);
            // Look up the encoded digest from the manifest file
            String hexdigest = manifest.getProperty(filename);
            // Compute the digest for the file.
            byte[] digest;
            try { digest = getFileDigest(filename, md); }
            catch (IOException e) {
                System.out.println("\nSkipping " + filename + ": " + e);
                continue;
            }

            // Encode the computed digest and compare it to the encoded digest
            // from the manifest.  If they are not equal, print an error
            // message.
            if (!hexdigest.equals(hexEncode(digest)))
                System.out.println("\nFile '" + filename +
                                   "' failed verification.");

            // Send one dot of output for each file we process.  Since
            // computing message digests takes some time, this lets the user
            // know that the program is functioning and making progress
            System.out.print(".");
            System.out.flush();
        }
        // And tell the user we're done with verification.
        System.out.println("done.");
    }

    /**
     * This convenience method is used by both create() and verify().  It
     * reads the contents of a named file and computes a message digest
     * for it, using the specified MessageDigest object.
     **/
    public static byte[] getFileDigest(String filename, MessageDigest md)
        throws IOException {
        // Make sure there is nothing left behind in the MessageDigest
        md.reset();

        // Create a stream to read from the file and compute the digest
        DigestInputStream in =
            new DigestInputStream(new FileInputStream(filename),md);

        // Read to the end of the file, discarding everything we read.
```

Example 6-4: Manifest.java (continued)

```
        // The DigestInputStream automatically passes all the bytes read to
        // the update() method of the MessageDigest
        while(in.read(buffer) != -1) /* do nothing */ ;

        // Finally, compute and return the digest value.
        return md.digest();
    }

    /** This static buffer is used by getFileDigest() above */
    public static byte[] buffer = new byte[4096];

    /** This array is used to convert from bytes to hexadecimal numbers */
    static final char[] digits = { '0', '1', '2', '3', '4', '5', '6', '7',
                                   '8', '9', 'a', 'b', 'c', 'd', 'e', 'f'};

    /**
     * A convenience method to convert an array of bytes to a String.  We do
     * this simply by converting each byte to two hexadecimal digits.
     * Something like Base 64 encoding is more compact, but harder to encode.
     **/
    public static String hexEncode(byte[] bytes) {
        StringBuffer s = new StringBuffer(bytes.length * 2);
        for(int i = 0; i < bytes.length; i++) {
            byte b = bytes[i];
            s.append(digits[(b& 0xf0) >> 4]);
            s.append(digits[b& 0x0f]);
        }
        return s.toString();
    }

    /**
     * A convenience method to convert in the other direction, from a string
     * of hexadecimal digits to an array of bytes.
     **/
    public static byte[] hexDecode(String s) throws IllegalArgumentException {
        try {
            int len = s.length();
            byte[] r = new byte[len/2];
            for(int i = 0; i < r.length; i++) {
                int digit1 = s.charAt(i*2), digit2 = s.charAt(i*2 + 1);
                if ((digit1 >= '0') && (digit1 <= '9')) digit1 -= '0';
                else if ((digit1 >= 'a')&& (digit1 <= 'f')) digit1 -= 'a' - 10;
                if ((digit2 >= '0') && (digit2 <= '9')) digit2 -= '0';
                else if ((digit2 >= 'a')&& (digit2 <= 'f')) digit2 -= 'a' - 10;
                r[i] = (byte)((digit1 << 4) + digit2);
            }
            return r;
        }
        catch (Exception e) {
            throw new IllegalArgumentException("hexDecode(): invalid input");
        }
    }
}
```

Cryptography

The core Java platform doesn't include support for encryption and decryption of data because of strict U.S. export regulations. The Java Cryptography Extension, or JCE, does support these technologies, however. To enable them, you simply have to download and install the JCE from *http://java.sun.com/products/jce/*. Note that JCE 1.2.1 (in beta at this writing) is available in a globally exportable version that allows only weak encryption using reduced key sizes. If you are outside the United States and Canada, you can use this version of the JCE, or you can obtain some other implementation that has been developed outside of the United States and is therefore free from restrictive regulation.

To install the JCE, simply copy all the JAR files that come with it to the *jre/lib/ext/* directory of your Java distribution. Next, to make the JCE algorithms automatically available to all Java programs, edit the *jre/lib/security/java.security* file to include a line like the following:

```
security.provider.3=com.sun.crypto.provider.SunJCE
```

Read the comments in the *java.security* file for more information about what this line does.

Example 6-5 is a program that allows you to encrypt and decrypt files using the TripleDES encryption algorithm and to generate TripleDES keys that are stored in files. It uses the JCE classes in javax.crypto and its subpackages. The key classes are Cipher, which represents an encryption or decryption algorithm, and SecretKey, which represents the encryption and decryption key used by the algorithm. You can find an API quick-reference for the JCE classes in *Java in a Nutshell*. You can also learn more about cryptography and the JCE from *Java Cryptography* by Jonathan Knudsen (O'Reilly).

Example 6-5: TripleDES.java

```
package com.davidflanagan.examples.security;
import javax.crypto.*;
import javax.crypto.spec.*;
import java.security.*;
import java.security.spec.*;
import java.io.*;

/**
 * This class defines methods for encrypting and decrypting using the Triple
 * DES algorithm and for generating, reading and writing Triple DES keys.
 * It also defines a main() method that allows these methods to be used
 * from the command line.
 **/
public class TripleDES {
    /**
     * The program.  The first argument must be -e, -d, or -g to encrypt,
     * decrypt, or generate a key.  The second argument is the name of a file
     * from which the key is read or to which it is written for -g.  The
     * -e and -d arguments cause the program to read from standard input and
     * encrypt or decrypt to standard output.
     **/
    public static void main(String[] args) {
        try {
```

Example 6–5: TripleDES.java (continued)

```
                // Check to see whether there is a provider that can do TripleDES
                // encryption.  If not, explicitly install the SunJCE provider.
                try { Cipher c = Cipher.getInstance("DESede"); }
                catch(Exception e) {
                    // An exception here probably means the JCE provider hasn't
                    // been permanently installed on this system by listing it
                    // in the $JAVA_HOME/jre/lib/security/java.security file.
                    // Therefore, we have to install the JCE provider explicitly.
                    System.err.println("Installing SunJCE provider.");
                    Provider sunjce = new com.sun.crypto.provider.SunJCE();
                    Security.addProvider(sunjce);
                }

                // This is where we'll read the key from or write it to
                File keyfile = new File(args[1]);

                // Now check the first arg to see what we're going to do
                if (args[0].equals("-g")) {          // Generate a key
                    System.out.print("Generating key. This may take some time...");
                    System.out.flush();
                    SecretKey key = generateKey();
                    writeKey(key, keyfile);
                    System.out.println("done.");
                    System.out.println("Secret key written to " + args[1] +
                                    ". Protect that file carefully!");
                }
                else if (args[0].equals("-e")) {  // Encrypt stdin to stdout
                    SecretKey key = readKey(keyfile);
                    encrypt(key, System.in, System.out);
                }
                else if (args[0].equals("-d")) {  // Decrypt stdin to stdout
                    SecretKey key = readKey(keyfile);
                    decrypt(key, System.in, System.out);
                }
        }
        catch(Exception e) {
            System.err.println(e);
            System.err.println("Usage: java " + TripleDES.class.getName() +
                            " -d|-e|-g <keyfile>");
        }
    }

    /** Generate a secret TripleDES encryption/decryption key */
    public static SecretKey generateKey() throws NoSuchAlgorithmException {
        // Get a key generator for Triple DES (a.k.a. DESede)
        KeyGenerator keygen = KeyGenerator.getInstance("DESede");
        // Use it to generate a key
        return keygen.generateKey();
    }

    /** Save the specified TripleDES SecretKey to the specified file */
    public static void writeKey(SecretKey key, File f)
        throws IOException, NoSuchAlgorithmException, InvalidKeySpecException
    {
        // Convert the secret key to an array of bytes like this
        SecretKeyFactory keyfactory = SecretKeyFactory.getInstance("DESede");
        DESedeKeySpec keyspec =
            (DESedeKeySpec)keyfactory.getKeySpec(key, DESedeKeySpec.class);
```

Example 6-5: TripleDES.java (continued)

```java
        byte[] rawkey = keyspec.getKey();

        // Write the raw key to the file
        FileOutputStream out = new FileOutputStream(f);
        out.write(rawkey);
        out.close();
    }

    /** Read a TripleDES secret key from the specified file */
    public static SecretKey readKey(File f)
        throws IOException, NoSuchAlgorithmException,
                InvalidKeyException, InvalidKeySpecException
    {
        // Read the raw bytes from the keyfile
        DataInputStream in = new DataInputStream(new FileInputStream(f));
        byte[] rawkey = new byte[(int)f.length()];
        in.readFully(rawkey);
        in.close();

        // Convert the raw bytes to a secret key like this
        DESedeKeySpec keyspec = new DESedeKeySpec(rawkey);
        SecretKeyFactory keyfactory = SecretKeyFactory.getInstance("DESede");
        SecretKey key = keyfactory.generateSecret(keyspec);
        return key;
    }

    /**
     * Use the specified TripleDES key to encrypt bytes from the input stream
     * and write them to the output stream.  This method uses
     * CipherOutputStream to perform the encryption and write bytes at the
     * same time.
     **/
    public static void encrypt(SecretKey key, InputStream in, OutputStream out)
        throws NoSuchAlgorithmException, InvalidKeyException,
                NoSuchPaddingException, IOException
    {
        // Create and initialize the encryption engine
        Cipher cipher = Cipher.getInstance("DESede");
        cipher.init(Cipher.ENCRYPT_MODE, key);

        // Create a special output stream to do the work for us
        CipherOutputStream cos = new CipherOutputStream(out, cipher);

        // Read from the input and write to the encrypting output stream
        byte[] buffer = new byte[2048];
        int bytesRead;
        while((bytesRead = in.read(buffer)) != -1) {
            cos.write(buffer, 0, bytesRead);
        }
        cos.close();

        // For extra security, don't leave any plaintext hanging around memory.
        java.util.Arrays.fill(buffer, (byte) 0);
    }

    /**
     * Use the specified TripleDES key to decrypt bytes ready from the input
     * stream and write them to the output stream.  This method uses
```

Example 6–5: TripleDES.java (continued)

```
 * Cipher directly to show how it can be done without
 * CipherInputStream and CipherOutputStream.
 **/
public static void decrypt(SecretKey key, InputStream in, OutputStream out)
    throws NoSuchAlgorithmException, InvalidKeyException, IOException,
           IllegalBlockSizeException, NoSuchPaddingException,
           BadPaddingException
{
    // Create and initialize the decryption engine
    Cipher cipher = Cipher.getInstance("DESede");
    cipher.init(Cipher.DECRYPT_MODE, key);

    // Read bytes, decrypt, and write them out.
    byte[] buffer = new byte[2048];
    int bytesRead;
    while((bytesRead = in.read(buffer)) != -1) {
        out.write(cipher.update(buffer, 0, bytesRead));
    }

    // Write out the final bunch of decrypted bytes
    out.write(cipher.doFinal());
    out.flush();
}
}
```

Exercises

6-1. Write a PasswordManager class that associates usernames with passwords and has methods for creating and deleting username/password pairs, changing the password associated with a username, and authenticating a user by verifying a supplied password. PasswordManager should store the usernames and passwords in a file (or in a database, if you've already read Chapter 17, *Database Access with SQL).*

Note, however, that the class should not store the passwords as plain text as that would allow an intruder who broke into the PasswordManager system to obtain full access to all passwords. To prevent this, it is common to use a one-way function to encrypt passwords. Message digests, such as those used in Example 6-4, provide exactly this kind of a one-way function. Computing a message digest for a password is relatively easy, but going in the opposite direction from digest to password is very difficult or impossible.

Design the PasswordManager class so that instead of storing the actual password, it stores only a message digest of the password. To verify a user's password, your class should compute a digest for the supplied password and compare it to the stored digest. If the digests match, you can assume that the passwords match also. (There is actually an infinitesimally small chance that two different passwords will produce the same message digest, but you can disregard this possibility.)

6-2. Write a network service and client that allows a user to change his current password that is registered with your PasswordManager class. If you've read Chapter 16, *Remote Method Invocation,* modify PasswordManager so that it runs as a RMI remote object and write a client program that uses the remote object to change a password. If you have not read that chapter yet, write the password-changing service to run under the Server class developed in Chapter 5 and use the GenericClient class from that same chapter to interact with the service. In either case, create a security policy file that defines the set of permissions required by your network service, and use this policy file to enable your service to run with the -Djava.security.manager option to the Java interpreter.

6-3. The TripleDES class of Example 6-5 uses the DESede algorithm in the default ECB (electronic code book) mode. This encryption mode is more vulnerable to certain decryption attacks than CBC (cipher block chaining) mode. Modify the example so that it uses CBC mode. You specify the mode as part of the algorithm name: in this case, instead of specifying "DESede" as the algorithm, specify "DESede/CBC/PKCS5Padding".

To encrypt using CBC mode, the Cipher object creates an initialization vector (IV) of random bytes, which is also required when decrypting. Modify the encrypt() method so that it obtains the IV with the getIV() method of the Cipher object and writes the bytes (and the length) of the IV array to the output stream before it writes out the encrypted bytes. To do this, you may want to modify encrypt() so that it doesn't use the CipherOutputStreamx but instead works with the Cipher class directly, the way decrypt() does. Modify the decrypt() method so that it reads the bytes of the IV and uses them to create a javax.crypto.spec.IvParameterSpec object, which it then passes (as an AlgorithmParameterSpec) to one of the init() methods of the Cipher object.

6-4. The TripleDES program stores and reads secret keys from unprotected files, which is not a very secure way to work with important keys. Modify the program so that it uses a KeyStore object to store (and retrieve) the key in password-protected form. The KeyStore class was demonstrated in Example 6-4, where it was used to store PublicKey and PrivateKey objects for digital signatures. A KeyStore can also store SecretKey objects, however. Simply pass the SecretKey to the setKeyEntry() method, specifying a name for the key and a password to protect it with. Since the key is not a PrivateKey, you should pass null for the Certificate[] argument to this method.

CHAPTER 7

Internationalization

Internationalization is the process of making a program flexible enough to run correctly in any locale. The required corollary to internationalization is localization—the process of arranging for a program to run in a specific locale.

There are several distinct steps to the task of internationalization. Java (1.1 and later) addresses these steps with several different mechanisms:

- A program must be able to read, write, and manipulate localized text. Java uses the Unicode character encoding, which by itself is a huge step towards internationalization. In addition, the InputStreamReader and Output-StreamWriter classes convert text from a locale-specific encoding to Unicode and from Unicode to a locale-specific encoding, respectively.

- A program must conform to local customs when displaying dates and times, formatting numbers, and sorting strings. Java addresses these issues with the classes in the java.text package.

- A program must display all user-visible text in the local language. Translating the messages a program displays is always one of the main tasks in localizing a program. A more important task is writing the program so that all user-visible text is fetched at runtime, rather than hardcoded directly into the program. Java facilitates this process with the ResourceBundle class and its subclasses in the java.util package.

This chapter discusses all three aspects of internationalization.

A Word About Locales

A *locale* represents a geographic, political, or cultural region. In Java, locales are represented by the java.util.Locale class. A locale is frequently defined by a language, which is represented by its standard lowercase two-letter code, such as en (English) or fr (French). Sometimes, however, language alone is not sufficient to uniquely specify a locale, and a country is added to the specification. A country is represented by an uppercase two-letter code. For example, the United States

English locale (en_US) is distinct from the British English locale (en_GB), and the French spoken in Canada (fr_CA) is different from the French spoken in France (fr_FR). Occasionally, the scope of a locale is further narrowed with the addition of a system-dependent variant string.

The Locale class maintains a static default locale, which can be set and queried with Locale.setDefault() and Locale.getDefault(). Locale-sensitive methods in Java typically come in two forms. One uses the default locale, and the other uses a Locale object that is explicitly specified as an argument. A program can create and use any number of nondefault Locale objects, although it is more common simply to rely on the default locale, which is inherited from the underlying default locale on the native platform. Locale-sensitive classes in Java often provide a method to query the list of locales that they support.

Finally, note that AWT and Swing GUI components (see Chapter 10, *Graphical User Interfaces*) have a locale property, so it is possible for different components to use different locales. (Most components, however, are not locale-sensitive; they behave the same in any locale.)

Unicode

Java uses the Unicode character encoding. (Java 1.3 uses Unicode Version 2.1. Support for Unicode 3.0 will be included in Java 1.4 or another future release.) Unicode is a 16-bit character encoding established by the Unicode Consortium, which describes the standard as follows (see *http://unicode.org*):

> The Unicode Standard defines codes for characters used in the major languages written today. Scripts include the European alphabetic scripts, Middle Eastern right-to-left scripts, and scripts of Asia. The Unicode Standard also includes punctuation marks, diacritics, mathematical symbols, technical symbols, arrows, dingbats, etc. ... In all, the Unicode Standard provides codes for 49,194 characters from the world's alphabets, ideograph sets, and symbol collections.

In the canonical form of the Unicode encoding, which is what Java char and String types use, every character occupies two bytes. The Unicode characters \u0020 to \u007E are equivalent to the ASCII and ISO8859-1 (Latin-1) characters 0x20 through 0x7E. The Unicode characters \u00A0 to \u00FF are identical to the ISO8859-1 characters 0xA0 to 0xFF. Thus, there is a trivial mapping between Latin-1 and Unicode characters. A number of other portions of the Unicode encoding are based on preexisting standards, such as ISO8859-5 (Cyrillic) and ISO8859-8 (Hebrew), though the mappings between these standards and Unicode may not be as trivial as the Latin-1 mapping.

Note that Unicode support may be limited on many platforms. One of the difficulties with the use of Unicode is the poor availability of fonts to display all the Unicode characters. Figure 7-1 shows some of the characters that are available in the standard fonts that ship with Sun's Java 1.3 SDK for Linux. (Note that these fonts do not ship with the Java JRE, so even if they are available on your development platform, they may not be available on your target platform.) Note the special box glyph that indicates undefined characters.

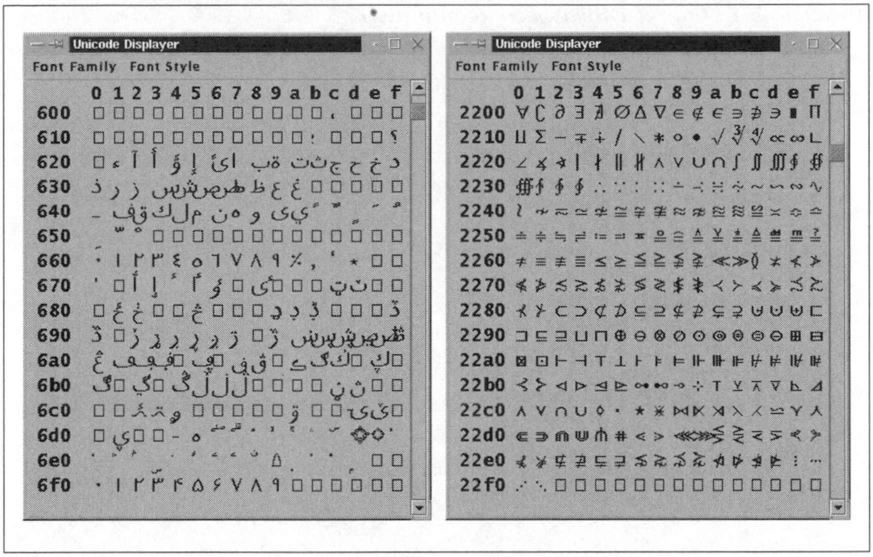

Figure 7–1. Some Unicode characters and their encodings

Example 7-1 lists code used to create the displays of Figure 7-1. Because Unicode characters are integrated so fundamentally into the Java language, this Uni-codeDisplay program does not perform any sophisticated internationalization techniques to display Unicode glyphs. Thus, you'll find that Example 7-1 is more of a Swing GUI example rather than an internationalization example. If you haven't read Chapter 10 yet, you may not understand all the code in this example.

Example 7–1: UnicodeDisplay.java

```
package com.davidflanagan.examples.i18n;
import javax.swing.*;
import java.awt.*;
import java.awt.event.*;

/**
 * This program displays Unicode glyphs using user-specified fonts
 * and font styles.
 **/
public class UnicodeDisplay extends JFrame implements ActionListener {
    int page = 0;
    UnicodePanel p;
    JScrollBar b;
    String fontfamily = "Serif";
    int fontstyle = Font.PLAIN;

    /**
     * This constructor creates the frame, menubar, and scrollbar
     * that work along with the UnicodePanel class, defined below
     **/
    public UnicodeDisplay(String name) {
        super(name);
        p = new UnicodePanel();                 // Create the panel
        p.setBase((char)(page * 0x100));        // Initialize it
        getContentPane().add(p, "Center");      // Center it
```

Example 7-1: UnicodeDisplay.java (continued)

```
        // Create and set up a scrollbar, and put it on the right
        b = new JScrollBar(Scrollbar.VERTICAL, 0, 1, 0, 0xFF);
        b.setUnitIncrement(1);
        b.setBlockIncrement(0x10);
        b.addAdjustmentListener(new AdjustmentListener() {
                public void adjustmentValueChanged(AdjustmentEvent e) {
                    page = e.getValue();
                    p.setBase((char)(page * 0x100));
                }
            });
        getContentPane().add(b, "East");

        // Set things up so we respond to window close requests
        this.addWindowListener(new WindowAdapter() {
                public void windowClosing(WindowEvent e) { System.exit(0); }
            });

        // Handle Page Up and Page Down and the up and down arrow keys
        this.addKeyListener(new KeyAdapter() {
                public void keyPressed(KeyEvent e) {
                    int code = e.getKeyCode();
                    int oldpage = page;
                    if ((code == KeyEvent.VK_PAGE_UP) ||
                        (code == KeyEvent.VK_UP)) {
                        if (e.isShiftDown()) page -= 0x10;
                        else page -= 1;
                        if (page < 0) page = 0;
                    }
                    else if ((code == KeyEvent.VK_PAGE_DOWN) ||
                             (code == KeyEvent.VK_DOWN)) {
                        if (e.isShiftDown()) page += 0x10;
                        else page += 1;
                        if (page > 0xff) page = 0xff;
                    }
                    if (page != oldpage) {       // if anything has changed...
                        p.setBase((char) (page * 0x100)); // update the display
                        b.setValue(page);        // and update scrollbar to match
                    }
                }
            });

        // Set up a menu system to change fonts.  Use a convenience method.
        JMenuBar menubar = new JMenuBar();
        this.setJMenuBar(menubar);
        menubar.add(makemenu("Font Family",
                        new String[] {"Serif", "SansSerif", "Monospaced"},
                        this));
        menubar.add(makemenu("Font Style",
                        new String[]{
                            "Plain","Italic","Bold","BoldItalic"
                        }, this));
    }

    /** This method handles the items in the menubars */
    public void actionPerformed(ActionEvent e) {
        String cmd = e.getActionCommand();
        if (cmd.equals("Serif")) fontfamily = "Serif";
        else if (cmd.equals("SansSerif")) fontfamily = "SansSerif";
```

Example 7-1: UnicodeDisplay.java (continued)

```
            else if (cmd.equals("Monospaced")) fontfamily = "Monospaced";
            else if (cmd.equals("Plain")) fontstyle = Font.PLAIN;
            else if (cmd.equals("Italic")) fontstyle = Font.ITALIC;
            else if (cmd.equals("Bold")) fontstyle = Font.BOLD;
            else if (cmd.equals("BoldItalic")) fontstyle = Font.BOLD + Font.ITALIC;
            p.setFont(fontfamily, fontstyle);
    }

    /** A convenience method to create a Menu from an array of items */
    private JMenu makemenu(String name, String[] itemnames,
                           ActionListener listener)
    {
        JMenu m = new JMenu(name);
        for(int i = 0; i < itemnames.length; i++) {
            JMenuItem item = new JMenuItem(itemnames[i]);
            item.addActionListener(listener);
            item.setActionCommand(itemnames[i]);  // okay here, though
            m.add(item);
        }
        return m;
    }

    /** The main() program just creates a window, packs it, and shows it */
    public static void main(String[] args) {
        UnicodeDisplay f = new UnicodeDisplay("Unicode Displayer");
        f.pack();
        f.show();
    }

    /**
     * This nested class is the one that displays one "page" of Unicode
     * glyphs at a time.  Each "page" is 256 characters, arranged into 16
     * rows of 16 columns each.
     **/
    public static class UnicodePanel extends JComponent {
        protected char base;  // What character we start the display at
        protected Font font = new Font("serif", Font.PLAIN, 18);
        protected Font headingfont = new Font("monospaced", Font.BOLD, 18);
        static final int lineheight = 25;
        static final int charspacing = 20;
        static final int x0 = 65;
        static final int y0 = 40;

        /** Specify where to begin displaying, and re-display */
        public void setBase(char base) { this.base = base; repaint(); }

        /** Set a new font name or style, and redisplay */
        public void setFont(String family, int style) {
            this.font = new Font(family, style, 18);
            repaint();
        }

        /**
         * The paintComponent() method actually draws the page of glyphs
         **/
        public void paintComponent(Graphics g) {
            int start = (int)base & 0xFFF0; // Start on a 16-character boundary
```

Example 7–1: UnicodeDisplay.java (continued)

```
        // Draw the headings in a special font
        g.setFont(headingfont);

        // Draw 0..F on top
        for(int i=0; i < 16; i++) {
            String s = Integer.toString(i, 16);
            g.drawString(s, x0 + i*charspacing, y0-20);
        }

        // Draw column down left.
        for(int i = 0; i < 16; i++) {
            int j = start + i*16;
            String s = Integer.toString(j, 16);
            g.drawString(s, 10, y0+i*lineheight);
        }

        // Now draw the characters
        g.setFont(font);
        char[] c = new char[1];
        for(int i = 0; i < 16; i++) {
            for(int j = 0; j < 16; j++) {
                c[0] = (char)(start + j*16 + i);
                g.drawChars(c, 0, 1, x0 + i*charspacing, y0+j*lineheight);
            }
        }
    }

    /** Custom components like this one should always have this method */
    public Dimension getPreferredSize() {
        return new Dimension(x0 + 16*charspacing,
                             y0 + 16*lineheight);
    }
    }
}
```

Character Encodings

Text representation has traditionally been one of the most difficult problems of internationalization. Java, however, solves this problem quite elegantly and hides the difficult issues. Java uses Unicode internally, so it can represent essentially any character in any commonly used written language. As I noted earlier, the remaining task is to convert Unicode to and from locale-specific encodings. Java includes quite a few internal byte-to-char and char-to-byte converters that handle converting locale-specific character encodings to Unicode and vice versa. While the converters themselves are not public, they are accessible through the InputStreamReader and OutputStreamWriter classes, which are character streams included in the java.io package.

Any program can automatically handle locale-specific encodings simply by using these character stream classes to do their textual input and output. Note that the FileReader and FileWriter classes use these streams to automatically read and write text files that use the platform's default encoding.

Example 7-2 shows a simple program that works with character encodings. It converts a file from one specified encoding to another by converting from the first encoding to Unicode and then from Unicode to the second encoding. Note that most of the program is taken up with the mechanics of parsing argument lists, handling exceptions, and so on. Only a few lines are required to create the Input-StreamReader and OutputStreamWriter classes that perform the two halves of the conversion. Also note that exceptions are handled by calling LocalizedError.display(). This method is not part of the Java API; it is a custom method shown in Example 7-5 at the end of this chapter.

Example 7-2: ConvertEncoding.java

```
package com.davidflanagan.examples.i18n;
import java.io.*;

/** A program to convert from one character encoding to another */
public class ConvertEncoding {
    public static void main(String[] args) {
        String from = null, to = null;
        String infile = null, outfile = null;
        for(int i = 0; i < args.length; i++) { // Parse command-line arguments.
            if (i == args.length-1) usage();    // All args require another.
            if (args[i].equals("-from")) from = args[++i];
            else if (args[i].equals("-to")) to = args[++i];
            else if (args[i].equals("-in")) infile = args[++i];
            else if (args[i].equals("-out")) outfile = args[++i];
            else usage();
        }

        try { convert(infile, outfile, from, to); }  // Attempt conversion.
        catch (Exception e) {                        // Handle exceptions.
            LocalizedError.display(e);  // Defined at the end of this chapter.
            System.exit(1);
        }
    }

    public static void usage() {
        System.err.println("Usage: java ConvertEncoding <options>\n" +
                           "Options:\n\t-from <encoding>\n\t" +
                           "-to <encoding>\n\t" +
                           "-in <file>\n\t-out <file>");
        System.exit(1);
    }

    public static void convert(String infile, String outfile,
                               String from, String to)
            throws IOException, UnsupportedEncodingException
    {
        // Set up byte streams.
        InputStream in;
        if (infile != null) in = new FileInputStream(infile);
        else in = System.in;
        OutputStream out;
        if (outfile != null) out = new FileOutputStream(outfile);
        else out = System.out;

        // Use default encoding if no encoding is specified.
        if (from == null) from = System.getProperty("file.encoding");
        if (to == null) to = System.getProperty("file.encoding");
```

Example 7-2: ConvertEncoding.java (continued)

```
        // Set up character streams.
        Reader r = new BufferedReader(new InputStreamReader(in, from));
        Writer w = new BufferedWriter(new OutputStreamWriter(out, to));

        // Copy characters from input to output. The InputStreamReader
        // converts from the input encoding to Unicode, and the
        // OutputStreamWriter converts from Unicode to the output encoding.
        // Characters that cannot be represented in the output encoding are
        // output as '?'
        char[] buffer = new char[4096];
        int len;
        while((len = r.read(buffer)) != -1)    // Read a block of input.
            w.write(buffer, 0, len);           // And write it out.
        r.close();                             // Close the input.
        w.close();                             // Flush and close output.
    }
}
```

Handling Local Customs

The second problem of internationalization is the task of following local customs and conventions in areas such as date and time formatting. The java.text package defines classes to help with this duty.

The NumberFormat class formats numbers, monetary amounts, and percentages in a locale-dependent way for display to the user. This is necessary because different locales have different conventions for number formatting. For example, in France, a comma is used as a decimal separator instead of a period, as in many English-speaking countries. A NumberFormat object can use the default locale or any locale you specify.

The DateFormat class formats dates and times in a locale-dependent way for display to the user. Different countries have different conventions. Should the month or day be displayed first? Should periods or colons separate fields of the time? What are the names of the months in the language of the locale? A DateFormat object can simply use the default locale, or it can use any locale you specify. The DateFormat class is used in conjunction with the TimeZone and Calendar classes of java.util. The TimeZone object tells the DateFormat what time zone the date should be interpreted in, while the Calendar object specifies how the date itself should be broken down into days, weeks, months, and years. Almost all locales use the standard GregorianCalendar.

The Collator class compares strings in a locale-dependent way. This is necessary because different languages alphabetize strings in different ways (and some languages don't even use alphabets). In traditional Spanish, for example, the letters "ch" are treated as a single character that comes between "c" and "d" for the purposes of sorting. When you need to sort strings or search for a string within Unicode text, you should use a Collator object, either one created to work with the default locale or one created for a specified locale.

The BreakIterator class allows you to locate character, word, line, and sentence boundaries in a locale-dependent way. This is useful when you need to recognize such boundaries in Unicode text, such as when you are implementing a word-wrapping algorithm.

Example 7-3 shows a class that uses the NumberFormat and DateFormat classes to display a hypothetical stock portfolio to the user following local conventions. The program uses various NumberFormat and DateFormat object to format (using the format() method) different types of numbers and dates. These Format objects all operate using the default locale but could have been created with an explicitly specified locale. The program displays information about a hypothetical stock portfolio, formatting dates and numbers and monetary values according to the current or the specified locale. The following listing shows the output of this program in American, British, and French locales:

```
% java com.davidflanagan.examples.i18n.Portfolio en US
Portfolio value at July 9, 2000 9:08:48 PM PDT:
Symbol  Shares  Purchased    At      Quote   Change
XXX     400     Feb 3, 2000  $11.90  $13.00  9%
YYY     1,100   Mar 2, 2000  $71.09  $27.25  -62%
ZZZ     6,000   May 17, 2000 $23.37  $89.12  281%

% java com.davidflanagan.examples.i18n.Portfolio en GB
Portfolio value at 09 July 2000 21:08:55 PDT:
Symbol  Shares  Purchased    At      Quote   Change
XXX     400     03-Feb-00    £11.90  £13.00  9%
YYY     1,100   02-Mar-00    £71.09  £27.25  -62%
ZZZ     6,000   17-May-00    £23.37  £89.12  281%

% java com.davidflanagan.examples.i18n.Portfolio fr FR
Portfolio value at 9 juillet 2000 21:09:03 PDT:
Symbol  Shares  Purchased    At        Quote     Change
XXX     400     3 févr. 00   11,90 F   13,00 F   9%
YYY     1 100   2 mars 00    71,09 F   27,25 F   -62%
ZZZ     6 000   17 mai 00    23,37 F   89,12 F   281%
```

Example 7–3: Portfolio.java

```java
package com.davidflanagan.examples.i18n;
import java.text.*;
import java.util.*;
import java.io.*;

/**
 * A partial implementation of a hypothetical stock portfolio class.
 * We use it only to demonstrate number and date internationalization.
 **/
public class Portfolio {
    EquityPosition[] positions;
    Date lastQuoteTime = new Date();

    public Portfolio(EquityPosition[] positions, Date lastQuoteTime) {
        this.positions = positions;
        this.lastQuoteTime = lastQuoteTime;
    }

    public void print(PrintWriter out) {
        // Obtain NumberFormat and DateFormat objects to format our data.
        NumberFormat number = NumberFormat.getInstance();
        NumberFormat price = NumberFormat.getCurrencyInstance();
        NumberFormat percent = NumberFormat.getPercentInstance();
```

Example 7–3: Portfolio.java (continued)

```
        DateFormat shortdate = DateFormat.getDateInstance(DateFormat.MEDIUM);
        DateFormat fulldate = DateFormat.getDateTimeInstance(DateFormat.LONG,
                                                          DateFormat.LONG);

        // Print some introductory data.
        out.println("Portfolio value at " +
                    fulldate.format(lastQuoteTime) + ":");
        out.println("Symbol\tShares\tPurchased\tAt\t" +
                    "Quote\tChange");

        // Display the table using the format() methods of the Format objects.
        for(int i = 0; i < positions.length; i++) {
            out.print(positions[i].name + "\t");
            out.print(number.format(positions[i].shares) + "\t");
            out.print(shortdate.format(positions[i].purchased) + "\t");
            out.print(price.format(positions[i].bought) + "\t");
            out.print(price.format(positions[i].current) + "\t");
            double change =
                (positions[i].current-positions[i].bought)/positions[i].bought;
            out.println(percent.format(change));
            out.flush();
        }
    }

    static class EquityPosition {
        String name;            // Name of the stock.
        int shares;             // Number of shares held.
        Date purchased;         // When purchased.
        double bought;          // Purchase price per share
        double current;         // Current price per share
        EquityPosition(String n, int s, Date when, double then, double now) {
            name = n; shares = s; purchased = when;
            bought = then; current = now;
        }
    }

    /**
     * This is a test program that demonstrates the class
     **/
    public static void main(String[] args) {
        // This is the portfolio to display.  Note we use a deprecated
        // Date() constructor here for convenience. It represents the year
        // offset from 1900, and will cause a warning message when compiling.
        EquityPosition[] positions = new EquityPosition[] {
            new EquityPosition("XXX", 400, new Date(100,1,3),11.90,13.00),
            new EquityPosition("YYY", 1100, new Date(100,2,2),71.09,27.25),
            new EquityPosition("ZZZ", 6000, new Date(100,4,17),23.37,89.12)
        };

        // Create the portfolio from these positions
        Portfolio portfolio = new Portfolio(positions, new Date());

        // Set the default locale using the language code and country code
        // specified on the command line.
        if (args.length == 2) Locale.setDefault(new Locale(args[0], args[1]));

        // Now print the portfolio
        portfolio.print(new PrintWriter(System.out));
```

Example 7–3: Portfolio.java (continued)

```
    }
}
```

Setting the Locale

Example 7-3 contains code that explicitly sets the locale using the language code and the country code specified on the command line. If these arguments are not specified, it uses the default locale for your system. When experimenting with internationalization, you may want to change the default locale for the entire platform, so you can see what happens. How you do this is platform-dependent. On Unix platforms, you typically set the locale by setting the LANG environment variable. For example, to set the locale for Canadian French, using a Unix *csh*-style shell, use this command:

```
% setenv LANG fr_CA
```

Or, to set the locale to English as spoken in Great Britain when using a Unix *sh*-style shell, use this command:

```
$ export LANG=en_GB
```

To set the locale in Windows, use the Regional Settings control on the Windows Control Panel.

Localizing User-Visible Messages

The third task of internationalization involves ensuring that there are no user-visible strings that are hardcoded in an application; instead, strings should be looked up based on the locale. In Example 7-3, for example, the strings "Portfolio value", "Symbol", "Shares", and others are hardcoded in the application and appear in English, even when the program is run in the French locale. The only way to prevent this is to fetch all user-visible messages at runtime and to translate every message into each languages your application must support.

Java helps you handle this task with the ResourceBundle class of the java.util package. This class represents a bundle of resources that can be looked up by name. You define a localized resource bundle for each locale you want to support, and Java loads the correct bundle for the default (or specified) locale. With the correct bundle loaded, you can look up the resources (typically strings) your program needs at runtime.

Working with Resource Bundles

To define a bundle of localized resources, you create a subclass of ResourceBundle and provide definitions for the handleGetObject() and getKeys() methods. handleGetObject() is passed the name of a resource; it should return an appropriate localized version of that resource. getKeys() should return an Enumeration object that gives the user a list of all resource names defined in the ResourceBundle. Instead of subclassing ResourceBundle directly, however, it is often easier to subclass `ListResourceBundle`. You can also simply provide a property file (see the `java.util.Properties` class) that `ResourceBundle.getBundle()` uses to create an instance of `PropertyResourceBundle`.

To use localized resources from a `ResourceBundle` in a program, you should first call the static `getBundle()` method, which dynamically loads and instantiates a `ResourceBundle`, as described shortly. The returned `ResourceBundle` has the name you specify and is appropriate for the specified locale (or for the default locale, if no locale is explicitly specified). Once you have obtained a `ResourceBundle` object with `getBundle()`, use the `getObject()` method to look up resources by name. Note that there is a convenience method, `getString()`, that simply casts the value returned by `getObject()` to be a `String` object.

When you call `getBundle()`, you specify the base name of the desired `Resource-Bundle` and a desired locale (if you don't want to rely on the default locale). Recall that a `Locale` is specified with a two-letter language code, an optional two-letter country code, and an optional variant string. `getBundle()` looks for an appropriate `ResourceBundle` class for the locale by appending this locale information to the base name for the bundle. The method looks for an appropriate class with the following algorithm:

1. Search for a class with the following name:

    basename_language_country_variant

    If no such class is found, or no variant string is specified for the locale, it goes to the next step.

2. Search for a class with the following name:

    basename_language_country

    If no such class is found, or no country code is specified for the locale, it goes to the next step.

3. Search for a class with the following name:

    basename_language

    If no such class is found, it goes to the final step.

4. Search for a class which has the same name as the basename, or in other words, search for a class with the following name:

    basename

    This represents a default resource bundle used by any locale that is not explicitly supported.

At each step in this process, `getBundle()` checks first for a class file with the given name. If no class file is found, it uses the `getResourceAsStream()` method of `ClassLoader` to look for a `Properties` file with the same name as the class and a *.properties* extension. If such a properties file is found, its contents are used to create a `Properties` object and `getBundle()` instantiates and returns a `Property-ResourceBundle` that exports the properties in the `Properties` file through the `ResourceBundle` API.

If `getBundle()` cannot find a class or properties file for the specified locale in any of the four previous search steps, it repeats the search using the default locale instead of the specified locale. If no appropriate `ResourceBundle` is found in this search either, `getBundle()` throws a `MissingResourceException`.

Any `ResourceBundle` object can have a parent `ResourceBundle` specified for it. When you look up a named resource in a `ResourceBundle`, `getObject()` first looks in the specified bundle, but if the named resource is not defined in that bundle, it recursively looks in the parent bundle. Thus, every `ResourceBundle` inherits the resources of its parent and may choose to override some, or all, of these resources. (Note that we are using the terms "inherit" and "override" in a different sense than we do when talking about classes that inherit and override methods in their superclass.) What this means is that every `ResourceBundle` you define does not have to define every resource required by your application. For example, you might define a `ResourceBundle` of messages to display to French-speaking users. Then you might define a smaller and more specialized `ResourceBundle` that overrides a few of these messages so that they are appropriate for French-speaking users who live in Canada.

Your application is not required to find and set up the parent objects for the `ResourceBundle` objects it uses. The `getBundle()` method actually does this for you. When `getBundle()` finds an appropriate class or properties file as described above, it does not immediately return the `ResourceBundle` it has found. Instead, it continues through the remaining steps in the previous search process, looking for less-specific class or properties files from which the `ResourceBundle` may inherit resources. If and when `getBundle()` finds these less-specific resource bundles, it sets them up as the appropriate ancestors of the original bundle. Only once it has checked all possibilities does it return the original `ResourceBundle` object that it created.

To continue the example begun earlier, when a program runs in Quebec, `getBundle()` might first find a small specialized `ResourceBundle` class that has only a few specific Quebecois resources. Next, it looks for a more general `ResourceBundle` that contains French messages, and it sets this bundle as the parent of the original Quebecois bundle. Finally, `getBundle()` looks for (and probably finds) a class the defines a default set of resources, probably written in English (assuming that English is the native tongue of the original programmer). This default bundle is set as the parent of the French bundle (which makes it the grandparent of the Quebecois bundle). When the application looks up a named resource, the Quebecois bundle is searched first. If the resource isn't defined there, the French bundle is searched, and any named resource not found in the French bundle is looked up in the default bundle.

ResourceBundle Example

Examining some code makes this discussion of resource bundles much clearer. Example 7-4 is a convenience routine for creating Swing menu panes. Given a list of menu item names, it looks up labels and menu shortcuts for those named menu items in a resource bundle and creates a localized menu pane. The example has a simple test program attached.

Figure 7-2 shows the menus it creates in the American, British, and French locales. This program cannot run, of course, without localized resource bundles from which the localized menu labels are looked up.

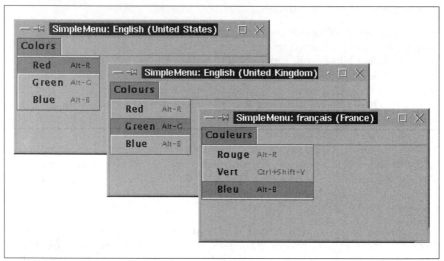

Figure 7-2. Localized menu panes

Example 7-4: SimpleMenu.java

```
package com.davidflanagan.examples.i18n;
import javax.swing.*;
import java.awt.*;
import java.awt.event.*;
import java.util.Locale;
import java.util.ResourceBundle;
import java.util.MissingResourceException;

/** A convenience class to automatically create localized menu panes */
public class SimpleMenu {
    /** The convenience method that creates menu panes */
    public static JMenu create(ResourceBundle bundle,
                               String menuname, String[] itemnames,
                               ActionListener listener)
    {
        // Get the menu title from the bundle.  Use name as default label.
        String menulabel;
        try { menulabel = bundle.getString(menuname + ".label"); }
        catch(MissingResourceException e) { menulabel = menuname; }

        // Create the menu pane.
        JMenu menu = new JMenu(menulabel);

        // For each named item in the menu.
        for(int i = 0; i < itemnames.length; i++) {
            // Look up the label for the item, using name as default.
            String itemlabel;
            try {
                itemlabel =
                    bundle.getString(menuname+"."+itemnames[i]+".label");
            }
```

Example 7-4: SimpleMenu.java (continued)

```
            catch (MissingResourceException e) { itemlabel = itemnames[i]; }

            JMenuItem item = new JMenuItem(itemlabel);

            // Look up an accelerator for the menu item
            try {
                String acceleratorText =
                    bundle.getString(menuname+"."+itemnames[i]+".accelerator");
                item.setAccelerator(KeyStroke.getKeyStroke(acceleratorText));
            }
            catch (MissingResourceException e) {}

            // Register an action listener and command for the item.
            if (listener != null) {
                item.addActionListener(listener);
                item.setActionCommand(itemnames[i]);
            }

            // Add the item to the menu.
            menu.add(item);
        }

        // Return the automatically created localized menu.
        return menu;
    }

    /** A simple test program for the above code */
    public static void main(String[] args) {
        // Get the locale: default, or specified on command-line
        Locale locale;
        if (args.length == 2) locale = new Locale(args[0], args[1]);
        else locale = Locale.getDefault();

        // Get the resource bundle for that Locale.  This will throw an
        // (unchecked) MissingResourceException if no bundle is found.
        ResourceBundle bundle =
            ResourceBundle.getBundle("com.davidflanagan.examples.i18n.Menus",
                                     locale);

        // Create a simple GUI window to display the menu with
        final JFrame f = new JFrame("SimpleMenu: " +   // Window title
                            locale.getDisplayName(Locale.getDefault()));
        JMenuBar menubar = new JMenuBar();             // Create a menubar.
        f.setJMenuBar(menubar);                        // Add menubar to window

        // Define an action listener for that our menu will use.
        ActionListener listener = new ActionListener() {
                public void actionPerformed(ActionEvent e) {
                    String s = e.getActionCommand();
                    Component c = f.getContentPane();
                    if (s.equals("red")) c.setBackground(Color.red);
                    else if (s.equals("green")) c.setBackground(Color.green);
                    else if (s.equals("blue")) c.setBackground(Color.blue);
                }
            };

        // Now create a menu using our convenience routine with the resource
        // bundle and action listener we've created
```

Example 7-4: SimpleMenu.java (continued)

```
        JMenu menu = SimpleMenu.create(bundle, "colors",
                                new String[] {"red", "green", "blue"},
                                listener);

        // Finally add the menu to the GUI, and pop it up
        menubar.add(menu);        // Add the menu to the menubar
        f.setSize(300, 150);      // Set the window size.
        f.setVisible(true);       // Pop the window up.
    }
}
```

As I've already said, this example does not stand alone. It relies on resource bundles to localize the menu. The following listing shows three property files that serve as resource bundles for this example. Note that this single listing contains the bodies of three separate files:

```
# The file Menus.properties is the default "Menus" resource bundle.
# As an American programmer, I made my own locale the default.
colors.label=Colors
colors.red.label=Red
colors.red.accelerator=alt R
colors.green.label=Green
colors.green.accelerator=alt G
colors.blue.label=Blue
colors.blue.accelerator=alt B

# This is the file Menus_en_GB.properties.  It is the resource bundle for
# British English.  Note that it overrides only a single resource definition
# and simply inherits the rest from the default (American) bundle.
colors.label=Colours

# This is the file Menus_fr.properties.  It is the resource bundle for all
# French-speaking locales.  It overrides most, but not all, of the resources
# in the default bundle.
colors.label=Couleurs
colors.red.label=Rouge
colors.green.label=Vert
colors.green.accelerator=control shift V
colors.blue.label=Bleu
```

Formatted Messages

We've seen that in order to internationalize programs, you must place all user-visible messages into resource bundles. This is straightforward when the text to be localized consists of simple labels such as those on buttons and menu items. It is trickier, however, with messages that are composed partially of static text and partially of dynamic values. For example, a compiler might have to display a message such as "Error at line 5 of file "hello.java"", in which the line number and filename are dynamic and locale-independent, while the rest of the message is static and needs to be localized.

The MessageFormat class of the java.text package helps tremendously with these types of messages. To use it, you store only the static parts of a message in the ResourceBundle and include special characters that indicate where the dynamic parts of the message are to be placed. For example, one resource bundle might contain the message: "Error at line {0} of file {1}." And another resource bundle might contain a "translation" that looks like this: "Erreur: {1}: {0}."

To use such a localized message, you create a MessageFormat object from the static part of the message and then call its format() method, passing in an array of the values to be substituted. In this case, the array contains an Integer object that specifies the line number and a String object that specifies the filename. The MessageFormat class knows about other Format classes defined in java.text. It creates and uses NumberFormat objects to format numbers and DateFormat objects to format dates and times. In addition, you can design messages that create Choice-Format objects to convert from numbers to strings. This is useful when working with enumerated types, such as numbers that correspond to month names, or when you need to use the singular or plural form of a word based on the value of some number.

Example 7-5 demonstrates this kind of MessageFormat usage. It is a convenience class with a single static method for the localized display of exception and error message. When invoked, the code attempts to load a ResourceBundle with the basename "Errors". If found, it looks up a message resource using the class name of the exception object that was passed. If such a resource is found, it displays the error message. An array of five values is passed to the format() method. The localized error message can include any or all of these arguments.

The LocalizedError.display() method defined in this example was used in Example 7-2 at the beginning of this chapter. The default *Errors.properties* resource bundle used in conjunction with this example is shown following the code listing. Error message display for the program is nicely internationalized. Porting the program's error message to a new locale is simply a matter of translating (localizing) the *Errors.properties* file.

Example 7–5: LocalizedError.java

```
package com.davidflanagan.examples.i18n;
import java.text.*;
import java.io.*;
import java.util.*;

/**
 * A convenience class that can display a localized exception message
 * depending on the class of the exception.  It uses a MessageFormat,
 * and passes five arguments that the localized message may include:
 *    {0}: the message included in the exception or error.
 *    {1}: the full class name of the exception or error.
 *    {2}: a guess at what file the exception was caused by.
 *    {3}: a line number in that file.
 *    {4}: the current date and time.
 * Messages are looked up in a ResourceBundle with the basename
 * "Errors", using a the full class name of the exception object as
 * the resource name.  If no resource is found for a given exception
 * class, the superclasses are checked.
 **/
public class LocalizedError {
    public static void display(Throwable error) {
        ResourceBundle bundle;
        // Try to get the resource bundle.
```

Example 7-5: LocalizedError.java (continued)

```
        // If none, print the error in a non-localized way.
        try { bundle = ResourceBundle.getBundle("Errors"); }
        catch (MissingResourceException e) {
            error.printStackTrace(System.err);
            return;
        }

        // Look up a localized message resource in that bundle, using the
        // classname of the error (or its superclasses) as the resource name.
        // If no resource was found, display the error without localization.
        String message = null;
        Class c = error.getClass();
        while((message == null) && (c != Object.class)) {
            try { message = bundle.getString(c.getName()); }
            catch (MissingResourceException e) { c = c.getSuperclass(); }
        }
        if (message == null) { error.printStackTrace(System.err);  return; }

        // Try to figure out the filename and line number of the
        // exception.  Output the error's stack trace into a string, and
        // use the heuristic that the first line number that appears in
        // the stack trace is after the first or  second colon.  We assume that
        // this stack frame is the first one the programmer has any control
        // over, and so report it as the location of the exception.
        // Note that this is implementation-dependent and not robust...
        String filename = "";
        int linenum = 0;
        try {
            StringWriter sw = new StringWriter(); // Output stream to a string.
            PrintWriter out=new PrintWriter(sw);  // PrintWriter wrapper.
            error.printStackTrace(out);           // Print stacktrace.
            String trace = sw.toString();         // Get it as a string.
            int pos = trace.indexOf(':');         // Look for first colon.
            if (error.getMessage() != null)       // If the error has a message
                pos = trace.indexOf(':', pos+1);  // look for second colon.
            int pos2 = trace.indexOf(')', pos);   // Look for end of line #
            linenum = Integer.parseInt(trace.substring(pos+1,pos2)); // line #
            pos2 = trace.lastIndexOf('(', pos);   // Back to start of filename.
            filename = trace.substring(pos2+1, pos); // Get filename.
        }
        catch (Exception e) { ; }                 // Ignore exceptions.

        // Set up an array of arguments to use with the message
        String errmsg = error.getMessage();
        Object[] args = {
            ((errmsg!= null)?errmsg:""), error.getClass().getName(),
            filename, new Integer(linenum), new Date()
        };
        // Finally, display the localized error message, using
        // MessageFormat.format() to substitute the arguments into the message.
        System.out.println(MessageFormat.format(message, args));
    }

    /**
     * This is a simple test program that demonstrates the display() method.
     * You can use it to generate and display a FileNotFoundException or an
     * ArrayIndexOutOfBoundsException
     **/
```

Example 7–5: LocalizedError.java (continued)

```
public static void main(String[] args) {
    try { FileReader in = new FileReader(args[0]); }
    catch(Exception e) { LocalizedError.display(e); }
}
}
```

The following listing shows the resource bundle properties file used to localize the set of possible error messages that can be thrown by the ConvertEncoding class shown at the beginning of this chapter:

```
#
# This is the file Errors.properties
# One property for each class of exceptions that our program might
# report.  Note the use of backslashes to continue long lines onto the
# next.  Also note the use of \n and \t for newlines and tabs
#
java.io.FileNotFoundException: \
Error: File "{0}" not found\n\t\
Error occurred at line {3} of file "{2}"\n\tat {4}

java.io.UnsupportedEncodingException: \
Error: Specified encoding not supported\n\t\
Error occurred at line {3} of file "{2}"\n\tat {4,time} on {4,date}

java.io.CharConversionException:\
Error: Character conversion failure.  Input data is not in specified format.

# A generic resource.  Display a message for any error or exception that
# is not handled by a more specific resource.
java.lang.Throwable:\
Error: {1}: {0}\n\t\
Error occurred at line {3} of file "{2}"\n\t{4,time,long} {4,date,long}
```

With a resource bundle like this, ConvertEncoding produces error messages like the following:

```
Error: File "myfile (No such file or directory)" not found
        Error occurred at line 64 of file "FileInputStream.java"
        at 7/9/00 9:28 PM
```

Or, if the current locale is fr_FR:

```
Error: File "myfile (Aucun fichier ou répertoire de ce type)" not found
        Error occurred at line 64 of file "FileInputStream.java"
        at 09/07/00 21:28
```

Exercises

7-1. Several internationalization-related classes, such as NumberFormat and Date-Format, have static methods named getAvailableLocales() that return an array of the Locale objects they support. You can look up the name of the country of a given Locale object with the getDisplayCountry() method. Note that this method has two variants. One takes no arguments and displays the country name as appropriate in the default locale. The other version of getDisplayCountry() expects a Locale argument and displays the country name in the language of the specified locale.

Write a program that displays the country names for all locales returned by NumberFormat.getAvailableLocales(). Using the static locale constants defined by the Locale class, display each country name in English, French, German, and Italian.

7-2. Modify the Portfolio class of Example 7-3 to remove all hardcoded display strings. Instead, use the ResourceBundle and MessageFormat classes as demonstrated in Example 7-4 and Example 7-5.

7-3. Write a multicity digital clock program that displays the current date and time in the cities Washington, London, Paris, Bonn, Beijing, and Tokyo. Display the dates and times using the customary formats for those cities. You'll want to read about the java.util.TimeZone class and the DateFormat.setTimeZone() method. Consult a map or search the Internet to determine the time zones for each of the cities. Write the program as an AWT or Swing application or as an applet after you have read Chapter 10 and Chapter 15, *Applets*. You may want to base the program on the Clock applet from Example 15-2.

7-4. Example 7-4 shows how you can use a ResourceBundle to internationalize the text that appears within menus in your application. One feature of Swing that discourages internationalization is that the JButton, JMenu, and JMenuItem constructors, among others, are passed the labels they are to display. This makes it very tempting for programmers to hardcode these labels into their programs. Create internationalized subclasses of these components, named IButton, IMenu, and IMenuItem, that instead take resource names as their constructor arguments. Each class should look up a resource bundle named "Labels" and use this bundle to look up the button or menu label that corresponds to the resource name passed to the constructor. If the bundle does not exist, or if a given resource is not defined in it, the IButton, IMenu, and IMenuItem classes should default to using the resource names as their labels. Write a simple test program (and some test property files) that demonstrate these new classes under two or three different locales. You'll probably want to read Chapter 10 before working on this exercise.

CHAPTER 8

Reflection

The Reflection API allows a Java program to inspect and manipulate itself; it comprises the java.lang.Class class and the java.lang.reflect package, which represents the members of a class with Method, Constructor, and Field objects.

Reflection can obtain information about a class and its members. This is the technique that the JavaBeans (see Chapter 14, *JavaBeans*) introspection mechanism uses to determine the properties, events, and methods that are supported by a bean, for example. Reflection can also manipulate objects in Java. You can use the Field class to query and set the values of fields, the Method class to invoke methods, and the Constructor class to create new objects. The examples in this chapter demonstrate both object inspection and manipulation using the Reflection API.

In addition to the examples in this chapter, the Java Reflection API is also used by an example in Chapter 17, *Database Access with SQL.*

Obtaining Class and Member Information

Example 8-1 shows a program that uses the Class, Constructor, Field, and Method classes to display information about a specified class. The program's output is similar to the class synopses that appear in *Java in a Nutshell.* (You might notice that the names of method arguments are not shown; argument names are not stored in class files, so they are not available through the Reflection API.)

Here is the output from using ShowClass on itself:

```
public class ShowClass extends Object {
    // Constructors
    public ShowClass();
    // Fields
    // Methods
    public static void main(String[]) throws ClassNotFoundException;
    public static String modifiers(int);
    public static void print_class(Class);
    public static String typename(Class);
    public static void print_field(Field);
```

```
        public static void print_method_or_constructor(Member);
    }
```

The code for this example is quite straightforward. It uses the Class.forName() method to dynamically load the named class, and then calls various methods of Class object to look up the superclass, interfaces, and members of the class. The example uses Constructor, Field, and Method objects to obtain information about each member of the class.

Example 8-1: ShowClass.java

```
package com.davidflanagan.examples.reflect;
import java.lang.reflect.*;

/** A program that displays a class synopsis for the named class */
public class ShowClass {
    /** The main method.  Print info about the named class */
    public static void main(String[] args) throws ClassNotFoundException {
        Class c = Class.forName(args[0]);
        print_class(c);
    }

    /**
     * Display the modifiers, name, superclass and interfaces of a class
     * or interface. Then go and list all constructors, fields, and methods.
     **/
    public static void print_class(Class c)
    {
        // Print modifiers, type (class or interface), name and superclass.
        if (c.isInterface()) {
            // The modifiers will include the "interface" keyword here...
            System.out.print(Modifier.toString(c.getModifiers()) + " " +
                                typename(c));
        }
        else if (c.getSuperclass() != null) {
            System.out.print(Modifier.toString(c.getModifiers()) + " class " +
                                typename(c) +
                                " extends " + typename(c.getSuperclass()));
        }
        else {
            System.out.print(Modifier.toString(c.getModifiers()) + " class " +
                                typename(c));
        }

        // Print interfaces or super-interfaces of the class or interface.
        Class[] interfaces = c.getInterfaces();
        if ((interfaces != null) && (interfaces.length > 0)) {
            if (c.isInterface()) System.out.print(" extends ");
            else System.out.print(" implements ");
            for(int i = 0; i < interfaces.length; i++) {
                if (i > 0) System.out.print(", ");
                System.out.print(typename(interfaces[i]));
            }
        }

        System.out.println(" {");              // Begin class member listing.

        // Now look up and display the members of the class.
        System.out.println("  // Constructors");
        Constructor[] constructors = c.getDeclaredConstructors();
```

Example 8-1: ShowClass.java (continued)

```
        for(int i = 0; i < constructors.length; i++)   // Display constructors.
            print_method_or_constructor(constructors[i]);

        System.out.println("  // Fields");
        Field[] fields = c.getDeclaredFields();         // Look up fields.
        for(int i = 0; i < fields.length; i++)          // Display them.
            print_field(fields[i]);

        System.out.println("  // Methods");
        Method[] methods = c.getDeclaredMethods();      // Look up methods.
        for(int i = 0; i < methods.length; i++)         // Display them.
            print_method_or_constructor(methods[i]);

        System.out.println("}");                        // End class member listing.
    }

    /** Return the name of an interface or primitive type, handling arrays. */
    public static String typename(Class t) {
        String brackets = "";
        while(t.isArray()) {
            brackets += "[]";
            t = t.getComponentType();
        }
        String name = t.getName();
        int pos = name.lastIndexOf('.');
        if (pos != -1) name = name.substring(pos+1);
        return name + brackets;
    }

    /** Return a string version of modifiers, handling spaces nicely. */
    public static String modifiers(int m) {
        if (m == 0) return "";
        else return Modifier.toString(m) + " ";
    }

    /** Print the modifiers, type, and name of a field */
    public static void print_field(Field f) {
        System.out.println("  " + modifiers(f.getModifiers()) +
                          typename(f.getType()) + " " + f.getName() + ";");
    }

    /**
     * Print the modifiers, return type, name, parameter types and exception
     * type of a method or constructor.  Note the use of the Member interface
     * to allow this method to work with both Method and Constructor objects.
     **/
    public static void print_method_or_constructor(Member member) {
        Class returntype=null, parameters[], exceptions[];
        if (member instanceof Method) {
            Method m = (Method) member;
            returntype = m.getReturnType();
            parameters = m.getParameterTypes();
            exceptions = m.getExceptionTypes();
            System.out.print("  " + modifiers(member.getModifiers()) +
                            typename(returntype) + " " + member.getName() +
                            "(");
        } else {
            Constructor c = (Constructor) member;
```

Example 8-1: ShowClass.java (continued)

```
                    parameters = c.getParameterTypes();
                    exceptions = c.getExceptionTypes();
                    System.out.print("   " + modifiers(member.getModifiers()) +
                                  typename(c.getDeclaringClass()) + "(");
            }

        for(int i = 0; i < parameters.length; i++) {
            if (i > 0) System.out.print(", ");
            System.out.print(typename(parameters[i]));
        }
        System.out.print(")");
        if (exceptions.length > 0) System.out.print(" throws ");
        for(int 1 = 0; 1 < exceptions.length; i++) {
            if (i > 0) System.out.print(", ");
            System.out.print(typename(exceptions[i]));
        }
        System.out.println(";");
    }
}
```

Invoking a Named Method

Example 8-2 defines the Command class, which demonstrates another use of the Reflection API. A Command object encapsulates a Method object, an object on which the method is to be invoked, and an array of arguments to pass to the method. The invoke() method invokes the method on the specified object using the specified arguments. The actionPerformed() method does the same thing. If you've read Chapter 10, *Graphical User Interfaces*, you know that this method implements the java.awt.event.ActionListener interface, which means that Command objects can be used as action listeners to respond to button presses, menu selections, and other events within a graphical user interface. GUI programs typically create a slew of ActionListener implementations to handle events. With the Command class, simple action listeners can be defined without creating lots of new classes.

The most useful feature (and the most complicated code) in the Command class is the parse() method, which parses a string that contains a method name and list of arguments to create a Command object. This is useful because it allows Command objects to be read from configuration files, for example. We'll use this feature of the Command class in Chapter 10.

Java does not allow methods to be passed directly as data values, but the Reflection API makes it possible for methods passed by name to be invoked indirectly. Note that this technique is not particularly efficient. For asynchronous event handling in a GUI, though, it is certainly efficient enough: indirect method invocation through the Reflection API is much faster than the response time required by the limits of human perception. Invoking a method by name is not an appropriate technique, however, when repetitive calls are required or when the computer is not waiting for human input. Thus, you should not use this technique for passing a comparison method to a sorting routine or passing a filename filter to a directory listing method, for example. In cases like these, you should use the standard technique of implementing a class that contains the desired method and passing an instance of the class to the appropriate routine.

Example 8-2: Command.java

```
package com.davidflanagan.examples.reflect;
import java.awt.event.*;
import java.beans.*;
import java.lang.reflect.*;
import java.io.*;
import java.util.*;

/**
 * This class represents a Method, the list of arguments to be passed
 * to that method, and the object on which the method is to be invoked.
 * The invoke() method invokes the method.  The actionPerformed() method
 * does the same thing, allowing this class to implement ActionListener
 * and be used to respond to ActionEvents generated in a GUI or elsewhere.
 * The static parse() method parses a string representation of a method
 * and its arguments.
 **/
public class Command implements ActionListener {
    Method m;        // The method to be invoked
    Object target;   // The object to invoke it on
    Object[] args;   // The arguments to pass to the method

    // An empty array; used for methods with no arguments at all.
    static final Object[] nullargs = new Object[] {};

    /** This constructor creates a Command object for a no-arg method */
    public Command(Object target, Method m) { this(target, m, nullargs); }

    /**
     * This constructor creates a Command object for a method that takes the
     * specified array of arguments.  Note that the parse() method provides
     * another way to create a Command object
     **/
    public Command(Object target, Method m, Object[] args) {
        this.target = target;
        this.m = m;
        this.args = args;
    }

    /**
     * Invoke the Command by calling the method on its target, and passing
     * the arguments.  See also actionPerformed() which does not throw the
     * checked exceptions that this method does.
     **/
    public void invoke()
        throws IllegalAccessException, InvocationTargetException
    {
        m.invoke(target, args);  // Use reflection to invoke the method
    }

    /**
     * This method implements the ActionListener interface.  It is like
     * invoke() except that it catches the exceptions thrown by that method
     * and rethrows them as an unchecked RuntimeException
     **/
    public void actionPerformed(ActionEvent e) {
        try {
            invoke();                             // Call the invoke method
        }
```

Example 8-2: Command.java (continued)

```java
        catch (InvocationTargetException ex) {  // but handle the exceptions
            throw new RuntimeException("Command: " +
                                      ex.getTargetException().toString());
        }
        catch (IllegalAccessException ex) {
            throw new RuntimeException("Command: " + ex.toString());
        }
    }

    /**
     * This static method creates a Command using the specified target object,
     * and the specified string.  The string should contain method name
     * followed by an optional parenthesized comma-separated argument list and
     * a semicolon.  The arguments may be boolean, integer or double literals,
     * or double-quoted strings.  The parser is lenient about missing commas,
     * semicolons and quotes, but throws an IOException if it cannot parse the
     * string.
     **/
    public static Command parse(Object target, String text) throws IOException
    {
        String methodname;                     // The name of the method
        ArrayList args = new ArrayList();  // Hold arguments as we parse them.
        ArrayList types = new ArrayList(); // Hold argument types.

        // Convert the string into a character stream, and use the
        // StreamTokenizer class to convert it into a stream of tokens
        StreamTokenizer t = new StreamTokenizer(new StringReader(text));

        // The first token must be the method name
        int c = t.nextToken();  // read a token
        if (c != t.TT_WORD)     // check the token type
            throw new IOException("Missing method name for command");
        methodname = t.sval;    // Remember the method name

        // Now we either need a semicolon or a open paren
        c = t.nextToken();
        if (c == '(') { // If we see an open paren, then parse an arg list
            for(;;) {                         // Loop 'till end of arglist
                c = t.nextToken();            // Read next token

                if (c == ')') {               // See if we're done parsing arguments.
                    c = t.nextToken();  // If so, parse an optional semicolon
                    if (c != ';') t.pushBack();
                    break;                    // Now stop the loop.
                }

                // Otherwise, the token is an argument; figure out its type
                if (c == t.TT_WORD) {
                    // If the token is an identifier, parse boolean literals,
                    // and treat any other tokens as unquoted string literals.
                    if (t.sval.equals("true")) {       // Boolean literal
                        args.add(Boolean.TRUE);
                        types.add(boolean.class);
                    }
                    else if (t.sval.equals("false")) { // Boolean literal
                        args.add(Boolean.FALSE);
                        types.add(boolean.class);
                    }
```

Example 8-2: Command.java (continued)

```
                    else {                          // Assume its a string
                        args.add(t.sval);
                        types.add(String.class);
                    }
                }
                else if (c == '"') {        // If the token is a quoted string
                    args.add(t.sval);
                    types.add(String.class);
                }
                else if (c == t.TT_NUMBER) { // If the token is a number
                    int i = (int) t.nval;
                    if (i == t.nval) {          // Check if its an integer
                        // Note: this code treats a token like "2.0" as an int!
                        args.add(new Integer(i));
                        types.add(int.class);
                    }
                    else {                          // Otherwise, its a double
                        args.add(new Double(t.nval));
                        types.add(double.class);
                    }
                }
                else {                          // Any other token is an error
                    throw new IOException("Unexpected token " + t.sval +
                                    " in argument list of " +
                                    methodname + "().");
                }

                // Next should be a comma, but we don't complain if its not
                c = t.nextToken();
                if (c != ',') t.pushBack();
            }
        }
        else if (c != ';') { // if a method name is not followed by a paren
            t.pushBack();    // then allow a semi-colon but don't require it.
        }

        // We've parsed the argument list.
        // Next, convert the lists of argument values and types to arrays
        Object[] argValues = args.toArray();
        Class[] argtypes = (Class[])types.toArray(new Class[argValues.length]);

        // At this point, we've got a method name, and arrays of argument
        // values and types.  Use reflection on the class of the target object
        // to find a method with the given name and argument types.  Throw
        // an exception if we can't find the named method.
        Method method;
        try { method = target.getClass().getMethod(methodname, argtypes); }
        catch (Exception e) {
            throw new IOException("No such method found, or wrong argument " +
                            "types: " + methodname);
        }

        // Finally, create and return a Command object, using the target object
        // passed to this method, the Method object we obtained above, and
        // the array of argument values we parsed from the string.
        return new Command(target, method, argValues);
    }
```

Reflection

Example 8-2: Command.java (continued)

```
/**
 * This simple program demonstrates how a Command object can be parsed from
 * a string and used as an ActionListener object in a Swing application.
 **/
static class Test {
    public static void main(String[] args) throws IOException {
        javax.swing.JFrame f = new javax.swing.JFrame("Command Test");
        javax.swing.JButton b1 = new javax.swing.JButton("Tick");
        javax.swing.JButton b2 = new javax.swing.JButton("Tock");
        javax.swing.JLabel label = new javax.swing.JLabel("Hello world");
        java.awt.Container pane = f.getContentPane();

        pane.add(b1, java.awt.BorderLayout.WEST);
        pane.add(b2, java.awt.BorderLayout.EAST);
        pane.add(label, java.awt.BorderLayout.NORTH);

        b1.addActionListener(Command.parse(label, "setText(\"tick\");"));
        b2.addActionListener(Command.parse(label, "setText(\"tock\");"));

        f.pack();
        f.show();
    }
}
}
```

Exercises

8-1. Write a program that takes the name of a Java class as a command-line argument and uses the `Class` class to print out all the superclasses of that class. For example, if invoked with the argument "java.awt.Applet", the program prints the following: `java.lang.Object java.awt.Component java.awt.Container java.awt.Panel`.

8-2. Modify the program you wrote in Exercise 8-1 so that it prints out all interfaces implemented by a specified class or by any of its superclasses. Check for the case of classes that implement interfaces that extend other interfaces. For example, if a class implements `java.awt.LayoutManager2`, the `LayoutManager2` interface and `LayoutManager`, its superinterface, should be listed.

8-3. Define a class named `Assignment` that is modeled on the `Command` class shown in Example 8-2. Instead of invoking a named method, as `Command` does, `Assignment` should assign a value to a named field of an object. Give your class a constructor with the following signature:

```
public Assignment(Object target, Field field, Object value)
```

Also give it an `assign()` method that, when invoked, assigns the specified value to the specified field of the specified object. `Assignment` should implement `ActionListener` and define an `actionPerformed()` method that also performs the assignment. Write a static `parse()` method for `Assignment` that is similar to the `parse()` method of `Command`. It should parse strings of the form *fieldname=value* and be able to parse boolean, numeric, and string values.

CHAPTER 9

Object Serialization

Object serialization is the ability of a Serializable class to output the state of an object instance to a byte stream and, at some later time, read that state back in, creating a copy of the original object. When an object is serialized, the entire object graph of all the objects it refers to are serialized along with it. This means it's possible to serialize complex data structures such as binary trees. It's also possible to serialize applets and complete GUI component hierarchies.

Simple Serialization

Despite the power and importance of serialization, it is performed using a simple API that forms part of the java.io package: an object is serialized by the write-Object() method of the ObjectOutputStream class and deserialized by the read-Object() method of the ObjectInputStream class. These classes are byte streams like the various other streams we saw in Chapter 3, *Input/Output*. They implement the ObjectOutput and ObjectInput interfaces, respectively, and these interfaces extend the DataOutput and DataInput interfaces. This means that ObjectOutput-Stream defines the same methods as DataOutputStream for writing primitive values, while ObjectInputStream defines the same methods as DataInputStream for reading primitive values. The methods we're interested in here, however, are writeObject() and readObject(), which write and read objects.

Only objects that implement the java.io.Serializable interface may be serialized. Serializable is a marker interface; it doesn't define any methods that need to be implemented. Nevertheless, for security reasons, some classes don't want their private state to be exposed by the serialization mechanism. Therefore, a class must explicitly declare itself to be serializable by implementing this interface.

An object is serialized by passing it to the writeObject() method of an ObjectOutputStream. This writes out the values of all of its fields, including private fields and fields inherited from superclasses. The values of primitive fields are simply written to the stream as they would be with a DataOutputStream. When a field in an object refers to another object, an array, or a string, however, the write-Object() method is invoked recursively to serialize that object as well. If that object (or an array element) refers to another object, writeObject() is again invoked recursively. Thus, a single call to writeObject() may result in an entire object graph being serialized. When two or more objects each refer to the other, the serialization algorithm is careful to only output each object once; write-Object() can't enter infinite recursion.

Deserializing an object simply follows the reverse of this process. An object is read from a stream of data by calling the readObject() method of an ObjectInput-Stream. This recreates the object in the state it was in when serialized. If the object refers to other objects, they are recursively deserialized as well.

Example 9-1 demonstrates the basics of serialization. The example defines generic methods that can store and retrieve any serializable object's state to and from a file. It also includes an interesting deepclone() method that uses serialization to copy an object graph. The example includes a Serializable inner class and a test class that demonstrates the methods at work.

Example 9–1: Serializer.java

```java
package com.davidflanagan.examples.serialization;
import java.io.*;

/**
 * This class defines utility routines that use Java serialization.
 **/
public class Serializer {
    /**
     * Serialize the object o (and any Serializable objects it refers to) and
     * store its serialized state in File f.
     **/
    static void store(Serializable o, File f) throws IOException {
        ObjectOutputStream out =    // The class for serialization
            new ObjectOutputStream(new FileOutputStream(f));
        out.writeObject(o);         // This method serializes an object graph
        out.close();
    }

    /**
     * Deserialize the contents of File f and return the resulting object
     **/
    static Object load(File f) throws IOException, ClassNotFoundException {
        ObjectInputStream in =      // The class for de-serialization
            new ObjectInputStream(new FileInputStream(f));
        return in.readObject();     // This method deserializes an object graph
    }

    /**
     * Use object serialization to make a "deep clone" of the object o.
     * This method serializes o and all objects it refers to, and then
     * deserializes that graph of objects, which means that everything is
     * copied.  This differs from the clone() method of an object which is
     * usually implemented to produce a "shallow" clone that copies references
     * to other objects, instead of copying all referenced objects.
     **/
    static Object deepclone(final Serializable o)
        throws IOException, ClassNotFoundException
    {
        // Create a connected pair of "piped" streams.
```

Example 9–1: Serializer.java (continued)

```java
        // We'll write bytes to one, and read them from the other one.
        final PipedOutputStream pipeout = new PipedOutputStream();
        PipedInputStream pipein = new PipedInputStream(pipeout);

        // Now define an independent thread to serialize the object and write
        // its bytes to the PipedOutputStream
        Thread writer = new Thread() {
                public void run() {
                    ObjectOutputStream out = null;
                    try {
                        out = new ObjectOutputStream(pipeout);
                        out.writeObject(o);
                    }
                    catch(IOException e) {}
                    finally {
                        try { out.close(); } catch (Exception e) {}
                    }
                }
            };
        writer.start();  // Make the thread start serializing and writing

        // Meanwhile, in this thread, read and deserialize from the piped
        // input stream.  The resulting object is a deep clone of the original.
        ObjectInputStream in = new ObjectInputStream(pipein);
        return in.readObject();
    }

    /**
     * This is a simple serializable data structure that we use below for
     * testing the methods above
     **/
    public static class DataStructure implements Serializable {
        String message;
        int[] data;
        DataStructure other;
        public String toString() {
            String s = message;
            for(int i = 0; i < data.length; i++)
                s += " " + data[i];
            if (other != null) s += "\n\t" + other.toString();
            return s;
        }
    }

    /** This class defines a main() method for testing */
    public static class Test {
        public static void main(String[] args)
            throws IOException, ClassNotFoundException
        {
            // Create a simple object graph
            DataStructure ds = new DataStructure();
            ds.message = "hello world";
            ds.data = new int[] { 1, 2, 3, 4 };
            ds.other = new DataStructure();
            ds.other.message = "nested structure";
            ds.other.data = new int[] { 9, 8, 7 };

            // Display the original object graph
```

Example 9-1: Serializer.java (continued)

```
            System.out.println("Original data structure: " + ds);

            // Output it to a file
            File f = new File("datastructure.ser");
            System.out.println("Storing to a file...");
            Serializer.store(ds, f);

            // Read it back from the file, and display it again
            ds = (DataStructure) Serializer.load(f);
            System.out.println("Read from the file: " + ds);

            // Create a deep clone and display that.  After making the copy
            // modify the original to prove that the clone is "deep".
            DataStructure ds2 = (DataStructure) Serializer.deepclone(ds);
            ds.other.message = null; ds.other.data = null; // Change original
            System.out.println("Deep clone: " + ds2);
        }
    }
}
```

Custom Serialization

Not every piece of program state can, or should be, serialized. Such things as `FileDescriptor` objects are inherently platform-specific or virtual machine-dependent. If a `FileDescriptor` were serialized, for example, it would have no meaning when deserialized in a different virtual machine. For this reason, and also for important the security reasons described earlier, not all objects can be serialized.

Even when an object is serializable, it may not make sense for it to serialize all its state. Some fields may be "scratch" fields that can hold temporary or precomputed values but don't actually hold state needed to restore a serialized object. Consider a GUI component. It may define fields that store the coordinates of the last mouse click it received. This information is never of interest when the component is deserialized, so there's no need to bother saving the values of these fields as part of the component's state. To tell the serialization mechanism that a field shouldn't be saved, simply declare it `transient`:

```
    protected transient short last_x, last_y; // Temporary fields for mouse pos
```

There are also situations where a field is not transient (i.e., it does contain an important part of an object's state), but for some reason it can't be successfully serialized. Consider another GUI component that computes its preferred size based on the size of the text it displays. Because fonts have slight size variations from platform to platform, this precomputed preferred size isn't valid if the component is serialized on one type of platform and deserialized on another. Since the preferred size fields will not be reliable when deserialized, they should be declared `transient`, so that they don't take up space in the serialized object. But in this case, their values must be recomputed when the object is deserialized.

A class can define custom serialization and deserialization behavior (such as recomputing a preferred size) for its objects by implementing `writeObject()` and `readObject()` methods. Surprisingly, these methods are not defined by any interface, and they must be declared `private`. If a class defines these methods, the appropriate one is invoked by the `ObjectOutputStream` or `ObjectInputStream` when an object is serialized or deserialized.

For example, a GUI component might define a `readObject()` method to give it an opportunity to recompute its preferred size upon deserialization. The method might look like this:

```
private void readObject(ObjectInputStream in)
            throws IOException, ClassNotFoundException
{
    in.defaultReadObject();     // Deserialize the component in the usual way.
    this.computePreferredSize(); // But then go recompute its size.
}
```

This method calls the `defaultReadObject()` method of the `ObjectInputStream` to deserialize the object as normal and then takes care of the postprocessing it needs to perform.

Example 9-2 is a more complete example of custom serialization. It shows a class that implements a growable array of integers. This class defines a `writeObject()` method to do some preprocessing before being serialized and a `readObject()` method to do postprocessing after deserialization.

Example 9–2: IntList.java

```
package com.davidflanagan.examples.serialization;
import java.io.*;

/**
 * A simple class that implements a growable array of ints, and knows
 * how to serialize itself as efficiently as a non-growable array.
 **/
public class IntList implements Serializable {
    protected int[] data = new int[8]; // An array to store the numbers.
    protected transient int size = 0;  // Index of next unused element of array

    /** Return an element of the array */
    public int get(int index) throws ArrayIndexOutOfBoundsException {
        if (index >= size) throw new ArrayIndexOutOfBoundsException(index);
        else return data[index];
    }

    /** Add an int to the array, growing the array if necessary */
    public void add(int x) {
        if (data.length==size) resize(data.length*2);  // Grow array if needed.
        data[size++] = x;                               // Store the int in it.
    }

    /** An internal method to change the allocated size of the array */
    protected void resize(int newsize) {
        int[] newdata = new int[newsize];            // Create a new array
        System.arraycopy(data, 0, newdata, 0, size); // Copy array elements.
        data = newdata;                              // Replace old array
    }

    /** Get rid of unused array elements before serializing the array */
    private void writeObject(ObjectOutputStream out) throws IOException {
        if (data.length > size) resize(size);  // Compact the array.
```

Example 9–2: IntList.java (continued)

```
            out.defaultWriteObject();              // Then write it out normally.
    }

    /** Compute the transient size field after deserializing the array */
    private void readObject(ObjectInputStream in)
        throws IOException, ClassNotFoundException
    {
        in.defaultReadObject();                    // Read the array normally.
        size = data.length;                        // Restore the transient field.
    }

    /**
     * Does this object contain the same values as the object o?
     * We override this Object method so we can test the class.
     **/
    public boolean equals(Object o) {
        if (!(o instanceof IntList)) return false;
        IntList that = (IntList) o;
        if (this.size != that.size) return false;
        for(int i = 0; i < this.size; i++)
            if (this.data[i] != that.data[i]) return false;
        return true;
    }

    /** A main() method to prove that it works */
    public static void main(String[] args) throws Exception {
        IntList list = new IntList();
        for(int i = 0; i < 100; i++) list.add((int)(Math.random()*40000));
        IntList copy = (IntList)Serializer.deepclone(list);
        if (list.equals(copy)) System.out.println("equal copies");
        Serializer.store(list, new File("intlist.ser"));
    }
}
```

Externalizable Classes

The Externalizable interface extends Serializable and defines the write-
External() and readExternal() methods. An Externalizable object may be serialized as other Serializable objects are, but the serialization mechanism calls
writeExternal() and readExternal() to perform the serialization and deserialization. Unlike the readObject() and writeObject() methods in Example 9-2, the
readExternal() and writeExternal() methods can't call the defaultReadOb-
ject() and defaultWriteObject() methods: they must read and write the complete state of the object by themselves.

It is useful to declare an object Externalizable when the object already has an
existing file format or when you want to accomplish something that is simply not
possible with the standard serialization methods. Example 9-3 defines the CompactIntList class, an Externalizable subclass of the IntList class from the previous example. CompactIntList makes the assumption that it is typically used to
store many small numbers; it implements Externalizable so it can define a serialized form that is more compact than the format used by ObjectOutputStream and
ObjectInputStream.

Example 9-3: CompactIntList.java

```
package com.davidflanagan.examples.serialization;
import java.io.*;

/**
 * This subclass of IntList assumes that most of the integers it contains are
 * less than 32,000.  It implements Externalizable so that it can define a
 * compact serialization format that takes advantage of this fact.
 **/
public class CompactIntList extends IntList implements Externalizable {
    /**
     * This version number is here in case a later revision of this class wants
     * to modify the externalization format, but still retain compatibility
     * with externalized objects written by this version
     **/
    static final byte version = 1;

    /**
     * This method from the Externalizable interface is responsible for saving
     * the complete state of the object to the specified stream.  It can write
     * anything it wants as long as readExternal() can read it.
     **/
    public void writeExternal(ObjectOutput out) throws IOException {
        if (data.length > size) resize(size);  // Compact the array.

        out.writeByte(version);  // Start with our version number.
        out.writeInt(size);      // Output the number of array elements
        for(int i = 0; i < size; i++) {  // Now loop through the array
            int n = data[i];             // The array element to write
            if ((n < Short.MAX_VALUE) && (n > Short.MIN_VALUE+1)) {
                // If n fits in a short and is not Short.MIN_VALUE, then write
                // it out as a short, saving ourselves two bytes
                out.writeShort(n);
            }
            else {
                // Otherwise write out the special value Short.MIN_VALUE to
                // signal that the number does not fit in a short, and then
                // output the number using a full 4 bytes, for 6 bytes total
                out.writeShort(Short.MIN_VALUE);
                out.writeInt(n);
            }
        }
    }

    /**
     * This Externalizable method is responsible for completely restoring the
     * state of the object.  A no-arg constructor will be called to re-create
     * the object, and this method must read the state written by
     * writeExternal() to restore the object's state.
     **/
    public void readExternal(ObjectInput in)
        throws IOException, ClassNotFoundException
    {
        // Start by reading and verifying the version number.
        byte v = in.readByte();
        if (v != version)
            throw new IOException("CompactIntList: unknown version number");

        // Read the number of array elements, and make array that big
```

Example 9-3: CompactIntList.java (continued)

```
        int newsize = in.readInt();
        resize(newsize);
        this.size = newsize;

        // Now read that many values from the stream
        for(int i = 0; i < newsize; i++) {
            short n = in.readShort();
            if (n != Short.MIN_VALUE) data[i] = n;
            else data[i] = in.readInt();
        }
    }

    /** A main() method to prove that it works */
    public static void main(String[] args) throws Exception {
        CompactIntList list = new CompactIntList();
        for(int i = 0; i < 100; i++) list.add((int)(Math.random()*40000));
        CompactIntList copy = (CompactIntList)Serializer.deepclone(list);
        if (list.equals(copy)) System.out.println("equal copies");
        Serializer.store(list, new File("compactintlist.ser"));
    }
}
```

Serialization and Class Versioning

One of the features of Example 9-3 is that it includes a version number in the serialization stream it writes. This is useful if the class evolves in the future and needs to use a new serialization format. The version number allows future versions of the class to recognize serialized objects written by this version of the class.

For Serializable objects that are not Externalizable, the Serialization API handles versioning itself. When an object is serialized, some information about the object's class must obviously be serialized with it, so that the correct class file can be loaded when the object is deserialized. This information about the class is represented by the java.io.ObjectStreamClass class. It contains the fully qualified name of the class and a version number for the class. The version number is very important because an early version of a class may not be able to deserialize a serialized instance created by a later version of the same class. The version number for a class is a long value. By default, the serialization mechanism creates a unique version number by computing a hash of the name of the class, the name of its superclass and any interfaces it implements, the name and type of its fields, and the name and type of its nonprivate methods. Thus, whenever you add a new method, change the name of a field, or make even minor modifications to the API or implementation of a class, its computed version number changes. When an object is serialized by one version of a class, it can't be deserialized by a version that has a different version number.

Thus, when you make changes to a serializable class, even minor changes that don't affect the serialization format, you break serialization compatibility between versions. For example, our IntList class really ought to have a set() method that sets the value of a specified element of the list. But if you add this method, the new version of the class can't deserialize objects serialized by the old version. The way to prevent this problem is to explicitly declare a version number for your class. You do this by giving the class a constant field named serialVersionUID.

The value of this field doesn't matter; it must simply be the same for all versions of the class that have a compatible serialization format. Since the original IntList class shown in Example 9-2 doesn't have a serialVersionUID field, its version number was implicitly computed based on the API of the class. In order to give the new version of IntList a version number that matches the original version, use the *serialver* command that comes with the Java SDK:

```
% serialver com.davidflanagan.examples.serialization.IntList
IntList:    static final long serialVersionUID = 4538804519406678841L;
```

Now run *serialver* and specify the name of the original version of the class. *serialver* prints a field definition suitable for inclusion in the modified version of the class. By including this constant field in the modified class, you retain serialization compatibility between it and the original version.

Advanced Versioning

Sometimes you make changes to a class that alters the way the class stores its state. Imagine a Rectangle class that represents the rectangle as the coordinate of the upper-left corner, plus a width and a height. Now suppose that the class is reimplemented so that it maintains exactly the same public API, but the rectangle is now represented by two points: the coordinates of the upper-left corner and the lower-right corner. The internal private fields of the class have changed, so it would appear that serialization compatibility between the two implementations of the class is simply not possible.

In Java 1.2 and later, however, the serialization mechanism has been updated to allow the serialization format to be totally decoupled from the fields used by a particular implementation or version of the class. A class can now declare a private field named serialPersistentFields that refers to an array of java.io.Object-StreamField objects. Each of these objects defines a field name and a field type. These fields need not have any relationship to the fields implemented by the class; they are the fields of the serialized form of the class. By defining this array of ObjectStreamField objects, the class is specifying its serialization format. When a new version of the class is defined, that new version must be able to save and restore its state in the format defined by the serialPersistentFields array.

The techniques for reading and writing the serialization fields declared by the serialPersistentFields array are beyond the scope of this chapter. For more information, check the putFields() and writeFields() methods of ObjectOutputStream and the readFields() method of ObjectInputStream. See also the advanced serialization examples supplied as part of the Java SDK documentation.

Serialized Applets

One particularly interesting application of object serialization is serialized applets (see Chapter 15, *Applets*). As of Java 1.1, the HTML <APPLET> tag has a new attribute, OBJECT, that can be used in place of the CODE attribute to specify a serialized object file instead of a class file. When such an <APPLET> tag is encountered, the applet viewer or web browser creates the applet by deserializing it.

The reason that this is interesting is that it allows an applet to be shipped in a preinitialized state. The code for the applet need not even include the code that performed the initialization. For example, imagine a GUI builder tool that allows a programmer to build a GUI using a point-and-click interface. Such a tool could create a tree of AWT components within an Applet panel and then serialize the applet, including all the GUI components it contains. When deserialized, the applet would have a complete GUI, despite the fact that the applet's class file doesn't contain any code to create the GUI.

You can experiment with applet serialization with the *appletviewer* program. Start an applet running in *appletviewer* in the usual way. This loads the applet and runs its init() and start() methods. Next, select the **Stop** item from the menu to stop the applet. Now use the **Save** menu item to serialize the applet to a file. By convention, your serialized applet file should be given a *.ser* extension. If the applet refers to any nonserializable objects, you may not be able to serialize it. For example, you may encounter problems serializing applets that use threads or images.

Once you serialize an applet, create an HTML file with an <APPLET> tag like this:

```
<APPLET OBJECT="MyApplet.ser" WIDTH=400 HEIGHT=200></APPLET>
```

Finally, you can use *appletviewer* with this new HTML file. It should deserialize and display the applet. When created in this way, the applet's init() method is not called (since it was called before serialization), but its start() method is called (because the applet should have been stopped before serialization).

Exercises

9-1. The java.util.Properties class is essentially a hashtable that maps string keys to string values. It defines store() and load() methods that save and load its contents to and from a byte stream. These methods save the Properties object in a human-readable text format despite the fact that they use byte streams. Properties inherits the Serializable interface from its superclass, java.util.Hashtable. Define a subclass of Properties that implements storeBinary() and loadBinary() methods that use object serialization to save and load the contents of the Properties object in binary form. You may also want to use java.util.zip.GZIPOutputStream and java.util.zip.GZIPInputStream in your methods to make the binary format particularly compact. Use the *serialver* program to obtain a serialVersionUID value for your class.

9-2. As noted in the previous exercise, the Properties object has store() and load() methods that allow it to save and restore its state. Define an Externalizable subclass of Properties that uses these store() and load() methods as the basis for its writeExternal() and readExternal() methods. In order to make this work, the writeExternal() method needs to determine the number of bytes written by the store() method and write this value into the stream before writing the bytes themselves. This allows the readExternal() method to know when to stop reading. Also include a version number in the externalizable data format you use.

PART II

Graphics and GUIs

Part II contains examples that use the graphical user interface and graphics features of Java. These examples correspond to the portion of Java that is covered in *Java Foundation Classes in a Nutshell.*

CHAPTER 10

Graphical User Interfaces

Graphical user interfaces, or GUIs, represent an excellent example of software modularity and reuse. GUIs are almost always assembled from libraries of prede-fined building blocks. To Motif programmers on Unix systems, these GUI building blocks are known as *widgets*. To Windows programmers, they are known as *con-trols*. In Java, they are known as by the generic term *components*, because they are all subclasses of java.awt.Component.*

In Java 1.0 and 1.1, the standard library of GUI components was the Abstract Win-dowing Toolkit (AWT)—the package java.awt and its subpackages. In addition to GUI components, the AWT includes facilities for drawing graphics, performing cut-and-paste-style data transfer, and other related operations. On most platforms, AWT components are implemented using the operating-system native GUI system. That is, AWT components are implemented on top of Windows controls on Win-dows operating systems, on top of Motif widgets on Unix systems, and so on. This implementation style led to a least-common denominator toolkit, and, as a result, the AWT API is not as complete and full featured as it should be.

Java 1.2 introduced a new library of GUI components known as Swing. Swing consists of the javax.swing package and its subpackages. Unlike the AWT, Swing has a platform-independent implementation and a state-of-the-art set of features. Although Swing first became a core part of the Java platform in Java 1.2, a version of Swing is available for use with Java 1.1 platforms. Swing has largely replaced the AWT for the creation of GUIs, so we'll focus on Swing in this chapter.† Note that Swing defines a new, more powerful set of GUI components but retains the same underlying GUI programming model used by the AWT. Thus, if you learn to create GUIs with Swing components, you can do the same with AWT components.

---

* Except for menu-related AWT components, which are all subclasses of java.awt.MenuComponent.

† The exception is with applets, which, for compatibility with the existing installed base of web browsers that do not support Swing, often use AWT components.

There are four basic steps to creating a GUI in Java:

1. *Create and configure the components*

    You create a GUI component just like any other object in Java, by calling the constructor. You'll need to consult the documentation for individual components to determine what arguments a constructor expects. For example, to create a Swing JButton component that displays the label "Quit", simply write:

    ```
    JButton quit = new JButton("Quit");
    ```

    Once you have created a component, you may want to configure it by setting one or more properties. For example, to specify the font a JButton component should use, you can write:

    ```
    quit.setFont(new Font("sansserif", Font.BOLD, 18));
    ```

    Again, consult the documentation for the component you are using to determine what methods you can use to configure the component.

2. *Add the components to a container*

    All components must be placed within a *container*. Containers in Java are all subclasses of java.awt.Container. Commonly used containers include JFrame and JDialog classes, which represent top-level windows and dialog boxes, respectively. The java.applet.Applet class, which is subclassed to create applets, is also a container and can therefore contain and display GUI components. A container is a type of component, so containers can be, and commonly are, nested within other containers. JPanel is a container that is often used in this manner. In developing a GUI, you are really creating a containment hierarchy: the top-level window or applet contains containers that may contain other containers, which in turn contain components. To add a component to a container, you simply pass the component to the add() method of the container. For example, you can add a quit button to a "button box" container with code like the following:

    ```
    buttonbox.add(quit);
    ```

3. *Arrange, or lay out, the components*

    In addition to specifying which components are placed inside of which containers, you must also specify the position and size of each component within its container, so that the GUI has a pleasing appearance. While it is possible to hardcode the position and size of each component, it is more common to use a LayoutManager object to lay out the components of a container automatically according to certain layout rules defined by the particular LayoutManager you have chosen. We'll learn more about layout management later in this chapter.

4. *Handle the events generated by the components*

    The steps described so far are sufficient to create a GUI that looks good on the screen, but our graphical "user interface" is not complete, because it does not yet respond to the user. As the user interacts with the components that make up your GUI using the keyboard and mouse, those components generate, or fire, events. An *event* is simply an object that contains information about a user interaction. The final step in GUI creation is the addition of *event listeners*—objects that are notified when an event is generated and respond to the event in an appropriate way. For example, the **Quit** button needs an event listener that causes the application to exit.

We'll look at each of these topics in more detail in the first few sections of this chapter. Then we'll move on to more advanced GUI examples that highlight particular Swing components or specific GUI programming techniques. As usual, you'll want to have access to AWT and Swing reference material as you study the examples. One such reference is *Java Foundation Classes in a Nutshell*. You may also find it helpful to read this chapter in conjunction with Chapters 2 and 3 of that book.

Components

As we've just discussed, the first step in creating a GUI is to create and configure the components that comprise it. To do this, you need to be familiar with the components that are available to you and their methods. Chapter 2 of *Java Foundation Classes in a Nutshell* contains tables that list the available AWT and Swing components. You can also find this information by looking at a listing of the classes in the java.awt and javax.swing packages; it is particularly easy to identify Swing components, since their names all begin with the letter J.

Every component defines a set of properties you can use to configure it. A *property* is a named attribute of a component whose value you can set. Typical component properties have such names as font, background, and alignment. You set a property value with a *setter* method and query it with a *getter* method. Setter and getter methods are collectively called *property accessor methods*, and their names usually begin with the words "set" and "get". The notion of component properties is formally defined by the JavaBeans specification; we'll see more about them in Chapter 14, *JavaBeans*. For now, however, an informal understanding will suffice: components can be configured by invoking various methods whose names begin with "set". Remember that components inherit many methods from their superclasses, notably java.awt.Component and javax.swing.JComponent, so just because a component class does not define a setter method directly does not mean that the component does not support a particular property.

Example 10-1 is a listing of *ShowComponent.java*. This program provides a simple way to experiment with AWT and Swing components and their properties. You can invoke it with the name of one or more component classes on the command line. Each class name may be followed by zero or more property specifications of the form *name=value*. The program creates an instance of each named class and configures it by setting the specified properties to the given values. The program then displays the components using a Swing JTabbedPane container within a JFrame window. For example, to create the window displayed in Figure 10-1, I invoked `ShowComponent` as follows (this is one long command-line that has been wrapped onto multiple lines:

```
% java com.davidflanagan.examples.gui.ShowComponent javax.swing.JButton
'text=Hello World!' font=helvetica-bold-48 javax.swing.JRadioButton
'text=pick me' java.awt.Button label=Hello javax.swing.JSlider
```

Figure 10–1. Components displayed by ShowComponent

One of the powerful features of the Swing component library is its use of a plug-gable look-and-feel architecture, which enables an entire GUI to change its appearance. The default appearance, known as the "Metal" look-and-feel, is the same across all platforms. However, a program can choose any installed look-and-feel, including ones that simulate the appearance of native OS applications. One of the interesting features of the `ShowComponent` program is its pulldown menu labeled **Look and Feel**. It allows you to choose from any of the installed look-and-feels.*

Many examples in this chapter take the form of component subclasses. In addition to using the `ShowComponent` program as a way to experiment with predefined Swing and AWT components, we'll also use it as a viewer to display other examples. But `ShowComponent` isn't just a utility program; it is an interesting example in its own right. It demonstrates the basic steps of creating a simple Swing GUI complete with `JFrame`, `JMenuBar`, and `JTabbedPane` components. If you study the `main()` method, you'll see how the window is created, configured, and popped up. `createPlafMenu()` demonstrates the creation and configuration of a pulldown menu. The remainder of Example 10-1, the `getComponentsFromArgs()` method, is a sophisticated example of using Java reflection (and also JavaBeans introspection) to work with GUIs. This code is interesting, although it is not directly relevant to this chapter.

Example 10–1: ShowComponent.java

```
package com.davidflanagan.examples.gui;
import java.awt.*;
import java.awt.event.*;
```

---

* Although the Windows look-and-feel comes standard with the Java distribution, legal issues prevent its use on any OS other than Windows. So, although this choice appears in the menu, you can't use it if you are not using a Microsoft operating system. Also, an implementation that emulates the MacOS look-and-feel is available from Apple, and a Java implementation of Apple's new "Aqua" look-and-feel is also expected.

Example 10–1: ShowComponent.java (continued)

```
import javax.swing.*;
import java.beans.*;
import java.lang.reflect.*;
import java.util.Vector;

/**
 * This class is a program that uses reflection and JavaBeans introspection to
 * create a set of named components, set named properties on those components,
 * and display them.  It allows the user to view the components using any
 * installed look-and-feel.  It is intended as a simple way to experiment with
 * AWT and Swing components, and to view a number of the other examples
 * developed in this chapter.  It also demonstrates frames, menus, and the
 * JTabbedPane component.
 **/
public class ShowComponent {
    // The main program
    public static void main(String[] args) {
        // Process the command line to get the components to display
        Vector components = getComponentsFromArgs(args);

        // Create a frame (a window) to display them in
        JFrame frame = new JFrame("ShowComponent");

        // Handle window close requests by exiting the VM
        frame.addWindowListener(new WindowAdapter() { // Anonymous inner class
                public void windowClosing(WindowEvent e) { System.exit(0); }
            });

        // Set up a menu system that allows the user to select the
        // look-and-feel of the component from a list of installed PLAFs
        JMenuBar menubar = new JMenuBar();       // Create a menubar
        frame.setJMenuBar(menubar);              // Tell the frame to display it
        JMenu plafmenu = createPlafMenu(frame);  // Create a menu
        menubar.add(plafmenu);                   // Add the menu to the menubar

        // Create a JTabbedPane to display each of the components
        JTabbedPane pane = new JTabbedPane();

        // Now add each component as a tab of the tabbed pane
        // Use the unqualified component classname as the tab text
        for(int i = 0; i < components.size(); i++) {
            Component c = (Component)components.elementAt(i);
            String classname = c.getClass().getName();
            String tabname = classname.substring(classname.lastIndexOf('.')+1);
            pane.addTab(tabname, c);
        }

        // Add the tabbed pane to the frame.  Note the call to getContentPane()
        // This is required for JFrame, but not for most Swing components
        frame.getContentPane().add(pane);

        // Set the frame size and pop it up
        frame.pack();                 // Make frame as big as its kids need
        frame.setVisible(true);       // Make the frame visible on the screen

        // The main() method exits now but the Java VM keeps running because
        // all AWT programs automatically start an event-handling thread.
    }
```

Example 10-1: ShowComponent.java (continued)

```
/**
 * This static method queries the system to find out what Pluggable
 * Look-and-Feel (PLAF) implementations are available.  Then it creates a
 * JMenu component that lists each of the implementations by name and
 * allows the user to select one of them using JRadioButtonMenuItem
 * components.  When the user selects one, the selected menu item
 * traverses the component hierarchy and tells all components to use the
 * new PLAF.
 **/
public static JMenu createPlafMenu(final JFrame frame) {
    // Create the menu
    JMenu plafmenu = new JMenu("Look and Feel");

    // Create an object used for radio button mutual exclusion
    ButtonGroup radiogroup = new ButtonGroup();

    // Look up the available look and feels
    UIManager.LookAndFeelInfo[] plafs =
        UIManager.getInstalledLookAndFeels();

    // Loop through the plafs, and add a menu item for each one
    for(int i = 0; i < plafs.length; i++) {
        String plafName = plafs[i].getName();
        final String plafClassName = plafs[i].getClassName();

        // Create the menu item
        JMenuItem item = plafmenu.add(new JRadioButtonMenuItem(plafName));

        // Tell the menu item what to do when it is selected
        item.addActionListener(new ActionListener() {
                public void actionPerformed(ActionEvent e) {
                    try {
                        // Set the new look and feel
                        UIManager.setLookAndFeel(plafClassName);
                        // Tell each component to change its look-and-feel
                        SwingUtilities.updateComponentTreeUI(frame);
                        // Tell the frame to resize itself to the its
                        // children's new desired sizes
                        frame.pack();
                    }
                    catch(Exception ex) { System.err.println(ex); }
                }

            });

        // Only allow one menu item to be selected at once
        radiogroup.add(item);
    }
    return plafmenu;
}

/**
 * This method loops through the command line arguments looking for
 * class names of components to create and property settings for those
 * components in the form name=value.  This method demonstrates
 * reflection and JavaBeans introspection as they can be applied to
 * dynamically created GUIs
 **/
```

Example 10-1: ShowComponent.java (continued)

```java
    public static Vector getComponentsFromArgs(String[] args) {
        Vector components = new Vector();          // List of components to return
        Component component = null;                // The current component
        PropertyDescriptor[] properties = null;    // Properties of the component
        Object[] methodArgs = new Object[1];       // We'll use this below

    nextarg:  // This is a labeled loop
        for(int i = 0; i < args.length; i++) {    // Loop through all arguments
            // If the argument does not contain an equal sign, then it is
            // a component class name.  Otherwise it is a property setting
            int equalsPos = args[i].indexOf('=');
            if (equalsPos == -1) {  // Its the name of a component
                try {
                    // Load the named component class
                    Class componentClass = Class.forName(args[i]);
                    // Instantiate it to create the component instance
                    component = (Component)componentClass.newInstance();
                    // Use JavaBeans to introspect the component
                    // And get the list of properties it supports
                    BeanInfo componentBeanInfo =
                        Introspector.getBeanInfo(componentClass);
                    properties = componentBeanInfo.getPropertyDescriptors();
                }
                catch(Exception e) {
                    // If any step failed, print an error and exit
                    System.out.println("Can't load, instantiate, " +
                                        "or introspect: " + args[i]);
                    System.exit(1);
                }

                // If we succeeded, store the component in the vector
                components.addElement(component);
            }
            else { // The arg is a name=value property specification
                String name =args[i].substring(0, equalsPos); // property name
                String value =args[i].substring(equalsPos+1); // property value

                // If we don't have a component to set this property on, skip!
                if (component == null) continue nextarg;

                // Now look through the properties descriptors for this
                // component to find one with the same name.
                for(int p = 0; p < properties.length; p++) {
                    if (properties[p].getName().equals(name)) {
                        // Okay, we found a property of the right name.
                        // Now get its type, and the setter method
                        Class type = properties[p].getPropertyType();
                        Method setter = properties[p].getWriteMethod();

                        // Check if property is read-only!
                        if (setter == null) {
                            System.err.println("Property " + name+
                                                " is read-only");
                            continue nextarg;  // continue with next argument
                        }

                        // Try to convert the property value to the right type
                        // We support a small set of common property types here
```

Example 10–1: ShowComponent.java (continued)

```
                    // Store the converted value in an Object[] so it can
                    // be easily passed when we invoke the property setter
                    try {
                        if (type == String.class) { // no conversion needed
                            methodArgs[0] = value;
                        }
                        else if (type == int.class) {      // String to int
                            methodArgs[0] = Integer.valueOf(value);
                        }
                        else if (type == boolean.class) { // to boolean
                            methodArgs[0] = Boolean.valueOf(value);
                        }
                        else if (type == Color.class) {    // to Color
                            methodArgs[0] = Color.decode(value);
                        }
                        else if (type == Font.class) {    // String to Font
                            methodArgs[0] = Font.decode(value);
                        }
                        else {
                            // If we can't convert, ignore the property
                            System.err.println("Property " + name +
                                               " is of unsupported type " +
                                               type.getName());
                            continue nextarg;
                        }
                    }
                    catch (Exception e) {
                        // If conversion failed, continue with the next arg
                        System.err.println("Can't convert  '" + value +
                                           "' to type " + type.getName() +
                                           " for property " + name);
                        continue nextarg;
                    }

                    // Finally, use reflection to invoke the property
                    // setter method of the component we created, and pass
                    // in the converted property value.
                    try { setter.invoke(component, methodArgs); }
                    catch (Exception e) {
                        System.err.println("Can't set property: " + name);
                    }

                    // Now go on to next command-line arg
                    continue nextarg;
                }
            }

            // If we get here, we didn't find the named property
            System.err.println("Warning: No such property: " + name);
        }
    }

    return components;
    }
}
```

Containers

The second step in creating a GUI is to place the components you have created and configured into appropriate containers. Chapter 2 of *Java Foundation Classes in a Nutshell* contains tables that list the container classes available in the AWT and Swing packages. Many of these container classes have specialized uses. JFrame is a top-level window, for example, and JTabbedPane displays the components it contains in individual tabbed panes. Example 10-1 demonstrated the use of these containers. But Swing and the AWT also define generic container classes, such as JPanel.

Example 10-2 is a listing of *Containers.java*. This class is a subclass of JPanel. Its constructor method creates a number of other nested JPanel instances, as well as a number of JButton objects contained by those JPanel classes. Example 10-2 illustrates the concept of the containment hierarchy of a GUI, using color to represent the nesting depth of the hierarchy. Figure 10-2 shows what the Containers class looks like when displayed with the ShowComponent program as follows (another single long command-line that has been wrapped onto two lines):

```
% java com.davidflanagan.examples.gui.ShowComponent \
com.davidflanagan.examples.gui.Containers
```

For variety, Figure 10-2 uses the Motif look-and-feel and shows the contents of the **Look and Feel** menu.

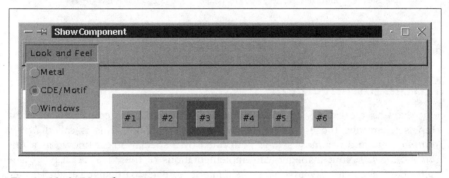

Figure 10-2. Nested containers

Example 10-2: Containers.java

```
package com.davidflanagan.examples.gui;
import javax.swing.*;
import java.awt.*;

/**
 * A component subclass that demonstrates nested containers and components.
 * It creates the hierarchy shown below, and uses different colors to
 * distinguish the different nesting levels of the containers
 *
 *   containers---panel1----button1
 *        |           |---panel2----button2
 *        |           |              |----panel3----button3
 *        |           |---panel4----button4
 *        |                          |----button5
 *        |---button6
 */
```

Example 10-2: Containers.java (continued)

```
*/
public class Containers extends JPanel {
    public Containers() {
        this.setBackground(Color.white);            // This component is white
        this.setFont(new Font("Dialog", Font.BOLD, 24));

        JPanel p1 = new JPanel();
        p1.setBackground(new Color(200, 200, 200)); // Panel1 is darker
        this.add(p1);                   // p1 is contained by this component
        p1.add(new JButton("#1"));      // Button 1 is contained in p1

        JPanel p2 = new JPanel();
        p2.setBackground(new Color(150, 150, 150)); // p2 is darker than p2
        p1.add(p2);                     // p2 is contained in p1
        p2.add(new JButton("#2"));      // Button 2 is contained in p2

        JPanel p3 = new JPanel();
        p3.setBackground(new Color(100, 100, 100)); // p3 is darker than p2
        p2.add(p3);                     // p3 is contained in p2
        p3.add(new JButton("#3"));      // Button 3 is contained in p3

        JPanel p4 = new JPanel();
        p4.setBackground(new Color(150, 150, 150)); // p4 is darker than p1
        p1.add(p4);                     // p4 is contained in p1
        p4.add(new JButton("#4"));      // Button4 is contained in p4
        p4.add(new JButton("#5"));      // Button5 is also contained in p4

        this.add(new JButton("#6")); // Button6 is contained in this component
    }
}
```

Layout Management

Once you have created your components and added them to containers, the next step is to arrange those components within the container. This is called *layout management* and is almost always performed by a special object known as a *layout manager*. Layout managers are implementations of the java.awt.LayoutManager interface or its LayoutManager2 subinterface. Each particular LayoutManager implementation enforces a specific layout policy and automatically arranges the components within a container according to that policy. The sections that follow demonstrate the use of each the AWT and Swing layout managers. Note that BoxLayout is the only layout manager defined by Swing. Although Swing defines many new components, Swing GUIs typically rely on AWT layout managers.

You create a layout manager as you would any other object. Different layout manager classes take different constructor arguments to specify the parameters of their layout policy. Once you create a layout manager, you do not usually invoke its methods. Instead, you pass the layout manager object to the setLayout() method of the container that is to be managed; the container invokes the various Layout-Manager methods when necessary. Once you have set the layout manager, you can usually forget about it.

As you'll see in the following sections, most of the predefined AWT layout managers have fairly simple layout policies that may not seem like much use on their own. Their power becomes apparent when combined, however. For example, you can use a GridLayout to arrange 10 buttons into two columns within a container, and then use a BorderLayout to position those two columns against the left edge of another container.

The following sections demonstrate all the important layout managers, using a short example and a screen shot of the layout produced by the example. The figures are produced using the ShowComponent class from Example 10-1; you can use this program to experiment with the examples yourself. Pay particular attention to the way the layouts change when you resize the window.

FlowLayout

The FlowLayout layout manager arranges its children like words on a page: from left to right in a row and top to bottom. When there is not enough space remaining in the current row for the next component, the FlowLayout "wraps" and places the component in a new row. When you create a FlowLayout, you can specify whether the rows should be left-justified, centered, or right-justified. You can also specify the amount of horizontal and vertical space the layout manager leaves between components. FlowLayout makes no attempt to fit its components into the container; it leaves each component at its preferred size. If there is extra space, FlowLayout leaves it blank. If there is not enough room in the container, some components simply do not appear. Note that FlowLayout is the default layout manager for JPanel containers. If you do not specify a different layout manager, a panel uses a FlowLayout that centers its rows and leaves five pixels between components, both horizontally and vertically.

Example 10-3 is a short program that arranges buttons using a FlowLayout layout manager; Figure 10-3 shows the resulting output.

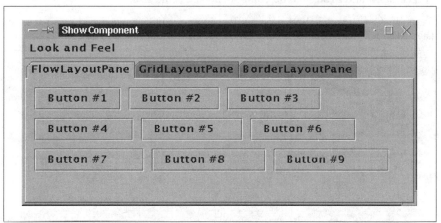

Figure 10–3. Components laid out with a FlowLayout

Example 10-3: FlowLayoutPane.java

```
package com.davidflanagan.examples.gui;
import java.awt.*;
import javax.swing.*;
```

Example 10–3: FlowLayoutPane.java (continued)

```
public class FlowLayoutPane extends JPanel {
    public FlowLayoutPane() {
        // Use a FlowLayout layout manager.  Left justify rows.
        // Leave 10 pixels of horizontal and vertical space between components.
        this.setLayout(new FlowLayout(FlowLayout.LEFT, 10, 10));

        // Add some buttons to demonstrate the layout.
        String spaces = "";  // Used to make the buttons different
        for(int i = 1; i <= 9; i++) {
            this.add(new JButton("Button #" + i + spaces));
            spaces += " ";
        }

        // Give ourselves a default size
        this.setPreferredSize(new Dimension(500, 200));
    }
}
```

GridLayout

GridLayout is a heavy-handed layout manager that arranges components left to right and top to bottom in an evenly spaced grid of specified dimensions. When you create a GridLayout, you can specify the number of rows and columns in the grid, as well as the horizontal and vertical space the GridLayout should leave between the components. Typically, you specify only the desired number of rows or columns, leaving the other dimension set to 0. This allows the GridLayout to pick the appropriate number of rows or columns based on the number of components. GridLayout does not honor the preferred sizes of its components. Instead, it divides the size of the container into the specified number of equally sized rows and columns and makes all the components the same size.

Example 10-4 shows a short program that arranges buttons in a grid using a GridLayout layout manager. Figure 10-4 shows the resulting output.

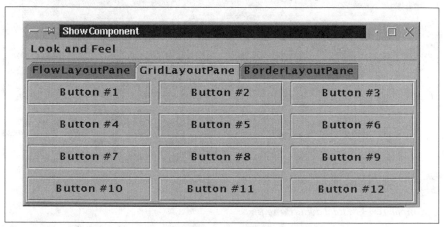

Figure 10–4. Components laid out with a GridLayout

Example 10–4: GridLayoutPane.java

```
package com.davidflanagan.examples.gui;
import java.awt.*;
import javax.swing.*;

public class GridLayoutPane extends JPanel {
  public GridLayoutPane() {
    // Layout components into a grid three columns wide, with the number
    // of rows depending on the number of components.  Leave 10 pixels
    // of horizontal and vertical space between components
    this.setLayout(new GridLayout(0, 3, 10, 10));
    // Add some components
    for(int i = 1; i <= 12; i++) this.add(new JButton("Button #" + i));
  }
}
```

BorderLayout

The BorderLayout layout manager arranges up to five components within a container. Four of the components are laid out against specific edges of the container, and one is placed in the center. When you add a component to a container that is managed by BorderLayout, you must specify where you want the component placed. You do this with the two-argument version of add(), passing one of the constants NORTH, EAST, SOUTH, WEST, or CENTER defined by BorderLayout as the second argument. These constants are called *layout constraints*; you use use them with code like the following:

```
    this.add(b, BorderLayout.SOUTH);
```

Remember that BorderLayout can lay out only one component in each of these positions.

BorderLayout does not honor the preferred sizes of the components it manages. Components specified laid out NORTH or SOUTH are made as wide as the container and retain their preferred height. EAST and WEST components are made as high as the container (minus the heights of the top and bottom components, if any) and retain their preferred width. The CENTER component is made as large as whatever space remains in the center of the container, after the specified number of pixels of horizontal and vertical space are allocated. You do not have to specify the full five children. For example, the BorderLayout class is often used to place a fixed-size child (such as a JToolBar) against one edge of a container, with a variable-sized child (such as a JTextArea) in whatever space remains in the center.

BorderLayout is the default layout manager for the content panes of JFrame and JDialog containers. If you do not explicitly specify a layout manager for these content panes, they use a BorderLayout configured to leave no horizontal or vertical space between components.

Example 10-5 lists a program that arranges five buttons using a BorderLayout layout manager; Figure 10-5 shows the resulting output.

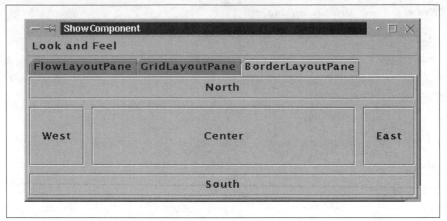

Figure 10–5. Components laid out with a BorderLayout

Example 10–5: BorderLayoutPane.java

```
package com.davidflanagan.examples.gui;
import java.awt.*;
import javax.swing.*;

public class BorderLayoutPane extends JPanel {
    String[] borders = {"North", "East", "South", "West", "Center"};
    public BorderLayoutPane() {
        // Use a BorderLayout with 10-pixel margins between components
        this.setLayout(new BorderLayout(10, 10));
        for(int i = 0; i < 5; i++) {          // Add children to the pane
            this.add(new JButton(borders[i]),   // Add this component
                borders[i]);                    // Using this constraint
        }
    }
}
```

Box and BoxLayout

javax.swing.BoxLayout is a simple but versatile layout manager that arranges its children into a row or a column. The javax.swing.Box container uses BoxLayout; it is much more common to work with the Box class than to use BoxLayout directly. What gives Box containers their versatility is the ability to add stretchy space (*glue*) and rigid space (*struts*) to the layout. The Box class defines static methods that make it particularly easy to create rows, columns, glue, and struts.

Example 10-6 creates several Box containers that demonstrate the capabilities of BoxLayout. The various boxes are themselves laid out using a BorderLayout. The program output is shown in Figure 10-6. To keep you on your toes, Example 10-6 also demonstrates the use of Swing borders to add margins and decorations around the outside of certain containers. Note that these borders can be added around any Swing component or container; they are part of the javax.swing.border package and have nothing to do with the BorderLayout layout manager. See javax.swing.border.Border and the setBorder() method of JComponent.

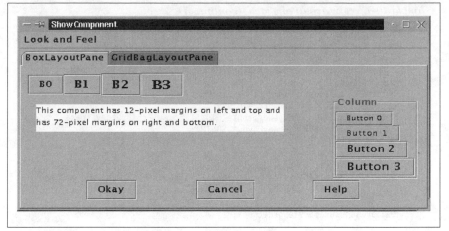

Figure 10-6. Components laid out with a BoxLayout

Example 10-6: BoxLayoutPane.java

```java
package com.davidflanagan.examples.gui;
import java.awt.*;
import javax.swing.*;
import javax.swing.border.*;

public class BoxLayoutPane extends JPanel {
    public BoxLayoutPane() {
        // Use a BorderLayout layout manager to arrange various Box components
        this.setLayout(new BorderLayout());

        // Give the entire panel a margin by adding an empty border
        // We could also do this by overriding getInsets()
        this.setBorder(new EmptyBorder(10,10,10,10));

        // Add a plain row of buttons along the top of the pane
        Box row = Box.createHorizontalBox();
        for(int i = 0; i < 4; i++) {
            JButton b = new JButton("B" + i);
            b.setFont(new Font("serif", Font.BOLD, 12+i*2));
            row.add(b);
        }
        this.add(row, BorderLayout.NORTH);

        // Add a plain column of buttons along the right edge
        // Use BoxLayout with a different kind of Swing container
        // Give the column a border: can't do this with the Box class
        JPanel col = new JPanel();
        col.setLayout(new BoxLayout(col, BoxLayout.Y_AXIS));
        col.setBorder(new TitledBorder(new EtchedBorder(), "Column"));
        for(int i = 0; i < 4; i++) {
            JButton b = new JButton("Button " + i);
            b.setFont(new Font("sansserif", Font.BOLD, 10+i*2));
            col.add(b);
        }
        this.add(col, BorderLayout.EAST); // Add column to right of panel

        // Add a button box along the bottom of the panel.
        // Use "Glue" to space the buttons evenly
```

Example 10–6: BoxLayoutPane.java (continued)

```
        Box buttonbox = Box.createHorizontalBox();
        buttonbox.add(Box.createHorizontalGlue());      // stretchy space
        buttonbox.add(new JButton("Okay"));
        buttonbox.add(Box.createHorizontalGlue());      // stretchy space
        buttonbox.add(new JButton("Cancel"));
        buttonbox.add(Box.createHorizontalGlue());      // stretchy space
        buttonbox.add(new JButton("Help"));
        buttonbox.add(Box.createHorizontalGlue());      // stretchy space
        this.add(buttonbox, BorderLayout.SOUTH);

        // Create a component to display in the center of the panel
        JTextArea textarea = new JTextArea();
        textarea.setText("This component has 12-pixel margins on left and top"+
                        " and has 72-pixel margins on right and bottom.");
        textarea.setLineWrap(true);
        textarea.setWrapStyleWord(true);

        // Use Box objects to give the JTextArea an unusual spacing
        // First, create a column with 3 kids.  The first and last kids
        // are rigid spaces.  The middle kid is the text area
        Box fixedcol = Box.createVerticalBox();
        fixedcol.add(Box.createVerticalStrut(12));  // 12 rigid pixels
        fixedcol.add(textarea);                 // Component fills in the rest
        fixedcol.add(Box.createVerticalStrut(72));  // 72 rigid pixels

        // Now create a row.  Give it rigid spaces on the left and right,
        // and put the column from above in the middle.
        Box fixedrow = Box.createHorizontalBox();
        fixedrow.add(Box.createHorizontalStrut(12));
        fixedrow.add(fixedcol);
        fixedrow.add(Box.createHorizontalStrut(72));

        // Now add the JTextArea in the column in the row to the panel
        this.add(fixedrow, BorderLayout.CENTER);
    }
}
```

GridBagLayout

GridBagLayout is the most flexible and powerful of the AWT layout managers but is also the most complicated, and sometimes the most frustrating. It arranges components according to a number of constraints, which are stored in a GridBagConstraints object. In Java 1.1 and later, you pass a GridBagConstraints object as the second argument to the add() method, along with the component to be added. With Java 1.0, however, you must specify the constraints object for a component by calling the setConstraints() method of the GridBagLayout itself.

The basic GridBagLayout layout policy is to arrange components at specified positions in a grid. The grid may be of arbitrary size, and the rows and columns of the grid may be of arbitrary heights and widths. A component laid out in this grid may occupy more than one row or column. The gridx and gridy fields of GridBagConstraints specify the position of the component in the grid, and the gridwidth and gridheight fields specify the number of columns and rows, respectively, that the component occupies in the grid. The insets field specifies the margins that should be left around each individual component, while fill specifies whether and how a component should grow when there is more space available for it than it needs for its default size. The anchor field specifies how a component should be positioned when there is more space available than it uses. GridBagConstraints defines a number of constants that are legal values for these last two fields. Finally, weightx and weighty specify how extra horizontal and vertical space should be distributed among the components when the container is resized. Consult reference material on GridBagConstraints for more details.

Example 10-7 shows a short program that uses a GridBagLayout layout manager to produce the layout pictured in Figure 10-7. Note that the program reuses a single GridBagConstraints object, which is perfectly legal.

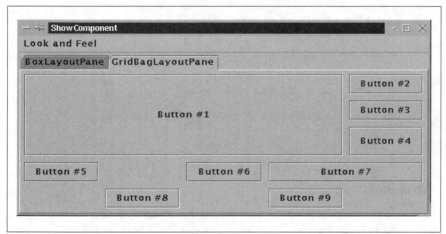

Figure 10–7. Components laid out with a GridBagLayout

Example 10–7: GridBagLayoutPane.java

```
package com.davidflanagan.examples.gui;
import java.awt.*;
import javax.swing.*;

public class GridBagLayoutPane extends JPanel {
    public GridBagLayoutPane() {
        // Create and specify a layout manager
        this.setLayout(new GridBagLayout());

        // Create a constraints object, and specify some default values
        GridBagConstraints c = new GridBagConstraints();
        c.fill = GridBagConstraints.BOTH; // components grow in both dimensions
        c.insets = new Insets(5,5,5,5);   // 5-pixel margins on all sides

        // Create and add a bunch of buttons, specifying different grid
        // position, and size for each.
        // Give the first button a resize weight of 1.0 and all others
        // a weight of 0.0.  The first button will get all extra space.
        c.gridx = 0; c.gridy = 0; c.gridwidth = 4; c.gridheight=4;
        c.weightx = c.weighty = 1.0;
        this.add(new JButton("Button #1"), c);

        c.gridx = 4; c.gridy = 0; c.gridwidth = 1; c.gridheight=1;
        c.weightx = c.weighty = 0.0;
```

Example 10–7: GridBagLayoutPane.java (continued)

```
            this.add(new JButton("Button #2"), c);

            c.gridx = 4; c.gridy = 1; c.gridwidth = 1; c.gridheight=1;
            this.add(new JButton("Button #3"), c);

            c.gridx = 4; c.gridy = 2; c.gridwidth = 1; c.gridheight=2;
            this.add(new JButton("Button #4"), c);

            c.gridx = 0; c.gridy = 4; c.gridwidth = 1; c.gridheight=1;
            this.add(new JButton("Button #5"), c);

            c.gridx = 2; c.gridy = 4; c.gridwidth = 1; c.gridheight=1;
            this.add(new JButton("Button #6"), c);

            c.gridx = 3; c.gridy = 4; c.gridwidth = 2; c.gridheight=1;
            this.add(new JButton("Button #7"), c);

            c.gridx = 1; c.gridy = 5; c.gridwidth = 1; c.gridheight=1;
            this.add(new JButton("Button #8"), c);

            c.gridx = 3; c.gridy = 5; c.gridwidth = 1; c.gridheight=1;
            this.add(new JButton("Button #9"), c);
    }
}
```

Hardcoded Layout

All AWT and Swing containers have a default layout manager. If you set this manager to null, however, you can arrange components within a container however you like. You do this by calling the setBounds() method of each component, or, in Java 1.0, by calling the now deprecated reshape() method. Note that this technique does not work if any layout manager is specified because the layout manager resizes and repositions all the components in a container.

Before using this technique, you should understand that there are a number of good reasons not to hardcode component sizes and positions. First, since components can have a platform-dependent look-and-feel, they may have different sizes on different platforms. Similarly, fonts differ somewhat from platform to platform, and this can affect the sizes of components. And finally, hardcoding component sizes and positions doesn't allow for customization (using the user's preferred font, for example) or internationalization (translating text in your GUI into other languages).

Nevertheless, there may be times when layout management becomes frustrating enough that you resort to hardcoded component sizes and positions. Example 10-8 is a simple program that does this; the layout it produces is shown in Figure 10-8. Note that this example overrides the getPreferredSize() method to report the preferred size of the container. This is functionality usually provided by the layout manager, but in the absence of a manager, you must determine the preferred size of the container yourself. Since a Swing container is being used, overriding getPreferredSize() isn't strictly necessary; try calling setPreferredSize() instead.

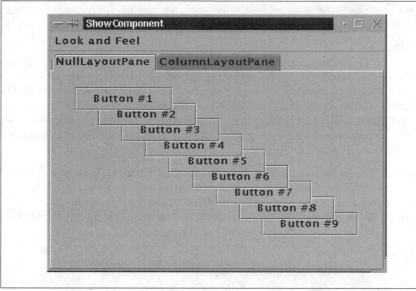

Figure 10–8. Hardcoded component positions

Example 10–8: NullLayoutPane.java

```java
package com.davidflanagan.examples.gui;
import java.awt.*;
import javax.swing.*;

public class NullLayoutPane extends JPanel {
    public NullLayoutPane() {
        // Get rid of the default layout manager.
        // We'll arrange the components ourselves.
        this.setLayout(null);

        // Create some buttons and set their sizes and positions explicitly
        for(int i = 1; i <= 9; i++) {
            JButton b = new JButton("Button #" + i);
            b.setBounds(i*30, i*20, 125, 30); // use reshape() in Java 1.0
            this.add(b);
        }
    }

    // Specify how big the panel should be.
    public Dimension getPreferredSize() { return new Dimension(425, 250); }
}
```

Creating Custom Layout Managers

When none of the predefined AWT layout managers is appropriate for the GUI
you want to implement, you have the option of writing your own custom layout
manager by implementing LayoutManager or LayoutManager2. This is actually easier to do that it might seem. The primary method of interest is layoutContainer(),
which the container calls when it wants the components it contains to be laid out.
This method should loop through the components contained in that container and

set the size and position of each one, using setBounds(). layoutContainer() can call preferredSize() on each component to determine the size it would like to be.

The other important method is preferredLayoutSize(). This method should return the preferred size of the container. Typically this is the size required to arrange all the components at their preferred sizes. The minimumLayoutSize() method is similar, in that it should return the minimum allowable size for the container. Finally, if your layout manager is interested in constraints specified when the add() method is called to add a component to a container, it can define the addLayoutComponent() method.

Example 10-9 shows a listing of *ColumnLayout.java*, an implementation of the LayoutManager2 interface that arranges components in a column. ColumnLayout differs from BoxLayout in that it allows a horizontal alignment to be specified for the components in the column. Example 10-10 is a simple program that uses ColumnLayout to produce the output shown in Figure 10-9.

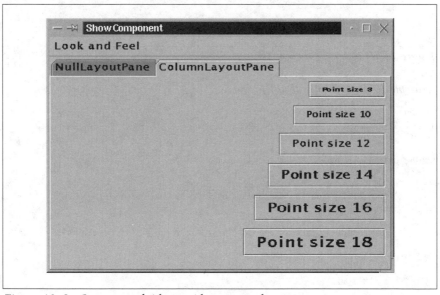

Figure 10–9. Component laid out with a custom layout manager

Example 10–9: ColumnLayout.java

```
package com.davidflanagan.examples.gui;
import java.awt.*;

/**
 * This LayoutManager arranges the components into a column.
 * Components are always given their preferred size.
 *
 * When you create a ColumnLayout, you may specify four values:
 *    margin_height -- how much space to leave on top and bottom
 *    margin_width -- how much space to leave on left and right
 *    spacing -- how much vertical space to leave between items
 *    alignment -- the horizontal position of the components:
```

Example 10-9: ColumnLayout.java (continued)

```
*       ColumnLayout.LEFT -- left-justify the components
*       ColumnLayout.CENTER -- horizontally center the components
*       ColumnLayout.RIGHT -- right-justify the components
*
* You never call the methods of a ColumnLayout object.  Just create one
* and make it the layout manager for your container by passing it to
* the addLayout() method of the Container object.
*/
public class ColumnLayout implements LayoutManager2 {
    protected int margin_height;
    protected int margin_width;
    protected int spacing;
    protected int alignment;

    // Constants for the alignment argument to the constructor.
    public static final int LEFT = 0;
    public static final int CENTER = 1;
    public static final int RIGHT = 2;

    /** The constructor.  See comment above for meanings of these arguments */
    public ColumnLayout(int margin_height, int margin_width,
                        int spacing, int alignment)  {
        this.margin_height = margin_height;
        this.margin_width = margin_width;
        this.spacing = spacing;
        this.alignment = alignment;
    }

    /**
     * A default constructor that creates a ColumnLayout using 5-pixel
     * margin width and height, 5-pixel spacing, and left alignment
     **/
    public ColumnLayout() { this(5, 5, 5, LEFT); }

    /**
     * The method that actually performs the layout.
     * Called by the Container
     **/
    public void layoutContainer(Container parent) {
        Insets insets = parent.getInsets();
        Dimension parent_size = parent.getSize();
        Component kid;
        int nkids = parent.getComponentCount();
        int x0 = insets.left + margin_width;  // The base X position
        int x;
        int y = insets.top + margin_height;   // Start at the top of the column

        for(int i = 0; i < nkids; i++) {      // Loop through the kids
            kid = parent.getComponent(i);     // Get the kid
            if (!kid.isVisible()) continue;   // Skip hidden ones
            Dimension pref = kid.getPreferredSize();  // How big is it?
            switch(alignment) {               // Compute X coordinate
            default:
            case LEFT:   x = x0; break;
            case CENTER: x = (parent_size.width - pref.width)/2; break;
            case RIGHT:
                x = parent_size.width-insets.right-margin_width-pref.width;
                break;
```

Example 10-9: ColumnLayout.java (continued)

```
            }
            // Set the size and position of this kid
            kid.setBounds(x, y, pref.width, pref.height);
            y += pref.height + spacing;        // Get Y position of the next one
        }
    }

    /** The Container calls this to find out how big the layout should to be */
    public Dimension preferredLayoutSize(Container parent) {
        return layoutSize(parent, 1);
    }
    /** The Container calls this to find out how big the layout must be */
    public Dimension minimumLayoutSize(Container parent) {
        return layoutSize(parent, 2);
    }
    /** The Container calls this to find out how big the layout can be */
    public Dimension maximumLayoutSize(Container parent) {
        return layoutSize(parent, 3);
    }

    // Compute min, max, or preferred size of all the visible children
    protected Dimension layoutSize(Container parent, int sizetype) {
        int nkids = parent.getComponentCount();
        Dimension size = new Dimension(0,0);
        Insets insets = parent.getInsets();
        int num_visible_kids = 0;

        // Compute maximum width and total height of all visible kids
        for(int i = 0; i < nkids; i++) {
            Component kid = parent.getComponent(i);
            Dimension d;
            if (!kid.isVisible()) continue;
            num_visible_kids++;
            if (sizetype == 1) d = kid.getPreferredSize();
            else if (sizetype == 2) d = kid.getMinimumSize();
            else d = kid.getMaximumSize();
            if (d.width > size.width) size.width = d.width;
            size.height += d.height;
        }

        // Now add in margins and stuff
        size.width += insets.left + insets.right + 2*margin_width;
        size.height += insets.top + insets.bottom + 2*margin_height;
        if (num_visible_kids > 1)
            size.height += (num_visible_kids - 1) * spacing;
        return size;
    }

    // Other LayoutManager(2) methods that are unused by this class
    public void addLayoutComponent(String constraint, Component comp) {}
    public void addLayoutComponent(Component comp, Object constraint) {}
    public void removeLayoutComponent(Component comp) {}
    public void invalidateLayout(Container parent) {}
    public float getLayoutAlignmentX(Container parent) { return 0.5f; }
    public float getLayoutAlignmentY(Container parent) { return 0.5f; }
}
```

Example 10-10: ColumnLayoutPane.java

```java
package com.davidflanagan.examples.gui;
import java.awt.*;
import javax.swing.*;

public class ColumnLayoutPane extends JPanel {
    public ColumnLayoutPane() {
        // Get rid of the default layout manager.
        // We'll arrange the components ourselves.
        this.setLayout(new ColumnLayout(5, 5, 10, ColumnLayout.RIGHT));

        // Create some buttons and set their sizes and positions explicitly
        for(int i = 0; i < 6; i++) {
            int pointsize = 8 + i*2;
            JButton b = new JButton("Point size " + pointsize);
            b.setFont(new Font("helvetica", Font.BOLD, pointsize));
            this.add(b);
        }
    }
}
```

Event Handling

In the previous section on layout management, there were a number of examples that arranged JButton components in interesting ways. If you ran the examples, however, you probably noticed that nothing interesting happened when you clicked on the buttons. The fourth step in creating a GUI is hooking up the event handling that makes components respond to user input. As of Java 1.1 and later, AWT and Swing components use the event-handling API defined by the JavaBeans component model. Prior to Java 1.1, the AWT used a different API that is not covered in this chapter. We'll see some examples of event handling using the old model when we study applets (see Chapter 15, *Applets*), where this model is still sometimes used for backwards compatibility with old web browsers.

In Java 1.1 and later, the event-handling API is based on events and event listeners. Like everything else in Java, events are objects. An event object is an instance of a class that extends java.util.EventObject. The java.awt.event package defines a number event classes commonly used by AWT and Swing components. The javax.swing.event package defines additional events used by Swing components, but not by AWT components. And the java.beans package defines a couple of JavaBeans event classes also used by Swing components. Event classes usually define methods (or fields) that provide details about the event that occurred. For example, the java.awt.event.MouseEvent class defines a getX() method that returns the X coordinate of the location of the mouse when the event occurred.

An EventListener is an object that is interested in being notified when an event of a particular type occurs. An object that generates events (an *event source*, such as a JButton component) maintains a list of listeners and provides methods that allow listeners to be added to or removed from this list. When an event of the appropriate type occurs, the event source notifies all registered event listeners. To notify the listeners, it first creates an event object that describes the event and then passes that event object to a method defined by the event listeners. The particular method that is invoked depends on the type of event; different event listener types define different methods.

All event listener types are interfaces that extend the `java.util.EventListener` interface. This is a marker interface; it does not define any methods of its own, but exists so that you can use the `instanceof` operator to distinguish event listeners from other object types. The `java.awt.event`, `javax.swing.event`, and `java.beans` packages define a number of event-listener interfaces that extend the generic `EventListener` interface. Each listener is specific to a particular type of event and defines one or more methods that are invoked in particular circumstances (e.g., `java.awt.MouseListener`). The only special feature of an event-listener method is that it always takes an event object as its single argument.

Note that the `java.awt.event` and `javax.swing.event` packages define only event listener *interfaces*, not event listener *classes*. A GUI must define its own custom implementation of an event listener, as it is this implementation that provides the actual Java code executed in response to an event. These packages do define some Java classes however: event adapter classes. An *event adapter* is an implementation of an event listener interface that consists entirely of empty methods. Many listener interfaces define multiple methods, but often you are interested in using only one of these methods at a time. In this case, it is easier to subclass an adapter, overriding only the method you are interested in, instead of implementing the interface directly and having to define all its methods.

Every AWT and Swing application has an automatically created thread, called the *event dispatch thread*, that invokes the methods of event listeners. When an application starts, the main thread builds the GUI, and then it often exits. From then on, everything that happens takes place in the event dispatch thread, in response to the invocation of event listener methods. One important side-effect of this implementation is that AWT and Swing components are not thread-safe, for performance reasons. Thus, if you are writing a multithreaded program, you must be careful to call component methods only from the event dispatch thread. Calling component methods from other threads may cause intermittent and difficult-to-diagnose bugs. If you need to perform some kind of animation or repetitive task with Swing, use a `javax.swing.Timer` instead of using a separate thread. If another thread really needs to interact with a Swing component, use the `java.awt.EventQueue` invoke-Later() and invokeAndWait() methods.

Chapter 2 of *Java Foundation Classes in a Nutshell* describes the event-handling API in more detail and also contains tables that list the various types of AWT and Swing event listeners, their methods, and the components that use those listener interfaces. The following sections contain some examples that illustrate different ways of using the Java event-handling API, as well as an example that demonstrate an API for handling certain types of input events using a lower-level API.

Handling Mouse Events

Example 10-11 is a listing of *ScribblePanel1.java*, a simple `JPanel` subclass that implements the `MouseListener` and a `MouseMotionListener` interfaces in order to receive mouse-click and mouse-drag events. It responds to these events by drawing lines, allowing the user to "scribble" in the pane. Figure 10-10 shows the

ScribblePanel example (and a sample scribble) running within the ShowComponent program developed at the start of this chapter.

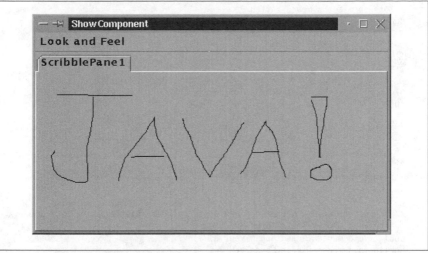

Figure 10–10. A scribble in ScribblePanel

Note that the ScribblePanel class is both the source of mouse events (they are generated by the java.awt.Component superclass) and the event listener. This can be seen most clearly in the constructor method where the component passes itself to its own addMouseListener() and addMouseMotionListener() methods. The mouseDragged() method is the key to scribbling: it uses the drawLine() method of the Graphics object to draw a line from the previous mouse position to the current mouse position.

Example 10–11: ScribblePanel.java

```
package com.davidflanagan.examples.gui;
import javax.swing.*;        // For JPanel component
import java.awt.*;           // For Graphics object
import java.awt.event.*;     // For Event and Listener objects

/**
 * A simple JPanel subclass that uses event listeners to allow the user
 * to scribble with the mouse.  Note that scribbles are not saved or redrawn.
 **/
public class ScribblePanel extends JPanel
    implements MouseListener, MouseMotionListener {
    protected int last_x, last_y;  // Previous mouse coordinates

    public ScribblePanel() {
        // This component registers itself as an event listener for
        // mouse events and mouse motion events.
        this.addMouseListener(this);
        this.addMouseMotionListener(this);

        // Give the component a preferred size
        setPreferredSize(new Dimension(450,200));
    }
```

Example 10-11: ScribblePane1.java (continued)

```java
    // A method from the MouseListener interface.  Invoked when the
    // user presses a mouse button.
    public void mousePressed(MouseEvent e) {
        last_x = e.getX();  // remember the coordinates of the click
        last_y = e.getY();
    }

    // A method from the MouseMotionListener interface.  Invoked when the
    // user drags the mouse with a button pressed.
    public void mouseDragged(MouseEvent e) {
        int x = e.getX();    // Get the current mouse position
        int y = e.getY();
        // Draw a line from the saved coordinates to the current position
        this.getGraphics().drawLine(last_x, last_y, x, y);
        last_x = x;          // Remember the current position
        last_y = y;
    }

    // The other, unused methods of the MouseListener interface.
    public void mouseReleased(MouseEvent e) {}
    public void mouseClicked(MouseEvent e) {}
    public void mouseEntered(MouseEvent e) {}
    public void mouseExited(MouseEvent e) {}

    // The other, unused, method of the MouseMotionListener interface.
    public void mouseMoved(MouseEvent e) {}
}
```

More Mouse Events

Example 10-12 shows a listing of *ScribblePane2.java.* which is much like Scrib-blePane1 except that it uses anonymous inner classes to define its event listeners. This is a common GUI programming idiom in Java, and, in fact, it was one of the primary reasons that anonymous inner classes were added to the language. Note that the inner classes subclass event adapter classes, rather than implement the event listeners directly; this means that unused methods don't have to be implemented.

ScribblePane2 also includes a KeyListener that clears the scribble when the user types the C key and defines a color property (with setColor() and getColor() as its property accessor methods) that specifies the color in which to scribble. Recall that the ShowComponent program allows you to specify property values. It understands colors specified using hexadecimal RGB notation, so to use this example to scribble with blue lines, you can use a command like this:

```
% java com.davidflanagan.examples.gui.ShowComponent \
    com.davidflanagan.examples.gui.ScribblePane2 color=#0000ff
```

A final point to note about this example is that the scribbling functionality has been cleaned up and placed into moveto(), lineto(), and clear() methods. This allows the methods to be invoked by other components and allows the component to be subclassed more cleanly.

Example 10–12: ScribblePane2.java

```java
package com.davidflanagan.examples.gui;
import javax.swing.*;        // For JPanel component
import java.awt.*;           // For Graphics object
import java.awt.event.*;     // For Event and Listener objects

/**
 * A simple JPanel subclass that uses event listeners to allow the user
 * to scribble with the mouse.  Note that scribbles are not saved or redrawn.
 **/
public class ScribblePane2 extends JPanel {
    public ScribblePane2() {
        // Give the component a preferred size
        setPreferredSize(new Dimension(450,200));

        // Register a mouse event handler defined as an inner class
        // Note the call to requestFocus().  This is required in order for
        // the component to receive key events.
        addMouseListener(new MouseAdapter() {
                public void mousePressed(MouseEvent e) {
                    moveto(e.getX(), e.getY());  // Move to click position
                    requestFocus();              // Take keyboard focus
                }
            });

        // Register a mouse motion event handler defined as an inner class
        // By subclassing MouseMotionAdapter rather than implementing
        // MouseMotionListener, we only override the method we're interested
        // in and inherit default (empty) implementations of the other methods.
        addMouseMotionListener(new MouseMotionAdapter() {
                public void mouseDragged(MouseEvent e) {
                    lineto(e.getX(), e.getY());  // Draw to mouse position
                }
            });

        // Add a keyboard event handler to clear the screen on key 'C'
        addKeyListener(new KeyAdapter() {
                public void keyPressed(KeyEvent e) {
                    if (e.getKeyCode() == KeyEvent.VK_C) clear();
                }
            });
    }

    /** These are the coordinates of the the previous mouse position */
    protected int last_x, last_y;

    /** Remember the specified point */
    public void moveto(int x, int y) {
        last_x = x;
        last_y = y;
    }

    /** Draw from the last point to this point, then remember new point */
    public void lineto(int x, int y) {
        Graphics g = getGraphics();          // Get the object to draw with
        g.setColor(color);                   // Tell it what color to use
        g.drawLine(last_x, last_y, x, y);    // Tell it what to draw
        moveto(x, y);                        // Save the current point
    }
```

Example 10–12: ScribblePane2.java (continued)

```
/**
 * Clear the drawing area, using the component background color.  This
 * method works by requesting that the component be redrawn.  Since this
 * component does not have a paintComponent() method, nothing will be
 * drawn.  However, other parts of the component, such as borders or
 * sub-components will be drawn correctly.
 **/
public void clear() { repaint(); }

/** This field holds the current drawing color property */
Color color = Color.black;
/** This is the property "setter" method for the color property */
public void setColor(Color color) { this.color = color; }
/** This is the property "getter" method for the color property */
public Color getColor() { return color; }
```

```
}
```

Handling Component Events

The two previous examples have shown how to handle mouse and keyboard events. These are low-level input events generated by the system and reported to event listeners by code in the java.awt.Component class. Usually, when you are building a GUI, you do not handle these low-level events yourself; instead, you use predefined components to interpret the raw input events and generate higher-level semantic events. For example, when the JButton component detects a low-level mouse click and mouse release, it generates a higher-level java.awt.event.ActionEvent to notify any interested listeners that the user clicked on the button to activate it. Similarly, the JList component generates a javax.swing.event.ListSelectionEvent when the user makes a selection from the list.

Example 10-13 is a listing of *ScribblePane3.java*. This example extends ScribblePane2 and adds a JButton and a JList to its user interface. The user can clear the screen by clicking on the button and change the drawing color by selecting from the list. You can see these new components in Figure 10-11. The example demonstrates implementing the ActionListener and ListSelection Listener interfaces to respond to the events generated by these Swing components.

When you run Example 10-13, notice it allows you to scribble on top of the JButton and JList components. Swing components are "lightweight" components, which means that they are drawn directly within the window of the component that contains them. This is quite different from the "heavyweight" AWT components that use nested, but independent, windows.

Example 10–13: ScribblePane3.java

```
package com.davidflanagan.examples.gui;
import java.awt.*;          // For Graphics object and colors
import javax.swing.*;       // For JPanel component
import java.awt.event.*;    // For ActionListener interface
import javax.swing.event.*; // For ListSelectionListener interface
```

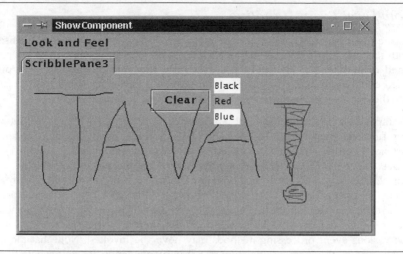

Figure 10–11. Swing components in ScribblePane3

Example 10–13: ScribblePane3.java (continued)

```java
/**
 * This scribble component includes a JButton to clear the screen, and
 * a JList that lets the user select a drawing color.  It uses
 * event listener objects to handle events from those sub-components.
 **/
public class ScribblePane3 extends ScribblePane2 {
    // These are colors the user can choose from
    Color[] colors = new Color[] { Color.black, Color.red, Color.blue };
    // These are names for those colors
    String[] colorNames = new String[] { "Black", "Red", "Blue" };

    // Add JButton and JList components to the panel.
    public ScribblePane3() {
        // Implicit super() call here invokes the superclass constructor

        // Add a "Clear" button to the panel.
        // Handle button events with an action listener
        JButton clear = new JButton("Clear");
        clear.addActionListener(new ActionListener() {
                public void actionPerformed(ActionEvent e) { clear(); }
            });
        this.add(clear);

        // Add a JList to allow color choices.
        // Handle list selection events with a ListSelectionListener.
        final JList colorList = new JList(colorNames);
        colorList.addListSelectionListener(new ListSelectionListener() {
                public void valueChanged(ListSelectionEvent e) {
                    setColor(colors[colorList.getSelectedIndex()]);
                }
            });
        this.add(colorList);
    }
}
```

Low-Level Event Handling

As we just discussed, graphical user interfaces do not usually concern themselves with the details of low-level mouse and keyboard events. Instead, they use predefined components to interpret these events for them. By the same token, predefined components that handle frequent mouse and keyboard events do not usually use the high-level event listener API to handle these low-level events.

Example 10-14 shows a listing of *ScribblePane4.java*, a final reimplementation of our scribble component. This version does not use event listeners at all, but instead overrides the processMouseEvent(), processMouseMotionEvent(), and processKeyEvent() methods defined by its java.awt.Component superclass.* Event objects are passed to these methods directly, without any requirement to register event listeners. What is required, however, is that the constructor call enableEvents() to specify the kinds of events in which it is interested. If the constructor does not do this, the system may not deliver events of those types, and the various event processing methods may never be invoked. Note that the event processing methods invoke the superclass' implementation for any events they do not handle themselves. This allows the superclass to dispatch these events to any listener objects that may have been registered.

Example 10–14: ScribblePane4.java

```
package com.davidflanagan.examples.gui;
import javax.swing.*;        // For JPanel component
import java.awt.*;           // For Graphics object
import java.awt.event.*;     // For Event and Listener objects

/**
 * Another scribble class.  This one overrides the low-level event processing
 * methods of the component instead of registering event listeners.
 **/
public class ScribblePane4 extends JPanel {
    public ScribblePane4() {
        // Give the component a preferred size
        setPreferredSize(new Dimension(450,200));

        // Tell the system what kind of events the component is interested in
        enableEvents(AWTEvent.MOUSE_EVENT_MASK |
                     AWTEvent.MOUSE_MOTION_EVENT_MASK |
                     AWTEvent.KEY_EVENT_MASK);
    }

    public void processMouseEvent(MouseEvent e) {
        if (e.getID() == MouseEvent.MOUSE_PRESSED) {
            moveto(e.getX(), e.getY());
            requestFocus();
        }
        else super.processMouseEvent(e); // pass unhandled events to superclass
    }

    public void processMouseMotionEvent(MouseEvent e) {
        if (e.getID() == MouseEvent.MOUSE_DRAGGED) lineto(e.getX(), e.getY());
```

---

* This same technique can be used with the processFocusEvent(), processComponentEvent(), and processWindowEvent methods of Component.

Example 10–14: ScribblePane4.java (continued)

```
        else super.processMouseMotionEvent(e);
    }

    public void processKeyEvent(KeyEvent e) {
        if ((e.getID() == KeyEvent.KEY_PRESSED) &&
            (e.getKeyCode() == KeyEvent.VK_C)) clear();
        else super.processKeyEvent(e);    // Give superclass a chance to handle
    }

    /** These are the coordinates of the the previous mouse position */
    protected int last_x, last_y;

    /** Remember the specified point */
    public void moveto(int x, int y) {
        last_x = x;
        last_y = y;
    }

    /** Draw from the last point to this point, then remember new point */
    public void lineto(int x, int y) {
        getGraphics().drawLine(last_x, last_y, x, y);
        moveto(x, y);
    }

    /** Clear the drawing area, using the component background color */
    public void clear() { repaint(); }
}
```

Custom Events and Event Listeners

Although Swing and the AWT define quite a few event classes and event listener interfaces, there is no reason you cannot define custom event and listener types of your own. The class shown in Example 10-15 does exactly that: it defines its own custom event and listener types using inner classes.

The Swing component set provides a number of ways to allow the user to select an item from a list of items. You can present such a choice with a JList component, a JComboBox component, or a group of cooperating JRadioButton components. The APIs for creating, manipulating, and responding to events with these components differ substantially. Example 10-15 is a listing of an ItemChooser class that abstracts away the differences between these three presentation types. When you create an ItemChooser component, you specify the name of the choice being presented, a list of items to be chosen among, the currently chosen item, and a presentation type. The presentation type determines how the choice is presented to the user, but the API you use to work with the ItemChooser component is independent of the presentation.

The ItemChooser class includes an inner class named Demo. ItemChooser.Demo has a main() method that demonstrates the ItemChooser component, as shown in Figure 10-12. The demo program gets the choice labels from command-line arguments, so you can run it with a command like the following:

```
% java com.davidflanagan.examples.gui.ItemChooser\$Demo Fourscore and twenty \
  years ago
```

Note that on Unix systems, you have to escape the $ in the inner class name with a backslash. On Windows systems, the backslash is not necessary. We'll see another use of ItemChooser in Example 10-18.

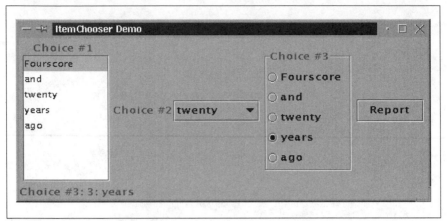

Figure 10–12. A demonstration of the ItemChooser component

The interesting thing about ItemChooser is that it defines its own event and event listener types as inner classes. You should pay attention to the definitions of these types and study how they are used within the ItemChooser Demo classes, as this example demonstrates both sides of the event architecture: event generation and event handling. This example shows you how to work with JList, JComboBox, and JRadioButton components; it is particularly interesting because it listens for and responds to the events generated by those internal components and translates those internal events into its own event type. Once you understand how Item-Chooser works, you'll have a thorough understanding of the AWT and Swing event architecture.

Example 10–15: ItemChooser.java

```
package com.davidflanagan.examples.gui;
import java.awt.*;
import java.awt.event.*;
import javax.swing.*;
import javax.swing.event.*;
import javax.swing.border.*;
import java.util.*;

/**
 * This class is a Swing component that presents a choice to the user.  It
 * allows the choice to be presented in a JList, in a JComboBox, or with a
 * bordered group of JRadioButton components.  Additionally, it displays the
 * name of the choice with a JLabel.  It allows an arbitrary value to be
 * associated with each possible choice.  Note that this component only allows
 * one item to be selected at a time.  Multiple selections are not supported.
 **/
public class ItemChooser extends JPanel {
    // These fields hold property values for this component
    String name;           // The overall name of the choice
    String[] labels;       // The text for each choice option
```

Example 10-15: ItemChooser.java (continued)

```
Object[] values;        // Arbitrary values associated with each option
int selection;          // The selected choice
int presentation;       // How the choice is presented

// These are the legal values for the presentation field
public static final int LIST = 1;
public static final int COMBOBOX = 2;
public static final int RADIOBUTTONS = 3;

// These components are used for each of the 3 possible presentations
JList list;                    // One type of presentation
JComboBox combobox;            // Another type of presentation
JRadioButton[] radiobuttons;   // Yet another type

// The list of objects that are interested in our state
ArrayList listeners = new ArrayList();

// The constructor method sets everything up
public ItemChooser(String name, String[] labels, Object[] values,
                   int defaultSelection, int presentation)
{
    // Copy the constructor arguments to instance fields
    this.name = name;
    this.labels = labels;
    this.values = values;
    this.selection = defaultSelection;
    this.presentation = presentation;

    // If no values were supplied, use the labels
    if (values == null) this.values = labels;

    // Now create content and event handlers based on presentation type
    switch(presentation) {
    case LIST: initList(); break;
    case COMBOBOX: initComboBox(); break;
    case RADIOBUTTONS: initRadioButtons(); break;
    }
}

// Initialization for JList presentation
void initList() {
    list = new JList(labels);           // Create the list
    list.setSelectedIndex(selection);   // Set initial state

    // Handle state changes
    list.addListSelectionListener(new ListSelectionListener() {
            public void valueChanged(ListSelectionEvent e) {
                ItemChooser.this.select(list.getSelectedIndex());
            }
        });

    // Lay out list and name label vertically
    this.setLayout(new BoxLayout(this, BoxLayout.Y_AXIS)); // vertical
    this.add(new JLabel(name));         // Display choice name
    this.add(new JScrollPane(list));    // Add the JList
}

// Initialization for JComboBox presentation
```

Example 10–15: ItemChooser.java (continued)

```
    void initComboBox() {
        combobox = new JComboBox(labels);          // Create the combo box
        combobox.setSelectedIndex(selection);      // Set initial state

        // Handle changes to the state
        combobox.addItemListener(new ItemListener() {
                public void itemStateChanged(ItemEvent e) {
                    ItemChooser.this.select(combobox.getSelectedIndex());
                }
            });

        // Lay out combo box and name label horizontally
        this.setLayout(new BoxLayout(this, BoxLayout.X_AXIS));
        this.add(new JLabel(name));
        this.add(combobox);
    }

    // Initialization for JRadioButton presentation
    void initRadioButtons() {
        // Create an array of mutually exclusive radio buttons
        radiobuttons = new JRadioButton[labels.length];    // the array
        ButtonGroup radioButtonGroup = new ButtonGroup(); // used for exclusion
        ChangeListener listener = new ChangeListener() {  // A shared listener
                public void stateChanged(ChangeEvent e) {
                    JRadioButton b = (JRadioButton)e.getSource();
                    if (b.isSelected()) {
                        // If we received this event because a button was
                        // selected, then loop through the list of buttons to
                        // figure out the index of the selected one.
                        for(int i = 0; i < radiobuttons.length; i++) {
                            if (radiobuttons[i] == b) {
                                ItemChooser.this.select(i);
                                return;
                            }
                        }
                    }
                }
            };

        // Display the choice name in a border around the buttons
        this.setBorder(new TitledBorder(new EtchedBorder(), name));
        this.setLayout(new BoxLayout(this, BoxLayout.Y_AXIS));

        // Create the buttons, add them to the button group, and specify
        // the event listener for each one.
        for(int i = 0; i < labels.length; i++) {
            radiobuttons[i] = new JRadioButton(labels[i]);
            if (i == selection) radiobuttons[i].setSelected(true);
            radiobuttons[i].addChangeListener(listener);
            radioButtonGroup.add(radiobuttons[i]);
            this.add(radiobuttons[i]);
        }
    }

    // These simple property accessor methods just return field values
    // These are read-only properties.  The values are set by the constructor
    // and may not be changed.
    public String getName() { return name; }
```

Example 10–15: ItemChooser.java (continued)

```java
public int getPresentation() { return presentation; }
public String[] getLabels() { return labels; }
public Object[] getValues() { return values; }

/** Return the index of the selected item */
public int getSelectedIndex() { return selection; }

/** Return the object associated with the selected item */
public Object getSelectedValue() { return values[selection]; }

/**
 * Set the selected item by specifying its index.  Calling this
 * method changes the on-screen display but does not generate events.
 **/
public void setSelectedIndex(int selection) {
    switch(presentation) {
    case LIST: list.setSelectedIndex(selection); break;
    case COMBOBOX: combobox.setSelectedIndex(selection); break;
    case RADIOBUTTONS: radiobuttons[selection].setSelected(true); break;
    }
    this.selection = selection;
}

/**
 * This internal method is called when the selection changes.  It stores
 * the new selected index, and fires events to any registered listeners.
 * The event listeners registered on the JList, JComboBox, or JRadioButtons
 * all call this method.
 **/
protected void select(int selection) {
    this.selection = selection;  // Store the new selected index
    if (!listeners.isEmpty()) {  // If there are any listeners registered
        // Create an event object to describe the selection
        ItemChooser.Event e =
            new ItemChooser.Event(this, selection, values[selection]);
        // Loop through the listeners using an Iterator
        for(Iterator i = listeners.iterator(); i.hasNext();) {
            ItemChooser.Listener l = (ItemChooser.Listener)i.next();
            l.itemChosen(e);  // Notify each listener of the selection
        }
    }
}

// These methods are for event listener registration and deregistration
public void addItemChooserListener(ItemChooser.Listener l) {
    listeners.add(l);
}
public void removeItemChooserListener(ItemChooser.Listener l) {
    listeners.remove(l);
}

/**
 * This inner class defines the event type generated by ItemChooser objects
 * The inner class name is Event, so the full name is ItemChooser.Event
 **/
public static class Event extends java.util.EventObject {
    int selectedIndex;      // index of the selected item
    Object selectedValue;   // the value associated with it
```

Example 10–15: ItemChooser.java (continued)

```
        public Event(ItemChooser source,
                     int selectedIndex, Object selectedValue) {
            super(source);
            this.selectedIndex = selectedIndex;
            this.selectedValue = selectedValue;
        }

        public ItemChooser getItemChooser() { return (ItemChooser)getSource();}
        public int getSelectedIndex() { return selectedIndex; }
        public Object getSelectedValue() { return selectedValue; }
    }

    /**
     * This inner interface must be implemented by any object that wants to be
     * notified when the current selection in a ItemChooser component changes.
     **/
    public interface Listener extends java.util.EventListener {
        public void itemChosen(ItemChooser.Event e);
    }

    /**
     * This inner class is a simple demonstration of the ItemChooser component
     * It uses command-line arguments as ItemChooser labels and values.
     **/
    public static class Demo {
        public static void main(String[] args) {
            // Create a window, arrange to handle close requests
            final JFrame frame = new JFrame("ItemChooser Demo");
            frame.addWindowListener(new WindowAdapter() {
                    public void windowClosing(WindowEvent e) {System.exit(0);}
                });

            // A "message line" to display results in
            final JLabel msgline = new JLabel(" ");

            // Create a panel holding three ItemChooser components
            JPanel chooserPanel = new JPanel();
            final ItemChooser c1 = new ItemChooser("Choice #1", args, null, 0,
                                                   ItemChooser.LIST);
            final ItemChooser c2 = new ItemChooser("Choice #2", args, null, 0,
                                                   ItemChooser.COMBOBOX);
            final ItemChooser c3 = new ItemChooser("Choice #3", args, null, 0,
                                                   ItemChooser.RADIOBUTTONS);

            // An event listener that displays changes on the message line
            ItemChooser.Listener l = new ItemChooser.Listener() {
                    public void itemChosen(ItemChooser.Event e) {
                        msgline.setText(e.getItemChooser().getName() + ": " +
                                        e.getSelectedIndex() + ": " +
                                        e.getSelectedValue());
                    }
                };
            c1.addItemChooserListener(l);
            c2.addItemChooserListener(l);
            c3.addItemChooserListener(l);

            // Instead of tracking every change with a ItemChooser.Listener,
            // applications can also just query the current state when
```

Example 10–15: ItemChooser.java (continued)

```
            // they need it.  Here's a button that does that.
            JButton report = new JButton("Report");
            report.addActionListener(new ActionListener() {
                public void actionPerformed(ActionEvent e) {
                    // Note the use of multi-line italic HTML text
                    // with the JOptionPane message dialog box.
                    String msg = "<html><i>" +
                        c1.getName() + ": " + c1.getSelectedValue() + "<br>"+
                        c2.getName() + ": " + c2.getSelectedValue() + "<br>"+
                        c3.getName() + ": " + c3.getSelectedValue() + "</i>";
                    JOptionPane.showMessageDialog(frame, msg);
                }
            });

        // Add the 3 ItemChooser objects, and the Button to the panel
        chooserPanel.add(c1);
        chooserPanel.add(c2);
        chooserPanel.add(c3);
        chooserPanel.add(report);

        // Add the panel and the message line to the window
        Container contentPane = frame.getContentPane();
        contentPane.add(chooserPanel, BorderLayout.CENTER);
        contentPane.add(msgline, BorderLayout.SOUTH);

        // Set the window size and pop it up.
        frame.pack();
        frame.show();
    }
  }
}
```

A Complete GUI

We've looked separately at components, containers, layout management, and event handling, so now it is time to tie these pieces together and add the additional details required to create a complete graphical user interface. Example 10-16 lists *Scribble.java*, a simple paint-style application, pictured in Figure 10-13.

This application relies on the scribbling capabilities of the ScribblePane2 class of Example 10-12. It places a ScribblePane2 instance within a JFrame container to create the main application window and then adds a JMenuBar and two JToolBar components to allow the user to control the application. Scribble uses a JColor-Chooser to let the user select a drawing color and a JOptionPane to display a confirmation dialog when the user asks to quit. You should pay particular attention to how these five Swing components are used; most full-featured applications use them in similar ways. Note that Example 10-16 is a complete application; it is designed to be run standalone, not to be viewed using the ShowComponent program. However, the Scribble class is designed as a subclass of JFrame, so that other applications can instantiate Scribble windows of their own, if they so choose.

This example also introduces the Action interface, which is a subinterface of ActionListener. Any Action object can be used as an ActionListener to respond

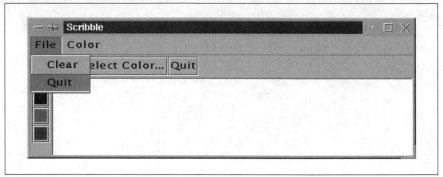

Figure 10-13. The Scribble application

to an ActionEvent generated by a component. What the Action interface adds to the ActionListener interface is the ability to associate arbitrary properties with an Action object. The Action interface also defines standard property names that can specify the name, icon, and description of the action performed by the listener. Action objects are particularly convenient to use because they can be added directly to JMenu and JToolBar components; the components use the action name and/or icon to automatically create appropriate menu items or toolbar buttons to represent the action. (In Java 1.3, Action objects can also be passed directly to the constructor methods of components such as JButton.) Action objects can also be enabled or disabled. When an action is disabled, any component that has been created to represent it is also disabled, preventing the user from attempting to perform the action.

Example 10-16: Scribble.java

```
package com.davidflanagan.examples.gui;
import java.awt.*;
import java.awt.event.*;
import javax.swing.*;
import javax.swing.border.*;

/**
 * This JFrame subclass is a simple "paint" application.
 **/
public class Scribble extends JFrame {
    /**
     * The main method instantiates an instance of the class, sets it size,
     * and makes it visible on the screen
     **/
    public static void main(String[] args) {
        Scribble scribble = new Scribble();
        scribble.setSize(500, 300);
        scribble.setVisible(true);
    }

    // The scribble application relies on the ScribblePane2 component developed
    // earlier.  This field holds the ScribblePane2 instance it uses.
    ScribblePane2 scribblePane;

    /**
     * This constructor creates the GUI for this application.
```

Example 10–16: Scribble.java (continued)

```
     **/
    public Scribble() {
        super("Scribble");  // Call superclass constructor and set window title

        // Handle window close requests
        this.addWindowListener(new WindowAdapter() {
                public void windowClosing(WindowEvent e) { System.exit(0); }
            });

        // All content of a JFrame (except for the menubar) goes in the
        // Frame's internal "content pane", not in the frame itself.
        // The same is true for JDialog and similar top-level containers.
        Container contentPane = this.getContentPane();

        // Specify a layout manager for the content pane
        contentPane.setLayout(new BorderLayout());

        // Create the main scribble pane component, give it a border, and
        // a background color, and add it to the content pane
        scribblePane = new ScribblePane2();
        scribblePane.setBorder(new BevelBorder(BevelBorder.LOWERED));
        scribblePane.setBackground(Color.white);
        contentPane.add(scribblePane, BorderLayout.CENTER);

        // Create a menubar and add it to this window.  Note that JFrame
        // handles menus specially and has a special method for adding them
        // outside of the content pane.
        JMenuBar menubar = new JMenuBar();  // Create a menubar
        this.setJMenuBar(menubar);          // Display it in the JFrame

        // Create menus and add to the menubar
        JMenu filemenu = new JMenu("File");
        JMenu colormenu = new JMenu("Color");
        menubar.add(filemenu);
        menubar.add(colormenu);

        // Create some Action objects for use in the menus and toolbars.
        // An Action combines a menu title and/or icon with an ActionListener.
        // These Action classes are defined as inner classes below.
        Action clear = new ClearAction();
        Action quit = new QuitAction();
        Action black = new ColorAction(Color.black);
        Action red = new ColorAction(Color.red);
        Action blue = new ColorAction(Color.blue);
        Action select = new SelectColorAction();

        // Populate the menus using Action objects
        filemenu.add(clear);
        filemenu.add(quit);
        colormenu.add(black);
        colormenu.add(red);
        colormenu.add(blue);
        colormenu.add(select);

        // Now create a toolbar, add actions to it, and add it to the
        // top of the frame (where it appears underneath the menubar)
        JToolBar toolbar = new JToolBar();
        toolbar.add(clear);
```

Example 10–16: Scribble.java (continued)

```
        toolbar.add(select);
        toolbar.add(quit);
        contentPane.add(toolbar, BorderLayout.NORTH);

        // Create another toolbar for use as a color palette and add to
        // the left side of the window.
        JToolBar palette = new JToolBar();
        palette.add(black);
        palette.add(red);
        palette.add(blue);
        palette.setOrientation(SwingConstants.VERTICAL);
        contentPane.add(palette, BorderLayout.WEST);
    }

    /** This inner class defines the "clear" action that clears the scribble */
    class ClearAction extends AbstractAction {
        public ClearAction() {
            super("Clear");  // Specify the name of the action
        }
        public void actionPerformed(ActionEvent e) { scribblePane.clear(); }
    }

    /** This inner class defines the "quit" action to quit the program */
    class QuitAction extends AbstractAction {
        public QuitAction() { super("Quit"); }
        public void actionPerformed(ActionEvent e) {
            // Use JOptionPane to confirm that the user really wants to quit
            int response =
                JOptionPane.showConfirmDialog(Scribble.this, "Really Quit?");
            if (response == JOptionPane.YES_OPTION) System.exit(0);
        }
    }

    /**
     * This inner class defines an Action that sets the current drawing color
     * of the ScribblePane2 component.  Note that actions of this type have
     * icons rather than labels
     **/
    class ColorAction extends AbstractAction {
        Color color;
        public ColorAction(Color color) {
            this.color = color;
            putValue(Action.SMALL_ICON, new ColorIcon(color)); // specify icon
        }
        public void actionPerformed(ActionEvent e) {
            scribblePane.setColor(color);  // Set current drawing color
        }
    }

    /**
     * This inner class implements Icon to draw a solid 16x16 block of the
     * specified color.  Most icons are instances of ImageIcon, but since
     * we're only using solid colors here, it is easier to implement this
     * custom Icon type
     **/
    static class ColorIcon implements Icon {
        Color color;
        public ColorIcon(Color color) { this.color = color; }
```

Example 10–16: Scribble.java (continued)

```
            // These two methods specify the size of the icon
            public int getIconHeight() { return 16; }
            public int getIconWidth() { return 16; }
            // This method draws the icon
            public void paintIcon(Component c, Graphics g, int x, int y) {
                g.setColor(color);
                g.fillRect(x, y, 16, 16);
            }
        }

        /**
         * This inner class defines an Action that uses JColorChooser to allow
         * the user to select a drawing color
         **/
        class SelectColorAction extends AbstractAction {
            public SelectColorAction() { super("Select Color..."); }
            public void actionPerformed(ActionEvent e) {
                Color color = JColorChooser.showDialog(Scribble.this,
                                                       "Select Drawing Color",
                                                       scribblePane.getColor());
                if (color != null) scribblePane.setColor(color);
            }
        }
    }
```

Actions and Reflection

Example 10-16 demonstrated the use of `Action` objects, which allow an application's command set to be easily presented to the user in menubars, toolbars, and so on. The awkward part about working with `Action` objects, however, is that each one must usually be defined as a class of its own. If you are willing to use the Java Reflection API, however, there is an easier alternative. In Example 8-2 in Chapter 8, *Reflection*, we saw the `Command` class—a class that encapsulates a `java.lang.reflect.Method` object, an array of arguments for the method, and the object upon which the method is to be invoked. Calling the `invoke()` method of a `Command` object invokes the method. The most powerful feature of the `Command` class, however, is its static `parse()` method, which can create a `Command` by parsing a textual representation of the method name and argument list.

The `Command` class implements the `ActionListener` interface, so `Command` objects can be used as simple action listeners. But a `Command` is not an `Action`. Example 10-17 addresses this; it is a listing of *CommandAction.java*, a subclass of `AbstractAction` that uses a `Command` object to perform the action. Since the `Command` class does the hard work, the code for `CommandAction` is relatively simple.

Example 10–17: CommandAction.java

```
package com.davidflanagan.examples.gui;
import com.davidflanagan.examples.reflect.*;
import javax.swing.*;
import java.awt.event.*;

public class CommandAction extends AbstractAction {
    Command command;   // The command to execute in response to an ActionEvent
```

Example 10–17: CommandAction.java (continued)

```
/**
 * Create an Action object that has the various specified attributes,
 * and invokes the specified Command object in response to ActionEvents
 **/
public CommandAction(Command command, String label,
                     Icon icon, String tooltip,
                     KeyStroke accelerator, int mnemonic,
                     boolean enabled)
{
    this.command = command;  // Remember the command to invoke

    // Set the various action attributes with putValue()
    if (label != null) putValue(NAME, label);
    if (icon != null) putValue(SMALL_ICON, icon);
    if (tooltip != null) putValue(SHORT_DESCRIPTION, tooltip);
    if (accelerator != null) putValue(ACCELERATOR_KEY, accelerator);
    if (mnemonic != KeyEvent.VK_UNDEFINED)
        putValue(MNEMONIC_KEY, new Integer(mnemonic));

    // Tell the action whether it is currently enabled or not
    setEnabled(enabled);
}

/**
 * This method implements ActionListener, which is a super-interface of
 * Action.  When a component generates an ActionEvent, it is passed to
 * this method.  This method simply passes it on to the Command object
 * which is also an ActionListener object
 **/
public void actionPerformed(ActionEvent e) { command.actionPerformed(e); }

// These constants are defined by Action in Java 1.3.
// For compatibility with Java 1.2, we re-define them here.
public static final String ACCELERATOR_KEY = "AcceleratorKey";
public static final String MNEMONIC_KEY = "MnemonicKey";
}
```

Custom Dialogs

The Scribble program of Example 10-16 displayed two kinds of dialogs: a confirmation dialog created by JOptionPane and a color selection dialog created by JColorChooser. These Swing components support many basic dialog box needs. The JOptionPane class makes it easy to display simple (and not-so-simple) information, confirmation, and selection dialogs, while JColorChooser and JFileChooser provide color and file selection capabilities. Most nontrivial applications, however, need to create custom dialogs that go beyond these standard components. This is easy to do with the JDialog component.

Example 10-18 shows the FontChooser class. It subclasses JDialog and uses the ItemChooser class developed in Example 10-15 to display font families, styles, and sizes to the user. A FontChooser dialog is pictured in Figure 10-14. The inner class FontChooser.Demo is a simple demonstration application you can use to experiment with the FontChooser dialog.

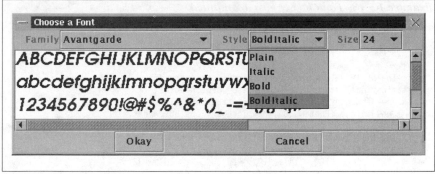

Figure 10–14. The FontChooser dialog

JDialog is a RootPaneContainer like JFrame, which means you can't add children to it directly. You must instead add them to the container returned by getContent-Pane(). FontChooser creates a modal dialog, which means that the show() method blocks and does not return to the caller until the user dismisses the dialog. Finally, FontChooser is implemented as a subclass of JDialog, so that it can be reused by many applications. When you need to create a custom dialog specific to a single application, you can simply create a JDialog instance and populate it with whatever child components you need; in other words, you do not need to write a custom subclass to define a new dialog.

Example 10–18: FontChooser.java

```
package com.davidflanagan.examples.gui;
import java.awt.*;
import java.awt.event.*;
import javax.swing.*;
import javax.swing.event.*;
import com.davidflanagan.examples.gui.ItemChooser;

/**
 * This is a JDialog subclass that allows the user to select a font, in any
 * style and size, from the list of available fonts on the system.  The
 * dialog is modal. Display it with show(); this method does not return
 * until the user dismisses the dialog.  When show() returns, call
 * getSelectedFont() to obtain the user's selection.  If the user clicked the
 * dialog's "Cancel" button, getSelectedFont() will return null.
 **/
public class FontChooser extends JDialog {
    // These fields define the component properties
    String family;         // The name of the font family
    int style;             // The font style
    int size;              // The font size
    Font selectedFont;     // The Font they correspond to

    // This is the list of all font families on the system
    String[] fontFamilies;

    // The various Swing components used in the dialog
    ItemChooser families, styles, sizes;
    JTextArea preview;
    JButton okay, cancel;
```

Example 10–18: FontChooser.java (continued)

```java
    // The names to appear in the "Style" menu
    static final String[] styleNames = new String[] {
        "Plain", "Italic", "Bold", "BoldItalic"
    };
    // The style values that correspond to those names
    static final Integer[] styleValues = new Integer[] {
        new Integer(Font.PLAIN), new Integer(Font.ITALIC),
        new Integer(Font.BOLD), new Integer(Font.BOLD+Font.ITALIC)
    };
    // The size "names" to appear in the size menu
    static final String[] sizeNames = new String[] {
        "8", "10", "12", "14", "18", "20", "24", "28", "32",
        "40", "48", "56", "64", "72"
    };

    // This is the default preview string displayed in the dialog box
    static final String defaultPreviewString =
        "ABCDEFGHIJKLMNOPQRSTUVWXYZ\n" +
        "abcdefghijklmnopqrstuvwxyz\n" +
        "1234567890!@#$%^&*()_-=+[]{}<,.>\n" +
        "The quick brown fox jumps over the lazy dog";

    /** Create a font chooser dialog for the specified frame. */
    public FontChooser(Frame owner) {
        super(owner, "Choose a Font");  // Set dialog frame and title

        // This dialog must be used as a modal dialog.  In order to be used
        // as a modeless dialog, it would have to fire a PropertyChangeEvent
        // whenever the selected font changed, so that applications could be
        // notified of the user's selections.
        setModal(true);

        // Figure out what fonts are available on the system
        GraphicsEnvironment env =
            GraphicsEnvironment.getLocalGraphicsEnvironment();
        fontFamilies = env.getAvailableFontFamilyNames();

        // Set initial values for the properties
        family = fontFamilies[0];
        style = Font.PLAIN;
        size = 18;
        selectedFont = new Font(family, style, size);

        // Create ItemChooser objects that allow the user to select font
        // family, style, and size.
        families = new ItemChooser("Family", fontFamilies, null, 0,
                                   ItemChooser.COMBOBOX);
        styles = new ItemChooser("Style", styleNames, styleValues, 0,
                                 ItemChooser.COMBOBOX);
        sizes = new ItemChooser("Size", sizeNames,null,4,ItemChooser.COMBOBOX);

        // Now register event listeners to handle selections
        families.addItemChooserListener(new ItemChooser.Listener() {
                public void itemChosen(ItemChooser.Event e) {
                    setFontFamily((String)e.getSelectedValue());
                }
            });
        styles.addItemChooserListener(new ItemChooser.Listener() {
```

Example 10–18: FontChooser.java (continued)

```java
                public void itemChosen(ItemChooser.Event e) {
                    setFontStyle(((Integer)e.getSelectedValue()).intValue());
                }
        });
        sizes.addItemChooserListener(new ItemChooser.Listener() {
                public void itemChosen(ItemChooser.Event e) {
                    setFontSize(Integer.parseInt((String)e.getSelectedValue()));
                }
        });

        // Create a component to preview the font.
        preview = new JTextArea(defaultPreviewString, 5, 40);
        preview.setFont(selectedFont);

        // Create buttons to dismiss the dialog, and set handlers on them
        okay = new JButton("Okay");
        cancel = new JButton("Cancel");
        okay.addActionListener(new ActionListener() {
                public void actionPerformed(ActionEvent e) { hide(); }
        });
        cancel.addActionListener(new ActionListener() {
                public void actionPerformed(ActionEvent e) {
                    selectedFont = null;
                    hide();
                }
        });

        // Put the ItemChoosers in a Box
        Box choosersBox = Box.createHorizontalBox();
        choosersBox.add(Box.createHorizontalStrut(15));
        choosersBox.add(families);
        choosersBox.add(Box.createHorizontalStrut(15));
        choosersBox.add(styles);
        choosersBox.add(Box.createHorizontalStrut(15));
        choosersBox.add(sizes);
        choosersBox.add(Box.createHorizontalStrut(15));
        choosersBox.add(Box.createGlue());

        // Put the dismiss buttons in another box
        Box buttonBox = Box.createHorizontalBox();
        buttonBox.add(Box.createGlue());
        buttonBox.add(okay);
        buttonBox.add(Box.createGlue());
        buttonBox.add(cancel);
        buttonBox.add(Box.createGlue());

        // Put the choosers at the top, the buttons at the bottom, and
        // the preview in the middle.
        Container contentPane = getContentPane();
        contentPane.add(new JScrollPane(preview), BorderLayout.CENTER);
        contentPane.add(choosersBox, BorderLayout.NORTH);
        contentPane.add(buttonBox, BorderLayout.SOUTH);

        // Set the dialog size based on the component size.
        pack();
    }

    /**
```

Example 10–18: FontChooser.java (continued)

```
    * Call this method after show() to obtain the user's selection.  If the
    * user used the "Cancel" button, this will return null
    **/
    public Font getSelectedFont() { return selectedFont; }


    // These are other property getter methods
    public String getFontFamily() { return family; }
    public int getFontStyle() { return style; }
    public int getFontSize() { return size; }

    // The property setter methods are a little more complicated.
    // Note that none of these setter methods update the corresponding
    // ItemChooser components as they ought to.
    public void setFontFamily(String name) {
        family = name;
        changeFont();
    }
    public void setFontStyle(int style) {
        this.style = style;
        changeFont();
    }
    public void setFontSize(int size) {
        this.size = size;
        changeFont();
    }
    public void setSelectedFont(Font font) {
        selectedFont = font;
        family = font.getFamily();
        style = font.getStyle();
        size = font.getSize();
        preview.setFont(font);
    }

    // This method is called when the family, style, or size changes
    protected void changeFont() {
        selectedFont = new Font(family, style, size);
        preview.setFont(selectedFont);
    }

    // Override this inherited method to prevent anyone from making us modeless
    public boolean isModal() { return true; }

    /** This inner class demonstrates the use of FontChooser */
    public static class Demo {
        public static void main(String[] args) {
            // Create some components and a FontChooser dialog
            final JFrame frame = new JFrame("demo");
            final JButton button = new JButton("Push Me!");
            final FontChooser chooser = new FontChooser(frame);

            // Handle button clicks
            button.addActionListener(new ActionListener() {
                    public void actionPerformed(ActionEvent e) {
                        // Pop up the dialog
                        chooser.show();
                        // Get the user's selection
                        Font font = chooser.getSelectedFont();
```

Example 10-18: FontChooser.java (continued)

```
                        // If not cancelled, set the button font
                        if (font != null) button.setFont(font);
                }
        });

        // Display the demo
        frame.getContentPane().add(button);
        frame.setSize(200, 100);
        frame.show();
    }
  }
}
```

Displaying Tables

Now that we've seen how to assemble a prototypical Swing GUI, we can move on and start studying some more advanced Swing programming topics. We'll start with examples of some of the more powerful, and therefore complicated, components. The JTable class displays tabular data. It is particularly easy to use if your data happens to be organized into arrays of arrays. If this is not the case, however, you must implement the javax.swing.table.TableModel interface to serve as a translator between your data and the JTable component.

Example 10-19, which is a listing of *PropertyTable.java*, does exactly this. PropertyTable is a subclass of JTable that uses a custom TableModel implementation to display a table of the properties defined by a specified JavaBeans class. The example includes a main() method so you can run it as a standalone application. Figure 10-15 shows the PropertyTable class in action. When studying this example, pay particular attention to the TableModel implementation; the TableModel is the key to working with the JTable component. Also note the PropertyTable constructor method that uses the TableColumnModel to modify the default appearance of the columns in the table.

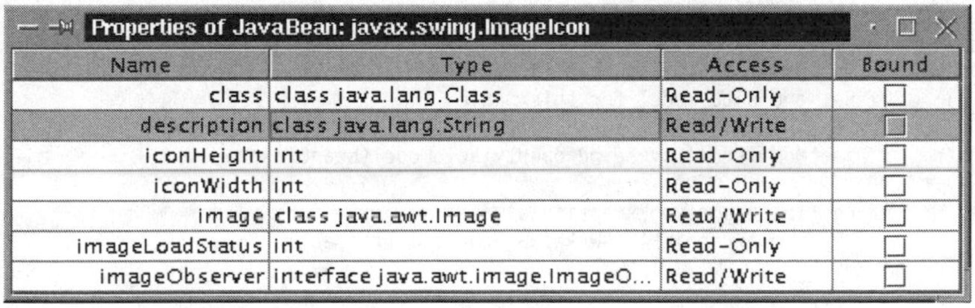

Name	Type	Access	Bound
class	class java.lang.Class	Read-Only	☐
description	class java.lang.String	Read/Write	☐
iconHeight	int	Read-Only	☐
iconWidth	int	Read-Only	☐
image	class java.awt.Image	Read/Write	☐
imageLoadStatus	int	Read-Only	☐
imageObserver	interface java.awt.image.ImageO...	Read/Write	☐

Properties of JavaBean: javax.swing.ImageIcon

Figure 10-15. The PropertyTable application

Example 10-19: PropertyTable.java

```
package com.davidflanagan.examples.gui;
import java.awt.*;
import javax.swing.*;
import javax.swing.table.*;    // TableModel and other JTable-related classes
```

Example 10–19: PropertyTable.java (continued)

```java
import java.beans.*;          // For JavaBean introspection
import java.util.*;           // For array sorting

/**
 * This class is a JTable subclass that displays a table of the JavaBeans
 * properties of any specified class.
 **/
public class PropertyTable extends JTable {
    /** This main method allows the class to be demonstrated  standalone */
    public static void main(String[] args) {
        // Specify the name of the class as a command-line argument
        Class beanClass = null;
        try {
            // Use reflection to get the Class from the classname
            beanClass = Class.forName(args[0]);
        }
        catch (Exception e) {  // Report errors
            System.out.println("Can't find specified class: "+e.getMessage());
            System.out.println("Usage: java TableDemo <JavaBean class name>");
            System.exit(0);
        }

        // Create a table to display the properties of the specified class
        JTable table = new PropertyTable(beanClass);

        // Then put the table in a scrolling window, put the scrolling
        // window into a frame, and pop it all up on to the screen
        JScrollPane scrollpane = new JScrollPane(table);
        JFrame frame = new JFrame("Properties of JavaBean: " + args[0]);
        frame.getContentPane().add(scrollpane);
        frame.setSize(500, 400);
        frame.setVisible(true);
    }

    /**
     * This constructor method specifies what data the table will display
     * (the table model) and uses the TableColumnModel to customize the
     * way that the table displays it.  The hard work is done by the
     * TableModel implementation below.
     **/
    public PropertyTable(Class beanClass) {
        // Set the data model for this table
        try {
            setModel(new JavaBeanPropertyTableModel(beanClass));
        }
        catch (IntrospectionException e) {
            System.err.println("WARNING: can't introspect: " + beanClass);
        }

        // Tweak the appearance of the table by manipulating its column model
        TableColumnModel colmodel = getColumnModel();

        // Set column widths
        colmodel.getColumn(0).setPreferredWidth(125);
        colmodel.getColumn(1).setPreferredWidth(200);
        colmodel.getColumn(2).setPreferredWidth(75);
        colmodel.getColumn(3).setPreferredWidth(50);
```

Example 10-19: PropertyTable.java (continued)

```
        // Right justify the text in the first column
        TableColumn namecol = colmodel.getColumn(0);
        DefaultTableCellRenderer renderer = new DefaultTableCellRenderer();
        renderer.setHorizontalAlignment(SwingConstants.RIGHT);
        namecol.setCellRenderer(renderer);
    }


    /**
     * This class implements TableModel and represents JavaBeans property data
     * in a way that the JTable component can display.  If you've got some
     * type of tabular data to display, implement a TableModel class to
     * describe that data, and the JTable component will be able to display it.
     **/
    static class JavaBeanPropertyTableModel extends AbstractTableModel {
        PropertyDescriptor[] properties;  // The properties to display

        /**
         * The constructor: use the JavaBeans introspector mechanism to get
         * information about all the properties of a bean.  Once we've got
         * this information, the other methods will interpret it for JTable.
         **/
        public JavaBeanPropertyTableModel(Class beanClass)
            throws java.beans.IntrospectionException
        {
            // Use the introspector class to get "bean info" about the class.
            BeanInfo beaninfo = Introspector.getBeanInfo(beanClass);
            // Get the property descriptors from that BeanInfo class
            properties = beaninfo.getPropertyDescriptors();
            // Now do a case-insensitive sort by property name
            // The anonymous Comparator implementation specifies how to
            // sort PropertyDescriptor objects by name
            Arrays.sort(properties, new Comparator() {
                    public int compare(Object p, Object q) {
                        PropertyDescriptor a = (PropertyDescriptor) p;
                        PropertyDescriptor b = (PropertyDescriptor) q;
                        return a.getName().compareToIgnoreCase(b.getName());
                    }
                    public boolean equals(Object o) { return o == this; }
                });
        }

        // These are the names of the columns represented by this TableModel
        static final String[] columnNames = new String[] {
            "Name", "Type", "Access", "Bound"
        };

        // These are the types of the columns represented by this TableModel
        static final Class[] columnTypes = new Class[] {
            String.class, Class.class, String.class, Boolean.class
        };

        // These simple methods return basic information about the table
        public int getColumnCount() { return columnNames.length; }
        public int getRowCount() { return properties.length; }
        public String getColumnName(int column) { return columnNames[column]; }
        public Class getColumnClass(int column) { return columnTypes[column]; }

        /**
```

Example 10-19: PropertyTable.java (continued)

```
            * This method returns the value that appears at the specified row and
            * column of the table
            **/
           public Object getValueAt(int row, int column) {
               PropertyDescriptor prop = properties[row];
               switch(column) {
               case 0: return prop.getName();
               case 1: return prop.getPropertyType();
               case 2: return getAccessType(prop);
               case 3: return new Boolean(prop.isBound());
               default: return null;
               }
           }

           // A helper method called from getValueAt() above
           String getAccessType(PropertyDescriptor prop) {
               java.lang.reflect.Method reader = prop.getReadMethod();
               java.lang.reflect.Method writer = prop.getWriteMethod();
               if ((reader != null) && (writer != null)) return "Read/Write";
               else if (reader != null) return "Read-Only";
               else if (writer != null) return "Write-Only";
               else return "No Access";  // should never happen
           }
       }
   }
```

Displaying Trees

The JTree component is used to display tree-structured data. If your data is in the
form of nested arrays, vectors, or hashtables, you can simply pass the root node of
the data structure to the JTree constructor, and it displays it. Tree data is not typically in this form, however. In order to display data that is in another form, you
must implement the javax.swing.Tree.TreeModel interface to interpret the data in
a way the JTree component can use it.

Example 10-20 shows a listing of *ComponentTree.java*, a JTree subclass that uses
a custom TreeModel implementation to display the containment hierarchy of an
AWT or Swing GUI in tree form. The class includes a main() method that uses the
ComponentTree class to display its own component hierarchy, as shown in Figure
10-16. As with the previous JTable example, the key to this example is the
TreeModel implementation. The main() method also illustrates a technique for
responding to tree node selection events.

Example 10-20: ComponentTree.java

```
package com.davidflanagan.examples.gui;
import java.awt.*;
import java.awt.event.*;
import javax.swing.*;
import javax.swing.event.*;
import javax.swing.tree.*;

/**
 * This class is a JTree subclass that displays the tree of AWT or Swing
 * component that make up a GUI.
```

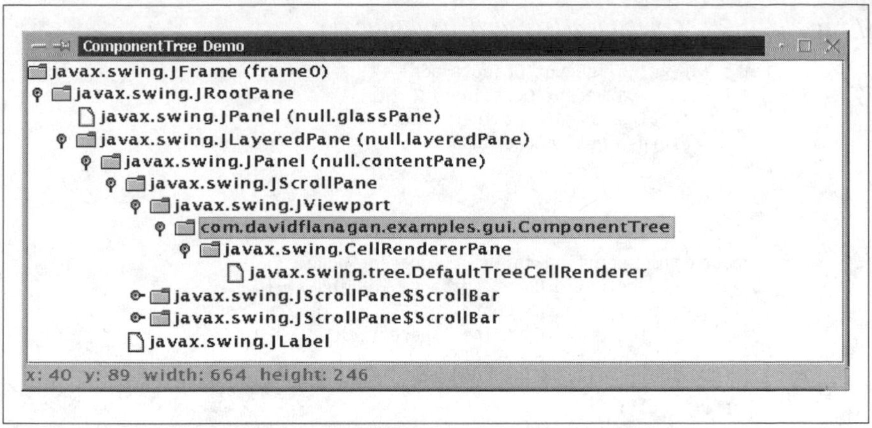

Figure 10–16. The ComponentTree application

Example 10–20: ComponentTree.java (continued)

```
**/
public class ComponentTree extends JTree {
    /**
     * All this constructor method has to do is set the TreeModel and
     * TreeCellRenderer objects for the tree.  It is these classes (defined
     * below) that do all the real work.
     **/
    public ComponentTree(Component c) {
        super(new ComponentTreeModel(c));
        setCellRenderer(new ComponentCellRenderer(getCellRenderer()));
    }

    /**
     * The TreeModel class puts hierarchical data in a form that the JTree
     * can display.  This implementation interprets the containment hierarchy
     * of a Component for display by the ComponentTree class.  Note that any
     * kind of Object can be a node in the tree, as long as the TreeModel knows
     * how to handle it.
     **/
    static class ComponentTreeModel implements TreeModel {
        Component root;    // The root object of the tree

        // Constructor: just remember the root object
        public ComponentTreeModel(Component root) { this.root = root; }

        // Return the root of the tree
        public Object getRoot() { return root; }

        // Is this node a leaf? (Leaf nodes are displayed differently by JTree)
        // Any node that isn't a container is a leaf, since they cannot have
        // children.  We also define containers with no children as leaves.
        public boolean isLeaf(Object node) {
            if (!(node instanceof Container)) return true;
            Container c = (Container) node;
            return c.getComponentCount() == 0;
        }

        // How many children does this node have?
```

Example 10–20: ComponentTree.java (continued)

```
        public int getChildCount(Object node) {
            if (node instanceof Container) {
                Container c = (Container) node;
                return c.getComponentCount();
            }
            return 0;
        }

        // Return the specified child of a parent node.
        public Object getChild(Object parent, int index) {
            if (parent instanceof Container) {
                Container c = (Container) parent;
                return c.getComponent(index);
            }
            return null;
        }

        // Return the index of the child node in the parent node
        public int getIndexOfChild(Object parent, Object child) {
            if (!(parent instanceof Container)) return -1;
            Container c = (Container) parent;
            Component[] children = c.getComponents();
            if (children == null) return -1;
            for(int i = 0; i < children.length; i++) {
                if (children[i] == child) return i;
            }
            return -1;
        }

        // This method is only required for editable trees, so it is not
        // implemented here.
        public void valueForPathChanged(TreePath path, Object newvalue) {}

        // This TreeModel never fires any events (since it is not editable)
        // so event listener registration methods are left unimplemented
        public void addTreeModelListener(TreeModelListener l) {}
        public void removeTreeModelListener(TreeModelListener l) {}
    }


    /**
     * A TreeCellRenderer displays each node of a tree.  The default renderer
     * displays arbitrary Object nodes by calling their toString() method.
     * The Component.toString() method returns long strings with extraneous
     * information.  Therefore, we use this "wrapper" implementation of
     * TreeCellRenderer to convert nodes from Component objects to useful
     * String values before passing those String values on to the default
     * renderer.
     **/
    static class ComponentCellRenderer implements TreeCellRenderer {
        TreeCellRenderer renderer;  // The renderer we are a wrapper for
        // Constructor: just remember the renderer
        public ComponentCellRenderer(TreeCellRenderer renderer) {
            this.renderer = renderer;
        }

        // This is the only TreeCellRenderer method.
        // Compute the string to display, and pass it to the wrapped renderer
```

Example 10-20: ComponentTree.java (continued)

```
      public Component getTreeCellRendererComponent(JTree tree, Object value,
                                                    boolean selected,
                                                    boolean expanded,
                                                    boolean leaf, int row,
                                                    boolean hasFocus) {
          String newvalue = value.getClass().getName();    // Component type
          String name = ((Component)value).getName();       // Component name
          if (name != null) newvalue += " (" + name + ")"; // unless null
          // Use the wrapped renderer object to do the real work
          return renderer.getTreeCellRendererComponent(tree, newvalue,
                                                        selected, expanded,
                                                        leaf, row, hasFocus);
      }
  }
}


/**
 * This main() method demonstrates the use of the ComponentTree class: it
 * puts a ComponentTree component in a Frame, and uses the ComponentTree
 * to display its own GUI hierarchy.  It also adds a TreeSelectionListener
 * to display additional information about each component as it is selected
 **/
public static void main(String[] args) {
    // Create a frame for the demo, and handle window close requests
    JFrame frame = new JFrame("ComponentTree Demo");
    frame.addWindowListener(new WindowAdapter() {
            public void windowClosing(WindowEvent e) { System.exit(0); }
        });

    // Create a scroll pane and a "message line" and add them to the
    // center and bottom of the frame.
    JScrollPane scrollpane = new JScrollPane();
    final JLabel msgline = new JLabel(" ");
    frame.getContentPane().add(scrollpane, BorderLayout.CENTER);
    frame.getContentPane().add(msgline, BorderLayout.SOUTH);

    // Now create the ComponentTree object, specifying the frame as the
    // component whose tree is to be displayed.  Also set the tree's font.
    JTree tree = new ComponentTree(frame);
    tree.setFont(new Font("SanssSerif", Font.BOLD, 12));

    // Only allow a single item in the tree to be selected at once
    tree.getSelectionModel().setSelectionMode(
                    TreeSelectionModel.SINGLE_TREE_SELECTION);

    // Add an event listener for notifications when
    // the tree selection state changes.
    tree.addTreeSelectionListener(new TreeSelectionListener() {
            public void valueChanged(TreeSelectionEvent e) {
                // Tree selections are referred to by "path"
                // We only care about the last node in the path
                TreePath path = e.getPath();
                Component c = (Component) path.getLastPathComponent();
                // Now we know what component was selected, so
                // display some information about it in the message line
                if (c.isShowing()) {
                    Point p = c.getLocationOnScreen();
                    msgline.setText("x: " + p.x + "  y: " + p.y +
                            "  width: " + c.getWidth() +
```

Example 10-20: ComponentTree.java (continued)

```
                                      "  height: " + c.getHeight());
                }
                else {
                    msgline.setText("component is not showing");
                }
            }
        });

    // Now that we've set up the tree, add it to the scrollpane
    scrollpane.setViewportView(tree);

    // Finally, set the size of the main window, and pop it up.
    frame.setSize(600, 400);
    frame.setVisible(true);
    }
}
```

A Simple Web Browser

The two previous examples have shown us the powerful JTable and JTree components. A third powerful Swing component is javax.swing.text.JTextComponent and its various subclasses, which include JTextField, JTextArea, and JEditor-Pane. JEditorPane is a particularly interesting component that makes it easy to display (or edit) HTML text.

As an aside, it is worth noting here that you do not have to create a JEditorPane to display static HTML text. In Java 1.2.2 and later, the JLabel, JButton, and other similar components can all display multiline, multifont formatted HTML labels. The trick is to begin the label with the string "<html>". This tells the component to treat the rest of the label string as formatted HTML text and display it (using an internal JTextComponent) in that way. You can experiment with the feature using the ShowComponent program; use it to create a JButton component and set the text property to a value that begins with "<html>".

Example 10-21 is a listing of *WebBrowser.java*, a JFrame subclass that implements the simple web browser shown in Figure 10-17. The WebBrowser class uses the power of the java.net.URL class to download HTML documents from the Web and the JEditorPane component to display the contents of those documents. Although defined as a reusable component, the WebBrowser class includes a main() method so that it can be run as a standalone application.

Example 10-21 is intended as a demonstration of the power of the JEditorPane component. The truth is, however, that using JEditorPane is quite trivial: simply pass a URL to the setPage() method or a string of HTML text to the setText() method. So, when you study the code for this example, don't focus too much on the JEditorPane. You should instead look at WebBrowser as an example of pulling together many Swing components and programming techniques to create a fairly substantial GUI. Points of interest include the enabling and disabling of Action objects and the use of the JFileChooser component. The example also uses a JLabel as an application message line, with a javax.swing.Timer that performs a simple text-based animation in that message line.

Figure 10–17. The WebBrowser component

Another thing to notice about this example is that it demonstrates several other example classes that are developed later in this chapter. GUIResourceBundle, which is developed in Example 10-22, is the primary one. This class allows common GUI resources (such as colors and fonts) to be read from textual descriptions stored in a properties file, which therefore allows the resources to be customized and localized. When GUIResourceBundle is extended with ResourceParser implementations, it can parse more complex "resources," such as entire JMenuBar and JToolBar components. WebBrowser defers the creation of its menus and toolbars to GUIResourceBundle.

The WebBrowser class uses the default Metal look-and-feel, but it allows the user to select "theme" (a color and font combination) for use within that look-and-feel. This functionality is provided by the ThemeManager class, which is developed in Example 10-28. The printing capability of the web browser is provided by the PrintableDocument class, which is developed in Chapter 12, *Printing*.

Example 10–21: WebBrowser.java

```
package com.davidflanagan.examples.gui;
import java.awt.*;               // LayoutManager stuff
import javax.swing.*;            // Swing components
import java.awt.event.*;         // AWT event handlers
```

Example 10-21: WebBrowser.java (continued)

```
import javax.swing.event.*;        // Swing event handlers
import java.beans.*;               // JavaBeans event handlers
import java.awt.print.*;           // Printing functionality
import java.io.*;                  // Input/output
import java.net.*;                 // Networking with URLs
import java.util.*;                // Hashtables and other utilities
// Import this class by name.  JFileChooser uses it, and its name conflicts
// with java.io.FileFilter
import javax.swing.filechooser.FileFilter;
// Import a class for printing Swing documents.  See printing chapter.
import com.davidflanagan.examples.print.PrintableDocument;

/**
 * This class implements a simple web browser using the HTML
 * display capabilities of the JEditorPane component.
 **/
public class WebBrowser extends JFrame
    implements HyperlinkListener, PropertyChangeListener
{
    /**
     * A simple main() method that allows the WebBrowser class to be used
     * as a stand-alone application.
     **/
    public static void main(String[] args) throws IOException {
        // End the program when there are no more open browser windows
        WebBrowser.setExitWhenLastWindowClosed(true);
        WebBrowser browser = new WebBrowser();  // Create a browser window
        browser.setSize(800, 600);              // Set its size
        browser.setVisible(true);               // Make it visible.

        // Tell the browser what to display.  This method is defined below.
        browser.displayPage((args.length > 0) ? args[0] : browser.getHome());
    }

    // This class uses GUIResourceBundle to create its menubar and toolbar
    // This static initializer performs one-time registration of the
    // required ResourceParser classes.
    static {
        GUIResourceBundle.registerResourceParser(new MenuBarParser());
        GUIResourceBundle.registerResourceParser(new MenuParser());
        GUIResourceBundle.registerResourceParser(new ActionParser());
        GUIResourceBundle.registerResourceParser(new CommandParser());
        GUIResourceBundle.registerResourceParser(new ToolBarParser());
    }

    // These are the Swing components that the browser uses
    JEditorPane textPane;          // Where the HTML is displayed
    JLabel messageLine;            // Displays one-line messages
    JTextField urlField;           // Displays and edits the current URL
    JFileChooser fileChooser;      // Allows the user to select a local file

    // These are Actions that are used in the menubar and toolbar.
    // We obtain explicit references to them from the GUIResourceBundle
    // so we can enable and disable them.
    Action backAction, forwardAction;

    // These fields are used to maintain the browsing history of the window
    java.util.List history = new ArrayList();  // The history list
```

Example 10–21: WebBrowser.java (continued)

```
int currentHistoryPage = -1;                 // Current location in it
public static final int MAX_HISTORY = 50;    // Trim list when over this size

// These static fields control the behavior of the close() action
static int numBrowserWindows = 0;
static boolean exitWhenLastWindowClosed = false;

// This is where the "home()" method takes us.  See also setHome()
String home = "http://www.davidflanagan.com";  // A default value

/** Create and initialize a new WebBrowser window */
public WebBrowser() {
    super();                               // Chain to JFrame constructor

    textPane = new JEditorPane();          // Create HTML window
    textPane.setEditable(false);           // Don't allow the user to edit it

    // Register action listeners.  The first is to handle hyperlinks.
    // The second is to receive property change notifications, which tell
    // us when a document is done loading.  This class implements these
    // EventListener interfaces, and the methods are defined below
    textPane.addHyperlinkListener(this);
    textPane.addPropertyChangeListener(this);

    // Put the text pane in a JScrollPane in the center of the window
    this.getContentPane().add(new JScrollPane(textPane),
                              BorderLayout.CENTER);

    // Now create a message line and place it at the bottom of the window
    messageLine = new JLabel(" ");
    this.getContentPane().add(messageLine, BorderLayout.SOUTH);

    // Read the file WebBrowserResources.properties (and any localized
    // variants appropriate for the current Locale) to create a
    // GUIResourceBundle from which we'll get our menubar and toolbar.
    GUIResourceBundle resources =
        new GUIResourceBundle(this,"com.davidflanagan.examples.gui." +
                              "WebBrowserResources");

    // Read a menubar from the resource bundle and display it
    JMenuBar menubar = (JMenuBar) resources.getResource("menubar",
                                                        JMenuBar.class);
    this.setJMenuBar(menubar);

    // Read a toolbar from the resource bundle.  Don't display it yet.
    JToolBar toolbar =
        (JToolBar) resources.getResource("toolbar", JToolBar.class);

    // Create a text field that the user can enter a URL in.
    // Set up an action listener to respond to the ENTER key in that field
    urlField = new JTextField();
    urlField.addActionListener(new ActionListener() {
            public void actionPerformed(ActionEvent e) {
                displayPage(urlField.getText());
            }
        });

    // Add the URL field and a label for it to the end of the toolbar
```

Example 10-21: WebBrowser.java (continued)

```
            toolbar.add(new JLabel("          URL:"));
            toolbar.add(urlField);

            // And add the toolbar to the top of the window
            this.getContentPane().add(toolbar, BorderLayout.NORTH);

            // Read cached copies of two Action objects from the resource bundle
            // These actions are used by the menubar and toolbar, and enabling and
            // disabling them enables and disables the menu and toolbar items.
            backAction = (Action)resources.getResource("action.back",Action.class);
            forwardAction =
                (Action)resources.getResource("action.forward", Action.class);

            // Start off with both actions disabled
            backAction.setEnabled(false);
            forwardAction.setEnabled(false);

            // Create a ThemeManager for this frame,
            // and add a Theme menu to the menubar
            ThemeManager themes = new ThemeManager(this, resources);
            menubar.add(themes.getThemeMenu());

            // Keep track of how many web browser windows are open
            WebBrowser.numBrowserWindows++;
        }

        /** Set the static property that controls the behavior of close() */
        public static void setExitWhenLastWindowClosed(boolean b) {
            exitWhenLastWindowClosed = b;
        }

        /** These are accessor methods for the home property. */
        public void setHome(String home) { this.home = home; }
        public String getHome() { return home; }

        /**
         * This internal method attempts to load and display the specified URL.
         * It is called from various places throughout the class.
         **/
        boolean visit(URL url) {
            try {
                String href = url.toString();
                // Start animating.  Animation is stopped in propertyChanged()
                startAnimation("Loading " + href + "...");
                textPane.setPage(url);    // Load and display the URL
                this.setTitle(href);      // Display URL in window titlebar
                urlField.setText(href);   // Display URL in text input field
                return true;              // Return success
            }
            catch (IOException ex) {      // If page loading fails
                stopAnimation();
                messageLine.setText("Can't load page: " + ex.getMessage());
                return false;             // Return failure
            }
        }

        /**
         * Ask the browser to display the specified URL, and put it in the
```

Example 10-21: WebBrowser.java (continued)

GUIs

```java
 * history list.
 **/
public void displayPage(URL url) {
    if (visit(url)) {      // go to the specified url, and if we succeed:
        history.add(url);        // Add the url to the history list
        int numentries = history.size();
        if (numentries > MAX_HISTORY+10) {  // Trim history when too large
            history = history.subList(numentries-MAX_HISTORY, numentries);
            numentries = MAX_HISTORY;
        }
        currentHistoryPage = numentries-1;  // Set current history page
        // If we can go back, then enable the Back action
        if (currentHistoryPage > 0) backAction.setEnabled(true);
    }
}

/** Like displayPage(URL), but takes a string instead */
public void displayPage(String href) {
    try {
        displayPage(new URL(href));
    }
    catch (MalformedURLException ex) {
        messageLine.setText("Bad URL: " + href);
    }
}

/** Allow the user to choose a local file, and display it */
public void openPage() {
    // Lazy creation: don't create the JFileChooser until it is needed
    if (fileChooser == null) {
        fileChooser = new JFileChooser();
        // This javax.swing.filechooser.FileFilter displays only HTML files
        FileFilter filter = new FileFilter() {
                public boolean accept(File f) {
                    String fn = f.getName();
                    if (fn.endsWith(".html") || fn.endsWith(".htm"))
                        return true;
                    else return false;
                }
                public String getDescription() { return "HTML Files"; }
            };
        fileChooser.setFileFilter(filter);
        fileChooser.addChoosableFileFilter(filter);
    }

    // Ask the user to choose a file.
    int result = fileChooser.showOpenDialog(this);
    if (result == JFileChooser.APPROVE_OPTION) {
        // If they didn't click "Cancel", then try to display the file.
        File selectedFile = fileChooser.getSelectedFile();
        String url = "file://" + selectedFile.getAbsolutePath();
        displayPage(url);
    }
}

/** Go back to the previously displayed page. */
public void back() {
    if (currentHistoryPage > 0)  // go back, if we can
```

Example 10–21: WebBrowser.java (continued)

```
            visit((URL)history.get(--currentHistoryPage));
        // Enable or disable actions as appropriate
        backAction.setEnabled((currentHistoryPage > 0));
        forwardAction.setEnabled((currentHistoryPage < history.size()-1));
    }

    /** Go forward to the next page in the history list */
    public void forward() {
        if (currentHistoryPage < history.size()-1)  // go forward, if we can
            visit((URL)history.get(++currentHistoryPage));
        // Enable or disable actions as appropriate
        backAction.setEnabled((currentHistoryPage > 0));
        forwardAction.setEnabled((currentHistoryPage < history.size()-1));
    }

    /** Reload the current page in the history list */
    public void reload() {
        if (currentHistoryPage != -1)
            visit((URL)history.get(currentHistoryPage));
    }

    /** Display the page specified by the "home" property */
    public void home() { displayPage(getHome()); }

    /** Open a new browser window */
    public void newBrowser() {
        WebBrowser b = new WebBrowser();
        b.setSize(this.getWidth(), this.getHeight());
        b.setVisible(true);
    }

    /**
     * Close this browser window.  If this was the only open window,
     * and exitWhenLastBrowserClosed is true, then exit the VM
     **/
    public void close() {
        this.setVisible(false);                 // Hide the window
        this.dispose();                         // Destroy the window
        synchronized(WebBrowser.class) {        // Synchronize for thread-safety
            WebBrowser.numBrowserWindows--; // There is one window fewer now
            if ((numBrowserWindows==0) && exitWhenLastWindowClosed)
                System.exit(0);                 // Exit if it was the last one
        }
    }

    /**
     * Exit the VM.  If confirm is true, ask the user if they are sure.
     * Note that showConfirmDialog() displays a dialog, waits for the user,
     * and returns the user's response (i.e. the button the user selected).
     **/
    public void exit(boolean confirm) {
        if (!confirm ||
            (JOptionPane.showConfirmDialog(this,  // dialog parent
                /* message to display */  "Are you sure you want to quit?",
                /* dialog title */        "Really Quit?",
                /* dialog buttons */      JOptionPane.YES_NO_OPTION) ==
             JOptionPane.YES_OPTION))  // If Yes button was clicked
            System.exit(0);
```

Example 10-21: WebBrowser.java (continued)

```
    }

    /**
     * Print the contents of the text pane using the java.awt.print API
     * Note that this API does not work efficiently in Java 1.2
     * All the hard work is done by the PrintableDocument class.
     **/
    public void print() {
        // Get a PrinterJob object from the system
        PrinterJob job = PrinterJob.getPrinterJob();
        // This is the object that we are going to print
        PrintableDocument pd = new PrintableDocument(textPane);
        // Tell the PrinterJob what we want to print
        job.setPageable(pd);
        // Display a print dialog, asking the user what pages to print, what
        // printer to print to, and giving the user a chance to cancel.
        if (job.printDialog()) {  // If the user did not cancel
            try { job.print(); }  // Start printing!
            catch(PrinterException ex) {  // display errors nicely
                messageLine.setText("Couldn't print: " + ex.getMessage());
            }
        }
    }

    /**
     * This method implements HyperlinkListener.  It is invoked when the user
     * clicks on a hyperlink, or move the mouse onto or off of a link
     **/
    public void hyperlinkUpdate(HyperlinkEvent e) {
        HyperlinkEvent.EventType type = e.getEventType();  // what happened?
        if (type == HyperlinkEvent.EventType.ACTIVATED) {      // Click!
            displayPage(e.getURL());   // Follow the link; display new page
        }
        else if (type == HyperlinkEvent.EventType.ENTERED) {  // Mouse over!
            // When mouse goes over a link, display it in the message line
            messageLine.setText(e.getURL().toString());
        }
        else if (type == HyperlinkEvent.EventType.EXITED) {   // Mouse out!
            messageLine.setText(" ");  // Clear the message line
        }
    }

    /**
     * This method implements java.beans.PropertyChangeListener.  It is
     * invoked whenever a bound property changes in the JEditorPane object.
     * The property we are interested in is the "page" property, because it
     * tells us when a page has finished loading.
     **/
    public void propertyChange(PropertyChangeEvent e) {
        if (e.getPropertyName().equals("page")) // If the page property changed
            stopAnimation();                     // Then stop the loading... animation
    }

    /**
     * The fields and methods below implement a simple animation in the
     * web browser message line; they are used to provide user feedback
     * while web pages are loading.
     **/
```

Example 10–21: WebBrowser.java (continued)

```
String animationMessage;   // The "loading..." message to display
int animationFrame = 0;    // What "frame" of the animation are we on
String[] animationFrames = new String[] {  // The content of each "frame"
    "-", "\\", "|", "/", "-", "\\", "|", "/",
    ",", ".", "o", "O", "0", "#", "*", "+"
};

/** This object calls the animate() method 8 times a second */
javax.swing.Timer animator =
    new javax.swing.Timer(125, new ActionListener() {
            public void actionPerformed(ActionEvent e) { animate(); }
        });

/** Display the next frame. Called by the animator timer */
void animate() {
    String frame = animationFrames[animationFrame++];    // Get next frame
    messageLine.setText(animationMessage + " " + frame); // Update msgline
    animationFrame = animationFrame % animationFrames.length;
}

/** Start the animation.  Called by the visit() method. */
void startAnimation(String msg) {
    animationMessage = msg;    // Save the message to display
    animationFrame = 0;        // Start with frame 0 of the animation
    animator.start();          // Tell the timer to start firing.
}

/** Stop the animation.  Called by propertyChanged() method. */
void stopAnimation() {
    animator.stop();           // Tell the timer to stop firing events
    messageLine.setText(" ");  // Clear the message line
}
}
```

Describing GUIs with Properties

At its core, the task of specifying a graphical user interface is a descriptive one. This descriptive task does not map well onto a procedural and algorithm-based programming language such as Java. You end up writing lots of code that creates components, sets properties, and adds components to containers. Instead of simply describing the structure of the GUI you want, you must write the step-by-step code to build the GUI.

One way to avoid writing this tedious GUI construction code is to create a GUI-description language of some sort, then write code that can read that language and automatically create the described GUI. One common approach is to describe a GUI using an XML grammar. In this chapter, we'll rely on the simpler syntax of Java properties files as used by the ResourceBundle class. (See Chapter 7, *Internationalization* for examples using java.util.ResourceBundle.)

A java.util.Properties object is a hashtable that maps string keys to string values. The Properties class can read and write a simple text file format in which each *name:value* line defines a single property. Furthermore, a Properties object can have a parent Properties object. When you look up the value of a property

---

that does not exist in the child `Properties` object, the parent `Properties` object is searched (and this continues recursively). The `ResourceBundle` class provides an internationalization layer around properties files that allows properties to be customized for use in different locales. Internationalization is an important consideration for GUI-based applications, which makes the `ResourceBundle` class useful for describing GUI resources.

Handling Basic GUI Resources

Because properties files are text-based, one limitation to working with `Resource-Bundle` objects that are based on properties files is that they support only `String` resources. The `GUIResourceBundle` class, presented in Example 10-22, is a subclass of `ResourceBundle` that adds additional methods for reading string resources and converting them to objects of the types commonly used in GUI programming, such as `Color` and `Font`.

The `GUIResourceBundle` code is straightforward. The `ResourceParser` interface provides an extension mechanism; we'll look at that next. Note that the `MalformedResourceException` class used in this example is not a standard Java class; it is a custom subclass of `MissingResourceException` that was developed for this example. Because it is a trivial subclass, its code is not shown here, but you'll find the code in the online example archive.

Example 10-22: GUIResourceBundle.java

```
package com.davidflanagan.examples.gui;
import java.io.*;
import java.util.*;
import java.awt.*;

/**
 * This class extends ResourceBundle and adds methods to retrieve types of
 * resources commonly used in GUIs.  Additionally, it adds extensibility
 * by allowing ResourceParser objects to be registered to parse other
 * resource types.
 **/
public class GUIResourceBundle extends ResourceBundle {
    // The root object.  Required to parse certain resource types like Commands
    Object root;

    // The resource bundle that actually contains the textual resources
    // This class is a wrapper around this bundle
    ResourceBundle bundle;

    /** Create a GUIResourceBundle wrapper around a specified bundle */
    public GUIResourceBundle(Object root, ResourceBundle bundle) {
        this.root = root;
        this.bundle = bundle;
    }

    /**
     * Load a named bundle and create a GUIResourceBundle around it.  This
     * constructor takes advantage of the internationalization features of
     * the ResourceBundle.getBundle() method.
     **/
    public GUIResourceBundle(Object root, String bundleName)
```

Example 10-22: GUIResourceBundle.java (continued)

```java
        throws MissingResourceException
    {
        this.root = root;
        this.bundle = ResourceBundle.getBundle(bundleName);
    }

    /**
     * Create a PropertyResourceBundle from the specified stream and then
     * create a GUIResourceBundle wrapper for it
     **/
    public GUIResourceBundle(Object root, InputStream propertiesStream)
        throws IOException
    {
        this.root = root;
        this.bundle = new PropertyResourceBundle(propertiesStream);
    }

    /**
     * Create a PropertyResourceBundle from the specified properties file and
     * then create a GUIResourceBundle wrapper for it.
     **/
    public GUIResourceBundle(Object root, File propertiesFile)
        throws IOException
    {
        this(root, new FileInputStream(propertiesFile));
    }

    /** This is one of the abstract methods of ResourceBundle */
    public Enumeration getKeys() { return bundle.getKeys(); }

    /** This is the other abstract method of ResourceBundle */
    protected Object handleGetObject(String key)
        throws MissingResourceException
    {
        return bundle.getObject(key);  // simply defer to the wrapped bundle
    }

    /** This is a property accessor method for our root object */
    public Object getRoot() { return root; }

    /**
     * This method is like the inherited getString() method, except that
     * when the named resource is not found, it returns the specified default
     * instead of throwing an exception
     **/
    public String getString(String key, String defaultValue) {
        try { return bundle.getString(key); }
        catch(MissingResourceException e) { return defaultValue; }
    }

    /**
     * Look up the named resource and parse it as a list of strings separated
     * by spaces, tabs, or commas.
     **/
    public java.util.List getStringList(String key)
        throws MissingResourceException
    {
        String s = getString(key);
```

Example 10–22: GUIResourceBundle.java (continued)

```
        StringTokenizer t = new StringTokenizer(s, ", \t", false);
        ArrayList list = new ArrayList();
        while(t.hasMoreTokens()) list.add(t.nextToken());
        return list;
    }

    /** Like above, but return a default instead of throwing an exception */
    public java.util.List getStringList(String key,
                                        java.util.List defaultValue) {
        try { return getStringList(key); }
        catch(MissingResourceException e) { return defaultValue; }
    }

    /** Look up the named resource and try to interpret it as a boolean. */
    public boolean getBoolean(String key) throws MissingResourceException {
        String s = bundle.getString(key);
        s = s.toLowerCase();
        if (s.equals("true")) return true;
        else if (s.equals("false")) return false;
        else if (s.equals("yes")) return true;
        else if (s.equals("no")) return false;
        else if (s.equals("on")) return true;
        else if (s.equals("off")) return false;
        else {
            throw new MalformedResourceException("boolean", key);
        }
    }

    /** As above, but return the default instead of throwing an exception */
    public boolean getBoolean(String key, boolean defaultValue) {
        try { return getBoolean(key); }
        catch(MissingResourceException e) {
            if (e instanceof MalformedResourceException)
                System.err.println("WARNING: " + e.getMessage());
            return defaultValue;
        }
    }

    /** Like getBoolean(), but for integers */
    public int getInt(String key) throws MissingResourceException {
        String s = bundle.getString(key);

        try {
            // Use decode() instead of parseInt() so we support octal
            // and hexadecimal numbers
            return Integer.decode(s).intValue();
        } catch (NumberFormatException e) {
            throw new MalformedResourceException("int", key);
        }
    }

    /** As above, but with a default value */
    public int getInt(String key, int defaultValue) {
        try { return getInt(key); }
        catch(MissingResourceException e) {
            if (e instanceof MalformedResourceException)
                System.err.println("WARNING: " + e.getMessage());
            return defaultValue;
```

Example 10–22: GUIResourceBundle.java (continued)

```
            }
        }

        /** Return a resource of type double */
        public double getDouble(String key) throws MissingResourceException {
            String s = bundle.getString(key);

            try {
                return Double.parseDouble(s);
            } catch (NumberFormatException e) {
                throw new MalformedResourceException("double", key);
            }
        }

        /** As above, but with a default value */
        public double getDouble(String key, double defaultValue) {
            try { return getDouble(key); }
            catch(MissingResourceException e) {
                if (e instanceof MalformedResourceException)
                    System.err.println("WARNING: " + e.getMessage());
                return defaultValue;
            }
        }

        /** Look up the named resource and convert to a Font */
        public Font getFont(String key) throws MissingResourceException {
            // Font.decode() always returns a Font object, so we can't check
            // whether the resource value was well-formed or not.
            return Font.decode(bundle.getString(key));
        }

        /** As above, but with a default value */
        public Font getFont(String key, Font defaultValue) {
            try { return getFont(key); }
            catch (MissingResourceException e) { return defaultValue; }
        }

        /** Look up the named resource, and convert to a Color */
        public Color getColor(String key) throws MissingResourceException {
            try {
                return Color.decode(bundle.getString(key));
            }
            catch (NumberFormatException e) {
                // It would be useful to try to parse color names here as well
                // as numeric color specifications
                throw new MalformedResourceException("Color", key);
            }
        }

        /** As above, but with a default value */
        public Color getColor(String key, Color defaultValue) {
            try { return getColor(key); }
            catch(MissingResourceException e) {
                if (e instanceof MalformedResourceException)
                    System.err.println("WARNING: " + e.getMessage());
                return defaultValue;
            }
        }
```

Example 10–22: GUIResourceBundle.java (continued)

```
/** A hashtable for mapping resource types to resource parsers */
static HashMap parsers = new HashMap();

/** An extension mechanism: register a parser for new resource types */
public static void registerResourceParser(ResourceParser parser) {
    // Ask the ResourceParser what types it can parse
    Class[] supportedTypes = parser.getResourceTypes();
    // Register it in the hashtable for each of those types
    for(int i = 0; i < supportedTypes.length; i++)
        parsers.put(supportedTypes[i], parser);
}

/** Look up a ResourceParser for the specified resource type */
public static ResourceParser getResourceParser(Class type) {
    return (ResourceParser) parsers.get(type);
}

/**
 * Look for a ResourceParser for the named type, and if one is found,
 * ask it to parse and return the named resource
 **/
public Object getResource(String key, Class type)
    throws MissingResourceException
{
    // Get a parser for the specified type
    ResourceParser parser = (ResourceParser)parsers.get(type);
    if (parser == null)
        throw new MissingResourceException(
                "No ResourceParser registered for " +
                type.getName() + " resources",
                type.getName(), key);

    try {  // Ask the parser to parse the resource
        return parser.parse(this, key, type);
    }
    catch(MissingResourceException e) {
        throw e;  // Rethrow MissingResourceException exceptions
    }
    catch(Exception e) {
        // If any other type of exception occurs, convert it to
        // a MalformedResourceException
        String msg = "Malformed " + type.getName() + " resource: " +
            key + ": " + e.getMessage();
        throw new MalformedResourceException(msg, type.getName(), key);
    }
}

/**
 * Like the 2-argument version of getResource, but return a default value
 * instead of throwing a MissingResourceException
 **/
public Object getResource(String key, Class type, Object defaultValue) {
    try {  return getResource(key, type); }
    catch (MissingResourceException e) {
        if (e instanceof MalformedResourceException)
            System.err.println("WARNING: " + e.getMessage());
        return defaultValue;
    }
```

GUIs

Example 10–22: GUIResourceBundle.java (continued)

```
        }
}
```

An Extension Mechanism for Complex Resources

As we just saw, Example 10-22 uses the ResourceParser interface to provide an extension mechanism that allows it to handle more complex resource types. Example 10-23 is a listing of this simple interface. We'll see some interesting implementations of the interface in the sections that follow.

Example 10–23: ResourceParser.java

```
package com.davidflanagan.examples.gui;

/**
 * This interface defines an extension mechanism that allows GUIResourceBundle
 * to parse arbitrary resource types
 **/
public interface ResourceParser {
    /**
     * Return an array of classes that specify what kind of resources
     * this parser can handle
     **/
    public Class[] getResourceTypes();

    /**
     * Read the property named by key from the specified bundle, convert
     * it to the specified type, and return it.  For complex resources,
     * the parser may need to read more than one property from the bundle;
     * typically it may a number of properties whose names begin with the
     * specified key.
     **/
    public Object parse(GUIResourceBundle bundle, String key, Class type)
        throws Exception;
}
```

Parsing Commands and Actions

For our first ResourceParser implementation, we'll add the ability to parse Action objects. As we've seen, Action objects are commonly used in GUIs; an Action includes a number of attributes, such as a description, an icon, and a tooltip, that may need to be localized. Our ActionParser implementation is based on the CommandAction class shown in Example 10-17, which in turn relies on the reflection capabilities of the Command class shown in Example 8-2.

In order to implement the ActionParser class, you need to parse Command objects from a properties file. So let's start with the CommandParser class, shown in Example 10-24. This class is quite simple because it relies on the parsing capabilities of the Command class. The ActionParser listing follows in Example 10-25.

To help you understand how these parser classes work, consider the following properties, excerpted from the *WebBrowserResources.properties* file used by the WebBrowser class of Example 10-21:

```
action.home: home();
action.home.label: Home
action.home.description: Go to home page
action.oreilly: displayPage("http://www.oreilly.com");
action.oreilly.label: O'Reilly
action.oreilly.description: O'Reilly & Associates home page
```

These properties describe two actions, one named by the key "action.home" and the other by "action.oreilly".

Example 10-24: CommandParser.java

```
package com.davidflanagan.examples.gui;
import com.davidflanagan.examples.reflect.Command;

/**
 * This class parses a Command object from a GUIResourceBundle.  It uses
 * the Command.parse() method to perform all the actual parsing work.
 **/
public class CommandParser implements ResourceParser {
    static final Class[] supportedTypes = new Class[] { Command.class };
    public Class[] getResourceTypes() { return supportedTypes;}

    public Object parse(GUIResourceBundle bundle, String key, Class type)
        throws java.util.MissingResourceException, java.io.IOException
    {
        String value = bundle.getString(key);  // look up the command text
        return Command.parse(bundle.getRoot(), value);  // parse it!
    }
}
```

Example 10-25: ActionParser.java

```
package com.davidflanagan.examples.gui;
import com.davidflanagan.examples.reflect.*;
import java.awt.event.*;
import javax.swing.*;
import java.util.*;

/**
 * This class parses an Action object from a GUIResourceBundle.
 * The specified key is used to look up the Command string for the action.
 * The key is also used as a prefix for other resource names that specify
 * other attributes (such as the label and icon) associated with the Action.
 * An action named "zoomOut" might be specified like this:
 *
 *      zoomOut: zoom(0.5);
 *      zoomOut.label: Zoom Out
 *      zoomOut.description: Zoom out by a factor of 2
 *
 * Because Action objects are often reused by an application (for example
 * in a toolbar and a menu system, this ResourceParser caches the Action
 * objects it returns.  By sharing Action objects, you can disable and enable
 * an action and that change will affect the entire GUI.
 **/
public class ActionParser implements ResourceParser {
    static final Class[] supportedTypes = new Class[] { Action.class };
    public Class[] getResourceTypes() { return supportedTypes; }

    HashMap bundleToCacheMap = new HashMap();
```

Example 10–25: ActionParser.java (continued)

```
public Object parse(GUIResourceBundle bundle, String key, Class type)
    throws java.util.MissingResourceException
{
    // Look up the Action cache associated with this bundle
    HashMap cache = (HashMap) bundleToCacheMap.get(bundle);
    if (cache == null) {  // If there isn't one, create one and save it
        cache = new HashMap();
        bundleToCacheMap.put(bundle, cache);
    }
    // Now look up the Action associated with the key in the cache.
    Action action = (Action) cache.get(key);
    // If we found a cached action, return it.
    if (action != null) return action;

    // If there was no cached action create one.  The command is
    // the only required resource.  It will throw an exception if
    // missing or malformed.
    Command command = (Command) bundle.getResource(key, Command.class);

    // The remaining calls all supply default values, so they will not
    // throw exceptions, even if ResourceParsers haven't been registered
    // for types like Icon and KeyStroke
    String label = bundle.getString(key + ".label", null);
    Icon icon = (Icon) bundle.getResource(key + ".icon", Icon.class, null);
    String tooltip = bundle.getString(key + ".description", null);
    KeyStroke accelerator =
        (KeyStroke) bundle.getResource(key + ".accelerator",
                                       KeyStroke.class, null);
    int mnemonic = bundle.getInt(key + ".mnemonic", KeyEvent.VK_UNDEFINED);
    boolean enabled = bundle.getBoolean(key + ".enabled", true);

    // Create a CommandAction object with these values
    action = new CommandAction(command, label, icon, tooltip,
                               accelerator, mnemonic, enabled);

    // Save it in the cache, then return it
    cache.put(key, action);
    return action;
    }
}
```

Parsing Menus

We've seen that the GUIResourceBundle class makes it easy to read simple GUI resources, such as colors and fonts, from a properties file. We've also seen how to extend GUIResourceBundle to parse more complex resources, such as Action objects. Fonts, colors, and actions are resources that are used by the components that make up a GUI. With a small conceptual leap, however, we can start to think of GUI components themselves as resources to be used by the larger application.

Example 10-26 and Example 10-27 show how this can work. These examples list the MenuBarParser and MenuParser classes, which read JMenuBar and JMenu objects, respectively, from a properties file. MenuBarParser relies on MenuParser to obtain the JMenu objects that populate the menubar, and MenuParser relies on the

ActionParser class listed previously to obtain the Action objects that represent the individual menu items in each JMenu.

MenuParser and MenuBarParser read menu descriptions from properties files using a simple grammar illustrated by the following lines from the *WebBrowser-Resource.properties* file:

```
# The menubar contains two menus, named "menu.file" and "menu.go"
menubar: menu.file menu.go

# The "menu.file" menu has the label "File".  It contains five items
# specified as action objects, and these items are separated into two
# groups by a separator
menu.file: File: action.new action.open action.print - action.close action.exit

# The "menu.go" menu has the label "Go", and contains four items
menu.go: Go: action.back action.forward action.reload action.home
```

These lines describe a menubar with the property name "menubar" and all its submenus. Note that I've omitted the properties that define the actions contained by the individual menu panes.

As you can see, the menubar grammar is quite simple: it is just a list of the property names of the menus contained by the menubar. For this reason, the MenuBarParser code in Example 10-26 is quite simple. The grammar that describes menus is somewhat more complicated, which is reflected in Example 10-27.

You may recall that the WebBrowser example also uses the GUIResourceBundle to read a JToolBar from the properties file. This is done using a ToolBarParser class. The code for that class is quite similar to the code for MenuBarParser and is not listed here. It is available in the online example archive, however.

Example 10–26: MenuBarParser.java

```java
package com.davidflanagan.examples.gui;
import javax.swing.*;
import java.util.*;

/**
 * Parse a JMenuBar from a ResourceBundle.  A menubar is represented
 * simply as a list of menu property names.  E.g.:
 *      menubar: menu.file menu.edit menu.view menu.help
 **/
public class MenuBarParser implements ResourceParser {
    static final Class[] supportedTypes = new Class[] { JMenuBar.class };
    public Class[] getResourceTypes() { return supportedTypes; }

    public Object parse(GUIResourceBundle bundle, String key, Class type)
        throws java.util.MissingResourceException
    {
        // Get the value of the key as a list of strings
        List menuList = bundle.getStringList(key);

        // Create a MenuBar
        JMenuBar menubar = new JMenuBar();

        // Create a JMenu for each of the menu property names,
        // and add it to the bar
        int nummenus = menuList.size();
```

Example 10–26: MenuBarParser.java (continued)

```
        for(int i = 0; i < nummenus; i++) {
            menubar.add((JMenu) bundle.getResource((String)menuList.get(i),
                                                    JMenu.class));
        }

        return menubar;
    }
}
```

Example 10–27: MenuParser.java

```
package com.davidflanagan.examples.gui;
import com.davidflanagan.examples.reflect.*;
import java.awt.event.*;
import javax.swing.*;
import java.util.StringTokenizer;

/**
 * This class parses a JMenu or JPopupMenu from textual descriptions found in
 * a GUIResourceBundle.  The grammar is straightforward: the menu label
 * followed by a colon and a list of menu items.  Menu items that begin with
 * a '>' character are submenus.  Menu items that begin with a '-' character
 * are separators.  All other items are action names.
 **/
public class MenuParser implements ResourceParser {
    static final Class[] supportedTypes = new Class[] {
        JMenu.class, JPopupMenu.class  // This class handles two resource types
    };

    public Class[] getResourceTypes() { return supportedTypes; }

    public Object parse(GUIResourceBundle bundle, String key, Class type)
        throws java.util.MissingResourceException
    {
        // Get the string value of the key
        String menudef = bundle.getString(key);

        // Break it up into words, ignoring whitespace, colons and commas
        StringTokenizer st = new StringTokenizer(menudef, " \t:,");

        // The first word is the label of the menu
        String menuLabel = st.nextToken();

        // Create either a JMenu or JPopupMenu
        JMenu menu = null;
        JPopupMenu popup = null;
        if (type == JMenu.class) menu = new JMenu(menuLabel);
        else popup = new JPopupMenu(menuLabel);

        // Then loop through the rest of the words, creating a JMenuItem
        // for each one.  Accumulate these items in a list
        while(st.hasMoreTokens()) {
            String item = st.nextToken();     // the next word
            char firstchar = item.charAt(0);  // determines type of menu item
            switch(firstchar) {
            case '-':     // words beginning with - add a separator to the menu
                if (menu != null) menu.addSeparator();
                else popup.addSeparator();
                break;
```

Example 10–27: MenuParser.java (continued)

```
            case '>':    // words beginning with > are submenu names
                // strip off the > character, and recurse to parse the submenu
                item = item.substring(1);
                // Parse a submenu and add it to the list of items
                JMenu submenu = (JMenu)parse(bundle, item, JMenu.class);
                if (menu != null) menu.add(submenu);
                else popup.add(submenu);
                break;
            case '!': // words beginning with ! are action names
                item = item.substring(1);    // strip off the ! character
                /* falls through */          // fall through to the next case
            default:   // By default all other words are taken as action names
                // Look up the named action and add it to the menu
                Action action = (Action)bundle.getResource(item, Action.class);
                if (menu != null) menu.add(action);
                else popup.add(action);
                break;
            }
        }

        // Finally, return the menu or the popup menu
        if (menu != null) return menu;
        else return popup;
    }
}
```

Themes and the Metal Look-and-Feel

The default platform-independent look-and-feel for Swing applications is known as the Metal look-and-feel. One of the powerful but little-known features of Metal is that the fonts and colors it uses are easily customizable. All you have to do is pass a `MetalTheme` object to the static `setCurrentTheme()` method of `Metal-LookAndFeel`. (These classes are defined in the infrequently used `javax.swing.plaf.metal` package.)

The `MetalTheme` class is abstract, so, in practice, you work with `DefaultMetalTheme`. This class has six methods that return the basic theme colors (really three shades each of a primary and a secondary color) and four methods that return the basic theme fonts. To define a new theme, all you have to do is subclass `DefaultMetalTheme` and override these methods to return the fonts and colors you want. (If you want more customizability than this, you have to subclass `MetalTheme` directly.)

Example 10-28 is a listing of *ThemeManager.java*. This example includes a subclass of `DefaultMetalTheme`, but defines it as an inner class of `ThemeManager`. The `ThemeManager` class provides the ability to read theme definitions (i.e., color and font specifications) from a `GUIResourceBundle`. It also defines methods for reading the name of a default theme and a list of names of all available themes from the bundle. Finally, `ThemeManager` can return a `JMenu` component that displays a list of available themes to the user and switches the current theme based on the user's selection.

ThemeManager, and the JMenu component it creates, were used in the WebBrowser class of Example 10-21. Before you examine the ThemeManager code, take a look at the following lines excerpted from the WebBrowserResources.properties file, which define the set of available themes for the web browser:

```
# This property defines the property names of all available themes.
themelist: theme.metal theme.rose, theme.lime, theme.primary, theme.bigfont
# This property defines the name of the default property
defaultTheme: theme.metal

# This theme only has a name.  All font and color values are unchanged from
# the default Metal theme
theme.metal.name: Default Metal

# This theme uses shades of red/pink
theme.rose.name: Rose
theme.rose.primary: #905050
theme.rose.secondary: #906050

# This theme uses lime green colors
theme.lime.name: Lime
theme.lime.primary: #509050
theme.lime.secondary: #506060

# This theme uses bright primary colors
theme.primary.name: Primary Colors
theme.primary.primary: #202090
theme.primary.secondary: #209020

# This theme uses big fonts and the default colors
theme.bigfont.name: Big Fonts
theme.bigfont.controlFont: sansserif-bold-18
theme.bigfont.menuFont: sansserif-bold-18
theme.bigfont.smallFont: sansserif-plain-14
theme.bigfont.systemFont: sansserif-plain-14
theme.bigfont.userFont: sansserif-plain-14
theme.bigfont.titleFont: sansserif-bold-18
```

With these theme definitions, you should have no trouble understanding the resource parsing code of ThemeManager. getThemeMenu() creates a JMenu populated by JRadioButtonMenuItem objects, rather than JMenuItem or Action objects, as we've seen earlier in this chapter. This emphasizes the fact that only one theme can be selected at a time. When the theme is changed, the setTheme() method uses a SwingUtilities method to propagate the change to all components within the frame. Finally, note that the Theme inner class doesn't use Font and Color objects, but FontUIResource and ColorUIResource objects instead. These classes are part of the javax.swing.plaf package and are trivial subclasses of Font and Color that implement the UIResource marker interface. This interface allows components to distinguish between property values assigned by the look-and-feel, which all implement UIResource, and property values assigned by the application. Based on this distinction, application settings can override look-and-feel settings, even when the look-and-feel (or theme) changes while the application is running.

Example 10–28: ThemeManager.java

```
package com.davidflanagan.examples.gui;
import java.awt.*;
import java.awt.event.*;
import javax.swing.*;
import javax.swing.plaf.*;
import javax.swing.plaf.metal.MetalLookAndFeel;
import javax.swing.plaf.metal.DefaultMetalTheme;

/**
 * This class reads theme descriptions from a GUIResourceBundle and uses them
 * to specify colors and fonts for the Metal look-and-feel.
 **/
public class ThemeManager {
    JFrame frame;                    // The frame which themes are applied to
    GUIResourceBundle resources;     // Properties describing the themes

    /**
     * Build a ThemeManager for the frame and resource bundle.  If there
     * is a default theme specified, apply it to the frame
     **/
    public ThemeManager(JFrame frame, GUIResourceBundle resources) {
        this.frame = frame;
        this.resources = resources;
        String defaultName = getDefaultThemeName();
        if (defaultName != null) setTheme(defaultName);
    }

    /** Look up the named theme, and apply it to the frame */
    public void setTheme(String themeName) {
        // Look up the theme in the resource bundle
        Theme theme = new Theme(resources, themeName);
        // Make it the current theme
        MetalLookAndFeel.setCurrentTheme(theme);
        // Re-apply the Metal look-and-feel to install new theme
        try { UIManager.setLookAndFeel(new MetalLookAndFeel()); }
        catch(UnsupportedLookAndFeelException e) {}
        // Propagate the new l&f across the entire component tree of the frame
        SwingUtilities.updateComponentTreeUI(frame);
    }

    /** Get the "display name" or label of the named theme */
    public String getDisplayName(String themeName) {
        return resources.getString(themeName + ".name", null);
    }

    /** Get the name of the default theme, or null */
    public String getDefaultThemeName() {
        return resources.getString("defaultTheme", null);
    }

    /**
     * Get the list of all known theme names.  The returned values are
     * theme property names, not theme display names.
     **/
    public String[] getAllThemeNames() {
        java.util.List names = resources.getStringList("themelist");
        return (String[]) names.toArray(new String[names.size()]);
    }
```

Example 10–28: ThemeManager.java (continued)

```java
/**
 * Get a JMenu that lists all known themes by display name and
 * installs any selected theme.
 **/
public JMenu getThemeMenu() {
    String[] names = getAllThemeNames();
    String defaultName = getDefaultThemeName();
    JMenu menu = new JMenu("Themes");
    ButtonGroup buttongroup = new ButtonGroup();
    for(int i = 0; i < names.length; i++) {
        final String themeName = names[i];
        String displayName = getDisplayName(themeName);
        JMenuItem item = menu.add(new JRadioButtonMenuItem(displayName));
        buttongroup.add(item);
        if (themeName.equals(defaultName)) item.setSelected(true);
        item.addActionListener(new ActionListener() {
                public void actionPerformed(ActionEvent event) {
                    setTheme(themeName);
                }
            });
    }
    return menu;
}


/**
 * This class extends the DefaultMetalTheme class to return Color and
 * Font values read from a GUIResourceBundle
 **/
public static class Theme extends DefaultMetalTheme {
    // These fields are the values returned by this Theme
    String displayName;
    FontUIResource controlFont, menuFont, smallFont;
    FontUIResource systemFont, userFont, titleFont;
    ColorUIResource primary1, primary2, primary3;
    ColorUIResource secondary1, secondary2, secondary3;

    /**
     * This constructor reads all the values it needs from the
     * GUIResourceBundle.  It uses intelligent defaults if properties
     * are not specified.
     **/
    public Theme(GUIResourceBundle resources, String name) {
        // Use this theme object to get default font values from
        DefaultMetalTheme defaultTheme = new DefaultMetalTheme();

        // Look up the display name of the theme
        displayName = resources.getString(name + ".name", null);

        // Look up the fonts for the theme
        Font control = resources.getFont(name + ".controlFont", null);
        Font menu = resources.getFont(name + ".menuFont", null);
        Font small = resources.getFont(name + ".smallFont", null);
        Font system = resources.getFont(name + ".systemFont", null);
        Font user = resources.getFont(name + ".userFont", null);
        Font title = resources.getFont(name + ".titleFont", null);

        // Convert fonts to FontUIResource, or get defaults
        if (control != null) controlFont = new FontUIResource(control);
```

Example 10–28: ThemeManager.java (continued)

```
        else controlFont = defaultTheme.getControlTextFont();
        if (menu != null) menuFont = new FontUIResource(menu);
        else menuFont = defaultTheme.getMenuTextFont();
        if (small != null) smallFont = new FontUIResource(small);
        else smallFont = defaultTheme.getSubTextFont();
        if (system != null) systemFont = new FontUIResource(system);
        else systemFont = defaultTheme.getSystemTextFont();
        if (user != null) userFont = new FontUIResource(user);
        else userFont = defaultTheme.getUserTextFont();
        if (title != null) titleFont = new FontUIResource(title);
        else titleFont = defaultTheme.getWindowTitleFont();

        // Look up primary and secondary colors
        Color primary = resources.getColor(name + ".primary", null);
        Color secondary = resources.getColor(name + ".secondary", null);

        // Derive all six colors from these two, using defaults if needed
        if (primary != null) primary1 = new ColorUIResource(primary);
        else primary1 = new ColorUIResource(102, 102, 153);
        primary2 = new ColorUIResource(primary1.brighter());
        primary3 = new ColorUIResource(primary2.brighter());
        if (secondary != null) secondary1 = new ColorUIResource(secondary);
        else secondary1 = new ColorUIResource(102, 102, 102);
        secondary2 = new ColorUIResource(secondary1.brighter());
        secondary3 = new ColorUIResource(secondary2.brighter());
    }

    // These methods override DefaultMetalTheme and return the property
    // values we looked up and computed for this theme
    public String getName() { return displayName; }
    public FontUIResource getControlTextFont() { return controlFont;}
    public FontUIResource getSystemTextFont() { return systemFont;}
    public FontUIResource getUserTextFont() { return userFont;}
    public FontUIResource getMenuTextFont() { return menuFont;}
    public FontUIResource getWindowTitleFont() { return titleFont;}
    public FontUIResource getSubTextFont() { return smallFont;}
    protected ColorUIResource getPrimary1() { return primary1; }
    protected ColorUIResource getPrimary2() { return primary2; }
    protected ColorUIResource getPrimary3() { return primary3; }
    protected ColorUIResource getSecondary1() { return secondary1; }
    protected ColorUIResource getSecondary2() { return secondary2; }
    protected ColorUIResource getSecondary3() { return secondary3; }
    }
}
```

Custom Components

Most examples in this chapter have been subclasses of JFrame, JPanel, or some other Swing component. In this sense, they have all been "custom components." The ItemChooser class is a particularly useful example of this kind of component. Most of these examples, however, have not handled their own low-level mouse and keyboard events or done their own drawing; they've relied on superclasses to handle low-level events and subcomponents to provide a visual appearance.

There is another kind of lower-level custom component, though; one that provides its own "look" by drawing itself with a Graphics object and its own "feel" by directly handling mouse and keyboard events that occur in it. The AppletMenuBar class, listed in Example 10-29, is a custom component of this type. As its name implies, this component can display a menubar in an applet. Most web browsers (at least at the time of this writing) do not have the Swing components preinstalled. So, for compatibility with these browsers, many applets are written using only AWT components. One of the shortcomings of the AWT is that only Frame objects can have menubars; the Applet class cannot display a java.awt.Menubar. Therefore, the AppletMenuBar component is a custom AWT component that simulates a menubar. It provides a paint() method that draws the menubar, primarily the menu labels, and defines low-level event handling methods that track the mouse, perform "rollover" effects, and popup menus (using the java.awt.Popup-Menu class) when appropriate. The AppletMenuBar class also includes an inner class named Demo that implements a demonstration applet.

In order to understand the AppletMenuBar component, it may help to see how the component might be used in an applet. The following lines show a simple init() method for an applet that uses the class:

```java
public void init() {
    AppletMenuBar menubar = new AppletMenuBar();   // Create the menubar
    menubar.setForeground(Color.black);            // Set properties on it
    menubar.setHighlightColor(Color.red);
    menubar.setFont(new Font("helvetica", Font.BOLD, 12));
    this.setLayout(new BorderLayout());
    this.add(menubar, BorderLayout.NORTH);         // Add it at the applet top

    // Create a couple of popup menus and add dummy items to them
    PopupMenu file = new PopupMenu();
    file.add("New..."); file.add("Open..."); file.add("Save As...");
    PopupMenu edit = new PopupMenu();
    edit.add("Cut"); edit.add("Copy"); edit.add("Paste");

    // Add the popup menus (with labels) to the menubar
    menubar.addMenu("File", file);
    menubar.addMenu("Edit", edit);
}
```

When you study AppletMenuBar, there are a number of things to notice. The paint() method is the heart of the component, as it does all of the drawing. The processMouseEvent() method, which handles all the mouse events, is equally important. Both methods override standard methods inherited from the Component class, and both rely on the measure() method, which precomputes the size and position of each of the menu labels. AppletMenuBar defines various property accessor methods, and many of the property setter methods respond to property changes by causing the menubar to redraw or remeasure itself. The other overridden methods, getPreferedSize(), getMinimumSize(), and isFocusTraversable(), all provide important information about the component that is used by the component's container. Finally, notice that AppletMenuBar does not fire any events or define event listener registration methods. The MenuItem objects in the popup menus do all the event handling, so there is simply no need for them here. Still, generating events is a common task for custom components, as we saw with ItemChooser.

By necessity, AppletMenuBar is an AWT component. Developing custom Swing components is similar, but there are a few key differences. For instance, Swing components draw themselves in the paintComponent() method, not the paint() method. If you want your custom Swing component to support pluggable look-and-feels, you have to define a javax.swing.plaf.ComponentUI for it. You can read more about custom Swing components at the end of Chapter 4 of *Java Foundation Classes in a Nutshell*. Finally, although you can use AppletMenuBar in Swing GUIs, you should not. First, there is no need. Second, its look-and-feel does not match that of other Swing components. And third, mixing "heavyweight" components such as this one with "lightweight" Swing components can cause layout and redisplay problems.

Example 10–29: AppletMenuBar.java

```java
package com.davidflanagan.examples.gui;
import java.awt.*;
import java.awt.event.*;
import java.util.Vector;

public class AppletMenuBar extends Panel {
    // Menubar contents
    Vector labels = new Vector();
    Vector menus = new Vector();

    // Properties
    Insets margins = new Insets(3, 10, 3, 10); // top, left, bottom, right
    int spacing = 10;               // Space between menu labels
    Color highlightColor;           // Rollover color for labels

    // internal stuff
    boolean remeasure = true;       // Whether the labels need to be remeasured
    int[] widths;                           // The width of each label
    int[] startPositions;                   // Where each label starts
    int ascent, descent;                    // Font metrics
    Dimension prefsize = new Dimension();   // How big do we want to be?
    int highlightedItem = -1;               // Which item is the mouse over?

    /**
     * Create a new component that simulates a menubar by displaying
     * the specified labels.  Whenever the user clicks the specified label,
     * popup the PopupMenu specified in the menus array.
     * Elements of the menus array may be a static PopupMenu object, or
     * a PopupMenuFactory object for dynamically creating menus.
     * Perhaps we'll also provide some other kind of constructor or factory
     * method that reads popup menus out of a config file.
     */
    public AppletMenuBar() {
        // We'd like these kinds of events to be delivered
        enableEvents(AWTEvent.MOUSE_EVENT_MASK |
                     AWTEvent.MOUSE_MOTION_EVENT_MASK);
    }

    /** Add a popup menu to the menubar */
    public void addMenu(String label, PopupMenu menu) {
        insertMenu(label, menu, -1);
    }

    /** Insert a popup menu into the menubar */
```

Example 10–29: AppletMenuBar.java (continued)

```java
public void insertMenu(String label, PopupMenu menu, int index) {
    if (index < 0) index += labels.size()+1;  // Position to put it at
    this.add(menu);                            // Popup belongs to us
    labels.insertElementAt(label, index);      // Remember the label
    menus.insertElementAt(menu, index);        // Remember the menu
    remeasure = true;                          // Remeasure everything
    invalidate();                              // Container must relayout
}

/** Property accessor methods for margins property */
public Insets getMargins() { return (Insets) margins.clone(); }
public void setMargins(Insets margins) {
    this.margins = margins;
    remeasure = true;
    invalidate();
}

/** Property accessor methods for spacing property */
public int getSpacing() { return spacing; }
public void setSpacing(int spacing) {
    if (this.spacing != spacing) {
        this.spacing = spacing;
        remeasure = true;
        invalidate();
    }
}

/** Accessor methods for highlightColor property */
public Color getHighlightColor() {
    if (highlightColor == null) return getForeground();
    else return highlightColor;
}
public void setHighlightColor(Color c) {
    if (highlightColor != c) {
        highlightColor = c;
        repaint();
    }
}

/** We override the setFont() method so we can remeasure */
public void setFont(Font f) {
    super.setFont(f);
    remeasure = true;
    invalidate();
}

/** Override these color property setter method so we can repaint */
public void setForeground(Color c) {
    super.setForeground(c);
    repaint();
}
public void setBackground(Color c) {
    super.setBackground(c);
    repaint();
}

/**
 * This method is called to draw tell the component to redraw itself.
```

Example 10-29: AppletMenuBar.java (continued)

```
 * If we were implementing a Swing component, we'd override
 * paintComponent() instead
 **/
public void paint(Graphics g) {
    if (remeasure) measure();   // Remeasure everything first, if needed

    // Figure out Y coordinate to draw at
    Dimension size = getSize();
    int baseline = size.height - margins.bottom - descent;
    // Set the font to draw with
    g.setFont(getFont());
    // Loop through the labels
    int nummenus = labels.size();
    for(int i = 0; i < nummenus; i++) {
        // Set the drawing color.  Highlight the current item
        if ((i == highlightedItem) && (highlightColor != null))
            g.setColor(getHighlightColor());
        else
            g.setColor(getForeground());

        // Draw the menu label at the position computed in measure()
        g.drawString((String)labels.elementAt(i),
                    startPositions[i], baseline);
    }

    // Now draw a groove at the bottom of the menubar.
    Color bg = getBackground();
    g.setColor(bg.darker());
    g.drawLine(0, size.height-2, size.width, size.height-2);
    g.setColor(bg.brighter());
    g.drawLine(0, size.height-1, size.width, size.height-1);
}

/** Called when a mouse event happens over the menubar */
protected void processMouseEvent(MouseEvent e) {
    int type = e.getID();               // What type of event?
    int item = findItemAt(e.getX());    // Over which menu label?

    if (type == MouseEvent.MOUSE_PRESSED) {
        // If it was a mouse down event, then pop up the menu
        if (item == -1) return;
        Dimension size = getSize();
        PopupMenu pm = (PopupMenu) menus.elementAt(item);
        if (pm != null) pm.show(this, startPositions[item]-3, size.height);

    }
    else if (type == MouseEvent.MOUSE_EXITED) {
        // If the mouse left the menubar, then unhighlight
        if (highlightedItem != -1) {
            highlightedItem = -1;
            if (highlightColor != null) repaint();
        }
    }
    else if ((type == MouseEvent.MOUSE_MOVED) ||
            (type == MouseEvent.MOUSE_ENTERED)) {
        // If the mouse moved, change the highlighted item, if necessary
        if (item != highlightedItem) {
            highlightedItem = item;
```

Example 10–29: AppletMenuBar.java (continued)

```
                    if (highlightColor != null) repaint();
            }
        }
    }


    /** This method is called when the mouse moves */
    protected void processMouseMotionEvent(MouseEvent e) {
        processMouseEvent(e);
    }


    /** This utility method converts an X coordinate to a menu label index */
    protected int findItemAt(int x) {
        // This could be a more efficient search...
        int nummenus = labels.size();
        int halfspace = spacing/2-1;
        int i;
        for(i = nummenus-1; i >= 0; i--) {
            if ((x >= startPositions[i]-halfspace) &&
                (x <= startPositions[i]+widths[i]+halfspace)) break;
        }
        return i;
    }



    /**
     * Measure the menu labels, and figure out their positions, so we
     * can determine when a click happens, and so we can redraw efficiently.
     **/
    protected void measure() {
        // Get information about the font
        FontMetrics fm = this.getFontMetrics(getFont());
        // Remember the basic font size
        ascent = fm.getAscent();
        descent = fm.getDescent();
        // Create arrays to hold the measurements and positions
        int nummenus = labels.size();
        widths = new int[nummenus];
        startPositions = new int[nummenus];

        // Measure the label strings and
        // figure out the starting position of each label
        int pos = margins.left;
        for(int i = 0; i < nummenus; i++) {
            startPositions[i] = pos;
            String label = (String)labels.elementAt(i);
            widths[i] = fm.stringWidth(label);
            pos += widths[i] + spacing;
        }

        // Compute our preferred size from this data
        prefsize.width = pos - spacing + margins.right;
        prefsize.height = ascent + descent + margins.top + margins.bottom;

        // We've don't need to be remeasured anymore.
        remeasure = false;
    }

    /**
```

Example 10-29: AppletMenuBar.java (continued)

```
 * These methods tell the container how big the menubar wants to be.
 *
 **/
public Dimension getMinimumSize() { return getPreferredSize(); }
public Dimension getPreferredSize() {
    if (remeasure) measure();
    return prefsize;
}
/** @deprecated Here for compatibility with Java 1.0 */
public Dimension minimumSize() { return getPreferredSize(); }
/** @deprecated Here for compatibility with Java 1.0 */
public Dimension preferredSize() { return getPreferredSize(); }

/**
 * This method is called when the underlying AWT component is created.
 * We can't measure ourselves (no font metrics) until this is called.
 **/
public void addNotify() {
    super.addNotify();
    measure();
}

/** This method tells the container not to give us keyboard focus */
public boolean isFocusTraversable() { return false; }
}
```

Exercises

10-1.   Take a look again at Figure 10-7. Write a class that produces a sample layout like GridBagLayoutPane, without using the GridBagLayout layout manager. You'll probably want to use BorderLayout and the Box container or BoxLayout layout manager.

10-2.   The ScribblePane2 class has a serious shortcoming: the scribbles are erased whenever the window is obscured and then uncovered. Modify ScribblePane2 so that it remembers the user's scribble. You need to modify the lineto() method so that in addition to drawing a line, it also stores the coordinates and color of the line (using a Vector or ArrayList, perhaps). JComponent calls its paintComponent() method whenever the component needs to be redrawn. Read the documentation for this method, then override it to redraw the scribble using the saved coordinates. Finally, you also need to modify the clear() method to work with this new system.

10-3.   The ItemChooser class allows items to be specified only when the component is created. Add methods that allow items to be added and removed. Make the methods work regardless of the presentation type in use.

10-4.   The Scribble application defines and uses a ColorAction class to allow the user to select the current drawing color. Add a LineWidthAction class that lets the user select the line width. To accomplish this, give the ScribblePane2 component a setLineWidth() method so that it can draw using wide lines. See java.awt.BasicStroke to learn how to draw with wide lines.

10-5.   One shortcoming of the FontChooser class is that when you call setSelectedFont(), the ItemChooser components are not updated to match the current font. Modify FontChooser so that it does update these selections. You'll probably want to modify ItemChooser so that, in addition to its setSelectedIndex() method, it also has setSelectedLabel() and setSelectedValue() methods that specify the selected item by label or by value.

10-6.   Modify the ShowComponent program to add a **Show Properties** ... command to the menu. When the user selects this menu item, the program should use the PropertyTable component (in a separate window) to display the list of properties defined by the currently displayed component. To enable this, you need to keep track of the displayed components, and you have to query the JTabbedPane to find which component is currently displayed.

        Once you can display the table of properties correctly, add a menu item to the property display window. This item, when selected, should find the selected row of the table (use getSelectedRow()), and then allow the user to set that property. Use one of the static methods of JOptionPane to display a dialog that allows the user to enter a property value (as a string), then parse that value and set the specified property.

10-7.   Modify ShowComponent again so that it has a **Containment Hierarchy** ... menu item. When the user selects this item, the program should use a ComponentTree component (in a separate window) to display the containment hierarchy of the currently displayed component.

10-8.   A common feature of web browsers is a **Go** menu that lists the last 10 or 15 URLs that have been visited and provides a quick way to revisit those sites. Add this feature to the WebBrowser class. Note that WebBrowser already tracks its browsing history. You need to add a **Go** menu to the JMenuBar that is read from the GUIResourceBundle. The contents of the **Go** menu depends on the current browsing history. One technique is to change the contents of the menu each time the browser visits a new page. Alternately, you can use a MenuListener object to receive notification just before the menu is popped up, and then, from the menuSelected() method of the listener, add the appropriate items to the menu.

10-9.   The GUIResourceBundle class and the ResourceParser extension interface provide a powerful mechanism for describing a GUI in a properties file. Implement more ResourceParser classes to support other resource types. In particular, write parsers for the ImageIcon and KeyStroke classes; support for these two types is required to fully support the ActionParser class.

10-10. Modify the ShowComponent class to use the ThemeManager class (with an appropriate properties file) and the **Themes** menu it can create. Ideally, you should make the **Themes** menu a submenu of the **Look and Feel** menu the program already displays.

10-11. Modify the `AppletMenuBar` component so that, in addition to displaying menus, it can also display buttons (i.e., make it work as a combination menubar/toolbar). Add an `addCommand()` method that is analogous to the `addMenu()` method. Instead of taking a string and a `PopupMenu`, this new method should take a string label and a `ActionListener` object. If the user clicks on the specified label, the component should call the `actionPerformed()` method of the specified listener. When testing the class, recall that the `Command` class from Chapter 8 implements the `ActionListener` interface.

CHAPTER 11

Graphics

Java 1.0 and 1.1 provided rudimentary graphics capabilities through the java.awt.Graphics class and associated classes, such as java.awt.Color and java.awt.Font. In Java 1.2 and later, the Java 2D API provides state-of-the-art, two-dimensional graphics facilities using the java.awt.Graphics2D class (a subclass of Graphics) and associated classes, such as java.awt.BasicStroke, java.awt.GradientPaint, java.awt.TexturePaint, java.awt.AffineTransform, and java.awt.AlphaComposite.

This chapter demonstrates using all these classes; it shows how you can draw graphics with and without the Java 2D API. The key class for all graphics operations is Graphics (or in the Java 2D API, its subclass, Graphics2D). The purpose of this class is threefold:

It defines the drawing surface
A Graphics object can represent the on-screen drawing area within an AWT (or Swing) component. It can also represent an off-screen image you can draw into or a piece of paper to be printed on a printer.

It defines drawing methods
All primitive graphics operations, such as drawing lines, filling shapes, and displaying text, are performed using methods of the Graphics class.

It defines attributes used by the drawing methods
Various methods of the Graphics class can set the font, color, clipping region, and other attributes used when performing graphics operations, such as drawing lines, filling shapes, and displaying text. The values of these graphical attributes are often instances of AWT classes, such as Color, Font, Stroke, AffineTransform, and so on.

The graphics capabilities of Java are intimately wed with the Abstract Windowing Toolkit (AWT). As such, the Graphics and Graphics2D classes are part of the java.awt package, as are all the associated classes that define graphical attributes. As we discussed in Chapter 10, *Graphical User Interfaces*, the central class of the AWT is java.awt.Component. Component is the basic building block of all graphical user interfaces in Java. A Graphics object represents a drawing surface, but Java doesn't allow you to draw directly to the computer screen. Instead, it restricts you to drawing within the confines of a Component, using a Graphics object that represents the drawing surface of that component. Thus, to do graphics in Java, you must have a Component (or a java.applet.Applet, a Component subclass) to draw into. Drawing is usually done by subclassing a specific component and defining a paint() method (or a paintComponent() method, for Swing components). The examples in this chapter have been structured to focus on the mechanics of drawing, rather than the mechanics of GUI creation, but you will still see some code that handles GUI-related tasks.

Graphics Before Java 1.2

Prior to the introduction of the Java 2D API in Java 1.2, the java.awt.Graphics class provided only rudimentary graphics capabilities. It allowed you to draw lines, draw and fill simple shapes, display text, and draw images and perform basic image manipulation. You could specify a drawing color, a font, a clipping region, and the location of the origin. Notably missing, however, was the ability to specify a line width or rotate or scale drawings. Example 11-1 is a listing of the Graphics-Sampler applet that demonstrates all the pre-Java 1.2 basic drawing primitives and attributes. The output of this applet is shown in Figure 11-1.

If you have read Chapter 15, *Applets*, you should understand the structure of this code. This is a very simple applet, however, so you should be able to understand it even before you read that chapter. The init() method is called once, when the applet first starts up, and performs one-time initialization. The paint() method displays the content of the applet. The Graphics object passed to this method represents the drawing surface of the applet; it allows you to draw anywhere within the bounds of the Applet object. tile() and centerText() are utility methods defined for the convenience of the paint() method. They demonstrate important graphics drawing techniques, but have nothing to do with the applet API.

It is important to understand that the paint() method may be called many times. The drawing done in this method doesn't necessarily persist: if the applet is covered by another window and then uncovered, the graphics contained in the applet may well be lost (whether this actually happens depends on the underlying operating system and other factors.) In order to restore the graphics, the system invokes the paint() method again. Thus, all drawing should be done in the paint() method. If you draw anything in the init() method, those graphics may be erased and never reappear. (This is one of the serious shortcomings of Example 10-11 and related examples in Chapter 10.)

Example 11-1: GraphicsSampler.java

```
package com.davidflanagan.examples.graphics;
import java.applet.*;
import java.awt.*;

/**
 * An applet that demonstrates most of the graphics primitives in
 * java.awt.Graphics.
 **/
public class GraphicsSampler extends Applet {
```

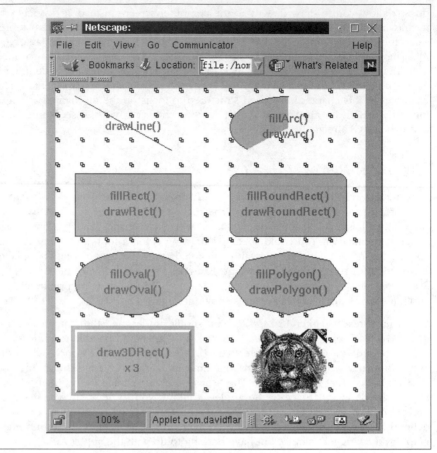

Figure 11-1. A sampling of graphics primitives

Example 11-1: GraphicsSampler.java (continued)

```java
    Color fill, outline, textcolor;  // The various colors we use
    Font font;                       // The font we use for text
    FontMetrics metrics;             // Information about font size
    Image image, background;         // Some images we draw with

    // This method is called when the applet is first created.
    // It performs initialization, such as creating the resources
    // (graphics attribute values) used by the paint() method.
    public void init() {
        // Initialize color resources.  Note the use of the Color() constructor
        // and the use of pre-defined color constants.
        fill = new Color(200, 200, 200); // Equal red, green, and blue == gray
        outline = Color.blue;            // Same as new Color(0, 0, 255)
        textcolor = Color.red;           // Same as new Color(255, 0, 0)

        // Create a font for use in the paint() method.  Get its metrics, too.
        font = new Font("sansserif", Font.BOLD, 14);
        metrics = this.getFontMetrics(font);
```

Example 11-1: GraphicsSampler.java (continued)

```
        // Load some Image objects for use in the paint() method.
        image = this.getImage(this.getDocumentBase(), "tiger.gif");
        background = this.getImage(this.getDocumentBase(), "background.gif");

        // Set a property that tells the applet its background color
        this.setBackground(Color.lightGray);
    }

    // This method is called whenever the applet needs to be drawn or redrawn
    public void paint(Graphics g) {
        g.setFont(font);  // Specify the font we'll be using throughout

        // Draw a background by tiling an image tile() is defined below
        tile(g, this, background);

        // Draw a line
        g.setColor(outline);              // Specify the drawing color
        g.drawLine(25, 10, 150, 80);      // Draw a line from (25,10) to (150,80)
        // Draw some text.  See the centerText() method below.
        centerText("drawLine()", null, g, textcolor, 25, 10, 150, 80);

        // Draw and fill an arc
        g.setColor(fill);
        g.fillArc(225, 10, 150, 80, 90, 135);
        g.setColor(outline);
        g.drawArc(225, 10, 150, 80, 90, 135);
        centerText("fillArc()", "drawArc()", g, textcolor,225,10,150,80);

        // Draw and fill a rectangle
        g.setColor(fill);
        g.fillRect(25, 110, 150, 80);
        g.setColor(outline);
        g.drawRect(25, 110, 150, 80);
        centerText("fillRect()", "drawRect()", g, textcolor, 25, 110, 150, 80);

        // Draw and fill a rounded rectangle
        g.setColor(fill);
        g.fillRoundRect(225, 110, 150, 80, 20, 20);
        g.setColor(outline);
        g.drawRoundRect(225, 110, 150, 80, 20, 20);
        centerText("fillRoundRect()", "drawRoundRect()", g, textcolor,
                   225, 110, 150, 80);

        // Draw and fill an oval
        g.setColor(fill);
        g.fillOval(25, 210, 150, 80);
        g.setColor(outline);
        g.drawOval(25, 210, 150, 80);
        centerText("fillOval()", "drawOval()", g, textcolor, 25, 210, 150, 80);

        // Define an octagon using arrays of X and Y coordinates
        int numpoints = 8;
        int[] xpoints = new int[numpoints+1];
        int[] ypoints = new int[numpoints+1];
        for(int i=0; i < numpoints; i++) {
            double angle = 2*Math.PI * i / numpoints;
            xpoints[i] = (int)(300 + 75*Math.cos(angle));
            ypoints[i] = (int)(250 - 40*Math.sin(angle));
```

Example 11-1: GraphicsSampler.java (continued)

```
        }

        // Draw and fill the polygon
        g.setColor(fill);
        g.fillPolygon(xpoints, ypoints, numpoints);
        g.setColor(outline);
        g.drawPolygon(xpoints, ypoints, numpoints);
        centerText("fillPolygon()", "drawPolygon()", g, textcolor,
                   225, 210, 150, 80);

        // Draw a 3D rectangle (clear an area for it first)
        g.setColor(fill);
        g.fillRect(20, 305, 160, 90);
        g.draw3DRect(25, 310, 150, 80, true);
        g.draw3DRect(26, 311, 148, 78, true);
        g.draw3DRect(27, 312, 146, 76, true);
        centerText("draw3DRect()", "x 3", g, textcolor, 25, 310, 150, 80);

        // Draw an image (centered within an area)
        int w = image.getWidth(this);
        int h = image.getHeight(this);
        g.drawImage(image, 225 + (150-w)/2, 310 + (80-h)/2, this);
        centerText("drawImage()", null, g, textcolor,  225, 310, 150, 80);
    }

    // Utility method to tile an image on the background of the component
    protected void tile(Graphics g, Component c, Image i) {
        // Use bounds() instead of getBounds() if you want
        // compatibility with Java 1.0 and old browsers like Netscape 3
        Rectangle r = c.getBounds();              // How big is the component?
        int iw = i.getWidth(c);                   // How big is the image?
        int ih = i.getHeight(c);
        if ((iw <= 0) || (ih <= 0)) return;
        for(int x=0; x < r.width; x += iw)        // Loop horizontally
            for(int y=0; y < r.height; y += ih)   // Loop vertically
                g.drawImage(i, x, y, c);          // Draw the image
    }

    // Utility method to center two lines of text in a rectangle.
    // Relies on the FontMetrics obtained in the init() method.
    protected void centerText(String s1, String s2, Graphics g, Color c,
                              int x, int y, int w, int h)
    {
        int height = metrics.getHeight();   // How tall is the font?
        int ascent = metrics.getAscent();   // Where is the font baseline?
        int width1=0, width2 = 0, x0=0, x1=0, y0=0, y1=0;
        width1 = metrics.stringWidth(s1);   // How wide are the strings?
        if (s2 != null) width2 = metrics.stringWidth(s2);
        x0 = x + (w - width1)/2;            // Center the strings horizontally
        x1 = x + (w - width2)/2;
        if (s2 == null)                     // Center one string vertically
            y0 = y + (h - height)/2 + ascent;
        else {                              // Center two strings vertically
            y0 = y + (h - (int)(height * 2.2))/2 + ascent;
            y1 = y0 + (int)(height * 1.2);
        }
        g.setColor(c);                     // Set the color
        g.drawString(s1, x0, y0);          // Draw the strings
```

Example 11-1: GraphicsSampler.java (continued)

```
        if (s2 != null) g.drawString(s2, x1, y1);
    }
}
```

Running the Applet

If you have not yet read Chapter 15, you may not know how to run the applet listed in Example 11-1. All you need to do is include the following <applet> tag in an HTML file, place the file in the same directory as the GraphicsSampler class file, and load the HTML file into a web browser:

```
<applet code="com/davidflanagan/examples/graphics/GraphicsSampler.class"
        codebase="../../../.."
        width=400 height=400>
</applet>
```

You'll find this tag in a file named *GraphicsSampler.html* in this book's online example archive.

Note that GraphicsSampler calls the Java 1.1 method getBounds(), so you must use a browser that supports Java 1.1, such as Netscape Navigator 4.0 or later. You can also use the *appletviewer* application that comes with the Java SDK:

```
% appletviewer GraphicsSampler.html
```

Fonts

To enhance cross-platform portability, Java 1.0 and 1.1 defined only a handful of fonts (as we'll see later, Java 1.2 allows you to use any font available on the underlying system). In Java 1.0, these fonts were TimesRoman, Helvetica, and Courier. In Java 1.1, the fonts were given preferred logical names: Serif, SansSerif, and Monospaced. Each font is available in four styles and any number of sizes. Example 11-2 shows the listing of the FontList applet, which displays each of the standard fonts in each of the available styles. Its output is shown in Figure 11-2.

Example 11-2: FontList.java

```
package com.davidflanagan.examples.graphics;
import java.applet.*;
import java.awt.*;

/**
 * An applet that displays the standard fonts and styles available in Java 1.1
 **/
public class FontList extends Applet {
    // The available font families
    String[] families = {"Serif",         // "TimesRoman" in Java 1.0
                         "SansSerif",      // "Helvetica" in Java 1.0
                         "Monospaced"};    // "Courier" in Java 1.0

    // The available font styles and names for each one
    int[] styles = {Font.PLAIN, Font.ITALIC, Font.BOLD, Font.ITALIC+Font.BOLD};
    String[] stylenames = {"Plain", "Italic", "Bold", "Bold Italic"};
```

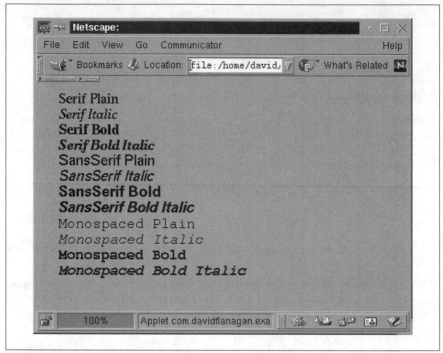

Figure 11-2. The standard fonts and styles

Example 11-2: FontList.java (continued)

```
// Draw the applet.
public void paint(Graphics g) {
    for(int f=0; f < families.length; f++) {          // for each family
        for(int s = 0; s < styles.length; s++) {       // for each style
            Font font = new Font(families[f],styles[s],18); // create font
            g.setFont(font);                              // set font
            String name = families[f] + " " +stylenames[s]; // create name
            g.drawString(name, 20, (f*4 + s + 1) * 20);   // display name
        }
    }
}
}
```

Colors

A color in Java is represented by the java.awt.Color class. The Color class defines a number of constants that refer to predefined Color objects for commonly used colors, such as Color.black and Color.white. You can also create your own custom Color object by specifying the red, green, and blue components of the color. These components may be specified as integers between 0 and 255 or as float values between 0.0 and 1.0. Additionally, the static getHSBColor() method allows you to create a Color object based on hue, saturation, and brightness values. As of Java 1.1, the java.awt.SystemColor subclass of Color defines a number of constant SystemColor objects that represent standard colors in the system desktop palette. You can use these colors to make your application match the desktop color scheme.

Example 11-3 lists the `ColorGradient` applet, which uses `Color` objects to produce the color gradient shown in Figure 11-3. This applet uses applet parameters in the HTML file to specify the starting and ending colors of the gradient. You can use the applet with HTML tags like the following:

```
<applet code="com/davidflanagan/examples/graphics/ColorGradient.class"
        codebase="../../../../" width=525 height=150>
    <param name="startColor" value="#a06060"> <!-- light red -->
    <param name="endColor" value="#ffffff">   <!-- white -->
</applet>
```

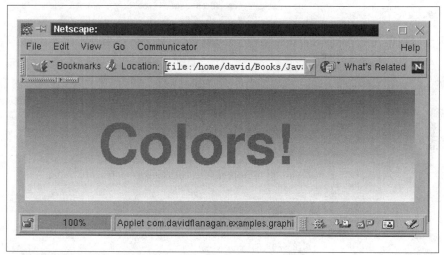

Figure 11-3. A color gradient

Example 11-3: ColorGradient.java

```
package com.davidflanagan.examples.graphics;
import java.applet.*;
import java.awt.*;

/** An applet that demonstrates the Color class */
public class ColorGradient extends Applet {
    Color startColor, endColor;   // Start and end color of the gradient
    Font bigFont;                 // A font we'll use

    /**
     * Get the gradient start and end colors as applet parameter values, and
     * parse them using Color.decode().  If they are malformed, use white.
     **/
    public void init() {
        try {
            startColor = Color.decode(getParameter("startColor"));
            endColor = Color.decode(getParameter("endColor"));
        }
        catch (NumberFormatException e) {
            startColor = endColor = Color.white;
        }
```

Example 11–3: ColorGradient.java (continued)

```java
        bigFont = new Font("Helvetica", Font.BOLD, 72);
    }

    /** Draw the applet.  The interesting code is in fillGradient() below */
    public void paint(Graphics g) {
        fillGradient(this, g, startColor, endColor);  // display the gradient
        g.setFont(bigFont);                           // set a font
        g.setColor(new Color(100, 100, 200));         // light blue
        g.drawString("Colors!", 100, 100);            // draw something interesting
    }

    /**
     * Draw a color gradient from the top of the specified component to the
     * bottom.  Start with the start color and change smoothly to the end
     **/
    public void fillGradient(Component c, Graphics g, Color start, Color end) {
        Rectangle bounds = this.getBounds();  // How big is the component?
        // Get the red, green, and blue components of the start and end
        // colors as floats between 0.0 and 1.0.  Note that the Color class
        // also works with int values between 0 and 255
        float r1 = start.getRed()/255.0f;
        float g1 = start.getGreen()/255.0f;
        float b1 = start.getBlue()/255.0f;
        float r2 = end.getRed()/255.0f;
        float g2 = end.getGreen()/255.0f;
        float b2 = end.getBlue()/255.0f;
        // Figure out how much each component should change at each y value
        float dr = (r2-r1)/bounds.height;
        float dg = (g2-g1)/bounds.height;
        float db = (b2-b1)/bounds.height;

        // Now loop once for each row of pixels in the component
        for(int y = 0; y < bounds.height; y++) {
            g.setColor(new Color(r1, g1, b1));     // Set the color of the row
            g.drawLine(0, y, bounds.width-1, y);   // Draw the row
            r1 += dr; g1 += dg; b1 += db;          // Increment color components
        }
    }
}
```

Simple Animation

Animation is nothing more than the rapid drawing of a graphic, with small changes between "frames," so the object being drawn appears to move. Example 11-4 shows the listing for an applet that performs a simple animation: it moves a red circle around the screen. The applet uses a Thread object to trigger the redraws. The technique used here is quite simple: when you run the applet, you may notice that it flickers as the ball moves.

Later in this chapter, I'll show you another animation example that uses more advanced techniques to prevent flickering and produce smoother animation.

Example 11-4: BouncingCircle.java

```java
package com.davidflanagan.examples.graphics;
import java.applet.*;
import java.awt.*;

/** An applet that displays a simple animation */
public class BouncingCircle extends Applet implements Runnable {
    int x = 150, y = 50, r = 50;  // Position and radius of the circle
    int dx = 11, dy = 7;          // Trajectory of circle
    Thread animator;              // The thread that performs the animation
    volatile boolean pleaseStop;  // A flag to ask the thread to stop

    /** This method simply draws the circle at its current position */
    public void paint(Graphics g) {
        g.setColor(Color.red);
        g.fillOval(x-r, y-r, r*2, r*2);
    }

    /**
     * This method moves (and bounces) the circle and then requests a redraw.
     * The animator thread calls this method periodically.
     **/
    public void animate() {
        // Bounce if we've hit an edge.
        Rectangle bounds = getBounds();
        if ((x - r + dx < 0) || (x + r + dx > bounds.width)) dx = -dx;
        if ((y - r + dy < 0) || (y + r + dy > bounds.height)) dy = -dy;

        // Move the circle.
        x += dx;   y += dy;

        // Ask the browser to call our paint() method to draw the circle
        // at its new position.
        repaint();
    }

    /**
     * This method is from the Runnable interface.  It is the body of the
     * thread that performs the animation.  The thread itself is created
     * and started in the start() method.
     **/
    public void run() {
        while(!pleaseStop) {                    // Loop until we're asked to stop
            animate();                          // Update and request redraw
            try { Thread.sleep(100); }          // Wait 100 milliseconds
            catch(InterruptedException e) {} // Ignore interruptions
        }
    }

    /** Start animating when the browser starts the applet */
    public void start() {
        animator = new Thread(this);   // Create a thread
        pleaseStop = false;            // Don't ask it to stop now
        animator.start();              // Start the thread.
        // The thread that called start now returns to its caller.
        // Meanwhile, the new animator thread has called the run() method
    }

    /** Stop animating when the browser stops the applet */
```

Example 11-4: BouncingCircle.java (continued)

```
    public void stop() {
        // Set the flag that causes the run() method to end
        pleaseStop = true;
    }
}
```

The Java 2D API

We now turn to the Java 2D API, which is available in Java 1.2 and later. Features of this API include:

- The `Graphics2D` class, which is a subclass of `Graphics` that defines additional graphics primitives and attributes.

- The `Shape` interface, which Java 2D uses to define many graphics primitives and other operations. The `java.awt.geom` package contains a number of useful implementations of `Shape`.

- The `Stroke` interface, which describes how lines are drawn (or stroked). The `BasicStroke` class implements this interface and supports the drawing of wide and dashed lines.

- The `Paint` interface, which describes how shapes are filled. The `Gradient-Paint` implementation allows filling with color gradients, while `TexturePaint` supports tiling with images. Also, as of Java 1.2, the `Color` class implements the `Paint` interface, to allow shapes to be filled with a solid color.

- The `Composite` interface, which defines how colors being drawn are combined with the colors already on the drawing surface. The `AlphaComposite` class allows colors to be combined based on the rules of alpha transparency. The `Color` class also has new constructors and methods that support translucent colors.

- The `RenderingHints` class, which allows an application to request particular types of drawing, such as antialiased drawing. Antialiasing uses transparent colors and compositing to smooth the edges of text and other shapes, preventing "jaggies."

- The `java.awt.geom.AffineTransform` class, which defines coordinate-system transformations and allows shapes (and entire coordinate systems) to be translated, scaled, rotated, and sheared.

  Because `AffineTransform` allows coordinate-system transformations, including scaling, the Java 2D API distinguishes between the coordinate system of the device (i.e., device space) and the (possibly) transformed user coordinate system (i.e., user space). Coordinates in user space can be specified using `float` and `double` values, and graphics drawn using Java 2D are resolution-independent.

In addition, in Java 1.2 and later, your applications are no longer restricted to using a fixed set of logical fonts; you can now use any font installed on the system. Finally, the Java 2D API includes an easy-to-use image-processing API.

The rest of this chapter is devoted to examples that demonstrate these features of the Java 2D API. Most of the examples are implementations of the GraphicsExample interface, which is shown in Example 11-5.

Example 11-5: GraphicsExample.java

```
package com.davidflanagan.examples.graphics;
import java.awt.*;

/**
 * This interface defines the methods that must be implemented by an
 * object that is to be displayed by the GraphicsExampleFrame object
 */
public interface GraphicsExample {
    public String getName();                    // Return the example name
    public int getWidth();                      // Return its width
    public int getHeight();                     // Return its height
    public void draw(Graphics2D g, Component c); // Draw the example
}
```

You can run these examples using the GraphicsExampleFrame frame program, which is shown at the end of the chapter. This program creates a simple GUI, instantiates the classes listed on the command line, and displays them in a window. For example, to display the Shapes example we'll see in the next section, you can use GraphicsExampleFrame as follows:

```
% java com.davidflanagan.examples.graphics.GraphicsExampleFrame Shapes
```

Many of the figures shown in the chapter are drawn at high resolution; they are not typical screenshots of a running program. GraphicsExampleFrame includes printing functionality that generated these figures. Even though GraphicsExample-Frame doesn't do any graphics drawing of its own and is therefore more of an example of Java's printing capabilities, it is still listed in Example 11-18 in this chapter.

Drawing and Filling Shapes

Example 11-6 lists a GraphicsExample implementation that shows how various Shape objects can be defined, drawn, and filled. The example produces the output shown in Figure 11-4. Although the Java 2D API allows basic shapes to be drawn and filled using the methods demonstrated in Example 11-1, this example uses a different approach. It defines each shape as a Shape object, using various classes, mostly from java.awt.geom.

Each Shape is drawn using the draw() method of the Graphics2D class and filled using the fill() method. Note that each Shape object is defined with one corner at (or near) the origin, rather than at the location where it is displayed on the screen. This creates position-independent objects that can easily be reused. To draw the shapes at particular locations, the example uses the translate() method of Graphics2D to move the origin of the coordinate system. Finally, the call to set-Stroke() specifies that drawing be done with a two-pixel-wide line, while the call to setRenderingHint() requests that drawing be done using antialiasing.

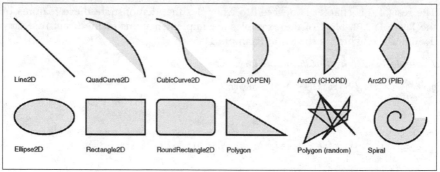

Figure 11-4. Drawing and filling shapes with the Java 2D API

Example 11-6: Shapes.java

```java
package com.davidflanagan.examples.graphics;
import java.awt.*;
import java.awt.geom.*;
import java.awt.font.*;
import java.awt.image.*;

/** A demonstration of Java2D shapes */
public class Shapes implements GraphicsExample {
    static final int WIDTH = 725, HEIGHT = 250;    // Size of our example
    public String getName() {return "Shapes";}      // From GraphicsExample
    public int getWidth() { return WIDTH; }          // From GraphicsExample
    public int getHeight() { return HEIGHT; }        // From GraphicsExample

    Shape[] shapes = new Shape[] {
        // A straight line segment
        new Line2D.Float(0, 0, 100, 100),
        // A quadratic bezier curve.  Two end points and one control point
        new QuadCurve2D.Float(0, 0, 80, 15, 100, 100),
        // A cubic bezier curve.  Two end points and two control points
        new CubicCurve2D.Float(0, 0, 80, 15, 10, 90, 100, 100),
        // A 120 degree portion of an ellipse
        new Arc2D.Float(-30, 0, 100, 100, 60, -120, Arc2D.OPEN),
        // A 120 degree portion of an ellipse, closed with a chord
        new Arc2D.Float(-30, 0, 100, 100, 60, -120, Arc2D.CHORD),
        // A 120 degree pie slice of an ellipse
        new Arc2D.Float(-30, 0, 100, 100, 60, -120, Arc2D.PIE),
        // An ellipse
        new Ellipse2D.Float(0, 20, 100, 60),
        // A rectangle
        new Rectangle2D.Float(0, 20, 100, 60),
        // A rectangle with rounded corners
        new RoundRectangle2D.Float(0, 20, 100, 60, 15, 15),
        // A triangle
        new Polygon(new int[] { 0, 0, 100 }, new int[] {20, 80, 80}, 3),
        // A random polygon, initialized in code below
        null,
        // A spiral: an instance of a custom Shape implementation
        new Spiral(50, 50, 5, 0, 50, 4*Math.PI),
    };

    {  // Initialize the null shape above as a Polygon with random points
        Polygon p = new Polygon();
```

Example 11–6: Shapes.java (continued)

```
        for(int i = 0; i < 10; i++)
            p.addPoint((int)(100*Math.random()), (int)(100*Math.random()));
        shapes[10] = p;
    }

    // These are the labels for each of the shapes
    String[] labels = new String[] {
        "Line2D", "QuadCurve2D", "CubicCurve2D", "Arc2D (OPEN)",
        "Arc2D (CHORD)", "Arc2D (PIE)", "Ellipse2D", "Rectangle2D",
        "RoundRectangle2D", "Polygon", "Polygon (random)", "Spiral"
    };

    /** Draw the example */
    public void draw(Graphics2D g, Component c) {
        // Set basic drawing attributes
        g.setFont(new Font("SansSerif", Font.PLAIN, 10));     // select font
        g.setStroke(new BasicStroke(2.0f));                   // 2 pixel lines
        g.setRenderingHint(RenderingHints.KEY_ANTIALIASING,   // antialiasing
                        RenderingHints.VALUE_ANTIALIAS_ON);
        g.translate(10, 10);                                  // margins

        // Loop through each shape
        for(int i = 0; i < shapes.length; i++) {
            g.setColor(Color.yellow);           // Set a color
            g.fill(shapes[i]);                  // Fill the shape with it
            g.setColor(Color.black);            // Switch to black
            g.draw(shapes[i]);                  // Outline the shape with it
            g.drawString(labels[i], 0, 110);    // Label the shape
            g.translate(120, 0);                // Move over for next shape
            if (i % 6 == 5) g.translate(-6*120, 120);  // Move down after 6
        }
    }
}
```

Transforms

The AffineTransform class can transform a shape (or coordinate system) by translating, scaling, rotating, or shearing it, using any combination of these individual transformation types. Figure 11-5 illustrates the results of various types of coordinate-system transformations on the appearance of one shape, drawn multiple times. Example 11-7 shows the Java code that generates the figure.

An *affine transformation* is a linear transformation that has two important properties: all straight lines remain straight, and all parallel lines remain parallel. The AffineTransform class can perform a great variety of transformations, but it can't produce nonlinear effects, such as distorting a figure as through a fisheye lens. That kind of effect can be achieved only with image-processing techniques. For a further discussion of transformations and of the linear algebra behind the Affine-Transform class, see Chapter 4 of *Java Foundation Classes in a Nutshell*.

Example 11–7: Transforms.java

```
package com.davidflanagan.examples.graphics;
import java.awt.*;
import java.awt.geom.*;
```

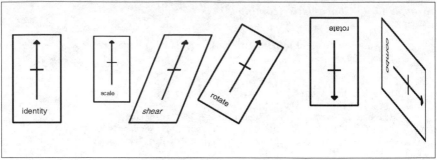

Figure 11–5. Transformed shapes

Example 11–7: Transforms.java (continued)

```java
/** A demonstration of Java2D transformations */
public class Transforms implements GraphicsExample {
    public String getName() { return "Transforms"; } // From GraphicsExample
    public int getWidth() { return 750; }             // From GraphicsExample
    public int getHeight() { return 250; }            // From GraphicsExample

    Shape shape;                    // The shape to draw
    AffineTransform[] transforms;   // The ways to transform it
    String[] transformLabels;       // Labels for each transform

    /**
     * This constructor sets up the Shape and AffineTransform objects we need
     **/
    public Transforms() {
        GeneralPath path = new GeneralPath();   // Create a shape to draw
        path.append(new Line2D.Float(0.0f, 0.0f, 0.0f, 100.0f), false);
        path.append(new Line2D.Float(-10.0f, 50.0f, 10.0f, 50.0f), false);
        path.append(new Polygon(new int[] { -5, 0, 5 },
                                new int[] { 5, 0, 5 }, 3), false);
        this.shape = path;  // Remember this shape

        // Set up some transforms to alter the shape
        this.transforms = new AffineTransform[6];
        // 1) the identity transform
        transforms[0] = new AffineTransform();
        // 2) A scale tranform: 3/4 size
        transforms[1] = AffineTransform.getScaleInstance(0.75, 0.75);
        // 3) A shearing transform
        transforms[2] = AffineTransform.getShearInstance(-0.4, 0.0);
        // 4) A 30 degree clockwise rotation about the origin of the shape
        transforms[3] = AffineTransform.getRotateInstance(Math.PI*2/12);
        // 5) A 180 degree rotation about the midpoint of the shape
        transforms[4] = AffineTransform.getRotateInstance(Math.PI, 0.0, 50.0);
        // 6) A combination transform
        transforms[5] = AffineTransform.getScaleInstance(0.5, 1.5);
        transforms[5].shear(0.0, 0.4);
        transforms[5].rotate(Math.PI/2, 0.0, 50.0);  // 90 degrees

        // Define names for the transforms
        transformLabels = new String[] {
            "identity", "scale", "shear", "rotate", "rotate", "combo"
        };
    }
```

Example 11–7: Transforms.java (continued)

```
/** Draw the defined shape and label, using each transform */
public void draw(Graphics2D g, Component c) {
    // Define basic drawing attributes
    g.setColor(Color.black);                                    // black
    g.setStroke(new BasicStroke(2.0f, BasicStroke.CAP_SQUARE,   // 2-pixel
                                BasicStroke.JOIN_BEVEL));
    g.setRenderingHint(RenderingHints.KEY_ANTIALIASING,         // antialias
                       RenderingHints.VALUE_ANTIALIAS_ON);

    // Now draw the shape once using each of the transforms we've defined
    for(int i = 0; i < transforms.length; i++) {
        AffineTransform save = g.getTransform();    // save current state
        g.translate(i*125 + 50, 50);                // move origin
        g.transform(transforms[i]);                 // apply transform
        g.draw(shape);                              // draw shape
        g.drawString(transformLabels[i], -25, 125); // draw label
        g.drawRect(-40, -10, 80, 150);              // draw box
        g.setTransform(save);                       // restore transform
    }
}
}
```

Line Styles with BasicStroke

In the last couple of examples, we've used the BasicStroke class to draw lines that are wider than the one-pixel lines supported by the Graphics class. Wide lines are more complicated than thin lines, however, so BasicStroke allows you to specify other line attributes as well: the *cap style* of a line specifies how the end-points of lines look, and the *join style* specifies how the corners, or vertices, of shapes look. These style options for endpoints and vertices are shown in Figure 11-6. The figure also illustrates the use of a dot-dashed patterned line, which is another feature of BasicStroke. The figure was produced using the code listed in Example 11-8, which demonstrates how to use BasicStroke to draw wide lines with a variety of cap and join styles and to draw patterned lines.

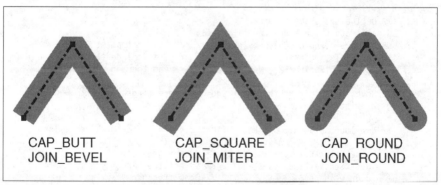

Figure 11–6. Line styles with BasicStroke

Example 11-8: LineStyles.java

```java
package com.davidflanagan.examples.graphics;
import java.awt.*;
import java.awt.geom.*;

/** A demonstration of Java2D line styles */
public class LineStyles implements GraphicsExample {
    public String getName() { return "LineStyles"; }  // From GraphicsExample
    public int getWidth() { return 450; }              // From GraphicsExample
    public int getHeight() { return 180; }             // From GraphicsExample

    int[] xpoints = new int[] { 0, 50, 100 };  // X coordinates of our shape
    int[] ypoints = new int[] { 75, 0, 75 };   // Y coordinates of our shape

    // Here are three different line styles we will demonstrate
    // They are thick lines with different cap and join styles
    Stroke[] linestyles = new Stroke[] {
        new BasicStroke(25.0f, BasicStroke.CAP_BUTT, BasicStroke.JOIN_BEVEL),
        new BasicStroke(25.0f, BasicStroke.CAP_SQUARE, BasicStroke.JOIN_MITER),
        new BasicStroke(25.0f, BasicStroke.CAP_ROUND, BasicStroke.JOIN_ROUND),
    };

    // Another line style: a 2 pixel-wide dot-dashed line
    Stroke thindashed = new BasicStroke(2.0f,  // line width
        /* cap style */                BasicStroke.CAP_BUTT,
        /* join style, miter limit */  BasicStroke.JOIN_BEVEL, 1.0f,
        /* the dash pattern */         new float[] {8.0f, 3.0f, 2.0f, 3.0f},
        /* the dash phase */           0.0f);   /* on 8, off 3, on 2, off 3 */

    // Labels to appear in the diagram, and the font to use to display them.
    Font font = new Font("Helvetica", Font.BOLD, 12);
    String[] capNames = new String[] {"CAP_BUTT", "CAP_SQUARE","CAP_ROUND"};
    String[] joinNames = new String[] {"JOIN_BEVEL","JOIN_MITER","JOIN_ROUND"};

    /** This method draws the example figure */
    public void draw(Graphics2D g, Component c) {
        // Use anti-aliasing to avoid "jaggies" in the lines
        g.setRenderingHint(RenderingHints.KEY_ANTIALIASING,
                           RenderingHints.VALUE_ANTIALIAS_ON);

        // Define the shape to draw
        GeneralPath shape = new GeneralPath();
        shape.moveTo(xpoints[0], ypoints[0]);  // start at point 0
        shape.lineTo(xpoints[1], ypoints[1]);  // draw a line to point 1
        shape.lineTo(xpoints[2], ypoints[2]);  // and then on to point 2

        // Move the origin to the right and down, creating a margin
        g.translate(20,40);

        // Now loop, drawing our shape with the three different line styles
        for(int i = 0; i < linestyles.length; i++) {
            g.setColor(Color.gray);          // Draw a gray line
            g.setStroke(linestyles[i]);      // Select the line style to use
            g.draw(shape);                   // Draw the shape

            g.setColor(Color.black);         // Now use black
            g.setStroke(thindashed);         // And the thin dashed line
            g.draw(shape);                   // And draw the shape again.
```

Example 11–8: LineStyles.java (continued)

```
                 // Highlight the location of the vertexes of the shape
                 // This accentuates the cap and join styles we're demonstrating
                 for(int j = 0; j < xpoints.length; j++)
                     g.fillRect(xpoints[j]-2, ypoints[j]-2, 5, 5);

                 g.drawString(capNames[i], 5, 105);   // Label the cap style
                 g.drawString(joinNames[i], 5, 120);  // Label the join style

                 g.translate(150, 0); // Move over to the right before looping again
            }
        }
    }
```

Graphics

Stroking Lines

The BasicStroke class is an implementation of the Stroke interface. This interface is responsible for defining how lines are drawn, or stroked, in Java 2D. Filling arbitrary shapes is the fundamental graphics operation defined by Java 2D. The Stroke interface defines the API by which line drawing operations are transformed into area-filling operations, as illustrated in Figure 11-7. Example 11-9 shows the code used to produce this figure. (Once you understand how the Stroke interface converts a shape to a stroked shape suitable for filling, you can define interesting custom Stroke implementations, as we'll do later in this chapter, in Example 11-15).

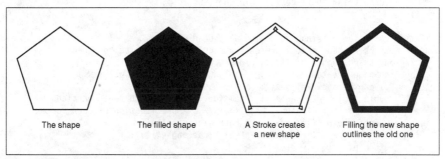

| The shape | The filled shape | A Stroke creates a new shape | Filling the new shape outlines the old one |

Figure 11–7. How lines are drawn in Java 2D

Example 11–9: Stroking.java

```
package com.davidflanagan.examples.graphics;
import java.awt.*;
import java.awt.geom.*;

/** A demonstration of how Stroke objects work */
public class Stroking implements GraphicsExample {
    static final int WIDTH = 725, HEIGHT = 250;  // Size of our example
    public String getName() {return "Stroking";} // From GraphicsExample
    public int getWidth() { return WIDTII; }      // From GraphicsExample
    public int getHeight() { return HEIGHT; }     // From GraphicsExample

    /** Draw the example */
    public void draw(Graphics2D g, Component c) {
        // Create the shape we'll work with.  See convenience method below.
```

Example 11–9: Stroking.java (continued)

```
        Shape pentagon = createRegularPolygon(5, 75);

        // Set up basic drawing attributes
        g.setColor(Color.black);                          // Draw in black
        g.setStroke(new BasicStroke(1.0f));               // Use thin lines
        g.setFont(new Font("SansSerif", Font.PLAIN, 12)); // Basic small font

        g.translate(100, 100);                     // Move to position
        g.draw(pentagon);                          // Outline the shape
        g.drawString("The shape", -30, 90);        // Draw the caption

        g.translate(175, 0);                       // Move over
        g.fill(pentagon);                          // Fill the shape
        g.drawString("The filled shape", -50, 90); // Another caption

        // Now use a Stroke object to create a "stroked shape" for our shape
        BasicStroke wideline = new BasicStroke(10.0f);
        Shape outline = wideline.createStrokedShape(pentagon);

        g.translate(175, 0);                       // Move over
        g.draw(outline);                           // Draw the stroked shape
        g.drawString("A Stroke creates",-50,90);   // Draw the caption
        g.drawString("a new shape", -35, 105);

        g.translate(175,0);                        // Move over
        g.fill(outline);                           // Fill the stroked shape
        g.drawString("Filling the new shape",-65,90); // Draw the caption
        g.drawString("outlines the old one",-65,105);
    }

    // A convenience method to define a regular polygon.
    // Returns a shape that represents a regular polygon with the specified
    // radius and number of sides, and centered at the origin.
    public Shape createRegularPolygon(int numsides, int radius) {
        Polygon p = new Polygon();
        double angle = 2 * Math.PI / numsides;   // Angle between vertices
        for(int i = 0; i < numsides; i++)  // Compute location of each vertex
            p.addPoint((int)(radius * Math.sin(angle*i)),
                       (int)(radius * -Math.cos(angle*i)));
        return p;
    }
}
```

Filling Shapes with Paint

We've just seen that line drawing in Java 2D is defined in terms of the more fundamental operation of area filling. In previous examples, we've used the fill() method of Graphics2D to fill the interior of a Shape with whatever solid color was previously passed to the setColor() method. The Java 2D API generalizes the notion of color, however, and allows you to fill an area using any implementation of the Paint interface. The Paint implementation is responsible for specifying the colors to use in the area filling (or line drawing) operation. In Java 1.2 and later, the Color class implements the Paint method, allowing shapes to be filled with solid colors. Java 2D also defines two other Paint implementations: Gradient-Paint, which fills a shape with a color gradient, and TexturePaint, which fills a shape by tiling an image. These classes can be used to achieve some of the fill effects shown in Figure 11-8.

Figure 11-8. Filling shapes with Paint objects

Example 11-10 shows the code that generates Figure 11-8. In addition to using the GradientPaint and TexturePaint classes, this example demonstrates a variety of other Java 2D capabilities: translucent colors, font glyphs as Shape objects that create "text art," an AffineTransform and a translucent color that produce a shadow effect, and a BufferedImage that performs off-screen drawing. Example 11-10 also illustrates the use of GenericPaint, a custom Paint implementation that we'll see in Example 11-16.

Example 11-10: Paints.java

```
package com.davidflanagan.examples.graphics;
import java.awt.*;
import java.awt.geom.*;
import java.awt.font.*;
import java.awt.image.*;

/** A demonstration of Java2D transformations */
public class Paints implements GraphicsExample {
    static final int WIDTH = 800, HEIGHT = 375;  // Size of our example

    public String getName() { return "Paints"; } // From GraphicsExample
    public int getWidth() { return WIDTH; }       // From GraphicsExample
    public int getHeight() { return HEIGHT; }     // From GraphicsExample

    /** Draw the example */
    public void draw(Graphics2D g, Component c) {
        // Paint the entire background using a GradientPaint.
        // The background color varies diagonally from deep red to pale blue
        g.setPaint(new GradientPaint(0, 0, new Color(150, 0, 0),
                                     WIDTH, HEIGHT, new Color(200, 200, 255)));
        g.fillRect(0, 0, WIDTH, HEIGHT);          // fill the background

        // Use a different GradientPaint to draw a box.
        // This one alternates between deep opaque green and transparent green.
```

Example 11-10: Paints.java (continued)

```
// Note: the 4th arg to Color() constructor specifies color opacity
g.setPaint(new GradientPaint(0, 0, new Color(0, 150, 0),
                             20, 20, new Color(0, 150, 0, 0), true));
g.setStroke(new BasicStroke(15));           // use wide lines
g.drawRect(25, 25, WIDTH-50, HEIGHT-50);  // draw the box

// The glyphs of fonts can be used as Shape objects, which enables
// us to use Java2D techniques with letters Just as we would with
// any other shape.  Here we get some letter shapes to draw.
Font font = new Font("Serif", Font.BOLD, 10);  // a basic font
Font bigfont =                              // a scaled up version
    font.deriveFont(AffineTransform.getScaleInstance(30.0, 30.0));
GlyphVector gv = bigfont.createGlyphVector(g.getFontRenderContext(),
                                           "JAV");
Shape jshape = gv.getGlyphOutline(0);    // Shape of letter J
Shape ashape = gv.getGlyphOutline(1);    // Shape of letter A
Shape vshape = gv.getGlyphOutline(2);    // Shape of letter V

// We're going to outline the letters with a 5-pixel wide line
g.setStroke(new BasicStroke(5.0f));

// We're going to fake shadows for the letters using the
// following Paint and AffineTransform objects
Paint shadowPaint = new Color(0, 0, 0, 100);      // Translucent black
AffineTransform shadowTransform =
    AffineTransform.getShearInstance(-1.0, 0.0); // Shear to the right
shadowTransform.scale(1.0, 0.5);                  // Scale height by 1/2

// Move to the baseline of our first letter
g.translate(65, 270);

// Draw the shadow of the J shape
g.setPaint(shadowPaint);
g.translate(15,20);      // Compensate for the descender of the J
// transform the J into the shape of its shadow, and fill it
g.fill(shadowTransform.createTransformedShape(jshape));
g.translate(-15,-20);   // Undo the translation above

// Now fill the J shape with a solid (and opaque) color
g.setPaint(Color.blue);        // Fill with solid, opaque blue
g.fill(jshape);                // Fill the shape
g.setPaint(Color.black);       // Switch to solid black
g.draw(jshape);                // And draw the outline of the J

// Now draw the A shadow
g.translate(75, 0);            // Move to the right
g.setPaint(shadowPaint);       // Set shadow color
g.fill(shadowTransform.createTransformedShape(ashape)); // draw shadow

// Draw the A shape using a solid transparent color
g.setPaint(new Color(0, 255, 0, 125));  // Transparent green as paint
g.fill(ashape);                          // Fill the shape
g.setPaint(Color.black);                 // Switch to solid back
g.draw(ashape);                          // Draw the outline

// Move to the right and draw the shadow of the letter V
g.translate(175, 0);
g.setPaint(shadowPaint);
```

Example 11-10: Paints.java (continued)

```
        g.fill(shadowTransform.createTransformedShape(vshape));

        // We're going to fill the next letter using a TexturePaint, which
        // repeatedly tiles an image. The first step is to obtain the image.
        // We could load it from an image file, but here we create it
        // ourselves by drawing a into an off-screen image.  Note that we use
        // a GradientPaint to fill the off-screen image, so the fill pattern
        // combines features of both Paint classes.
        BufferedImage tile =                    // Create an image
            new BufferedImage(50, 50, BufferedImage.TYPE_INT_RGB);
        Graphics2D tg = tile.createGraphics(); // Get its Graphics for drawing
        tg.setColor(Color.pink);
        tg.fillRect(0, 0, 50, 50);      // Fill tile background with pink
        tg.setPaint(new GradientPaint(40, 0, Color.green,  // diagonal gradient
                                    0, 40, Color.gray)); // green to gray
        tg.fillOval(5, 5, 40, 40);      // Draw a circle with this gradient

        // Use this new tile to create a TexturePaint and fill the letter V
        g.setPaint(new TexturePaint(tile, new Rectangle(0, 0, 50, 50)));
        g.fill(vshape);                 // Fill letter shape
        g.setPaint(Color.black);        // Switch to solid black
        g.draw(vshape);                 // Draw outline of letter

        // Move to the right and draw the shadow of the final A
        g.translate(160, 0);
        g.setPaint(shadowPaint);
        g.fill(shadowTransform.createTransformedShape(ashape));

        // For the last letter, use a custom Paint class to fill with a
        // complex mathematically defined pattern.  The GenericPaint
        // class is defined later in the chapter.
        g.setPaint(new GenericPaint() {
                public int computeRed(double x, double y) { return 128; }
                public int computeGreen(double x, double y) {
                    return (int)((Math.sin(x/7) + Math.cos(y/5) + 2)/4 *255);
                }
                public int computeBlue(double x, double y) {
                    return ((int)(x*y))%256;
                }
                public int computeAlpha(double x, double y) {
                    return ((int)x%25*8+50) + ((int)y%25*8+50);
                }
            });
        g.fill(ashape);                 // Fill letter A
        g.setPaint(Color.black);        // Revert to solid black
        g.draw(ashape);                 // Draw the outline of the A
    }
}
```

Antialiasing

As we've already seen, you can request that Java 2D perform antialiasing when it draws text and graphics. Antialiasing smoothes the edges of shapes (such as text glyphs) and lines and reduces jaggies. Antialiased drawing is necessary because the outline of a shape drawn on a computer monitor can never be perfectly smooth; a mathematically perfect shape can't be mapped precisely onto a grid of discrete pixels. When the shape is drawn, the pixels inside the shape are filled, while the pixels outside are not. The outline of a shape rarely falls on perfect pixel boundaries, however, so approximations are made at the edges. The result is jagged lines that approximate the abstract shape you wish to represent.

Antialiasing is simply a technique for improving these approximations using translucent colors. For example, if a pixel at the edge of a shape is half covered by the shape, the pixel is filled using a color that is half opaque. If only one-fifth of the pixel is covered, the pixel is one-fifth opaque. This technique works quite well to reduce jaggies. Figure 11-9 illustrates the process of antialiasing: it shows an antialiased figure that has been artificially enlarged to show the translucent colors used at the edges of shapes and text glyphs. The figure is generated by the straightforward code in Example 11-11.

Figure 11-9. Antialiasing enlarged

Example 11-11: AntiAlias.java

```
package com.davidflanagan.examples.graphics;
import java.awt.*;
import java.awt.geom.*;
import java.awt.image.*;

/** A demonstration of anti-aliasing */
public class AntiAlias implements GraphicsExample {
    static final int WIDTH = 650, HEIGHT = 350;        // Size of our example
    public String getName() {return "AntiAliasing";}   // From GraphicsExample
    public int getWidth() { return WIDTH; }            // From GraphicsExample
    public int getHeight() { return HEIGHT; }          // From GraphicsExample

    /** Draw the example */
    public void draw(Graphics2D g, Component c) {
        BufferedImage image =                          // Create an off-screen image
            new BufferedImage(65, 35, BufferedImage.TYPE_INT_RGB);
        Graphics2D ig = image.createGraphics(); // Get its Graphics for drawing

        // Set the background to a gradient fill.  The varying color of
```

Example 11-11: AntiAlias.java (continued)

```
                // the background helps to demonstrate the anti-aliasing effect
                ig.setPaint(new GradientPaint(0,0,Color.black,65,35,Color.white));
                ig.fillRect(0, 0, 65, 35);

                // Set drawing attributes for the foreground.
                // Most importantly, turn on anti-aliasing.
                ig.setStroke(new BasicStroke(2.0f));                    // 2-pixel lines
                ig.setFont(new Font("Serif", Font.BOLD, 18));           // 18-point font
                ig.setRenderingHint(RenderingHints.KEY_ANTIALIASING,    // Anti-alias!
                                    RenderingHints.VALUE_ANTIALIAS_ON);

                // Now draw pure blue text and a pure red oval
                ig.setColor(Color.blue);
                ig.drawString("Java", 9, 22);
                ig.setColor(Color.red);
                ig.drawOval(1, 1, 62, 32);

                // Finally, scale the image by a factor of 10 and display it
                // in the window.  This will allow us to see the anti-aliased pixels
                g.drawImage(image, AffineTransform.getScaleInstance(10, 10), c);

                // Draw the image one more time at its original size, for comparison
                g.drawImage(image, 0, 0, c);
        }
}
```

Combining Colors with AlphaComposite

As I've just explained, antialiasing works by drawing with translucent colors at the edges of a shape. But what exactly does it mean to draw with a translucent color? Take another look at Figure 11-9, or, better yet, run the example using the GraphicsExampleFrame program, so you can see the example in full color. When you draw with a translucent color, whatever color is below it "shows through." In Figure 11-9, the background gray colors show through the pure translucent red and blue colors, resulting in reddish and bluish grays. At the hardware level, of course, there is no such thing as a translucent color; drawing with a translucent color is simulated by combining the drawing color with the existing color beneath it.

Combining colors in this way is called *compositing* and is the job of the Composite interface. You can pass a Composite object to the setComposite() method of a Graphics2D object to tell it how to combine a drawing color (the source color) with the colors that are already on the drawing surface (the destination colors). Java 2D defines one implementation of the Composite interface, AlphaComposite, that combines colors based on their alpha transparency values.

The default AlphaComposite object used by Graphics2D is sufficient for most drawing, so you don't often need to create AlphaComposite objects. Still, there are interesting effects you can achieve with AlphaComposite. Example 11-12 demonstrates these effects (and an unrelated clipping effect), which are shown in Figure 11-10.

The example does much of its drawing into an off-screen image, then copies the contents of that image onto the screen. This is because many compositing effects can only be achieved when working with a drawing surface (such as an off-screen

Figure 11-10. Effects created with AlphaComposite

image) that has an "alpha channel" and supports transparent colors. Be sure to check out how this off-screen BufferedImage is created.

Example 11-12 also illustrates the type of effects that are possible when you set a clipping region. Java 2D allows any Shape to be used as a clipping region; graphics are displayed only if they fall within this shape. The example uses the java.awt.geom.Area class to define a complex shape, combining two ellipses and a rectangle, and then uses this shape as a clipping region.

Example 11-12: CompositeEffects.java

```java
package com.davidflanagan.examples.graphics;
import java.awt.*;
import java.awt.geom.*;
import java.awt.image.*;

public class CompositeEffects implements GraphicsExample {
    Image cover;  // The image we'll be displaying, and its size
    static final int COVERWIDTH = 127, COVERHEIGHT = 190;

    /** This constructor loads the cover image */
    public CompositeEffects() {
        java.net.URL imageurl = this.getClass().getResource("cover.gif");
        cover = new javax.swing.ImageIcon(imageurl).getImage();
    }

    // These are basic GraphicsExample methods
    public String getName() {return "Composite Effects";}
    public int getWidth() { return 6*COVERWIDTH + 70; }
    public int getHeight() { return COVERHEIGHT + 35; }

    /** Draw the example */
    public void draw(Graphics2D g, Component c) {
        // fill the background
        g.setPaint(new Color(175, 175, 175));
        g.fillRect(0, 0, getWidth(), getHeight());

        // Set text attributes
        g.setColor(Color.black);
        g.setFont(new Font("SansSerif", Font.BOLD, 12));

        // Draw the unmodified image
```

Example 11–12: CompositeEffects.java (continued)

```
g.translate(10, 10);
g.drawImage(cover, 0, 0, c);
g.drawString("SRC_OVER", 0, COVERHEIGHT+15);

// Draw the cover again, using AlphaComposite to make the opaque
// colors of the image 50% translucent
g.translate(COVERWIDTH+10, 0);
g.setComposite(AlphaComposite.getInstance(AlphaComposite.SRC_OVER,
                              0.5f));
g.drawImage(cover, 0, 0, c);

// Restore the pre-defined default Composite for the screen, so
// opaque colors stay opaque.
g.setComposite(AlphaComposite.SrcOver);
// Label the effect
g.drawString("SRC_OVER, 50%", 0, COVERHEIGHT+15);

// Now get an offscreen image to work with.  In order to achieve
// certain compositing effects, the drawing surface must support
// transparency. Onscreen drawing surfaces cannot, so we have to do the
// compositing in an offscreen image that is specially created to have
// an "alpha channel", then copy the final result to the screen.
BufferedImage offscreen =
    new BufferedImage(COVERWIDTH, COVERHEIGHT,
                      BufferedImage.TYPE_INT_ARGB);

// First, fill the image with a color gradient background that varies
// left-to-right from opaque to transparent yellow
Graphics2D osg = offscreen.createGraphics();
osg.setPaint(new GradientPaint(0, 0, Color.yellow,
                               COVERWIDTH, 0,
                               new Color(255, 255, 0, 0)));
osg.fillRect(0,0, COVERWIDTH, COVERHEIGHT);

// Now copy the cover image on top of this, but use the DstOver rule
// which draws it "underneath" the existing pixels, and allows the
// image to show depending on the transparency of those pixels.
osg.setComposite(AlphaComposite.DstOver);
osg.drawImage(cover, 0, 0, c);

// And display this composited image on the screen.  Note that the
// image is opaque and that none of the screen background shows through
g.translate(COVERWIDTH+10, 0);
g.drawImage(offscreen, 0, 0, c);
g.drawString("DST_OVER", 0, COVERHEIGHT+15);

// Now start over and do a new effect with the off-screen image.
// First, fill the offscreen image with a new color gradient.  We
// don't care about the colors themselves; we just want the
// translucency of the background to vary.  We use opaque black to
// transparent black. Note that since we've already used this offscreen
// image, we set the composite to Src, we can fill the image and
// ignore anything that is already there.
osg.setComposite(AlphaComposite.Src);
osg.setPaint(new GradientPaint(0, 0, Color.black,
                               COVERWIDTH, COVERHEIGHT,
                               new Color(0, 0, 0, 0)));
osg.fillRect(0,0, COVERWIDTH, COVERHEIGHT);
```

Example 11–12: CompositeEffects.java (continued)

```
        // Now set the compositing type to SrcIn, so colors come from the
        // source, but translucency comes from the destination
        osg.setComposite(AlphaComposite.SrcIn);

        // Draw our loaded image into the off-screen image, compositing it.
        osg.drawImage(cover, 0, 0, c);

        // And then copy our off-screen image to the screen.  Note that the
        // image is translucent and some of the image shows through.
        g.translate(COVERWIDTH+10, 0);
        g.drawImage(offscreen, 0, 0, c);
        g.drawString("SRC_IN", 0, COVERHEIGHT+15);

        // If we do the same thing but use SrcOut, then the resulting image
        // will have the inverted translucency values of the destination
        osg.setComposite(AlphaComposite.Src);
        osg.setPaint(new GradientPaint(0, 0, Color.black,
                                 COVERWIDTH, COVERHEIGHT,
                                 new Color(0, 0, 0, 0)));
        osg.fillRect(0,0, COVERWIDTH, COVERHEIGHT);
        osg.setComposite(AlphaComposite.SrcOut);
        osg.drawImage(cover, 0, 0, c);
        g.translate(COVERWIDTH+10, 0);
        g.drawImage(offscreen, 0, 0, c);
        g.drawString("SRC_OUT", 0, COVERHEIGHT+15);

        // Here's a cool effect; it has nothing to do with compositing, but
        // uses an arbitrary shape to clip the image.  It uses Area to combine
        // shapes into more complicated ones.
        g.translate(COVERWIDTH+10, 0);
        Shape savedClip = g.getClip();  // Save current clipping region
        // Create a shape to use as the new clipping region.
        // Begin with an ellipse
        Area clip = new Area(new Ellipse2D.Float(0,0,COVERWIDTH,COVERHEIGHT));
        // Intersect with a rectangle, truncating the ellipse.
        clip.intersect(new Area(new Rectangle(5,5,
                                     COVERWIDTH-10,COVERHEIGHT-10)));
        // Then subtract an ellipse from the bottom of the truncated ellipse.
        clip.subtract(new Area(new Ellipse2D.Float(COVERWIDTH/2-40,
                                     COVERHEIGHT-20, 80, 40)));
        // Use the resulting shape as the new clipping region
        g.clip(clip);
        // Then draw the image through this clipping region
        g.drawImage(cover, 0, 0, c);
        // Restore the old clipping region so we can label the effect
        g.setClip(savedClip);
        g.drawString("Clipping", 0, COVERHEIGHT+15);
    }
}
```

Image Processing

Both Java 1.0 and 1.1 included a complex API for filtering images on the fly as they were downloaded over a network connection. Although this API is still available in later versions of Java, it is not commonly used, nor is it demonstrated in this book. Java 2D defines a simpler API based on the BufferedImageOp interface of the `java.awt.image` package. This package also includes several versatile implementations of the interface that can generate the image-processing effects illustrated in Figure 11-11. Example 11-13 shows the code used to produce Figure 11-11. The code is straightforward: to process a `BufferedImage`, simply pass it to the `filter()` method of a `BufferedImageOp`.

Figure 11–11. Image processing with BufferedImageOp

Example 11–13: ImageOps.java

```
package com.davidflanagan.examples.graphics;
import java.awt.*;
import java.awt.geom.*;
import java.awt.image.*;
import java.awt.color.*;

/** A demonstration of various image processing filters */
public class ImageOps implements GraphicsExample {
    static final int WIDTH = 600, HEIGHT = 675;        // Size of our example
```

Example 11-13: ImageOps.java (continued)

```
public String getName() {return "Image Processing";}// From GraphicsExample
public int getWidth() { return WIDTH; }             // From GraphicsExample
public int getHeight() { return HEIGHT; }           // From GraphicsExample

Image image;

/** This constructor loads the image we will manipulate */
public ImageOps() {
    java.net.URL imageurl = this.getClass().getResource("cover.gif");
    image = new javax.swing.ImageIcon(imageurl).getImage();
}

// These arrays of bytes are used by the LookupImageOp image filters below
static byte[] brightenTable = new byte[256];
static byte[] thresholdTable = new byte[256];
static {  // Initialize the arrays
    for(int i = 0; i < 256; i++) {
        brightenTable[i] = (byte)(Math.sqrt(i/255.0)*255);
        thresholdTable[i] = (byte)((i < 225)?0:i);
    }
}

// This AffineTransform is used by one of the image filters below
static AffineTransform mirrorTransform;
static {  // Create and initialize the AffineTransform
    mirrorTransform = AffineTransform.getTranslateInstance(127, 0);
    mirrorTransform.scale(-1.0, 1.0);  // flip horizontally
}

// These are the labels we'll display for each of the filtered images
static String[] filterNames = new String[] {
    "Original", "Gray Scale",  "Negative",  "Brighten (linear)",
    "Brighten (sqrt)", "Threshold", "Blur", "Sharpen",
    "Edge Detect", "Mirror", "Rotate (center)", "Rotate (lower left)"
};

// The following BufferedImageOp image filter objects perform
// different types of image processing operations.
static BufferedImageOp[] filters = new BufferedImageOp[] {
    // 1) No filter here.  We'll display the original image
    null,
    // 2) Convert to Grayscale color space
    new ColorConvertOp(ColorSpace.getInstance(ColorSpace.CS_GRAY), null),
    // 3) Image negative.  Multiply each color value by -1.0 and add 255
    new RescaleOp(-1.0f, 255f, null),
    // 4) Brighten using a linear formula that increases all color values
    new RescaleOp(1.25f, 0, null),
    // 5) Brighten using the lookup table defined above
    new LookupOp(new ByteLookupTable(0, brightenTable), null),
    // 6) Threshold using the lookup table defined above
    new LookupOp(new ByteLookupTable(0, thresholdTable), null),
    // 7) Blur by "convolving" the image with a matrix
    new ConvolveOp(new Kernel(3, 3, new float[] {
       .1111f,.1111f,.1111f,
       .1111f,.1111f,.1111f,
       .1111f,.1111f,.1111f,})),
    // 8) Sharpen by using a different matrix
    new ConvolveOp(new Kernel(3, 3, new float[] {
```

Example 11–13: ImageOps.java (continued)

```
                0.0f, -0.75f, 0.0f,
                -0.75f, 4.0f, -0.75f,
                0.0f, -0.75f, 0.0f})),
        // 9) Edge detect using yet another matrix
        new ConvolveOp(new Kernel(3, 3, new float[] {
                0.0f,  -0.75f, 0.0f,
                -0.75f, 3.0f, -0.75f,
                0.0f,  -0.75f, 0.0f})),
        // 10) Compute a mirror image using the transform defined above
        new AffineTransformOp(mirrorTransform,AffineTransformOp.TYPE_BILINEAR),
        // 11) Rotate the image 180 degrees about its center point
        new AffineTransformOp(AffineTransform.getRotateInstance(Math.PI,64,95),
                          AffineTransformOp.TYPE_NEAREST_NEIGHBOR),
        // 12) Rotate the image 15 degrees about the bottom left
        new AffineTransformOp(AffineTransform.getRotateInstance(Math.PI/12,
                                                          0, 190),
                          AffineTransformOp.TYPE_NEAREST_NEIGHBOR),
    };

    /** Draw the example */
    public void draw(Graphics2D g, Component c) {
        // Create a BufferedImage big enough to hold the Image loaded
        // in the constructor.  Then copy that image into the new
        // BufferedImage object so that we can process it.
        BufferedImage bimage = new BufferedImage(image.getWidth(c),
                                                 image.getHeight(c),
                                                 BufferedImage.TYPE_INT_RGB);
        Graphics2D ig = bimage.createGraphics();
        ig.drawImage(image, 0, 0, c);  // copy the image

        // Set some default graphics attributes
        g.setFont(new Font("SansSerif", Font.BOLD, 12));  // 12pt bold text
        g.setColor(Color.green);                          // Draw in green
        g.translate(10, 10);                              // Set some margins

        // Loop through the filters
        for(int i = 0; i < filters.length; i++) {
            // If the filter is null, draw the original image, otherwise,
            // draw the image as processed by the filter
            if (filters[i] == null) g.drawImage(bimage, 0, 0, c);
            else g.drawImage(filters[i].filter(bimage, null), 0, 0, c);
            g.drawString(filterNames[i], 0, 205);      // Label the image
            g.translate(137, 0);                       // Move over
            if (i % 4 == 3) g.translate(-137*4, 215);  // Move down after 4
        }
    }
}
```

A Custom Shape

Figure 11-4 showed how Java 2D can be used to draw and fill various types of shapes. One of the shapes shown in that figure is a spiral, which was drawn using the Spiral class, a custom Shape implementation shown in Example 11-14.

The Shape interface defines three important methods (some of which have multiple overloaded versions) that all shapes must implement. The contains() methods determine whether a shape contains a point or a rectangle; a Shape has to be able to tell its inside from its outside. Because our spiral is a curve that doesn't enclose an area, there is no inside, and these methods always return false. The intersects() methods determine whether any part of the shape intersects a specified rectangle. Since this is hard to compute exactly for a spiral, the code approximates the spiral with a circle for the purposes of these methods.

The getPathIterator() methods are the heart of any Shape implementation. Each method returns a PathIterator object that describes the outline of the shape in terms of line and curve segments. Java 2D relies on PathIterator objects to draw and fill shapes. The key methods of the SpiralIterator implementation are currentSegment(), which returns one line segment of the spiral, and next(), which moves the iterator to the next segment. next() uses some hairy mathematics to make sure that the line segment approximation of the spiral is good enough.

Example 11–14: Spiral.java

```java
package com.davidflanagan.examples.graphics;
import java.awt.*;
import java.awt.geom.*;

/** This Shape implementation represents a spiral curve */
public class Spiral implements Shape {
    double centerX, centerY;          // The center of the spiral
    double startRadius, startAngle;   // The spiral starting point
    double endRadius, endAngle;       // The spiral ending point
    double outerRadius;               // the bigger of the two radii
    int angleDirection;               // 1 if angle increases, -1 otherwise

    /**
     * The constructor.  It takes arguments for the center of the shape, the
     * start point, and the end point.  The start and end points are specified
     * in terms of angle and radius.  The spiral curve is formed by varying
     * the angle and radius smoothly between the two end points.
     **/
    public Spiral(double centerX, double centerY,
                  double startRadius, double startAngle,
                  double endRadius, double endAngle)
    {
        // Save the parameters that describe the spiral
        this.centerX = centerX;          this.centerY = centerY;
        this.startRadius = startRadius;  this.startAngle = startAngle;
        this.endRadius = endRadius;      this.endAngle = endAngle;

        // figure out the maximum radius, and the spiral direction
        this.outerRadius = Math.max(startRadius, endRadius);
        if (startAngle < endAngle) angleDirection = 1;
        else angleDirection = -1;

        if ((startRadius < 0) || (endRadius < 0))
            throw new IllegalArgumentException("Spiral radii must be >= 0");
    }

    /**
     * The bounding box of a Spiral is the same as the bounding box of a
     * circle with the same center and the maximum radius
     **/
    public Rectangle getBounds() {
```

Example 11-14: Spiral.java (continued)

```
        return new Rectangle((int)(centerX-outerRadius),
                             (int)(centerY-outerRadius),
                             (int)(outerRadius*2), (int)(outerRadius*2));
    }

    /** Same as getBounds(), but with floating-point coordinates */
    public Rectangle2D getBounds2D() {
        return new Rectangle2D.Double(centerX-outerRadius, centerY-outerRadius,
                                      outerRadius*2, outerRadius*2);
    }

    /**
     * A spiral is an open curve, not a not a closed area; it does not have an
     * inside and an outsize, so the contains() methods always return false.
     **/
    public boolean contains(double x, double y) { return false; }
    public boolean contains(Point2D p) { return false; }
    public boolean contains(Rectangle2D r) { return false; }
    public boolean contains(double x, double y, double w, double h) {
        return false;
    }

    /**
     * This method is allowed to approximate if it would be too computationally
     * intensive to determine an exact answer.  Therefore, we check whether
     * the rectangle intersects a circle of the outer radius.  This is a good
     * guess for a tight spiral, but less good for a "loose" spiral.
     **/
    public boolean intersects(double x, double y, double w, double h) {
        Shape approx = new Ellipse2D.Double(centerX-outerRadius,
                                            centerY-outerRadius,
                                            outerRadius*2, outerRadius*2);
        return approx.intersects(x, y, w, h);
    }

    /** This version of intersects() just calls the one above */
    public boolean intersects(Rectangle2D r) {
        return intersects(r.getX(), r.getY(), r.getWidth(), r.getHeight());
    }

    /**
     * This method is the heart of all Shape implementations.  It returns a
     * PathIterator that describes the shape in terms of the line and curve
     * segments that comprise it.  Our iterator implementation approximates
     * the shape of the spiral using line segments only.  We pass in a
     * "flatness" argument that tells it how good the approximation must be.
     * (smaller numbers mean a better approximation).
     */
    public PathIterator getPathIterator(AffineTransform at) {
        return new SpiralIterator(at, outerRadius/500.0);
    }

    /**
     * Return a PathIterator that describes the shape in terms of line
     * segments only, with an approximation quality specified by flatness.
     **/
    public PathIterator getPathIterator(AffineTransform at, double flatness) {
        return new SpiralIterator(at, flatness);
```

Example 11–14: Spiral.java (continued)

```
    }

    /**
     * This inner class is the PathIterator for our Spiral shape.  For
     * simplicity, it does not describe the spiral path in terms of Bezier
     * curve segments, but simply approximates it with line segments.  The
     * flatness property specifies how far the approximation is allowed to
     * deviate from the true curve.
     **/
    class SpiralIterator implements PathIterator {
        AffineTransform transform;      // How to transform generated coordinates
        double flatness;                // How close an approximation
        double angle = startAngle;      // Current angle
        double radius = startRadius;    // Current radius
        boolean done = false;           // Are we done yet?

        /** A simple constructor.  Just store the parameters into fields */
        public SpiralIterator(AffineTransform transform, double flatness) {
            this.transform = transform;
            this.flatness = flatness;
        }

        /**
         * All PathIterators have a "winding rule" that helps to specify what
         * is the inside of a area and what is the outside.  If you fill a
         * spiral (which you're not supposed to do) the winding rule returned
         * here yields better results than the alternative, WIND_EVEN_ODD
         **/
        public int getWindingRule() { return WIND_NON_ZERO; }

        /** Returns true if the entire path has been iterated */
        public boolean isDone() { return done; }

        /**
         * Store the coordinates of the current segment of the path into the
         * specified array, and return the type of the segment.  Use
         * trigonometry to compute the coordinates based on the current angle
         * and radius.  If this was the first point, return a MOVETO segment,
         * otherwise return a LINETO segment.  Also, check to see if we're done.
         **/
        public int currentSegment(float[] coords) {
            // given the radius and the angle, compute the point coords
            coords[0] = (float)(centerX + radius*Math.cos(angle));
            coords[1] = (float)(centerY - radius*Math.sin(angle));

            // If a transform was specified, use it on the coordinates
            if (transform != null) transform.transform(coords, 0, coords, 0,1);

            // If we've reached the end of the spiral remember that fact
            if (angle == endAngle) done = true;

            // If this is the first point in the spiral then move to it
            if (angle == startAngle) return SEG_MOVETO;

            // Otherwise draw a line from the previous point to this one
            return SEG_LINETO;
        }
```

Example 11–14: Spiral.java (continued)

```
    /** This method is the same as above, except using double values */
    public int currentSegment(double[] coords) {
        coords[0] = centerX + radius*Math.cos(angle);
        coords[1] = centerY - radius*Math.sin(angle);
        if (transform != null) transform.transform(coords, 0, coords, 0,1);
        if (angle == endAngle) done = true;
        if (angle == startAngle) return SEG_MOVETO;
        else return SEG_LINETO;
    }

    /**
     * Move on to the next segment of the path.  Compute the angle and
     * radius values for the next point in the spiral.
     **/
    public void next() {
        if (done) return;

        // First, figure out how much to increment the angle.  This
        // depends on the required flatness, and also upon the current
        // radius.  When drawing a circle (which we'll use as our
        // approximation) of radius r, we can maintain a flatness f by
        // using angular increments given by this formula:
        //      a = acos(2*(f/r)*(f/r) - 4*(f/r) + 1)
        // Use this formula to figure out how much we can increment the
        // angle for the next segment.  Note that the formula does not
        // work well for very small radii, so we special case those.
        double x = flatness/radius;
        if (Double.isNaN(x) || (x > .1))
            angle += Math.PI/4*angleDirection;
        else {
            double y = 2*x*x - 4*x + 1;
            angle += Math.acos(y)*angleDirection;
        }

        // Check whether we've gone past the end of the spiral
        if ((angle-endAngle)*angleDirection > 0) angle = endAngle;

        // Now that we know the new angle, we can use interpolation to
        // figure out what the corresponding radius is.
        double fractionComplete = (angle-startAngle)/(endAngle-startAngle);
        radius = startRadius + (endRadius-startRadius)*fractionComplete;
    }
  }
}
```

Custom Strokes

As we saw in Example 11-9, the Stroke class converts a line-drawing operation into an area filling operation by taking the Shape whose outline is to be drawn and returning a stroked shape that represents the outline itself. Because Stroke is such a simple interface, it is relatively easy to implement custom Stroke classes that perform interesting graphical effects. Example 11-15 includes four custom Stroke implementations that it uses along with a simple BasicStroke object to produce the output shown in Figure 11-12.

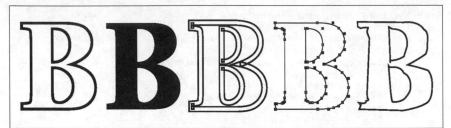

Figure 11–12. Special effects with custom Stroke classes

You should pay particular attention to the ControlPointsStroke and SloppyStroke implementations. These classes are interesting because they use a PathIterator object to break a shape down into its component line and curve segments (just the opposite of what was done in the Spiral class shown in Example 11-14). These two custom Stroke classes also use the GeneralPath class of java.awt.geom to build a custom shape out of arbitrary line and curve segments (which shows how closely linked the GeneralPath class and the PathIterator interface are).

Example 11–15: CustomStrokes.java

```
package com.davidflanagan.examples.graphics;
import java.awt.*;
import java.awt.geom.*;
import java.awt.font.*;

/** A demonstration of writing custom Stroke classes */
public class CustomStrokes implements GraphicsExample {
    static final int WIDTH = 750, HEIGHT = 200;        // Size of our example
    public String getName() {return "Custom Strokes";} // From GraphicsExample
    public int getWidth() { return WIDTH; }            // From GraphicsExample
    public int getHeight() { return HEIGHT; }          // From GraphicsExample

    // These are the various stroke objects we'll demonstrate
    Stroke[] strokes = new Stroke[] {
        new BasicStroke(4.0f),          // The standard, predefined stroke
        new NullStroke(),               // A Stroke that does nothing
        new DoubleStroke(8.0f, 2.0f),   // A Stroke that strokes twice
        new ControlPointsStroke(2.0f),  // Shows the vertices & control points
        new SloppyStroke(2.0f, 3.0f)    // Perturbs the shape before stroking
    };

    /** Draw the example */
    public void draw(Graphics2D g, Component c) {
        // Get a shape to work with.  Here we'll use the letter B
        Font f = new Font("Serif", Font.BOLD, 200);
        GlyphVector gv = f.createGlyphVector(g.getFontRenderContext(), "B");
        Shape shape = gv.getOutline();

        // Set drawing attributes and starting position
        g.setColor(Color.black);
        g.setRenderingHint(RenderingHints.KEY_ANTIALIASING,
                           RenderingHints.VALUE_ANTIALIAS_ON);
        g.translate(10, 175);

        // Draw the shape once with each stroke
        for(int i = 0; i < strokes.length; i++) {
```

Example 11–15: CustomStrokes.java (continued)

```
            g.setStroke(strokes[i]);    // set the stroke
            g.draw(shape);              // draw the shape
            g.translate(140,0);         // move to the right
        }
    }
}

/**
 * This Stroke implementation does nothing.  Its createStrokedShape()
 * method returns an unmodified shape.  Thus, drawing a shape with
 * this Stroke is the same as filling that shape!
 **/
class NullStroke implements Stroke {
    public Shape createStrokedShape(Shape s) { return s; }
}

/**
 * This Stroke implementation applies a BasicStroke to a shape twice.
 * If you draw with this Stroke, then instead of outlining the shape,
 * you're outlining the outline of the shape.
 **/
class DoubleStroke implements Stroke {
    BasicStroke stroke1, stroke2;    // the two strokes to use
    public DoubleStroke(float width1, float width2) {
        stroke1 = new BasicStroke(width1);  // Constructor arguments specify
        stroke2 = new BasicStroke(width2);  // the line widths for the strokes
    }

    public Shape createStrokedShape(Shape s) {
        // Use the first stroke to create an outline of the shape
        Shape outline = stroke1.createStrokedShape(s);
        // Use the second stroke to create an outline of that outline.
        // It is this outline of the outline that will be filled in
        return stroke2.createStrokedShape(outline);
    }
}

/**
 * This Stroke implementation strokes the shape using a thin line, and
 * also displays the end points and Bezier curve control points of all
 * the line and curve segments that make up the shape.  The radius
 * argument to the constructor specifies the size of the control point
 * markers. Note the use of PathIterator to break the shape down into
 * its segments, and of GeneralPath to build up the stroked shape.
 **/
class ControlPointsStroke implements Stroke {
    float radius;  // how big the control point markers should be
    public ControlPointsStroke(float radius) { this.radius = radius; }

    public Shape createStrokedShape(Shape shape) {
        // Start off by stroking the shape with a thin line.  Store the
        // resulting shape in a GeneralPath object so we can add to it.
        GeneralPath strokedShape =
            new GeneralPath(new BasicStroke(1.0f).createStrokedShape(shape));

        // Use a PathIterator object to iterate through each of the line and
        // curve segments of the shape.  For each one, mark the endpoint and
        // control points (if any) by adding a rectangle to the GeneralPath
```

Example 11–15: CustomStrokes.java (continued)

```
        float[] coords = new float[6];
        for(PathIterator i=shape.getPathIterator(null); !i.isDone();i.next()) {
            int type = i.currentSegment(coords);
            Shape s = null, s2 = null, s3 = null;
            switch(type) {
            case PathIterator.SEG_CUBICTO:
                markPoint(strokedShape, coords[4], coords[5]); // falls through
            case PathIterator.SEG_QUADTO:
                markPoint(strokedShape, coords[2], coords[3]); // falls through
            case PathIterator.SEG_MOVETO:
            case PathIterator.SEG_LINETO:
                markPoint(strokedShape, coords[0], coords[1]); // falls through
            case PathIterator.SEG_CLOSE:
                break;
            }
        }

        return strokedShape;
    }

    /** Add a small square centered at (x,y) to the specified path */
    void markPoint(GeneralPath path, float x, float y) {
        path.moveTo(x-radius, y-radius);  // Begin a new sub-path
        path.lineTo(x+radius, y-radius);  // Add a line segment to it
        path.lineTo(x+radius, y+radius);  // Add a second line segment
        path.lineTo(x-radius, y+radius);  // And a third
        path.closePath();                 // Go back to last moveTo position
    }
}

/**
 * This Stroke implementation randomly perturbs the line and curve segments
 * that make up a Shape, and then strokes that perturbed shape.  It uses
 * PathIterator to loop through the Shape and GeneralPath to build up the
 * modified shape.  Finally, it uses a BasicStroke to stroke the modified
 * shape.  The result is a "sloppy" looking shape.
 **/
class SloppyStroke implements Stroke {
    BasicStroke stroke;
    float sloppiness;
    public SloppyStroke(float width, float sloppiness) {
        this.stroke = new BasicStroke(width); // Used to stroke modified shape
        this.sloppiness = sloppiness;         // How sloppy should we be?
    }

    public Shape createStrokedShape(Shape shape) {
        GeneralPath newshape = new GeneralPath();  // Start with an empty shape

        // Iterate through the specified shape, perturb its coordinates, and
        // use them to build up the new shape.
        float[] coords = new float[6];
        for(PathIterator i=shape.getPathIterator(null); !i.isDone();i.next()) {
            int type = i.currentSegment(coords);
            switch(type) {
            case PathIterator.SEG_MOVETO:
                perturb(coords, 2);
                newshape.moveTo(coords[0], coords[1]);
                break;
```

Example 11–15: CustomStrokes.java (continued)

```
                    case PathIterator.SEG_LINETO:
                        perturb(coords, 2);
                        newshape.lineTo(coords[0], coords[1]);
                        break;
                    case PathIterator.SEG_QUADTO:
                        perturb(coords, 4);
                        newshape.quadTo(coords[0], coords[1], coords[2], coords[3]);
                        break;
                    case PathIterator.SEG_CUBICTO:
                        perturb(coords, 6);
                        newshape.curveTo(coords[0], coords[1], coords[2], coords[3],
                                         coords[4], coords[5]);
                        break;
                    case PathIterator.SEG_CLOSE:
                        newshape.closePath();
                        break;
                }
            }

        // Finally, stroke the perturbed shape and return the result
        return stroke.createStrokedShape(newshape);
    }

    // Randomly modify the specified number of coordinates, by an amount
    // specified by the sloppiness field.
    void perturb(float[] coords, int numCoords) {
        for(int i = 0; i < numCoords; i++)
            coords[i] += (float)((Math.random()*2-1.0)*sloppiness);
    }
}
```

Graphics

Custom Paint

Figure 11-8 showed a variety of shape-filling techniques; it included a large letter A filled with a complex pattern defined by the GenericPaint class. Example 11-16 shows the implementation of this class. You may want to take another look at Example 11-10 to see how the GenericPaint class is used, before you dive into the code listed here.

The GenericPaint class itself is pretty simple: it defines both the abstract color computation methods that subclasses implement and a createContext() method that returns a PaintContext. The implementation of PaintContext does all the hard work. This is pretty low-level stuff, so don't be dismayed if you don't understand everything. The code should at least give you a basic idea of how painting works in Java 2D.

Example 11–16: GenericPaint.java

```
package com.davidflanagan.examples.graphics;
import java.awt.*;
import java.awt.geom.*;
import java.awt.image.*;

/**
 * This is an abstract Paint implementation that computes the color of each
```

Example 11–16: GenericPaint.java (continued)

```
 * point to be painted by passing the coordinates of the point to the calling
 * the abstract methods computeRed(), computeGreen(), computeBlue() and
 * computeAlpha().  Subclasses must implement these three methods to perform
 * whatever type of painting is desired.  Note that while this class provides
 * great flexibility, it is not very efficient.
 **/
public abstract class GenericPaint implements Paint {
    /** This is the main Paint method;  all it does is return a PaintContext */
    public PaintContext createContext(ColorModel cm,
                                      Rectangle deviceBounds,
                                      Rectangle2D userBounds,
                                      AffineTransform xform,
                                      RenderingHints hints) {
        return new GenericPaintContext(xform);
    }

    /** This paint class allows translucent painting */
    public int getTransparency() { return TRANSLUCENT; }

    /**
     * These three methods return the red, green, blue, and alpha values of
     * the pixel at appear at the specified user-space coordinates.  The return
     * value of each method should be between 0 and 255.
     **/
    public abstract int computeRed(double x, double y);
    public abstract int computeGreen(double x, double y);
    public abstract int computeBlue(double x, double y);
    public abstract int computeAlpha(double x, double y);

    /**
     * The PaintContext class does all the work of painting
     **/
    class GenericPaintContext implements PaintContext {
        ColorModel model;  // The color model
        Point2D origin, unitVectorX, unitVectorY;  // For device-to-user xform

        public GenericPaintContext(AffineTransform userToDevice) {
            // Our color model packs ARGB values into a single int
            model = new DirectColorModel(32, 0x00ff0000,0x0000ff00,
                                             0x000000ff, 0xff000000);
            // The specified transform converts user to device pixels
            // We need to figure out the reverse transformation, so we
            // can compute the user space coordinates of each device pixel
            try {
                AffineTransform deviceToUser = userToDevice.createInverse();
                origin = deviceToUser.transform(new Point(0,0), null);
                unitVectorX = deviceToUser.deltaTransform(new Point(1,0),null);
                unitVectorY = deviceToUser.deltaTransform(new Point(0,1),null);
            }
            catch (NoninvertibleTransformException e) {
                // If we can't invert the transform, just use device space
                origin = new Point(0,0);
                unitVectorX = new Point(1,0);
                unitVectorY = new Point(0, 1);
            }
        }

        /** Return the color model used by this Paint implementation */
```

Example 11–16: GenericPaint.java (continued)

```
        public ColorModel getColorModel() { return model; }

        /**
         * This is the main method of PaintContext.  It must return a Raster
         * that contains fill data for the specified rectangle.  It creates a
         * raster of the specified size, and loops through the device pixels.
         * For each one, it converts the coordinates to user space, then calls
         * the computeRed(), computeGreen() and computeBlue() methods to
         * obtain the appropriate color for the device pixel.
         **/
        public Raster getRaster(int x, int y, int w, int h) {
            WritableRaster raster = model.createCompatibleWritableRaster(w,h);
            int[] colorComponents = new int[4];
            for(int j = 0; j < h; j++) {        // Loop through rows of raster
                int deviceY = y + j;
                for(int i = 0; i < w; i++) {  // Loop through columns
                    int deviceX = x + i;
                    // Convert device coordinate to user-space coordinate
                    double userX = origin.getX() +
                        deviceX * unitVectorX.getX() +
                        deviceY * unitVectorY.getX();
                    double userY = origin.getY() +
                        deviceX * unitVectorX.getY() +
                        deviceY * unitVectorY.getY();
                    // Compute the color components of the pixel
                    colorComponents[0] = computeRed(userX, userY);
                    colorComponents[1] = computeGreen(userX, userY);
                    colorComponents[2] = computeBlue(userX, userY);
                    colorComponents[3] = computeAlpha(userX, userY);
                    // Set the color of the pixel
                    raster.setPixel(i, j, colorComponents);
                }
            }
            return raster;
        }

        /** Called when the PaintContext is no longer needed. */
        public void dispose() {}
    }
}
```

Advanced Animation

Way back in Example 11-4, we saw a simple animation technique that suffered, unfortunately, from flickering. Example 11-17 is a program that performs a more graphics-intensive animation but doesn't flicker, because it uses a technique known as *double-buffering*: it draws each frame of the animation off-screen, then copies the frame onto the screen all at once. This example also has better performance because it requests redraws of only the relatively small portion of the screen that needs to be redrawn.

Another interesting feature of this example is its use of the javax.swing.Timer class to call the actionPerformed() method of a specified ActionListener object at specified intervals. The Timer class is used here so that you don't have to create a Thread. (Note that Java 1.3 includes java.util.Timer, a class that is similar to, but quite distinct from, javax.swing.Timer.)

Example 11-17: Hypnosis.java

```java
package com.davidflanagan.examples.graphics;
import java.awt.*;
import java.awt.event.*;
import java.awt.image.*;
import javax.swing.*;
import javax.swing.Timer;  // Import explicitly because of java.util.Timer

/**
 * A Swing component that smoothly animates a spiral in a hypnotic way.
 **/
public class Hypnosis extends JComponent implements ActionListener {
    double x, y;            // The center of the spiral
    double r1, r2;          // The inner and outer radii of the spiral
    double a1, a2;          // The start and end angles of the spiral
    double deltaA;          // How much the angle changes each frame
    double deltaX, deltaY;  // The trajectory of the center
    float linewidth;        // How wide the lines are
    Timer timer;            // The object that triggers the animation
    BufferedImage buffer;   // The image we use for double-buffering
    Graphics2D osg;         // Graphics2D object for drawing into the buffer

    public Hypnosis(double x, double y, double r1, double r2,
                    double a1, double a2, float linewidth, int delay,
                    double deltaA, double deltaX, double deltaY)
    {
        this.x = x; this.y = y;
        this.r1 = r1; this.r2 = r2;
        this.a1 = a1; this.a2 = a2;
        this.linewidth = linewidth;
        this.deltaA = deltaA;
        this.deltaX = deltaX;
        this.deltaY = deltaY;

        // Set up a timer to call actionPerformed() every delay milliseconds
        timer = new Timer(delay, this);

        // Create a buffer for double-buffering
        buffer = new BufferedImage((int)(2*r2+linewidth),
                                   (int)(2*r2+linewidth),
                                   BufferedImage.TYPE_INT_RGB);

        // Create a Graphics object for the buffer, and set the linewidth
        // and request antialiasing when drawing with it
        osg = buffer.createGraphics();
        osg.setStroke(new BasicStroke(linewidth, BasicStroke.CAP_ROUND,
                                      BasicStroke.JOIN_ROUND));
        osg.setRenderingHint(RenderingHints.KEY_ANTIALIASING,
                             RenderingHints.VALUE_ANTIALIAS_ON);
    }

    // Start and stop the animation by starting and stopping the timer
    public void start() { timer.start(); }
    public void stop() { timer.stop(); }

    /**
```

Example 11-17: Hypnosis.java (continued)

```
     * Swing calls this method to ask the component to redraw itself.
     * This method uses double-buffering to make the animation smoother.
     * Swing does double-buffering automatically, so this may not actually
     * make much difference, but it is important to understand the technique.
     **/
    public void paintComponent(Graphics g) {
        // Clear the background of the off-screen image
        osg.setColor(getBackground());
        osg.fillRect(0, 0, buffer.getWidth(), buffer.getHeight());

        // Now draw a black spiral into the off-screen image
        osg.setColor(Color.black);
        osg.draw(new Spiral(r2+linewidth/2, r2+linewidth/2, r1, a1, r2, a2));

        // Now copy that off-screen image onto the screen
        g.drawImage(buffer, (int)(x-r2), (int)(y-r2), this);
    }


    /**
     * This method implements the ActionListener interface.  Our Timer object
     * calls this method periodically.  It updates the position and angles
     * of the spiral and requests a redraw.  Instead of redrawing the entire
     * component, however, this method requests a redraw only for the
     * area that has changed.
     **/
    public void actionPerformed(ActionEvent e) {
        // Ask to have the old bounding box of the spiral redrawn.
        // Nothing else has anything drawn in it, so it doesn't need a redraw
        repaint((int)(x-r2-linewidth), (int)(y-r2-linewidth),
                (int)(2*(r2+linewidth)), (int)(2*(r2+linewidth)));

        // Now animate: update the position and angles of the spiral

        // Bounce if we've hit an edge
        Rectangle bounds = getBounds();
        if ((x - r2 + deltaX < 0) || (x + r2 + deltaX > bounds.width))
            deltaX = -deltaX;
        if ((y - r2 + deltaY < 0) || (y + r2 + deltaY > bounds.height))
            deltaY = -deltaY;

        // Move the center of the spiral
        x += deltaX;
        y += deltaY;

        // Increment the start and end angles;
        a1 += deltaA;
        a2 += deltaA;
        if (a1 > 2*Math.PI) {  // Don't let them get too big
            a1 -= 2*Math.PI;
            a2 -= 2*Math.PI;
        }

        // Now ask to have the new bounding box of the spiral redrawn.  This
        // rectangle will be intersected with the redraw rectangle requested
        // above, and only the combined region will be redrawn
        repaint((int)(x-r2-linewidth), (int)(y-r2-linewidth),
                (int)(2*(r2+linewidth)), (int)(2*(r2+linewidth)));
    }
```

Example 11–17: Hypnosis.java (continued)

```java
    /** Tell Swing not to double-buffer for us, since we do our own */
    public boolean isDoubleBuffered() { return false; }

    /** This is a main() method for testing the component */
    public static void main(String[] args) {
        JFrame f = new JFrame("Hypnosis");
        Hypnosis h = new Hypnosis(200, 200, 10, 100, 0, 11*Math.PI, 7, 100,
                                  2*Math.PI/30, 3, 5);
        f.getContentPane().add(h, BorderLayout.CENTER);
        f.setSize(400, 400);
        f.show();
        h.start();
    }
}
```

Displaying Graphics Examples

Example 11-18 shows the GraphicsExampleFrame class we've been using to display GraphicsExample implementations throughout this chapter. This program mainly demonstrates the Swing and Printing APIs, but is included here for completeness. The paintComponent() method of the GraphicsExamplePane inner class is where the draw() method of each GraphicsExample object is invoked. Although paint-Component() is declared as taking a Graphics object, in Java 1.2 and later it is always passed a Graphics2D object, which can be safely cast to that type.

Example 11–18: GraphicsExampleFrame.java

```java
package com.davidflanagan.examples.graphics;
import java.awt.*;
import java.awt.event.*;
import javax.swing.*;
import javax.swing.event.*;
import java.awt.print.*;

/**
 * This class displays one or more GraphicsExample objects in a
 * Swing JFrame and a JTabbedPane
 */
public class GraphicsExampleFrame extends JFrame {
    public GraphicsExampleFrame(final GraphicsExample[] examples) {
        super("GraphicsExampleFrame");

        Container cpane = getContentPane();    // Set up the frame
        cpane.setLayout(new BorderLayout());
        final JTabbedPane tpane = new JTabbedPane(); // And the tabbed pane
        cpane.add(tpane, BorderLayout.CENTER);

        // Add a menubar
        JMenuBar menubar = new JMenuBar();           // Create the menubar
        this.setJMenuBar(menubar);                   // Add it to the frame
        JMenu filemenu = new JMenu("File");          // Create a File menu
        menubar.add(filemenu);                       // Add to the menubar
        JMenuItem print = new JMenuItem("Print");    // Create a Print item
        filemenu.add(print);                         // Add it to the menu
        JMenuItem quit = new JMenuItem("Quit");      // Create a Quit item
        filemenu.add(quit);                          // Add it to the menu
```

Example 11–18: GraphicsExampleFrame.java (continued)

```java
        // Tell the Print menu item what to do when selected
        print.addActionListener(new ActionListener() {
            public void actionPerformed(ActionEvent e) {
                // Get the currently displayed example, and call
                // the print method (defined below)
                print(examples[tpane.getSelectedIndex()]);
            }
        });

        // Tell the Quit menu item what to do when selected
        quit.addActionListener(new ActionListener() {
            public void actionPerformed(ActionEvent e) { System.exit(0); }
        });

        // In addition to the Quit menu item, also handle window close events
        this.addWindowListener(new WindowAdapter() {
            public void windowClosing(WindowEvent e) { System.exit(0); }
        });

        // Insert each of the example objects into the tabbed pane
        for(int i = 0; i < examples.length; i++) {
            GraphicsExample e = examples[i];
            tpane.addTab(e.getName(), new GraphicsExamplePane(e));
        }
    }

    /**
     * This inner class is a custom Swing component that displays
     * a GraphicsExample object.
     */
    public class GraphicsExamplePane extends JComponent {
        GraphicsExample example;  // The example to display
        Dimension size;           // How much space it requires

        public GraphicsExamplePane(GraphicsExample example) {
            this.example = example;
            size = new Dimension(example.getWidth(), example.getHeight());
        }

        /** Draw the component and the example it contains */
        public void paintComponent(Graphics g) {
            g.setColor(Color.white);                    // set the background
            g.fillRect(0, 0, size.width, size.height);  // to white
            g.setColor(Color.black);                  // set a default drawing color
            example.draw((Graphics2D) g, this);  // ask example to draw itself
        }

        // These methods specify how big the component must be
        public Dimension getPreferredSize() { return size; }
        public Dimension getMinimumSize() { return size; }
    }

    /** This method is invoked by the Print menu item */
    public void print(final GraphicsExample example) {
        // Start off by getting a printer job to do the printing
        PrinterJob job = PrinterJob.getPrinterJob();
        // Wrap the example in a Printable object (defined below)
        // and tell the PrinterJob that we want to print it
```

Example 11–18: GraphicsExampleFrame.java (continued)

```
            job.setPrintable(new PrintableExample(example));

        // Display the print dialog to the user
        if (job.printDialog()) {
            // If they didn't cancel it, then tell the job to start printing
            try {
                job.print();
            }
            catch(PrinterException e) {
                System.out.println("Couldn't print: " + e.getMessage());
            }
        }
    }

    /**
     * This inner class implements the Printable interface in order to print
     * a GraphicsExample object.
     **/
    class PrintableExample implements Printable  {
        GraphicsExample example;  // The example to print

        // The constructor.  Just remember the example
        public PrintableExample(GraphicsExample example) {
            this.example = example;
        }

        /**
         * This method is called by the PrinterJob to print the example
         **/
        public int print(Graphics g, PageFormat pf, int pageIndex) {
            // Tell the PrinterJob that there is only one page
            if (pageIndex != 0) return NO_SUCH_PAGE;

            // The PrinterJob supplies us a Graphics object to draw with.
            // Anything drawn with this object will be sent to the printer.
            // The Graphics object can safely be cast to a Graphics2D object.
            Graphics2D g2 = (Graphics2D)g;

            // Translate to skip the left and top margins.
            g2.translate(pf.getImageableX(), pf.getImageableY());

            // Figure out how big the printable area is, and how big
            // the example is.
            double pageWidth = pf.getImageableWidth();
            double pageHeight = pf.getImageableHeight();
            double exampleWidth = example.getWidth();
            double exampleHeight = example.getHeight();

            // Scale the example if needed
            double scalex = 1.0, scaley = 1.0;
            if (exampleWidth > pageWidth) scalex = pageWidth/exampleWidth;
            if (exampleHeight > pageHeight) scaley = pageHeight/exampleHeight;
            double scalefactor = Math.min(scalex, scaley);
            if (scalefactor != 1) g2.scale(scalefactor, scalefactor);

            // Finally, call the draw() method of the example, passing in
            // the Graphics2D object for the printer
            example.draw(g2, GraphicsExampleFrame.this);
```

Example 11–18: GraphicsExampleFrame.java (continued)

```java
            // Tell the PrinterJob that we successfully printed the page
            return PAGE_EXISTS;
        }
    }

    /**
     * The main program.  Use Java reflection to load and instantiate
     * the specified GraphicsExample classes, then create a
     * GraphicsExampleFrame to display them.
     **/
    public static void main(String[] args) {
        GraphicsExample[] examples = new GraphicsExample[args.length];

        // Loop through the command line arguments
        for(int i=0; i < args.length; i++) {
            // The class name of the requested example
            String classname = args[i];

            // If no package is specified, assume it is in this package
            if (classname.indexOf('.') == -1)
                classname = "com.davidflanagan.examples.graphics."+args[i];

            // Try to instantiate the named GraphicsExample class
            try {
                Class exampleClass = Class.forName(classname);
                examples[i] = (GraphicsExample) exampleClass.newInstance();
            }
            catch (ClassNotFoundException e) {  // unknown class
                System.err.println("Couldn't find example: " + classname);
                System.exit(1);
            }
            catch (ClassCastException e) {       // wrong type of class
                System.err.println("Class " + classname +
                                   " is not a GraphicsExample");
                System.exit(1);
            }
            catch (Exception e) {  // class doesn't have a public constructor
                // catch InstantiationException,IllegalAccessException
                System.err.println("Couldn't instantiate example: " +
                                   classname);
                System.exit(1);
            }
        }

        // Now create a window to display the examples in, and make it visible
        GraphicsExampleFrame f = new GraphicsExampleFrame(examples);
        f.pack();
        f.setVisible(true);
    }
}
```

Exercises

11-1. Example 11-1 contains a centerText() method that centers one or two lines of text within a rectangle. Write a modified version of this method that positions a single line of text according to two new method parameters. One parameter should specify the horizontal positioning: left-, center-, or right-justified. The other parameter should specify the vertical position: at the top of the rectangle, centered, or at the bottom of the rectangle. You can use the FontMetrics class, as Example 11-1 does, or the Java 2D getStringBounds() method of the Font class. Write a GraphicsExample class that demonstrates all nine possible positioning types supported by your method.

11-2. Use the animation techniques demonstrated in this chapter to write an applet that scrolls a textual message across the screen. The text to scroll and the scrolling speed should be read from applet parameters specified with <PARAM> tags in an HTML file.

11-3. Experiment with the graphics capabilities of the Graphics and Graphics2D classes and write an applet or application that displays some kind of interesting and dynamic graphics. You may want to take your inspiration from one of the many screensaver programs on the market. For example, you might draw filled rectangles on the screen, using random sizes, positions, and colors. (See Math.random() and java.util.Random for ways to generate random numbers.) Feel free to use any of the custom Shape, Stroke, or Paint classes developed in this chapter. Be creative!

11-4. One of the things that makes graphics so powerful is that it gives us the ability to visualize patterns. Look back at Example 1-15. This program computes prime numbers with the "Sieve of Eratosthenes" algorithm, whereby prime numbers are located by ruling out multiples of all previous prime numbers. As part of this algorithm, you maintain an array that specifies whether a number is prime or not. Write a graphical version of the Sieve program. It should display the array as a 2D matrix; cells in the matrix that represent prime numbers should be displayed in one color; non-primes should be displayed in another color. Write your program as a standalone application or as a GraphicsExample implementation, if you prefer.

Now extend your program again. When computing primes, don't simply store a boolean value to indicate whether a number is prime or not. Instead, store an int value that specifies, for non-prime numbers, the prime number that was used to rule this one out. After computing a set of primes, display the contents of your array as a rectangular grid, using a different color to indicate the multiples of each prime. The patterns that emerge look best when viewed in a square grid with a prime number as its height and width. For example, if you compute all the primes up to 361, you can graphically display your results in a square grid with 19 cells per side. Study the patterns you see. Does it give you insight into the workings of the algorithm? Does it help you understand why it is called a "sieve"?

11-5. Example 11-10 demonstrates how font glyphs can be used as Shape objects and shows how those Shape objects can be transformed with an arbitrary AffineTransform object. Write a custom Stroke object that is initialized with a Font and a string of text. When this Stroke class is used to draw a shape, it should display the specified text, using the specified font, along the outline of the specified shape. The text should hug the outline of the shape as closely as possible, which means that each font glyph has to be rotated, positioned, and drawn independently of the other glyphs. Use the two-argument version of Shape.getPathIterator() to obtain a FlatteningPathIterator that approximates the shape using straight line segments. You'll need to use geometry to compute the slope of each line segment and trigonometry to convert the slope to a rotation angle for each font glyph (you may find Math.atan2() helpful). Write a GraphicsExample class that displays some text art that demonstrates your new Stroke object.

CHAPTER 12

Printing

The Graphics and Graphics2D objects represent a "drawing surface"; in Chapter 11, *Graphics*, we saw examples of using both the screen and an off-screen buffer as drawing surfaces. Printing in Java is simply a matter of obtaining a Graphics object that uses a printer as a drawing surface. Once you have a Graphics object, you can print text and draw graphics to the printer just as you do onscreen. The only trick is in obtaining the Graphics object for a printer. Java 1.1 introduced one API for doing this, and then Java 1.2 introduced a new and different API.* This chapter includes examples of printing components and multipage documents using both APIs.

Printing with the Java 1.1 API

Example 12-1 harks back to the "scribble" programs of Chapter 10, *Graphical User Interfaces*; it is a GUI component that allows the user to scribble with the mouse. The example stores the coordinates of the mouse scribbles, and when the user clicks the **Print** button, it prints the scribble out. This example uses the AWT (not Swing) and the Java 1.1 Printing API. The printScribble() method shows the steps required to use this API. The actual printing occurs in the paint() method, which is the method that also does onscreen drawing.

Example 12–1: ScribblePrinter1.java

```
package com.davidflanagan.examples.print;
import java.awt.*;
import java.awt.event.*;
import java.util.*;

/**
 * A "scribble" application that remembers the scribble and allows the user
 * to print it.  It displays an AWT API and uses the Java 1.1 printing API.
 **/
```

---

* Then Java 1.3 added enhancements to the Java 1.1 API, in the form of the JobAttributes and PageAttributes classes. And Java 1.4 is expected to enhance the Java 1.2 Printing API.

Example 12-1: ScribblePrinter1.java (continued)

```java
public class ScribblePrinter1 extends Panel {
    private short last_x = 0, last_y = 0;          // last click posistion
    private Vector lines = new Vector(256,256);     // store the scribble
    private Properties printprefs = new Properties(); // store user preferences
    private Frame frame;

    public ScribblePrinter1(Frame frame) {
        // Remember the frame: we'll need it to create a PrintJob
        this.frame = frame;

        // Register event types we're interested in for scribbling
        enableEvents(AWTEvent.MOUSE_EVENT_MASK |
                     AWTEvent.MOUSE_MOTION_EVENT_MASK);

        // Add a print button to he layout, and respond to it by printing
        Button b = new Button("Print");
        b.addActionListener(new ActionListener() {
                public void actionPerformed(ActionEvent e) { printScribble(); }
            });
        this.setLayout(new FlowLayout(FlowLayout.RIGHT, 5, 5));
        this.add(b);
    }

    /** Redraw (or print) the scribble based on stored lines */
    public void paint(Graphics g) {
        for(int i = 0; i < lines.size(); i++) {
            Line l = (Line)lines.elementAt(i);
            g.drawLine(l.x1, l.y1, l.x2, l.y2);
        }
    }

    /** Print out the scribble */
    public void printScribble() {
        // Obtain a PrintJob
        Toolkit toolkit = this.getToolkit();
        PrintJob job = toolkit.getPrintJob(frame, "ScribblePrinter1", printprefs);

        // If the user clicked Cancel in the print dialog, don't print
        if (job == null) return;

        // Get the Graphics object we use to draw to the printer
        Graphics g = job.getGraphics();

        // Give the output a larger top and left margin.  Otherwise it will
        // be scrunched up in the upper-left corner of the page.
        g.translate(100, 100);

        // Draw a border around the output area.
        Dimension size = this.getSize();
        g.drawRect(-1, -1, size.width+2, size.height+2);

        // Set a clipping region so our scribbles don't go outside the border
        // On-screen this happens automatically, but not on paper.
        g.setClip(0, 0, size.width, size.height);

        // Print this component and all components it contains
        // This will invoke the paint() method, and will paint the button too.
        // Use print() instead of printAll() if you don't the button to show.
```

Example 12–1: ScribblePrinter1.java (continued)

```
        this.printAll(g);

        // Finish up.
        g.dispose();        // End the current page
        job.end();          // End the print job
    }

    /** Called when the user clicks to begin a scribble */
    public void processMouseEvent(MouseEvent e) {
        if (e.getID() == MouseEvent.MOUSE_PRESSED) {
            last_x = (short)e.getX();          // remember click position
            last_y = (short)e.getY();
        }
        else super.processMouseEvent(e);
    }

    /** Called when the the user drags the mouse: does the scribbling */
    public void processMouseMotionEvent(MouseEvent e) {
        if (e.getID() == MouseEvent.MOUSE_DRAGGED) {
            Graphics g = getGraphics();
            g.drawLine(last_x, last_y, e.getX(), e.getY());  // draw the line
            lines.addElement(new Line(last_x, last_y,        // and save it
                                 (short) e.getX(), (short)e.getY()));
            last_x = (short) e.getX();
            last_y = (short) e.getY();
        }
        else super.processMouseMotionEvent(e);
    }

    /** The main method.  Create a ScribblePrinter1 object and away we go! */
    public static void main(String[] args) {
        Frame frame = new Frame("ScribblePrinter1");
        ScribblePrinter1 s = new ScribblePrinter1(frame);
        frame.add(s, BorderLayout.CENTER);
        frame.setSize(400, 400);
        frame.show();
    }

    /**
     * This inner class stores the coordinates of one line of the scribble.
     **/
    class Line {
        public short x1, y1, x2, y2;
        public Line(short x1, short y1, short x2, short y2) {
            this.x1 = x1; this.y1 = y1; this.x2 = x2; this.y2 = y2;
        }
    }
}
```

Printing with the Java 1.2 API

Example 12-2 does the same thing as Example 12-1 but has been modified to use
Swing, Java 2D, and the Java 1.2 Printing API. The Java 1.2 API is contained in the
java.awt.print package. Note that it uses the java.awt.print.PrinterJob class,
not the java.awt.PrintJob class of the Java 1.1 API. Our example class implements the java.awt.print.Printable interface, which means that it defines a

print() method that allows it to be printed by a `PrinterJob`. `printScribble()` starts things off by obtaining a `PrinterJob` object and telling it what to print, and the print() method does the rest. Like the previous example, this one uses the component's own drawing method, `paintComponent()` in this case, to do the actual printing. You can find another example of the Java 1.2 Printing API in Example 11-18.

Example 12-2: ScribblePrinter2.java

```
package com.davidflanagan.examples.print;
import java.awt.*;
import java.awt.event.*;
import java.awt.print.*;
import java.awt.geom.*;
import javax.swing.*;
import java.util.*;


/**
 * A "scribble" application that remembers the scribble and allows the user
 * to print it.  It displays a Swing API and uses the Java 1.2 printing API.
 * It also uses Java2D features to draw and represent the scribble.
 **/
public class ScribblePrinter2 extends JComponent implements Printable {
    Stroke linestyle = new BasicStroke(3.0f); // Draw with wide lines
    GeneralPath scribble = new GeneralPath(); // Holds the scribble

    public ScribblePrinter2() {
        // Register event types we're interested in for scribbling
        enableEvents(AWTEvent.MOUSE_EVENT_MASK |
                     AWTEvent.MOUSE_MOTION_EVENT_MASK);

        // Add a print button to he layout, and respond to it by printing
        JButton b = new JButton("Print");
        b.addActionListener(new ActionListener() {
                public void actionPerformed(ActionEvent e) { printScribble(); }
            });
        this.setLayout(new FlowLayout(FlowLayout.LEFT, 5, 5));
        this.add(b);
    }

    /** Redraw (or print) the scribble based on stored lines */
    public void paintComponent(Graphics g) {
        super.paintComponent(g);   // Allow the superclass to draw itself
        Graphics2D g2 = (Graphics2D) g;
        g2.setStroke(linestyle);   // Specify wide lines
        g2.draw(scribble);         // Draw the scribble
    }

    /**
     * Print out the scribble.  This is the method invoked by the Print button;
     * it is not part of the Printable interface
     **/
    public void printScribble() {
        // Obtain a java.awt.print.PrinterJob  (not java.awt.PrintJob)
        PrinterJob job = PrinterJob.getPrinterJob();

        // Tell the PrinterJob to print us (since we implement Printable)
        // using the default page layout
        job.setPrintable(this, job.defaultPage());
```

Example 12-2: ScribblePrinter2.java (continued)

```
    // Display the print dialog that allows the user to set options.
    // The method returns false if the user cancelled the print request
    if (job.printDialog()) {
        // If not cancelled, start printing!  This will call the print()
        // method defined by the Printable interface.
        try { job.print(); }
        catch (PrinterException e) { System.err.println(e);  }
    }
}

/**
 * This is the method defined by the Printable interface.  It prints the
 * scribble to the specified Graphics object, respecting the paper size
 * and margins specified by the PageFormat.  If the specified page number
 * is not page 0, it returns a code saying that printing is complete.  The
 * method must be prepared to be called multiple times per printing request
 **/
public int print(Graphics g, PageFormat format, int pagenum) {
    // We are only one page long; reject any other page numbers
    if (pagenum > 0) return Printable.NO_SUCH_PAGE;

    // The Java 1.2 printing API passes us a Graphics object, but we
    // can always cast it to a Graphics2D object
    Graphics2D g2 = (Graphics2D) g;

    // Translate to accommodate the requested top and left margins.
    g2.translate(format.getImageableX(), format.getImageableY());

    // Figure out how big the drawing is, and how big the page
    // (excluding margins) is
    Dimension size = this.getSize();                     // Scribble size
    double pageWidth = format.getImageableWidth();     // Page width
    double pageHeight = format.getImageableHeight();   // Page height

    // If the scribble is too wide or tall for the page, scale it down
    if (size.width > pageWidth) {
        double factor = pageWidth/size.width;   // How much to scale
        g2.scale(factor, factor);               // Adjust coordinate system
        pageWidth /= factor;                    // Adjust page size up
        pageHeight /= factor;
    }
    if (size.height > pageHeight) {   // Do the same thing for height
        double factor = pageHeight/size.height;
        g2.scale(factor, factor);
        pageWidth /= factor;
        pageHeight /= factor;
    }

    // Now we know the scribble will fit on the page.  Center it by
    // translating as necessary.
    g2.translate((pageWidth-size.width)/2,(pageHeight-size.height)/2);

    // Draw a line around the outside of the drawing area
    g2.drawRect(-1, -1, size.width+2, size.height+2);

    // Set a clipping region so the scribbles don't go out of bounds
    g2.setClip(0, 0, size.width, size.height);
```

Example 12-2: ScribblePrinter2.java (continued)

```
        // Finally, print the component by calling the paintComponent() method.
        // Or, call paint() to paint the component, its background, border, and
        // children, including the Print JButton
        this.paintComponent(g);

        // Tell the PrinterJob that the page number was valid
        return Printable.PAGE_EXISTS;
    }

    /** Called when the user clicks to begin a scribble */
    public void processMouseEvent(MouseEvent e) {
        if (e.getID() == MouseEvent.MOUSE_PRESSED) {
            scribble.moveTo(e.getX(), e.getY());  // Start a new line
        }
        else super.processMouseEvent(e);
    }

    /** Called when the the user drags the mouse: does the scribbling */
    public void processMouseMotionEvent(MouseEvent e) {
        if (e.getID() == MouseEvent.MOUSE_DRAGGED) {
            scribble.lineTo(e.getX(), e.getY());  // Add a line to the scribble
            repaint();  // Redraw the whole scribble. Clean but a little slow
        }
        else super.processMouseMotionEvent(e);
    }

    /** The main method.  Create a ScribblePrinter2 object and away we go! */
    public static void main(String[] args) {
        JFrame frame = new JFrame("ScribblePrinter2");
        ScribblePrinter2 s = new ScribblePrinter2();
        frame.getContentPane().add(s, BorderLayout.CENTER);
        frame.setSize(400, 400);
        frame.setVisible(true);
    }
}
```

Printing Multipage Text Documents

The two printing examples we've seen so far print GUI components on a single page. Printing multipage documents is more interesting, but also trickier, because we have to decide where to place the page breaks. Example 12-3 shows how this can be done. This HardcopyWriter class is a custom java.io.Writer stream that uses the Java 1.1 Printing API to print the characters sent through it, inserting line breaks and page breaks as necessary.

The HardcopyWriter class includes two demonstration programs as inner classes. The first, PrintFile, reads a specified text file and prints it by sending its contents to a HardcopyWriter stream. The second, Demo, prints a demonstration page that shows off the font and tabbing capabilities of the class, as shown in Figure 12-1.

Example 12-3 is long but worth studying. In addition to demonstrating the Java 1.1 Printing API again, it shows an approach to paginating a text document. It is also a useful example of a custom Writer stream.

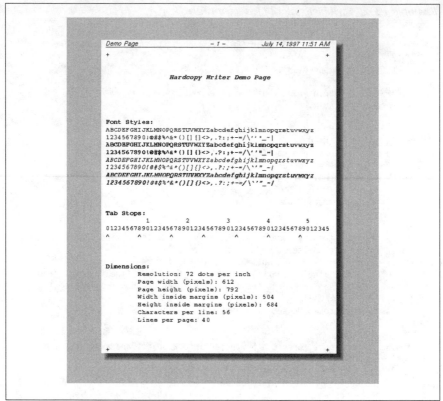

Figure 12-1. Demonstration page printed by HardcopyWriter

Example 12-3: HardcopyWriter.java

```java
package com.davidflanagan.examples.print;
import java.awt.*;
import java.awt.event.*;
import java.io.*;
import java.text.*;
import java.util.*;

/**
 * A character output stream that sends output to a printer.
 **/
public class HardcopyWriter extends Writer {
    // These are the instance variables for the class
    protected PrintJob job;                   // The PrintJob object in use
    protected Graphics page;                  // Graphics object for current page
    protected String jobname;                 // The name of the print job
    protected int fontsize;                   // Point size of the font
    protected String time;                    // Current time (appears in header)
    protected Dimension pagesize;             // Size of the page (in dots)
    protected int pagedpi;                    // Page resolution in dots per inch
    protected Font font, headerfont;          // Body font and header font
    protected FontMetrics metrics;            // Metrics for the body font
    protected FontMetrics headermetrics;      // Metrics for the header font
    protected int x0, y0;                     // Upper-left corner inside margin
```

Example 12-3: HardcopyWriter.java (continued)

```
protected int width, height;        // Size (in dots) inside margins
protected int headery;              // Baseline of the page header
protected int charwidth;            // The width of each character
protected int lineheight;           // The height of each line
protected int lineascent;           // Offset of font baseline
protected int chars_per_line;       // Number of characters per line
protected int lines_per_page;       // Number of lines per page
protected int charnum = 0, linenum = 0; // Current column and line position
protected int pagenum = 0;          // Current page number

// A field to save state between invocations of the write() method
private boolean last_char_was_return = false;

// A static variable that holds user preferences between print jobs
protected static Properties printprops = new Properties();

/**
 * The constructor for this class has a bunch of arguments:
 * The frame argument is required for all printing in Java.
 * The jobname appears left justified at the top of each printed page.
 * The font size is specified in points, as on-screen font sizes are.
 * The margins are specified in inches (or fractions of inches).
 **/
public HardcopyWriter(Frame frame, String jobname, int fontsize,
                      double leftmargin, double rightmargin,
                      double topmargin, double bottommargin)
    throws HardcopyWriter.PrintCanceledException
{
    // Get the PrintJob object with which we'll do all the printing.
    // The call is synchronized on the static printprops object, which
    // means that only one print dialog can be popped up at a time.
    // If the user clicks Cancel in the print dialog, throw an exception.
    Toolkit toolkit = frame.getToolkit();   // get Toolkit from Frame
    synchronized(printprops) {
        job = toolkit.getPrintJob(frame, jobname, printprops);
    }
    if (job == null)
        throw new PrintCanceledException("User cancelled print request");

    pagesize = job.getPageDimension();      // query the page size
    pagedpi = job.getPageResolution();      // query the page resolution

    // Bug Workaround:
    // On windows, getPageDimension() and getPageResolution don't work, so
    // we've got to fake them.
    if (System.getProperty("os.name").regionMatches(true,0,"windows",0,7)){
        // Use screen dpi, which is what the PrintJob tries to emulate
        pagedpi = toolkit.getScreenResolution();
        // Assume a 8.5" x 11" page size.  A4 paper users must change this.
        pagesize = new Dimension((int)(8.5 * pagedpi), 11*pagedpi);
        // We also have to adjust the fontsize.  It is specified in points,
        // (1 point = 1/72 of an inch) but Windows measures it in pixels.
        fontsize = fontsize * pagedpi / 72;
    }

    // Compute coordinates of the upper-left corner of the page.
    // I.e. the coordinates of (leftmargin, topmargin).  Also compute
    // the width and height inside of the margins.
```

Example 12–3: HardcopyWriter.java (continued)

```java
        x0 = (int)(leftmargin * pagedpi);
        y0 = (int)(topmargin * pagedpi);
        width = pagesize.width - (int)((leftmargin + rightmargin) * pagedpi);
        height = pagesize.height - (int)((topmargin + bottommargin) * pagedpi);

        // Get body font and font size
        font = new Font("Monospaced", Font.PLAIN, fontsize);
        metrics = frame.getFontMetrics(font);
        lineheight = metrics.getHeight();
        lineascent = metrics.getAscent();
        charwidth = metrics.charWidth('0');  // Assumes a monospaced font!

        // Now compute columns and lines will fit inside the margins
        chars_per_line = width / charwidth;
        lines_per_page = height / lineheight;

        // Get header font information
        // And compute baseline of page header: 1/8" above the top margin
        headerfont = new Font("SansSerif", Font.ITALIC, fontsize);
        headermetrics = frame.getFontMetrics(headerfont);
        headery = y0 - (int)(0.125 * pagedpi) -
            headermetrics.getHeight() + headermetrics.getAscent();

        // Compute the date/time string to display in the page header
        DateFormat df = DateFormat.getDateTimeInstance(DateFormat.LONG,
                                            DateFormat.SHORT);
        df.setTimeZone(TimeZone.getDefault());
        time = df.format(new Date());

        this.jobname = jobname;                 // save name
        this.fontsize = fontsize;               // save font size
    }

    /**
     * This is the write() method of the stream.  All Writer subclasses
     * implement this.  All other versions of write() are variants of this one
     **/
    public void write(char[] buffer, int index, int len) {
        synchronized(this.lock) {  // For thread safety
            // Loop through all the characters passed to us
            for(int i = index; i < index + len; i++) {
                // If we haven't begun a page (or a new page), do that now.
                if (page == null) newpage();

                // If the character is a line terminator, then begin new line,
                // unless it is a \n immediately after a \r.
                if (buffer[i] == '\n') {
                    if (!last_char_was_return) newline();
                    continue;
                }
                if (buffer[i] == '\r') {
                    newline();
                    last_char_was_return = true;
                    continue;
                }
                else last_char_was_return = false;

                // If it some other non-printing character, ignore it.
```

Example 12-3: HardcopyWriter.java (continued)

```java
                    if (Character.isWhitespace(buffer[i]) &&
                        !Character.isSpaceChar(buffer[i]) && (buffer[i] != '\t'))
                        continue;

                    // If no more characters will fit on the line, start new line.
                    if (charnum >= chars_per_line) {
                        newline();
                        // Also start a new page, if necessary
                        if (page == null) newpage();
                    }

                    // Now print the character:
                    // If it is a space, skip one space, without output.
                    // If it is a tab, skip the necessary number of spaces.
                    // Otherwise, print the character.
                    // It is inefficient to draw only one character at a time, but
                    // because our FontMetrics don't match up exactly to what the
                    // printer uses we need to position each character individually
                    if (Character.isSpaceChar(buffer[i])) charnum++;
                    else if (buffer[i] == '\t') charnum += 8 - (charnum % 8);
                    else {
                        page.drawChars(buffer, i, 1,
                                       x0 + charnum * charwidth,
                                       y0 + (linenum*lineheight) + lineascent);
                        charnum++;
                    }
                }
            }
        }

    /**
     * This is the flush() method that all Writer subclasses must implement.
     * There is no way to flush a PrintJob without prematurely printing the
     * page, so we don't do anything.
     **/
    public void flush() { /* do nothing */ }

    /**
     * This is the close() method that all Writer subclasses must implement.
     * Print the pending page (if any) and terminate the PrintJob.
     */
    public void close() {
        synchronized(this.lock) {
            if (page != null) page.dispose();   // Send page to the printer
            job.end();                          // Terminate the job
        }
    }

    /**
     * Set the font style.  The argument should be one of the font style
     * constants defined by the java.awt.Font class.  All subsequent output
     * will be in that style.  This method relies on all styles of the
     * Monospaced font having the same metrics.
     **/
    public void setFontStyle(int style) {
        synchronized (this.lock) {
            // Try to set a new font, but restore current one if it fails
            Font current = font;
```

Example 12-3: HardcopyWriter.java (continued)

```
            try { font = new Font("Monospaced", style, fontsize); }
            catch (Exception e) { font = current; }
            // If a page is pending, set the new font. Otherwise newpage() will
            if (page != null) page.setFont(font);
        }
    }

    /** End the current page.  Subsequent output will be on a new page. */
    public void pageBreak() { synchronized(this.lock) { newpage(); } }

    /** Return the number of columns of characters that fit on the page */
    public int getCharactersPerLine() { return this.chars_per_line; }

    /** Return the number of lines that fit on a page */
    public int getLinesPerPage() { return this.lines_per_page; }

    /** This internal method begins a new line */
    protected void newline() {
        charnum = 0;                        // Reset character number to 0
        linenum++;                          // Increment line number
        if (linenum >= lines_per_page) {    // If we've reached the end of page
            page.dispose();                 //   send page to printer
            page = null;                    //   but don't start a new page yet.
        }
    }

    /** This internal method begins a new page and prints the header. */
    protected void newpage() {
        page = job.getGraphics();                   // Begin the new page
        linenum = 0; charnum = 0;                   // Reset line and char number
        pagenum++;                                  // Increment page number
        page.setFont(headerfont);                   // Set the header font.
        page.drawString(jobname, x0, headery);      // Print job name left justified

        String s = "- " + pagenum + " -";           // Print the page # centered.
        int w = headermetrics.stringWidth(s);
        page.drawString(s, x0 + (this.width - w)/2, headery);
        w = headermetrics.stringWidth(time);         // Print date right justified
        page.drawString(time, x0 + width - w, headery);

        // Draw a line beneath the header
        int y = headery + headermetrics.getDescent() + 1;
        page.drawLine(x0, y, x0+width, y);

        // Set the basic monospaced font for the rest of the page.
        page.setFont(font);
    }

    /**
     * This is the exception class that the HardcopyWriter constructor
     * throws when the user clicks "Cancel" in the print dialog box.
     **/
    public static class PrintCanceledException extends Exception {
        public PrintCanceledException(String msg) { super(msg); }
    }

    /**
     * A program that prints the specified file using HardcopyWriter
```

Example 12-3: HardcopyWriter.java (continued)

```
    **/
    public static class PrintFile {
        public static void main(String[] args) {
            try {
                if (args.length != 1)
                    throw new IllegalArgumentException("Wrong # of arguments");
                FileReader in = new FileReader(args[0]);
                HardcopyWriter out = null;
                Frame f = new Frame("PrintFile: " + args[0]);
                f.setSize(200, 50);
                f.show();
                try {
                    out = new HardcopyWriter(f, args[0], 10, .5, .5, .5, .5);
                }
                catch (HardcopyWriter.PrintCanceledException e) {
                    System.exit(0);
                }
                f.setVisible(false);
                char[] buffer = new char[4096];
                int numchars;
                while((numchars = in.read(buffer)) != -1)
                    out.write(buffer, 0, numchars);
                in.close();
                out.close();
            }
            catch (Exception e) {
                System.err.println(e);
                System.err.println("Usage: " +
                                   "java HardcopyWriter$PrintFile <filename>");
                System.exit(1);
            }
            System.exit(0);
        }
    }

    /**
     * A program that prints a demo page using HardcopyWriter
     **/
    public static class Demo extends Frame implements ActionListener {
        /** The main method of the program.  Create a test window */
        public static void main(String[] args) {
            Frame f = new Demo();
            f.show();
        }
        // Buttons used in this program
        protected Button print, quit;

        /** Constructor for the test program's window. */
        public Demo() {
            super("HardcopyWriter Test");          // Call frame constructor
            Panel p = new Panel();                  // Add a panel to the frame
            this.add(p, "Center");                  // Center it
            p.setFont(new Font("SansSerif",         // Set a default font
                               Font.BOLD, 18));
            print = new Button("Print Test Page"); // Create a Print button
            quit = new Button("Quit");              // Create a Quit button
            print.addActionListener(this);          // Specify that we'll handle
            quit.addActionListener(this);           //   button presses
```

Example 12-3: HardcopyWriter.java (continued)

```
            p.add(print);                           // Add the buttons to panel
            p.add(quit);
            this.pack();                            // Set the frame size
    }

    /** Handle the button presses */
    public void actionPerformed(ActionEvent e) {
        Object o = e.getSource();
        if (o == quit) System.exit(0);
        else if (o == print) printDemoPage();
    }

    /** Print the demo page */
    public void printDemoPage() {
        // Create a HardcopyWriter, using a 14 point font and 3/4" margins.
        HardcopyWriter hw;
        try { hw=new HardcopyWriter(this, "Demo Page",14,.75,.75,.75,.75);}
        catch (HardcopyWriter.PrintCanceledException e) { return; }

        // Send output to it through a PrintWriter stream
        PrintWriter out = new PrintWriter(hw);

        // Figure out the size of the page
        int rows = hw.getLinesPerPage(), cols = hw.getCharactersPerLine();

        // Mark upper left and upper-right corners
        out.print("+");                              // upper-left corner
        for(int i=0;i<cols-2;i++) out.print(" ");    // space over
        out.print("+");                              // upper-right corner

        // Display a title
        hw.setFontStyle(Font.BOLD + Font.ITALIC);
        out.println("\n\t\tHardcopy Writer Demo Page\n\n");

        // Demonstrate font styles
        hw.setFontStyle(Font.BOLD);
        out.println("Font Styles:");
        int[] styles = { Font.PLAIN, Font.BOLD,
                         Font.ITALIC, Font.ITALIC+Font.BOLD };
        for(int i = 0; i < styles.length; i++) {
            hw.setFontStyle(styles[i]);
            out.println("ABCDEFGHIJKLMNOPQRSTUVWXYZ" +
                        "abcdefghijklmnopqrstuvwxyz");
            out.println("1234567890!@#$%^&*()[]{}<>,.?:;+-=/\\`'\"_~|");
        }
        hw.setFontStyle(Font.PLAIN);
        out.println("\n");

        // Demonstrate tab stops
        hw.setFontStyle(Font.BOLD);
        out.println("Tab Stops:");
        hw.setFontStyle(Font.PLAIN);
        out.println("        1       2       3       4       5");
        out.println("0123456789012345678901234567890123456789012345678890");
        out.println("^\t^\t^\t^\t^\t^\t^\t^");
        out.println("\n");

        // Output some information about page dimensions and resolution
```

Example 12-3: HardcopyWriter.java (continued)

```
                hw.setFontStyle(Font.BOLD);
                out.println("Dimensions:");
                hw.setFontStyle(Font.PLAIN);
                out.println("\tResolution: " + hw.pagedpi + " dots per inch");
                out.println("\tPage width (pixels): " + hw.pagesize.width);
                out.println("\tPage height (pixels): " + hw.pagesize.height);
                out.println("\tWidth inside margins (pixels): " + hw.width);
                out.println("\tHeight inside margins (pixels): " + hw.height);
                out.println("\tCharacters per line: " + cols);
                out.println("\tLines per page: " + rows);

                // Skip down to the bottom of the page
                for(int i = 0; i < rows-30; i++) out.println();

                // And mark the lower left and lower right
                out.print("+");                          // lower-left
                for(int i=0;i<cols-2;i++) out.print(" "); // space-over
                out.print("+");                          // lower-right

                // Close the output stream, forcing the page to be printed
                out.close();
        }
    }
}
```

Printing Swing Documents

Example 10-21 in Chapter 10 demonstrated the power of javax.swing. text.JTextComponent to display complex documents, including HTML documents. One feature missing from JTextComponent, however, is the ability to print those documents. Example 10-21 included a printing feature based on a PrintableDocument class, which is listed in Example 12-4.

PrintableDocument uses the Java 1.2 Printing API. In addition to implementing the Printable interface, this example also implements the Pageable interface. Pageable represents a multipage document and defines three methods: getNumberOf-Pages(), which returns the number of pages in the document; getPageFormat(), which returns the size and orientation of each page of the document; and get-Printable(), which returns a Printable object that represents each page.

Beyond demonstrating the use of the Pageable and Printable interfaces, the example also shows the inner workings of the javax.swing.text package. In this package, Document objects are composed of nested Element objects, which are displayed on the screen (or a printer) by a parallel hierarchy of View objects. javax.swing.text is one of the more obscure areas of Swing, so don't worry if you don't understand all the details.

Unfortunately, the PrintableDocument class is not as robust and reliable as I would like. In my tests, I have found that it occasionally breaks a page in the middle of a line of text, placing half the line at the bottom of one page and the rest at the top of the next page. I am uncertain whether the bug lies in PrintableDocu-ment or the javax.swing.text package. Also, PrintableDocument doesn't handle unbreakable wide lines very well. When a document contains an unbreakable line that is wider than the requested page width (in an HTML <PRE> tag, for example), the Document class makes the entire document as wide as the widest line. Thus, it is not just wide lines within <PRE> tags that get truncated; the entire document is formatted to be too wide, causing all lines to get truncated at the right margin of the printed page.

Example 12–4: PrintableDocument.java

```java
package com.davidflanagan.examples.print;
import java.awt.*;
import java.awt.print.*;
import java.awt.geom.*;
import java.awt.font.*;
import javax.swing.*;
import javax.swing.text.*;
import java.util.*;


/**
 * This class implements the Pageable and Printable interfaces and allows
 * the contents of any JTextComponent to be printed using the java.awt.print
 * printing API.
 **/
public class PrintableDocument implements Pageable, Printable {
    View root;                  // The root View to be printed
    PageFormat format;          // Paper plus page orientation
    double scalefactor;         // How much to scale before printing
    int numPages;               // How many pages in the document
    double printX, printY;      // coordinates of upper-left of print area
    double printWidth;          // Width of the printable area
    double printHeight;         // Height of the printable area
    Rectangle drawRect;         // The rectangle in which the document is painted

    // How lenient are we with the bottom margin in widow/orphan prevention?
    static final double MARGIN_ADJUST = .97;

    // The font we use for printing page numbers
    static final Font headerFont = new Font("Serif", Font.PLAIN, 12);

    /**
     * This constructor allows printing the contents of any JTextComponent
     * using a default PageFormat and a default scale factor.  The default
     * scale factor is .75 because the default fonts are overly large.
     */
    public PrintableDocument(JTextComponent textComponent) {
        this(textComponent, new PageFormat(), .75);
    }


    /**
     * This constructor allows the contents of any JTextComponent to be
     * printed, using any specified PageFormat object and any scaling factor.
     **/
    public PrintableDocument(JTextComponent textComponent, PageFormat format,
                             double scalefactor)
    {
        // Remember the page format, and ask it for the printable area
        this.format = format;
        this.scalefactor = scalefactor;
        this.printX = format.getImageableX()/scalefactor;
        this.printY = format.getImageableY()/scalefactor;
        this.printWidth = format.getImageableWidth()/scalefactor;
```

Example 12-4: PrintableDocument.java (continued)

```
        this.printHeight = format.getImageableHeight()/scalefactor;
        double paperWidth = format.getWidth()/scalefactor;

        // Get the document and its root Element from the text component
        Document document = textComponent.getDocument();
        Element rootElement = document.getDefaultRootElement();
        // Get the EditorKit and its ViewFactory from the text component
        EditorKit editorKit =textComponent.getUI().getEditorKit(textComponent);
        ViewFactory viewFactory = editorKit.getViewFactory();

        // Use the ViewFactory to create a root View object for the document
        // This is the object we'll print.
        root = viewFactory.create(rootElement);

        // The Swing text architecture requires us to call setParent() on
        // our root View before we use it for anything.  In order to do this,
        // we need a View object that can serve as the parent.  We use a
        // custom implementation defined below.
        root.setParent(new ParentView(root, viewFactory, textComponent));

        // Tell the view how wide the page is; it has to format itself
        // to fit within this width.  The height doesn't really matter here
        root.setSize((float)printWidth, (float)printHeight);

        // Now that the view has formatted itself for the specified width,
        // Ask it how tall it is.
        double documentHeight = root.getPreferredSpan(View.Y_AXIS);

        // Set up the rectangle that tells the view where to draw itself
        // We'll use it in other methods of this class.
        drawRect = new Rectangle(0, 0, (int)printWidth, (int)documentHeight);

        // Now if the document is taller than one page, we have to
        // figure out where the page breaks are.
        if (documentHeight > printHeight) paginate(root, drawRect);

        // Once we've broken it into pages, figure out how many pages.
        numPages = pageLengths.size() + 1;
    }

    // This is the starting offset of the page we're currently working on
    double pageStart = 0;

    /**
     * This method loops through the children of the specified view,
     * recursing as necessary, and inserts pages breaks when needed.
     * It makes a rudimentary attempt to avoid "widows" and "orphans".
     **/
    protected void paginate(View v, Rectangle2D allocation) {
        // Figure out how tall this view is, and tell it to allocate
        // that space among its children
        double myheight = v.getPreferredSpan(View.Y_AXIS);
        v.setSize((float)printWidth, (float)myheight);

        // Now loop through each of the children
        int numkids = v.getViewCount();
        for(int i = 0; i < numkids; i++) {
            View kid = v.getView(i);  // this is the child we're working with
```

Example 12–4: PrintableDocument.java (continued)

```
                    // Figure out its size and location
                    Shape kidshape = v.getChildAllocation(i, allocation);
                    if (kidshape == null) continue;
                    Rectangle2D kidbox = kidshape.getBounds2D();

                    // This is the Y coordinate of the bottom of the child
                    double kidpos = kidbox.getY() + kidbox.getHeight() - pageStart;

                    // If this is the first child of a group, then we want to ensure
                    // that it doesn't get left by itself at the bottom of a page.
                    // I.e. we want to prevent "widows"
                    if ((numkids > 1) && (i == 0)) {
                        // If it is not near the end of the page, then just move
                        // on to the next child
                        if (kidpos < printY + printHeight*MARGIN_ADJUST) continue;

                        // Otherwise, the child is near the bottom of the page, so
                        // break the page before this child and place this child on
                        // the new page.
                        breakPage(kidbox.getY());
                        continue;
                    }

                    // If this is the last child of a group, we don't want it to
                    // appear by itself at the top of a new page, so allow it to
                    // squeeze past the bottom margin if necessary.  This helps to
                    // prevent "orphans"
                    if ((numkids > 1) && (i == numkids-1)) {
                        // If it fits normally, just move on to the next one
                        if (kidpos < printY + printHeight) continue;

                        // Otherwise, if it fits with extra space, then break the
                        // page at the end of the group
                        if (kidpos < printY + printHeight/MARGIN_ADJUST) {
                            breakPage(allocation.getY() + allocation.getHeight());
                            continue;
                        }
                    }

                    // If the child is not the first or last of a group, then we use
                    // the bottom margin strictly.  If the child fits on the page,
                    // then move on to the next child.
                    if (kidpos < printY+printHeight) continue;

                    // If we get here, the child doesn't fit on this page.  If it has
                    // no children, then break the page before this child and continue.
                    if (kid.getViewCount() == 0) {
                        breakPage(kidbox.getY());
                        continue;
                    }

                    // If we get here, then the child did not fit on the page, but it
                    // has kids of its own, so recurse to see if any of those kids
                    // will fit on the page.
                    paginate(kid, kidbox);
                }
            }
```

Example 12-4: PrintableDocument.java (continued)

```
// For a document of n pages, this list stores the lengths of pages
// 0 through n-2.  The last page is assumed to have a full length
ArrayList pageLengths = new ArrayList();

// For a document of n pages, this list stores the starting offset of
// pages 1 through n-1.  The offset of page 0 is always 0
ArrayList pageOffsets = new ArrayList();

/**
 * Break a page at the specified Y coordinate.  Store the necessary
 * information into the pageLengths and pageOffsets lists
 **/
void breakPage(double y) {
    double pageLength = y-pageStart-printY;
    pageStart = y-printY;
    pageLengths.add(new Double(pageLength));
    pageOffsets.add(new Double(pageStart));
}

/** Return the number of pages. This is a Pageable method.    */
public int getNumberOfPages() { return numPages; }

/**
 * Return the PageFormat object for the specified page.  This is a
 * Pageable method. This implementation uses the computed length of the
 * page in the returned PageFormat object.  The PrinterJob will use this
 * as a clipping region, which will prevent extraneous parts of the
 * document from being drawn in the top and bottom margins.
 **/
public PageFormat getPageFormat(int pagenum) {
    // On the last page, just return the user-specified page format
    if (pagenum == numPages-1) return format;

    // Otherwise, look up the height of this page and return an
    // appropriate PageFormat.
    double pageLength = ((Double)pageLengths.get(pagenum)).doubleValue();
    PageFormat f = (PageFormat) format.clone();
    Paper p = f.getPaper();
    if (f.getOrientation() == PageFormat.PORTRAIT)
        p.setImageableArea(printX*scalefactor, printY*scalefactor,
                            printWidth*scalefactor, pageLength*scalefactor);
    else
        p.setImageableArea(printY*scalefactor, printX*scalefactor,
                            pageLength*scalefactor, printWidth*scalefactor);
    f.setPaper(p);
    return f;
}

/**
 * This Pageable method returns the Printable object for the specified
 * page.  Since this class implements both Pageable and Printable, it just
 * returns this.
 **/
public Printable getPrintable(int pagenum) { return this; }

/**
 * This is the basic Printable method that prints a specified page
 **/
```

Example 12–4: PrintableDocument.java (continued)

```java
public int print(Graphics g, PageFormat format, int pageIndex) {
    // Return an error code on attempts to print past the end of the doc
    if (pageIndex >= numPages) return NO_SUCH_PAGE;

    // Cast the Graphics object so we can use Java2D operations
    Graphics2D g2 = (Graphics2D)g;

    // Translate to accommodate the top and left margins
    g2.translate(format.getImageableX(), format.getImageableY());

    // Scale the page by the specified scaling factor
    g2.scale(scalefactor, scalefactor);

    // Display a page number centered in the area of the top margin.
    // Set a new clipping region so we can draw into the top margin
    // But remember the original clipping region so we can restore it
    if (pageIndex > 0) {
        Shape originalClip = g.getClip();
        g.setClip(new Rectangle(0, (int)-printY,
                                (int)printWidth, (int)printY));
        // Compute the header to display, measure it, then display it
        String numString = "- " + (pageIndex+1) + " -";
        // Get string and font measurements
        FontRenderContext frc = g2.getFontRenderContext();
        Rectangle2D numBounds = headerFont.getStringBounds(numString, frc);
        LineMetrics metrics = headerFont.getLineMetrics(numString, frc);
        g.setFont(headerFont);     // Set the font
        g.setColor(Color.black);   // Print with black ink
        g.drawString(numString,    // Display the string
                    (int)((printWidth-numBounds.getWidth())/2),
                    (int)(-(printY-numBounds.getHeight())/2 +
                          metrics.getAscent()));
        g.setClip(originalClip);   // Restore the clipping region
    }

    // Get the staring position and length of the page within the document
    double pageStart = 0.0, pageLength = printHeight;
    if (pageIndex > 0)
        pageStart = ((Double)pageOffsets.get(pageIndex-1)).doubleValue();
    if (pageIndex < numPages-1)
        pageLength = ((Double)pageLengths.get(pageIndex)).doubleValue();

    // Scroll so that the appropriate part of the document is lined up
    // with the upper-left corner of the page
    g2.translate(0.0, -pageStart);

    // Now paint the entire document.  Because of the clipping region,
    // only the desired portion of the document will actually be drawn on
    // this sheet of paper.
    root.paint(g, drawRect);

    // Finally return a success code
    return PAGE_EXISTS;
}

/**
 * This inner class is a concrete implementation of View, with a
 * couple of key method implementations.  An instance of this class
```

Example 12-4: PrintableDocument.java (continued)

```
 * is used as the parent of the root View object we want to print
 **/
static class ParentView extends View {
    ViewFactory viewFactory; // The ViewFactory for the hierarchy of views
    Container container;      // The Container for the hierarchy of views

    public ParentView(View v, ViewFactory viewFactory, Container container)
    {
        super(v.getElement());
        this.viewFactory = viewFactory;
        this.container = container;
    }

    // These methods return key pieces of information required by
    // the View hierarchy.
    public ViewFactory getViewFactory() { return viewFactory; }
    public Container getContainer() { return container; }

    // These methods are abstract in View, so we've got to provide
    // dummy implementations of them here, even though they're never used.
    public void paint(Graphics g, Shape allocation) {}
    public float getPreferredSpan(int axis) { return 0.0f; }
    public int viewToModel(float x,float y,Shape a,Position.Bias[] bias) {
        return 0;
    }
    public Shape modelToView(int pos, Shape a, Position.Bias b)
        throws BadLocationException {
        return a;
    }
  }
}
```

Exercises

12-1. In Java 1.3, `java.awt.JobAttributes` and `java.awt.PageAttributes` are new classes that enhance the Java 1.1 Printing API. Read the documentation for these classes, then modify the `HardcopyWriter` class so that you can pass `PageAttributes` and `JobAttributes` objects to the `HardcopyWriter` constructor. Test your modification by writing a program that prints in landscape mode and uses duplex (two-sided) printing (if you have a printer that supports this feature).

12-2. With the Java 1.2 Printing API, the `print()` method of a `Printable` object may be called multiple times per page to facilitate the printing of high-resolution images and drawings. For this reason, it is not possible to print a character stream with the Java 1.2 API, as is done in with the Java 1.1 API in the `HardcopyWriter` class. Nevertheless, it is still possible to print multipage text documents using the Java 1.2 API. Write a program that reads a text file and prints its contents using the Java 1.2 API.

12-3. Modify your program from the previous exercise to support "2-up" printing—printing two reduced-size pages side by side in landscape mode. You'll want to use Java 2D scaling and rotation features to accomplish this.

CHAPTER 13

Data Transfer

In Java 1.1, the `java.awt.datatransfer` package provided interapplication data-transfer capabilities and support for the cut-and-paste data-transfer metaphor. Java 1.2 extended the data-transfer capabilities of GUI applications by adding the `java.awt.dnd` package, which supports the drag-and-drop data-transfer metaphor. This chapter demonstrates how you can add support for cut-and-paste and drag-and-drop to your AWT and Swing applications. It also shows how you can use the `DataFlavor` class and the `Transferable` interface to permit the transfer of custom data types between applications.

Data Transfer Architecture

Before we look at any data transfer examples, it is important that you understand the data transfer architecture used by `java.awt.datatransfer` (and by `java.awt.dnd`). The `java.awt.datatransfer.DataFlavor` class is perhaps the most central class; it represents the type of data to be transferred. Every data flavor consists of a human-readable name, a `Class` object that specifies the Java data type of the transferred data, and a MIME type that specifies the encoding used during data transfer. The `DataFlavor` class predefines a couple of commonly used flavors for transferring strings and lists of `File` objects. It also predefines several MIME types used with those flavors. For example, `DataFlavor.stringFlavor` can transfer Java `String` objects as Unicode text. It has a representation class of `java.lang.String` and a MIME type of:

```
application/x-java-serialized-object; class=java.lang.String
```

The `java.awt.datatransfer.Transferable` interface is another important piece of the data-transfer picture. This interface specifies three methods that should be implemented by any object that wants to make data available for transfer: `get-TransferDataFlavors()`, which returns an array of all the `DataFlavor` types it can use to transfer its data; `isDataFlavorSupported()`, which checks whether the `Transferable` object supports a given flavor; and the most important method, `get-TransferData()`, which actually returns the data in a format appropriate for the requested `DataFlavor`.

The data-transfer architecture relies on object serialization as one of its means of transferring data between applications, which makes the data-transfer architecture quite general and flexible. It was designed to allow arbitrary data to be transferred between independent Java virtual machines and even between Java applications and native-platform applications. Unfortunately, the data transfer architecture has apparently never been fully implemented, so data transfer between JVMs and between a JVM and a native application only works if you use the special predefined flavors, `DataFlavor.stringFlavor` and `DataFlavor.javaFileListFlavor`. Although you can define other `DataFlavor` objects to represent other serializable Java classes, these custom flavors work to transfer data only within a single JVM.

Simple Copy-and-Paste

While `DataFlavor` and `Transferable` provide the underlying infrastructure for data transfer, it is the `java.awt.datatransfer.Clipboard` class and `java.awt.data-transfer.ClipboardOwner` interface that support the cut-and-paste style of data transfer. A typical cut-and-paste scenario works like this:

- When the user issues a command to copy or cut something, the initiating application first obtains the system `Clipboard` object by calling the `getSys-temClipboard()` method of the `java.awt.Toolkit` object. Next, the application creates a `Transferable` object that represents the data to be transferred. Finally, it passes this transferable object to the clipboard by calling the `set-Contents()` method of the clipboard. The initiating application must also pass an object that implements the `ClipboardOwner` interface to `setContents()`. By doing so, the application becomes the clipboard owner and must maintain its `Transferable` object until it ceases to be the clipboard owner.

- When the user issues a command to paste, the receiving application first obtains the system `Clipboard` object in the same way the initiating application did. Then it calls the `getContents()` method of the system clipboard to receive the `Transferable` object stored there. Now it can use the methods defined by the `Transferable` interface to choose a `DataFlavor` for the data transfer and actually transfer the data.

- When the user copies or cuts some other piece of data, a new data transfer is initiated, and the new initiating application (it may be the same one) becomes the new clipboard owner. The previous owner is notified it is no longer the clipboard owner when the system invokes the `lostOwnership()` method of the `ClipboardOwner` object specified in the initiating call to `setContents()`.

Note that untrusted applets are not allowed to work with the system clipboard because there might be sensitive data on it from other applications. This means that applets can't participate in interapplication cut-and-paste. Instead, an applet must create a private clipboard object to use intraapplet data transfer.

Example 13-1 is a simple AWT program that demonstrates how to support `String` cut-and-paste capabilities in a program. It relies on the predefined `DataFla-vor.stringFlavor` and the `StringSelection` class, which implements the `Trans-ferable` interface for string data. The program also uses the Java 1.2 `DataFlavor.javaFileListFlavor` to allow filenames to be pasted. Note that the program performs a copy operation rather than a cut operation. To do a cut, simply delete the text from the source after copying it to the clipboard. The interesting code is in the copy() and paste() methods towards the end of the example. Also note that the example implements ClipboardOwner, so it is notified when its data is no longer on the clipboard. The best way to test this program is by starting two independent copies of it and transferring data between them. You can also try transferring data between an instance of this program and a native application on your platform.

Example 13-1: SimpleCutAndPaste.java

```java
package com.davidflanagan.examples.datatransfer;
import java.awt.*;
import java.awt.event.*;
import java.awt.datatransfer.*;

/**
 * This program demonstrates how to add simple copy-and-paste capabilities
 * to an application.
 **/
public class SimpleCutAndPaste extends Frame implements ClipboardOwner
{
    /** The main method creates a frame and pops it up. */
    public static void main(String[] args) {
        Frame f = new SimpleCutAndPaste();
        f.addWindowListener(new WindowAdapter() {
                public void windowClosing(WindowEvent e) { System.exit(0); }
            });
        f.pack();
        f.setVisible(true);
    }

    /** The text field that holds the text that is cut or pasted */
    TextField field;

    /**
     * The constructor builds a very simple test GUI, and registers this object
     * as the ActionListener for the buttons
     **/
    public SimpleCutAndPaste() {
        super("SimpleCutAndPaste");  // Window title
        this.setFont(new Font("SansSerif", Font.PLAIN, 18)); // Use a big font

        // Set up the Cut button
        Button copy = new Button("Copy");
        copy.addActionListener(new ActionListener() {
                public void actionPerformed(ActionEvent e) { copy(); }
            });
        this.add(copy, "West");

        // Set up the Paste button
        Button paste = new Button("Paste");
        paste.addActionListener(new ActionListener() {
                public void actionPerformed(ActionEvent e) { paste(); }
            });
        this.add(paste, "East");

        // Set up the text field that they both operate on
        field = new TextField();
```

Example 13–1: SimpleCutAndPaste.java (continued)

```
        this.add(field, "North");
}

/**
 * This method takes the current contents of the text field, creates a
 * StringSelection object to represent that string, and puts the
 * StringSelection onto the clipboard
 **/
public void copy() {
    // Get the currently displayed value
    String s = field.getText();

    // Create a StringSelection object to represent the text.
    // StringSelection is a pre-defined class that implements
    // Transferable and ClipboardOwner for us.
    StringSelection ss = new StringSelection(s);

    // Now set the StringSelection object as the contents of the clipboard
    // Also specify that we're the clipboard owner
    this.getToolkit().getSystemClipboard().setContents(ss, this);

    // Highlight the text to indicate it is on the clipboard.
    field.selectAll();
}

/**
 * Get the contents of the clipboard, and, if we understand the type,
 * display the contents.  This method understands strings and file lists.
 **/
public void paste() {
    // Get the clipboard
    Clipboard c = this.getToolkit().getSystemClipboard();

    // Get the contents of the clipboard, as a Transferable object
    Transferable t = c.getContents(this);

    // Find out what kind of data is on the clipboard
    try {
        if (t.isDataFlavorSupported(DataFlavor.stringFlavor)) {
            // If it is a string, then get and display the string
            String s = (String) t.getTransferData(DataFlavor.stringFlavor);
            field.setText(s);

        }
        else if (t.isDataFlavorSupported(DataFlavor.javaFileListFlavor)) {
            // If it is a list of File objects, get the list and display
            // the name of the first file on the list
            java.util.List files = (java.util.List)
                t.getTransferData(DataFlavor.javaFileListFlavor);
            java.io.File file = (java.io.File)files.get(0);
            field.setText(file.getName());
        }
    }
    // If anything goes wrong with the transfer, just beep and do nothing.
    catch (Exception e) { this.getToolkit().beep(); }
}

/**
```

Data
Transfer

Example 13-1: SimpleCutAndPaste.java (continued)

```
      * This method implements the ClipboardOwner interface.  It is called when
      * something else is placed on the clipboard.
      **/
     public void lostOwnership(Clipboard c, Transferable t) {
         // Un-highlight the text field, since we don't "own" the clipboard
         // anymore, and the text is no longer available to be pasted.
         field.select(0,0);
     }
}
```

A Transferable Data Type

The `java.awt.datatransfer.StringSelection` class makes it simple to transfer `String` values between applications. To transfer other types of data, however, you must create a custom implementation of the `Transferable` interface. Example 13-2 shows the `Scribble` class—a data type that represents a set of line segments. It implements the `Shape` interface, so it can be drawn with the Java 2D API (see Chapter 11, *Graphics*). More important, it implements the `Transferable` interface, so that scribbles can be transferred from one application to another.

The `Scribble` class actually supports data transfer using two data flavors. It defines a custom flavor that transfers serialized `Scribble` instances. However, as noted at the beginning of the chapter, custom flavors like these do not work for data transfer between independent JVMs (at least with Sun's Java implementations). Therefore, `Scribble` also allows itself to be transferred as a `String` and defines methods for converting scribbles to and from string form. Note that Example 13-2 doesn't demonstrate cut-and-paste or drag-and-drop data transfer; it simply defines the data-transfer infrastructure used by the cut-and-paste and drag-and-drop examples that follow. It's also worth studying as a custom `Shape` implementation.

Example 13-2: Scribble.java

```
package com.davidflanagan.examples.datatransfer;
import java.awt.*;
import java.awt.geom.*;
import java.awt.datatransfer.*;
import java.io.Serializable;
import java.util.StringTokenizer;

/**
 * This class represents a scribble composed of any number of "polylines".
 * Each "polyline" is set of connected line segments.  A scribble is created
 * through a series of calls to the moveto() and lineto() methods.  moveto()
 * specifies the starting point of a new polyline, and lineto() adds a new
 * point to the end of the current polyline().
 *
 * This class implements the Shape interface which means that it can be drawn
 * using the Java2D graphics API
 *
 * It also implements the Transferable interface, which means that it can
 * easily be used with cut-and-paste and drag-and-drop.  It defines a custom
 * DataFlavor, scribbleDataFlavor, which transfers Scribble objects as Java
 * objects.  However, it also supports cut-and-paste and drag-and-drop based
 * on a portable string representation of the scribble.  The toString()
```

Example 13-2: Scribble.java (continued)

```
 * and parse() methods write and read this string format
 **/
public class Scribble implements Shape, Transferable, Serializable, Cloneable {
    protected double[] points = new double[64]; // The scribble data
    protected int numPoints = 0;                 // The current number of points
    double maxX = Double.NEGATIVE_INFINITY;      // The bounding box
    double maxY = Double.NEGATIVE_INFINITY;
    double minX = Double.POSITIVE_INFINITY;
    double minY = Double.POSITIVE_INFINITY;

    /**
     * Begin a new polyline at (x,y).  Note the use of Double.NaN in the
     * points array to mark the beginning of a new polyline
     **/
    public void moveto(double x, double y) {
        if (numPoints + 3 > points.length) reallocate();
        // Mark this as the beginning of a new line
        points[numPoints++] = Double.NaN;
        // The rest of this method is just like lineto();
        lineto(x, y);
    }

    /**
     * Add the point (x,y) to the end of the current polyline
     **/
    public void lineto(double x, double y) {
        if (numPoints + 2 > points.length) reallocate();
        points[numPoints++] = x;
        points[numPoints++] = y;

        // See if the point enlarges our bounding box
        if (x > maxX) maxX = x;
        if (x < minX) minX = x;
        if (y > maxY) maxY = y;
        if (y < minY) minY = y;
    }

    /**
     * Append the Scribble s to this Scribble
     **/
    public void append(Scribble s) {
        int n = numPoints + s.numPoints;
        double[] newpoints = new double[n];
        System.arraycopy(points, 0, newpoints, 0, numPoints);
        System.arraycopy(s.points, 0, newpoints, numPoints, s.numPoints);
        points = newpoints;
        numPoints = n;
        minX = Math.min(minX, s.minX);
        maxX = Math.max(maxX, s.maxX);
        minY = Math.min(minY, s.minY);
        maxY = Math.max(maxY, s.maxY);
    }

    /**
     * Translate the coordinates of all points in the Scribble by x,y
     **/
    public void translate(double x, double y) {
        for(int i = 0; i < numPoints; i++) {
```

Example 13-2: Scribble.java (continued)

```
            if (Double.isNaN(points[i])) continue;
            points[i++] += x;
            points[i] += y;
        }
        minX += x; maxX += x;
        minY += y; maxY += y;
    }

    /** An internal method to make more room in the data array */
    protected void reallocate() {
        double[] newpoints = new double[points.length * 2];
        System.arraycopy(points, 0, newpoints, 0, numPoints);
        points = newpoints;
    }

    /** Clone a Scribble object and its internal array of data */
    public Object clone() {
        try {
            Scribble s = (Scribble) super.clone();   // make a copy of all fields
            s.points = (double[]) points.clone();    // copy the entire array
            return s;
        }
        catch (CloneNotSupportedException e) {   // This should never happen
            return this;
        }
    }

    /** Convert the scribble data to a textual format */
    public String toString() {
        StringBuffer b = new StringBuffer();
        for(int i = 0; i < numPoints; i++) {
            if (Double.isNaN(points[i])) {
                b.append("m ");
            }
            else {
                b.append(points[i]);
                b.append(' ');
            }
        }
        return b.toString();
    }

    /**
     * Create a new Scribble object and initialize it by parsing a string of
     * coordinate data in the format produced by toString()
     **/
    public static Scribble parse(String s) throws NumberFormatException {
        StringTokenizer st = new StringTokenizer(s);
        Scribble scribble = new Scribble();
        while(st.hasMoreTokens()) {
            String t = st.nextToken();
            if (t.charAt(0) == 'm') {
                scribble.moveto(Double.parseDouble(st.nextToken()),
                                Double.parseDouble(st.nextToken()));
            }
            else {
                scribble.lineto(Double.parseDouble(t),
                                Double.parseDouble(st.nextToken()));
```

Example 13-2: Scribble.java (continued)

```
            }
        }
        return scribble;
    }


    // ======== The following methods implement the Shape interface ========

    /** Return the bounding box of the Shape */
    public Rectangle getBounds() {
        return new Rectangle((int)(minX-0.5f), (int)(minY-0.5f),
                             (int)(maxX-minX+0.5f), (int)(maxY-minY+0.5f));
    }


    /** Return the bounding box of the Shape */
    public Rectangle2D getBounds2D() {
        return new Rectangle2D.Double(minX, minY, maxX-minX, maxY-minY);
    }


    /** Our shape is an open curve, so it never contains anything */
    public boolean contains(Point2D p) { return false; }
    public boolean contains(Rectangle2D r) { return false; }
    public boolean contains(double x, double y) { return false; }
    public boolean contains(double x, double y, double w, double h) {
        return false;
    }


    /**
     * Determine if the scribble intersects the specified rectangle by testing
     * each line segment individually
     **/
    public boolean intersects(Rectangle2D r) {
        if (numPoints < 4) return false;
        int i = 0;
        double x1, y1, x2 = 0.0, y2 = 0.0;
        while(i < numPoints) {
            if (Double.isNaN(points[i])) { // If we're beginning a new line
                i++;                       // Skip the NaN
                x2 = points[i++];
                y2 = points[i++];
            }
            else {
                x1 = x2;
                y1 = y2;
                x2 = points[i++];
                y2 = points[i++];
                if (r.intersectsLine(x1, y1, x2, y2)) return true;
            }
        }

        return false;
    }


    /** Test for intersection by invoking the method above */
    public boolean intersects(double x, double y, double w, double h){
        return intersects(new Rectangle2D.Double(x,y,w,h));
    }


    /**
```

Example 13-2: Scribble.java (continued)

```
   * Return a PathIterator object that tells Java2D how to draw this scribble
   **/
  public PathIterator getPathIterator(AffineTransform at) {
      return new ScribbleIterator(at);
  }

  /**
   * Return a PathIterator that doesn't include curves.  Ours never does.
   **/
  public PathIterator getPathIterator(AffineTransform at, double flatness) {
      return getPathIterator(at);
  }

  /**
   * This inner class implements the PathIterator interface to describe
   * the shape of a scribble.  Since a Scribble is composed of arbitrary
   * movetos and linetos, we simply return their coordinates
   **/
  public class ScribbleIterator implements PathIterator {
      protected int i = 0;                    // Position in array
      protected AffineTransform transform;

      public ScribbleIterator(AffineTransform transform) {
          this.transform = transform;
      }

      /** How to determine insideness and outsideness for this shape */
      public int getWindingRule() { return PathIterator.WIND_NON_ZERO; }

      /** Have we reached the end of the scribble path yet? */
      public boolean isDone() { return i >= numPoints; }

      /** Move on to the next segment of the path */
      public void next() {
          if (Double.isNaN(points[i])) i += 3;
          else i += 2;
      }

      /**
       * Get the coordinates of the current moveto or lineto as floats
       **/
      public int currentSegment(float[] coords) {
          int retval;
          if (Double.isNaN(points[i])) {          // If its a moveto
              coords[0] = (float)points[i+1];
              coords[1] = (float)points[i+2];
              retval = SEG_MOVETO;
          }
          else {
              coords[0] = (float)points[i];
              coords[1] = (float)points[i+1];
              retval = SEG_LINETO;
          }

          // If a transform was specified, use it on the coordinates
          if (transform != null) transform.transform(coords, 0, coords, 0,1);

          return retval;
```

Example 13-2: Scribble.java (continued)

```
        }

    /**
     * Get the coordinates of the current moveto or lineto as doubles
     **/
    public int currentSegment(double[] coords) {
        int retval;
        if (Double.isNaN(points[i])) {
            coords[0] = points[i+1];
            coords[1] = points[i+2];
            retval = SEG_MOVETO;
        }
        else {
            coords[0] = points[i];
            coords[1] = points[i+1];
            retval = SEG_LINETO;
        }
        if (transform != null) transform.transform(coords, 0, coords, 0,1);
        return retval;
    }
}


//===== The following methods implement the Transferable interface =====

// This is the custom DataFlavor for Scribble objects
public static DataFlavor scribbleDataFlavor =
    new DataFlavor(Scribble.class, "Scribble");

// This is a list of the flavors we know how to work with
public static DataFlavor[] supportedFlavors = {
    scribbleDataFlavor,
    DataFlavor.stringFlavor
};

/** Return the data formats or "flavors" we know how to transfer */
public DataFlavor[] getTransferDataFlavors() {
    return (DataFlavor[]) supportedFlavors.clone();
}

/** Check whether we support a given flavor */
public boolean isDataFlavorSupported(DataFlavor flavor) {
    return (flavor.equals(scribbleDataFlavor) ||
            flavor.equals(DataFlavor.stringFlavor));
}

/**
 * Return the scribble data in the requested format, or throw an exception
 * if we don't support the requested format
 **/
public Object getTransferData(DataFlavor flavor)
    throws UnsupportedFlavorException
{
    if (flavor.equals(scribbleDataFlavor)) { return this; }
    else if (flavor.equals(DataFlavor.stringFlavor)) { return toString(); }
    else throw new UnsupportedFlavorException(flavor);
}
}
```

Cutting and Pasting Scribbles

Example 13-3 is a Swing application that allows the user to scribble with the mouse and then transfer scribbles using cut-and-paste. It uses the Scribble class defined in Example 13-2 to store, draw, and transfer the scribbles. The cut-and-paste functionality is implemented in the cut(), copy(), and paste() methods, which the user accesses through a popup menu. Notice how the paste() method first attempts to transfer the data using the custom Scribble data flavor; if that fails, it tries again using the predefined string data flavor. To test the program, run two copies of it and transfer scribbles back and forth between the two copies.

Example 13–3: ScribbleCutAndPaste.java

```
package com.davidflanagan.examples.datatransfer;
import java.awt.*;
import java.awt.event.*;
import javax.swing.*;
import java.awt.datatransfer.*;  // Clipboard, Transferable, DataFlavor, etc.

/**
 * This component allows the user to scribble in a window, and to cut and
 * paste scribbles between windows.  It stores mouse coordinates in a Scribble
 * object, which is used to draw the scribble, and also to transfer the
 * scribble to and from the clipboard.  A JPopupMenu provides access to the
 * cut, copy, and paste commands.
 **/
public class ScribbleCutAndPaste extends JComponent
    implements ActionListener, ClipboardOwner
{
    Stroke linestyle = new BasicStroke(3.0f); // Draw with wide lines
    Scribble scribble = new Scribble();        // Holds our scribble
    Scribble selection;                        // A copy of the scribble as cut
    JPopupMenu popup;                          // A menu for cut-and-paste

    public ScribbleCutAndPaste() {
        // Create the popup menu.
        String[] labels = new String[] {   "Clear", "Cut", "Copy", "Paste" };
        String[] commands = new String[] { "clear", "cut", "copy", "paste" };
        popup = new JPopupMenu();                      // Create the menu
        popup.setLabel("Edit");
        for(int i = 0; i < labels.length; i++) {
            JMenuItem mi = new JMenuItem(labels[i]); // Create a menu item
            mi.setActionCommand(commands[i]);        // Set its action command
            mi.addActionListener(this);              // And its action listener
            popup.add(mi);                           // Add item to the menu
        }
        // Finally, register the popup menu with the component it appears over
        this.add(popup);

        // Add event listeners to do the drawing and handle the popup
        addMouseListener(new MouseAdapter() {
                public void mousePressed(MouseEvent e) {
                    if (e.isPopupTrigger())
                        popup.show((Component)e.getSource(),
                                   e.getX(), e.getY());
                    else
                        scribble.moveto(e.getX(), e.getY()); // start new line
                }
```

Example 13-3: ScribbleCutAndPaste.java (continued)

```
            });

        addMouseMotionListener(new MouseMotionAdapter() {
            public void mouseDragged(MouseEvent e) {
                // If this isn't mouse button 1, ignore it
                if ((e.getModifiers() & InputEvent.BUTTON1_MASK) == 0)
                    return;
                scribble.lineto(e.getX(), e.getY());    // Add a line
                repaint();
            }
        });
    }

    /**
     * Draw the component.
     * This method relies on Scribble which implements Shape.
     **/
    public void paintComponent(Graphics g) {
        super.paintComponent(g);
        Graphics2D g2 = (Graphics2D) g;
        g2.setStroke(linestyle);    // Specify wide lines
        g2.draw(scribble);          // Draw the scribble
    }

    /** This is the ActionListener method invoked by the popup menu items */
    public void actionPerformed(ActionEvent event) {
        String command = event.getActionCommand();
        if (command.equals("clear")) clear();
        else if (command.equals("cut")) cut();
        else if (command.equals("copy")) copy();
        else if (command.equals("paste")) paste();
    }

    /** Clear the scribble.  Invoked by popup menu */
    void clear() {
        scribble = new Scribble();   // Get a new, empty scribble
        repaint();                   // And redraw everything.
    }

    /**
     * Make a copy of the current Scribble and put it on the clipboard
     * We can do this because Scribble implements Transferable
     * The user invokes this method through the popup menu
     **/
    public void copy() {
        // Get system clipboard
        Clipboard c = this.getToolkit().getSystemClipboard();

        // Make a copy of the Scribble object to put on the clipboard
        selection = (Scribble) scribble.clone();

        // Put the copy on the clipboard
        c.setContents(selection,  // What to put on the clipboard
                      this);      // Who to notify when it is no longer there
    }

    /**
     * The cut action is just like the copy action, except that we erase the
```

Example 13–3: ScribbleCutAndPaste.java (continued)

```
      * current scribble after copying it to the clipboard
      **/
     public void cut() {
         copy();
         clear();
     }

     /**
      * The user invokes this method through the popup menu.
      * First, ask for the Transferable contents of the system clipboard.
      * Then ask that Transferable object for the scribble data it represents.
      * Try using both data flavors supported by the Scribble class.
      * If it doesn't work, beep to tell the user it failed.
      **/
     public void paste() {
         Clipboard c = this.getToolkit().getSystemClipboard(); // Get clipboard
         Transferable t = c.getContents(this);              // Get its contents

         // Now try to get a Scribble object from the transferrable
         Scribble pastedScribble = null;
         try {
             pastedScribble =
                 (Scribble)t.getTransferData(Scribble.scribbleDataFlavor);
         }
         catch (Exception e) { // UnsupportedFlavor, NullPointer, etc.
             // If that didn't work, try asking for a string instead.
             try {
                 String s = (String)t.getTransferData(DataFlavor.stringFlavor);
                 // We got a string, so try converting it to a Scribble
                 pastedScribble = Scribble.parse(s);
             }
             catch (Exception e2) { // UnsupportedFlavor, NumberFormat, etc.
                 // If we couldn't get and parse a string, give up
                 this.getToolkit().beep();    // Tell the user the paste failed
                 return;
             }
         }

         // If we get here, we've retrieved a Scribble object from the clipboard
         // Add it to the current scribble, and ask to be redrawn
         scribble.append(pastedScribble);
         repaint();
     }

     /**
      * This method implements the ClipboardOwner interface.  We specify a
      * ClipboardOwner when we copy a Scribble to the clipboard.  This method
      * will be invoked when something else is copied to the clipboard, and
      * bumps our data off the clipboard.  When this method is invoked we no
      * longer have to maintain our copied Scribble object, since it is no
      * longer available to be pasted.  Often, a component will highlight a
      * selected object while it is on the clipboard, and will use this method
      * to un-highlight the object when it is no longer on the clipboard.
      **/
     public void lostOwnership(Clipboard c, Transferable t) {
         selection = null;
     }
```

Example 13-3: ScribbleCutAndPaste.java (continued)

```java
    /** A simple main method to test the class. */
    public static void main(String[] args) {
        JFrame frame = new JFrame("ScribbleCutAndPaste");
        ScribbleCutAndPaste s = new ScribbleCutAndPaste();
        frame.getContentPane().add(s, BorderLayout.CENTER);
        frame.setSize(400, 400);
        frame.setVisible(true);
    }
}
```

Dragging and Dropping Scribbles

Java 1.2 adds support for data transfer through drag-and-drop. The drag-and-drop API is contained in the java.awt.dnd package and is built on top of the same DataFlavor and Transferable architecture as cut-and-paste. Example 13-4 is a Swing program that allows the user to scribble with the mouse in "draw" mode and drag-and-drop scribbles in "drag" mode.

The drag-and-drop API is substantially more complex than the cut-and-paste API, which is reflected in the length of this example. The key interfaces are DragGestureListener, which triggers a new drag, and DragSourceListener and DropTargetListener, which notify the source of a drag and the target of a drop of important events that occur during the drag-and-drop process. The example implements all three interfaces. Note that these interfaces define methods with similar names and use a confusing variety of event types. For a more detailed description of the drag-and-drop API, see *Java Foundation Classes in a Nutshell*.

While studying this example, you should pay particular attention to dragGestureRecognized(), which is where the drag is initiated, and drop(), which is where data is actually transferred from source to target. This example uses a List of Scribble objects; each Scribble object represents a single connected set of line segments. This differs from Example 13-3, which uses a single Scribble to represent the entire scribble, including connected and disjoint line segments.

To test the program, start one copy and draw some lines with the mouse. Then click on the **Drag** button and drag some lines with the mouse. Next, start another copy of the program and drag lines from one program to the other. Note that the Java drag-and-drop API can integrate with the native drag-and-drop system on your computer; it uses the same mouse and keyboard bindings as native applications do. Usually, the default drag-and-drop operation is a move. But, by holding down the appropriate modifier key, you can change it to a copy operation.

Example 13-4: ScribbleDragAndDrop.java

```java
package com.davidflanagan.examples.datatransfer;
import java.awt.*;
import java.awt.event.*;
import javax.swing.*;
import javax.swing.border.*;
import java.awt.datatransfer.*;   // Clipboard, Transferable, DataFlavor, etc.
import java.awt.dnd.*;
import java.util.ArrayList;
```

Example 13-4: ScribbleDragAndDrop.java (continued)

```java
/**
 * This component can operate in two modes.  In "draw mode", it allows the user
 * to scribble with the mouse.  In "drag mode", it allows the user to drag
 * scribbles with the mouse.  Regardless of the mode, it always allows
 * scribbles to be dropped on it from other applications.
 **/
public class ScribbleDragAndDrop extends JComponent
    implements DragGestureListener,    // For recognizing the start of drags
               DragSourceListener,     // For processing drag source events
               DropTargetListener,     // For processing drop target events
               MouseListener,          // For processing mouse clicks
               MouseMotionListener     // For processing mouse drags
{
    ArrayList scribbles = new ArrayList();  // A list of Scribbles to draw
    Scribble currentScribble;               // The scribble in progress
    Scribble beingDragged;                  // The scribble being dragged
    DragSource dragSource;                  // A central DnD object
    boolean dragMode;                       // Are we dragging or scribbling?

    // These are some constants we use
    static final int LINEWIDTH = 3;
    static final BasicStroke linestyle = new BasicStroke(LINEWIDTH);
    static final Border normalBorder = new BevelBorder(BevelBorder.LOWERED);
    static final Border dropBorder = new BevelBorder(BevelBorder.RAISED);

    /** The constructor: set up drag-and-drop stuff */
    public ScribbleDragAndDrop() {
        // Give ourselves a nice default border.
        // We'll change this border during drag-and-drop.
        setBorder(normalBorder);

        // Register listeners to handle drawing
        addMouseListener(this);
        addMouseMotionListener(this);

        // Create a DragSource and DragGestureRecognizer to listen for drags
        // The DragGestureRecognizer will notify the DragGestureListener
        // when the user tries to drag an object
        dragSource = DragSource.getDefaultDragSource();
        dragSource.createDefaultDragGestureRecognizer(this, // What component
                    DnDConstants.ACTION_COPY_OR_MOVE, // What drag types?
                                            this);// the listener

        // Create and set up a DropTarget that will listen for drags and
        // drops over this component, and will notify the DropTargetListener
        DropTarget dropTarget = new DropTarget(this,   // component to monitor
                                        this);  // listener to notify
        this.setDropTarget(dropTarget);  // Tell the component about it.
    }

    /**
     * The component draws itself by drawing each of the Scribble objects.
     **/
    public void paintComponent(Graphics g) {
        super.paintComponent(g);
        Graphics2D g2 = (Graphics2D) g;
        g2.setStroke(linestyle);    // Specify wide lines
```

Example 13-4: ScribbleDragAndDrop.java (continued)

```
        int numScribbles = scribbles.size();
        for(int i = 0; i < numScribbles; i++) {
            Scribble s = (Scribble)scribbles.get(i);
            g2.draw(s);              // Draw the scribble
        }
    }

    public void setDragMode(boolean dragMode) {
        this.dragMode = dragMode;
    }
    public boolean getDragMode() { return dragMode; }

    /**
     * This method, and the following four methods are from the MouseListener
     * interface.  If we're in drawing mode, this method handles mouse down
     * events and starts a new scribble.
     **/
    public void mousePressed(MouseEvent e) {
        if (dragMode) return;
        currentScribble = new Scribble();
        scribbles.add(currentScribble);
        currentScribble.moveto(e.getX(), e.getY());
    }
    public void mouseReleased(MouseEvent e) {}
    public void mouseClicked(MouseEvent e) {}
    public void mouseEntered(MouseEvent e) {}
    public void mouseExited(MouseEvent e) {}

    /**
     * This method and mouseMoved() below are from the MouseMotionListener
     * interface.  If we're in drawing mode, this method adds a new point
     * to the current scribble and requests a redraw
     **/
    public void mouseDragged(MouseEvent e) {
        if (dragMode) return;
        currentScribble.lineto(e.getX(), e.getY());
        repaint();
    }
    public void mouseMoved(MouseEvent e) {}

    /**
     * This method implements the DragGestureListener interface.  It will be
     * invoked when the DragGestureRecognizer thinks that the user has
     * initiated a drag.  If we're not in drawing mode, then this method will
     * try to figure out which Scribble object is being dragged, and will
     * initiate a drag on that object.
     **/
    public void dragGestureRecognized(DragGestureEvent e) {
        // Don't drag if we're not in drag mode
        if (!dragMode) return;

        // Figure out where the drag started
        MouseEvent inputEvent = (MouseEvent) e.getTriggerEvent();
        int x = inputEvent.getX();
        int y = inputEvent.getY();

        // Figure out which scribble was clicked on, if any by creating a
        // small rectangle around the point and testing for intersection.
```

Example 13–4: ScribbleDragAndDrop.java (continued)

```
            Rectangle r = new Rectangle (x-LINEWIDTH, y-LINEWIDTH,
                                         LINEWIDTH*2, LINEWIDTH*2);
        int numScribbles = scribbles.size();
        for(int i =  0; i < numScribbles; i++) {  // Loop through the scribbles
            Scribble s = (Scribble) scribbles.get(i);
            if (s.intersects(r)) {
                // The user started the drag on top of this scribble, so
                // start to drag it.

                // First, remember which scribble is being dragged, so we can
                // delete it later (if this is a move rather than a copy)
                beingDragged = s;

                // Next, create a copy that will be the one dragged
                Scribble dragScribble = (Scribble) s.clone();
                // Adjust the origin to the point the user clicked on.
                dragScribble.translate(-x, -y);

                // Choose a cursor based on the type of drag the user initiated
                Cursor cursor;
                switch(e.getDragAction()) {
                case DnDConstants.ACTION_COPY:
                    cursor = DragSource.DefaultCopyDrop;
                    break;
                case DnDConstants.ACTION_MOVE:
                    cursor = DragSource.DefaultMoveDrop;
                    break;
                default:
                    return;   // We only support move and copys
                }

                // Some systems allow us to drag an image along with the
                // cursor.  If so, create an image of the scribble to drag
                if (dragSource.isDragImageSupported()) {
                    Rectangle scribbleBox = dragScribble.getBounds();
                    Image dragImage = this.createImage(scribbleBox.width,
                                                       scribbleBox.height);
                    Graphics2D g = (Graphics2D)dragImage.getGraphics();
                    g.setColor(new Color(0,0,0,0));  // transparent background
                    g.fillRect(0, 0, scribbleBox.width, scribbleBox.height);
                    g.setColor(Color.black);
                    g.setStroke(linestyle);
                        g.translate(-scribbleBox.x, -scribbleBox.y);
                    g.draw(dragScribble);
                    Point hotspot = new Point(-scribbleBox.x, -scribbleBox.y);

                    // Now start dragging, using the image.
                    e.startDrag(cursor, dragImage, hotspot, dragScribble,this);
                }
                else {
                    // Or start the drag without an image
                    e.startDrag(cursor, dragScribble,this);
                }
                // After we've started dragging one scribble, stop looking
                return;
            }
        }
    }
```

Example 13-4: ScribbleDragAndDrop.java (continued)

```
/**
 * This method, and the four unused methods that follow it implement the
 * DragSourceListener interface.  dragDropEnd() is invoked when the user
 * drops the scribble she was dragging.  If the drop was successful, and
 * if the user did a "move" rather than a "copy", then we delete the
 * dragged scribble from the list of scribbles to draw.
 **/
public void dragDropEnd(DragSourceDropEvent e) {
    if (!e.getDropSuccess()) return;
    int action = e.getDropAction();
    if (action == DnDConstants.ACTION_MOVE) {
        scribbles.remove(beingDragged);
        beingDragged = null;
        repaint();
    }
}


// These methods are also part of DragSourceListener.
// They are invoked at interesting points during the drag, and can be
// used to perform "drag over" effects, such as changing the drag cursor
// or drag image.
public void dragEnter(DragSourceDragEvent e) {}
public void dragExit(DragSourceEvent e) {}
public void dropActionChanged(DragSourceDragEvent e) {}
public void dragOver(DragSourceDragEvent e) {}

// The next five methods implement DropTargetListener

/**
 * This method is invoked when the user first drags something over us.
 * If we understand the data type being dragged, then call acceptDrag()
 * to tell the system that we're receptive.  Also, we change our border
 * as a "drag under" effect to signal that we can accept the drop.
 **/
public void dragEnter(DropTargetDragEvent e) {
    if (e.isDataFlavorSupported(Scribble.scribbleDataFlavor) ||
        e.isDataFlavorSupported(DataFlavor.stringFlavor)) {
        e.acceptDrag(DnDConstants.ACTION_COPY_OR_MOVE);
        this.setBorder(dropBorder);
    }
}

/** The user is no longer dragging over us, so restore the border */
public void dragExit(DropTargetEvent e) { this.setBorder(normalBorder); }

/**
 * This is the key method of DropTargetListener.  It is invoked when the
 * user drops something on us.
 **/
public void drop(DropTargetDropEvent e) {
    this.setBorder(normalBorder);              // Restore the default border

    // First, check whether we understand the data that was dropped.
    // If we supports our data flavors, accept the drop, otherwise reject.
    if (e.isDataFlavorSupported(Scribble.scribbleDataFlavor) ||
        e.isDataFlavorSupported(DataFlavor.stringFlavor)) {
        e.acceptDrop(DnDConstants.ACTION_COPY_OR_MOVE);
    }
```

Example 13-4: ScribbleDragAndDrop.java (continued)

```
        else {
            e.rejectDrop();
            return;
        }

        // We've accepted the drop, so now we attempt to get the dropped data
        // from the Transferable object.
        Transferable t = e.getTransferable();  // Holds the dropped data
        Scribble droppedScribble;  // This will hold the Scribble object

        // First, try to get the data directly as a scribble object
        try {
            droppedScribble =
                (Scribble) t.getTransferData(Scribble.scribbleDataFlavor);
        }
        catch (Exception ex) {  // unsupported flavor, IO exception, etc.
            // If that doesn't work, try to get it as a String and parse it
            try {
                String s = (String) t.getTransferData(DataFlavor.stringFlavor);
                droppedScribble = Scribble.parse(s);
            }
            catch(Exception ex2) {
                // If we still couldn't get the data, tell the system we failed
                e.dropComplete(false);
                return;
            }
        }

        // If we get here, we've got the Scribble object
        Point p = e.getLocation();                // Where did the drop happen?
        droppedScribble.translate(p.getX(), p.getY());  // Move it there
        scribbles.add(droppedScribble);           // add to display list
        repaint();                                // ask for redraw
        e.dropComplete(true);                     // signal success!
    }

    // These are unused DropTargetListener methods
    public void dragOver(DropTargetDragEvent e) {}
    public void dropActionChanged(DropTargetDragEvent e) {}

    /**
     * The main method.  Creates a simple application using this class.  Note
     * the buttons for switching between draw mode and drag mode.
     **/
    public static void main(String[] args) {
        // Create a frame and put a scribble pane in it
        JFrame frame = new JFrame("ScribbleDragAndDrop");
        final ScribbleDragAndDrop scribblePane = new ScribbleDragAndDrop();
        frame.getContentPane().add(scribblePane, BorderLayout.CENTER);

        // Create two buttons for switching modes
        JToolBar toolbar = new JToolBar();
        ButtonGroup group = new ButtonGroup();
        JToggleButton draw = new JToggleButton("Draw");
        JToggleButton drag = new JToggleButton("Drag");
        draw.addActionListener(new ActionListener() {
                public void actionPerformed(ActionEvent e) {
                    scribblePane.setDragMode(false);
```

Example 13–4: ScribbleDragAndDrop.java (continued)

```
            }
        });
        drag.addActionListener(new ActionListener() {
                public void actionPerformed(ActionEvent e) {
                    scribblePane.setDragMode(true);
                }
        });
        group.add(draw); group.add(drag);
        toolbar.add(draw); toolbar.add(drag);
        frame.getContentPane().add(toolbar, BorderLayout.NORTH);

        // Start off in drawing mode
        draw.setSelected(true);
        scribblePane.setDragMode(false);

        // Pop up the window
        frame.setSize(400, 400);
        frame.setVisible(true);
    }
}
```

Exercises

13-1. Consider the `StringSelection` class: it implements the `Transferable` interface for the `String` class and makes it easy to transfer strings between applications. Write a class named `SimpleSelection` that implements the `Transferable` and `ClipboardOwner` interfaces just as `StringSelection` does. The constructor for your class should take an arbitrary serializable object as its sole argument; this object is the "selection" it should transfer. Construct a `DataFlavor` based on the representation class of this object (see `Object.getClass()`) and implement the methods of the `Transferable` interface using the `DataFlavor` you created.

Now modify Example 13-1 to use `SimpleSelection` to transfer `Integer` objects using cut-and-paste. Note that `SimpleSelection` will probably only work for intraapplication cut-and-paste.

13-2. Modify Example 13-4 so that it supports cut-and-paste in addition to drag-and-drop. Allow the user to select a scribble by double-clicking on it (see `MouseEvent.getClickCount()`). Allow the user to paste a scribble from the clipboard using a menu item, mouse gesture, or keyboard event of your choice. When the user double-clicks a scribble, highlight that scribble using a different color and keep it highlighted until something else replaces it on the clipboard.

CHAPTER 14

JavaBeans

The JavaBeans API provides a framework for defining reusable, embeddable, modular software components. The JavaBeans specification includes the following definition of a bean: "a reusable software component that can be manipulated visually in a builder tool." As you can see, this is a rather loose definition; beans can take a variety of forms. At the simplest level, individual GUI components are all beans, while at a much higher level, an embeddable spreadsheet application might also function as a bean. Most beans, however, probably fall somewhere between these two extremes.

One of the goals of the JavaBeans model is interoperability with similar component frameworks. So, for example, a native Windows program can, with an appropriate bridge or wrapper object, use a Java bean as if it were a COM or ActiveX component. The details of this sort of interoperability are beyond the scope of this chapter, however.

Beans can be used at three levels, by three different categories of programmers:

- If you are developing GUI editors, application builders, or other "beanbox" tools, you need the JavaBeans API to manipulate beans within these tools. *beanbox* is the name of the sample bean manipulation program provided by Sun in its JavaBeans Development Kit™ (BDK).* The term is a useful one, and I'll use it to describe any kind of graphical design tool or application builder that manipulates beans.

- If you are writing actual beans, you need the JavaBeans API to write code that can be used in any conforming beanbox.

- If you are writing applications that use beans developed by other programmers or using a beanbox tool to combine those beans into an application, you don't actually need to be familiar with the JavaBeans API. You only need to be familiar with the documentation for individual beans that you use.

---

* You can download the BDK from *http://java.sun.com/beans* if you do not already have a bean-enabled development environment.

This chapter explains how to use the JavaBeans API at the second level, or in other words, it describes how to write beans. It covers the following topics:

- Basic bean concepts and terminology

- Requirements for the simplest beans

- Packaging beans in JAR files

- Providing additional information about beans with the BeanInfo class

- Defining property editors to allow custom editing of bean properties

- Defining bean customizers to allow customization of an entire bean

Note that the bean examples in this chapter are AWT components, for use with Java 1.0 and 1.1. Although Swing components are now more commonly used than AWT components, there are already many examples of custom Swing components in Chapter 10, *Graphical User Interfaces*. Thus, the examples in this chapter do double-duty as AWT examples as well as JavaBeans examples.

Bean Basics

We begin our discussion of beans with some basic concepts and terminology. Any object that conforms to certain basic rules and naming conventions* can be a bean; there is no Bean class that all beans are required to subclass. Many beans are AWT components, but it is also quite possible, and often useful, to write "invisible" beans that don't have an onscreen appearance. (Just because a bean doesn't have an onscreen appearance in a finished application doesn't mean that it can't be visually manipulated by a beanbox tool, however.)

A bean exports properties, events, and methods. A *property* is a piece of the bean's internal state that can be programmatically set and queried, usually through a standard pair of get and set accessor methods. A bean may generate *events* in the same way that an AWT component, such as a Button, generates ActionEvent events. The JavaBeans API uses the same event model (in fact, it defines the event model) used by Swing and AWT GUIs in Java 1.1 and later. See Chapter 10 for a full discussion of this model. A bean defines an event by providing methods for adding and removing event listener objects from a list of interested listeners for that event. Finally, the *methods* exported by a bean are simply any public methods defined by the bean, excluding those methods used to get and set property values and register and remove event listeners.

In addition to the regular sort of properties just described, the JavaBeans API also provides support for indexed properties, bound properties, and constrained properties. An *indexed property* is any property that has an array value and for which the bean provides methods to get and set individual elements of the array, as well as methods to get and set the entire array. A *bound property* is one that sends out a notification event when its value changes, while a *constrained property* is one

---

* See Chapter 6 of *Java in a Nutshell* for a discussion of these rules and naming conventions. This overview of JavaBeans is excerpted from that chapter.

that sends out a notification event when its value changes and allows the change to be vetoed by listeners.

Because Java allows dynamic loading of classes, beanbox programs can load arbitrary beans. The beanbox tool determines the properties, events, and methods a bean supports with an introspection mechanism that is based on the `java.lang.reflect` reflection mechanism for obtaining information about the members of a class. A bean can also provide an auxiliary `BeanInfo` class that supplies additional information about the bean. The `BeanInfo` class provides this additional information in the form of a number of `FeatureDescriptor` objects, each of which describes a single feature of the bean. `FeatureDescriptor` has a number of subclasses: `BeanDescriptor`, `PropertyDescriptor`, `IndexedPropertyDescriptor`, `EventSetDescriptor`, `MethodDescriptor`, and `ParameterDescriptor`.

A primary task of a beanbox application is to allow the user to customize a bean by setting property values. A *beanbox* defines property editors for commonly used property types, such as numbers, strings, fonts, and colors. If a bean has a property of a more complicated type, however, it may need to define a `PropertyEditor` class that enables the beanbox to let the user set values for that property.

In addition, a complex bean may not be satisfied with the property-by-property customization mechanism provided by most beanboxes. Such a bean may want to define a `Customizer` class, which creates a graphical interface that allows the user to configure a bean in some useful way. A particularly complex bean may even define customizers that serve as "wizards" that guide the user step-by-step through the customization process.

A Simple Bean

As noted earlier, Swing and AWT components can all function as beans. When you write a custom GUI component, it is not difficult to make it function as a bean as well. Example 14-1 shows the definition of a custom JavaBeans component, `MultiLineLabel`, that displays one or more lines of static text. This is something the AWT `Label` component can't do.

What makes this component a bean is that all its properties have `get` and `set` accessor methods. Because `MultiLineLabel` doesn't respond to user input in any way, it doesn't define any events, so no event listener registration methods are required. `MultiLineLabel` also defines a no-argument constructor, so that it can be easily instantiated by beanboxes.

Example 14-1: MultiLineLabel.java

```
package com.davidflanagan.examples.beans;
import java.awt.*;
import java.util.*;

/**
 * A custom component that displays multiple lines of text with specified
 * margins and alignment.  In Java 1.1 we could also subclass Component,
 * making this a "lightweight" component.  Instead, we try to maintain
 * Java 1.0 compatibility for this component.  This means that you will see
 * deprecation warnings when you compile this class with Java 1.1 or later.
```

Example 14-1: MultiLineLabel.java (continued)

```java
**/
public class MultiLineLabel extends Canvas {
    // User-specified properties
    protected String label;             // The label, not broken into lines
    protected int margin_width;         // Left and right margins
    protected int margin_height;        // Top and bottom margins
    protected Alignment alignment;      // The alignment of the text.

    // Computed state values
    protected int num_lines;            // The number of lines
    protected String[] lines;           // The label, broken into lines
    protected int[] line_widths;        // How wide each line is
    protected int max_width;            // The width of the widest line
    protected int line_height;          // Total height of the font
    protected int line_ascent;          // Font height above baseline
    protected boolean measured = false; // Have the lines been measured?

    // Here are five versions of the constructor.
    public MultiLineLabel(String label, int margin_width,
                          int margin_height, Alignment alignment) {
        this.label = label;                  // Remember all the properties.
        this.margin_width = margin_width;
        this.margin_height = margin_height;
        this.alignment = alignment;
        newLabel();                          // Break the label up into lines.
    }

    public MultiLineLabel(String label, int margin_width, int margin_height) {
        this(label, margin_width, margin_height, Alignment.LEFT);
    }

    public MultiLineLabel(String label, Alignment alignment) {
        this(label, 10, 10, alignment);
    }

    public MultiLineLabel(String label) { this(label, 10, 10, Alignment.LEFT);}

    public MultiLineLabel() { this(""); }

    // Methods to set and query the various attributes of the component.
    // Note that some query methods are inherited from the superclass.
    public void setLabel(String label) {
        this.label = label;
        newLabel();             // Break the label into lines.
        measured = false;       // Note that we need to measure lines.
        repaint();              // Request a redraw.
    }

    public void setFont(Font f) {
        super.setFont(f);       // Tell our superclass about the new font.
        measured = false;       // Note that we need to remeasure lines.
        repaint();              // Request a redraw.
    }

    public void setForeground(Color c) {
        super.setForeground(c); // Tell our superclass about the new color.
        repaint();              // Request a redraw (size is unchanged).
    }
```

JavaBeans

Example 14-1: MultiLineLabel.java (continued)

```
public void setAlignment(Alignment a) { alignment = a; repaint(); }
public void setMarginWidth(int mw) { margin_width = mw; repaint(); }
public void setMarginHeight(int mh) { margin_height = mh; repaint(); }

// Property getter methods.  Note that getFont(), getForeground(), etc.
// are inherited from the superclass.
public String getLabel() { return label; }
public Alignment getAlignment() { return alignment; }
public int getMarginWidth() { return margin_width; }
public int getMarginHeight() { return margin_height; }

/**
 * This method is called by a layout manager when it wants to
 * know how big we'd like to be.  In Java 1.1, getPreferredSize() is
 * the preferred version of this method.  We use this deprecated version
 * so that this component can interoperate with 1.0 components.
 */
public Dimension preferredSize() {
    if (!measured) measure();
    return new Dimension(max_width + 2*margin_width,
                         num_lines * line_height + 2*margin_height);
}

/**
 * This method is called when the layout manager wants to know
 * the bare minimum amount of space we need to get by.
 * For Java 1.1, we'd use getMinimumSize().
 */
public Dimension minimumSize() { return preferredSize(); }

/**
 * This method draws the component.
 * Note that it handles the margins and the alignment, but that
 * it doesn't have to worry about the color or font--the superclass
 * takes care of setting those in the Graphics object we're passed.
 **/
public void paint(Graphics g) {
    int x, y;
    Dimension size = this.size();  // use getSize() in Java 1.1
    if (!measured) measure();
    y = line_ascent + (size.height - num_lines * line_height)/2;
    for(int i = 0; i < num_lines; i++, y += line_height) {
        if (alignment == Alignment.LEFT) x = margin_width;
        else if (alignment == Alignment.CENTER)
            x = (size.width - line_widths[i])/2;
        else x = size.width - margin_width - line_widths[i];
        g.drawString(lines[i], x, y);
    }
}

/**
 * This internal method breaks a specified label up into an array of lines.
 * It uses the StringTokenizer utility class.
 **/
protected synchronized void newLabel() {
    StringTokenizer t = new StringTokenizer(label, "\n");
    num_lines = t.countTokens();
    lines = new String[num_lines];
```

Example 14-1: MultiLineLabel.java (continued)

```
        line_widths = new int[num_lines];
        for(int i = 0; i < num_lines; i++) lines[i] = t.nextToken();
    }


    /**
     * This internal method figures out how the font is, and how wide each
     * line of the label is, and how wide the widest line is.
     **/
    protected synchronized void measure() {
        FontMetrics fm = this.getToolkit().getFontMetrics(this.getFont());
        line_height = fm.getHeight();
        line_ascent = fm.getAscent();
        max_width = 0;
        for(int i = 0; i < num_lines; i++) {
            line_widths[i] = fm.stringWidth(lines[i]);
            if (line_widths[i] > max_width) max_width = line_widths[i];
        }
        measured = true;
    }
}
```

The Alignment Class

MultiLineLabel uses an auxiliary class named Alignment to define three alignment constants. The definition of this class is shown in Example 14-2. The class defines three constants that hold three instances of itself and declares its constructor private, so that no other instances can be created. In this way, Alignment effectively creates an enumerated type. This is a useful technique that is not at all specific to JavaBeans.

Example 14-2: Alignment.java

```
package com.davidflanagan.examples.beans;

/** This class defines an enumerated type with three values */
public class Alignment {
    /** This private constructor prevents anyone from instantiating us */
    private Alignment() {};
    // The following three constants are the only instances of this class
    public static final Alignment LEFT = new Alignment();
    public static final Alignment CENTER = new Alignment();
    public static final Alignment RIGHT = new Alignment();
}
```

Packaging a Bean

To prepare a bean for use in a beanbox, you must package it in a JAR file, along with any other classes or resource files it requires. (JAR files are "Java archives"; you can read about the *jar* tool in *Java in a Nutshell*.) Because a single bean can have many auxiliary files, and because a JAR file can contain multiple beans, the manifest of the JAR file must define which JAR file entries are beans. You create a JAR file with the c option to the *jar* command. When you use the m option in conjunction with c, it tells *jar* to read a partial manifest file that you specify. *jar* uses the information in your partially specified manifest file when creating the complete manifest for the JAR file. To identify a class file as a bean, you simply add the following line to the file's manifest entry:

```
Java-Bean: true
```

To package the MultiLineLabel class in a JAR file, first create a manifest "stub" file. Create a file, perhaps named *manifest.stub*, with these contents:

```
Name: com/davidflanagan/examples/beans/MultiLineLabel.class
Java-Bean: true
```

Note that the forward slashes in the manifest file shouldn't be changed to backward slashes on Windows systems. The format of the JAR manifest file requires forward slashes to separate directories, regardless of the platform. Having created this partial manifest file, you can now create the JAR file:

```
% jar cfm MultiLineLabel.jar manifest.stub
   com/davidflanagan/examples/beans/MultiLineLabel.class
   com/davidflanagan/examples/beans/Alignment.class
```

Note that this is a single long command line that has been broken onto three lines. Also, on a Windows system, you do need to replace forward slashes with backslashes in this command line. If this bean required auxiliary files, you would specify them at the end of the *jar* command line, along with the class files for the bean.

Installing a Bean

The procedure for installing a bean depends on the beanbox tool you use. For the *beanbox* tool shipped with the BDK, all you need to do is copy the bean's JAR file into the *jars* directory within the BDK directory. Once you have done this, the bean appears on the palette of beans every time you start the application. Alternatively, you can load a bean's JAR file at runtime by selecting the **Load JAR** option from the **File** menu of *beanbox*.

A More Complex Bean

Example 14-3 shows another bean, YesNoPanel. This bean displays a message (using MultiLineLabel) and three buttons to the user. It fires an event when the user clicks on one of the buttons. YesNoPanel is intended for use within dialog boxes, as it provides an ideal way to ask the user yes/no questions. Figure 14-1 shows the YesNoPanel being manipulated in Sun's *beanbox* tool.

The YesNoPanel bean uses a custom AnswerEvent type to notify AnswerListener objects when the user has clicked on one of its three buttons. This new event class and listener interface are defined in the next section.

Notice that YesNoPanel doesn't use any classes from the java.beans package. One of the surprising things about beans is that they typically don't have to use any classes from this package. As you'll see later in this chapter, it's the auxiliary classes that are shipped with a bean that make heavy use of that package.

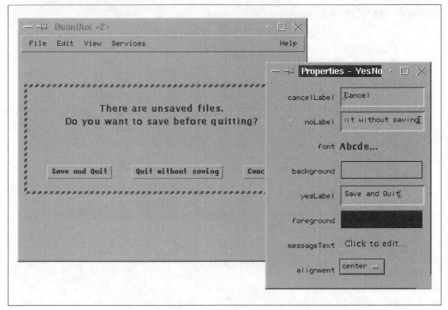

Figure 14-1. The YesNoPanel bean in beanbox

Example 14-3: YesNoPanel.java

```java
package com.davidflanagan.examples.beans;
import java.awt.*;
import java.awt.event.*;
import java.util.*;

/**
 * This JavaBean displays a multi-line message and up to three buttons.  It
 * fires an AnswerEvent when the user clicks on one of the buttons
 **/
public class YesNoPanel extends Panel {
    // Properties of the bean.
    protected String messageText;  // The message to display
    protected Alignment alignment; // The alignment of the message
    protected String yesLabel;     // Text for the yes, no, & cancel buttons
    protected String noLabel;
    protected String cancelLabel;

    // Internal components of the panel
    protected MultiLineLabel message;
    protected Button yes, no, cancel;

    /** The no-argument bean constructor, with default property values */
    public YesNoPanel() { this("Your\nMessage\nHere"); }

    public YesNoPanel(String messageText) {
        this(messageText, Alignment.LEFT, "Yes", "No", "Cancel");
    }

    /** A constructor for programmers using this class "by hand" */
    public YesNoPanel(String messageText, Alignment alignment,
                      String yesLabel, String noLabel, String cancelLabel)
```

Example 14–3: YesNoPanel.java (continued)

```
{
    // Create the components for this panel
    setLayout(new BorderLayout(15, 15));

    // Put the message label in the middle of the window.
    message = new MultiLineLabel(messageText, 20, 20, alignment);
    add(message, BorderLayout.CENTER);

    // Create a panel for the Panel buttons and put it at the bottom
    // of the Panel.  Specify a FlowLayout layout manager for it.
    Panel buttonbox = new Panel();
    buttonbox.setLayout(new FlowLayout(FlowLayout.CENTER, 25, 15));
    add(buttonbox, BorderLayout.SOUTH);

    // Create each specified button, specifying the action listener
    // and action command for each, and adding them to the buttonbox
    yes = new Button();                    // Create buttons
    no = new Button();
    cancel = new Button();
    // Add the buttons to the button box
    buttonbox.add(yes);
    buttonbox.add(no);
    buttonbox.add(cancel);

    // Register listeners for each button
    yes.addActionListener(new ActionListener() {
            public void actionPerformed(ActionEvent e) {
                fireEvent(new AnswerEvent(YesNoPanel.this,
                                          AnswerEvent.YES));
            }
        });

    no.addActionListener(new ActionListener() {
            public void actionPerformed(ActionEvent e) {
                fireEvent(new AnswerEvent(YesNoPanel.this,
                                          AnswerEvent.NO));
                }
        });
    cancel.addActionListener(new ActionListener() {
            public void actionPerformed(ActionEvent e) {
                fireEvent(new AnswerEvent(YesNoPanel.this,
                                          AnswerEvent.CANCEL));
            }
        });

    // Now call property setter methods to set the message and button
    // components to contain the right text
    setMessageText(messageText);
    setAlignment(alignment);
    setYesLabel(yesLabel);
    setNoLabel(noLabel);
    setCancelLabel(cancelLabel);
}

// Methods to query all of the bean properties.
public String getMessageText() { return messageText; }
public Alignment getAlignment() { return alignment; }
public String getYesLabel() { return yesLabel; }
```

Example 14-3: YesNoPanel.java (continued)

```java
    public String getNoLabel() { return noLabel; }
    public String getCancelLabel() { return cancelLabel; }

    // Methods to set all of the bean properties.
    public void setMessageText(String messageText) {
        this.messageText = messageText;
        message.setLabel(messageText);
        validate();
    }

    public void setAlignment(Alignment alignment) {
        this.alignment = alignment;
        message.setAlignment(alignment);
    }

    public void setYesLabel(String l) {
        yesLabel = l;
        yes.setLabel(l);
        yes.setVisible((l != null) && (l.length() > 0));
        validate();
    }

    public void setNoLabel(String l) {
        noLabel = l;
        no.setLabel(l);
        no.setVisible((l != null) && (l.length() > 0));
        validate();
    }

    public void setCancelLabel(String l) {
        cancelLabel = l;
        cancel.setLabel(l);
        cancel.setVisible((l != null) && (l.length() > 0));
        validate();
    }

    public void setFont(Font f) {
        super.setFont(f);      // Invoke the superclass method
        message.setFont(f);
        yes.setFont(f);
        no.setFont(f);
        cancel.setFont(f);
        validate();
    }

    /** This field holds a list of registered ActionListeners. */
    protected Vector listeners = new Vector();

    /** Register an action listener to be notified when a button is pressed */
    public void addAnswerListener(AnswerListener l) {
        listeners.addElement(l);
    }

    /** Remove an Answer listener from our list of interested listeners */
    public void removeAnswerListener(AnswerListener l) {
        listeners.removeElement(l);
    }
```

Example 14–3: YesNoPanel.java (continued)

```
    /** Send an event to all registered listeners */
    public void fireEvent(AnswerEvent e) {
        // Make a copy of the list and fire the events using that copy.
        // This means that listeners can be added or removed from the original
        // list in response to this event.  We ought to be able to just use an
        // enumeration for the vector, but that doesn't actually copy the list.
        Vector list = (Vector) listeners.clone();
        for(int i = 0; i < list.size(); i++) {
            AnswerListener listener = (AnswerListener)list.elementAt(i);
            switch(e.getID()) {
            case AnswerEvent.YES: listener.yes(e); break;
            case AnswerEvent.NO:  listener.no(e); break;
            case AnswerEvent.CANCEL: listener.cancel(e); break;
            }
        }
    }

    /** A main method that demonstrates the class */
    public static void main(String[] args) {
        // Create an instance of InfoPanel, with title and message specified:
        YesNoPanel p = new YesNoPanel("Do you really want to quit?");

        // Register an action listener for the Panel.  This one just prints
        // the results out to the console.
        p.addAnswerListener(new AnswerListener() {
                public void yes(AnswerEvent e) { System.exit(0); }
                public void no(AnswerEvent e) { System.out.println("No"); }
                public void cancel(AnswerEvent e) {
                    System.out.println("Cancel");
                }
            });

        Frame f = new Frame();
        f.add(p);
        f.pack();
        f.setVisible(true);
    }
}
```

Custom Events

Beans can use the standard event types defined in the java.awt.event and javax.swing.event packages, but they don't have to. Our YesNoPanel class defines its own event type, AnswerEvent. Defining a new event class is really quite simple; AnswerEvent is shown in Example 14-4.

Example 14–4: AnswerEvent.java

```
package com.davidflanagan.examples.beans;

/**
 * The YesNoPanel class fires an event of this type when the user clicks one
 * of its buttons.  The id field specifies which button the user pressed.
 **/
public class AnswerEvent extends java.util.EventObject {
    public static final int YES = 0, NO = 1, CANCEL = 2;  // Button constants
```

Example 14–4: AnswerEvent.java (continued)

```
    protected int id;                           // Which button was pressed?
    public AnswerEvent(Object source, int id) {
        super(source);
        this.id = id;
    }
    public int getID() { return id; }           // Return the button
}
```

Along with the AnswerEvent class, YesNoPanel also defines a new type of event listener interface, AnswerListener, that defines the methods that must be implemented by any object that wants to receive notification from a YesNoPanel. The
definition of AnswerListener is shown in Example 14-5.

Example 14–5: AnswerListener.java

```
package com.davidflanagan.examples.beans;

/**
 * Classes that want to be notified when the user clicks a button in a
 * YesNoPanel should implement this interface.  The method invoked depends
 * on which button the user clicked.
 **/
public interface AnswerListener extends java.util.EventListener {
    public void yes(AnswerEvent e);
    public void no(AnswerEvent e);
    public void cancel(AnswerEvent e);
}
```

Specifying Bean Information

The YesNoPanel class itself, as well as the MultiLineLabel, Alignment,
AnswerEvent, and AnswerListener classes it relies on, are all a required part of our
bean. When an application that uses the bean is shipped, it has to include all five
class files. There are other kinds of classes, however, that are often bundled with a
bean but not intended for use by the application developer. These classes are used
by the beanbox tool that manipulates the bean. The bean class itself doesn't refer
to any of these auxiliary beanbox classes, so it is not dependent on them, and they
don't have to be shipped with the bean in finished products.

The first of these optional, auxiliary classes is a BeanInfo class. As explained earlier, a beanbox discovers the properties, events, and methods exported by a bean
through introspection based on the Java Reflection API. A bean developer who
wants to provide additional information about a bean, or refine the (somewhat
rough) information available through introspection, should define a class that
implements the BeanInfo interface to provide that information. A BeanInfo class
typically subclasses SimpleBeanInfo, which provides a no-op implementation of
the BeanInfo interface. When you want to override only one or two methods, it is
easier to subclass SimpleBeanInfo than to implement BeanInfo directly. Beanbox
tools rely on a naming convention in order to find the BeanInfo class for a given
bean: a BeanInfo class should have the same name as the bean, with the string
"BeanInfo" appended. Example 14-6 shows an implementation of the YesNoPanel-
BeanInfo class.

This BeanInfo class specifies a number of pieces of information for our bean:

- An icon that represents the bean.

- A BeanDescriptor object, which includes a reference to a Customizer class for the bean. We'll see an implementation of this class later in the chapter.

- A list of the supported properties of the bean, along with a short description of each one. Some beanbox tools (but not Sun's *beanbox*) display these strings to the user in some useful way.

- A method that returns the most commonly customized property of the bean; this is called the "default" property.

- A reference to a PropertyEditor class for one of the properties. We'll see the implementation of this property editor class later in the chapter.

Besides specifying this information, a BeanInfo class can also provide information about the methods it defines and the events it generates. The various Feature-Descriptor objects that provide information about such things as properties and methods can also include other information not provided by YesNoPanelBeanInfo, such as a localized display name that is distinct from the programmatic name.

Example 14–6: YesNoPanelBeanInfo.java

```
package com.davidflanagan.examples.beans;
import java.beans.*;
import java.lang.reflect.*;
import java.awt.*;

/**
 * This BeanInfo class provides additional information about the YesNoPanel
 * bean in addition to what can be obtained through  introspection alone.
 **/
public class YesNoPanelBeanInfo extends SimpleBeanInfo {
    /**
     * Return an icon for the bean.  We should really check the kind argument
     * to see what size icon the beanbox wants, but since we only have one
     * icon to offer, we just return it and let the beanbox deal with it
     **/
    public Image getIcon(int kind) { return loadImage("YesNoPanelIcon.gif"); }

    /**
     * Return a descriptor for the bean itself.  It specifies a customizer
     * for the bean class.  We could also add a description string here
     **/
    public BeanDescriptor getBeanDescriptor() {
        return new BeanDescriptor(YesNoPanel.class,
                                  YesNoPanelCustomizer.class);
    }

    /** This is a convenience method for creating PropertyDescriptor objects */
    static PropertyDescriptor prop(String name, String description) {
        try {
            PropertyDescriptor p =
                new PropertyDescriptor(name, YesNoPanel.class);
            p.setShortDescription(description);
            return p;
        }
```

Example 14-6: YesNoPanelBeanInfo.java (continued)

```
        catch(IntrospectionException e) { return null; }
}

// Initialize a static array of PropertyDescriptor objects that provide
// additional information about the properties supported by the bean.
// By explicitly specifying property descriptors, we are able to provide
// simple help strings for each property; these would not be available to
// the beanbox through simple introspection.  We are also able to register
// a special property editors for the messageText property
static PropertyDescriptor[] props = {
    prop("messageText", "The message text that appears in the bean body"),
    prop("alignment", "The alignment of the message text"),
    prop("yesLabel", "The label for the Yes button"),
    prop("noLabel", "The label for the No button"),
    prop("cancelLabel","The label for the Cancel button"),
    prop("font", "The font for the message and buttons"),
    prop("background", "The background color"),
    prop("foreground", "The foreground color"),
};
static {
    props[0].setPropertyEditorClass(YesNoPanelMessageEditor.class);
}

/** Return the property descriptors for this bean */
public PropertyDescriptor[] getPropertyDescriptors() { return props; }

/** The message property is most often customized; make it the default */
public int getDefaultPropertyIndex() { return 0; }
}
```

Defining a Simple Property Editor

A bean can also provide auxiliary PropertyEditor classes for use by a beanbox tool. PropertyEditor is a flexible interface that allows a bean to tell a beanbox how to display and edit the values of certain types of properties.

A beanbox tool always provides simple property editors for common property types, such as strings, numbers, fonts, and colors. If your bean has a property of a nonstandard type, however, you should register a property editor for that type. The easiest way to "register" a property editor is through a simple naming convention. If your type is defined by the class *X*, the editor for it should be defined in the class *X* Editor. Alternatively, you can register a property editor by calling the PropertyEditorManager.registerEditor() method, probably from the constructor of your BeanInfo class. If you call this method from the bean itself, the bean then depends on the property editor class, so the editor has to be bundled with the bean in applications, which is not desirable. Another way to register a property editor is by using a PropertyDescriptor object in a BeanInfo class to specify the PropertyEditor for a specific property. The YesNoPanelBeanInfo class does this for the messageText property, for example.

The PropertyEditor interface can seem confusing at first. Its methods allow you to define three techniques for displaying the value of a property and two techniques for allowing the user to edit the value of a property. The value of a property can be displayed:

As a string

> If you define the getAsText() method, a beanbox can convert a property to a string and display that string to the user.

As an enumerated value

> If a property can take only on values from a fixed set of values, you can define the getTags() method to allow a beanbox to display a dropdown menu of allowed values for the property.

In a graphical display

> If you define paintValue(), a beanbox can ask the property editor to display the value using some natural graphical format, such as a color swatch for colors. You also need to define isPaintable() to specify that a graphical format is supported.

The two editing techniques are:

String editing

> If you define the setAsText() method, a beanbox knows it can simply have the user type a value into a text field and pass that value to setAsText(). If your property editor defines getTags(), it should also define setAsText(), so that a beanbox can set the property value using the individual tag values.

Custom editing

> If your property editor defines getCustomEditor(), a beanbox can call it to obtain some kind of GUI component that can be displayed in a dialog box and serve as a custom editor for the property. You also need to define supportsCustomEditor() to specify that custom editing is supported.

The setValue() method of a PropertyEditor is called to specify the current value of the property. It is this value that should be converted to a string or graphical representation by getAsText() or paintValue().

A property editor must maintain a list of event listeners that are interested in changes to the value of the property. The addPropertyChangeListener() and removePropertyChangeListener() methods are standard event listener registration and removal methods. When a property editor changes the value of a property, either through setAsText() or through a custom editor, it must send a PropertyChangeEvent to all registered listeners.

PropertyEditor defines the getJavaInitializationString() for use by beanbox tools that generate Java code. This method should return a fragment of Java code that can initialize a variable to the current property value.

Finally, a class that implements the PropertyEditor interface must have a no-argument constructor, so it can be dynamically loaded and instantiated by a beanbox.

Most property editors can be much simpler than this detailed description suggests. In many cases, you can subclass PropertyEditorSupport instead of implementing the PropertyEditor interface directly. This useful class provides no-op implementations of most `PropertyEditor` methods. It also implements the methods for adding and removing event listeners.

A property that has an enumerated value requires a simple property editor. The `alignment` property of the `YesNoPanel` bean is an example of this common type of property. The property has only the three legal values defined by the `Alignment` class. The `AlignmentEditor` class shown in Example 14-7 is a property editor that tells a beanbox how to display and edit the value of this property. Because `AlignmentEditor` follows a JavaBeans naming convention, a beanbox automatically uses it for any property of type `Alignment`.

Example 14-7: AlignmentEditor.java

```
package com.davidflanagan.examples.beans;
import java.beans.*;
import java.awt.*;

/**
 * This PropertyEditor defines the enumerated values of the alignment property
 * so that a bean box or IDE can present those values to the user for selection
 **/
public class AlignmentEditor extends PropertyEditorSupport {
    /** Return the list of value names for the enumerated type. */
    public String[] getTags() {
        return new String[] { "left", "center", "right" };
    }

    /** Convert each of those value names into the actual value. */
    public void setAsText(String s) {
        if (s.equals("left")) setValue(Alignment.LEFT);
        else if (s.equals("center")) setValue(Alignment.CENTER);
        else if (s.equals("right")) setValue(Alignment.RIGHT);
        else throw new IllegalArgumentException(s);
    }

    /** This is an important method for code generation. */
    public String getJavaInitializationString() {
        Object o = getValue();
        if (o == Alignment.LEFT)
            return "com.davidflanagan.examples.beans.Alignment.LEFT";
        if (o == Alignment.CENTER)
            return "com.davidflanagan.examples.beans.Alignment.CENTER";
        if (o == Alignment.RIGHT)
            return "com.davidflanagan.examples.beans.Alignment.RIGHT";
        return null;
    }
}
```

Defining a Complex Property Editor

There is another `YesNoPanel` property value that requires a property editor. The `messageText` property of `YesNoPanel` can specify a multiline message to be displayed in the panel. This property requires a property editor because the *beanbox* program doesn't distinguish between single-line and multiline string types; the `TextField` objects it uses for text input don't allow the user to enter multiple lines of text. For this reason, you define the `YesNoPanelMessageEditor` class and register it with the `PropertyDescriptor` for the message property, as shown in Example 14-6.

Example 14-8 shows the definition of this property editor. This is a more complex editor that supports the creation of a custom editor component and graphical display of the value. Note that this example implements `PropertyEditor` directly, which means that it must handle registration and notification of `PropertyChange-Listener` objects. `getCustomEditor()` returns an editor component for multiline strings. Figure 14-2 shows this custom editor placed within a dialog box created by the *beanbox* program. Note that the **Done** button in this figure is part of the *beanbox* dialog, not part of the property editor itself.

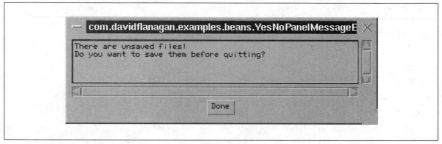

Figure 14-2. A custom property editor dialog

The `paintValue()` method displays the value of the `messageText` property. This multiline value doesn't typically fit in the small rectangle of screen space allowed for the property, so `paintValue()` displays instructions for popping up the custom editor, which allows the user to inspect and edit the property value.

Example 14-8: YesNoPanelMessageEditor.java

```java
package com.davidflanagan.examples.beans;
import java.beans.*;
import java.awt.*;
import java.awt.event.*;

/**
 * This class is a custom editor for the messageText property of the
 * YesNoPanel bean.  It is necessary because the default editor for
 * properties of type String does not allow multi-line strings
 * to be entered.
 */
public class YesNoPanelMessageEditor implements PropertyEditor {
    protected String value;  // The value we will be editing.

    public void setValue(Object o) {  value = (String) o; }
    public Object getValue() { return value; }
    public void setAsText(String s) { value = s; }
    public String getAsText() { return value; }
    public String[] getTags() { return null; }  // not enumerated; no tags

    // Say that we allow custom editing.
    public boolean supportsCustomEditor() { return true; }

    // Return the custom editor.  This just creates and returns a TextArea
    // to edit the multi-line text.  But it also registers a listener on the
```

Example 14–8: YesNoPanelMessageEditor.java (continued)

```
    // text area to update the value as the user types and to fire the
    // property change events that property editors are required to fire.
    public Component getCustomEditor() {
        final TextArea t = new TextArea(value);
        t.setSize(300, 150); // TextArea has no preferred size, so set one
        t.addTextListener(new TextListener() {
                public void textValueChanged(TextEvent e) {
                    value = t.getText();
                    listeners.firePropertyChange(null, null, null);
                }
            });
        return t;
    }

    // Visual display of the value, for use with the custom editor.
    // Just print some instructions and hope they fit in the in the box.
    // This could be more sophisticated.
    public boolean isPaintable() { return true; }
    public void paintValue(Graphics g, Rectangle r) {
        g.setClip(r);
        g.drawString("Click to edit...", r.x+5, r.y+15);
    }

    // Important method for code generators.  Note that it really ought to
    // escape any quotes or backslashes in value before returning the string.
    public String getJavaInitializationString() { return "\"" + value + "\""; }

    // This code uses the PropertyChangeSupport class to maintain a list of
    // listeners interested in the edits we make to the value.
    protected PropertyChangeSupport listeners =new PropertyChangeSupport(this);
    public void addPropertyChangeListener(PropertyChangeListener l) {
        listeners.addPropertyChangeListener(l);
    }
    public void removePropertyChangeListener(PropertyChangeListener l) {
        listeners.removePropertyChangeListener(l);
    }
}
```

Defining a Bean Customizer

A bean may want to provide some way for the user of a beanbox program to customize its properties other than by setting them one at a time. A bean can do this by creating a Customizer class for itself and registering the customizer class with the BeanDescriptor object returned by its BeanInfo class, as in Example 14-6.

A customizer must be some kind of GUI component that is suitable for display in a dialog box created by the beanbox. Therefore, a customizer class is typically a subclass of Panel. In addition, a customizer must implement the Customizer interface. This interface consists of methods for adding and removing property change event listeners and a setObject() method that the beanbox calls to tell the customizer what bean object it is customizing. Whenever the user makes a change to the bean through the customizer, the customizer sends a PropertyChangeEvent to any interested listeners. Finally, like a property editor, a customizer must have a no-argument constructor, so it can easily be instantiated by a beanbox.

Example 14-9 shows a customizer for our `YesNoPanel` bean. This customizer displays a panel that has the same layout as a `YesNoPanel`, but it substitutes a `TextArea` object for the message display and three `TextField` objects for the three buttons that the dialog can display. These text entry areas allow the user to enter values for the `messageText`, `yesLabel`, `noLabel`, and `cancelLabel` properties. Figure 14-3 shows this customizer panel displayed within a dialog box created by the *beanbox* program. Again, note that the **Done** button is part of the *beanbox* dialog, not part of the customizer itself.

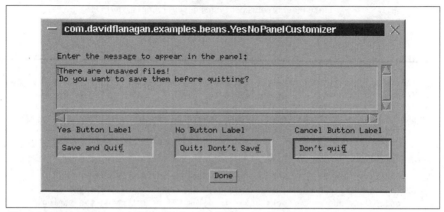

Figure 14-3. The customizer dialog for the YesNoPanel bean

Example 14-9: YesNoPanelCustomizer.java

```java
package com.davidflanagan.examples.beans;
import java.awt.*;
import java.awt.event.*;
import java.beans.*;

/**
 * This class is a customizer for the YesNoPanel bean.  It displays a
 * TextArea and three TextFields where the user can enter the main message
 * and the labels for each of the three buttons.  It does not allow the
 * alignment property to be set.
 **/
public class YesNoPanelCustomizer extends Panel
    implements Customizer, TextListener
{
    protected YesNoPanel bean;    // The bean being customized
    protected TextArea message;   // For entering the message
    protected TextField fields[]; // For entering button text

    // The bean box calls this method to tell us what object to customize.
    // This method will always be called before the customizer is displayed,
    // so it is safe to create the customizer GUI here.
    public void setObject(Object o) {
        bean = (YesNoPanel)o;    // save the object we're customizing

        // Put a label at the top of the panel.
        this.setLayout(new BorderLayout());
        this.add(new Label("Enter the message to appear in the panel:"),
                "North");
```

Example 14-9: YesNoPanelCustomizer.java (continued)

```
        // And a big text area below it for entering the message.
        message = new TextArea(bean.getMessageText());
        message.addTextListener(this);
        // TextAreas don't know how big they want to be.  You must tell them.
        message.setSize(400, 200);
        this.add(message, "Center");

        // Then add a row of textfields for entering the button labels.
        Panel buttonbox = new Panel();                       // The row container
        buttonbox.setLayout(new GridLayout(1, 0, 25, 10)); // Equally spaced
        this.add(buttonbox, "South");                        // Put row on bottom

        // Now go create three TextFields to put in this row.  But actually
        // position a Label above each, so create an container for each
        // TextField+Label combination.
        fields = new TextField[3];            // Array of TextFields.
        String[] labels = new String[] {      // Labels for each.
            "Yes Button Label", "No Button Label", "Cancel Button Label"};
        String[] values = new String[] {      // Initial values of each.
            bean.getYesLabel(), bean.getNoLabel(), bean.getCancelLabel()};
        for(int i = 0; i < 3; i++) {
            Panel p = new Panel();                      // Create a container.
            p.setLayout(new BorderLayout());            // Give it a BorderLayout.
            p.add(new Label(labels[i]), "North");       // Put a label on the top.
            fields[i] = new TextField(values[i]);       // Create the text field.
            p.add(fields[i], "Center");                 // Put it below the label.
            fields[i].addTextListener(this);            // Set the event listener.
            buttonbox.add(p);                           // Add container to row.
        }
    }
    // Add some space around the outside of the panel.
    public Insets getInsets() { return new Insets(10, 10, 10, 10); }

    // This is the method defined by the TextListener interface.  Whenever the
    // user types a character in the TextArea or TextFields, this will get
    // called.  It updates the appropriate property of the bean and fires a
    // property changed event, as all customizers are required to do.
    // Note that we are not required to fire an event for every keystroke.
    // Instead we could include an "Apply" button that would make all the
    // changes at once, with a single property changed event.
    public void textValueChanged(TextEvent e) {
        TextComponent t = (TextComponent)e.getSource();
        String s = t.getText();
        if (t == message) bean.setMessageText(s);
        else if (t == fields[0]) bean.setYesLabel(s);
        else if (t == fields[1]) bean.setNoLabel(s);
        else if (t == fields[2]) bean.setCancelLabel(s);
        listeners.firePropertyChange(null, null, null);
    }

    // This code uses the PropertyChangeSupport class to maintain a list of
    // listeners interested in the edits we make to the bean.
    protected PropertyChangeSupport listeners =new PropertyChangeSupport(this);
    public void addPropertyChangeListener(PropertyChangeListener l) {
        listeners.addPropertyChangeListener(l);
    }
    public void removePropertyChangeListener(PropertyChangeListener l) {
        listeners.removePropertyChangeListener(l);
```

JavaBeans

Example 14–9: YesNoPanelCustomizer.java (continued)

```
    }
}
```

Exercises

14-1. Chapters 10, 12, and 13 contain examples of AWT and Swing components that allow the user to scribble with the mouse. Choose one of these classes, rename it to `ScribbleBean`, and package it in a JAR file, (along with any other example classes it may require). Now install it in a beanbox application of your choice, to demonstrate that it works. Give your bean an `erase()` method that erases the scribbles and use the beanbox to create a push button of some sort that invokes this method.

14-2. Modify your `ScribbleBean` bean so that it has color and line-width properties that specify the color and width of the lines used for the scribbles. Repackage the bean and test the properties in a beanbox.

14-3. An application that uses a `ScribbleBean` bean might want to be notified each time the user completes a single stroke of the scribble (i.e., each time the user clicks, drags, and then releases the mouse). For example, an application might make an off-screen copy of the scribble after each stroke, so that it could implement an undo facility. In order to provide this kind of notification, modify your `ScribbleBean` bean to support a "stroke" event. Define a simple `StrokeEvent` class and `StrokeListener` interface. Modify the `ScribbleBean` bean so that it allows registration and removal of `StrokeListener` objects, and so that it notifies all registered listeners each time a stroke of the scribble is complete. Regenerate the bean's JAR file so that it includes the `StrokeEvent` and `StrokeListener` class files.

14-4. Define a `BeanInfo` subclass for the `ScribbleBean` bean. This class should provide information about the `erase()` method, the color and width properties, and the stroke event defined by the bean. The `BeanInfo` class should use the `FeatureDescriptor.setShortDescription()` method to provide simple descriptive strings for the bean itself and its method, properties, and event.

CHAPTER 15

Applets

This chapter demonstrates the techniques of applet writing. It proceeds from a trivial "Hello World" applet to more sophisticated applets. Along the way, it explains how to:

- Draw graphics in your applet

- Handle and respond to simple user input

- Read and use values of applet parameters, allowing customization of an applet

- Load and display images and load and play sounds

- Package an applet and related files into a JAR file

Introduction to Applets

An applet, as the name implies, is a kind of mini-application, designed to be run by a web browser or in the context of some other "applet viewer." Applets differ from regular applications in a number of ways. One of the most important is that there are a number of security restrictions on what applets are allowed to do. An applet often consists of untrusted code, so it cannot be allowed access to the local filesystem, for example.

All applets subclass `java.applet.Applet`, which inherits from `java.awt.Panel` and `java.awt.Component`. So creating an applet is more like subclassing a GUI component than it is like writing an application. In particular, an applet does not have a `main()` method or other single entry point from which the program starts running. Instead, to write an applet, you subclass `Applet` and override a number of standard methods. At appropriate times, under well-defined circumstances, the web browser or applet viewer invokes the methods you have defined. The applet is not in control of the thread of execution; it simply responds when the browser or viewer tells it to. For this reason, the methods you write must take the necessary action and return promptly; they are not allowed to enter time-consuming (or infinite) loops. To perform a time-consuming or repetitive task, such as animation, an applet must create its own thread, over which it does have complete control.

The task of writing an applet, then, comes down to defining the appropriate methods. A number of these methods are defined by the `Applet` class:

`init()`
> Called when the applet is first loaded into the browser or viewer. It typically performs applet initialization, in preference to a constructor method. (The web browser doesn't pass any arguments to an applet's constructor method, so defining one isn't too useful.)

`destroy()`
> Called when the applet is about to be unloaded from the browser or viewer. It should free any resources, other than memory, the applet has allocated.

`start()`
> Called when the applet becomes visible and should start doing whatever it does. Often used with animation and with threads.

`stop()`
> Called when the applet becomes temporarily invisible, for example, when the user has scrolled it off the screen. Tells the applet to stop performing an animation or other task.

`getAppletInfo()`
> Called to get information about the applet. Should return a string suitable for display in a dialog box.

`getParameterInfo()`
> Called to obtain information about the parameters the applet responds to. Should return strings describing those parameters.

In addition to these `Applet` methods, there are a number of other methods, inherited from superclasses of `Applet`, that the browser invokes at appropriate times, and which an applet should override. The most obvious of these methods is `paint()`, which the browser or viewer invokes to ask the applet to draw itself on the screen. A related method is `print()`, which an applet should override if it wants to display itself on paper differently than it does on the screen. There are quite a few other methods applets should override to respond to events. For example, if an applet wants to respond to mouse clicks, it should override `mouseDown()`. (We'll see more about event handling in applets later in this chapter.)

The `Applet` class also defines some methods that are commonly used (but not overridden) by applets:

`getImage()`
> Loads an image file from the network and returns a `java.awt.Image` object.

`getAudioClip()`
> Loads a sound clip from the network and returns a `java.applet.AudioClip` object.

`getParameter()`

Looks up and returns the value of a named parameter, specified in the HTML file that refers to the applet with the <PARAM> tag.

`getCodeBase()`

Returns the base URL from which the applet class file was loaded.

`getDocumentBase()`

Returns the base URL of the HTML file that refers to the applet.

`showStatus()`

Displays a message in the status line of the browser or applet viewer.

`getAppletContext()`

Returns the `java.applet.AppletContext` object for the applet. `AppletContext` defines the useful `showDocument()` method that asks the browser to load and display a new web page.

A First Applet

Example 15-1 shows what is probably the simplest possible applet you can write in Java. Figure 15-1 shows the output it produces. This example introduces the `paint()` method, which is invoked by the applet viewer (or web browser) when the applet needs to be drawn. This method should perform graphical output—such as drawing text or lines or displaying images—for your applet. The argument to `paint()` is a `java.awt.Graphics` object that you use to do the drawing.

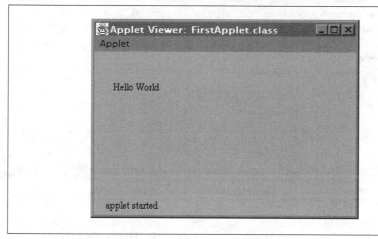

Figure 15-1. A simple applet

Example 15-1: FirstApplet.java

```
package com.davidflanagan.examples.applet;
import java.applet.*;   // Don't forget this import statement!
import java.awt.*;      // Or this one for the graphics!

/** This applet just says "Hello World! */
public class FirstApplet extends Applet {
```

Example 15–1: FirstApplet.java (continued)

```
    // This method displays the applet.
    public void paint(Graphics g) {
        g.drawString("Hello World", 25, 50);
    }
}
```

To display an applet, you need an HTML file that references it. Here is an HTML fragment that can be used with this first applet:

```
<applet code="com.davidflanagan.examples.applet.FirstApplet.class"
        codebase="../../../../"
        width=150 height=100>
</applet>
```

With an HTML file that references the applet, you can now view the applet with an applet viewer or web browser. Note that the WIDTH and HEIGHT attributes of this HTML tag are required. For most applet examples in this book, I show only the Java code, not the corresponding HTML file that goes with it. Typically, that HTML file contains a tag as simple as the one shown here.

A Clock Applet

Example 15-2 is an applet that displays the current time, as shown in Figure 15-2, and updates it once a second. Unlike Example 15-1, which defines a paint() method and does its own text drawing with Graphics.drawString(), this example uses a java.awt.Label component to do the drawing. While it is common for applets to do their own drawing with a paint() method, it is also important to remember that applets extend java.awt.Panel and can contain any type of GUI components. Clock defines an init() method that creates and configures the Label component.

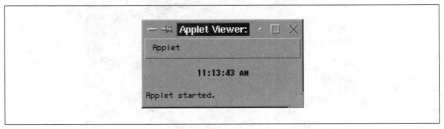

Figure 15–2. A clock applet

In order to update the time every second, Clock implements the Runnable inter-face and creates a Thread that runs the run() method. The applet's start() and stop() methods are invoked by the browser when the applet becomes visible or is hidden; they start and stop the thread. (Although the example is written to use Java 1.1, it does not rely on the Thread.stop() method, which was deprecated in Java 1.2.)

Finally, the Clock applet implements getAppletInfo() to provide information about the applet. Some applet viewers provide an interface for displaying this information.

Example 15-2: Clock.java

```java
package com.davidflanagan.examples.applet;
import java.applet.*;         // Don't forget this import statement!
import java.awt.*;            // Or this one for the graphics!
import java.util.Date;        // To obtain the current time
import java.text.DateFormat;  // For displaying the time

/**
 * This applet displays the time, and updates it every second
 **/
public class Clock extends Applet implements Runnable {
    Label time;                 // A component to display the time in
    DateFormat timeFormat;      // This object converts the time to a string
    Thread timer;               // The thread that updates the time
    volatile boolean running;   // A flag used to stop the thread

    /**
     * The init method is called when the browser first starts the applet.
     * It sets up the Label component and obtains a DateFormat object
     **/
    public void init() {
        time = new Label();
        time.setFont(new Font("helvetica", Font.BOLD, 12));
        time.setAlignment(Label.CENTER);
        setLayout(new BorderLayout());
        add(time, BorderLayout.CENTER);
        timeFormat = DateFormat.getTimeInstance(DateFormat.MEDIUM);
    }

    /**
     * This browser calls this method to tell the applet to start running.
     * Here, we create and start a thread that will update the time each
     * second.  Note that we take care never to have more than one thread
     **/
    public void start() {
        running = true;                     // Set the flag
        if (timer == null) {                // If we don't already have a thread
            timer = new Thread(this);       // Then create one
            timer.start();                  // And start it running
        }
    }

    /**
     * This method implements Runnable.  It is the body of the thread.  Once
     * a second, it updates the text of the Label to display the current time
     **/
    public void run() {
        while(running) {        // Loop until we're stopped
            // Get current time, convert to a String, and display in the Label
            time.setText(timeFormat.format(new Date()));
            // Now wait 1000 milliseconds
            try { Thread.sleep(1000); }
            catch (InterruptedException e) {}
        }
        // If the thread exits, set it to null so we can create a new one
        // if start() is called again.
        timer = null;
    }
```

Example 15–2: Clock.java (continued)

```
/**
 * The browser calls this method to tell the applet that it is not visible
 * and should not run.  It sets a flag that tells the run() method to exit
 **/
public void stop() { running = false; }

/**
 * Returns information about the applet for display by the applet viewer
 **/
public String getAppletInfo() {
    return "Clock applet Copyright (c) 2000 by David Flanagan";
}
}
```

Applets and the Java 1.0 Event Model

The AWT event model changed dramatically between Java 1.0 and 1.1. Chapter 10, *Graphical User Interfaces* described the Java 1.1 event handling model exclusively, since the Java 1.0 event model is now deprecated. However, because there is still a large installed base of web browsers (including Netscape 3.0 and 4.0) that support only the Java 1.0 event model, applets are sometimes still written using this model. This section briefly describes Java 1.0 event handling and includes an example applet that uses the model.*

In Java 1.0, all events are represented by the java.awt.Event class. This class has a number of instance fields that describe the event. One of these fields, id, specifies the type of the event. Event defines a number of constants that are the possible values for the id field. The target field specifies the object (typically a Component) that generated the event, or on which the event occurred (i.e., the source of the event). The other fields may or may not be used, depending on the type of the event. For example, the x and y fields are defined when id is BUT-TON_EVENT but not when it is ACTION_EVENT. The arg field can provide additional type-dependent data.

Java 1.0 events are dispatched first to the handleEvent() method of the Component on which they occurred. The default implementation of this method checks the id field of the Event object and dispatches the most commonly used types of events to various type-specific methods, listed in Table 15-1.

Table 15–1. Java 1.0 Event Processing Methods of Component

action()	lostFocus()	mouseExit()
gotFocus()	mouseDown()	mouseMove()
keyDown()	mouseDrag()	mouseUp()
keyUp()	mouseEnter()	

The methods listed in Table 15-1 are defined by the Component class. One of the primary characteristics of the Java 1.0 event model is that you must override these

---

* Note that this section and its example are excerpted from *Java Foundation Classes in a Nutshell*.

methods to process events. This means that you must create a subclass to define custom event-handling behavior, which is exactly what you do when you write an applet, for example. Notice, however, that not all the event types are dispatched by `handleEvent()` to more specific methods. So, if you are interested in `LIST_SELECT` or `WINDOW_ICONIFY` events, for example, you have to override `handleEvent()` itself, rather than one of the more specific methods. If you do this, you should usually invoke `super.handleEvent()` to continue dispatching events of other types in the default way.

The `handleEvent()` method, and all the type-specific methods, return `boolean` values. If an event-handling method returns `false`, as they all do by default, it means that the event was not handled, so it should be passed to the container of the current component to see if that container is interested in processing it. If a method returns `true`, on the other hand, it is a signal that the event *has* been handled, and no further processing is needed.

The fact that unhandled events are passed up the containment hierarchy is important. It means that you can override the `action()` method (for example) in an applet in order to handle the `ACTION_EVENT` events that are generated by the buttons within the applet. If they were not propagated up as they are, you would have to create a custom subclass of `Button` for every button you wanted to add to an interface.

In the Java 1.0 model, there is no de facto way to know what types of events are generated by what GUI components, nor to know what fields of the `Event` object are filled in for what types of events. You simply have to look up this information in the documentation of individual AWT components.

Many event types use the `modifiers` field of the `Event` object to report which keyboard modifier keys were depressed when the event occurred. This field contains a bitmask of the `SHIFT_MASK`, `CTRL_MASK`, `META_MASK`, and `ALT_MASK` constants defined by the `Event` class. The `shiftDown()`, `controlDown()`, and `metaDown()` methods can test for the various modifiers. When a mouse event occurs, the `Event` class does not have a special field to indicate which mouse button was pressed. Instead, this information is provided by reusing the keyboard modifier constants. This allows such systems as the Macintosh that use a one-button mouse to simulate other mouse buttons by using keyboard modifiers. If the left mouse button is in use, no keyboard modifiers are reported. If the right button is used, the `META_MASK` bit is set in the `modifiers` field. And if the middle button is down, the `ALT_MASK` bit is set.

When a keyboard event occurs, you should check the `id` field of the `Event` object to determine what kind of key was pressed. If the event type is `KEY_PRESS` or `KEY_RELEASE`, the keyboard key has an ASCII or Unicode representation and the `key` field of the event object contains the encoding of the key. On the other hand, if `id` is `KEY_ACTION` or `KEY_ACTION_RELEASE`, the key is a function key of some sort, and the `key` field contains one of the keyboard constants defined by the `Event` class, such as `Event.F1` or `Event.LEFT`.

Keep this quick introduction to the Java 1.0 event model in mind as you read over Example 15-3. This applet allows the user to produce simple drawings by scribbling with the mouse. It also allows the user to erase those drawings by clicking on a button or typing the E key. As you'll see, the applet overrides methods to handle mouse events, keyboard events, and action events generated by the Button component. In particular, note the boolean return values of these event handling methods. This applet does not define a paint() method. For simplicity, it does its drawing directly in response to the events it receives and does not store the coordinates. This means that it cannot regenerate the user's drawing if it is scrolled off the screen and then scrolled back on.

Example 15–3: Scribble.java

```java
package com.davidflanagan.examples.applet;
import java.applet.*;
import java.awt.*;

/**
 * This applet lets the user scribble with the mouse.
 * It demonstrates the Java 1.0 event model.
 **/
public class Scribble extends Applet {
    private int lastx, lasty;    // Remember last mouse coordinates.
    Button erase_button;         // The Erase button.

    /** Initialize the erase button, ask for keyboard focus */
    public void init() {
        erase_button = new Button("Erase");
        this.add(erase_button);
        this.setBackground(Color.white);  // Set background color for scribble
        this.requestFocus();  // Ask for keyboard focus so we get key events
    }

    /** Respond to mouse clicks */
    public boolean mouseDown(Event e, int x, int y) {
        lastx = x; lasty = y;              // Remember where the click was
        return true;
    }

    /** Respond to mouse drags */
    public boolean mouseDrag(Event e, int x, int y) {
        Graphics g = getGraphics();
        g.drawLine(lastx, lasty, x, y);    // Draw from last position to here
        lastx = x; lasty = y;              // And remember new last position
        return true;
    }

    /** Respond to key presses: Erase drawing when user types 'e' */
    public boolean keyDown(Event e, int key) {
        if ((e.id == Event.KEY_PRESS) && (key == 'e')) {
            Graphics g = getGraphics();
            g.setColor(this.getBackground());
            g.fillRect(0, 0, bounds().width, bounds().height);
            return true;
        }
        else return false;
    }

    /** Respond to Button clicks: erase drawing when user clicks button */
    public boolean action(Event e, Object arg) {
        if (e.target == erase_button) {
            Graphics g = getGraphics();
```

Example 15-3: Scribble.java (continued)

```
                g.setColor(this.getBackground());
                g.fillRect(0, 0, bounds().width, bounds().height);
                return true;
        }
        else return false;
    }
}
```

Java 1.0 Event Details

Example 15-4 shows an applet that handles all user input events that can occur in an applet and displays the event details. These are mouse and keyboard events primarily; the program does not define any GUI components, so it does not handle the higher-level semantic events those components generate. This example is interesting because it shows how to interpret modifiers and how to make sense of the various types of key events. If you find yourself writing complex event handling code, you may want to model pieces of it after this example.

Example 15-4: EventTester.java

```
package com.davidflanagan.examples.applet;
import java.applet.*;
import java.awt.*;
import java.util.*;

/** An applet that gives details about Java 1.0 events */
public class EventTester extends Applet {
    // Handle mouse events
    public boolean mouseDown(Event e, int x, int y)  {
        showLine(mods(e.modifiers) +  "Mouse Down: [" + x + "," + y + "]");
        return true;
    }
    public boolean mouseUp(Event e, int x, int y) {
        showLine(mods(e.modifiers) + "Mouse Up: [" + x + "," + y + "]");
        return true;
    }
    public boolean mouseDrag(Event e, int x, int y)  {
        showLine(mods(e.modifiers) + "Mouse Drag: [" + x + "," + y + "]");
        return true;
    }
    public boolean mouseMove(Event e, int x, int y) {
        showLine(mods(e.modifiers) + "Mouse Move: [" + x + "," + y + "]");
        return true;
    }
    public boolean mouseEnter(Event e, int x, int y)  {
        showLine("Mouse Enter: [" + x + "," + y + "]"); return true;
    }
    public boolean mouseExit(Event e, int x, int y)  {
        showLine("Mouse Exit: [" + x + "," + y + "]"); return true;
    }

    // Handle focus events
    public boolean gotFocus(Event e, Object what)  {
        showLine("Got Focus"); return true;
    }
    public boolean lostFocus(Event e, Object what)  {
```

Example 15-4: EventTester.java (continued)

```
        showLine("Lost Focus"); return true;
    }

    // Handle key down and key up events
    // This gets more confusing because there are two types of key events
    public boolean keyDown(Event e, int key) {
        int flags = e.modifiers;
        if (e.id == Event.KEY_PRESS)                    // a regular key
            showLine("Key Down: " + mods(flags) + key_name(e));
        else if (e.id == Event.KEY_ACTION)             // a function key
            showLine("Function Key Down: " + mods(flags) +
                        function_key_name(key));
        return true;
    }
    public boolean keyUp(Event e, int key)  {
        int flags = e.modifiers;
        if (e.id == Event.KEY_RELEASE)                  // a regular key
            showLine("Key Up: " + mods(flags) + key_name(e));
        else if (e.id == Event.KEY_ACTION_RELEASE)    // a function key
            showLine("Function Key Up: " + mods(flags) +
                        function_key_name(key));
        return true;
    }

    // The remaining methods help us sort out the various modifiers and keys

    // Return the current list of modifier keys
    private String mods(int flags) {
        String s = "[ ";
        if (flags == 0) return "";
        if ((flags & Event.SHIFT_MASK) != 0) s += "Shift ";
        if ((flags & Event.CTRL_MASK) != 0) s += "Control ";
        if ((flags & Event.META_MASK) != 0) s += "Meta ";
        if ((flags & Event.ALT_MASK) != 0) s += "Alt ";
        s += "] ";
        return s;
    }

    // Return the name of a regular (non-function) key.
    private String key_name(Event e) {
        char c = (char) e.key;
        if (e.controlDown()) {  // If CTRL flag is set, handle control chars.
            if (c < ' ') {
                c += '@';
                return "^" + c;
            }
        }
        else {                      // If CTRL flag is not set, then certain ASCII
            switch (c) {            // control characters have special meaning.
            case '\n': return "Return";
            case '\t': return "Tab";
            case '^[': return "Escape";
            case '^H': return "Backspace";
            }
        }
        // Handle the remaining possibilities.
        if (c == '^?') return "Delete";
        else if (c == ' ') return "Space";
```

Example 15-4: EventTester.java (continued)

```
            else return String.valueOf(c);
    }

    // Return the name of a function key.  Just compare the key to the
    // constants defined in the Event class.
    private String function_key_name(int key) {
        switch(key) {
        case Event.HOME: return "Home";       case Event.END: return "End";
        case Event.PGUP: return "Page Up";    case Event.PGDN: return"Page Down";
        case Event.UP: return "Up";           case Event.DOWN: return "Down";
        case Event.LEFT: return "Left";       case Event.RIGHT: return "Right";
        case Event.F1: return "F1";           case Event.F2: return "F2";
        case Event.F3: return "F3";           case Event.F4: return "F4";
        case Event.F5: return "F5";           case Event.F6: return "F6";
        case Event.F7: return "F7";           case Event.F8: return "F8";
        case Event.F9: return "F9";           case Event.F10: return "F10";
        case Event.F11: return "F11";         case Event.F12: return "F12";
        }
        return "Unknown Function Key";
    }

    /** A list of lines to display in the window */
    protected Vector lines = new Vector();
    /** Add a new line to the list of lines, and redisplay */
    protected void showLine(String s) {
        if (lines.size() == 20) lines.removeElementAt(0);
        lines.addElement(s);
        repaint();
    }
    /** This method repaints the text in the window */
    public void paint(Graphics g) {
        for(int i = 0; i < lines.size(); i++)
            g.drawString((String)lines.elementAt(i), 20, i*16 + 50);
    }
}
```

Reading Applet Parameters

Example 15-5 shows an extension to our Scribble applet. The ColorScribble class is a subclass of Scribble that adds the ability to scribble in a configurable foreground color over a configurable background color.

ColorScribble has an init() method that reads the value of two applet parameters that can be optionally specified with the <PARAM> tag in the applet's HTML file. The String values returned by getParameter() are converted to colors and specified as the default foreground and background colors for the applet. Note that the init() method invokes its superclass' init() method, so that the superclass has the opportunity to initialize itself.

This example also demonstrates the getAppletInfo() and getParameterInfo() methods. These methods provide textual information about the applet (its author, its version, its copyright, etc.) and the parameters that it can accept (the parameter names, their types, and their meanings). An applet should generally define these methods, although the current generation of web browsers do not actually ever make use of them. (The *appletviewer* application in the JDK does call these methods, however.)

Example 15–5: ColorScribble.java

```java
package com.davidflanagan.examples.applet;
import java.applet.*;
import java.awt.*;

/**
 * A version of the Scribble applet that reads two applet parameters
 * to set the foreground and background colors.  It also returns
 * information about itself when queried.
 **/
public class ColorScribble extends Scribble {
    // Read in two color parameters and set the colors.
    public void init() {
        super.init();  // Let the superclass initialize itself
        Color foreground = getColorParameter("foreground");
        Color background = getColorParameter("background");
        if (foreground != null) this.setForeground(foreground);
        if (background != null) this.setBackground(background);
    }

    // Read the specified parameter.  Interpret it as a hexadecimal
    // number of the form RRGGBB and convert it to a color.
    protected Color getColorParameter(String name) {
        String value = this.getParameter(name);
        try { return new Color(Integer.parseInt(value, 16)); }
        catch (Exception e) { return null; }
    }

    // Return information suitable for display in an About dialog box.
    public String getAppletInfo() {
        return "ColorScribble v. 0.03.  Written by David Flanagan.";
    }

    // Return info about the supported parameters.  Web browsers and applet
    // viewers should display this information, and may also allow users to
    // set the parameter values.
    public String[][] getParameterInfo() { return info; }

    // Here's the information that getParameterInfo() returns.
    // It is an array of arrays of strings describing each parameter.
    // Format: parameter name, parameter type, parameter description
    private String[][] info = {
        {"foreground", "hexadecimal color value", "foreground color"},
        {"background", "hexadecimal color value", "background color"}
    };
}
```

The following HTML fragment references the applet, and demonstrates how parameter values can be set with the <PARAM> tag:

```html
<applet code="com.davidflanagan.examples.applet.ColorScribble.class"
        codebase="../../../../"    width=400 height=400>
  <param name="foreground" value="FF0000">
  <param name="background" value="CCFFCC">
</applet>
```

Images and Sounds

Example 15-6 shows a Java applet that implements a simple client-side imagemap that can highlight the "hot spots" in the image and play a sound clip when the user clicks on the image. Figure 15-3 shows what this applet might look like, when configured with an appropriate image.

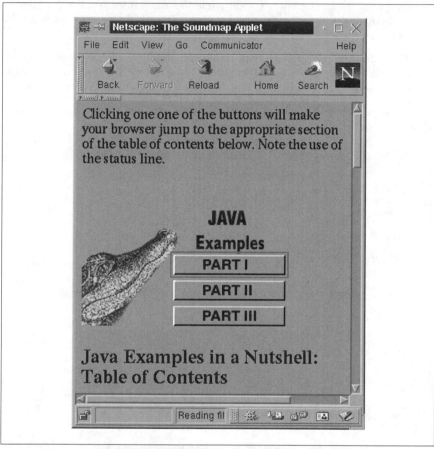

Figure 15-3. An imagemap applet

This applet demonstrates quite a few important applet techniques:

- The getParameter() method looks up the name of the image to display and the audio clip to play when the user clicks, and it also reads a list of rectangles and URLs that define the hot spots and hyperlinks of the imagemap.

- The getImage() and getDocumentBase() methods load the image (an Image object) in the init() method, and Graphics.drawImage() displays the image in the paint() method.

- The getAudioClip() method loads a sound file (an AudioClip object) in the init() method, and AudioClip.play() plays the sound in the mouse-Pressed() method.

- Events are handled using the Java 1.1 event model.

- The showStatus() method displays the destination URL when the user presses the mouse button over a hot spot, while the AppletContext.showDocument() method makes the browser display that URL when the user releases the mouse button.

- The individual hot spots are represented by instances of ImagemapRectangle, an inner class. The java.util.Vector class stores the list of hot-spot objects, and java.util.StringTokenizer parses the descriptions of those hot spots.

The following HTML fragment is an excerpt from *Soundmap.html* and shows an example of the properties read by this applet:

```
<APPLET code="com/davidflanagan/examples/applet/Soundmap.class"
        codebase="../../../../"
        width=288 height=288>
  <PARAM name="image" value="java_parts.gif">
  <PARAM name="sound" value="chirp.au">
  <PARAM name="rect0" value="114,95,151,33,#p1">
  <PARAM name="rect1" value="114,128,151,33,#p2">
  <PARAM name="rect2" value="114,161,151,33,#p3">
  <PARAM name="rect3" value="114,194,151,33,#p4">
  <PARAM name="rect4" value="114,227,151,33,#p5">
</APPLET>
```

Example 15–6: Soundmap.java

```
package com.davidflanagan.examples.applet;
import java.applet.*;
import java.awt.*;
import java.awt.event.*;
import java.net.*;
import java.util.*;

/**
 * A Java applet that simulates a client-side imagemap.
 * Plays a sound whenever the user clicks on one of the hyperlinks.
 */
public class Soundmap extends Applet implements MouseListener {
    protected Image image;      // The image to display.
    protected Vector rects;     // A list of rectangles in it.
    protected AudioClip sound; // A sound to play on user clicks in a rectangle
    protected ImagemapRectangle highlight; // Which rectangle is highlighted

    /** Initialize the applet */
    public void init() {
        // Look up the name of the image, relative to a base URL, and load it.
        // Note the use of three Applet methods in this one line.
        image = this.getImage(this.getDocumentBase(),
                              this.getParameter("image"));

        // Lookup and parse a list of rectangular areas and their URLs.
        // The convenience routine getRectangleParameter() is defined below.
        rects = new Vector();
```

Example 15-6: Soundmap.java (continued)

```
        ImagemapRectangle r;
        for(int i = 0; (r = getRectangleParameter("rect" + i)) != null; i++)
            rects.addElement(r);

        // Look up a sound to play when the user clicks one of those areas.
        sound = this.getAudioClip(this.getDocumentBase(),
                                  this.getParameter("sound"));

        // Specify an "event listener" object to respond to mouse button
        // presses and releases.  Note that this is the Java 1.1 event model.
        this.addMouseListener(this);
    }

    /**
     * Called when the applet is being unloaded from the system.
     * We use it here to "flush" the image we no longer need. This may
     * result in memory and other resources being freed more quickly.
     **/
    public void destroy() { image.flush(); }

    /**
     * To display the applet, we simply draw the image, and highlight the
     * current rectangle if any.
     **/
    public void paint(Graphics g) {
        g.drawImage(image, 0, 0, this);
        if (highlight != null) {
            g.setColor(Color.red);
            g.drawRect(highlight.x, highlight.y,
                       highlight.width, highlight.height);
            g.drawRect(highlight.x+1, highlight.y+1,
                       highlight.width-2, highlight.height-2);
        }
    }

    /**
     * We override this method so that it doesn't clear the background
     * before calling paint().  No clear is necessary, since paint() overwrites
     * everything with an image.  Causes less flickering this way.
     **/
    public void update(Graphics g) { paint(g); }

    /**
     * Parse a comma-separated list of rectangle coordinates and a URL.
     * Used to read the imagemap rectangle definitions from applet parameters
     **/
    protected ImagemapRectangle getRectangleParameter(String name) {
        int x, y, w, h;
        URL url;
        String value = this.getParameter(name);
        if (value == null) return null;

        try {
            StringTokenizer st = new StringTokenizer(value, ",");
            x = Integer.parseInt(st.nextToken());
            y = Integer.parseInt(st.nextToken());
            w = Integer.parseInt(st.nextToken());
            h = Integer.parseInt(st.nextToken());
```

Example 15–6: Soundmap.java (continued)

```
            url = new URL(this.getDocumentBase(), st.nextToken());
        }
        catch (NoSuchElementException e) { return null; }
        catch (NumberFormatException e) { return null; }
        catch (MalformedURLException e) { return null; }

        return new ImagemapRectangle(x, y, w, h, url);
    }

    /** Called when a mouse button is pressed. */
    public void mousePressed(MouseEvent e) {
        // On button down, check if we're inside one of the rectangles.
        // If so, highlight the rectangle, display a message, and play a sound.
        // The utility routine findrect() is defined below.
        ImagemapRectangle r = findrect(e);
        // If a rectangle is found, and is not already highlighted
        if (r != null && r != highlight) {
            highlight = r;                    // Remember which rectangle it is
            showStatus("To: " + r.url);    // display its URL in status line
            sound.play();                     // play the sound
            repaint();                        // request a redraw to highlight it
        }
    }

    /** Called when a mouse button is released. */
    public void mouseReleased(MouseEvent e) {
        // If the user releases the mouse button over a highlighted
        // rectangle, tell the browser to display its URL.  Also,
        // erase the highlight and clear status
        if (highlight != null) {
            ImagemapRectangle r = findrect(e);
            if (r == highlight)  getAppletContext().showDocument(r.url);
            showStatus("");     // clear the message.
            highlight = null;   // forget the highlight
            repaint();          // request a redraw
        }
    }

    /** Unused methods of the MouseListener interface */
    public void mouseEntered(MouseEvent e) {}
    public void mouseExited(MouseEvent e) {}
    public void mouseClicked(MouseEvent e) {}

    /** Find the rectangle we're inside. */
    protected ImagemapRectangle findrect(MouseEvent e) {
        int i, x = e.getX(), y = e.getY();
        for(i = 0; i < rects.size(); i++)  {
            ImagemapRectangle r = (ImagemapRectangle) rects.elementAt(i);
            if (r.contains(x, y)) return r;
        }
        return null;
    }

    /**
     * A helper class.  Just like java.awt.Rectangle, but with a URL field.
     * Note the use of a nested toplevel class for neatness.
     **/
    static class ImagemapRectangle extends Rectangle {
```

Example 15-6: Soundmap.java (continued)

```
        URL url;
        public ImagemapRectangle(int x, int y, int w, int h, URL url) {
            super(x, y, w, h);
            this.url = url;
        }
    }
}
```

JAR Files

The Soundmap applet defined in the previous section requires four files to operate: the class file for the applet itself, the class file for the nested class it contains, the image file, and the sound clip file. It can be loaded using an <APPLET> tag like this:

```
<APPLET code="com/davidflanagan/examples/applet/Soundmap.class"
        codebase="../../../../" width=288 height=288>
    ...
</APPLET>
```

When the applet is loaded in this manner, however, each of the four files is transferred in uncompressed form using a separate HTML request. As you might imagine, this is quite inefficient.

As of Java 1.1, you can instead combine the four files into a single JAR file. This single, compressed file (it is a ZIP file) can be transferred from web server to browser much more efficiently. To create a JAR file, use the *jar* tool, which has a syntax reminiscent of the Unix *tar* command:

```
% jar cf applets.jar com/davidflanagan/examples/applet
```

This command creates a new file, *applets.jar*, that contains all the files in the *com/davidflanagan/examples/applet* directory.

To use a JAR file, you specify it as the value of the ARCHIVE attribute of the <APPLET> tag:

```
<APPLET code="com/davidflanagan/examples/applet/Soundmap.class"
        archive="applets.jar" width=288 height=288>
    ...
</APPLET>
```

Note that the ARCHIVE attribute does not replace the CODE attribute. ARCHIVE specifies where to look for files, but CODE is still required to tell the browser which file in the archive is the applet class file to be executed. The ARCHIVE attribute may actually specify a comma-separated list of JAR files. The web browser or applet viewer searches these archives for any files the applet requires. If a file is not found in an archive, however, the browser falls back on its old behavior and attempts to load the file from the web server using a separate HTTP request.

Applets

Exercises

15-1. Modify FirstApplet to take advantage of the features of the Graphics class, so that it displays the "Hello World" message in a more visually interesting way.

15-2. Modify the Clock applet so that it is configurable via applet parameters. Your modified applet should read parameters that specify the update frequency for the time display, as well as the font, color, and format of the time display. (See java.text.SimpleDateFormat for a way to format dates and times according to a specified pattern). Also, add a getParameterInfo() method that describes the applet parameters you define and modify getApInfo() to include a message describing your contribution to the applet.

15-3. Modify the Soundmap applet so that it responds to mouse-motion events as well as mouse presses and releases. Your modified applet should highlight whatever rectangle the mouse is over, even if the mouse button is not pressed.

15-4. Write an applet that displays an arbitrary set of lines described through one or more applet parameters. Test your applet by having it draw something interesting. You may want to look at Example 13-2 for a way to encode a set of line segments in a textual form suitable to use as an applet parameter.

PART III

Enterprise Java

Part III contains examples that illustrate key enterprise APIs in Java. These examples correspond to the portion of Java covered in *Java Enterprise in a Nutshell*.

CHAPTER 16

Remote Method Invocation

This chapter presents examples of using the remote method invocation (RMI) capabilities of the `java.rmi` and `java.rmi.server` packages. Remote method invocation is a powerful technology for developing networked applications without having to worry about the low-level networking details. RMI transcends the client/ server model of computing with a more general remote object model. In this model, the server defines objects that clients can use remotely. Clients invoke methods of a remote object exactly as if it were a local object running in the same virtual machine as the client. RMI hides the underlying mechanism for transporting method arguments and return values across the network. An argument or return value can be a primitive value or any `Serializable` object.

To develop an RMI-based application, you need to follow these steps:

- Create an interface that extends the `java.rmi.Remote` interface. This interface defines the exported methods that the remote object implements (i.e., the methods the server implements and clients can invoke remotely). Each method in this interface must be declared to throw a `java.rmi.RemoteExcep-tion`, which is the superclass of many more specific RMI exception classes. Every remote method must declare that it can throw a `RemoteException`, because there are quite a few things that can go wrong during the remote method invocation process over a network.

- Define a subclass of `java.rmi.server.UnicastRemoteObject` (or sometimes a related class) that implements your `Remote` interface. This class represents the remote object (or server object). Other than declaring its remote methods to throw `RemoteException` objects, the remote object doesn't need to do anything special to allow its methods to be invoked remotely. The `Unicast-RemoteObject` and the rest of the RMI infrastructure handle this automatically.

- Write a program (a server) that creates an instance of your remote object. Export the object, making it available for use by clients, by registering the object by name with a registry service. This is usually done with the `java.rmi.Naming` class and the *rmiregistry* program. A server program may also act as its own registry server by using the `LocateRegistry` class and `Reg-istry` interface of the `java.rmi.registry` package.

- After you compile the server program with *javac*, use *rmic* to generate a stub and a skeleton for the remote object. With RMI, the client and server don't communicate directly. On the client side, the client's reference to a remote object is implemented as an instance of a stub class. When the client invokes a remote method, it is a method of this stub object that is actually called. The stub does the necessary networking to pass that invocation to a skeleton class on the server. This skeleton translates the networked request into a method invocation on the server object, and passes the return value back to the stub, which passes it back to the client. This can be a complicated system, but fortunately, application programmers never have to think about stubs and skeletons; they are generated automatically by the *rmic* tool. Invoke *rmic* with the name of the remote object class (not the interface) on the command line. It creates and compiles two new classes with the suffixes `_Stub` and `_Skel`.

- If the server uses the default registry service provided by the `Naming` class, you must run the registry server, if it is not already running. You can run the registry server by invoking the *rmiregistry* program.

- Now you can write a client program to use the remote object exported by the server. The client must first obtain a reference to the remote object by using the `Naming` class to look up the object by name; the name is typically an *rmi:* URL. The remote reference that is returned is an instance of the `Remote` interface for the object (or more specifically, a stub object for the remote object). Once the client has this remote object, it can invoke methods on it exactly as it would invoke the methods of a local object. The only thing that it must be aware of is that all remote methods can throw `RemoteException` objects, and that in the presence of network errors, this can happen at unexpected times.

- Finally, start up the server program, and run the client!

The following sections of this chapter provides two complete RMI examples that follow the steps outlined here. The first example is a fairly simple remote banking program, while the second example is a complex and lengthy multiuser domain (MUD) system.

Remote Banking

Example 16-1 shows a class, `Bank`, that contains inner classes and interfaces for a remote bank client/server example. In this example, the `RemoteBank` interface defines remote methods to open and close accounts, deposit and withdraw money, check the account balance, and obtain the transaction history for an account. The `Bank` class contains all of the classes and interfaces required for the example except for the server class; the class that actually implements the `Remote-Bank` interface. This server class is shown in Example 16-2.

Example 16-1 defines the following inner classes and interfaces:

RemoteBank

> The Remote interface implemented by the bank server and used by the bank client.

FunnyMoney

> A trivial class that represents money in this banking example. It is nothing more than a wrapper around an int, but it serves to demonstrate that Serializable objects can be passed as arguments to remote methods and returned by remote methods.

BankingException

> A simple exception subclass that represents banking-related exceptions, such as "Insufficient funds." It demonstrates that remote method implementations on a server can throw exceptions that are transported across the network and thrown in the client program.

Client

> This class is a standalone program that serves as a simple client to the bank server. It uses Naming.lookup() to look up the desired RemoteBank object in the system registry and then invokes various methods of that RemoteBank object, depending on its command-line arguments. It is really as simple as that; the use of RMI is almost transparent.

A session using the Bank.Client class might look as follows (note that the command-line argument "david" is the account name and "javanut" is the password that protects the account):

```
% java com.davidflanagan.examples.rmi.Bank\$Client open david javanut
Account opened.
% java com.davidflanagan.examples.rmi.Bank\$Client deposit david javanut 1000
Deposited 1000 wooden nickels.
% java com.davidflanagan.examples.rmi.Bank\$Client withdraw david javanut 100
Withdrew 100 wooden nickels.
% java com.davidflanagan.examples.rmi.Bank\$Client balance david javanut
You have 900 wooden nickels in the bank.
% java com.davidflanagan.examples.rmi.Bank\$Client history david javanut
Account opened at Wed Jul 12 15:30:12 PDT 2000
Deposited 1000 on Wed Jul 12 15:30:31 PDT 2000
Withdrew 100 on Wed Jul 12 15:30:39 PDT 2000
% java com.davidflanagan.examples.rmi.Bank\$Client close david javanut
900 wooden nickels returned to you.
Thanks for banking with us.
```

In this example session, the bank client is running on the same host as the server. This need not be the case; the Client class looks for a system property named bank to determine which bank server to connect to. So you could invoke the client program like this (one long command line that has been broken into two lines):

```
% java -Dbank=rmi://bank.trustme.com/TrustyBank \
com.davidflanagan.examples.rmi.Bank\$Client open david javanut
```

Example 16-1: Bank.java

```
package com.davidflanagan.examples.rmi;
import java.rmi.*;
import java.util.List;
```

Example 16-1: Bank.java (continued)

```java
/**
 * This class is a placeholder that simply contains other classes and
 * for interfaces remote banking.
 **/
public class Bank {
    /**
     * This is the interface that defines the exported methods of the
     * bank server.
     **/
    public interface RemoteBank extends Remote {
        /** Open a new account, with the specified name and password */
        public void openAccount(String name, String password)
            throws RemoteException, BankingException;

        /** Close the named account */
        public FunnyMoney closeAccount(String name, String password)
            throws RemoteException, BankingException;

        /** Deposit money into the named account */
        public void deposit(String name, String password, FunnyMoney money)
            throws RemoteException, BankingException;

        /** Withdraw the specified amount of money from the named account */
        public FunnyMoney withdraw(String name, String password, int amount)
            throws RemoteException, BankingException;

        /** Return the amount of money in the named account */
        public int getBalance(String name, String password)
            throws RemoteException, BankingException;

        /**
         * Return a List of Strings that list the transaction history
         * of the named account
         **/
        public List getTransactionHistory(String name, String password)
            throws RemoteException, BankingException;
    }

    /**
     * This simple class represents a monetary amount.  This implementation
     * is really nothing more than a wrapper around an integer.  It is a useful
     * to demonstrate that RMI can accept arbitrary non-String objects as
     * arguments and return them as values, as long as they are Serializable.
     * A more complete implementation of this FunnyMoney class might bear
     * a serial number, a digital signature, and other security features to
     * ensure that it is unique and non-forgeable.
     **/
    public static class FunnyMoney implements java.io.Serializable {
        public int amount;
        public FunnyMoney(int amount) { this.amount = amount; }
    }

    /**
     * This is a type of exception used to represent exceptional conditions
     * related to banking, such as "Insufficient Funds" and  "Invalid Password"
     **/
    public static class BankingException extends Exception {
        public BankingException(String msg) { super(msg); }
```

Example 16-1: Bank.java (continued)

```
}

/**
 * This class is a simple stand-alone client program that interacts
 * with a RemoteBank server.  It invokes different RemoteBank methods
 * depending on its command-line arguments, and demonstrates just how
 * simple it is to interact with a server using RMI.
 **/
public static class Client {
    public static void main(String[] args) {
        try {
            // Figure out what RemoteBank to connect to by reading a system
            // property (specified on the command line with a -D option to
            // java) or, if it is not defined, use a default URL.  Note
            // that by default this client tries to connect to a server on
            // the local machine
            String url = System.getProperty("bank", "rmi:///FirstRemote");

            // Now look up that RemoteBank server using the Naming object,
            // which contacts the rmiregistry server.  Given the url, this
            // call returns a RemoteBank object whose methods may be
            // invoked remotely
            RemoteBank bank = (RemoteBank) Naming.lookup(url);

            // Convert the user's command to lower case
            String cmd = args[0].toLowerCase();

            // Now, go test the command against a bunch of possible options
            if (cmd.equals("open")) {           // Open an account
                bank.openAccount(args[1], args[2]);
                System.out.println("Account opened.");
            }
            else if (cmd.equals("close")) {     // Close an account
                FunnyMoney money = bank.closeAccount(args[1], args[2]);
                // Note: our currency is denominated in wooden nickels
                System.out.println(money.amount +
                                 " wooden nickels returned to you.");
                System.out.println("Thanks for banking with us.");
            }
            else if (cmd.equals("deposit")) {   // Deposit money
                FunnyMoney money=new FunnyMoney(Integer.parseInt(args[3]));
                bank.deposit(args[1], args[2], money);
                System.out.println("Deposited " + money.amount +
                                 " wooden nickels.");
            }
            else if (cmd.equals("withdraw")) {  // Withdraw money
                FunnyMoney money = bank.withdraw(args[1], args[2],
                                                Integer.parseInt(args[3]));
                System.out.println("Withdrew " + money.amount +
                                " wooden nickels.");
            }
            else if (cmd.equals("balance")) {   // Check account balance
                int amt = bank.getBalance(args[1], args[2]);
                System.out.println("You have " + amt +
                                 " wooden nickels in the bank.");
            }
            else if (cmd.equals("history")) {   // Get transaction history
                List transactions =
```

Example 16–1: Bank.java (continued)

```
                · bank.getTransactionHistory(args[1], args[2]);
             for(int i = 0; i < transactions.size(); i++)
                 System.out.println(transactions.get(i));
          }
          else System.out.println("Unknown command");
        }
        // Catch and display RMI exceptions
        catch (RemoteException e) { System.err.println(e); }
        // Catch and display Banking related exceptions
        catch (BankingException e) { System.err.println(e.getMessage()); }
        // Other exceptions are probably user syntax errors, so show usage.
        catch (Exception e) {
            System.err.println(e);
            System.err.println("Usage: java [-Dbank=<url>] Bank$Client " +
                              "<cmd> <name> <password> [<amount>]");
            System.err.println("where cmd is: open, close, deposit, " +
                              "withdraw, balance, history");
        }
      }
    }
  }
}
```

A Bank Server

Example 16-1 defined a RemoteBank interface and a bank client program. Example 16-2 is a RemoteBankServer class that implements the RemoteBank interface and acts as a server for the Bank.Client program. This class includes a main() method so it can be run as a standalone program. This method creates a Remote-BankServer object and registers it with Naming.rebind(), so that clients can look it up. It reads the system property bankname to determine what name to use to register the bank but uses the name FirstRemote by default. (This is the same name that the Bank.Client uses by default as well.)

RemoteBankServer implements the RemoteBank interface, so it provides implementations for all remote methods defined by that interface. It also defines some utility methods that are not remote methods, but that are used by the remote methods. Note that RemoteBankServer includes an inner Account class that stores all the information about a single bank account. It maintains a hashtable that maps from account names to Account objects. The various remote methods look up the named account, verify the password, and operate on the account in some way. Any RMI remote object must be able to handle multiple, concurrent method invocations because multiple clients can be using the object at the same time. Remote-BankServer uses synchronized methods and synchronized statements to prevent two clients from opening, closing, or modifying the same account at the same time.

Before you can run this RemoteBankServer program, you must compile it, generate stub and skeleton classes, and start the *rmiregistry* service (if it is not already running). You might do all this with commands like the following (on a Unix system). Note the -d argument to *rmic*: it tells the RMI compiler where to put the stub and skeleton classes. Assuming the *RemoteBankServer.class* file is in the current directory, the usage shown here puts the generated classes in the same directory.

```
% javac RemoteBankServer.java
% rmic -d ../../../../ com.davidflanagan.examples.rmi.RemoteBankServer
% rmiregistry &
% java com.davidflanagan.examples.rmi.RemoteBankServer
FirstRemote is open and ready for customers.
```

Note that Example 16-2 contains a fatal flaw: if the bank server crashes, all bank account data is lost, which is likely to result in angry customers! Chapter 17, *Database Access with SQL*, includes another implementation of the RemoteBank interface. This implementation uses a database to store account data in a more persistent way.

Example 16–2: RemoteBankServer.java

```java
package com.davidflanagan.examples.rmi;
import java.rmi.*;
import java.rmi.server.*;
import java.util.*;
import Bank.*;

/**
 * This class implements the remote methods defined by the RemoteBank
 * interface.  It has a serious shortcoming, though: all account data is
 * lost when the server goes down.
 **/
public class RemoteBankServer extends UnicastRemoteObject implements RemoteBank
{
    /**
     * This nested class stores data for a single account with the bank
     **/
    class Account {
        String password;                        // account password
        int balance;                            // account balance
        List transactions = new ArrayList();    // account transaction history
        Account(String password) {
            this.password = password;
            transactions.add("Account opened at " + new Date());
        }
    }

    /**
     * This hashtable stores all open accounts and maps from account name
     * to Account object. Methods that use this object are synchronized
     * to prevent concurrent access by more than one thread.
     **/
    Map accounts = new HashMap();

    /**
     * This constructor doesn't do anything, but because the superclass
     * constructor throws an exception, the exception must be declared here
     **/
    public RemoteBankServer() throws RemoteException { super(); }

    /**
     * Open a bank account with the specified name and password
     * This method is synchronized to make it thread safe, since it
     * manipulates the accounts hashtable.
     **/
    public synchronized void openAccount(String name, String password)
        throws RemoteException, BankingException
```

Example 16-2: RemoteBankServer.java (continued)

```
{
    // Check if there is already an account under that name
    if (accounts.get(name) != null)
        throw new BankingException("Account already exists.");
    // Otherwise, it doesn't exist, so create it.
    Account acct = new Account(password);
    // And register it
    accounts.put(name, acct);
}

/**
 * This internal method is not a remote method.  Given a name and password
 * it checks to see if an account with that name and password exists.  If
 * so, it returns the Account object.  Otherwise, it throws an exception.
 * This method is synchronized because it uses the accounts hashtable.
 **/
synchronized Account verify(String name, String password) throws BankingException {
        Account acct = (Account)accounts.get(name);
        if (acct == null) throw new BankingException("No such account");
        if (!password.equals(acct.password))
            throw new BankingException("Invalid password");
        return acct;
    }
}

/**
 * Close the named account.  This method is synchronized to make it
 * thread safe, since it manipulates the accounts hashtable.
 **/
public synchronized FunnyMoney closeAccount(String name, String password)
    throws RemoteException, BankingException
{
    Account acct;
    acct = verify(name, password);
    accounts.remove(name);
    // Before changing the balance or transactions of any account, we first
    // have to obtain a lock on that account to be thread safe.
    synchronized (acct) {
        int balance = acct.balance;
        acct.balance = 0;
        return new FunnyMoney(balance);
    }
}

/** Deposit the specified FunnyMoney to the named account */
public void deposit(String name, String password, FunnyMoney money)
    throws RemoteException, BankingException
{
    Account acct = verify(name, password);
    synchronized(acct) {
        acct.balance += money.amount;
        acct.transactions.add("Deposited " + money.amount +
                              " on " + new Date());
    }
}

/** Withdraw the specified amount from the named account */
public FunnyMoney withdraw(String name, String password, int amount)
```

Example 16-2: RemoteBankServer.java (continued)

```
        throws RemoteException, BankingException
    {
        Account acct = verify(name, password);
        synchronized(acct) {
            if (acct.balance < amount)
                throw new BankingException("Insufficient Funds");
            acct.balance -= amount;
            acct.transactions.add("Withdrew " + amount + " on "+new Date());
            return new FunnyMoney(amount);
        }
    }

    /** Return the current balance in the named account */
    public int getBalance(String name, String password)
        throws RemoteException, BankingException
    {
        Account acct = verify(name, password);
        synchronized(acct) { return acct.balance; }
    }

    /**
     * Return a Vector of strings containing the transaction history
     * for the named account
     **/
    public List getTransactionHistory(String name, String password)
        throws RemoteException, BankingException
    {
        Account acct = verify(name, password);
        synchronized(acct) { return acct.transactions; }
    }

    /**
     * The main program that runs this RemoteBankServer.
     * Create a RemoteBankServer object and give it a name in the registry.
     * Read a system property to determine the name, but use "FirstRemote"
     * as the default name.  This is all that is necessary to set up the
     * service.  RMI takes care of the rest.
     **/
    public static void main(String[] args) {
        try {
            // Create a bank server object
            RemoteBankServer bank = new RemoteBankServer();
            // Figure out what to name it
            String name = System.getProperty("bankname", "FirstRemote");
            // Name it that
            Naming.rebind(name, bank);
            // Tell the world we're up and running
            System.out.println(name + " is open and ready for customers.");
        }
        catch (Exception e) {
            System.err.println(e);
            System.err.println("Usage: java [-Dbankname=<name>] " +
                               "com.davidflanagan.examples.rmi.RemoteBankServer");
            System.exit(1); // Force exit because there may be RMI threads
        }
    }
}
```

RMI

A Multiuser Domain

A multiuser domain, or MUD, is a program (a server) that allows multiple people (clients) to interact with each other and with a shared virtual environment. The environment is typically a series of rooms or places linked to each other by various exits. Each room or place has a textual description that serves as the backdrop and sets the tone for the interactions between users. Many early MUDs were set in dungeons, with place descriptions reflecting the dark, underground nature of that imaginary environment. In fact, the MUD acronym originally stood for "multiuser dungeon." Some MUDs serve primarily as chat rooms for their clients, while others have more of the flavor of old-style adventure games, where the focus is on exploring the environment and problem solving. Others are exercises in creativity and group dynamics, allowing users to add new places and items to the MUD.

Example 16-3 through Example 16-7 show classes and interfaces that define a simple user-extensible MUD system. A program like this MUD example clearly demonstrates how the RMI programming paradigm transcends the client/server model. As we'll see, MudServer and MudPlace are server objects that create the MUD environment within which users interact. But at the same time, each user within the MUD is represented by a MudPerson remote object that acts as a server when interacting with other users. Rather than having a single server and a set of clients, then, this system is really a distributed network of remote objects, all communicating with each other. Which objects are servers and which are clients really depends on your point of view.

In order to understand the MUD system, an overview of its architecture is useful. The MudServer class is a simple remote object (and standalone server program) that defines the entrance to a MUD and keeps track of the names of all the places within a MUD. Despite its name, the MudServer object doesn't provide the services most users think of as "the MUD." That is the job of the MudPlace class.

Each MudPlace object represents a single place within the MUD. Each place has a name, a description, lists the items in the place, the people (users) currently in the place, the exits from the place, and the other places to which those exits lead. An exit may lead to an adjoining MudPlace on the same server, or it may lead to a MudPlace object in a different MUD on a different server altogether. Thus, the MUD environment that a user interacts with is really a network of MudPlace objects. It is the descriptions of places and items, and the complexity of the linkages between places, that give the MUD the richness that make it interesting to a user.

The users, or people, in a MUD are represented by MudPerson objects. MudPerson is a remote object that defines two methods. One method returns a description of the person (i.e., what other people see when they look at this person) and the other method delivers a message to the person (or to the user that the MudPerson represents). These methods allow users to look at each other and to talk to each other. When two users run into each other in a given MudPlace and begin to talk to each other, the MudPlace and the server on which the MUD is running are no longer relevant; the two MudPerson objects can communicate directly with each other through the power of RMI.

The examples that follow are long and somewhat complex, but are worth studying carefully. Given the complexity of the MUD system being developed, however, the classes and interfaces defined below are actually surprisingly simple. As you'll see, remote method invocation techniques are very powerful in systems like this one.

Remote MUD Interfaces

Example 16-3 is a Mud class that serves as a placeholder for inner classes and interfaces (and one constant) used by the rest of the MUD system. Most importantly, Mud defines three Remote interfaces: RemoteMudServer, RemoteMudPerson, and RemoteMudPlace. These define the remote methods that are implemented by the MudServer, MudPerson, and MudPlace objects, respectively.

Example 16-3: Mud.java

```
package com.davidflanagan.examples.rmi;
import java.rmi.*;
import java.util.Vector;
import java.io.IOException;

/**
 * This class defines three nested Remote interfaces for use by our MUD game.
 * It also defines a bunch of exception subclasses, and a constant string
 * prefix used to create unique names when registering MUD servers
 **/
public class Mud {
    /**
     * This interface defines the exported methods of the MUD server object
     **/
    public interface RemoteMudServer extends Remote {
        /** Return the name of this MUD */
        public String getMudName() throws RemoteException;

        /** Return the main entrance place for this MUD */
        public RemoteMudPlace getEntrance() throws RemoteException;

        /** Look up and return some other named place in this MUD */
        public RemoteMudPlace getNamedPlace(String name)
            throws RemoteException, NoSuchPlace;

        /**
         * Dump the state of the server to a file so that it can be restored
         * later All places, and their exits and things are dumped, but the
         * "people" in them are not.
         **/
        public void dump(String password, String filename)
            throws RemoteException, BadPassword, IOException;
    }

    /**
     * This interface defines the methods exported by a "person" object that
     * is in the MUD.
     **/
    public interface RemoteMudPerson extends Remote {
        /** Return a full description of the person */
        public String getDescription() throws RemoteException;
```

Example 16-3: Mud.java (continued)

```
        /** Deliver a message to the person */
        public void tell(String message) throws RemoteException;
}

/**
 * This is the most important remote interface for the MUD.  It defines the
 * methods exported by the "places" or "rooms" within a MUD.  Each place
 * has a name and a description, and also maintains a list of "people" in
 * the place, things in the place, and exits from the place.  There are
 * methods to get a list of names for these people, things, and exits.
 * There are methods to get the RemoteMudPerson object for a named person,
 * to get a description of a named thing, and to go through a named exit.
 * There are methods for interacting with other people in the MUD.  There
 * are methods for building the MUD by creating and destroying things,
 * adding new places (and new exits to those places), for linking a place
 * through a new exit to some other place (possibly on another MUD server),
 * and for closing down an existing exit.
 **/
public interface RemoteMudPlace extends Remote {
        /** Look up the name of this place */
        public String getPlaceName() throws RemoteException;

        /** Get a description of this place */
        public String getDescription() throws RemoteException;

        /** Find out the names of all people here */
        public Vector getNames() throws RemoteException;

        /** Get the names of all things here */
        public Vector getThings() throws RemoteException;

        /** Get the names of all ways out of here */
        public Vector getExits() throws RemoteException;

        /** Get the RemoteMudPerson object for the named person. */
        public RemoteMudPerson getPerson(String name)
            throws RemoteException, NoSuchPerson;

        /** Get more details about a named thing */
        public String examineThing(String name)
            throws RemoteException,NoSuchThing;

        /** Use the named exit */
        public RemoteMudPlace go(RemoteMudPerson who, String direction)
            throws RemoteException,NotThere,AlreadyThere,NoSuchExit,LinkFailed;

        /** Send a message of the form "David: hi everyone" */
        public void speak(RemoteMudPerson speaker, String msg)
            throws RemoteException, NotThere;

        /** Send a message of the form "David laughs loudly" */
        public void act(RemoteMudPerson speaker, String msg)
            throws RemoteException, NotThere;

        /** Add a new thing in this place */
        public void createThing(RemoteMudPerson who, String name,
                                String description)
            throws RemoteException, NotThere, AlreadyThere;
```

Example 16–3: Mud.java (continued)

```
    /** Remove a thing from this place */
    public void destroyThing(RemoteMudPerson who, String thing)
        throws RemoteException, NotThere, NoSuchThing;

    /**
     * Create a new place, bi-directionally linked to this one by an exit
     **/
    public void createPlace(RemoteMudPerson creator,
                            String exit, String entrance,
                            String name, String description)
        throws RemoteException,NotThere,
               ExitAlreadyExists,PlaceAlreadyExists;

    /**
     * Link this place (unidirectionally) to some existing place.  The
     * destination place may even be on another server.
     **/
    public void linkTo(RemoteMudPerson who, String exit,
                       String hostname, String mudname, String placename)
        throws RemoteException, NotThere, ExitAlreadyExists, NoSuchPlace;

    /** Remove an existing exit */
    public void close(RemoteMudPerson who, String exit)
        throws RemoteException, NotThere, NoSuchExit;

    /**
     * Remove this person from this place, leaving them nowhere.
     * Send the specified message to everyone left in the place.
     **/
    public void exit(RemoteMudPerson who, String message)
        throws RemoteException, NotThere;

    /**
     * Put a person in a place, assigning their name, and sending the
     * specified message to everyone else in the place.  The client should
     * not make this method available to the user.  They should use go()
     * instead.
     **/
    public void enter(RemoteMudPerson who, String name, String message)
        throws RemoteException, AlreadyThere;

    /**
     * Return the server object of the MUD that "contains" this place
     * This method should not be directly visible to the player
     **/
    public RemoteMudServer getServer() throws RemoteException;
}

/**
 * This is a generic exception class that serves as the superclass
 * for a bunch of more specific exception types
 **/
public static class MudException extends Exception {}

/**
 * These specific exception classes are thrown in various contexts.
 * The exception class name contains all the information about the
 * exception; no detail messages are provided by these classes.
```

RMI

Example 16-3: Mud.java (continued)

```
     **/
     public static class NotThere extends MudException {}
     public static class AlreadyThere extends MudException {}
     public static class NoSuchThing extends MudException {}
     public static class NoSuchPerson extends MudException {}
     public static class NoSuchExit extends MudException {}
     public static class NoSuchPlace extends MudException {}
     public static class ExitAlreadyExists extends MudException {}
     public static class PlaceAlreadyExists extends MudException {}
     public static class LinkFailed extends MudException {}
     public static class BadPassword extends MudException {}

     /**
      * This constant is used as a prefix to the MUD name when the server
      * registers the mud with the RMI Registry, and when the client looks
      * up the MUD in the registry.  Using this prefix helps prevent the
      * possibility of name collisions.
      **/
     static final String mudPrefix = "com.davidflanagan.examples.rmi.Mud.";
}
```

The MUD Server

Example 16-4 shows the MudServer class. This class is a standalone program that starts a MUD running; it also provides the implementation of the RemoteMudServer interface. As noted before, a MudServer object merely serves as the entrance to a MUD: it is not the MUD itself. Therefore, this is a fairly simple class. One of its most interesting features is the use of the serialization classes of java.io and the compression classes of java.util.zip to save the state the MUD, so that it can be restored later.

Example 16-4: MudServer.java

```
package com.davidflanagan.examples.rmi;
import java.rmi.*;
import java.rmi.server.*;
import java.rmi.registry.*;
import java.io.*;
import java.util.Hashtable;
import java.util.zip.*;
import com.davidflanagan.examples.rmi.Mud.*;

/**
 * This class implements the RemoteMudServer interface.  It also defines a
 * main() method so you can run it as a standalone program that will
 * set up and initialize a MUD server.  Note that a MudServer maintains an
 * entrance point to a MUD, but it is not the MUD itself.  Most of the
 * interesting MUD functionality is defined by the RemoteMudPlace interface
 * and implemented by the RemotePlace class.  In addition to being a remote
 * object, this class is also Serializable, so that the state of the MUD
 * can be saved to a file and later restored.  Note that the main() method
 * defines two ways of starting a MUD: one is to start it from scratch with
 * a single initial place, and another is to restore an existing MUD from a
 * file.
 **/
public class MudServer extends UnicastRemoteObject
```

Example 16-4: MudServer.java (continued)

```
    implements RemoteMudServer, Serializable
{
    MudPlace entrance;   // The standard entrance to this MUD
    String password;     // The password required to dump() the state of the MUD
    String mudname;      // The name that this MUD is registered under
    Hashtable places;    // A mapping of place names to places in this MUD

    /**
     * Start a MUD from scratch, with the given name and password.  Create
     * an initial MudPlace object as the entrance, giving it the specified
     * name and description.
     **/
    public MudServer(String mudname, String password,
                     String placename, String description)
        throws RemoteException
    {
        this.mudname = mudname;
        this.password = password;
        this.places = new Hashtable();
        // Create the entrance place
        try { this.entrance = new MudPlace(this, placename, description); }
        catch (PlaceAlreadyExists e) {} // Should never happen
    }

    /** For serialization only.  Never call this constructor. */
    public MudServer() throws RemoteException {}

    /** This remote method returns the name of the MUD */
    public String getMudName() throws RemoteException { return mudname; }

    /** This remote method returns the entrance place of the MUD */
    public RemoteMudPlace getEntrance() throws RemoteException {
        return entrance;
    }

    /**
     * This remote method returns a RemoteMudPlace object for the named place.
     * In this sense, a MudServer acts as like an RMI Registry object,
     * returning remote objects looked up by name.  It is simpler to do it this
     * way than to use an actual Registry object.  If the named place does not
     * exist, it throws a NoSuchPlace exception
     **/
    public RemoteMudPlace getNamedPlace(String name)
            throws RemoteException, NoSuchPlace
    {
        RemoteMudPlace p = (RemoteMudPlace) places.get(name);
        if (p == null) throw new NoSuchPlace();
        return p;
    }

    /**
     * Define a new placename to place mapping in our hashtable.
     * This is not a remote method.  The MudPlace() constructor calls it
     * to register the new place it is creating.
     **/
    public void setPlaceName(RemoteMudPlace place, String name)
        throws PlaceAlreadyExists
    {
```

RMI

Example 16-4: MudServer.java (continued)

```
    if (places.containsKey(name)) throw new PlaceAlreadyExists();
    places.put(name, place);
}

/**
 * This remote method serializes and compresses the state of the MUD
 * to a named file, if the specified password matches the one specified
 * when the MUD was initially created.  Note that the state of a MUD
 * consists of all places in the MUD, with all things and exits in those
 * places.  The people in the MUD are not part of the state that is saved.
 **/
public void dump(String password, String f)
    throws RemoteException, BadPassword, IOException
{
    if ((this.password != null) && !this.password.equals(password))
        throw new BadPassword();
    ObjectOutputStream out = new ObjectOutputStream(
                        new GZIPOutputStream(new FileOutputStream(f)));
    out.writeObject(this);
    out.close();
}

/**
 * This main() method defines the standalone program that starts up a MUD
 * server.  If invoked with a single argument, it treats that argument as
 * the name of a file containing the serialized and compressed state of an
 * existing MUD, and recreates it.  Otherwise, it expects four command-line
 * arguments: the name of the MUD, the password, the name of the entrance
 * place for the MUD, and a description of that entrance place.
 * Besides creating the MudServer object, this program sets an appropriate
 * security manager, and uses the default rmiregistry to register the
 * the MudServer under its given name.
 **/
public static void main(String[] args) {
    try {
        MudServer server;
        if (args.length == 1) {
            // Read the MUD state in from a file
            FileInputStream f = new FileInputStream(args[0]);
            ObjectInputStream in =
                new ObjectInputStream(new GZIPInputStream(f));
            server = (MudServer) in.readObject();
        }
        // Otherwise, create an initial MUD from scratch
        else server = new MudServer(args[0], args[1], args[2], args[3]);

        Naming.rebind(Mud.mudPrefix + server.mudname, server);
    }
    // Display an error message if anything goes wrong.
    catch (Exception e) {
        System.out.println(e);
        System.out.println("Usage: java MudServer <savefile>\n" +
                        " or: java MudServer <mudname> <password> " +
                        "<placename> <description>");
        System.exit(1);
    }
}
```

Example 16–4: MudServer.java (continued)

```
    /** This constant is a version number for serialization */
    static final long serialVersionUID = 7453281245880199453L;
}
```

The MudPlace Class

Example 16-5 is the MudPlace class that implements the RemoteMudPlace interface and acts as a server for a single place or room within the MUD. It is this class that holds the description of a place and maintains the lists of the people and items in a place and the exits from a place. This is a long class, but many of the remote methods it defines have simple or even trivial implementations. The go(), create-Place(), and linkTo() methods are among the more complex and interesting methods; they manage the network of connections between MudPlace objects.

Note that the MudPlace class is Serializable, so that a MudPlace (and all places it is connected to) can be serialized along with the MudServer that refers to them. However, the names and people fields are declared transient, so they are not serialized along with the place.

Example 16–5: MudPlace.java

```
package com.davidflanagan.examples.rmi;
import java.rmi.*;
import java.rmi.server.*;
import java.rmi.registry.*;
import java.io.*;
import java.util.*;
import com.davidflanagan.examples.rmi.Mud.*;

/**
 * This class implements the RemoteMudPlace interface and exports a
 * bunch of remote methods that are at the heart of the MUD.  The
 * MudClient interacts primarily with these methods.  See the comment
 * for RemoteMudPlace for an overview.
 * The MudPlace class is Serializable so that places can be saved to disk
 * along with the MudServer that contains them.  Note, however that the
 * names and people fields are marked transient, so they are not serialized
 * along with the place (because it wouldn't make sense to try to save
 * RemoteMudPerson objects, even if they could be serialized).
 **/
public class MudPlace extends UnicastRemoteObject
    implements RemoteMudPlace, Serializable
{
    String placename, description;        // information about the place
    Vector exits = new Vector();          // names of exits from this place
    Vector destinations = new Vector();   // where the exits go to
    Vector things = new Vector();         // names of things in this place
    Vector descriptions = new Vector();   // descriptions of those things
    transient Vector names = new Vector();  // names of people in this place
    transient Vector people = new Vector(); // the RemoteMudPerson objects
    MudServer server;                     // the server for this place

    /** A no-arg constructor for de-serialization only.  Do not call it */
    public MudPlace() throws RemoteException { super(); }
```

Example 16–5: MudPlace.java (continued)

```java
/**
 * This constructor creates a place, and calls a server method
 * to register the object so that it will be accessible by name
 **/
public MudPlace(MudServer server, String placename, String description)
    throws RemoteException, PlaceAlreadyExists
{
    this.server = server;
    this.placename = placename;
    this.description = description;
    server.setPlaceName(this, placename);  // Register the place
}

/** This remote method returns the name of this place */
public String getPlaceName() throws RemoteException { return placename; }

/** This remote method returns the description of this place */
public String getDescription() throws RemoteException {
    return description;
}

/** This remote method returns a Vector of names of people in this place */
public Vector getNames() throws RemoteException { return names; }

/** This remote method returns a Vector of names of things in this place */
public Vector getThings() throws RemoteException { return things; }

/** This remote method returns a Vector of names of exits from this place*/
public Vector getExits() throws RemoteException { return exits; }

/**
 * This remote method returns a RemoteMudPerson object corresponding to
 * the specified name, or throws an exception if no such person is here
 **/
public RemoteMudPerson getPerson(String name)
    throws RemoteException, NoSuchPerson
{
    synchronized(names) {
        // What about when there are 2 of the same name?
        int i = names.indexOf(name);
        if (i == -1) throw new NoSuchPerson();
        return (RemoteMudPerson) people.elementAt(i);
    }
}

/**
 * This remote method returns a description of the named thing, or
 * throws an exception if no such thing is in this place.
 **/
public String examineThing(String name) throws RemoteException, NoSuchThing
{
    synchronized(things) {
        int i = things.indexOf(name);
        if (i == -1) throw new NoSuchThing();
        return (String) descriptions.elementAt(i);
    }
}
```

Example 16-5: MudPlace.java (continued)

```java
/**
 * This remote method moves the specified RemoteMudPerson from this place
 * in the named direction (i.e. through the named exit) to whatever place
 * is there.  It throws exceptions if the specified person isn't in this
 * place to begin with, or if they are already in the place through the
 * exit or if the exit doesn't exist, or if the exit links to another MUD
 * server and the server is not functioning.
 **/
public RemoteMudPlace go(RemoteMudPerson who, String direction)
    throws RemoteException, NotThere, AlreadyThere, NoSuchExit, LinkFailed
{
    // Make sure the direction is valid, and get destination if it is
    Object destination;
    synchronized(exits) {
        int i = exits.indexOf(direction);
        if (i == -1) throw new NoSuchExit();
        destination = destinations.elementAt(i);
    }

    // If destination is a string, it is a place on another server, so
    // connect to that server.  Otherwise, it is a place already on this
    // server.  Throw an exception if we can't connect to the server.
    RemoteMudPlace newplace;
    if (destination instanceof String) {
        try {
            String t = (String) destination;
            int pos = t.indexOf('@');
            String url = t.substring(0, pos);
            String placename = t.substring(pos+1);
            RemoteMudServer s = (RemoteMudServer) Naming.lookup(url);
            newplace = s.getNamedPlace(placename);
        }
        catch (Exception e) { throw new LinkFailed(); }
    }
    // If the destination is not a string, then it is a Place
    else newplace = (RemoteMudPlace) destination;

    // Make sure the person is here and get their name.
    // Throw an exception if they are not here
    String name = verifyPresence(who);

    // Move the person out of here, and tell everyone who remains about it.
    this.exit(who, name + " has gone " + direction);

    // Put the person into the new place.
    // Send a message to everyone already in that new place
    String fromwhere;
    if (newplace instanceof MudPlace) // going to a local place
        fromwhere = placename;
    else
        fromwhere = server.getMudName() + "." + placename;
    newplace.enter(who, name, name + " has arrived from: " + fromwhere);

    // Return the new RemoteMudPlace object to the client so they
    // know where they are now at.
    return newplace;
}
```

Example 16–5: MudPlace.java (continued)

```
/**
 * This remote method sends a message to everyone in the room.  Used to
 * say things to everyone.  Requires that the speaker be in this place.
 **/
public void speak(RemoteMudPerson speaker, String msg)
    throws RemoteException, NotThere
{
    String name = verifyPresence(speaker);
    tellEveryone(name + ":" + msg);
}


/**
 * This remote method sends a message to everyone in the room.  Used to
 * do things that people can see. Requires that the actor be in this place.
 **/
public void act(RemoteMudPerson actor, String msg)
    throws RemoteException, NotThere
{
    String name = verifyPresence(actor);
    tellEveryone(name + " " + msg);
}


/**
 * This remote method creates a new thing in this room.
 * It requires that the creator be in this room.
 **/
public void createThing(RemoteMudPerson creator,
                        String name, String description)
    throws RemoteException, NotThere, AlreadyThere
{
    // Make sure the creator is here
    String creatorname = verifyPresence(creator);
    synchronized(things) {
        // Make sure there isn't already something with this name.
        if (things.indexOf(name) != -1) throw new AlreadyThere();
        // Add the thing name and descriptions to the appropriate lists
        things.addElement(name);
        descriptions.addElement(description);
    }
    // Tell everyone about the new thing and its creator
    tellEveryone(creatorname + " has created a " + name);
}


/**
 * Remove a thing from this room.  Throws exceptions if the person
 * who removes it isn't themselves in the room, or if there is no
 * such thing here.
 **/
public void destroyThing(RemoteMudPerson destroyer, String thing)
    throws RemoteException, NotThere, NoSuchThing
{
    // Verify that the destroyer is here
    String name = verifyPresence(destroyer);
    synchronized(things) {
        // Verify that there is a thing by that name in this room
        int i = things.indexOf(thing);
        if (i == -1) throw new NoSuchThing();
        // And remove its name and description from the lists
```

Example 16–5: MudPlace.java (continued)

```
            things.removeElementAt(i);
            descriptions.removeElementAt(i);
        }
        // Let everyone know of the demise of this thing.
        tellEveryone(name + " had destroyed the " + thing);
    }


    /**
     * Create a new place in this MUD, with the specified name an description.
     * The new place is accessible from this place through
     * the specified exit, and this place is accessible from the new place
     * through the specified entrance.  The creator must be in this place
     * in order to create a exit from this place.
     **/
    public void createPlace(RemoteMudPerson creator,
                            String exit, String entrance, String name,
                            String description)
        throws RemoteException,NotThere,ExitAlreadyExists,PlaceAlreadyExists
    {
        // Verify that the creator is actually here in this place
        String creatorname = verifyPresence(creator);
        synchronized(exits) {  // Only one client may change exits at a time
            // Check that the exit doesn't already exist.
            if (exits.indexOf(exit) != -1) throw new ExitAlreadyExists();
            // Create the new place, registering its name with the server
            MudPlace destination = new MudPlace(server, name, description);
            // Link from there back to here
            destination.exits.addElement(entrance);
            destination.destinations.addElement(this);
            // And link from here to there
            exits.addElement(exit);
            destinations.addElement(destination);
        }
        // Let everyone know about the new exit, and the new place beyond
        tellEveryone(creatorname + " has created a new place: " + exit);
    }


    /**
     * Create a new exit from this mud, linked to a named place in a named
     * MUD on a named host (this can also be used to link to a named place in
     * the current MUD, of course).  Because of the possibilities of deadlock,
     * this method only links from here to there; it does not create a return
     * exit from there to here.  That must be done with a separate call.
     **/
    public void linkTo(RemoteMudPerson linker, String exit,
                       String hostname, String mudname, String placename)
        throws RemoteException, NotThere, ExitAlreadyExists, NoSuchPlace
    {
        // Verify that the linker is actually here
        String name = verifyPresence(linker);

        // Check that the link target actually exists.  Throw NoSuchPlace if
        // not.  Note that NoSuchPlace may also mean "NoSuchMud" or
        // "MudNotResponding".
        String url = "rmi://" + hostname + '/' + Mud.mudPrefix + mudname;
        try {
            RemoteMudServer s = (RemoteMudServer) Naming.lookup(url);
            RemoteMudPlace destination = s.getNamedPlace(placename);
```

RMI

Example 16–5: MudPlace.java (continued)

```
        }
        catch (Exception e) { throw new NoSuchPlace(); }

        synchronized(exits) {
            // Check that the exit doesn't already exist.
            if (exits.indexOf(exit) != -1) throw new ExitAlreadyExists();
            // Add the exit, to the list of exit names
            exits.addElement(exit);
            // And add the destination to the list of destinations.  Note that
            // the destination is stored as a string rather than as a
            // RemoteMudPlace.  This is because if the remote server goes down
            // then comes back up again, a RemoteMudPlace is not valid, but the
            // string still is.
            destinations.addElement(url + '@' + placename);
        }
        // Let everyone know about the new exit and where it leads
        tellEveryone(name + " has linked " + exit + " to " +
                         "'" + placename + "' in MUD '" + mudname +
                         "' on host " + hostname);
    }

    /**
     * Close an exit that leads out of this place.
     * It does not close the return exit from there back to here.
     * Note that this method does not destroy the place that the exit leads to.
     * In the current implementation, there is no way to destroy a place.
     **/
    public void close(RemoteMudPerson who, String exit)
        throws RemoteException, NotThere, NoSuchExit
    {
        // check that the person closing the exit is actually here
        String name = verifyPresence(who);
        synchronized(exits) {
            // Check that the exit exists
            int i = exits.indexOf(exit);
            if (i == -1) throw new NoSuchExit();
            // Remove it and its destination from the lists
            exits.removeElementAt(i);
            destinations.removeElementAt(i);
        }
        // Let everyone know that the exit doesn't exist anymore
        tellEveryone(name + " has closed exit " + exit);
    }

    /**
     * Remove a person from this place.  If there is a message, send it to
     * everyone who is left in this place.  If the specified person is not here
     * this method does nothing and does not throw an exception.  This method
     * is called by go(), and the client should call it when the user quits.
     * The client should not allow the user to invoke it directly, however.
     **/
    public void exit(RemoteMudPerson who, String message)
        throws RemoteException
    {
        String name;
        synchronized(names) {
            int i = people.indexOf(who);
            if (i == -1) return;
```

Example 16–5: MudPlace.java (continued)

```
            names.removeElementAt(i);
            people.removeElementAt(i);
        }
        if (message != null) tellEveryone(message);
    }


    /**
     * This method puts a person into this place, assigning them the
     * specified name, and displaying a message to anyone else who is in
     * that place.  This method is called by go(), and the client should
     * call it to initially place a person into the MUD.  Once the person
     * is in the MUD, however, the client should restrict them to using go()
     * and should not allow them to call this method directly.
     * If there have been networking problems, a client might call this method
     * to restore a person to this place, in case they've been bumped out.
     * (A person will be bumped out of a place if the server tries to send
     * a message to them and gets a RemoteException.)
     **/
    public void enter(RemoteMudPerson who, String name, String message)
        throws RemoteException, AlreadyThere
    {
        // Send the message to everyone who is already here.
        if (message != null) tellEveryone(message);

        // Add the person to this place.
        synchronized (names) {
            if (people.indexOf(who) != -1) throw new AlreadyThere();
            names.addElement(name);
            people.addElement(who);
        }
    }


    /**
     * This final remote method returns the server object for the MUD in which
     * this place exists.  The client should not allow the user to invoke this
     * method.
     **/
    public RemoteMudServer getServer() throws RemoteException {
        return server;
    }


    /**
     * Create and start a thread that sends out a message everyone in this
     * place.  If it gets a RemoteException talking to a person, it silently
     * removes that person from this place.  This is not a remote method, but
     * is used internally by a number of remote methods.
     **/
    protected void tellEveryone(final String message) {
        // If there is no-one here, don't bother sending the message!
        if (people.size() == 0) return;
        // Make a copy of the people here now.  The message is sent
        // asynchronously and the list of people in the room may change before
        // the message is sent to everyone.
        final Vector recipients = (Vector) people.clone();
        // Create and start a thread to send the message, using an anonymous
        // class.  We do this because sending the message to everyone in this
        // place might take some time, (particularly on a slow or flaky
        // network) and we don't want to wait.
```

Example 16-5: MudPlace.java (continued)

```
          new Thread() {
               public void run() {
                   // Loop through the recipients
                   for(int i = 0; i < recipients.size(); i++) {
                       RemoteMudPerson person =
                           (RemoteMudPerson)recipients.elementAt(i);
                       // Try to send the message to each one.
                       try { person.tell(message); }
                       // If it fails, assume that that person's client or
                       // network has failed, and silently remove them from
                       // this place.
                       catch (RemoteException e) {
                           try { MudPlace.this.exit(person, null); }
                           catch (Exception ex) {}
                       }
                   }
               }
          }.start();
     }

     /**
      * This convenience method checks whether the specified person is here.
      * If so, it returns their name.  If not it throws a NotThere exception
      **/
     protected String verifyPresence(RemoteMudPerson who) throws NotThere {
         int i = people.indexOf(who);
         if (i == -1) throw new NotThere();
         else return (String) names.elementAt(i);
     }

     /**
      * This method is used for custom de-serialization.  Since the vectors of
      * people and of their names are transient, they are not serialized with
      * the rest of this place.  Therefore, when the place is de-serialized,
      * those vectors have to be recreated (empty).
      **/
     private void readObject(ObjectInputStream in)
         throws IOException, ClassNotFoundException {
         in.defaultReadObject();  // Read most of the object as normal
         names = new Vector();    // Then recreate the names vector
         people = new Vector();   // and recreate the people vector
     }

     /** This constant is a version number for serialization */
     static final long serialVersionUID = 5090967989223703026L;
}
```

The MudPerson Class

Example 16-6 shows the MudPerson class. This is the simplest of the remote objects in the MUD system. It implements the two remote methods defined by the RemoteMudPerson interface and also defines a few nonremote methods used by the MudClient class of Example 16-7. The remote methods are quite simple: one simply returns a description string to the caller,x and the other writes a message to a stream where the user can see it.

Example 16-6: MudPerson.java

```java
package com.davidflanagan.examples.rmi;
import java.rmi.*;
import java.rmi.server.*;
import java.io.*;
import com.davidflanagan.examples.rmi.Mud.*;

/**
 * This is the simplest of the remote objects that we implement for the MUD.
 * It maintains only a little bit of state, and has only two exported
 * methods
 **/
public class MudPerson extends UnicastRemoteObject implements RemoteMudPerson {
    String name;            // The name of the person
    String description;     // The person's description
    PrintWriter tellStream; // Where to send messages we receive to

    public MudPerson(String n, String d, PrintWriter out)
        throws RemoteException
    {
        name = n;
        description = d;
        tellStream = out;
    }

    /** Return the person's name.  Not a remote method */
    public String getName() { return name; }

    /** Set the person's name.  Not a remote method */
    public void setName(String n) { name = n; }

    /** Set the person's description.  Not a remote method */
    public void setDescription(String d) { description = d; }

    /** Set the stream that messages to us should be written to. Not remote. */
    public void setTellStream(PrintWriter out) { tellStream = out; }

    /** A remote method that returns this person's description */
    public String getDescription() throws RemoteException {
        return description;
    }

    /**
     * A remote method that delivers a message to the person.
     * I.e. it delivers a message to the user controlling the "person"
     **/
    public void tell(String message) throws RemoteException {
        tellStream.println(message);
        tellStream.flush();
    }
}
```

A MUD Client

Example 16-7 is a client program for the MUD system developed in the previous examples. It uses the `Naming.lookup()` method to look up the `RemoteMudServer` object that represents a named MUD on a specified host. The program then calls `getEntrance()` or `getNamedPlace()` method of this `RemoteMudServer` object to obtain an initial `MudPlace` object into which to insert the user. Next, the program asks the user for a name and description of the `MudPerson` that will represent her in the MUD, creates a `MudPerson` object with that name and description, and then places it in the initial `RemoteMudPlace`. Finally, the program enters a loop that prompts the user to enter a command and processes the command. Most of the commands that this client supports simply invoke one of the remote methods of the `RemoteMudPlace` that represents the user's current location in the MUD. The end of the command loop consists of a number of `catch` clauses that handle the large number of things that can go wrong.

In order to use the `MudClient` class, you must first have a `MudServer` up and running. You should be able to accomplish that with commands like the following:

```
% cd com/davidflanagan/examples/rmi
% javac Mud*.java
% rmic -d ../../../../ com.davidflanagan.examples.rmi.MudServer
% rmic -d ../../../../ com.davidflanagan.examples.rmi.MudPlace
% rmic -d ../../../../ com.davidflanagan.examples.rmi.MudPerson
% rmiregistry &
% java com.davidflanagan.examples.rmi.MudServer MyMud muddy Lobby \
     'A large marble lobby with ficus trees'
```

Having started the server with these commands, you can then run the client with a command like this:

```
% java com.davidflanagan.examples.rmi.MudClient localhost MyMud
```

Example 16-7: MudClient.java

```java
package com.davidflanagan.examples.rmi;
import java.rmi.*;
import java.rmi.server.*;
import java.rmi.registry.*;
import java.io.*;
import java.util.*;
import com.davidflanagan.examples.rmi.Mud.*;

/**
 * This class is a client program for the MUD.  The main() method sets up
 * a connection to a RemoteMudServer, gets the initial RemoteMudPlace object,
 * and creates a MudPerson object to represent the user in the MUD.  Then it
 * calls runMud() to put the person in the place, begins processing
 * user commands.  The getLine() and getMultiLine() methods are convenience
 * methods used throughout to get input from the user.
 **/
public class MudClient {
    /**
     * The main program.  It expects two or three arguments:
     *    0) the name of the host on which the mud server is running
     *    1) the name of the MUD on that host
     *    2) the name of a place within that MUD to start at (optional).
```

Example 16–7: MudClient.java (continued)

```
 *
 * It uses the Naming.lookup() method to obtain a RemoteMudServer object
 * for the named MUD on the specified host.  Then it uses the getEntrance()
 * or getNamedPlace() method of RemoteMudServer to obtain the starting
 * RemoteMudPlace object.  It prompts the user for a their name and
 * description, and creates a MudPerson object.  Finally, it passes
 * the person and the place to runMud() to begin interaction with the MUD.
 **/
public static void main(String[] args) {
    try {
        String hostname = args[0]; // Each MUD is uniquely identified by a
        String mudname = args[1];  //    host and a MUD name.
        String placename = null;    // Each place in a MUD has a unique name
        if (args.length > 2) placename = args[2];

        // Look up the RemoteMudServer object for the named MUD using
        // the default registry on the specified host.  Note the use of
        // the Mud.mudPrefix constant to help prevent naming conflicts
        // in the registry.
        RemoteMudServer server =
            (RemoteMudServer)Naming.lookup("rmi://" + hostname + "/" +
                                           Mud.mudPrefix + mudname);

        // If the user did not specify a place in the mud, use
        // getEntrance() to get the initial place.  Otherwise, call
        // getNamedPlace() to find the initial place.
        RemoteMudPlace location = null;
        if (placename == null) location = server.getEntrance();
        else location = (RemoteMudPlace) server.getNamedPlace(placename);

        // Greet the user and ask for their name and description.
        // This relies on getLine() and getMultiLine() defined below.
        System.out.println("Welcome to " + mudname);
        String name = getLine("Enter your name: ");
        String description = getMultiLine("Please describe what " +
                                  "people see when they look at you:");

        // Define an output stream that the MudPerson object will use to
        // display messages sent to it to the user.  We'll use the console.
        PrintWriter myout = new PrintWriter(System.out);

        // Create a MudPerson object to represent the user in the MUD.
        // Use the specified name and description, and the output stream.
        MudPerson me = new MudPerson(name, description, myout);

        // Lower this thread's priority one notch so that broadcast
        // messages can appear even when we're blocking for I/O.  This is
        // necessary on the Linux platform, but may not be necessary on all
        // platforms.
        int pri = Thread.currentThread().getPriority();
        Thread.currentThread().setPriority(pri-1);

        // Finally, put the MudPerson into the RemoteMudPlace, and start
        // prompting the user for commands.
        runMud(location, me);
    }
    // If anything goes wrong, print a message and exit.
    catch (Exception e) {
```

Example 16–7: MudClient.java (continued)

```
            System.out.println(e);
            System.out.println("Usage: java MudClient <host> <mud> [<place>]");
            System.exit(1);
        }
    }

    /**
     * This method is the main loop of the MudClient.  It places the person
     * into the place (using the enter() method of RemoteMudPlace).  Then it
     * calls the look() method to describe the place to the user, and enters a
     * command loop to prompt the user for a command and process the command
     **/
    public static void runMud(RemoteMudPlace entrance, MudPerson me)
        throws RemoteException
    {
        RemoteMudPlace location = entrance;  // The current place
        String myname = me.getName();        // The person's name
        String placename = null;             // The name of the current place
        String mudname = null;               // The name of the mud of that place

        try {
            // Enter the MUD
            location.enter(me, myname, myname + " has entered the MUD.");
            // Figure out where we are (for the prompt)
            mudname = location.getServer().getMudName();
            placename = location.getPlaceName();
            // Describe the place to the user
            look(location);
        }
        catch (Exception e) {
            System.out.println(e);
            System.exit(1);
        }

        // Now that we've entered the MUD, begin a command loop to process
        // the user's commands.  Note that there is a huge block of catch
        // statements at the bottom of the loop to handle all the things that
        // could go wrong each time through the loop.
        for(;;) {  // Loop until the user types "quit"
            try {    // Catch any exceptions that occur in the loop
                // Pause just a bit before printing the prompt, to give output
                // generated indirectly by the last command a chance to appear.
                try { Thread.sleep(200); } catch (InterruptedException e) {}

                // Display a prompt, and get the user's input
                String line = getLine(mudname + '.' + placename + "> ");

                // Break the input into a command and an argument that consists
                // of the rest of the line.  Convert the command to lowercase.
                String cmd, arg;
                int i = line.indexOf(' ');
                if (i == -1) { cmd = line; arg = null; }
                else {
                    cmd = line.substring(0, i).toLowerCase();
                    arg = line.substring(i+1);
                }
                if (arg == null) arg = "";
```

Example 16-7: MudClient.java (continued)

```java
        // Now go process the command.  What follows is a huge repeated
        // if/else statement covering each of the commands supported by
        // this client.  Many of these commands simply invoke one of
        // the remote methods of the current RemoteMudPlace object.
        // Some have to do a bit of additional processing.

        // LOOK: Describe the place and its things, people, and exits
        if (cmd.equals("look")) look(location);
        // EXAMINE: Describe a named thing
        else if (cmd.equals("examine"))
            System.out.println(location.examineThing(arg));
        // DESCRIBE: Describe a named person
        else if (cmd.equals("describe")) {
            try {
                RemoteMudPerson p = location.getPerson(arg);
                System.out.println(p.getDescription());
            }
            catch(RemoteException e) {
                System.out.println(arg + " is having technical " +
                                   "difficulties. No description " +
                                   "is available.");
            }
        }
        // GO: Go in a named direction
        else if (cmd.equals("go")) {
            location = location.go(me, arg);
            mudname = location.getServer().getMudName();
            placename = location.getPlaceName();
            look(location);
        }
        // SAY: Say something to everyone
        else if (cmd.equals("say")) location.speak(me, arg);
        // DO: Do something that will be described to everyone
        else if (cmd.equals("do")) location.act(me, arg);
        // TALK: Say something to one named person
        else if (cmd.equals("talk")) {
            try {
                RemoteMudPerson p = location.getPerson(arg);
                String msg = getLine("What do you want to say?: ");
                p.tell(myname + " says \"" + msg + "\"");
            }
            catch (RemoteException e) {
                System.out.println(arg + " is having technical " +
                                   "difficulties. Can't talk to them.");
            }
        }
        // CHANGE: Change my own description
        else if (cmd.equals("change"))
            me.setDescription(
                    getMultiLine("Describe yourself for others: "));
        // CREATE: Create a new thing in this place
        else if (cmd.equals("create")) {
            if (arg.length() == 0)
                throw new IllegalArgumentException("name expected");
            String desc = getMultiLine("Please describe the " +
                                       arg + ": ");
            location.createThing(me, arg, desc);
        }
```

Example 16-7: MudClient.java (continued)

```
                    // DESTROY: Destroy a named thing
                    else if (cmd.equals("destroy")) location.destroyThing(me, arg);
                    // OPEN: Create a new place and connect this place to it
                    // through the exit specified in the argument.
                    else if (cmd.equals("open")) {
                        if (arg.length() == 0)
                            throw new IllegalArgumentException("direction expected");
                        String name = getLine("What is the name of place there?: ");
                        String back = getLine("What is the direction from " +
                                              "there back to here?: ");
                        String desc = getMultiLine("Please describe " +
                                                   name + ":");
                        location.createPlace(me, arg, back, name, desc);
                    }
                    // CLOSE: Close a named exit.  Note: only closes an exit
                    // uni-directionally, and does not destroy a place.
                    else if (cmd.equals("close")) {
                        if (arg.length() == 0)
                            throw new IllegalArgumentException("direction expected");
                        location.close(me, arg);
                    }
                    // LINK: Create a new exit that connects to an existing place
                    // that may be in another MUD running on another host
                    else if (cmd.equals("link")) {
                        if (arg.length() == 0)
                            throw new IllegalArgumentException("direction expected");
                        String host = getLine("What host are you linking to?: ");
                        String mud =
                            getLine("What is the name of the MUD on that host?: ");
                        String place =
                            getLine("What is the place name in that MUD?: ");
                        location.linkTo(me, arg, host, mud, place);
                        System.out.println("Don't forget to make a link from " +
                                           "there back to here!");
                    }
                    // DUMP: Save the state of this MUD into the named file,
                    // if the password is correct
                    else if (cmd.equals("dump")) {
                        if (arg.length() == 0)
                            throw new IllegalArgumentException("filename expected");
                        String password = getLine("Password: ");
                        location.getServer().dump(password, arg);
                    }
                    // QUIT: Quit the game
                    else if (cmd.equals("quit")) {
                        try { location.exit(me, myname + " has quit."); }
                        catch (Exception e) {}
                        System.out.println("Bye.");
                        System.out.flush();
                        System.exit(0);
                    }
                    // HELP: Print out a big help message
                    else if (cmd.equals("help")) System.out.println(help);
                    // Otherwise, this is an unrecognized command.
                    else System.out.println("Unknown command.  Try 'help'.");
                }
                // Handle the many possible types of MudException
                catch (MudException e) {
```

Example 16-7: MudClient.java (continued)

```
                    if (e instanceof NoSuchThing)
                        System.out.println("There isn't any such thing here.");
                    else if (e instanceof NoSuchPerson)
                        System.out.println("There isn't anyone by that name here.");
                    else if (e instanceof NoSuchExit)
                        System.out.println("There isn't an exit in that direction.");
                    else if (e instanceof NoSuchPlace)
                        System.out.println("There isn't any such place.");
                    else if (e instanceof ExitAlreadyExists)
                        System.out.println("There is already an exit " +
                                            "in that direction.");
                    else if (e instanceof PlaceAlreadyExists)
                        System.out.println("There is already a place " +
                                            "with that name.");
                    else if (e instanceof LinkFailed)
                        System.out.println("That exit is not functioning.");
                    else if (e instanceof BadPassword)
                        System.out.println("Invalid password.");
                    else if (e instanceof NotThere)      // Shouldn't happen
                        System.out.println("You can't do that when " +
                                            "you're not there.");
                    else if (e instanceof AlreadyThere)  // Shouldn't happen
                        System.out.println("You can't go there; " +
                                            "you're already there.");
                }
                // Handle RMI exceptions
                catch (RemoteException e) {
                    System.out.println("The MUD is having technical difficulties.");
                    System.out.println("Perhaps the server has crashed:");
                    System.out.println(e);
                }
                // Handle everything else that could go wrong.
                catch (Exception e) {
                    System.out.println("Syntax or other error:");
                    System.out.println(e);
                    System.out.println("Try using the 'help' command.");
                }
            }
        }
    }

    /**
     * This convenience method is used in several places in the
     * runMud() method above.  It displays the name and description of
     * the current place (including the name of the mud the place is in),
     * and also displays the list of things, people, and exits in
     * the current place.
     **/
    public static void look(RemoteMudPlace p)
        throws RemoteException, MudException
    {
        String mudname = p.getServer().getMudName(); // Mud name
        String placename = p.getPlaceName();         // Place name
        String description = p.getDescription();     // Place description
        Vector things = p.getThings();               // List of things here
        Vector names = p.getNames();                 // List of people here
        Vector exits = p.getExits();                 // List of exits from here

        // Print it all out
```

RMI

Example 16–7: MudClient.java (continued)

```
        System.out.println("You are in: " + placename +
                           " of the Mud: " + mudname);
        System.out.println(description);
        System.out.print("Things here: ");
        for(int i = 0; i < things.size(); i++) {       // Display list of things
            if (i > 0) System.out.print(", ");
            System.out.print(things.elementAt(i));
        }
        System.out.print("\nPeople here: ");
        for(int i = 0; i < names.size(); i++) {        // Display list of people
            if (i > 0) System.out.print(", ");
            System.out.print(names.elementAt(i));
        }
        System.out.print("\nExits are: ");
        for(int i = 0; i < exits.size(); i++) {        // Display list of exits
            if (i > 0) System.out.print(", ");
            System.out.print(exits.elementAt(i));
        }
        System.out.println();                          // Blank line
        System.out.flush();                            // Make it appear now!
    }

    /** This static input stream reads lines from the console */
    static BufferedReader in =
        new BufferedReader(new InputStreamReader(System.in));

    /**
     * A convenience method for prompting the user and getting a line of
     * input.  It guarantees that the line is not empty and strips off
     * whitespace at the beginning and end of the line.
     **/
    public static String getLine(String prompt) {
        String line = null;
        do {                          // Loop until a non-empty line is entered
            try {
                System.out.print(prompt);               // Display prompt
                System.out.flush();                     // Display it right away
                line = in.readLine();                   // Get a line of input
                if (line != null) line = line.trim();   // Strip off whitespace
            } catch (Exception e) {}                    // Ignore any errors
        } while((line == null) || (line.length() == 0));
        return line;
    }

    /**
     * A convenience method for getting multi-line input from the user.
     * It prompts for the input, displays instructions, and guarantees that
     * the input is not empty.  It also allows the user to enter the name of
     * a file from which text will be read.
     **/
    public static String getMultiLine(String prompt) {
        String text = "";
        for(;;) {  // We'll break out of this loop when we get non-empty input
            try {
                BufferedReader br = in;       // The stream to read from
                System.out.println(prompt);   // Display the prompt
                // Display some instructions
                System.out.println("You can enter multiple lines.  " +
```

Example 16-7: MudClient.java (continued)

```
                            "End with a '.' on a line by itself.\n" +
                            "Or enter a '<<' followed by a filename");
            // Make the prompt and instructions appear now.
            System.out.flush();
            // Read lines
            String line;
            while((line = br.readLine()) != null) {      // Until EOF
                if (line.equals(".")) break;  // Or until a dot by itself
                // Or, if a file is specified, start reading from it
                // instead of from the console.
                if (line.trim().startsWith("<<")) {
                    String filename = line.trim().substring(2).trim();
                    br = new BufferedReader(new FileReader(filename));
                    continue;  // Don't count the << as part of the input
                }
                // Add the line to the collected input
                else text += line + "\n";
            }
            // If we got at least one line, return it.  Otherwise, chastise
            // the user and go back to the prompt and the instructions.
            if (text.length() > 0) return text;
            else System.out.println("Please enter at least one line.");
        }
        // If there were errors, for example an IO error reading a file,
        // display the error and loop again, displaying prompt and
        // instructions
        catch(Exception e) { System.out.println(e); }
    }
}

/** This is the usage string that explains the available commands */
static final String help =
    "Commands are:\n" +
    "look: Look around\n" +
    "examine <thing>: examine the named thing in more detail\n" +
    "describe <person>: describe the named person\n" +
    "go <direction>: go in the named direction (i.e. a named exit)\n" +
    "say <message>: say something to everyone\n" +
    "do <message>: tell everyone that you are doing something\n" +
    "talk <person>: talk to one person.  Will prompt for message\n" +
    "change: change how you are described.  Will prompt for input\n" +
    "create <thing>: create a new thing.  Prompts for description \n" +
    "destroy <thing>: destroy a thing.\n" +
    "open <direction>: create an adjoining place. Prompts for input\n"+
    "close <direction>: close an exit from this place.\n" +
    "link <direction>: create an exit to an existing place,\n" +
    "     perhaps on another server.  Will prompt for input.\n" +
    "dump <filename>: save server state.  Prompts for password\n" +
    "quit: leave the Mud\n" +
    "help: display this message";
}
```

Advanced RMI

There are several advanced features of RMI that are beyond the scope of this book, but that are important to know about. I'm only going to describe these features briefly here; you should consult *Java Enterprise in a Nutshell* for details.

Remote Class Loading

Ideally, a client of a remote object should need only direct access to the remote interface; it should not need to know anything about the implementation of that interface. In the examples we've seen in this chapter, however, the client requires access to the implementation stub class as well. (And in practice, you've probably run the client and the server on the same machine with the same class path, so they shared all classes.)

Having to distribute implementation stubs with RMI client programs can be a burden, especially when the server implementation changes. Fortunately, RMI provides a mechanism that allows a client to remotely load the stub classes it needs from a network server. Unfortunately, making this work takes a fair bit of effort. First, you must have a web server running and make the stub classes available for download from that server. Second, you must install a security manager in all your clients to protect against malicious code in the downloaded stub classes (and remember that an RMI server that uses other remote objects is itself a RMI client). Third, since you've installed a security manager, you must explicitly specify a security policy that allows your RMI clients to make the network connections they need to communicate with remote objects. See *Java Enterprise in a Nutshell* for all the details.

Activation

In the RMI examples of this chapter, the process that implements a remote object must be running all the time, waiting for connections from clients. As of Java 1.2, the RMI activation service enables you to define remote objects that don't run all the time, but that are instantiated and activated only when needed. Activation also enables persistent remote references that can remain valid even across server crashes.

In order to implement an activatable remote object, you extend the `java.rmi.activation.Activatable` class, rather than the `UnicastRemoteObject` class that we've used in this chapter. When you subclass `Activatable`, you must define an initialization constructor that specifies a location from which the class can be loaded. You must also define an activation constructor (with different arguments) that the activation service uses to activate your object when it is requested by a client.

Once you have implemented your activatable remote object, you can instantiate an initial instance of it and register it with the activation service, or you can create an `ActivationDesc` object that tells the activation service how to instantiate it when it is needed. In either case, the activation service itself must be running. You run this service with the *rmid* command that ships with the Java SDK in Java 1.2 and later. Conveniently, *rmid* can also perform the function of the *rmiregistry* as well.

All the details described here are server-side details: the client can't tell the difference between an activatable remote object and a regular remote object. This section has outlined only the process of creating activatable objects; see *Java Enterprise in a Nutshell* for more information.

CORBA Interoperability with RMI/IIOP

One of the weaknesses of traditional RMI remote objects is that they work only when Java is used for both the client and the server. (This is also a strength, in that it keeps the remote method infrastructure simple and easy to use.) A new technology called RMI-IIOP allows you to use RMI remote objects with the IIOP network protocol. IIOP is the Internet Inter-ORB Protocol: the protocol used by the CORBA distributed object standard. RMI-IIOP is implemented in the javax.rmi package, and is a standard part of Java 1.3 and later.

RMI remote objects can't automatically use the IIOP protocol: you must implement them specially by subclassing the javax.rmi.PortableRemoteObject class and following a number of other steps. Although there is extra work involved, using RMI-IIOP can be of great value if you are working in a heterogeneous environment and want to connect Java remote objects with legacy remote objects implemented using the CORBA standard. See *Java Enterprise in a Nutshell* for an overview and see *http://java.sun.com/products/rmi-iiop/* and the RMI-IIOP documentation in the Java SDK for complete details.

Exercises

16-1. Modify the remote banking example in this chapter so that bank customers are allowed to borrow money from the bank against some maximum line of credit and can also apply money from their account to pay off their debt. Add borrow() and repay() methods to the RemoteBank interface, implement these methods in the server, and modify the client so that it can call these methods when the user requests them.

16-2. The *rmiregistry* program provides a simple name service for RMI programs; it allows servers to register names for the remote objects they serve, and it allows clients to look up those remote objects by name. Because it is a global registry, shared by any number of remote services, there is a possibility of name collisions. For this reason, if a service needs to define names for a number of remote objects, it should usually provide its own custom registry. That way, a client can use the global registry to look up the service's custom naming registry, and then it can use this custom registry to look up particular named objects for that service.

Use RMI to write a server that provides such a custom naming service. It should export remote methods that correspond to the bind(), rebind(), unbind(), and lookup() methods of the Naming class. You will probably want to use a java.util.Map object to associate names with remote objects.

16-3. The MUD example of this chapter uses remote objects to represent the rooms or places in the MUD and the people interacting in the MUD. Things that appear in the MUD, however, are not remote objects; they are simply part of the state of each room in the MUD.

Modify the example so that things are true remote objects. Define a MudThing interface that extends Remote. It should have a getDescription() method that returns the description of a thing. Modify the MudPlace interface and RemoteMudPlace class to have methods that allow MudThing objects to be added to and removed from a place.

Define a trivial implementation of MudThing that simply returns a static string from its getDescription() method. Then, define another implementation of MudThing, named Clock. This class should have more dynamic behavior: whenever its getDescription() method is called, it should return a string that displays the current time. Modify the MUD server so that it places a Clock object in the entrance to the MUD.

16-4. Modify the MUD example again so that MudPerson objects can pick up MudThing objects they find in a MudPlace, carry them around, drop them in other places, and give them to other people. Implement at least three new methods: pickup(), drop(), and give(). Modify the MUD client so that it supports pickup, drop, and give commands.

CHAPTER 17

Database Access with SQL

This chapter shows how you can communicate with a database server using the JDBC API of the `java.sql` package. JDBC is an API that allows a Java program to communicate with a database server using SQL (Structured Query Language) commands. Note that JDBC is a SQL API, not an embedded SQL mechanism for Java.

The `java.sql` package provides a fairly straightforward mechanism for sending SQL queries to a database and for receiving query results. Thus, assuming that you already have experience working with databases and SQL, this chapter should be relatively easy to understand. On the other hand, if you have not worked with databases before, you'll need to learn basic SQL syntax and some general database programming concepts before you can really take advantage of the examples in this chapter and JDBC in general. I'll try to explain some of the basic concepts as I go along, so that you can get a sense of what is possible with JDBC, but full coverage of database programming is beyond the scope of this chapter. *Java Enterprise in a Nutshell* contains a more thorough introduction to JDBC, a SQL reference, and an API quick-reference for the `java.sql` package.

In order to run the examples in this chapter, you need access to a database, and you have to obtain and install a JDBC driver for it. If you don't already have a database server to work with, you can use one of the excellent open-source databases available today. The examples in this chapter have been tested with MySQL, an open-source database available from *http://www.mysql.com*, and with PostgreSQL, another open-source server available at *http://www.postgresql.org*. JDBC drivers for these database servers can be downloaded from the same sites. Note that database servers are complex pieces of software. Downloading and installing a database may require significant effort.

Once you've decided what database server to use, read the documentation that comes with it. Before running the examples in this chapter, you need to know how to administer the database server. In particular, you need to know how to create a test database (or you need to have your database administrator create one for you). If you are new to databases, figuring out how to do this can actually be more difficult than learning how to program with JDBC.

Accessing a Database

Example 17-1 shows a program that connects to a database and then loops, prompting the user for a SQL statement, sending that statement to the database, and displaying the results. It demonstrates the four most important techniques for JDBC programming: registering a database driver, using the DriverManager class to obtain a Connection object that represents a database connection, sending a SQL statement to the database using the Statement object, and retrieving the results of a query with a ResultSet object. Before we look at the specifics of the ExecuteSQL program, let's examine these basic techniques.

One of the interesting things about the java.sql package is that its most important members, such as Connection, Statement, and ResultSet, are interfaces instead of classes. The whole point of JDBC is to hide the specifics of accessing particular kinds of database systems and these interfaces make that possible. A JDBC driver is a set of classes that implement the interfaces for a particular database system; different database systems require different drivers. As an application programmer, you don't have to worry about the implementation of these underlying classes. All you have to worry about is writing code that uses the methods defined by the various interfaces.

The DriverManager class is responsible for keeping track of all the JDBC drivers that are available on a system. So the first task of a JDBC program is to register an appropriate driver for the type of database being used. By convention, JDBC driver classes register themselves with the DriverManager when they are first loaded, so, in practice, all you have to do is load the driver class, allowing it to register itself. The Class.forName() method provides one easy way of doing this. This method takes a String argument that specifies a class name, so it's simple to pass the driver name to the program on the command line, instead of hardcoding the driver class into your program. Note that this step simply loads a driver and registers it with the DriverManager; it doesn't specify that the program actually use that driver. If a program needs to use multiple databases, it can load multiple driver classes in this step. The driver selection step comes next, when the program actually connects to a database.

After the required driver is loaded (and has registered itself), a JDBC program can connect to the database by calling DriverManager.getConnection(). You specify the database to connect to with a *jdbc:* URL. This URL has this general syntax:

```
jdbc:subprotocol://host:port/databasename
```

The *subprotocol* of the URL identifies the particular database system that is being used. The DriverManager class uses that part of the URL to select an appropriate JDBC driver from the list of drivers that have been registered. If the DriverManager can't find a JDBC driver for the database, it throws a SQLException.

I used the MySQL database while developing the examples in this chapter, so I had to use a URL like the following to connect to my database:

```
jdbc:mysql://dbserver.mydomain.com:1234/mydb
```

This URL specifies that JDBC should connect to the database named "mydb" stored on a MySQL database server running on the host *dbserver.mydomain.com* and listening for connections on port 1234.

If you are running the database server on the same host your Java program is running on, you can omit the host name portion of the URL. If your database server is listening on its default port (which it usually does), you can omit the port number. Here's another *jdbc:* URL that works for PosgreSQL server:

```
jdbc:postgresql://dbserver.mydomain.com/mydb
```

Or, if you are connecting to a server on the local host:

```
jdbc:postgresql:mydb
```

`DriverManager.getConnection()` returns an object that implements the `Connection` interface. This object represents the connection to the database; you use it to interact with the database. The `createStatement()` method of the `Connection` object creates an object that implements the `Statement` interface, which is what you use to send SQL queries and updates to the database. The `executeQuery()` and `executeUpdate()` methods of the `Statement` object send queries and updates, respectively, while the general-purpose `execute()` method sends a statement that can be either a query or an update.

After you send a query to the database, use the `getResultSet()` method of `Statement` to retrieve an object that implements the `ResultSet` interface. This object represents the values returned by the SQL query; it is organized into columns and rows like a table. A `ResultSet` offers its data one row at a time; you use `next()` to move from the current row to the next row. `ResultSet` provides numerous `getX()` methods that allow you to retrieve the data from each column of the current row as a number of different types.

The JDBC API was updated in Java 1.2 to JDBC 2.0. In JDBC 2.0, result sets can be configured to be scrollable, which means that in addition to the `next()` method, you can also use the `previous()` method to move to the previous row, `first()` and `last()` to move to the first and last rows, respectively, and `absolute()` and `relative()` to move to an arbitrary row specified with an absolute or relative row number. If your database server supports scrollable result sets, and if you're using a JDBC 2.0-compliant driver, you can specify scrollable result sets when you create your `Statement` object. To do this, use the two-argument version of the `createStatement()` method, with code like this:

```
Statement s = connection.createStatement(ResultSet.TYPE_SCROLL_INSENSITIVE,
                                          ResultSet.CONCUR_READ_ONLY);
```

There are other possible values for the two arguments to `createStatement()`, but a discussion of them is beyond the scope of this chapter. See *Java Enterprise in a Nutshell* for further information.

Now that you understand the basic techniques used in a JDBC program, let's go on to Example 17-1. The `ExecuteSQL` program uses all the techniques just discussed to connect to a database, execute SQL statements, and display the results. The program parses its command-line arguments to determine the class name of the JDBC driver, the URL of the database, and other parameters necessary to connect to the database. For example, you might invoke the ExecuteSQL program and enter a simple query like this (note that this long Java command line has been broken in two here):

```
% java com.davidflanagan.examples.sql.ExecuteSQL -d org.gjt.mm.mysql.Driver \
      -u java -p nut jdbc:mysql://db.domain.com/api
sql> SELECT * FROM package WHERE name LIKE '%.rmi%'
+----+-------------------------------+
| id |              name             |
+----+-------------------------------+
| 14 | java.rmi                      |
| 15 | java.rmi.dgc                  |
| 16 | java.rmi.registry            |
| 17 | java.rmi.server              |
+----+-------------------------------+
sql> quit
```

Notice that ExecuteSQL uses the execute() method of its Statement object to execute SQL statements. Since the user can enter any kind of SQL statement, you have to use this general-purpose method. If execute() returns true, the SQL statement was a query, so the program retrieves the ResultSet and displays the results of the query. Otherwise, the statement was an update, so the program simply outputs information about how many rows in the database were affected by the update.

The printResultsTable() method handles displaying the results of a query. This method gets a ResultSetMetaData object to find out some information about the data returned by the query, so it can format the results appropriately.

There are two other important JDBC programming techniques to note in Example 17-1. The first is the handling of SQLException exceptions that are thrown. The SQLException object supports the standard exception message with getMessage(), but it may also contain an additional message sent by the database server. You obtain this message by calling the getSQLState() method of the exception object.

The second technique is the handling of warnings. The SQLWarning class is a subclass of SQLException, but warnings, unlike exceptions, are not thrown. When a SQL command is executed, any warnings reported by the server are stored in a linked list of SQLWarning objects. You obtain the first SQLWarning object in this list by calling the getWarnings() method of the Connection object. If there are any additional SQLWarning objects, you get the next one by calling the getNextWarning() method of the current SQLWarning object. In Example 17-1, these warnings are displayed using a finally clause, so that they appear both when an exception is thrown and when execution completes normally.

Example 17–1: ExecuteSQL.java

```
package com.davidflanagan.examples.sql;
import java.sql.*;
import java.io.*;

/**
 * A general-purpose SQL interpreter program.
 **/
public class ExecuteSQL {
    public static void main(String[] args) {
        Connection conn = null;  // Our JDBC connection to the database server
```

Example 17–1: ExecuteSQL.java (continued)

```
    try {
        String driver = null, url = null, user = "", password = "";

        // Parse all the command-line arguments
        for(int n = 0; n < args.length; n++) {
            if (args[n].equals("-d")) driver = args[++n];
            else if (args[n].equals("-u")) user = args[++n];
            else if (args[n].equals("-p")) password = args[++n];
            else if (url == null) url = args[n];
            else throw new IllegalArgumentException("Unknown argument.");
        }

        // The only required argument is the database URL.
        if (url == null)
            throw new IllegalArgumentException("No database specified");

        // If the user specified the classname for the DB driver, load
        // that class dynamically.  This gives the driver the opportunity
        // to register itself with the DriverManager.
        if (driver != null) Class.forName(driver);

        // Now open a connection the specified database, using the
        // user-specified username and password, if any.  The driver
        // manager will try all of the DB drivers it knows about to try to
        // parse the URL and connect to the DB server.
        conn = DriverManager.getConnection(url, user, password);

        // Now create the statement object we'll use to talk to the DB
        Statement s = conn.createStatement();

        // Get a stream to read from the console
        BufferedReader in =
            new BufferedReader(new InputStreamReader(System.in));

        // Loop forever, reading the user's queries and executing them
        while(true) {
            System.out.print("sql> ");   // prompt the user
            System.out.flush();          // make the prompt appear now.
            String sql = in.readLine();  // get a line of input from user

            // Quit when the user types "quit".
            if ((sql == null) || sql.equals("quit")) break;

            // Ignore blank lines
            if (sql.length() == 0) continue;

            // Now, execute the user's line of SQL and display results.
            try {
                // We don't know if this is a query or some kind of
                // update, so we use execute() instead of executeQuery()
                // or executeUpdate() If the return value is true, it was
                // a query, else an update.
                boolean status = s.execute(sql);

                // Some complex SQL queries can return more than one set
                // of results, so loop until there are no more results
                do {
                    if (status) { // it was a query and returns a ResultSet
```

Database Access

Example 17-1: ExecuteSQL.java (continued)

```
                                ResultSet rs = s.getResultSet();   // Get results
                                printResultsTable(rs, System.out); // Display them
                            }
                            else {
                                // If the SQL command that was executed was some
                                // kind of update rather than a query, then it
                                // doesn't return a ResultSet.  Instead, we just
                                // print the number of rows that were affected.
                                int numUpdates = s.getUpdateCount();
                                System.out.println("Ok. " + numUpdates +
                                                    " rows affected.");
                            }

                            // Now go see if there are even more results, and
                            // continue the results display loop if there are.
                            status = s.getMoreResults();
                        } while(status || s.getUpdateCount() != -1);
                    }
                    // If a SQLException is thrown, display an error message.
                    // Note that SQLExceptions can have a general message and a
                    // DB-specific message returned by getSQLState()
                    catch (SQLException e) {
                        System.err.println("SQLException: " + e.getMessage()+ ":" +
                                            e.getSQLState());
                    }
                    // Each time through this loop, check to see if there were any
                    // warnings.  Note that there can be a whole chain of warnings.
                    finally { // print out any warnings that occurred
                        SQLWarning w;
                        for(w=conn.getWarnings(); w != null; w=w.getNextWarning())
                            System.err.println("WARNING: " + w.getMessage() +
                                                ":" + w.getSQLState());
                    }
                }
            }
            // Handle exceptions that occur during argument parsing, database
            // connection setup, etc.  For SQLExceptions, print the details.
            catch (Exception e) {
                System.err.println(e);
                if (e instanceof SQLException)
                    System.err.println("SQL State: " +
                                        ((SQLException)e).getSQLState());
                System.err.println("Usage: java ExecuteSQL [-d <driver>] " +
                                    "[-u <user>] [-p <password>] <database URL>");
            }

            // Be sure to always close the database connection when we exit,
            // whether we exit because the user types 'quit' or because of an
            // exception thrown while setting things up.  Closing this connection
            // also implicitly closes any open statements and result sets
            // associated with it.
            finally {
                try { conn.close(); } catch (Exception e) {}
            }
        }

    /**
     * This method attempts to output the contents of a ResultSet in a
```

Example 17–1: ExecuteSQL.java (continued)

```
 * textual table.  It relies on the ResultSetMetaData class, but a fair
 * bit of the code is simple string manipulation.
 **/
static void printResultsTable(ResultSet rs, OutputStream output)
    throws SQLException
{
    // Set up the output stream
    PrintWriter out = new PrintWriter(output);

    // Get some "meta data" (column names, etc.) about the results
    ResultSetMetaData metadata = rs.getMetaData();

    // Variables to hold important data about the table to be displayed
    int numcols = metadata.getColumnCount(); // how many columns
    String[] labels = new String[numcols];   // the column labels
    int[] colwidths = new int[numcols];      // the width of each
    int[] colpos = new int[numcols];         // start position of each
    int linewidth;                           // total width of table

    // Figure out how wide the columns are, where each one begins,
    // how wide each row of the table will be, etc.
    linewidth = 1; // for the initial '|'.
    for(int i = 0; i < numcols; i++) {            // for each column
        colpos[i] = linewidth;                    // save its position
        labels[i] = metadata.getColumnLabel(i+1); // get its label
        // Get the column width.  If the db doesn't report one, guess
        // 30 characters.  Then check the length of the label, and use
        // it if it is larger than the column width
        int size = metadata.getColumnDisplaySize(i+1);
        if (size == -1) size = 30;  // Some drivers return -1...
        if (size > 500) size = 30;  // Don't allow unreasonable sizes
        int labelsize = labels[i].length();
        if (labelsize > size) size = labelsize;
        colwidths[i] = size + 1;              // save the column the size
        linewidth += colwidths[i] + 2;        // increment total size
    }

    // Create a horizontal divider line we use in the table.
    // Also create a blank line that is the initial value of each
    // line of the table
    StringBuffer divider = new StringBuffer(linewidth);
    StringBuffer blankline = new StringBuffer(linewidth);
    for(int i = 0; i < linewidth; i++) {
        divider.insert(i, '-');
        blankline.insert(i, " ");
    }
    // Put special marks in the divider line at the column positions
    for(int i=0; i<numcols; i++) divider.setCharAt(colpos[i]-1,'+');
    divider.setCharAt(linewidth-1, '+');

    // Begin the table output with a divider line
    out.println(divider);

    // The next line of the table contains the column labels.
    // Begin with a blank line, and put the column names and column
    // divider characters "|" into it.  overwrite() is defined below.
    StringBuffer line = new StringBuffer(blankline.toString());
    line.setCharAt(0, '|');
```

Example 17-1: ExecuteSQL.java (continued)

```
        for(int i = 0; i < numcols; i++) {
            int pos = colpos[i] + 1 + (colwidths[i]-labels[i].length())/2;
            overwrite(line, pos, labels[i]);
            overwrite(line, colpos[i] + colwidths[i], " |");
        }

        // Then output the line of column labels and another divider
        out.println(line);
        out.println(divider);

        // Now, output the table data.  Loop through the ResultSet, using
        // the next() method to get the rows one at a time. Obtain the
        // value of each column with getObject(), and output it, much as
        // we did for the column labels above.
        while(rs.next()) {
            line = new StringBuffer(blankline.toString());
            line.setCharAt(0, '|');
            for(int i = 0; i < numcols; i++) {
                Object value = rs.getObject(i+1);
                if (value != null)
                    overwrite(line, colpos[i] + 1, value.toString().trim());
                overwrite(line, colpos[i] + colwidths[i], " |");
            }
            out.println(line);
        }

        // Finally, end the table with one last divider line.
        out.println(divider);
        out.flush();
    }

    /** This utility method is used when printing the table of results */
    static void overwrite(StringBuffer b, int pos, String s) {
        int slen = s.length();                  // String length
        int blen = b.length();                  // Buffer length
        if (pos+slen > blen) slen = blen-pos;   // Does it fit?
        for(int i = 0; i < slen; i++)           // Copy string into buffer
            b.setCharAt(pos+i, s.charAt(i));
    }
}
```

Using Database Metadata

Sometimes, in addition to querying and updating the data in a database, you also want to retrieve information about the database itself and its contents. This information is called *metadata*. The DatabaseMetaData interface allows you to retrieve this kind of information. You can obtain an object that implements this interface by calling the getMetaData() method of the Connection object, as shown in Example 17-2.

After GetDBInfo opens a database Connection and obtains a DatabaseMetaData object, it displays some general information about the database server and JDBC driver. Then, if the user just specified a database name on the command line, the program lists all the tables in that database. If the user specified a database name and a table name, however, the program lists the name and data type of each column in that table.

An interesting feature of this `GetDBInfo` program is how it obtains the parameters needed to connect to the database. The example operates on the premise that at any given site, it is typically used to connect to the same database server, using the same database driver, and may also be used with the same database username and password. So, instead of requiring the user to type all this cumbersome information on the command line each time the program is run, the program reads default values from a file named *DB.props* that is stored in the same directory as the *GetDBInfo.class* file. In order to run Example 17-2, you have to create an appropriate *DB.props* file for your system. On my system, this file contains:

```
# The name of the JDBC driver class
driver=org.gjt.mm.mysql.Driver
# The URL that specifies the database server.
# It should not include the name of the database to connect to
server=jdbc:mysql://db.domain.com/
# The database account name
user=david
# The password for the specified account.  Not specified here
# Uncomment the line below to specify a password
#password=
```

Lines that begin with # are comments, obviously. The *name=value* format is the standard file format for the `java.util.Properties` object that is used to read the contents of this file.

After the program reads the default values from the *DB.props* file, it parses its command-line arguments, which can override the `driver`, `server`, `user`, and `password` properties specified in the file. The name of the database to connect to must be specified on the command line; the database name is simply appended to the server URL. The name of a table in the database can optionally be specified on the command line. For example, you might run the program as follows:

```
% java com.davidflanagan.examples.sql.GetDBInfo api class
DBMS: MySQL 3.22.32
JDBC Driver: Mark Matthews' MySQL Driver 2.0a
Database: jdbc:mysql://localhost/api
User: david
Columns of class:
        id : int
        packageId : int
        name : varchar
```

Example 17-2: GetDBInfo.java

```java
package com.davidflanagan.examples.sql;
import java.sql.*;
import java.util.Properties;

/**
 * This class uses the DatabaseMetaData class to obtain information about
 * the database, the JDBC driver, and the tables in the database, or about
 * the columns of a named table.
 **/
public class GetDBInfo {
```

Example 17–2: GetDBInfo.java (continued)

```java
public static void main(String[] args) {
    Connection c = null;  // The JDBC connection to the database server
    try {
        // Look for the properties file DB.props in the same directory as
        // this program.  It will contain default values for the various
        // parameters needed to connect to a database
        Properties p = new Properties();
        try { p.load(GetDBInfo.class.getResourceAsStream("DB.props")); }
        catch (Exception e) {}

        // Get default values from the properties file
        String driver = p.getProperty("driver");       // Driver class name
        String server = p.getProperty("server", ""); // JDBC URL for server
        String user = p.getProperty("user", "");       // db user name
        String password = p.getProperty("password", ""); // db password

        // These variables don't have defaults
        String database = null; // The db name (appended to server URL)
        String table = null;    // The optional name of a table in the db

        // Parse the command-line args to override the default values above
        for(int i = 0; i < args.length; i++) {
            if (args[i].equals("-d")) driver = args[++i];     //-d <driver>
            else if (args[i].equals("-s")) server = args[++i];//-s <server>
            else if (args[i].equals("-u")) user = args[++i];  //-u <user>
            else if (args[i].equals("-p")) password = args[++i];
            else if (database == null) database = args[i];    // <dbname>
            else if (table == null) table = args[i];          // <table>
            else throw new IllegalArgumentException("Unknown argument: "
                                                   +args[i]);
        }

        // Make sure that at least a server or a database were specified.
        // If not, we have no idea what to connect to, and cannot continue.
        if ((server.length() == 0) && (database.length() == 0))
            throw new IllegalArgumentException("No database specified.");

        // Load the db driver, if any was specified.
        if (driver != null) Class.forName(driver);

        // Now attempt to open a connection to the specified database on
        // the specified server, using the specified name and password
        c = DriverManager.getConnection(server+database, user, password);

        // Get the DatabaseMetaData object for the connection.  This is the
        // object that will return us all the data we're interested in here
        DatabaseMetaData md = c.getMetaData();

        // Display information about the server, the driver, etc.
        System.out.println("DBMS: " + md.getDatabaseProductName() +
                           " " + md.getDatabaseProductVersion());
        System.out.println("JDBC Driver: " + md.getDriverName() +
                           " " + md.getDriverVersion());
        System.out.println("Database: " + md.getURL());
        System.out.println("User: " + md.getUserName());

        // Now, if the user did not specify a table, then display a list of
        // all tables defined in the named database.  Note that tables are
```

Example 17–2: GetDBInfo.java (continued)

```
                // returned in a ResultSet, just like query results are.
                if (table == null) {
                    System.out.println("Tables:");
                    ResultSet r = md.getTables("", "", "%", null);
                    while(r.next()) System.out.println("\t" + r.getString(3));
                }

                // Otherwise, list all columns of the specified table.
                // Again, information about the columns is returned in a ResultSet
                else {
                    System.out.println("Columns of " + table + ": ");
                    ResultSet r = md.getColumns("", "", table, "%");
                    while(r.next())
                        System.out.println("\t" + r.getString(4) + " : " +
                                            r.getString(6));
                }
            }
        // Print an error message if anything goes wrong.
        catch (Exception e) {
            System.err.println(e);
            if (e instanceof SQLException)
                System.err.println(((SQLException)e).getSQLState());
            System.err.println("Usage: java GetDBInfo [-d <driver] " +
                               "[-s <dbserver>]\n" +
                               "\t[-u <username>] [-p <password>] <dbname>");
        }
        // Always remember to close the Connection object when we're done!
        finally {
            try { c.close(); } catch (Exception e) {}
        }
    }
}
```

Building a Database

Example 17-3 shows a program, MakeAPIDB, that takes a list of class names and uses the Java Reflection API to build a database of those classes, the packages they belong to, and all methods and fields defined by the classes. Example 17-4 shows a program that uses the database created by this example.

MakeAPIDB uses the SQL CREATE TABLE statement to add three tables, named package, class, and member, to the database. The program then inserts data into those tables using INSERT INTO statements. The program uses the same INSERT INTO statements repeatedly, as it iterates though the list of class names. In this type of situation, you can often increase the efficiency of your insertions if you use PreparedStatement objects to execute the statements.

A prepared statement is essentially a blueprint for the statements you need to execute. When you send a SQL statement to the database, the database interprets the SQL and creates a template for executing the statement. If you are sending the same SQL statement repeatedly, only with different input parameters, the database still has to interpret the SQL each time. On database platforms that support prepared statements, you can eliminate this inefficiency by sending a prepared statement to the database before you actually make any calls to the database. The

Database Access

database interprets the prepared statement and creates its template just once. Then, when you execute the prepared statement repeatedly with different input parameters, the database uses the template it has already created. JDBC provides the PreparedStatement class to support prepared statements, but it doesn't guarantee that the underlying database actually takes advantage of them.

You create a PreparedStatement with the prepareStatement() method of a Connection object, as shown in Example 17-3. MakeAPIDB passes a SQL statement to prepareStatement(), substituting ? placeholders for the variable parameters in the statement. Later, before the program executes the prepared statement, it binds values to these parameters using the various setX() methods (e.g., setInt() and setString()) of the PreparedStatement object. Each setX() method takes two arguments: a parameter index (starting with 1) and a value. Then the program calls the executeUpdate() method of the PreparedStatement to execute the statement. (PreparedStatement also provides execute() and executeQuery() methods, just like Statement.)

MakeAPIDB expects its first argument to be the name of a file that contains a list of classes to be placed into the database. The classes should be listed one to a line; each line must contain a fully qualified class name (i.e., it must specify both package name and class name). Such a file might contain lines like the following:

```
java.applet.Applet
java.applet.AppletContext
java.applet.AppletStub
        ...
java.util.zip.ZipOutputStream
```

The program reads database parameters from a Properties file named *APIDB.props* in the current directory or from an alternate Properties file specified as the second command-line argument. This Properties file is similar to, but not quite the same as, the one used in conjunction with Example 17-2; it should contain properties named driver, database, user, and password. On my system, the *APIDB.props* file looks as follows:

```
# The full classname of the JDBC driver to load: this is a MySQL driver
driver=org.gjt.mm.mysql.Driver
# The URL of the mysql server (localhost) and database (apidb) to connect to
database=jdbc:mysql:///apidb
# The name of the database user account
user=david
# The password for the database user account.
# Uncomment the line below to specify a password
#password=
```

Note that before you run this program, you must create the database for it on your database server. To do this, you have to follow the instructions provided by your database vendor. You can also use an existing database, as long as it doesn't already contain tables named package, class, or member.*

---

* This program performs a large number of database updates. In my tests, the MySQL server was significantly faster than the PostgreSQL server for this program. Also, PostgreSQL 6.5 did not recognize the standard BIT type used for the member table. If you plan to use PostgreSQL for this example, you have to change the type of the isField column of that table.

Example 17-3: MakeAPIDB.java

```
package com.davidflanagan.examples.sql;
import java.sql.*;
import java.lang.reflect.*;
import java.io.*;
import java.util.*;

/**
 * This class is a standalone program that reads a list of classes and
 * builds a database of packages, classes, and class fields and methods.
 **/
public class MakeAPIDB {
    public static void main(String args[]) {
        Connection c = null;        // The connection to the database
        try {
            // Read the classes to index from a file specified by args[0]
            ArrayList classnames = new ArrayList();
            BufferedReader in = new BufferedReader(new FileReader(args[0]));
            String name;
            while((name = in.readLine()) != null) classnames.add(name);

            // Now determine the values needed to set up the database
            // connection The program attempts to read a property file named
            // "APIDB.props", or optionally specified by args[1].  This
            // property file (if any) may contain "driver", "database", "user",
            // and "password" properties that specify the necessary values for
            // connecting to the db.  If the properties file does not exist, or
            // does not contain the named properties, defaults will be used.
            Properties p = new Properties();       // Empty properties
            try {
                p.load(new FileInputStream(args[1])); // Try to load properties
            }
            catch (Exception e1) {
                try { p.load(new FileInputStream("APIDB.props")); }
                catch (Exception e2) {}
            }

            // Read values from Properties file
            String driver = p.getProperty("driver");
            String database = p.getProperty("database");
            String user = p.getProperty("user", "");
            String password = p.getProperty("password", "");

            // The driver and database properties are mandatory
            if (driver == null)
                throw new IllegalArgumentException("No driver specified!");
            if (database == null)
                throw new IllegalArgumentException("No database specified!");

            // Load the driver.  It registers itself with DriverManager.
            Class.forName(driver);

            // And set up a connection to the specified database
            c = DriverManager.getConnection(database, user, password);

            // Create three new tables for our data
            // The package table contains a package id and a package name.
            // The class table contains a class id, a package id, and a name.
            // The member table contains a class id, a member name, and an bit
```

Example 17-3: MakeAPIDB.java (continued)

```java
            // that indicates whether the class member is a field or a method.
            Statement s = c.createStatement();
            s.executeUpdate("CREATE TABLE package " +
                            "(id INT, name VARCHAR(80))");
            s.executeUpdate("CREATE TABLE class " +
                            "(id INT, packageId INT, name VARCHAR(48))");
            s.executeUpdate("CREATE TABLE member " +
                            "(classId INT, name VARCHAR(48), isField BIT)");

            // Prepare some statements that will be used to insert records into
            // these three tables.
            insertpackage =
                c.prepareStatement("INSERT INTO package VALUES(?,?)");
            insertclass =
                c.prepareStatement("INSERT INTO class VALUES(?,?,?)");
            insertmember =
                c.prepareStatement("INSERT INTO member VALUES(?,?,?)");

            // Now loop through the list of classes and use reflection
            // to store them all in the tables
            int numclasses = classnames.size();
            for(int i = 0; i < numclasses; i++) {
                try {
                    storeClass((String)classnames.get(i));
                }
                catch(ClassNotFoundException e) {
                    System.out.println("WARNING: class not found: " +
                                        classnames.get(i) + "; SKIPPING");
                }
            }
        }
    catch (Exception e) {
        System.err.println(e);
        if (e instanceof SQLException)
            System.err.println("SQLState: " +
                                ((SQLException)e).getSQLState());
        System.err.println("Usage: java MakeAPIDB " +
                            "<classlistfile> <propfile>");
    }
    // When we're done, close the connection to the database
    finally { try { c.close(); } catch (Exception e) {} }
}

/**
 * This hash table records the mapping between package names and package
 * id.  This is the only one we need to store temporarily.  The others are
 * stored in the db and don't have to be looked up by this program
 **/
static Map package_to_id = new HashMap();

// Counters for the package and class identifier columns
static int packageId = 0, classId = 0;

// Some prepared SQL statements for use in inserting
// new values into the tables.  Initialized in main() above.
static PreparedStatement insertpackage, insertclass, insertmember;

/**
```

Example 17–3: MakeAPIDB.java (continued)

```
 * Given a fully qualified classname, this method stores the package name
 * in the package table (if it is not already there), stores the class name
 * in the class table, and then uses the Java Reflection API to look up all
 * methods and fields of the class, and stores those in the member table.
 **/
public static void storeClass(String name)
    throws SQLException, ClassNotFoundException
{
    String packagename, classname;

    // Dynamically load the class.
    Class c = Class.forName(name);

    // Display output so the user knows that the program is progressing
    System.out.println("Storing data for: " + name);

    // Figure out the packagename and the classname
    int pos = name.lastIndexOf('.');
    if (pos == -1) {
        packagename = "";
        classname = name;
    }
    else {
        packagename = name.substring(0,pos);
        classname = name.substring(pos+1);
    }

    // Figure out what the package id is.  If there is one, then this
    // package has already been stored in the database.  Otherwise, assign
    // an id, and store it and the packagename in the db.
    Integer pid;
    pid = (Integer)package_to_id.get(packagename);  // Check hashtable
    if (pid == null) {
        pid = new Integer(++packageId);          // Assign an id
        package_to_id.put(packagename, pid);     // Remember it
        insertpackage.setInt(1, packageId);      // Set statement args
        insertpackage.setString(2, packagename);
        insertpackage.executeUpdate();           // Insert into package db
    }

    // Now, store the classname in the class table of the database.
    // This record includes the package id, so that the class is linked to
    // the package that contains it.  To store the class, we set arguments
    // to the PreparedStatement, then execute that statement
    insertclass.setInt(1, ++classId);            // Set class identifier
    insertclass.setInt(2, pid.intValue());       // Set package identifier
    insertclass.setString(3, classname);         // Set class name
    insertclass.executeUpdate();                 // Insert the class record

    // Now, get a list of all non-private methods of the class, and
    // insert those into the "members" table of the database.  Each
    // record includes the class id of the containing class, and also
    // a value that indicates that these are methods, not fields.
    Method[] methods = c.getDeclaredMethods();   // Get a list of methods
    for(int i = 0; i < methods.length; i++) {    // For all non-private
        if (Modifier.isPrivate(methods[i].getModifiers())) continue;
        insertmember.setInt(1, classId);         // Set the class id
        insertmember.setString(2, methods[i].getName()); // Set method name
```

Database
Access

Example 17–3: MakeAPIDB.java (continued)

```
                insertmember.setBoolean(3, false);        // It is not a field
                insertmember.executeUpdate();             // Insert into db
        }

        // Do the same thing for the non-private fields of the class
        Field[] fields = c.getDeclaredFields();    // Get a list of fields
        for(int i = 0; i < fields.length; i++) {   // For each non-private
            if (Modifier.isPrivate(fields[i].getModifiers())) continue;
            insertmember.setInt(1, classId);       // Set the class id
            insertmember.setString(2, fields[i].getName()); // Set field name
            insertmember.setBoolean(3, true);      // It is a field
            insertmember.executeUpdate();          // Insert the record
        }
    }
}
```

Using the API Database

Example 17-4 displays a program, LookupAPI, that uses the database built by the MakeAPIDB program of Example 17-3. LookupAPI behaves as follows:

- When invoked with the name of a class member, it lists the full name (including package and class) of each field and/or method that has that name.

- When run with the name of a class, it lists the full name of every class in any package that has that name.

- When called with a portion of a package name, it lists the names of all the packages that contain that string.

- When invoked with the -l option and a class name, it lists every member of every class that has that name.

- When run with the -l option and a portion of a package name, it lists all the classes and interfaces in any package that matches that string.

LookupAPI reads the same *APIDB.props* property file MakeAPIDB does. Or, alternatively, it reads a property file specified on the command line following a -p flag. Using the database connection parameters in the property file, the program connects to a database and executes the necessary SQL queries to return the desired information. Note that it calls the setReadOnly() method of the Connection object. Doing this provides a hint that the program performs only queries and doesn't modify the database in any way. For some database systems, this may improve efficiency. Other than the setReadOnly() method, this example doesn't introduce any new JDBC features. It simply serves as a real-world application of a database and demonstrates some of the powerful database queries that can be expressed using SQL.

Example 17-4: LookupAPI.java

```
package com.davidflanagan.examples.sql;
import java.sql.*;
import java.io.FileInputStream;
import java.util.Properties;
```

Example 17-4: LookupAPI.java (continued)

```java
/**
 * This program uses the database created by MakeAPIDB.  It opens a connection
 * to a database using the same property file used by MakeAPIDB.  Then it
 * queries that database in several interesting ways to obtain useful
 * information about Java APIs.  It can be used to look up the fully qualified
 * name of a member, class, or package, or it can be used to list the members
 * of a class or package.
 **/
public class LookupAPI {
    public static void main(String[] args) {
        Connection c = null;              // JDBC connection to the database
        try {
            // Some default values
            String target = null;            // The name to look up
            boolean list = false;            // List members or lookup name?
            String propfile = "APIDB.props"; // The file of db parameters

            // Parse the command-line arguments
            for(int i = 0; i < args.length; i++) {
                if (args[i].equals("-l")) list = true;
                else if (args[i].equals("-p")) propfile = args[++i];
                else if (target != null)
                    throw new IllegalArgumentException("Unexpected argument: "
                                                      + args[i]);
                else target = args[i];
            }
            if (target == null)
                throw new IllegalArgumentException("No target specified");

            // Now determine the values needed to set up the database
            // connection The program attempts to read a property file
            // named "APIDB.props", or optionally specified with the
            // -p argument.  This property file may contain "driver",
            // "database", "user", and "password" properties that
            // specify the necessary values for connecting to the db.
            // If the properties file does not exist, or does not
            // contain the named properties, defaults will be used.
            Properties p = new Properties();             // Empty properties
            try { p.load(new FileInputStream(propfile)); } // Try to load props
            catch (Exception e) {}

            // Read values from Properties file
            String driver = p.getProperty("driver");
            String database = p.getProperty("database");
            String user = p.getProperty("user", "");
            String password = p.getProperty("password", "");

            // The driver and database properties are mandatory
            if (driver == null)
                throw new IllegalArgumentException("No driver specified!");
            if (database == null)
                throw new IllegalArgumentException("No database specified!");

            // Load the database driver
            Class.forName(driver);

            // And set up a connection to the specified database
            c = DriverManager.getConnection(database, user, password);
```

Example 17-4: LookupAPI.java (continued)

```
                // Tell it we will not do any updates.
                // This hint may improve efficiency.
                c.setReadOnly(true);

                // If the "-l" option was given, then list the members of
                // the named package or class.  Otherwise, lookup all
                // matches for the specified member, class, or package.
                if (list) list(c, target);
                else lookup(c, target);
            }
            // If anything goes wrong, print the exception and a usage message.  If
            // a SQLException is thrown, display the state message it includes.
            catch (Exception e) {
                System.out.println(e);
                if (e instanceof SQLException)
                    System.out.println(((SQLException) e).getSQLState());
                System.out.println("Usage: java LookupAPI [-l] [-p <propfile>] " +
                                   "target");
            }
            // Always close the DB connection when we're done with it.
            finally {
                try { c.close(); } catch (Exception e) {}
            }
    }


    /**
     * This method looks up all matches for the specified target string in the
     * database.  First, it prints the full name of any members by that name.
     * Then it prints the full name of any classes by that name.  Then it
     * prints the name of any packages that contain the specified name
     **/
    public static void lookup(Connection c, String target) throws SQLException
    {
        // Create the Statement object we'll use to query the database
        Statement s = c.createStatement();

        // Go find all class members with the specified name
        s.executeQuery("SELECT DISTINCT " +
                       "package.name, class.name, member.name, member.isField"+
                       " FROM package, class, member" +
                       " WHERE member.name='" + target + "'" +
                       "   AND member.classId=class.id " +
                       "   AND class.packageId=package.id");

        // Loop through the results, and print them out (if there are any).
        ResultSet r = s.getResultSet();
        while(r.next()) {
            String pkg = r.getString(1);       // package name
            String cls = r.getString(2);       // class name
            String member = r.getString(3);    // member name
            boolean isField = r.getBoolean(4); // is the member a field?
            // Display this match
            System.out.println(pkg + "." + cls + "." + member +
                               (isField?"":"()"));
        }

        // Now look for a class with the specified name
        s.executeQuery("SELECT package.name, class.name " +
```

Example 17-4: LookupAPI.java (continued)

```
                        "FROM package, class " +
                        "WHERE class.name='" + target + "' " +
                        "  AND class.packageId=package.id");
        // Loop through the results and print them out
        r = s.getResultSet();
        while(r.next()) System.out.println(r.getString(1) + "." +
                                            r.getString(2));

        // Finally, look for a package that matches a part of of the name.
        // Note the use of the SQL LIKE keyword and % wildcard characters
        s.executeQuery("SELECT name FROM package " +
                        "WHERE name='" + target + "' " +
                        "   OR name LIKE '%." + target + ".%' " +
                        "   OR name LIKE '" + target + ".%' " +
                        "   OR name LIKE '%." + target + "'");
        // Loop through the results and print them out
        r = s.getResultSet();
        while(r.next()) System.out.println(r.getString(1));

        // Finally, close the Statement object
        s.close();
    }

    /**
     * This method looks for classes with the specified name, or packages
     * that contain the specified name.  For each class it finds, it displays
     * all methods and fields of the class.  For each package it finds, it
     * displays all classes in the package.
     **/
    public static void list(Connection conn, String target) throws SQLException
    {
        // Create two Statement objects to query the database with
        Statement s = conn.createStatement();
        Statement t = conn.createStatement();

        // Look for a class with the given name
        s.executeQuery("SELECT package.name, class.name " +
                        "FROM package, class " +
                        "WHERE class.name='" + target + "' " +
                        "  AND class.packageId=package.id");
        // Loop through all matches
        ResultSet r = s.getResultSet();
        while(r.next()) {
            String p = r.getString(1);  // package name
            String c = r.getString(2);  // class name
            // Print out the matching class name
            System.out.println("class " + p + "." + c + " {");

            // Now query all members of the class
            t.executeQuery("SELECT DISTINCT member.name, member.isField " +
                        "FROM package, class, member " +
                        "WHERE package.name = '" + p + "' " +
                        "  AND class.name = '" + c + "' " +
                        "  AND member.classId=class.id " +
                        "  AND class.packageId=package.id " +
                        "ORDER BY member.isField, member.name");

            // Loop through the ordered list of all members, and print them out
```

Example 17–4: LookupAPI.java (continued)

```
                ResultSet r2 = t.getResultSet();
                while(r2.next()) {
                    String m = r2.getString(1);
                    int isField = r2.getInt(2);
                    System.out.println("   " + m + ((isField == 1)?"":"()"));
                }
                // End the class listing
                System.out.println("}");
            }


            // Now go look for a package that matches the specified name
            s.executeQuery("SELECT name FROM package " +
                        "WHERE name='" + target + "'" +
                        "   OR name LIKE '%." + target + ".%' " +
                        "   OR name LIKE '" + target + ".%' " +
                        "   OR name LIKE '%." + target + "'");
            // Loop through any matching packages
            r = s.getResultSet();
            while(r.next()) {
                // Display the name of the package
                String p = r.getString(1);
                System.out.println("Package " + p + ": ");

                // Get a list of all classes and interfaces in the package
                t.executeQuery("SELECT class.name FROM package, class " +
                            "WHERE package.name='" + p + "' " +
                            "   AND class.packageId=package.id " +
                            "ORDER BY class.name");
                // Loop through the list and print them out.
                ResultSet r2 = t.getResultSet();
                while(r2.next()) System.out.println("   " + r2.getString(1));
            }

            // Finally, close both Statement objects
            s.close(); t.close();
        }
    }
```

Atomic Transactions

By default, a newly created database Connection object is in auto-commit mode. That means that each update to the database is treated as a separate transaction and is automatically committed to the database. Sometimes, however, you want to group several updates into a single atomic transaction, with the property that either all the updates complete successfully or no updates occur at all. With a database system (and JDBC driver) that supports it, you can take the Connection out of auto-commit mode and explicitly call commit() to commit a batch of transactions or call rollback() to abort a batch of transactions, undoing the ones that have already been done.

Example 17-5 displays a class that uses atomic transactions to ensure database consistency. It is an implementation of the RemoteBank interface that was developed in Chapter 16, *Remote Method Invocation*. As you may recall, the Remote-BankServer class developed in that chapter didn't provide any form of persistent storage for its bank account data. Example 17-5 addresses this problem by implementing a RemoteBank that uses a database to store all user account information.

After the RemoteDBBankServer creates its Connection object, it calls setAutoCommit() with the argument false to turn off auto-commit mode. Then, for example, the openAccount() method groups three transactions into a single, atomic transaction: adding the account to the database, creating a table for the account history, and adding an initial entry into the history. If all three transactions are successful (i.e., they don't throw any exceptions), openAccount() calls commit() to commit the transactions to the database. However, if any one of the transactions throws an exception, the catch clause takes care of calling rollback() to roll back any transactions that succeeded. All remote methods in RemoteDBBankServer use this technique to keep the account database consistent.

In addition to demonstrating the techniques of atomic transaction processing, the RemoteDBBankServer class provides further examples of using SQL queries to interact with a database. In order to run this example, you need to create a properties file named *BankDB.props* with database connection information. Before you run the server for the first time, you also need to create an accounts table in the database. You can do this by using the ExecuteSQL program to execute this SQL statement:

```
CREATE TABLE accounts (name VARCHAR(20), password VARCHAR(20), balance INT);
```

Remember also that this is an RMI server. This means you must run the *rmic* compiler as described in Chapter 16 to generate stub and skeleton classes. You must also start the *rmiregistry* service before running this program.*

Example 17-5: RemoteDBBankServer.java

```java
package com.davidflanagan.examples.sql;
import java.rmi.*;
import java.rmi.server.*;
import java.rmi.registry.*;
import java.sql.*;
import java.io.*;
import java.util.*;
import java.util.Date; // import explicitly to disambiguate from java.sql.Date
import com.davidflanagan.examples.rmi.Bank.*;  // Import inner classes of Bank

/**
 * This class is another implementation of the RemoteBank interface.
 * It uses a database connection as its back end, so that client data isn't
 * lost if the server goes down.  Note that it takes the database connection
 * out of "auto commit" mode and explicitly calls commit() and rollback() to
 * ensure that updates happen atomically.
 **/
public class RemoteDBBankServer extends UnicastRemoteObject
    implements RemoteBank
{
    Connection db;    // The connection to the database that stores account info
```

---

* Also, note that versions of MySQL prior to 2.23.15 don't support transactions. If you are using one of these versions of MySQL, you may need to upgrade or switch to another database in order to run this example.

Example 17–5: RemoteDBBankServer.java (continued)

```java
/** The constructor.  Just save the database connection object away */
public RemoteDBBankServer(Connection db) throws RemoteException {
    this.db = db;
}

/** Open an account */
public synchronized void openAccount(String name, String password)
    throws RemoteException, BankingException
{
    // First, check if there is already an account with that name
    Statement s = null;
    try {
        s = db.createStatement();
        s.executeQuery("SELECT * FROM accounts WHERE name='" + name + "'");
        ResultSet r = s.getResultSet();
        if (r.next()) throw new BankingException("Account name in use.");

        // If it doesn't exist, go ahead and create it Also, create a
        // table for the transaction history of this account and insert an
        // initial transaction into it.
        s = db.createStatement();
        s.executeUpdate("INSERT INTO accounts VALUES ('" + name + "', '" +
                        password + "', 0)");
        s.executeUpdate("CREATE TABLE " + name +
                        "_history (msg VARCHAR(80))");
        s.executeUpdate("INSERT INTO " + name + "_history " +
                        "VALUES ('Account opened at " + new Date() + "')");

        // And if we've been successful so far, commit these updates,
        // ending the atomic transaction.  All the methods below also use
        // this atomic transaction commit/rollback scheme
        db.commit();
    }
    catch(SQLException e) {
        // If an exception was thrown, "rollback" the prior updates,
        // removing them from the database.  This also ends the atomic
        // transaction.
        try { db.rollback(); } catch (Exception e2) {}
        // Pass the SQLException on in the body of a BankingException
        throw new BankingException("SQLException: " + e.getMessage() +
                                   ": " + e.getSQLState());
    }
    // No matter what happens, don't forget to close the DB Statement
    finally { try { s.close(); } catch (Exception e) {} }
}

/**
 * This convenience method checks whether the name and password match
 * an existing account.  If so, it returns the balance in that account.
 * If not, it throws an exception.  Note that this method does not call
 * commit() or rollback(), so its query is part of a larger transaction.
 **/
public int verify(String name, String password)
    throws BankingException, SQLException
{
    Statement s = null;
    try {
        s = db.createStatement();
```

Example 17–5: RemoteDBBankServer.java (continued)

```
            s.executeQuery("SELECT balance FROM accounts " +
                        "WHERE name='" + name + "' " +
                        " AND password = '" + password + "'");
        ResultSet r = s.getResultSet();
        if (!r.next())
            throw new BankingException("Bad account name or password");
        return r.getInt(1);
    }
    finally { try { s.close(); } catch (Exception e) {} }
}

/** Close a named account */
public synchronized FunnyMoney closeAccount(String name, String password)
    throws RemoteException, BankingException
{
    int balance = 0;
    Statement s = null;
    try {
        balance = verify(name, password);
        s = db.createStatement();
        // Delete the account from the accounts table
        s.executeUpdate("DELETE FROM accounts " +
                        "WHERE name = '" + name + "' " +
                        " AND password = '" + password + "'");
        // And drop the transaction history table for this account
        s.executeUpdate("DROP TABLE " + name + "_history");
        db.commit();
    }
    catch (SQLException e) {
        try { db.rollback(); } catch (Exception e2) {}
        throw new BankingException("SQLException: " + e.getMessage() +
                                ": " + e.getSQLState());
    }
    finally { try { s.close(); } catch (Exception e) {} }

    // Finally, return whatever balance remained in the account
    return new FunnyMoney(balance);
}

/** Deposit the specified money into the named account */
public synchronized void deposit(String name, String password,
                        FunnyMoney money)
    throws RemoteException, BankingException
{
    int balance = 0;
    Statement s = null;
    try {
        balance = verify(name, password);
        s = db.createStatement();
        // Update the balance
        s.executeUpdate("UPDATE accounts " +
                        "SET balance = " + balance + money.amount + " " +
                        "WHERE name='" + name + "' " +
                        " AND password = '" + password + "'");
        // Add a row to the transaction history
        s.executeUpdate("INSERT INTO " + name + "_history " +
                        "VALUES ('Deposited " + money.amount +
                        " at " + new Date() + "')");
```

Example 17–5: RemoteDBBankServer.java (continued)

```
            db.commit();
        }
    catch (SQLException e) {
        try { db.rollback(); } catch (Exception e2) {}
        throw new BankingException("SQLException: " + e.getMessage() +
                                    ": " + e.getSQLState());
    }
    finally { try { s.close(); } catch (Exception e) {} }
}

/** Withdraw the specified amount from the named account */
public synchronized FunnyMoney withdraw(String name, String password,
                                        int amount)
    throws RemoteException, BankingException
{
    int balance = 0;
    Statement s = null;
    try {
        balance = verify(name, password);
        if (balance < amount)
            throw new BankingException("Insufficient Funds");
        s = db.createStatement();
        // Update the account balance
        s.executeUpdate("UPDATE accounts " +
                        "SET balance = " + (balance - amount) + " " +
                        "WHERE name='" + name + "' " +
                        "  AND password = '" + password + "'");
        // Add a row to the transaction history
        s.executeUpdate("INSERT INTO " + name + "_history " +
                        "VALUES ('Withdrew " + amount +
                        " at " + new Date() + "')");
        db.commit();
    }
    catch (SQLException e) {
        try { db.rollback(); } catch (Exception e2) {}
        throw new BankingException("SQLException: " + e.getMessage() +
                                    ": " + e.getSQLState());
    }
    finally { try { s.close(); } catch (Exception e) {} }

    return new FunnyMoney(amount);
}

/** Return the balance of the specified account */
public synchronized int getBalance(String name, String password)
    throws RemoteException, BankingException
{
    int balance;
    try {
        // Get the balance
        balance = verify(name, password);
        // Commit the transaction
        db.commit();
    }
    catch (SQLException e) {
        try { db.rollback(); } catch (Exception e2) {}
        throw new BankingException("SQLException: " + e.getMessage() +
                                    ": " + e.getSQLState());
```

Example 17–5: RemoteDBBankServer.java (continued)

```
        }
        // Return the balance
        return balance;
    }

    /** Get the transaction history of the named account */
    public synchronized List getTransactionHistory(String name,
                                                   String password)
        throws RemoteException, BankingException
    {
        Statement s = null;
        List list = new ArrayList();
        try {
            // Call verify to check the password, even though we don't
            // care what the current balance is.
            verify(name, password);
            s = db.createStatement();
            // Request everything out of the history table
            s.executeQuery("SELECT * from " + name + "_history");
            // Get the results of the query and put them in a Vector
            ResultSet r = s.getResultSet();
            while(r.next()) list.add(r.getString(1));
            // Commit the transaction
            db.commit();
        }
        catch (SQLException e) {
            try { db.rollback(); } catch (Exception e2) {}
            throw new BankingException("SQLException: " + e.getMessage() +
                                       ": " + e.getSQLState());
        }
        finally { try { s.close(); } catch (Exception e) {} }
        // Return the Vector of transaction history.
        return list;
    }

    /**
     * This main() method is the standalone program that figures out what
     * database to connect to with what driver, connects to the database,
     * creates a RemoteDBBankServer object, and registers it with the registry,
     * making it available for client use
     **/
    public static void main(String[] args) {
        try {
            // Create a new Properties object.  Attempt to initialize it from
            // the BankDB.props file or the file optionally specified on the
            // command line, ignoring errors.
            Properties p = new Properties();
            try { p.load(new FileInputStream(args[0])); }
            catch (Exception e) {
                try { p.load(new FileInputStream("BankDB.props")); }
                catch (Exception e2) {}
            }

            // The BankDB.props file (or file specified on the command line)
            // must contain properties "driver" and "database", and may
            // optionally contain properties "user" and "password".
            String driver = p.getProperty("driver");
            String database = p.getProperty("database");
```

Example 17–5: RemoteDBBankServer.java (continued)

```
                String user = p.getProperty("user", "");
                String password = p.getProperty("password", "");

                // Load the database driver class
                Class.forName(driver);

                // Connect to the database that stores our accounts
                Connection db = DriverManager.getConnection(database,
                                                      user, password);

                // Configure the database to allow multiple queries and updates
                // to be grouped into atomic transactions
                db.setAutoCommit(false);
                db.setTransactionIsolation(Connection.TRANSACTION_READ_COMMITTED);

                // Create a server object that uses our database connection
                RemoteDBBankServer bank = new RemoteDBBankServer(db);

                // Read a system property to figure out how to name this server.
                // Use "SecondRemote" as the default.
                String name = System.getProperty("bankname", "SecondRemote");

                // Register the server with the name
                Naming.rebind(name, bank);

                // And tell everyone that we're up and running.
                System.out.println(name + " is open and ready for customers.");
            }
        catch (Exception e) {
            System.err.println(e);
            if (e instanceof SQLException)
                System.err.println("SQL State: " +
                          ((SQLException)e).getSQLState());
            System.err.println("Usage: java [-Dbankname=<name>] " +
                      "com.davidflanagan.examples.sql.RemoteDBBankServer " +
                          "[<dbpropsfile>]");
            System.exit(1);
        }
      }
    }
}
```

Exercises

17-1. Before you begin using JDBC, you must first have a database server and a
      JDBC driver for it, and you must know how to administer the server in order
      to do such things as create new databases. If you are not already an experi-
      enced database programmer, learning to do all this is more difficult than
      actually programming with JDBC. For this first exercise, therefore, obtain
      and install a database server if you don't already have one. Obtain and
      install a JDBC driver for it. Read the documentation for both the server and
      the driver. Learn the basics of the SQL language, if you don't already know
      it, and make a note of what SQL subset or SQL extensions are supported by
      your server and JDBC driver.

17-2. Example 17-1 is a general-purpose SQL interpreter program that displays database query results in a rudimentary text-based table format. Modify the program so that it outputs query results using HTML table syntax, resulting in output suitable for display in a web browser. Test your program by issuing queries against some existing database.

17-3. If you are familiar with CGI programming, modify Example 17-1 again so that it can be used as a CGI script. Write an appropriate HTML frontend that communicates the user's SQL queries to the Java program on the backend and displays the HTML table output by your program.

17-4. Write a program to create a database table of all files and directories stored on your computer (or at least all files and directories beneath a specified directory). Each entry in the database table should include a filename, a size, a modification date, and a boolean value that indicates whether it is a file or a directory. Run this program to generate a database of files. Write a second program that allows a user to make useful queries against this database, such as "list all files larger than 1 megabyte that are older than 1 month," or "list all files with the extension *.java* that were modified today." Optionally, design and create a GUI that allows a user to issue this sort of complicated query without knowing SQL.

CHAPTER 18

Servlets and JSP

A *servlet* is a Java class that implements the `javax.servlet.Servlet` interface, or, more commonly, extends the abstract `javax.servlet.http.HttpServlet` class. Servlets, and the Java Servlet API, are an extension architecture for web servers.* Instead of serving only static web pages, a servlet-enabled web server can invoke servlet methods to dynamically generate content at runtime. This model offers a number of advantages over traditional CGI scripts. Notably, servlet instances can persist across client requests, so the server is not constantly spawning external processes.

JSP stands for JavaServer Pages; it is an architecture built on top of the Servlet API. A JSP page contains HTML output intermingled with Java source code, special JSP tags, and tags from imported "tag libraries." A JSP-enabled web server compiles JSP pages on the fly, turning JSP source into servlets that produce dynamic output.

This chapter includes examples of both servlets and JSP pages and concludes with an example that shows how servlets and JSP pages can be integrated into an easy-to-deploy web application. It begins, however, by describing the prerequisites for compiling, deploying, running, and serving servlets. For more detailed information about servlets, see O'Reilly & Associates' *Java Servlet Programming*, by Jason Hunter with William Crawford. O'Reilly also has a forthcoming book, *JavaServer Pages*, by Hans Bergsten, that will provide much more detail than is possible in this chapter.

Servlet Setup

In order to run the examples in this chapter, you need the following:

---

* The `javax.servlet` package can actually be used with any type of server that implements a request/ response protocol. Web servers are currently the only common usage of servlets, however, and this chapter discusses servlets in that context only.

- A web server to host the examples.

- A *servlet container*, or *servlet engine*, which the web server uses to run the servlets. In order to run the JSP examples, your servlet container must also support JSP pages.

- The class files for the Servlet API, so you can compile the examples.

- A *deployment descriptor* that tells your servlet container how to map URLs to servlet classes.

This list looks more daunting than it actually is, as you'll see in the sections that follow.

The Servlet Container

Just as there are many web servers available, there are numerous servlet containers to choose from. I use and recommend Tomcat, an open-source product of the Jakarta project. Jakarta is itself a project of the Apache Software Foundation, the organization that produces the open-source Apache web server. Tomcat has benefited from substantial contributions by Sun; it is the successor to Sun's Java Servlet Development Kit, which makes it the reference implementation for Version 2.2 of the Servlet API. The core of Tomcat is a servlet and JSP container that can be used with the Apache web server, as well as various commercial web servers. For servlet development, however, Tomcat also includes a simple, pure-Java web server you can run on your local machine.

If you choose to use Tomcat, you can download it from *http://jakarta.apache.org*. As of this writing, the current version of Tomcat is 3.1. That will probably change by the time you read this chapter, however, so be sure to download the latest version and read the installation and configuration directions that come with Tomcat.

To install Tomcat, you simply unzip the archive file you downloaded. To run Tomcat, simply change to the directory you installed it in and type a command like the following:

```
% bin/tomcat.sh run      # Unix/Linux
C:\> bin\tomcat.bat run   # Windows
```

By default, the Tomcat web server listens on port 8080, so once you have started Tomcat, point your web browser at *http://localhost:8080/* or *http://127.0.0.1:8080/*. If everything is working correctly, you should see an introductory page with information about Tomcat. Of course, you should read the instructions that come with your version for full details.

If you've already got a working web server and servlet container, go ahead and use it (after you've read the documentation carefully). Note, however, that the examples in this chapter are written to the Servlets 2.2 and JSP 1.1 specifications. If your servlet container does not support these versions of the specifications, some of the examples may not work.

Compiling Servlets

Your servlet container should come with a JAR file that contains the class files for the Servlet API. It will probably be in a file named *lib/servlets.jar*. You need this JAR file to be able to compile the classes in this chapter. Either edit your CLASS-PATH environment variable to include the file or place a copy of the file in the *lib/jre/ext/* directory of your Java SDK, where the Java VM can find it automatically. Once you have done this, you can compile servlet classes with *javac*, just as you would compile other Java classes. If you cannot find the Servlet API classes in your servlet container distribution, you should be able to download them from Sun's web site (*http://java.sun.com/products/servlet/*). Be careful to download a version that matches the specifications supported by your servlet container.

Installing and Running Servlets

Once you've compiled a servlet, you need to place the resulting class file (or files) where the web server can find them. In general, this is a server-specific deployment task, so you should read the documentation that comes with your servlet container to figure out how to do it.

Fortunately, however, Version 2.2 of the Servlet API has introduced the concept of a *web application*—a set of one or more cooperating servlets, along with all the auxiliary files they require—and standardized the techniques for deploying the servlets that comprise a web application. Every web application includes a file named *WEB-INF/web.xml* that provides all the necessary servlet deployment details. Web applications may be packaged into WAR archives using the JAR archive format. We'll discuss WAR archives and the *web.xml* file at the end of this chapter.

The online version of the examples for this chapter includes a prepackaged WAR file. If you are using Tomcat or another 2.2-compliant servlet container, you can deploy all the examples in this chapter simply by placing the WAR file at the location specified by your container's documentation. For Tomcat 3.1, you simply drop the WAR file into the *webapps/* directory and restart Tomcat. (When Tomcat 3.1 encounters a new web application deployed in a WAR archive, the first thing it does is extract all the files from the archive and store them in a subdirectory of the *webapps/* directory. This is convenient because it allows you to start with the prepackaged *javaexamples2.war* archive, and easily modify, recompile, and redeploy the examples without recreating the WAR file.)

With WAR archives, the name of the WAR file is used as a URL prefix for all the servlets and other files in the archive. For example, suppose you deploy the *javaexamples2.war* archive in Tomcat's *webapps/* directory. If the WAR archive contains a file named *index.html* at the root level, the URL for this file is:

```
http://localhost:8080/javaexamples2/index.html
```

Servlet URLs are similar. The *web.xml* file defines a mapping of servlet names to the names of the classes that implement them. For example, the *web.xml* file in *javaexamples2.war* contains a mapping from the name hello to the class `com.davidflanagan.examples.servlet.Hello.` To run this servlet, you simply point your browser at:

```
http://localhost:8080/javaexamples2/servlet/hello
```

When the Tomcat servlet container is told to run this servlet, it knows to look for the class in the WAR archive using the filename:

```
WEB-INF/classes/com/davidflanagan/examples/servlet/Hello.class
```

A Hello World Servlet

Example 18-1 is a listing of *Hello.java*, which implements a simple "Hello world" servlet, illustrated in Figure 18-1. The `Hello` servlet inherits from `javax.servlet.http.HttpServlet` and overrides the `doGet()` method to provide output in response to an HTTP GET request. It also overrides the `doPost()` method, so it can respond to POST requests in the same way. The `doGet()` method outputs a string of HTML text. By default, this string is "Hello World".

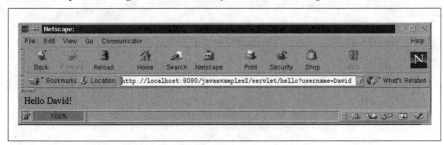

Figure 18–1. The output of the Hello servlet

If the `Hello` servlet can determine a username, however, it greets the user by name. The servlet looks for a username in two places, starting in the HTTP request (an `HttpServletRequest` object), as the value of a parameter named `username`. If the servlet cannot find a request parameter with this name, it looks for an `HttpSession` object associated with the request and sees if that object has an attribute named `username`. Servlet-enabled web servers (i.e., servlet containers) provide a session-tracking layer on top of the stateless HTTP protocol. The `HttpSession` object allows a servlet to set and query named attributes with a single client session. Later in the chapter, we'll see an example that takes advantage of the session-tracking ability of this `Hello` servlet.

Example 18–1: Hello.java

```
package com.davidflanagan.examples.servlet;
import javax.servlet.*;          // Basic servlet classes and interfaces
import javax.servlet.http.*;     // HTTP specific servlet stuff
import java.io.*;                // Servlets do IO and throw IOExceptions

/**
 * This simple servlet greets the user.  It looks in the request and session
 * objects in an attempt to greet the user by name.
 **/
public class Hello extends HttpServlet {
```

Example 18–1: Hello.java (continued)

```
    // This method is invoked when the servlet is the subject of an HTTP GET
    public void doGet(HttpServletRequest request, HttpServletResponse response)
        throws IOException
    {
        // See if the username is specified in the request
        String name = request.getParameter("username");

        // If not, look in the session object.  The web server or servlet
        // container performs session tracking automatically for the servlet,
        // and associates a HttpSession object with each session.
        if (name == null)
            name = (String)request.getSession().getAttribute("username");

        // If the username is not found in either place, use a default name.
        if (name == null) name = "World";

        // Specify the type of output we produce.  If this servlet is
        // included from within another servlet or JSP page, this setting
        // will be ignored.
        response.setContentType("text/html");

        // Get an stream that we can write the output to
        PrintWriter out = response.getWriter();

        // And, finally, do our output.
        out.println("Hello " + name + "!");
    }

    // This method is invoked when the servlet is the subject of an HTTP POST.
    // It calls the doGet() method so that this servlet works correctly
    // with either type of request.
    public void doPost(HttpServletRequest request,HttpServletResponse response)
        throws IOException
    {
        doGet(request, response);
    }
}
```

Running the Hello Servlet

Before you can run this servlet, you must compile and deploy it as described at the beginning of the chapter. To run a servlet, issue a request for it with a web browser. The URL you use depends on where the web server is running and how you deployed the servlet. If you are running Tomcat (or another 2.2-compliant servlet container) on your local machine, if the web server is listening on port 8080, and if you deploy the servlet as part of a web application named javaexamples2, you can run the servlet by pointing your browser at:

```
http://localhost:8080/javaexamples2/servlet/hello
```

This should display a web page that reads "Hello World". For slightly more sophisticated output, provide a request parameter with a URL like the following (which was used to produce the output in Figure 18-1):

```
http://localhost:8080/javaexamples2/servlet/hello?username=David
```

Servlet Initialization and Persistence: A Counter Servlet

Example 18-2 is a listing of *Counter.java*, a servlet that maintains any number of named counters. Each time the value of one of these counters is requested, the servlet increments the counter and outputs its new value. The servlet is suitable for use as a simple hit counter for multiple web pages but can also count any other type of event.

This servlet defines `init()` and `destroy()` methods and saves its state to a file, so it does not lose count when the web server (or servlet container) shuts down. To understand `init()` and `destroy()`, you have to understand something about the servlet life cycle. Servlet instances are not usually created anew for each client request. Instead, once a servlet is created, it can serve many requests before it is destroyed. A servlet such as `Counter` is typically not shut down unless the servlet container itself is shutting down, or the servlet is inactive and the container is trying to free up memory to make room for other servlets.

The `init()` method is invoked when the servlet container first instantiates the servlet, before any requests are serviced. The first thing this method does is look up the value of two *initialization parameters*: the filename of the file that contains the saved state and an integer value that specifies how often to save the state back into that file. Once the `init()` method has read these parameters, it reads the counts (using object serialization) from the specified file and is ready to begin serving requests. The values of the initialization parameters come from the *WEB-INF/web.xml* deployment file. Before running this example, you probably need to to edit that file to tell the servlet where to save its state. Look for these lines:

```
<init-param>
  <param-name>countfile</param-name>        <!-- where to save state -->
  <param-value>/tmp/counts.ser</param-value> <!-- adjust for your system-->
</init-param>
```

If the filename */tmp/counts.ser* does not make sense on your system, replace it with a filename that does.

The `destroy()` method is the companion to `init()`; it is invoked after the servlet has been taken out of service and there are no more requests being processed by the servlet. The `Counter` servlet uses this method to save its state, so it can be correctly restored when the servlet container starts the servlet up again. Note, however, that the `destroy()` method is invoked only when the servlet is shut down in a controlled way. In the case of a server crash or power outage, for example, there is no opportunity to save state. Thus, the `Counter` servlet also periodically saves it state from the `doGet()` method, so it never loses more than a small amount of data.

The `doGet()` method must first determine the name of the counter whose value is to be displayed. Since the `Counter` servlet is designed for use in a variety of ways, `doGet()` uses three techniques for obtaining the counter name. First, it checks for a parameter sent with the HTTP request. Next, it checks for a request attribute, which is a named value associated with the request by the servlet container or by another servlet that has invoked the `Counter` servlet. (You'll see an example of this later in the chapter.) Finally, if the servlet cannot find a counter name using either of these techniques, it uses the URL through which it was invoked as the counter name. As you'll see shortly, the servlet container can be configured to invoke the servlet in response to any URL that ends with the suffix *.count*.

Note that the doGet() method contains a synchronized block of code. The Servlet API allows multiple threads to execute the body of doGet() at the same time. Even though many threads representing many different user sessions may be running, they all share a single data structure—the hashtable of named counts. The synchronized block prevents the threads from accessing (and possibly corrupting) the shared data structure at the same time. Finally, note the use of the log() method. When asked to start counting with a counter name it has never used before, the servlet uses this method to produce a permanent record of the event in a log file.

Example 18-2: Counter.java

```
package com.davidflanagan.examples.servlet;
import javax.servlet.*;
import javax.servlet.http.*;
import java.io.*;
import java.util.*;

/**
 * This servlet maintains an arbitrary set of counter variables and increments
 * and displays the value of one named counter each time it is invoked.  It
 * saves the state of the counters to a disk file, so the counts are not lost
 * when the server shuts down.  It is suitable for counting page hits, or any
 * other type of event.  It is not typically invoked directly, but is included
 * within other pages, using JSP, SSI, or a RequestDispatcher
 **/
public class Counter extends HttpServlet {
    HashMap counts;        // A hash table: maps counter names to counts
    File countfile;        // The file that counts are saved in
    long saveInterval;     // How often (in ms) to save our state while running?
    long lastSaveTime;     // When did we last save our state?

    // This method is called when the web server first instantiates this
    // servlet.  It reads initialization parameters (which are configured
    // at deployment time in the web.xml file), and loads the initial state
    // of the counter variables from a file.
    public void init() throws ServletException {
        ServletConfig config = getServletConfig();
        try {
            // Get the save file.
            countfile = new File(config.getInitParameter("countfile"));
            // How often should we save our state while running?
            saveInterval =
                Integer.parseInt(config.getInitParameter("saveInterval"));
            // The state couldn't have changed before now.
            lastSaveTime = System.currentTimeMillis();
            // Now read in the count data
            loadState();
        }
        catch(Exception e) {
            // If something goes wrong, wrap the exception and rethrow it
            throw new ServletException("Can't init Counter servlet: " +
                                        e.getMessage(), e);
        }
```

Example 18–2: Counter.java (continued)

```
}

    // This method is called when the web server stops the servlet (which
    // happens when the web server is shutting down, or when the servlet is
    // not in active use.)  This method saves the counts to a file so they
    // can be restored when the servlet is restarted.
    public void destroy() {
        try { saveState(); }  // Try to save the state
        catch(Exception e) {} // Ignore any problems: we did the best we could
    }

    // These constants define the request parameter and attribute names that
    // the servlet uses to find the name of the counter to increment.
    public static final String PARAMETER_NAME = "counter";
    public static final String ATTRIBUTE_NAME =
        "com.davidflanagan.examples.servlet.Counter.counter";

    /**
     * This method is called when the servlet is invoked.  It looks for a
     * request parameter named "counter", and uses its value as the name of
     * the counter variable to increment.  If it doesn't find the request
     * parameter, then it uses the URL of the request as the name of the
     * counter.  This is useful when the servlet is mapped to a URL suffix.
     * This method also checks how much time has elapsed since it last saved
     * its state, and saves the state again if necessary.  This prevents it
     * from losing too much data if the server crashes or shuts down without
     * calling the destroy() method.
     **/
    public void doGet(HttpServletRequest request, HttpServletResponse response)
        throws IOException
    {
        // Get the name of the counter as a request parameter
        String counterName = request.getParameter(PARAMETER_NAME);

        // If we didn't find it there, see if it was passed to us as a
        // request attribute, which happens when the output of this servlet
        // is included by another servlet
        if (counterName == null)
            counterName = (String) request.getAttribute(ATTRIBUTE_NAME);

        // If it wasn't a parameter or attribute, use the request URL.
        if (counterName == null) counterName = request.getRequestURI();

        Integer count;  // What is the current count?

        // This block of code is synchronized because multiple requests may
        // be running at the same time in different threads.  Synchronization
        // prevents them from updating the counts hashtable at the same time
        synchronized(counts) {
            // Get the counter value from the hashtable
            count = (Integer)counts.get(counterName);

            // Increment the counter, or if it is new, log and start it at 1
            if (count != null) count = new Integer(count.intValue() + 1);
            else {
                // If this is a counter we haven't used before, send a message
                // to the log file, just so we can track what we're counting
                log("Starting new counter: " + counterName);
```

Example 18-2: Counter.java (continued)

```
                    // Start counting at 1!
                    count = new Integer(1);
            }

            // Store the incremented (or new) counter value into the hashtable
            counts.put(counterName, count);

            // Check whether saveInterval milliseconds have elapsed since we
            // last saved our state.  If so, save it again.  This prevents
            // us from losing more than saveInterval ms of data, even if the
            // server crashes unexpectedly.
            if (System.currentTimeMillis() - lastSaveTime > saveInterval) {
                saveState();
                lastSaveTime = System.currentTimeMillis();
            }
        } // End of synchronized block

        // Finally, output the counter value.  Since this servlet is usually
        // included within the output of other servlets, we don't bother
        // setting the content type.
        PrintWriter out = response.getWriter();
        out.print(count);
    }

    // The doPost method just calls doGet, so that this servlet can be
    // included in pages that are loaded with POST requests
    public void doPost(HttpServletRequest request,HttpServletResponse response)
        throws IOException
    {
        doGet(request, response);
    }

    // Save the state of the counters by serializing the hashtable to
    // the file specified by the initialization parameter.
    void saveState() throws IOException {
        ObjectOutputStream out = new ObjectOutputStream(
                    new BufferedOutputStream(new FileOutputStream(countfile)));
        out.writeObject(counts);  // Save the hashtable to the stream
        out.close();              // Always remember to close your files!
    }

    // Load the initial state of the counters by de-serializing a hashtable
    // from the file specified by the initialization parameter.  If the file
    // doesn't exist yet, then start with an empty hashtable.
    void loadState() throws IOException {
        if (!countfile.exists()) {
            counts = new HashMap();
            return;
        }
        ObjectInputStream in = null;
        try {
            in = new ObjectInputStream(
                    new BufferedInputStream(new FileInputStream(countfile)));
            counts = (HashMap) in.readObject();
        }
        catch(ClassNotFoundException e) {
            throw new IOException("Count file contains bad data: " +
                                e.getMessage());
```

Example 18-2: Counter.java (continued)

```
        }
        finally {
            try { in.close(); }
            catch (Exception e) {}
        }
    }
}
```

Running the Counter Servlet

Our *web.xml* file assigns the name `counter` to the `Counter` servlet. The servlet reads a request parameter also named `counter` to find the name of the counter variable to increment and display. Thus, you can test the servlet by pointing your browser to a URL like the following:

```
http://localhost:8080/javaexamples2/servlet/counter?counter=numhits
```

The *web.xml* file also specifies that the `Counter` servlet should be invoked whenever a file ending with the suffix *.count* (and beginning with the web application name) is requested from the web server. (You'll learn how the *web.xml* file specifies this later in the chapter.) In this case, `Counter` uses the URL itself as the name of the counter variable. Test this feature by entering a URL like the following:

```
http://localhost:8080/javaexamples2/index.html.count
```

By now, you've probably noticed that the `Counter` servlet doesn't produce very interesting output: it just displays a number. This servlet is not very useful when used on its own; it is intended, instead, to have its output included within the output of other servlets. (We'll explore a couple of ways to do this later in the chapter.) If your web server supports server-side includes (SSI) and the `<servlet>` tag, though, you can use this feature to include the output of the `Counter` servlet in web pages. (Tomcat does not support the SSI feature, probably because JSP technology makes SSI largely redundant and unnecessary.) To do so, you might create a *test.shtml* file that contains text like the following:

```
<p>This page has been accessed
  <servlet name='/servlet/counter'>
    <param name='counter' value='test.shtml'></param>
  </servlet>
times.
```

Database Access with Servlets

One common use of servlets (and web applications in general) is to provide a middle-tier of software that sits between the client and backend database servers. Thus, servlets often use the JDBC API to communicate with database servers. Example 18-3 is a listing of *Query.java*, a servlet that accepts a user-entered SQL query (using an HTML form), executes that query (using JDBC), and then displays the results of the query (using an HTML table). Figure 18-2 shows sample output from the servlet.

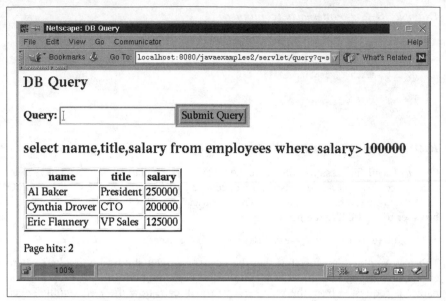

Figure 18–2. The output of the Query servlet

The code for this example is pretty straightforward. The init() method reads initialization parameters that specify the JDBC driver to use, the database to connect to, and the username and password to use when connecting. init() uses this information to establish a database connection that persists for the lifetime of the servlet; the connection is closed in the destroy() method. Creating a persistent connection means you don't have the overhead of establishing and closing a connection for each servlet request. It does assume, however, that the JDBC driver you use is thread-safe, and it only works if you limit yourself to database queries and simple updates that do not require transactions. If you need to work with transactions, you can synchronize the doGet() method to ensure that the servlet runs only one request at a time. Or, if you have a high-traffic web site, you can use a technique known as *connection pooling* to create connections in advance and distribute them to request threads as needed. This and related techniques are well explained in *Java Servlet Programming*.

The doGet() method uses standard JDBC code (see Chapter 17, *Database Access with SQL*) to send a SQL query to the database server and output the results in the form of an HTML table. (See an HTML reference such as O'Reilly's *HTML: The Definitive Guide*, by Chuck Musciano and Bill Kennedy, if you're not familiar with <table> and related HTML tags.) doGet() also displays the form that allows the user to enter the SQL query. When the user submits the form, the browser reloads the servlet, passing the user's SQL query as a request parameter. Including both form generation and form-processing code in the same servlet is a common and useful servlet programming technique.

Finally, note that the doGet() method uses a RequestDispatcher() object to invoke the Counter servlet and include the output of that servlet in its own output. doGet() uses setAttribute() to specify the counter name as a request attribute. The Counter servlet contains the corresponding call to getAttribute().

Example 18-3: Query.java

```java
package com.davidflanagan.examples.servlet;
import javax.servlet.*;
import javax.servlet.http.*;
import java.sql.*;
import java.io.*;

/**
 * This class demonstrates how JDBC can be used within a servlet.  It uses
 * initialization parameters (which come from the web.xml configuration file)
 * to create a single JDBC database connection, which is shared by all clients
 * of the servlet.
 ***/
public class Query extends HttpServlet {
    Connection db;  // This is the shared JDBC database connection

    public void init() throws ServletException {
        // Read initialization parameters from the web.xml file
        ServletConfig config = getServletConfig();
        String driverClassName = config.getInitParameter("driverClassName");
        String url = config.getInitParameter("url");
        String username = config.getInitParameter("username");
        String password = config.getInitParameter("password");

        // Use those init params to establish a connection to the database
        // If anything goes wrong, log it, wrap the exception and re-throw it
        try {
            Class.forName(driverClassName);
            db = DriverManager.getConnection(url, username, password);
        }
        catch (Exception e) {
            log("Can't create DB connection", e);
            throw new ServletException("Query: can't initialize: " +
                                       e.getMessage(), e);
        }
    }

    /** Close the database connection when the servlet is unloaded  */
    public void destroy() {
        try { db.close(); }        // Try to close the connection
        catch (SQLException e) {}  // Ignore errors; at least we tried!
    }

    public void doGet(HttpServletRequest request, HttpServletResponse response)
        throws IOException, ServletException
    {
        response.setContentType("text/html");    // We're outputting HTML
        PrintWriter out = response.getWriter();  // Where to output it to

        // Output document header and a form for entering SQL queries
        // When the form is submitted, this servlet is reloaded
        out.println("<head><title>DB Query</title></head>\n" +
                    "<body bgcolor=white><h1>DB Query</h1>\n" +
                    "<form><b>Query: </b><input name='q'>" +
                    "<input type=submit></form>");

        // See if a query was specified in this request.
        String query = request.getParameter("q");
        if (query != null) {
```

Example 18–3: Query.java (continued)

```
                    // display the query text as a page heading
                    out.println("<h1>" + query + "</h1>");

                    // Now try to execute the query and display the results in a table
                    Statement statement = null;  // An object to execute the query
                    try {
                        // Create a statement to use
                        statement = db.createStatement();
                        // Use it to execute the specified query, and get result set
                        ResultSet results = statement.executeQuery(query);
                        // Ask for extra information about the results
                        ResultSetMetaData metadata = results.getMetaData();
                        // How many columns are there in the results?
                        int numcols = metadata.getColumnCount();

                        // Begin a table, and output a header row of column names
                        out.println("<table border=2><tr>");
                        for(int i = 0; i < numcols; i++)
                            out.print("<th>" + metadata.getColumnLabel(i+1) + "</th>");
                        out.println("</tr>");

                        // Now loop through the "rows" of the result set
                        while(results.next()) {
                            // For each row, display the the values for each column
                            out.print("<tr>");
                            for(int i = 0; i < numcols; i++)
                                out.print("<td>" + results.getObject(i+1) + "</td>");
                            out.println("</tr>");
                        }
                        out.println("</table>");  // end the table

                    }
                    catch (SQLException e) {
                        // If anything goes wrong (usually a SQL error) display the
                        // error to the user so they can correct it.
                        out.println("SQL Error: " + e.getMessage());
                    }
                    finally { // Whatever happens, always close the Statement object
                        try { statement.close(); }
                        catch(Exception e) {}
                    }
                }

                // Now, display the number of hits on this page by invoking the
                // Counter servlet and including its output in this page.
                // This is done with a RequestDispatcher object.
                RequestDispatcher dispatcher =
                    request.getRequestDispatcher("/servlet/counter");
                if (dispatcher != null) {
                    out.println("<br>Page hits:");
                    // Add a request attribute that tells the servlet what to count.
                    // Use the attribute name defined by the Counter servlet, and
                    // use the name of this class as a unique counter name.
                    request.setAttribute(Counter.ATTRIBUTE_NAME,Query.class.getName());
                    // Tell the dispatcher to invoke its servlet and include the output
                    dispatcher.include(request, response);
                }
```

Example 18-3: Query.java (continued)

```
        // Finally, end the HTML output
        out.println("</body>");
    }
}
```

Running the Query Servlet

To run the Query servlet yourself, you have to edit the *WEB-INF/web.xml* file to set values for the various initialization parameters that tell it what JDBC driver to use, what database to connect to, and so on. Your servlet container must also be able to find the JDBC driver classes. You should be able to ensure this by placing a JAR file of driver classes in the *WEB-INF/lib/* directory of the web application, but, unfortunately, Tomcat 3.1 cannot find database driver classes in the *lib/* directory. (It can find servlet classes stored there, however, so this bug probably has something to do with the way the database driver is loaded using `Class.forName()`.) In any case, the solution is to place your JDBC driver JAR file in your CLASSPATH before starting Tomcat.

A Login Screen with JSP

Take another quick look at the `doGet()` method shown in Example 18-3; it contains a number of `println()` method calls that output HTML tags. One of the problems with servlets of this type is that they include hardcoded HTML tags locked inside Java classes where web designers and graphic artists cannot get at them. JavaServer Pages, or JSP, is an attempt to correct this situation. Instead of embedding HTML tags within Java code, JSP pages embed Java code within HTML pages.

Example 18-4 is a listing of the JSP page *login.jsp*. This page displays the login screen pictured in Figure 18-3 and performs trivial (and insecure) password verification before redirecting the user's browser to some other page (specified via a request parameter).

The first thing you'll notice about this JSP example is that it contains a lot of HTML-style tags that begin with <% and end with %>. These are JSP tags. The following table summarizes the types of JSP tags and their purposes:*

Tag	Purpose
<%- - . . . . - -%>	A JSP comment. Unlike HTML comments, JSP comments are stripped during the JSP compilation process and never appear in the output page.

---

* Note that I make no attempt here to document the complete JSP syntax. Consult a JSP reference, such as the O'Reilly's soon-to-be-published *JavaServer Pages*, for that purpose. You can also find documentation and tutorial information on Sun's web site (*http://java.sun.com/products/jsp*). One particularly useful item is a "JSP Syntax Reference Card" at *http://java.sun.com/products/jsp/pdf/card11a.pdf*.

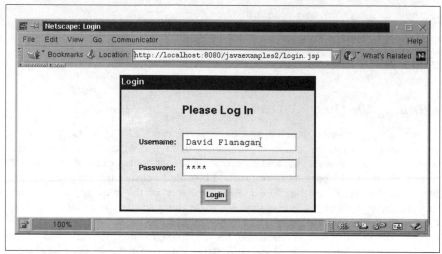

Figure 18-3. The output of login.jsp

Tag	Purpose
`<@page . . . %>`	The page directive. Every JSP page must have one. Common attributes specify the page language, the content type of the output, the page buffer size, and the list of packages to import.
`<%@include file="URL"%>`	Includes the specified file at compilation time.
`<%@taglib uri="taglibId"prefix="tagPrefix"%>`	Declares a tag library for the page. The `uri` attribute uniquely identifies the library, and the `prefix` attribute specifies the prefix by which it is known on the page.
`<%! . . . %>`	A declaration tag. These delimiters surround Java code that becomes methods and fields of the resulting servlet class.
`<%= . . . %>`	An expression tag. Contains a Java expression. The tag is replaced with the expression value at runtime.
`<% . . . %>`	A *scriptlet*. These delimiters surround Java code that becomes part of the `_jspService()` method, which is the JSP version of `goGet()` and `doPost()`.

You may also notice that the Java scriptlets and expressions in Example 18-4 use several local variables that are automatically declared by the JSP system. The following table shows available variables:

Name	Type
request	`javax.servlet.http.HttpServletRequest`
response	`javax.servlet.http.HttpServletResponse`
session	`javax.servlet.http.HttpSession`
config	`javax.servlet.ServletConfig`
application	`javax.servlet.ServletContext`
out	`javax.servlet.jsp.JspWriter`

Example 18-4 begins with @page and @taglib directives. These are followed by a declaration tag, which defines a simple password verification method.* The declaration is followed by a scriptlet tag, which includes Java code that runs each time the JSP page is requested. This code gets the login name and password from a previous form submission (unless this is the first time the page is requested) and attempts to verify the username and password. If the verification is successful, the scriptlet stores the username in the servlet's session object and sends a redirect to the user's browser, causing it to load whatever page was specified by the nextpage request parameter.

If password verification is not successful, the scriptlet tag ends and a block of HTML text follows. The HTML text creates the login form that allows the user to enter a name and a password. The HTML tags are interspersed occasionally with <%= . . . %> tags that contain Java expressions whose values are substituted into the HTML output. The HTML code also contains the custom <decor:box> and </decor:box> tags. This is an invocation of the box tag from the decor library imported at the top of the page by the <%@taglib . . . %> directive. This custom tag creates the bordered and titled box that appears in Figure 18-3. Later in the chapter (in Example 18-9), you'll see how this tag is implemented and made available to JSP pages. Note that JSP pages can also use a variety of tags with the jsp: prefix. No @taglib directive is required to use these tags. This example does not use them, but the next two examples do.

Example 18–4: login.jsp

```
<%--login.jsp
   The next two lines are JSP directives.  The page directive tells the JSP
   compiler that this page contains Java (instead of JavaScript e.g.) code and
   outputs HTML (instead of XML, e.g.). The second directive tells the JSP
   compiler that this page uses a "tag library" with the specified unique
   identifier and whose tags are prefixed (on this page) by the word "decor".
--%>
<%@page language='java' contentType='text/html'%>
<%@taglib uri='http://www.davidflanagan.com/tlds/decor_0_1.tld'
          prefix='decor'%>

<%--
   The code below is in a <%!...%> declaration block.  When this JSP page
   is compiled to a servlet, this code is used to define members of the
   Servlet class.
--%>
```

---

* This verify() method is included here to demonstrate how Java methods can be included in JSP pages. In production code, this method should be placed in an external class, independent of the page.

Example 18–4: login.jsp (continued)

```
<%! // Begin declaration block

// This method does very simple password verification. In a real application,
// this method would probably check a database of passwords.
public boolean verify(String username, String password) {
    // Accept any username as long as the password is "java"
    return ((username!=null) && (password!=null) && password.equals("java"));
}

%> <%-- End declaration block --%>

<%--
  The next block of code is between <% and %>, which mark it as a "scriptlet".
  When the JSP page is compiled, this code becomes part of the service()
  method of the servlet.  Scriptlet blocks are intermixed with HTML tags which
  are also compiled into the service() method and are output literally by the
  servlet.  Notice how this scriptlet ends in the middle of an else block.
  The HTML tags that follow it form part of the else{} block, and the block is
  closed in a scriptlet that comes later in the file.
--%>

<% // Begin scriptlet
// This request parameter is required.  It specifies what should be
// displayed if the login attempt is successful
String nextPage = request.getParameter("nextpage");

// This request parameter specifies a title for the login page
String title = request.getParameter("title");
if (title == null) title = "Please Log In"; // If not specified, use a default

// Look for username and password parameters in the request
String username = request.getParameter("username");
String password = request.getParameter("password");

// If the username and password are defined and  valid, then store
// the username in the session, and redirect to the specified page
// We do this without displaying any content of our own.
if ((username != null) && (password != null) && verify(username, password)) {
    session.setAttribute("username", username);
    response.sendRedirect(nextPage);
}
else {
    // Otherwise, we're going to have to display the login screen.
    // If the username and password properties are totally undefined,
    // then this is the first time, and all we display is the screen.
    // Otherwise, if they are defined, then we've just had a failed login
    // attempt, so display an additional "please try again" message.
    String message = "";
    if ((username != null) || (password != null)) {
        message = "Invalid username or password. Please try again";
    }
%>

    <%-- This is the body of the else block started above.  It displays --%>
    <%-- the login page.  It is straight HTML with only a few Java --%>
    <%-- expressions contained in <%= %> tags. It also contains tags --%>
    <%-- from a custom tag library, the subject of a later example --%>
    <head><title>Login</title></head>
```

Example 18-4: login.jsp (continued)

```
<body bgcolor='white'>
<br><br><br>          <%-- Space down from the top of the page a bit --%>
<%-- A custom tag: display a decorative box --%>
<decor:box color='yellow' margin='25' borderWidth='3' title='Login'>
<div align=center>  <%-- Center everything inside the box --%>
<%-- Display the login title and optional error message --%>
<font face='helvetica'><h1><%=title%></h1></font>
<font face='helvetica' color='red'><b><%=message%></b></font>
<%-- Now display an HTML form for the user to enter login information --%>
<form action='login.jsp' method='post'>
    <table>          <%-- Use a table to make the login form look nice --%>
        <tr>         <%-- First row: username --%>
            <td align='right'>
                <b><font face='helvetica'>Username:</font></b>
            </td>
            <td><input name='username'></td>
        </tr><tr>    <%-- Second row: password --%>
            <td align='right'>
                <b><font face='helvetica'>Password:</font></b>
            </td>
            <td><input type='password' name='password'></td>
        </tr><tr>    <%-- Third row: login button --%>
            <td align='center' colspan=2><font face='helvetica'><b>
            <input type=submit value='Login'>
            </b></font></td>
        </tr>
    </table>
    <%-- The form must also include some hidden fields so this page --%>
    <%-- can pass the nextpage and title parameters back to itself --%>
    <input type='hidden' name='nextpage' value='<%=nextPage%>'>
    <input type='hidden' name='title' value='<%=title%>'>
</form>
</div>
</decor:box> <%-- End of the custom box tag --%>
</body>      <%-- End of the HTML output --%>
<%
} // This is one final scriptlet to close the else block started above
%>
```

Running login.jsp

JSP files do not need to be compiled before they are run. The JSP container automatically performs the compilation the first time the JSP page is requested and whenever the page is subsequently modified. Unlike servlet class files, which must be placed in the *WEB-INF/classes* directory, JSP pages are treated just like HTML pages or images files and can be placed anywhere in the hierarchy of user-visible files for an application. In the sample WAR file, *login.jsp* is placed in the top-level directory and accessed with a URL like the following:

```
http://localhost:8080/javaexamples2/login.jsp
```

You may notice a delay the first time you request this URL, while your JSP container compiles the JSP file into a servlet.

In order for *login.jsp* to work correctly, it requires a request parameter named nextpage, so it can redirect the user's browser somewhere after the login succeeds. *login.jsp* stores the user's login name in the session object under the name username, which is exactly where the Hello servlet looks for it. Thus, you can use these servlets together with a URL like this:

```
http://localhost:8080/javaexamples2/login.jsp?nextpage=servlet/hello
```

Doing so obtains a username for the Hello servlet, but it does not provide any actual access control; the user can run Hello directly with a */servlet/hello* URL. In the next section, we'll see a technique that does require login.

Request Forwarding

Near the end of Example 18-3, we saw an example of using the RequestDispatcher class to include the output of one servlet within the output of another. In addition to its include() method, the RequestDispatcher class also has a forward() method, which transfers, or forwards, a request from one servlet to another. When this method is called, processing of the first servlet ends, and the second servlet takes over the job of producing output for the user. The only restriction on servlet forwarding is that the first servlet must not have already begun to produce output. A servlet that may forward to another servlet typically buffers its output in case it ends up having to forward to another page. JSP pages perform buffering automatically and allow a buffer size to be declared with the @page directive.

JSP provides an interface to the RequestDispatcher class through two custom tags that are part of the default JSP tag library. (This tag library is always available with the prefix jsp:; it does not need to be declared with a @taglib directive.) The <jsp:include> tag performs servlet (or JSP page) inclusion, and the <jsp:forward> tag does forwarding. Example 18-5 is a listing of *forcelogin.jsp*, which is a JSP page fragment that demonstrates the use of the <jsp:forward> tag.

forcelogin.jsp is not a complete JSP page; it is a page fragment that is intended to be statically included into another JSP page using an @include directive:

```
<%@include file="forcelogin.jsp"%>
```

It is important to understand that the @include directive performs static, compile-time file inclusion, rather than the dynamic, request-time inclusion performed by the <jsp:include> tag. Example 18-6 includes *forcelogin.jsp* with an @include directive in exactly this way.

The code in *forcelogin.jsp* checks to see if the session object has a username attribute defined. If not, it concludes that the user has not logged in and uses a <jsp:forward> tag to forward the user's request to the *login.jsp* page we saw in Example 18-4. It also uses a <jsp:param> tag to set the nextpage request parameter to tell *login.jsp* what page to come back to when the login is complete. Finally, because *forcelogin.jsp* is not a standalone JSP page, it does not have a URL of its own, so it uses the getRequestURI() method to figure out the URL for the page in which it has been included.

Example 18–5: forcelogin.jsp

```
<%--forcelogin.jsp
  This is a fragment of JSP code.  It cannot stand alone, but is
  intended to be included within other JSP pages.  It looks for a
  "username" attribute in the Session object, and if it does not find
  one, it forwards the request to the login.jsp page, which will
  authenticate the user and store their name in the session object.
  This code sends a "nextpage" request parameter to the login.jsp, so
  that the login page knows where to return to once the user has
  successfully logged in.  Note that request parameters passed to this
  page are not preserved when the login page redirects back to this page.
--%>
<%
// Check whether the username is already defined in the Session object
String _username = (String) session.getAttribute("username");
if (_username == null) {  // If the user has not already logged in
   String _page = request.getRequestURI();
%>
<%-- Invoke the login.jsp page.  The <jsp:forward> tag invokes the  --%>
<%-- page directly on the server side without sending a redirect --%>
<%-- to the client The <jsp:param> tags specify request parameters --%>
<%-- that are passed to login.jsp --%>
<jsp:forward page='login.jsp'>
    <jsp:param name='nextpage' value='<%=_page%>'/>
    <jsp:param name='title'
               value='<%= "You must log in to access " + _page%>'/>
</jsp:forward>
<%}%>
```

JSP Pages and JavaBeans

Example 18-6 is a listing of the JSP page *portal.jsp*. This example integrates many of the servlets and servlet programming techniques demonstrated in this chapter to create a very trivial Internet portal that displays customized content for its registered users. Figure 18-4 illustrates its output.

The major new feature of Example 18-6 is its use of a JavaBeans component (see Example 18-7) to move functionality (and the Java code that implements it) out of the JSP page into a separate Java class, thereby increasing the separation between Java and HTML code. *portal.jsp* uses the `<jsp:useBean>`, `<jsp:setProperty>`, and `<jsp:getProperty>` tags to instantiate and manipulate the bean. The `<jsp:useBean>` tag instantiates the bean and assigns the instance a name; this name can be used by the other JSP tags and by Java code in JSP expressions and scriptlets. The `scope="session"` attribute specifies that the bean instance should be associated with the user's session. In other words, the bean is instantiated when the user first visits the page. At that time, it is stored in the session object, so it can be retrieved on subsequent visits by that user during the same session.

The bean we create is an instance of `UserBean`, a simple class listed in Example 18-7. This class represents a single user of the portal and has methods for returning information about the user, such as his favorite color, and a string of customized HTML content that the portal should display.

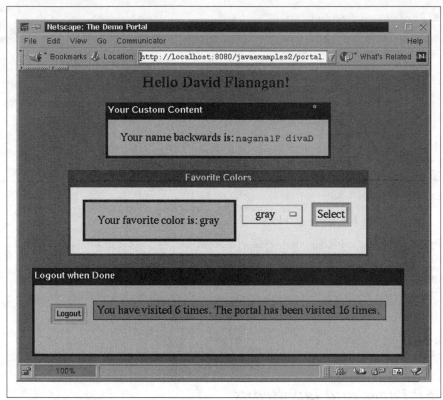

Figure 18–4. The output of portal.jsp

The *portal.jsp* page also demonstrates other useful JSP programming techniques. Like the *login.jsp* page, it has a `<%@taglib%>` directive and makes heavy use of the custom `<decor:box>` tag. It also uses the `<%@include%>` directive to statically include the *forcelogin.jsp* page at compile time. As we saw earlier, this forces the user to log in before any output is displayed. In addition, *portal.jsp* uses the `<jsp:include>` tag once at the top of the page to dynamically include the output of the Hello servlet and twice more at the end of the page to include output from the Counter servlet.

Note the code *portal.jsp* uses to dynamically generate the HTML `<select>` tag that lists color choices. This code surrounds HTML tags with Java scriptlets that form the beginning and end of a Java for loop. Each time through the loop, HTML tags are output. However, since the HTML tags include JSP expressions (`<%= . . . %>`), they expand differently each time through the loop. This is a relatively common and powerful JSP programming technique, although the tight coupling of Java and HTML code is not ideal.

Finally, note that *portal.jsp* includes an HTML form that displays a **logout** button. When clicked, this button loads the servlet servlet/logout. You'll see how this Logout servlet works in Example 18-8.

Example 18-6: portal.jsp

```
<%@page language='java' contentType='text/html'%>  <%-- On every JSP page --%>

<%-- Specify a tag library to use in this file --%>
<%@taglib uri='http://www.davidflanagan.com/tlds/decor_0_1.tld'
          prefix='decor'%>

<%-- Include the JSP code from forcelogin.jsp when this page is compiled --%>
<%-- The included file checks if the user is logged in, and if not, --%>
<%-- forwards to the login.jsp page to get a username and password. This --%>
<%-- ensures that the 'username' attribute is defined in the session. --%>
<%@include file='forcelogin.jsp'%>

<%-- Declare a new variable named 'user'. It is an instance of UserBean --%>
<%-- and it is associated with the session object. If this is a new --%>
<%-- session, then instantiate the bean and set its 'userName' property --%>
<%-- to the value of the username from the session. --%>
<jsp:useBean id='user' scope='session'
             class='com.davidflanagan.examples.servlet.UserBean'>
  <jsp:setProperty name='user' property='userName'
                   value='<%=(String)session.getAttribute("username")%>'/>
</jsp:useBean>

<%-- Each time this page is displayed, set the 'favoriteColor' property of --%>
<%-- the 'user' bean. Since no 'value' parameter is supplied, set the     --%>
<%-- property to the 'favoriteColor' parameter of the incoming request, if --%>
<%-- there is a parameter of that name; otherwise don't set the property.  --%>
<jsp:setProperty name='user' property='favoriteColor'/>

<%-- Begin to output the page. Note the use of the JSP to include a Java --%>
<%-- expression within the HTML <body> tag. This is an explicit use of   --%>
<%-- 'user' bean declared above. --%>
<head><title>The Demo Portal</title></head>
<body bgcolor='<%=user.getFavoriteColor()%>'>

<%-- Greet the user by invoking the hello servlet and including its output --%>
<%-- here. The hello servlet expects to find the username in the session --%>
<%-- where the login.jsp page stored it. Note the difference between --%>
<%-- this runtime jsp:include tag and the @include directive used above --%>
<%-- to include the forcelogin.jsp file at compile-time. --%>
<div align=center>
<h1><jsp:include page='servlet/hello' flush='true'/></h1>
</div>

<%-- Display a box using our 'decor' tag library, and as its content  %>
<%-- use the value of the 'customContent' property of the 'user' bean --%>
<%-- Hopefully, the bean will provide interesting content tailored --%>
<%-- to the specified user --%>
<decor:box title='Your Custom Content'>
  <jsp:getProperty name='user' property='customContent'/>
</decor:box>

<%-- Begin another box --%>
<%-- The content of this box is a table with 2 cells side-by-side --%>
<p>
<decor:box color='yellow' margin='15' borderColor='darkgreen'
           title='Favorite Colors' titleAlign='center' titleColor='#aaffaa'>
<table><tr><td>
<%-- The first cell is another box. It displays some text and the value--%>
```

Example 18–6: portal.jsp (continued)

```
<%-- of the 'favoriteColor' property of the 'user' bean --%>
<decor:box color='pink' margin='20'>
Your favorite color is:
<jsp:getProperty name='user' property='favoriteColor'/>
</decor:box>
</td>
<%-- This is the second cell of the table.  It contains a form for --%>
<%-- selecting a favorite color. Note the technique used to output the --%>
<%-- <select> element of the form. --%>
<td>
<form method='post'>                  <%-- Begin the form --%>
<select name='favoriteColor'>         <%-- Begin a <select> object --%>
<%                                     // Begin a Java scriptlet
// Ask the bean for the list of color choices, and the user's favorite
String[] colors = user.getColorChoices();
String favorite = user.getFavoriteColor();
// Now start looping through the list of colors.  The body of this loop
// is the HTML and JSP code below.
for(int i = 0; i < colors.length; i++) {
%>                                     <%-- End the scriptlet --%>
    <%-- Each time through the loop, we'll output an <option> element --%>
    <%-- Note the use of JSP <%=...%> expression tags to customize this --%>
    <%-- option tag for each iteration of the loop --%>
    <option value='<%=colors[i]%>'
        <%=(colors[i].equals(favorite))?"selected":""%>
    >
        <%=colors[i]%>                 <%-- Label of <option> element --%>
    </option>
<%}%>                                  <%-- End the for loop --%>
</select>                              <%-- End the <select> object --%>
<input type=submit value='Select'>  <%-- Submit button for the form --%>
</form>                                <%-- End the form--%>
</td></tr></table>                     <%-- End of 2nd cell and the table --%>
</decor:box>                           <%-- End of the box --%>

<%-- Begin a new box.  This one also contains a 2-cell table --%>
<br>
<decor:box title='Logout when Done' color='lightblue'>
<table><tr><td valign=top>

<%-- The first table cell is a simple form that allows the user to logout --%>
<%-- See Logout.java
for details --%>
<form action='servlet/logout' method='post'>
  <input type=hidden name='page' value='../portal.jsp'>
  <font face='helvetica'><b><input type='submit' value='Logout'></b></font>
</form>

<%-- The second item in the box is another box that displays counts --%>
<%-- We use jsp:include twice more to invoke the Counter servlet. --%>
<%-- Note that for the 2nd inclusion, we rely on the fact that the web.xml --%>
<%-- file maps any URL ending in ".count" to the Counter servlet --%>
</td><td valign=top>
<decor:box color='#a0a0c0' margin='5' borderWidth='1'>
You have visited
  <jsp:include page='servlet/counter' flush='true'>
      <jsp:param name='counter'
                 value='<%="portaluser_"+session.getAttribute("username")%>'/>
```

Example 18-6: portal.jsp (continued)

```
  </jsp:include>
times. The portal has been visited
  <jsp:include page='portal.jsp.count' flush='true'/>
times.
</decor:box>
</td></tr></table>
</decor:box>
```

Example 18-7 is a listing of *UserBean.java*, the JavaBeans class used by *portal.jsp*. It is a standard Java class, with getter and setter methods that follow the JavaBeans naming conventions. Note that the getCustomContent() method has a particularly unambitious implementation: a real web portal application would have to provide much more meaningful content than this method does.

One interesting feature of the UserBean class is that it implements HttpSession-BindingListener. This means that its valueBound() method is called when an instance is stored in a servlet's HttpSession object, and its valueUnbound() method is called when an instance is removed from the session. In the example, UserBean is removed from the session only when the session itself is being destroyed, either because the user logged out, the user became inactive, or because the server itself is shutting down. In any of these cases, the valueUnbound() method provides an opportunity for the bean to save its state to some kind of persistent storage, from which it can be restored by the setUserName() method. The valueUnbound() and setUserName() of this class do not currently save and restore state, but in a robust implementation they would.

Example 18-7: UserBean.java

```
package com.davidflanagan.examples.servlet;
import javax.servlet.http.*;

/**
 * This class is a simple non-visual JavaBean that defines properties that can
 * be used from a JSP page with the <jsp:useBean>, <jsp:setProperty> and
 * <jsp:getProperty> tags.  These JSP tags allow significant chunks of Java
 * code to be taken out of JSP pages and placed in Java files, where they are
 * easier to read, edit, and maintain.  This example only defines a few
 * trivial properties, but the class could do much more.
 *
 * This class is instantiated by portal.jsp and is bound in the Session object.
 * Therefore, it implements HttpSessionBindingListener so that it is notified
 * when the session is terminated (when the user logs out or the session
 * times out).
 **/
public class UserBean implements HttpSessionBindingListener {
    String username;               // The name of the user we represent
    String favorite = colors[0];   // The user's favorite color, with a default
    static final String[] colors = { "gray", "lightblue", "pink", "yellow" };

    // These are the getter and setter methods for the userName property
    // In a real program, setUserName() would probably look up information
    // about the user in a database of some kind.
    public String getUserName() { return username; }
    public void setUserName(String username) { this.username = username; }

    // These are the getter and setter methods for the favoriteColor property
```

Example 18–7: UserBean.java (continued)

```
public String getFavoriteColor() { return favorite; }
public void setFavoriteColor(String favorite) { this.favorite = favorite; }

// Return a list of colors the user is allowed to choose from
public String[] getColorChoices() { return colors; }

// This is a getter method for the "customContent" property.  In a more
// sophisticated example, this method might query a database and return
// current news clippings or stock quotes for the user.  Not here, though.
public String getCustomContent() {
    return "Your name backwards is: <tt>" +
        new StringBuffer(username).reverse() + "</tt>";
}


// This method implements HttpSessionBindingListener.  If an instance of
// this class is bound in a HttpSession object, then this method will
// be invoked when the instance becomes unbound, which typically happens
// when the session is invalidated because the user logged out or
// was inactive for too long.  In a real example, this method would
// probably save information about the user to a file or database.
public void valueUnbound(HttpSessionBindingEvent e) {
    System.out.println(username + " logged out or timed out." +
                       " Favorite color: " + favorite);
}

// Part of HttpSessionBindingListener; we don't care about it here
public void valueBound(HttpSessionBindingEvent e) {}
}
```

Ending a User Session

The portal example (Example 18-6) requires the user to log in the first time he visits and provides a **Logout** button that enables the user to log out. These login and logout events correspond to the creation and destruction of a javax.servlet. http.HttpSession object that maintains state for a single user of the web application. The HTTP protocol (the protocol of the Web) is a stateless protocol: every HTTP request is independent from every other one, and web servers do not maintain any state between requests. Because of the fundamentally stateless nature of the underlying protocol, one useful feature of servlet containers is that they perform session tracking, usually by placing a transient (and benign) cookie in the client's browser. The cookie contains a unique identifier the servlet container uses to identify the session.*

Sessions do not last forever: if a user does not issue a request to the web application within a specified session timeout period, the servlet container ends the session. The session timeout interval is one of the many configuration options that can be specified in the *WEB-INF/web.xml* deployment file (see Example 18-11).

---

* Session tracking can also be done if the end user has disabled cookies, with a technique called URL rewriting, in which the unique session identifier is added as a request parameter to all URLs in the web application. URLs are rewritten with the encodeURL() and encodeRedirectURL() methods of Http-ServletResponse.

Sessions can also be terminated explicitly, as shown in Example 18-8, a listing of *Logout.java*. This is the `Logout` servlet that is invoked from *portal.jsp* when the user clicks on the **Logout** button. The servlet ends the session by calling the `invalidate()` method of the `HttpSession` object. Then it reads the `page` request parameter and redirects the user's browser to that page. In the *portal.jsp* example, this `page` parameter was set to point the browser back to *portal.jsp*. Since the session was invalidated, however, the new request for the portal page is the first request of a new session, and the portal page forwards it to the *login.jsp* page.

Example 18–8: Logout.java

```
package com.davidflanagan.examples.servlet;
import javax.servlet.*;
import javax.servlet.http.*;

/**
 * This simple servlet ends the current session, and redirects the user's
 * browser to a URL specified by the "page" request parameter. It should be
 * suitable for use by any web application that requires the user to log in.
 **/
public class Logout extends HttpServlet {
    public void doGet(HttpServletRequest request, HttpServletResponse response)
        throws java.io.IOException
    {
        // Destroy the user's session
        request.getSession().invalidate();

        // Figure out what to display next
        String nextpage = request.getParameter("page");

        // And redirect the user's browser to that page
        response.sendRedirect(nextpage);
    }

    // doPost just invokes doGet
    public void doPost(HttpServletRequest request,HttpServletResponse response)
        throws java.io.IOException
    {
        doGet(request, response);
    }
}
```

Custom Tags

The *login.jsp* and *portal.jsp* files used the custom `<decor:box>` tag for drawing colored boxes with a border and optional title. The implementation of this tag consists of two parts. The first part is *DecorBox.java*, shown in Example 18-9, which contains the Java code that implements the tag. The second is *WEB-INF/tlds/decor_0_1.tld*, shown in Example 18-10, which is a tag library descriptor (TLD) file that describes the Decor tag library, the tags it contains, and the attributes supported by each tag. There is also one additional piece of the tag library puzzle: a mapping from the URI that uniquely names the tag library to the local copy of the TLD file. This mapping is part of the *WEB-INF/web.xml* deployment file for the web application; we'll see it in Example 18-11.

Defining a Custom Tag

DecorBox.java implements a simple custom tag. The doStartTag() method is called to output HTML text when the <decor:box> tag is encountered, and the doEndTag() method is called to output HTML when the closing </decor:box> tag is encountered. These methods use nested HTML tables to produce the desired box effect. Note that the class defines setter methods for a number of String properties. These properties define the supported attributes for the tag. For example, if a <decor:box> tag includes a margin="10" attribute, the setMargin() method is called with the string "10" before doStartTag() is called.

Example 18-9: DecorBox.java

```
package com.davidflanagan.examples.servlet;
import javax.servlet.jsp.*;          // JSP classes
import javax.servlet.jsp.tagext.*;   // Tag Library classes
import java.io.IOException;

/**
 * This Tag implementation is part of the "decor" tag library.  It uses HTML
 * tables to display a decorative box (with an optional title) around its
 * content.  The various properties correspond to the attributes supported by
 * the tag.
 **/
public class DecorBox extends TagSupport {
    // These fields contain values that control the appearance of the box
    String align;          // Alignment of the box
    String title;          // Title for the box
    String titleColor;     // Title foreground color
    String titleAlign;     // Title alignment relative to box
    String color;          // Box background color
    String borderColor;    // Border (and title background) color
    String margin;         // Pixels between box edge and content
    String borderWidth;    // Pixel width of the box border

    // The following property setter methods set the values of the fields above
    // When a JSP page uses this tag any tag attribute settings will be
    // translated into calls to these methods.
    public void setAlign(String value) { align = value; }
    public void setTitle(String value) { title = value; }
    public void setTitleColor(String value) { titleColor = value; }
    public void setTitleAlign(String value) { titleAlign = value; }
    public void setColor(String value) { this.color = value; }
    public void setBorderColor(String value) { borderColor = value; }
    public void setMargin(String value) { margin = value; }
    public void setBorderWidth(String value) { borderWidth = value; }

    /**
     * This inherited method is always the first property setter invoked
     * by the JSP container.  We don't care about the page context here, but
     * use this method to set the default values of the various properties.
     * They are initialized here in case the JSP container wants to reuse
     * this Tag object on multiple pages.
     **/
    public void setPageContext(PageContext context) {
        // Important!  Let the superclass save the page context object.
        // We'll need it in doStartTag() below.
        super.setPageContext(context);
```

Example 18-9: DecorBox.java (continued)

```java
            // Now set default values for all the other properties
            align = "center";
            title = null;
            titleColor = "white";
            titleAlign = "left";
            color = "lightblue";
            borderColor = "black";
            margin = "20";
            borderWidth = "4";
    }

    /**
     * This method is called when a <decor:box> tag is encountered.  Any
     * attributes will first be processed by calling the setter methods above.
     **/
    public int doStartTag() throws JspException {
        try {
            // Get the output stream from the PageContext object, which
            // will have been passed to the setPageContext() method.
            JspWriter out = pageContext.getOut();

            // Output the HTML tags necessary to display the box. The <div>
            // handles the alignment, and the <table> creates the border.
            out.print("<div align='" + align + "'>" +
                      "<table bgcolor='" + borderColor + "' " +
                      "border='0' cellspacing='0' " +
                      "cellpadding='" + borderWidth + "'>");

            // If there is a title, display it as a cell of the outer table
            if (title != null)
                out.print("<tr><td align='" + titleAlign + "'>" +
                          "<font face='helvetica' size='+1' " +
                          "color='" + titleColor + "'><b>" +
                          title + "</b></font></td></tr>");

            // Now begin an inner table that has a different color than
            // the border.
            out.print("<tr><td><table bgcolor='" + color + "' " +
                      "border='0' cellspacing='0' " +
                      "cellpadding='" + margin + "'><tr><td>");
        }
        catch (IOException e) {
            // Unlike a PrintWriter, a JspWriter can throw IOExceptions
            // We have to catch them and wrap them in a JSPException
            throw new JspException(e.getMessage());
        }

        // This return value tells the JSP class to process the body of the tag
        return EVAL_BODY_INCLUDE;
    }

    /**
     * This method is called when the closing </decor:box> tag is encountered
     **/
    public int doEndTag() throws JspException {
        // Try to output HTML to close the <table> and <div> tags.
        // Catch IOExceptions and rethrow them as JspExceptions
        try {
```

Example 18–9: DecorBox.java (continued)

```
            JspWriter out = pageContext.getOut();
            out.println("</td></tr></table></td></tr></table></div>");
        }
        catch (IOException e) { throw new JspException(e.getMessage()); }

        // This return value says to continue processing the JSP page.
        return EVAL_PAGE;
    }
}
```

Deploying a Custom Tag

Before you can use the custom tag defined by *DecorBox.java*, you must create a TLD for the custom tag library. Example 18-10 shows the TLD file for our tag library (which consists of the single box tag). As you can see, the TLD is an XML file. It provides information about the library, each of the tags it contains, and each of the attributes supported by each tag.

The <uri> tag near the top of the TLD is an important one. It defines a universally unique name by which the tag library is known. The name includes a version number so that this preliminary version of the the library can be distinguished from later versions. The purpose of the specified URI is to provide a name for the tag library; the URI may also, but is not required to, function as an official download location for the TLD file. This URI is the name that should identify the desired tag library in a JSP <%@taglib> directive. As you'll see, the *WEB-INF/web.xml* file allows you to define a mapping from tag library URIs to local TLD files.*

Example 18-10: WEB-INF/tlds/decor_0_1.tld

```
<?xml version="1.0" encoding="ISO-8859-1" ?>
<!DOCTYPE taglib
        PUBLIC "-//Sun Microsystems, Inc.//DTD JSP Tag Library 1.1//EN"
        "http://java.sun.com/j2ee/dtds/web-jsptaglib_1_1.dtd">

<!-- The tags above say that this is an XML document, and formally  -->
<!-- specify the document type. -->

<taglib>                         <!-- Define a tag library -->
  <tlibversion>0.1</tlibversion>   <!-- The version of this tag library -->
  <jspversion>1.1</jspversion>     <!-- The version of JSP -->
  <shortname>decor</shortname>     <!-- The common name for the library -->
  <uri>                            <!-- A URL that uniquely identifies it -->
    http://www.davidflanagan.com/tlds/decor_0_1.tld
  </uri>
  <info>                           <!-- A simple description of the library -->
    A simple tag library for decorative HTML output
  </info>
```

---

* There are other ways to specify the location of the TLD. If you abandon the idea of using a globally unique URI to identify the tag library, you can use a local URI in the <%@taglib%> directive to point directly to the local copy of the TLD. Or, instead of specifying the location of the TLD file itself, you can specify the location of a JAR file that contains the tag library implementation. In this case, the JSP container looks in the *META-INF/* directory for the TLD file. See the JSP specification for full details.

Example 18–10: WEB-INF/tlds/decor_0_1.tld (continued)

```
<!-- The <tag> tag defines a single tag of the tag library -->
<tag>
  <!-- First, define the tag name, implementation class, and description -->
  <name>box</name>
  <tagclass>com.davidflanagan.examples.servlet.DecorBox</tagclass>
  <info>Display a colored box with a border</info>

  <!-- Next, define each attribute that the tag supports -->
  <!-- For each, specify the name, whether it is required, and whether -->
  <!-- the tag value may be specified with a JSP <%= %> construct -->
  <attribute>
    <name>align</name>                 <!-- The 'align' attribute -->
    <required>false</required>         <!-- It is not required -->
    <rtexprvalue>true</rtexprvalue> <!-- It may have a <%= %> value -->
  </attribute>
  <attribute>                          <!-- Etc., etc., etc. -->
    <name>color</name>
    <required>false</required>
    <rtexprvalue>true</rtexprvalue>
  </attribute>
  <attribute>
    <name>borderColor</name>
    <required>false</required>
    <rtexprvalue>true</rtexprvalue>
  </attribute>
  <attribute>
    <name>margin</name>
    <required>false</required>
    <rtexprvalue>true</rtexprvalue>
  </attribute>
  <attribute>
    <name>borderWidth</name>
    <required>false</required>
    <rtexprvalue>true</rtexprvalue>
  </attribute>
  <attribute>
    <name>title</name>
    <required>false</required>
    <rtexprvalue>true</rtexprvalue>
  </attribute>
  <attribute>
    <name>titleColor</name>
    <required>false</required>
    <rtexprvalue>true</rtexprvalue>
  </attribute>
  <attribute>
    <name>titleAlign</name>
    <required>false</required>
    <rtexprvalue>true</rtexprvalue>
  </attribute>
</tag>
</taglib>
```

Deploying a Web Application

In this chapter, we've developed some servlets, some JSP pages, a JavaBeans component, and a tag library and its TLD. In order to tie all these examples together into a single "web application," you need to create the *WEB-INF/web.xml* file that describes the web application and place all the necessary files in all the appropriate places. An optional, but useful, next step is to archive all these files into a single WAR file that can be easily distributed and deployed.

Configuring Web Applications with web.xml

The *web.xml* file is listed in Example 18-11. It is an XML file that contains tags that provide various types of information about the web application. Version 2.2 of the Servlet specification contains complete details about the format and content of this file. The example demonstrates the most commonly used tags but omits a number of less-frequently used tags. The most important tags in a *web.xml* file are the <servlet> tags. A <servlet> tag specifies a mapping from a servlet name to a servlet class and defines the initialization parameters for the servlet. (Recall that servlets typically read their initialization parameters from the init() method.) To make this web application work on your system, you have to change the values of some of these initialization parameters. In particular, the countfile parameter of the counter servlet should be edited, and all the JDBC initialization parameters of the query servlet should be set to values appropriate for the database server you are using.

Note that it is perfectly legal to define multiple names for the same servlet implementation class. Each <servlet> tag defines a separate instance of the servlet class, and each instance can have a different set of initialization parameters. For example, if you wanted to use the Query servlet to talk to two different database servers, you could use two separate <servlet> tags that give the names queryDB1 and queryDB2 to two different instances of the Query class.

After all the <servlet> tags in the *web.xml* file comes a <servlet-mapping> tag.*
This tag is used to define a mapping from a URL prefix or suffix to a particular named servlet instance. When the web server receives a request for any URL that matches the specified pattern, it invokes the named servlet. In the example, I've used a <servlet-mapping> tag to map any URLs ending in *.count* to the counter servlet.

The <session-config> tag specifies session management information. In this example, it indicates that user sessions time out after 15 minutes without a request from the user. This tag is followed by a <taglib> tag that defines a mapping from the unique URI of the custom tag library to the local location of the TLD file for that library.

---

* The XML DTD for the *web.xml* file defines the required order of the tags. You are not free to rearrange them but must keep them in the order shown in this example.

Example 18-11: web.xml

```xml
<?xml version="1.0" encoding="ISO-8859-1"?>   <!-- This is an xml file -->
<!-- This is document type of the xml file -->
<!DOCTYPE web-app
    PUBLIC "-//Sun Microsystems, Inc.//DTD Web Application 2.2//EN"
    "http://java.sun.com/j2ee/dtds/web-app_2.2.dtd">

<!-- Define configuration and deployment information for a web application -->
<web-app>
  <!-- Each servlet tag defines information about a servlet.  This one -->
  <!-- defines a name for a specific Servlet implementation class.  It maps -->
  <!-- /servlet/hello (relative to the webapp root) to the specified class -->
  <servlet>
    <servlet-name>hello</servlet-name>
    <servlet-class>com.davidflanagan.examples.servlet.Hello</servlet-class>
  </servlet>

  <!-- Here's another servlet tag.  This one also defines initialization -->
  <!-- parameters that the servlet reads in its init() method. -->
  <servlet>  <!-- The counter servlet -->
    <servlet-name>counter</servlet-name>
    <servlet-class>com.davidflanagan.examples.servlet.Counter</servlet-class>
    <init-param>
      <param-name>countfile</param-name>          <!-- where to save state -->
      <param-value>/tmp/counts.ser</param-value> <!-- adjust for your system-->
    </init-param>
    <init-param>
      <param-name>saveInterval</param-name>       <!-- how often to save -->
      <param-value>30000</param-value>            <!-- every 30 seconds -->
    </init-param>
  </servlet>

  <servlet>  <!-- The query servlet -->
    <servlet-name>query</servlet-name>
    <servlet-class>com.davidflanagan.examples.servlet.Query</servlet-class>
    <!-- Configure all these init params for your database -->
    <init-param>
      <param-name>driverClassName</param-name>   <!-- JDBC driver classname -->
      <param-value>org.gjt.mm.mysql.Driver</param-value> <!-- mysql driver -->
    </init-param>
    <init-param>
      <param-name>url</param-name>                <!-- URL for the database -->
      <param-value>jdbc:mysql://dbserver.my.domain.com/dbname</param-value>
    </init-param>
    <init-param>
      <param-name>username</param-name>           <!-- Database username -->
      <param-value>david</param-value>
    </init-param>
    <init-param>
      <param-name>password</param-name>           <!-- Database password -->
      <param-value>secret</param-value>
    </init-param>
  </servlet>

  <!-- Note that you can define multiple named instances of a single -->
  <!-- servlet class.  If you have two different databases, for example, -->
  <!-- you could define another instance of the Query servlet using a -->
  <!-- with a different name and a different set of initialization params -->
  <servlet>  <!-- Another query servlet -->
```

Example 18–11: web.xml (continued)

```
    <servlet-name>queryOtherDatabase</servlet-name>
    <servlet-class>com.davidflanagan.examples.servlet.Query</servlet-class>
    <!-- Add init params here, or this servlet won't work right -->
  </servlet>

  <servlet>  <!-- The logout servlet -->
    <servlet-name>logout</servlet-name>
    <servlet-class>com.davidflanagan.examples.servlet.Logout</servlet-class>
  </servlet>

  <!-- A servlet mapping specifies URL prefixes or suffixes that cause a -->
  <!-- particular named servlet to be invoked.  This one specifies that any -->
  <!-- URL ending with ".count" will invoke the "counter" servlet -->
  <servlet-mapping>
    <servlet-name>counter</servlet-name>  <!-- A name from a <servlet> tag -->
    <url-pattern>*.count</url-pattern>    <!-- What URLs invoke it -->
  </servlet-mapping>

  <!-- This tag specifies session management information for our webapp -->
  <session-config>
    <session-timeout>15</session-timeout> <!-- timeout after 15 minutes idle-->
  </session-config>

  <!-- Mapping information about the tag libraries used in the webapp -->
  <taglib>
    <!-- When you see this unique identifier for a tag library... -->
    <taglib-uri>http://www.davidflanagan.com/tlds/decor_0_1.tld</taglib-uri>
    <!-- ...use this local copy of the Tag Library Descriptor file -->
    <taglib-location>tlds/decor_0_1.tld</taglib-location>
  </taglib>
</web-app>
```

Packaging Web Applications into WAR Files

As of Version 2.2 of the servlet specification, web applications can be portably distributed in WAR archives. A WAR archive is simply a JAR file that contains specific information for a web application, most notably the *WEB-INF/web.xml* file. Both the WAR and JAR archive formats use the standard ZIP archiving and compression format.

The root directory of the WAR archive and all of its subdirectories, except the *WEB-INF* directory, contain user-visible files the web server may display to the user. For example, you might place a static *index.html* file for your web application in the root directory. If the web application requires a lot of static content, you might want to organize it in subdirectories, such as an *images/* directory.

The root directory (and its subdirectories) is also where JSP pages are placed. The web server does not treat these as static files but defers them to the JSP container. If your application has a default *index.jsp* file, it should go here.

The */WEB-INF/* directory contains WEB application configuration INFormation and the Java classes needed to make the application run. As you've already seen, the */WEB-INF/web.xml* file is the main deployment descriptor for the application.

The */WEB-INF/classes/* directory contains any Java classes required by the web application. This includes servlet classes, JavaBeans, and custom tag implementations. Note that the classes must be in directories that correspond to their package names. Thus, in the example, the actual class files are in a subdirectory: */WEB-INF/classes/com/davidflanagan/examples/servlet/*.

The */WEB-INF/lib/* directory contains any JAR files required by the web application. It might contain a tag library implementation packaged in JAR format, for example. The */WEB-INF/tlds/* directory contains tag library descriptors, like the */WEB-INF/tlds/decor_0_1.tld* TLD file that describes the Decor custom tag library used by the JSP pages.

Creating a WAR file for a web application is largely a matter of getting all the files in the right place and packaging them up. Example 18-12 shows a Unix shell script that automates this task. Windows users should have no trouble transforming this script to a DOS batch file.

Example 18-12: makewar.sh: A Script for Packaging a Web Application

```
#!/bin/sh

# Delete all Java class files, and recompile everything
echo "Recompiling Java classes..."
rm *.class
javac *.java

# Create a temporary directory structure for the web application
echo "Creating WAR file..."
mkdir temp
mkdir temp/WEB-INF
mkdir temp/WEB-INF/tlds
mkdir temp/WEB-INF/classes
mkdir temp/WEB-INF/classes/com
mkdir temp/WEB-INF/classes/com/davidflanagan
mkdir temp/WEB-INF/classes/com/davidflanagan/examples
mkdir temp/WEB-INF/classes/com/davidflanagan/examples/servlet

# Now copy our files into those directories
cp *.jsp temp                       # JSP files go at the top level
cp WEB-INF/web.xml temp/WEB-INF     # Configuration files in WEB-INF/
cp WEB-INF/tlds/decor_0_1.tld temp/WEB-INF/tlds
# Java class files go under WEB-INF/classes
cp *.class temp/WEB-INF/classes/com/davidflanagan/examples/servlet

# At this point, the temporary directory contains all our files, so
# we can jar them up into a WAR file with the name javaexamples2.war
# This WAR file can now simply be dropped into the Tomcat webapps/ directory.
cd temp
jar cMf ../javaexamples2.war *

# Now delete the temporary directory hierarchy
cd ..
rm -rf temp
```

Exercises

18-1. Modify the `Hello` servlet so that it never offers a generic "Hello World" greeting. Instead, it should either greet the user by name or ask the user for a name, store that name in the session, and then greet the user by name. Although you are writing a single servlet, it should be able to display two distinct "pages" of output: a greeting page and a login page. The login page displays an HTML form, and the servlet should be able to handle submissions from this form. Use the HTML techniques shown in the `DecorBox` class to decorate the login page.

18-2. Modify the `Hello` servlet again, as in the last exercise. This time, however, do not hardcode the HTML for the greeting and login pages in the servlet itself. Instead, implement the contents of these pages in JSP files, and use the servlet as the controller that processes the input and decides when each page should be displayed. Your servlet class should use a `RequestDispatcher` to forward the request to the appropriate JSP page for display. It can use the session object or request attributes to pass data from the servlet to the JSP pages.

You may want to look at the *login.jsp* example for inspiration on the design of a login page. Note, however, that *login.jsp* displays the login page and also processes the results of submitting the form it displays. In this exercise, all the form-processing logic should be in the servlet itself, and the JSP pages should be pure presentation, containing as little Java code as possible.

18-3. Modify the `Counter` servlet to use a database rather than a local file as its persistence mechanism. Write a `CounterAdmin` servlet that is an administrative interface for the `Counter` servlet; it should display (but not update) each of the counts stored in the database. The `CounterAdmin` servlet should be password-protected and should display a JSP-based login page that requires the user to log in before the current counts are displayed. Use a servlet initialization parameter from the *web.xml* file to specify the password for the servlet.

18-4. The *login.jsp* and *portal.jsp* examples in this chapter demonstrate a number of ways JSP can be used: they show how Java code can be embedded directly within JSP and also how JavaBeans can be used with JSP. Another technique for using JSP that is becoming quite popular is the Model-View-Controller, or MVC, architecture. In this architecture, JavaBeans or other Java objects contain the relevant data; they are the "model." JSP pages provide a "view" of the data but contain very little Java code, so that they can be created and edited by graphic designers instead of by Java programmers. A web application may contain a number of different JSP pages to provide various views of the data. Finally, a central servlet acts as the "controller," deciding what view to display in response to each request and using a `RequestDispatcher` to forward the request to the appropriate JSP page.

For this exercise, redesign the *portal.jsp* example to use the MVC architecture. Write a single `Portal` servlet as the controller and define at least three JSP views: a login page, a main content page of the portal, and a page that allows the user to select a favorite color. Don't forget to include functionality that allows the user to logout. Use (or extend) the UserBean class as the model, but include a persistence mechanism (either a local file or a database) so the servlet can save its state. Remember that when a JSP page contains an HTML form, the servlet has to contain the logic for responding to submissions from that form. For form-based web applications like this one, a helpful technique is to include a HTML hidden field in each form that assigns a unique name to the form or the page, so that the controller servlet can determine what form data is being submitted and decide how to handle the submission.

18-5. Package the Portal servlet you created in Exercise 18-4 into a WAR file, along with the JSP pages and any other auxiliary files it requires. Use that WAR file to deploy your portal independently of the other examples from this chapter.

CHAPTER 19

XML

XML, or Extensible Markup Language, is a meta-language for marking up text documents with structural tags, similar to those found in HTML and SGML documents. XML has become popular because its structural markup allows documents to describe their own format and contents. XML enables "portable data," and it can be quite powerful when combined with the "portable code" enabled by Java.

Because of the popularity of XML, there are a number of tools for parsing and manipulating XML documents. And because XML documents are becoming more and more common, it is worth your time to learn how to use some of those tools to work with XML. The examples in this chapter introduce you to simple XML parsing and manipulation. If you are familiar with the basic structure of an XML file, you should have no problem understanding them. Note that there are many subtleties to working with XML; this chapter doesn't attempt to explain them all. To learn more about XML, try *Java and XML*, by Brett McLaughlin, or *XML Pocket Reference*, by Robert Eckstein, both from O'Reilly & Associates.

The world of XML and its affiliated technologies is moving so fast that it can be hard just keeping up with the acronyms, standards, APIs, and version numbers. I'll try to provide an overview of the state of various technologies in this chapter, but be warned that things may have changed, sometimes radically, by the time you read this material.

Parsing with JAXP and SAX 1

The first thing you want to do with an XML document is parse it. There are two commonly used approaches to XML parsing: they go by the acronyms SAX and DOM. We'll begin with SAX parsing; DOM parsing is covered later in the chapter. At the very end of the chapter, we'll also see a new, but very promising, Java-centric XML API known as JDOM.

SAX is the Simple API for XML. SAX is not a parser, but rather a Java API that describes how a parser operates. When parsing an XML document using the SAX API, you define a class that implements various "event" handling methods. As the parser encounters the various element types of the XML document, it invokes the corresponding event handler methods you've defined. Your methods take whatever actions are required to accomplish the desired task. In the SAX model, the parser converts an XML document into a sequence of Java method calls. The parser doesn't build a parse tree of any kind (although your methods can do this, if you want). SAX parsing is typically quite efficient and is therefore your best choice for most simple XML processing tasks.

The SAX API was created by David Megginson (*http://www.megginson.com/SAX/*). The Java implementation of the API is in the package org.xml.sax and its subpackages. SAX is a defacto standard but has not been standardized by any official body. SAX Version 1 has been in use for some time; SAX 2 was finalized in May 2000. There are numerous changes between the SAX 1 and SAX 2 APIs. Many Java-based XML parsers exist that conform to the SAX 1 or SAX 2 APIs.

With the SAX API, you can't completely abstract away the details of the XML parser implementation you are using: at a minimum, your code must supply the classname of the parser to be used. This is where JAXP comes in. JAXP is the Java API for XML Parsing. It is an "optional package" defined by Sun that consists of the javax.xml.parsers package. JAXP provides a thin layer on top of SAX (and on top of DOM, as we'll see) and standardizes an API for obtaining and using SAX (and DOM) parser objects. The JAXP package ships with default parser implementations but allows other parsers to be easily plugged in and configured using system properties. At this writing, the current version of JAXP is 1.0.1; it supports SAX 1, but not SAX 2. By the time you read this, however, JAXP 1.1, which will include support for SAX 2, may have become available.

Example 19-1 is a listing of *ListServlets1.java*, a program that uses JAXP and SAX to parse a web application deployment descriptor and list the names of the servlets configured by that file. If you haven't yet read Chapter 18, *Servlets and JSP*, you should know that servlet-based web applications are configured using an XML file named *web.xml*. This file contains <servlet> tags that define mappings between servlet names and the Java classes that implement them. To help you understand the task to be solved by the *ListServlets1.java* program, here is an excerpt from the *web.xml* file developed in Chapter 18:

```
<servlet>
  <servlet-name>hello</servlet-name>
  <servlet-class>com.davidflanagan.examples.servlet.Hello</servlet-class>
</servlet>

<servlet>
  <servlet-name>counter</servlet-name>
  <servlet-class>com.davidflanagan.examples.servlet.Counter</servlet-class>
  <init-param>
    <param-name>countfile</param-name>        <!-- where to save state -->
    <param-value>/tmp/counts.ser</param-value> <!-- adjust for your system -->
  </init-param>
  <init-param>
    <param-name>saveInterval</param-name>     <!-- how often to save -->
    <param-value>30000</param-value>          <!-- every 30 seconds -->
  </init-param>
</servlet>
```

```
<servlet>
  <servlet-name>logout</servlet-name>
  <servlet-class>com.davidflanagan.examples.servlet.Logout</servlet-class>
</servlet>
```

ListServlets1.java includes a main() method that uses the JAXP API to obtain a SAX parser instance. It then tells the parser what to parse and starts the parser running. The remaining methods of the class are invoked by the parser. Note that List-Servlets1 extends the SAX HandlerBase class. This superclass provides dummy implementations of all the SAX event handler methods. The example simply overrides the handlers of interest. The parser calls the startElement() method when it reads an XML tag; it calls endElement() when it finds a closing tag. characters() is invoked when the parser reads a string of plain text with no markup. Finally, the parser calls warning(), error(), or fatalError() when something goes wrong in the parsing process. The implementations of these methods are written specifically to extract the desired information from a *web.xml* file and are based on a knowledge of the structure of this type of file.

Note that *web.xml* files are somewhat unusual in that they don't rely on attributes for any of the XML tags. That is, servlet names are defined by a <servlet-name> tag nested within a <servlet> tag, instead of simply using a name attribute of the <servlet> tag itself. This fact makes the example program slightly more complex than it would otherwise be. The *web.xml* file does allow id attributes for all its tags. Although servlet engines are not expected to use these attributes, they may be useful to a configuration tool that parses and automatically generates *web.xml* files. For completeness, the startElement() method in Example 19-1 looks for an id attribute of the <servlet> tag. The value of that attribute, if it exists, is reported in the program's output.

Example 19–1: ListServlets1.java

```
package com.davidflanagan.examples.xml;
import javax.xml.parsers.*;          // The JAXP package
import org.xml.sax.*;                // The main SAX package
import java.io.*;

/**
 * Parse a web.xml file using JAXP and SAX1.  Print out the names
 * and class names of all servlets listed in the file.
 *
 * This class implements the HandlerBase helper class, which means
 * that it defines all the "callback" methods that the SAX parser will
 * invoke to notify the application.  In this example we override the
 * methods that we require.
 *
 * This example uses full package names in places to help keep the JAXP
 * and SAX APIs distinct.
 **/
public class ListServlets1 extends org.xml.sax.HandlerBase {
    /** The main method sets things up for parsing */
    public static void main(String[] args)
        throws IOException, SAXException, ParserConfigurationException
    {
        // Create a JAXP "parser factory" for creating SAX parsers
        javax.xml.parsers.SAXParserFactory spf=SAXParserFactory.newInstance();
```

Example 19-1: ListServlets1.java (continued)

```
        // Configure the parser factory for the type of parsers we require
        spf.setValidating(false);  // No validation required

        // Now use the parser factory to create a SAXParser object
        // Note that SAXParser is a JAXP class, not a SAX class
        javax.xml.parsers.SAXParser sp = spf.newSAXParser();

        // Create a SAX input source for the file argument
        org.xml.sax.InputSource input=new InputSource(new FileReader(args[0]));

        // Give the InputSource an absolute URL for the file, so that
        // it can resolve relative URLs in a <!DOCTYPE> declaration, e.g.
        input.setSystemId("file://" + new File(args[0]).getAbsolutePath());

        // Create an instance of this class; it defines all the handler methods
        ListServlets1 handler = new ListServlets1();

        // Finally, tell the parser to parse the input and notify the handler
        sp.parse(input, handler);

        // Instead of using the SAXParser.parse() method, which is part of the
        // JAXP API, we could also use the SAX1 API directly.  Note the
        // difference between the JAXP class javax.xml.parsers.SAXParser and
        // the SAX1 class org.xml.sax.Parser
        //
        // org.xml.sax.Parser parser = sp.getParser();  // Get the SAX parser
        // parser.setDocumentHandler(handler);           // Set main handler
        // parser.setErrorHandler(handler);              // Set error handler
        // parser.parse(input);                          // Parse!
    }

    StringBuffer accumulator = new StringBuffer();  // Accumulate parsed text
    String servletName;        // The name of the servlet
    String servletClass;       // The class name of the servlet
    String servletId;          // Value of id attribute of <servlet> tag

    // When the parser encounters plain text (not XML elements), it calls
    // this method, which accumulates them in a string buffer
    public void characters(char[] buffer, int start, int length) {
        accumulator.append(buffer, start, length);
    }

    // Every time the parser encounters the beginning of a new element, it
    // calls this method, which resets the string buffer
    public void startElement(String name, AttributeList attributes) {
        accumulator.setLength(0);  // Ready to accumulate new text
        // If its a servlet tag, look for id attribute
        if (name.equals("servlet"))
            servletId = attributes.getValue("id");
    }

    // When the parser encounters the end of an element, it calls this method
    public void endElement(String name) {
        if (name.equals("servlet-name")) {
            // After </servlet-name>, we know the servlet name saved up
            servletName = accumulator.toString().trim();
        }
        else if (name.equals("servlet-class")) {
```

Example 19-1: ListServlets1.java (continued)

```
                    // After </servlet-class>, we've got the class name accumulated
                    servletClass = accumulator.toString().trim();
            }
            else if (name.equals("servlet")) {
                    // Assuming the document is valid, then when we parse </servlet>,
                    // we know we've got a servlet name and class name to print out
                    System.out.println("Servlet " + servletName +
                                    ((servletId != null)?" (id="+servletId+")":"") +
                                    ": " + servletClass);
            }
    }

    /** This method is called when warnings occur */
    public void warning(SAXParseException exception) {
        System.err.println("WARNING: line " + exception.getLineNumber() + ": "+
                        exception.getMessage());
    }

    /** This method is called when errors occur */
    public void error(SAXParseException exception) {
        System.err.println("ERROR: line " + exception.getLineNumber() + ": " +
                        exception.getMessage());
    }

    /** This method is called when non-recoverable errors occur. */
    public void fatalError(SAXParseException exception) throws SAXException {
        System.err.println("FATAL: line " + exception.getLineNumber() + ": " +
                        exception.getMessage());
        throw(exception);
    }
}
```

Compiling and Running the Example

To run the previous example, you need the JAXP package from Sun. You can
download it by following the download links from *http://java.sun.com/xml/*. Once
you've downloaded the package, uncompress the archive it is packaged in and
install it somewhere convenient on your system. In Version 1.0.1 of JAXP, the
download bundle contains two JAR files: *jaxp.jar*, the JAXP API classes, and
parser.jar, the SAX and DOM APIs and default parser implementations. To compile
and run this example, you need both JAR files in your classpath. If you have any
other XML parsers, such as the Xerces parser, in your classpath, remove them or
make sure that the JAXP files are listed first; otherwise you may run into version-
skew problems between the different parsers. Note that you probably don't want
to permanently alter your classpath, since you'll have to change it again for the
next example. One simple solution with Java 1.2 and later is to temporarily drop
copies of the JAXP JAR files into the *jre/lib/ext/* directory of your Java installation.

With the two JAXP JAR files temporarily in your classpath, you can compile and
run *ListServlets1.java* as usual. When you run it, specify the name of a *web.xml* file
on the command line. You can use the sample file included with the downloadable examples for this book or specify one from your own servlet engine.

There is one complication to this example. Most *web.xml* files contain a <!DOC-TYPE> tag that specifies the document type (or DTD). Despite the fact that Example 19-1 specifies that the parser should not validate the document, a conforming XML parser must still read the DTD for any document that has a <!DOCTYPE> declaration. Most *web.xml* have a declaration like this:

```
<!DOCTYPE web-app
    PUBLIC "-//Sun Microsystems, Inc.//DTD Web Application 2.2//EN"
    "http://java.sun.com/j2ee/dtds/web-app_2.2.dtd">
```

In order to read the DTD, the parser must be able to read the specified URL. If your system is not connected to the Internet when you run the example, it will hang. One workaround is to replace the DTD URL with the name of a local copy of the DTD, which is what has been done in the sample *web.xml* file bundled with the downloadable examples. Another workaround to this DTD problem is to simply remove (or comment out) the <!DOCTYPE> declaration from the *web.xml* file you process with ListServlets1.

Parsing with SAX 2

Example 19-1 showed how you can parse an XML document using the SAX 1 API, which is what is supported by the current version of JAXP (at this writing). The SAX 1 API is out of date, however. So Example 19-2 shows how you can accomplish a similar parsing task using the SAX 2 API and the open-source Xerces parser available from the Apache Software Foundation.

Example 19-2 is a listing of the program *ListServlets2.java*. Like the *ListServlets1.java* example, this program reads a specified *web.xml* file and looks for <servlet> tags, so it can print out the servlet name-to-servlet class mappings. This example goes a little further than the last, however, and also looks for <servlet-mapping> tags, so it can also output the URL patterns that are mapped to named servlets. The example uses two hashtables to store the information as it accumulates it, then prints out all the information when parsing is complete.

The SAX 2 API is functionally similar to the SAX 1 API, but a number of classes and interfaces have new names and some methods have new signatures. Many of the changes were required for the addition of XML namespace support in SAX 2. As you read through Example 19-2, pay attention to the API differences from Example 19-1.

Example 19–2: ListServlets2.java

```
package com.davidflanagan.examples.xml;
import org.xml.sax.*;          // The main SAX package
import org.xml.sax.helpers.*;  // SAX helper classes
import java.io.*;              // For reading the input file
import java.util.*;            // Hashtable, lists, and so on

/**
 * Parse a web.xml file using the SAX2 API and the Xerces parser from the
 * Apache project.
 *
 * This class extends DefaultHandler so that instances can serve as SAX2
 * event handlers, and can be notified by the parser of parsing events.
```

Example 19–2: ListServlets2.java (continued)

```
 * We simply override the methods that receive events we're interested in
 **/
public class ListServlets2 extends org.xml.sax.helpers.DefaultHandler {
    /** The main method sets things up for parsing */
    public static void main(String[] args) throws IOException, SAXException {
        // Create the parser we'll use.  The parser implementation is a
        // Xerces class, but we use it only through the SAX XMLReader API
        org.xml.sax.XMLReader parser=new org.apache.xerces.parsers.SAXParser();

        // Specify that we don't want validation.  This is the SAX2
        // API for requesting parser features.  Note the use of a
        // globally unique URL as the feature name.  Non-validation is
        // actually the default, so this line isn't really necessary.
        parser.setFeature("http://xml.org/sax/features/validation", false);

        // Instantiate this class to provide handlers for the parser and
        // tell the parser about the handlers
        ListServlets2 handler = new ListServlets2();
        parser.setContentHandler(handler);
        parser.setErrorHandler(handler);

        // Create an input source that describes the file to parse.
        // Then tell the parser to parse input from that source
        org.xml.sax.InputSource input=new InputSource(new FileReader(args[0]));
        parser.parse(input);
    }

    HashMap nameToClass;      // Map from servlet name to servlet class name
    HashMap nameToPatterns;   // Map from servlet name to url patterns

    StringBuffer accumulator;                        // Accumulate text
    String servletName, servletClass, servletPattern; // Remember text

    // Called at the beginning of parsing.  We use it as an init() method
    public void startDocument() {
        accumulator = new StringBuffer();
        nameToClass = new HashMap();
        nameToPatterns = new HashMap();
    }

    // When the parser encounters plain text (not XML elements), it calls
    // this method, which accumulates them in a string buffer.
    // Note that this method may be called multiple times, even with no
    // intervening elements.
    public void characters(char[] buffer, int start, int length) {
        accumulator.append(buffer, start, length);
    }

    // At the beginning of each new element, erase any accumulated text.
    public void startElement(String namespaceURL, String localName,
                             String qname, Attributes attributes) {
        accumulator.setLength(0);
    }

    // Take special action when we reach the end of selected elements.
    // Although we don't use a validating parser, this method does assume
    // that the web.xml file we're parsing is valid.
    public void endElement(String namespaceURL, String localName, String qname)
```

Example 19-2: ListServlets2.java (continued)

```java
{
    if (localName.equals("servlet-name")) {        // Store servlet name
        servletName = accumulator.toString().trim();
    }
    else if (localName.equals("servlet-class")) {  // Store servlet class
        servletClass = accumulator.toString().trim();
    }
    else if (localName.equals("url-pattern")) {    // Store servlet pattern
        servletPattern = accumulator.toString().trim();
    }
    else if (localName.equals("servlet")) {        // Map name to class
        nameToClass.put(servletName, servletClass);
    }
    else if (localName.equals("servlet-mapping")) {// Map name to pattern
        List patterns = (List)nameToPatterns.get(servletName);
        if (patterns == null) {
            patterns = new ArrayList();
            nameToPatterns.put(servletName, patterns);
        }
        patterns.add(servletPattern);
    }
}

// Called at the end of parsing.  Used here to print our results.
public void endDocument() {
    List servletNames = new ArrayList(nameToClass.keySet());
    Collections.sort(servletNames);
    for(Iterator iterator = servletNames.iterator(); iterator.hasNext();) {
        String name = (String)iterator.next();
        String classname = (String)nameToClass.get(name);
        List patterns = (List)nameToPatterns.get(name);
        System.out.println("Servlet: " + name);
        System.out.println("Class: " + classname);
        if (patterns != null) {
            System.out.println("Patterns:");
            for(Iterator i = patterns.iterator(); i.hasNext(); ) {
                System.out.println("\t" + i.next());
            }
        }
        System.out.println();
    }
}

// Issue a warning
public void warning(SAXParseException exception) {
    System.err.println("WARNING: line " + exception.getLineNumber() + ": "+
                       exception.getMessage());
}

// Report a parsing error
public void error(SAXParseException exception) {
    System.err.println("ERROR: line " + exception.getLineNumber() + ": " +
                       exception.getMessage());
}

// Report a non-recoverable error and exit
public void fatalError(SAXParseException exception) throws SAXException {
    System.err.println("FATAL: line " + exception.getLineNumber() + ": " +
```

Example 19–2: ListServlets2.java (continued)

```
                            exception.getMessage());
        throw(exception);
    }
}
```

Compiling and Running the Example

The `ListServlets2` example uses the Xerces-J parser from the Apache XML Project. You can download this open-source parser by following the download links from *http://xml.apache.org/*. Once you have downloaded Xerces-J, unpack the distribution in a convenient location on your system. In that distribution, you should find a *xerces.jar* file. This file must be in your classpath to compile and run the *ListServlets2.java* example. Note that the *xerces.jar* file and the *parsers.jar* file from the JAXP distribution both contain versions of the SAX and DOM classes; you should avoid having both files in your classpath at the same time.

Parsing and Manipulating with JAXP and DOM

The first two examples in this chapter used the SAX API for parsing XML documents. We now turn to another commonly used parsing API, the DOM, or Document Object Model. The DOM API is a standard defined by the World Wide Web Consortium (W3C); its Java implementation consists of the `org.w3c.dom` package and its subpackages. The current version of the DOM standard is Level 1. As of this writing, the DOM Level 2 API is making its way through the standardization process at the W3C.

The Document Object Model defines the API of a parse tree for XML documents. The `org.xml.dom.Node` interface specifies the basic features of a node in this parse tree. Subinterfaces, such as `Document`, `Element`, `Entity`, and `Comment`, define the features of specific types of nodes. A program that uses the DOM parsing model is quite different from one that uses SAX. With the DOM, you have the parser read your XML document and transform it into a tree of `Node` objects. Once parsing is complete, you can traverse the tree to find the information you need. The DOM parsing model is useful if you need to make multiple passes through the tree, if you want to modify the structure of the tree, or if you need random access to an XML document, instead of the sequential access provided by the SAX model.

Example 19-3 is a listing of the program *WebAppConfig.java*. Like the first two examples in this chapter, `WebAppConfig` reads a *web.xml* web application deployment descriptor. This example uses a DOM parser to build a parse tree, then performs some operations on the tree to demonstrate how you can work with a tree of DOM nodes.

The `WebAppConfig()` constructor uses the JAXP API to obtain a DOM parser and then uses that parser to build a parse tree that represents the XML file. The root node of this tree is of type `Document`. This `Document` object is stored in an instance field of the `WebAppConfig` object, so it is available for traversal and modification by the other methods of the class. The class also includes a main() method that invokes these other methods.

The getServletClass() method looks for <servlet-name> tags and returns the text of the associated <servlet-class> tags. (These tags always come in pairs in a *web.xml* file.) This method demonstrates a number of features of the DOM parse tree, notably the getElementsByTagName() method. The addServlet() method inserts a new <servlet> tag into the parse tree. It demonstrates how to construct new DOM nodes and add them to an existing parse tree. Finally, the output() method uses an XMLDocumentWriter to traverse all the nodes of the parse tree and convert them back into XML format. The XMLDocumentWriter class is covered in the next section and listed in Example 19-4.

Example 19–3: WebAppConfig.java

```java
package com.davidflanagan.examples.xml;
import javax.xml.parsers.*;    // JAXP classes for parsing
import org.w3c.dom.*;          // W3C DOM classes for traversing the document
import org.xml.sax.*;          // SAX classes used for error handling by JAXP
import java.io.*;              // For reading the input file

/**
 * A WebAppConfig object is a wrapper around a DOM tree for a web.xml
 * file.  The methods of the class use the DOM API to work with the
 * tree in various ways.
 **/
public class WebAppConfig {
    /** The main method creates and demonstrates a WebAppConfig object */
    public static void main(String[] args)
        throws IOException, SAXException, ParserConfigurationException
    {
        // Create a new WebAppConfig object that represents the web.xml
        // file specified by the first command-line argument
        WebAppConfig config = new WebAppConfig(new File(args[0]));
        // Query the tree for the class name associated with the specified
        // servlet name
        System.out.println("Class for servlet " + args[1] + " is " +
                           config.getServletClass(args[1]));
        // Add a new servlet name-to-class mapping to the DOM tree
        config.addServlet("foo", "bar");
        // And write out an XML version of the DOM tree to standard out
        config.output(new PrintWriter(new OutputStreamWriter(System.out)));
    }

    org.w3c.dom.Document document;  // This field holds the parsed DOM tree

    /**
     * This constructor method is passed an XML file.  It uses the JAXP API to
     * obtain a DOM parser, and to parse the file into a DOM Document object,
     * which is used by the remaining methods of the class.
     **/
    public WebAppConfig(File configfile)
        throws IOException, SAXException, ParserConfigurationException
    {
        // Get a JAXP parser factory object
        javax.xml.parsers.DocumentBuilderFactory dbf =
            DocumentBuilderFactory.newInstance();
        // Tell the factory what kind of parser we want
        dbf.setValidating(false);
```

Example 19–3: WebAppConfig.java (continued)

```
        // Use the factory to get a JAXP parser object
        javax.xml.parsers.DocumentBuilder parser = dbf.newDocumentBuilder();

        // Tell the parser how to handle errors.  Note that in the JAXP API,
        // DOM parsers rely on the SAX API for error handling
        parser.setErrorHandler(new org.xml.sax.ErrorHandler() {
                public void warning(SAXParseException e) {
                    System.err.println("WARNING: " + e.getMessage());
                }
                public void error(SAXParseException e) {
                    System.err.println("ERROR: " + e.getMessage());
                }
                public void fatalError(SAXParseException e)
                    throws SAXException {
                    System.err.println("FATAL: " + e.getMessage());
                    throw e;    // re-throw the error
                }
            });

    // Finally, use the JAXP parser to parse the file.  This call returns
    // A Document object.  Now that we have this object, the rest of this
    // class uses the DOM API to work with it; JAXP is no longer required.
    document = parser.parse(configfile);
}


/**
 * This method looks for specific Element nodes in the DOM tree in order
 * to figure out the classname associated with the specified servlet name
 **/
public String getServletClass(String servletName) {
    // Find all <servlet> elements and loop through them.
    NodeList servletnodes = document.getElementsByTagName("servlet");
    int numservlets = servletnodes.getLength();
    for(int i = 0; i < numservlets; i++) {
        Element servletTag = (Element)servletnodes.item(i);
        // Get the first <servlet-name> tag within the <servlet> tag
        Element nameTag = (Element)
            servletTag.getElementsByTagName("servlet-name").item(0);
        if (nameTag == null) continue;

        // The <servlet-name> tag should have a single child of type
        // Text.  Get that child, and extract its text.  Use trim()
        // to strip whitespace from the beginning and end of it.
        String name =((Text)nameTag.getFirstChild()).getData().trim();

        // If this <servlet-name> tag has the right name
        if (servletName.equals(name)) {
            // Get the matching <servlet-class> tag
            Element classTag = (Element)
                servletTag.getElementsByTagName("servlet-class").item(0);
            if (classTag != null) {
                // Extract the tag's text as above, and return it
                Text classTagContent = (Text)classTag.getFirstChild();
                return classTagContent.getNodeValue().trim();
            }
        }
    }
```

Example 19-3: WebAppConfig.java (continued)

```
        // If we get here, no matching servlet name was found
        return null;
    }

    /**
     * This method adds a new name-to-class mapping in in the form of
     * a <servlet> sub-tree to the document.
     **/
    public void addServlet(String servletName, String className) {
        // Create the <servlet> tag
        Element newNode = document.createElement("servlet");
        // Create the <servlet-name> and <servlet-class> tags
        Element nameNode = document.createElement("servlet-name");
        Element classNode = document.createElement("servlet-class");
        // Add the name and classname text to those tags
        nameNode.appendChild(document.createTextNode(servletName));
        classNode.appendChild(document.createTextNode(className));
        // And add those tags to the servlet tag
        newNode.appendChild(nameNode);
        newNode.appendChild(classNode);

        // Now that we've created the new sub-tree, figure out where to put
        // it.  This code looks for another servlet tag and inserts the new
        // one right before it. Note that this code will fail if the document
        // does not already contain at least one <servlet> tag.
        NodeList servletnodes = document.getElementsByTagName("servlet");
        Element firstServlet = (Element)servletnodes.item(0);

        // Insert the new node before the first servlet node
        firstServlet.getParentNode().insertBefore(newNode, firstServlet);
    }

    /**
     * Output the DOM tree to the specified stream as an XML document.
     * See the XMLDocumentWriter example for the details.
     **/
    public void output(PrintWriter out) {
        XMLDocumentWriter docwriter = new XMLDocumentWriter(out);
        docwriter.write(document);
        docwriter.close();
    }
}
```

Compiling and Running the Example

The WebAppConfig class uses the JAXP and DOM APIs, so you must have the *jaxp.jar* and *parser.jar* files from the JAXP distribution in your classpath. You should avoid having the Xerces JAR file in your classpath at the same time, or you may run into version mismatch problems between the DOM Level 1 parser of JAXP 1.0 and the DOM Level 2 parser of Xerces. Compile *WebAppConfig.java* in the normal way. To run the program, specify the name of a *web.xml* file to parse as the first command-line argument and provide a servlet name as the second argument. When you run the program, it prints the class name (if any) that is mapped to the specified servlet name. Then it inserts a dummy <servlet> tag into the parse tree and prints out the modified parse tree in XML format to standard output. You'll probably want to pipe the output of the program to a paging program such as *more*.

Traversing a DOM Tree

The WebAppConfig class of Example 19-3 parses an XML file to a DOM tree, modifies the tree, then converts the tree back into an XML file. It does this using the class XMLDocumentWriter, which is listed in Example 19-4. The write() method of this class recursively traverses a DOM tree node by node and outputs the equivalent XML text to the specified PrintWriter stream. The code is relatively straightforward and helps illustrate the structure of a DOM tree. Note that XMLDocumentWriter is just an example. Among its shortcomings: it doesn't handle every possible type of DOM node, and it doesn't output a full <!DOCTYPE> declaration.

Example 19–4: XMLDocumentWriter.java

```
package com.davidflanagan.examples.xml;
import org.w3c.dom.*;          // W3C DOM classes for traversing the document
import java.io.*;

/**
 * Output a DOM Level 1 Document object to a java.io.PrintWriter as a simple
 * XML document.  This class does not handle every type of DOM node, and it
 * doesn't deal with all the details of XML like DTDs, character encodings and
 * preserved and ignored whitespace.  However, it does output basic
 * well-formed XML that can be parsed by a non-validating parser.
 **/
public class XMLDocumentWriter {
    PrintWriter out;  // the stream to send output to

    /** Initialize the output stream */
    public XMLDocumentWriter(PrintWriter out) { this.out = out; }

    /** Close the output stream. */
    public void close() { out.close(); }

    /** Output a DOM Node (such as a Document) to the output stream */
    public void write(Node node) { write(node, ""); }

    /**
     * Output the specified DOM Node object, printing it using the specified
     * indentation string
     **/
    public void write(Node node, String indent) {
        // The output depends on the type of the node
        switch(node.getNodeType()) {
        case Node.DOCUMENT_NODE: {       // If its a Document node
            Document doc = (Document)node;
            out.println(indent + "<?xml version='1.0'?>"); // Output header
            Node child = doc.getFirstChild();   // Get the first node
            while(child != null) {              // Loop 'till no more nodes
                write(child, indent);           // Output node
                child = child.getNextSibling(); // Get next node
            }
            break;
        }
```

Example 19–4: XMLDocumentWriter.java (continued)

```
        case Node.DOCUMENT_TYPE_NODE: {  // It is a <!DOCTYPE> tag
            DocumentType doctype = (DocumentType) node;
            // Note that the DOM Level 1 does not give us information about
            // the the public or system ids of the doctype, so we can't output
            // a complete <!DOCTYPE> tag here.  We can do better with Level 2.
            out.println("<!DOCTYPE " + doctype.getName() + ">");
            break;
        }
        case Node.ELEMENT_NODE: {         // Most nodes are Elements
            Element elt = (Element) node;
            out.print(indent + "<" + elt.getTagName());  // Begin start tag
            NamedNodeMap attrs = elt.getAttributes();     // Get attributes
            for(int i = 0; i < attrs.getLength(); i++) {  // Loop through them
                Node a = attrs.item(i);
                out.print(" " + a.getNodeName() + "='" +  // Print attr. name
                          fixup(a.getNodeValue()) + "'"); // Print attr. value
            }
            out.println(">");                             // Finish start tag

            String newindent = indent + "    ";           // Increase indent
            Node child = elt.getFirstChild();             // Get child
            while(child != null) {                        // Loop
                write(child, newindent);                  // Output child
                child = child.getNextSibling();           // Get next child
            }

            out.println(indent + "</" +                   // Output end tag
                        elt.getTagName() + ">");
            break;
        }
        case Node.TEXT_NODE: {                   // Plain text node
            Text textNode = (Text)node;
            String text = textNode.getData().trim();  // Strip off space
            if ((text != null) && text.length() > 0)  // If non-empty
                out.println(indent + fixup(text));    // print text
            break;
        }
        case Node.PROCESSING_INSTRUCTION_NODE: {  // Handle PI nodes
            ProcessingInstruction pi = (ProcessingInstruction)node;
            out.println(indent + "<?" + pi.getTarget() +
                        " " + pi.getData() + "?>");
            break;
        }
        case Node.ENTITY_REFERENCE_NODE: {        // Handle entities
            out.println(indent + "&" + node.getNodeName() + ";");
            break;
        }
        case Node.CDATA_SECTION_NODE: {           // Output CDATA sections
            CDATASection cdata = (CDATASection)node;
            // Careful! Don't put a CDATA section in the program itself!
            out.println(indent + "<" + "![CDATA[" + cdata.getData() +
                        "]]" + ">");
            break;
        }
        case Node.COMMENT_NODE: {                 // Comments
            Comment c = (Comment)node;
            out.println(indent + "<!--" + c.getData() + "-->");
            break;
```

Example 19–4: XMLDocumentWriter.java (continued)

```
        }
        default:   // Hopefully, this won't happen too much!
            System.err.println("Ignoring node: " + node.getClass().getName());
            break;
        }
    }

    // This method replaces reserved characters with entities.
    String fixup(String s) {
        StringBuffer sb = new StringBuffer();
        int len = s.length();
        for(int i = 0; i < len; i++) {
            char c = s.charAt(i);
            switch(c) {
            default: sb.append(c); break;
            case '<': sb.append("&lt;"); break;
            case '>': sb.append("&gt;"); break;
            case '&': sb.append("&amp;"); break;
            case '"': sb.append("&quot;"); break;
            case '\'': sb.append("&apos;"); break;
            }
        }
        return sb.toString();
    }
}
```

Traversing a Document with DOM Level 2

Example 19-5 is a listing of *DOMTreeWalkerTreeModel.java*, a class that demonstrates DOM tree traversal using the DOM Level 2 TreeWalker class. TreeWalker is part of the org.w3c.dom.traversal package. It allows you to traverse, or walk, a DOM tree using a simple API. More importantly, however, it lets you specify what type of nodes you want and automatically filters out all other nodes. It even allows you to provide a NodeFilter class that filters nodes based on any criteria you want.

The DOMTreeWalkerTreeModel implements the javax.swing.tree.TreeModel interface, which enables you to easily display a filtered DOM tree using a Swing JTree component. Figure 19-1 shows a filtered *web.xml* file being displayed in this way. What is interesting here is not the TreeModel methods themselves (refer to Chapter 10, *Graphical User Interfaces* for an explanation of TreeModel), but how the implementations of those methods use the TreeWalker API to traverse the DOM tree.

The main() method parses the XML document named on the command line, then creates a TreeWalker for the parse tree. The TreeWalker is configured to show all nodes except for comments and text nodes that contain only whitespace. Next, the main() method creates a DOMTreeWalkerTreeModel object for the TreeWalker. Finally, it creates a JTree component to display the tree described by the DOMTreeWalkerTreeModel.

Note that this example uses the Xerces parser because of its support for DOM Level 2 (which, at the time of this writing, is not supported by JAXP). Because the example uses Xerces, you must have the *xerces.jar* file in your classpath in order

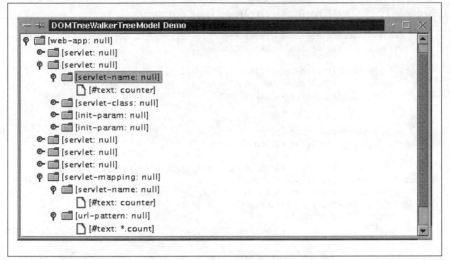

Figure 19–1. DOMTreeWalkerTreeModel display of a web.xml file

to compile and run the example. At the time of this writing, DOM Level 2 is rea-
sonably stable but is not yet an official standard. If the TreeWalker API changes
during the standardization process, it will probably break this example.

Example 19–5: DOMTreeWalkerTreeModel.java

```java
package com.davidflanagan.examples.xml;
import org.w3c.dom.*;                    // Core DOM classes
import org.w3c.dom.traversal.*;          // TreeWalker and related DOM classes
import org.apache.xerces.parsers.*;      // Apache Xerces parser classes
import org.xml.sax.*;                    // Xerces DOM parser uses some SAX classes
import javax.swing.*;                    // Swing classes
import javax.swing.tree.*;               // TreeModel and related classes
import javax.swing.event.*;              // Tree-related event classes
import java.io.*;                        // For reading the input XML file

/**
 * This class implements the Swing TreeModel interface so that the DOM tree
 * returned by a TreeWalker can be displayed in a JTree component.
 **/
public class DOMTreeWalkerTreeModel implements TreeModel {
    TreeWalker walker;  // The TreeWalker we're modeling for JTree

    /** Create a TreeModel for the specified TreeWalker */
    public DOMTreeWalkerTreeModel(TreeWalker walker) { this.walker = walker; }

    /**
     * Create a TreeModel for a TreeWalker that returns all nodes
     * in the specified document
     **/
    public DOMTreeWalkerTreeModel(Document document) {
        DocumentTraversal dt = (DocumentTraversal)document;
        walker = dt.createTreeWalker(document, NodeFilter.SHOW_ALL,null,false);
    }

    /**
```

Example 19–5: DOMTreeWalkerTreeModel.java (continued)

```java
 * Create a TreeModel for a TreeWalker that returns the specified
 * element and all of its descendant nodes.
 **/
public DOMTreeWalkerTreeModel(Element element) {
    DocumentTraversal dt = (DocumentTraversal)element.getOwnerDocument();
    walker = dt.createTreeWalker(element, NodeFilter.SHOW_ALL, null,false);
}

// Return the root of the tree
public Object getRoot() { return walker.getRoot(); }

// Is this node a leaf? (Leaf nodes are displayed differently by JTree)
public boolean isLeaf(Object node) {
    walker.setCurrentNode((Node)node);   // Set current node
    Node child = walker.firstChild();     // Ask for a child
    return (child == null);               // Does it have any?
}

// How many children does this node have?
public int getChildCount(Object node) {
    walker.setCurrentNode((Node)node);   // Set the current node
    // TreeWalker doesn't count children for us, so we count ourselves
    int numkids = 0;
    Node child = walker.firstChild();     // Start with the first child
    while(child != null) {                // Loop 'till there are no more
        numkids++;                        // Update the count
        child = walker.nextSibling();     // Get next child
    }
    return numkids;                       // This is the number of children
}

// Return the specified child of a parent node.
public Object getChild(Object parent, int index) {
    walker.setCurrentNode((Node)parent); // Set the current node
    // TreeWalker provides sequential access to children, not random
    // access, so we've got to loop through the kids one by one
    Node child = walker.firstChild();
    while(index-- > 0) child = walker.nextSibling();
    return child;
}

// Return the index of the child node in the parent node
public int getIndexOfChild(Object parent, Object child) {
    walker.setCurrentNode((Node)parent); // Set current node
    int index = 0;
    Node c = walker.firstChild();         // Start with first child
    while((c != child) && (c != null)) {  // Loop 'till we find a match
        index++;
        c = walker.nextSibling();         // Get the next child
    }
    return index;                         // Return matching position
}

// Only required for editable trees; unimplemented here.
public void valueForPathChanged(TreePath path, Object newvalue) {}

// This TreeModel never fires any events (since it is not editable)
// so event listener registration methods are left unimplemented
```

Example 19-5: DOMTreeWalkerTreeModel.java (continued)

```java
public void addTreeModelListener(TreeModelListener l) {}
public void removeTreeModelListener(TreeModelListener l) {}

/**
 * This main() method demonstrates the use of this class, the use of the
 * Xerces DOM parser, and the creation of a DOM Level 2 TreeWalker object.
 **/
public static void main(String[] args) throws IOException, SAXException {
    // Obtain an instance of a Xerces parser to build a DOM tree.
    // Note that we are not using the JAXP API here, so this
    // code uses Apache Xerces APIs that are not standards
    DOMParser parser = new org.apache.xerces.parsers.DOMParser();

    // Get a java.io.Reader for the input XML file and
    // wrap the input file in a SAX input source
    Reader in = new BufferedReader(new FileReader(args[0]));
    InputSource input = new org.xml.sax.InputSource(in);

    // Tell the Xerces parser to parse the input source
    parser.parse(input);

    // Ask the parser to give us our DOM Document.  Once we've got the DOM
    // tree, we don't have to use the Apache Xerces APIs any more; from
    // here on, we use the standard DOM APIs
    Document document = parser.getDocument();

    // If we're using a DOM Level 2 implementation, then our Document
    // object ought to implement DocumentTraversal
    DocumentTraversal traversal = (DocumentTraversal)document;

    // For this demonstration, we create a NodeFilter that filters out
    // Text nodes containing only space; these just clutter up the tree
    NodeFilter filter = new NodeFilter() {
        public short acceptNode(Node n) {
            if (n.getNodeType() == Node.TEXT_NODE) {
                // Use trim() to strip off leading and trailing space.
                // If nothing is left, then reject the node
                if (((Text)n).getData().trim().length() == 0)
                    return NodeFilter.FILTER_REJECT;
            }
            return NodeFilter.FILTER_ACCEPT;
        }
    };

    // This set of flags says to "show" all node types except comments
    int whatToShow = NodeFilter.SHOW_ALL & ~NodeFilter.SHOW_COMMENT;

    // Create a TreeWalker using the filter and the flags
    TreeWalker walker = traversal.createTreeWalker(document, whatToShow,
                                                   filter, false);

    // Instantiate a TreeModel and a JTree to display it
    JTree tree = new JTree(new DOMTreeWalkerTreeModel(walker));

    // Create a frame and a scrollpane to display the tree, and pop them up
    JFrame frame = new JFrame("DOMTreeWalkerTreeModel Demo");
    frame.getContentPane().add(new JScrollPane(tree));
    frame.setSize(500, 250);
```

Example 19–5: DOMTreeWalkerTreeModel.java (continued)

```
            frame.setVisible(true);
        }
    }
}
```

The JDOM API

Until now, this chapter has considered the official, standard ways of parsing and working with XML documents: DOM is a standard of the W3C, and SAX is a de facto standard by virtue of its nearly universal adoption. Both SAX and DOM were designed to be programming language-independent APIs, however. This generality means they can't take full advantage of the features of the Java language and platform, however. As I write this chapter, there is a new (still in beta release) but promising API targeted directly at Java programmers. As its name implies, JDOM is an XML document object model for Java. Like the DOM API, it creates a parse tree to represent an XML document. Unlike the DOM, however, the API is designed from the ground up for Java and is significantly easier to use than the DOM. JDOM is an open-source project initiated by Brett McLaughlin and Jason Hunter, who are the authors of the O'Reilly books *Java and XML* and *Java Servlet Programming*, respectively.

Example 19-6 shows how the JDOM API can be used to parse an XML document, to extract information from the resulting parse tree, to create new element nodes and add them to the parse tree, and, finally, to output the modified tree as an XML document. Compare this code to Example 19-3; the examples perform exactly the same task, but as you'll see, using the JDOM API makes the code simpler and cleaner. You should also notice that JDOM has its own built-in XMLOutputter class, obviating the need for the XMLDocumentWriter shown in Example 19-4.

Example 19–6: WebAppConfig2.java

```
package com.davidflanagan.examples.xml;
import java.io.*;
import java.util.*;
import org.jdom.*;
import org.jdom.input.SAXBuilder;
import org.jdom.output.XMLOutputter;

/**
 * This class is just like WebAppConfig, but it uses the JDOM (Beta 4) API
 * instead of the DOM and JAXP APIs
 **/
public class WebAppConfig2 {
    /** The main method creates and demonstrates a WebAppConfig2 object */
    public static void main(String[] args)
        throws IOException, JDOMException
    {
        // Create a new WebAppConfig object that represents the web.xml
        // file specified by the first command-line argument
        WebAppConfig2 config = new WebAppConfig2(new File(args[0]));

        // Query the tree for the class name associated with the servlet
        // name specified as the 2nd command-line argument
        System.out.println("Class for servlet " + args[1] + " is " +
```

Example 19–6: WebAppConfig2.java (continued)

```
                        config.getServletClass(args[1]));

    // Add a new servlet name-to-class mapping to the DOM tree
    config.addServlet("foo", "bar");

    // And write out an XML version of the DOM tree to standard out
    config.output(System.out);
}

/**
 * This field holds the parsed JDOM tree.  Note that this is a JDOM
 * Document, not a DOM Document.
 **/
protected org.jdom.Document document;

/**
 * Read the specified File and parse it to create a JDOM tree
 **/
public WebAppConfig2(File configfile) throws IOException, JDOMException {
    // JDOM can build JDOM trees from a variety of input sources.  One
    // of those input sources is a SAX parser.
    SAXBuilder builder =
        new SAXBuilder("org.apache.xerces.parsers.SAXParser");
    // Parse the specified file and convert it to a JDOM document
    document = builder.build(configfile);
}

/**
 * This method looks for specific Element nodes in the JDOM tree in order
 * to figure out the classname associated with the specified servlet name
 **/
public String getServletClass(String servletName) throws JDOMException {
    // Get the root element of the document.
    Element root = document.getRootElement();

    // Find all <servlet> elements in the document, and loop through them
    // to find one with the specified name.  Note the use of java.util.List
    // instead of org.w3c.dom.NodeList.
    List servlets = root.getChildren("servlet");
    for(Iterator i = servlets.iterator(); i.hasNext(); ) {
        Element servlet = (Element) i.next();
        // Get the text of the <servlet-name> tag within the <servlet> tag
        String name = servlet.getChild("servlet-name").getContent();
        if (name.equals(servletName)) {
            // If the names match, return the text of the <servlet-class>
            return servlet.getChild("servlet-class").getContent();
        }
    }
    return null;
}

/**
 * This method adds a new name-to-class mapping in the form of
 * a <servlet> sub-tree to the document.
 **/
public void addServlet(String servletName, String className)
    throws JDOMException
{
```

Example 19–6: WebAppConfig2.java (continued)

```
        // Create the new Element that represents our new servlet
        Element newServletName = new Element("servlet-name");
        newServletName.setContent(servletName);
        Element newServletClass = new Element("servlet-class");
        newServletClass.setContent(className);
        Element newServlet = new Element("servlet");
        newServlet.addChild(newServletName);
        newServlet.addChild(newServletClass);

        // find the first <servlet> child in the document
        Element root = document.getRootElement();
        Element firstServlet = root.getChild("servlet");

        // Now insert our new servlet tag before the one we just found.
        Element parent = firstServlet.getParent();
        List children = parent.getChildren();
        children.add(children.indexOf(firstServlet), newServlet);
    }

    /**
     * Output the JDOM tree to the specified stream as an XML document.
     **/
    public void output(OutputStream out) throws IOException {
        // JDOM can output JDOM trees in a variety of ways (such as converting
        // them to DOM trees or SAX event streams).  Here we use an "outputter"
        // that converts a JDOM tree to an XML document
        XMLOutputter outputter = new XMLOutputter("  ",      // indentation
                                                  true);     // use newlines
        outputter.output(document, out);
    }
}
```

Compiling and Running the Example

In order to compile and run Example 19-6, you must download the JDOM distribution, which is freely available from *http://www.jdom.org/*. This example was developed using the Beta 4 release of JDOM. Because of the beta status of JDOM, I'm not going to try to give explicit build instructions here. You need to have the JDOM classes in your classpath to compile and run the example. Additionally, since the example relies on the Xerces SAX 2 parser, you need to have the Xerces JAR file in your classpath to run the example. Xerces is conveniently bundled with JDOM (at least in the Beta 4 distribution). Finally, note that JDOM is undergoing rapid development, and the API may change somewhat from the Beta 4 version used here. If so, you may need to modify the example to get it to compile and run.

Exercises

19-1. Many of the examples in this chapter were designed to parse the *web.xml* files that configure web applications. If you use the Tomcat servlet container to run your servlets, you may know that Tomcat uses another XML file, *server.xml*, for server-level configuration information. In Tomcat 3.1, this file is located in the *conf* directory of the Tomcat distribution and contains a number of <Context> tags that use attributes to specify additional information about each web application. Write a program that uses a SAX parser (preferably SAX 2) to parse the *server.xml* file and output the values of the path and docBase attributes of each <Context> tag.

19-2. Using a DOM parser instead of a SAX parser, write a program that behaves identically to the program you developed in Exercise 19-1.

19-3. Rewrite the *server.xml* parser again, using the JDOM API this time.

19-4. Write a Swing-based web application configuration program that can read *web.xml* files, allow the user to modify them, and then write out the modified version. The program should allow the user to add new servlets to the web application and edit existing servlets. For each servlet, it should allow the user to specify the servlet name, class, initialization parameters, and URL pattern.

19-5. Design an XML grammar for representing a JavaBeans component and its property values. Write a class that can serialize an arbitrary bean to this XML format and deserialize, or recreate, a bean from the XML format. Use the Java Reflection API or the JavaBeans Introspector class to identify the properties of a bean. Assume that all properties of the bean are either primitive Java types, String objects, or other bean instances. (You may want to extend this list to include Font and Color objects as well.) Further assume that all bean classes define a no-argument constructor and all beans can be properly initialized by instantiating them and setting their public properties.

CHAPTER 20

Example Index

The following index allows you to look up a programming concept and find any examples in this book that demonstrate that concept. In addition, you can look up a Java class or method and see what examples use that class or method. Each index entry lists the example numbers for any relevant examples.

hexadecimal encoding, 6-4
HTML
    writing to browser, 3-8
HTMLWriter.java, 3-8
HTTP protocol
    client, 5-4
    server, 5-5
HttpClient.java, 5-4
HttpMirror.java, 5-5
HttpServlet, 18-1, 18-2, 18-3
HttpServletRequest, 18-1, 18-2, 18-3
HttpServletResponse, 18-1, 18-2, 18-3
HttpSession, 18-8
    invalidate(), 18-8
HttpSessionBindingEvent, 18-7
HttpSessionBindingListener, 18-7
HttpURLConnection, 5-2
HyperlinkListener, 10-21
Hypnosis.java, 11-17

I

I/O
    see input/output
I/O stream subclass, 3-7, 3-8
I/O streams, 3-2
I18N
    see internationalization
Icon, 10-16, 10-17
IllegalArgumentException, 1-9
Image, 11-1, 11-13
ImageIcon, 11-13
ImageOps.java, 11-13
immutable class, 2-5
InetAddress, 5-11
inheritance, 2-4
inner classes, 2-8
inner interfaces, 2-8
input/output
    archiving directories, 3-5
    compressing files, 3-5
    custom streams, 3-6, 3-7, 3-8, 12-3
    file copying, 3-2
    file deletion, 3-1
    listing directories, 3-4
    multiline console input, 16-7
    reading from console, 1-12, 16-7
    reading text files, 3-3
InputSource, 19-1, 19-2, 19-5
InputStream, 3-2

InputStreamReader, 7-2
InputStreamWriter, 7-2
Insets, 14-9
Integer, 1-11
    parseInt(), 1-11
interfaces, 2-8
internationalization
    character encodings, 7-2
    currency formats, 7-3
    date formats, 7-3
    localized formatting, 7-3
    localized messages, 7-5
    localizing GUI resources, 10-22
    menus, 7-4
    message formats, 7-5
    number formats, 7-3
    resource bundles, 7-4
    unicode, 7-1
IntList.java, 9-2
introspection, 10-1
Introspector, 10-1, 10-19
invoking methods, 8-2
ItemChooser.java, 10-15
ItemListener, 10-15

J

java.applet
    Applet, 15-1, 15-2, 15-3, 15-4, 15-5,
        15-6
    Applet.destroy(), 15-6
    Applet.getAppletInfo(), 15-2, 15-5
    Applet.getAudioClip(), 15-6
    Applet.getImage(), 15-6
    Applet.getParameter(), 15-5
    Applet.getParameterInfo(), 15-5
    Applet.init(), 15-2, 15-3, 15-5, 15-6
    Applet.paint(), 15-1, 15-4, 15-6
    Applet.start(), 15-2
    Applet.stop(), 15-2
    AudioClip, 15-6
java.awt
    AlphaComposite, 11-12
    BasicStroke, 11-8, 11-15
    BorderLayout, 10-5, 10-16, 10-21,
        14-9
    Button, 15-3
    Color, 10-28, 11-1, 11-3, 11-10
    Component.enableEvents(), 10-14

java.awt.Stroke
custom implementations, 11-15
java.beans
BeanDescriptor, 14-6
BeanInfo, 10-1, 10-19, 14-6
Customizer, 14-9
Introspector, 10-1, 10-19
PropertyChangeListener, 10-21
PropertyChangeSupport, 14-9
PropertyDescriptor, 10-1, 10-19,
14-6
PropertyEditor, 14-7, 14-8
PropertyEditorSupport, 14-7, 14-8
SimpleBeanInfo, 14-6
java.io
BufferedReader, 3-7, 7-2
BufferedWriter, 7-2
Externalizable, 9-3
File, 3-1, 3-2
File.delete(), 3-1
FileInputStream, 3-2
File.list(), 3-4
FileOutputStream, 3-2
FileReader, 3-3
FilterReader, 3-6
InputStream, 3-2
InputStreamReader, 7-2
InputStreamWriter, 7-2
ObjectInputStream, 9-1, 16-4, 18-2
ObjectOutputStream, 9-1, 16-4, 18-2
OutputStream, 3-2
PipedInputStream, 9-1
PipedOutputStream, 9-1
Reader, 7-2
Serializable, 16-4, 16-5
StreamTokenizer, 8-2
StringWriter, 4-2
Writer, 7-2, 12-3
java.lang
BufferedReader, 1-12
Class, 8-1, 8-2, 17-3
Class.forName(), 5-9, 8-1, 17-1
IllegalArgumentException, 1-9
Integer, 1-11
Integer.parseInt(), 1-11
Math, 1-15
Object.notify(), 4-5
Object.wait(), 4-5
Runnable, 15-2
SecurityException, 6-3

SecurityManager, 6-1
String, 1-5
StringBuffer, 1-13
System.arraycopy(), 13-2
System.currentTimeMillis(), 4-4,
4-5, 18-2
System.getProperty(), 6-3
System.in, 1-12, 16-7
System.out, 1-1, 16-7
Thread, 4-1, 4-2, 5-6, 5-8, 5-9, 5-10,
9-1, 11-4, 15-2, 16-5, 16-7
Thread.interrupt(), 5-9
Thread.join(), 4-1, 5-10
Thread.setPriority(), 4-1
Thread.start(), 4-1
Thread.yield(), 4-1
ThreadGroup, 4-2, 5-9
ThreadLocal, 4-1
Throwable.printStackTrace(), 7-5
java.lang.reflect
Constructor, 8-1
Field, 8-1, 17-3
Method, 8-1, 8-2, 17-3
Method.invoke(), 8-2
java.math
BigInteger, 1-10
java.net
DatagramPacket, 5-11, 5-12
DatagramSocket, 5-11, 5-12
DatagramSocket.receive(), 5-12
DatagramSocket.send(), 5-11
HttpURLConnection, 5-2
InetAddress, 5-11
ServerSocket, 5-5, 5-6, 5-9
ServerSocket.accept(), 5-5
ServerSocket.setSoTimeout(), 5-9
Socket, 5-4, 5-5, 5-6, 5-7, 5-8, 5-9
URL, 5-1, 5-2, 10-21
URL.openStream(), 5-1
URLClassLoader, 6-1
URLConnection, 5-2
java.rmi
Naming, 16-1, 16-2, 16-4, 16-7, 17-5
Remote, 16-1, 16-3
RemoteException, 16-1, 16-2
java.rmi.server
UnicastRemoteObject, 16-2, 16-4,
16-5, 16-6, 17-5

MenuParser.java, 10-27
menus
    from a resource bundle, 7-4
    internationalized, 7-4
    simplified creation, 7-4
message digests, 6-4
MessageDigest, 6-4
MessageFormat, 7-5
Method, 8-1, 8-2, 17-3
    invoke(), 8-2
modal dialogs, 10-18
modifiers
    volatile, 4-5
modulo, 1-2
MouseListener, 10-11, 10-12
MouseMotionListener, 10-11, 10-12
Mud.java, 16-3
MUD
    client program, 16-7
    RMI interfaces, 16-3
    RMI MudPerson implementation,
        16-6
    RMI MudPlace implementation,
        16-5
    RMI server implementation, 16-4
MudClient.java, 16-7
MudPerson.java, 16-6
MudPlace.java, 16-5
MudServer.java, 16-4
MultiLineLabel.java, 14-1
multithreaded
    see threads
multithreaded network server, 5-9
multithreaded proxy server, 5-10

N

NamedNodeMap, 19-4
Naming, 16-1, 16-2, 16-4, 16-7, 17-5
netscape.javascript
    JSObject, 3-8
networking
    dynamic loading of services, 5-9
    extensible multithreaded server, 5-9
    finger protocol, 5-7
    generic text-based client, 5-8
    getting URL information, 5-2
    HTTP client, 5-4
    line terminators, 5-8
    listening on a port, 5-5

multithreaded proxy server, 5-10
    proxy server, 5-6
    receiving datagrams, 5-12
    sending datagrams, 5-11
    sending email, 5-3
    simple HTTP server, 5-5
    with an applet, 5-7
    with ServerSocket, 5-5
    with Socket class, 5-4
    with UDP, 5-11, 5-12
    with URL class, 5-1
Node, 19-4, 19-5
NodeFilter, 19-5
NodeList, 19-3
NullLayoutPane.java, 10-8
number formats, 7-3
NumberFormat, 7-3

O

Object
    notify(), 4-5
    wait(), 4-5
ObjectInputStream, 9-1, 16-4, 18-2
ObjectInputStream.defaultReadOb-
        ject(), 9-2
ObjectOutputStream, 9-1, 16-4, 18-2
ObjectOutputStream.defaultWriteOb-
        ject(), 9-2
operators
    %, 1-2
    modulo, 1-2
org.apache.xerces.parsers
    DOMParser, 19-5
    SAXParser, 19-2
org.jdom
    Document, 19-6
    Element, 19-6
org.jdom.input
    SAXBuilder, 19-6
org.jdom.output
    XMLOutputter, 19-6
org.w3c.dom
    CDATASection, 19-4
    Comment, 19-4
    Document, 19-3, 19-4, 19-5
    DocumentType, 19-4
    DomParser, 19-5
    Element, 19-3, 19-4

Example Index

Y

YesNoPanel.java, 14-3
YesNoPanelBeanInfo.java, 14-6
YesNoPanelCustomizer.java, 14-9
YesNoPanelMessageEditor.java, 14-8

Z

zip files, 3-5
ZipOutputStream, 3-5

Index

About the Author

David Flanagan is a computer programmer who spends most of his time writing about Java. His other books with O'Reilly & Associates include the bestselling *Java in a Nutshell, Java Foundation Classes in a Nutshell, Java Enterprise in a Nutshell, Java Power Reference, JavaScript: The Definitive Guide*, and *JavaScript Pocket Reference*. David has a degree in computer science and engineering from the Massachusetts Institute of Technology. He lives with his partner Christie in the U.S. Pacific Northwest between the cities of Seattle, Washington and Vancouver, British Columbia.

Colophon

Our look is the result of reader comments, our own experimentation, and feedback from distribution channels. Distinctive covers complement our distinctive approach to technical topics, breathing personality and life into potentially dry subjects.

The animal featured on the cover of *Java Examples in a Nutshell, Second Edition*, is an alligator. There are only two species of alligator: the American alligator (*Alligator mississippiensis*), found in the southeastern coastal plain of the United States, and the smaller Chinese alligator (*Alligator sinensis*), found in the lower valley of the Yangtze River. Both alligators are related to the more widely distributed crocodile.

The alligator is a much-studied animal, and so a great deal is known about its life cycle. Female alligators lay 30 to 80 eggs at a time. The mother allows the sun to incubate the eggs, but stays nearby. After about 60 days the eggs hatch, and the young call out for their mother. The mother then carries or leads them to the water, where they live with her for a year.

Alligators eat a varied diet of insects, fish, shellfish, frogs, water birds, and small mammals. Alligator attacks on humans are rare. Although normally slow-moving animals, alligators can charge quickly for short distances when they or their young are in danger.

Alligators have been hunted extensively for their skin. The American alligator was placed on the endangered species list in 1969, then declared to be out of danger in 1987. The Chinese alligator remains on the endangered list.

Mary Anne Weeks Mayo was the copyeditor and production editor for *Java Examples in a Nutshell, Second Edition*. Emily Quill, Madeleine Newell, and Jane Ellin provided quality control. Ann Schirmer and Linley Dolby provided production assistance. Ellen Troutman-Zaig wrote the index.

Edie Freedman designed the cover of this book using a 19th-century engraving from the Dover Pictorial Archive. Emma Colby produced the cover layout with Quark-XPress 4.1 using Adobe's ITC Garamond font.

Alicia Cech and David Futato designed the interior layout based on a series design by Nancy Priest. The print version of this book was created by translating the DocBook SGML markup of its source files into a set of gtroff macros using a filter developed at

O'Reilly & Associates by Norman Walsh. Steve Talbott designed and wrote the underlying macro set on the basis of the GNU troff -gs macros; Lenny Muellner adapted them to SGML and implemented the book design. The GNU groff text formatter version 1.11.1 generated PostScript output. The text and heading fonts are ITC Garamond and Letter Gothic. The illustrations that appear in the book were produced by Robert Romano using Macromedia FreeHand 8 and Adobe Photoshop 5. This colophon was written by Clairemarie Fisher O'Leary.

Whenever possible, our books use a durable and flexible lay-flat binding. If the page count exceeds this binding's limit, perfect binding is used.